T0211012

Lecture Notes in Computer Science 11990

Dirk Beyer · Damien Zufferey (Eds.)

Verification, Model Checking, and Abstract Interpretation

21st International Conference, VMCAI 2020
New Orleans, LA, USA, January 16–21, 2020
Proceedings

 Springer

Editors
Dirk Beyer (iD)
Ludwig-Maximilians-Universität München
Munich, Germany

Damien Zufferey (iD)
Max Planck Institute for Software Systems
Kaiserslautern, Germany

ISSN 0302-9743   ISSN 1611-3349   (electronic)
Lecture Notes in Computer Science
ISBN 978-3-030-39321-2   ISBN 978-3-030-39322-9   (eBook)
https://doi.org/10.1007/978-3-030-39322-9

LNCS Sublibrary: SL1 – Theoretical Computer Science and General Issues

This Springer imprint is published by the registered company Springer Nature Switzerland AG
The registered company address is: Gewerbestrasse 11, 6330 Cham, Switzerland

Preface

Welcome to VMCAI 2020, the 21st International Conference on Verification, Model Checking, and Abstract Interpretation. VMCAI 2020 is part of the 47th ACM SIGPLAN Symposium on Principles of Programming Languages (POPL 2020), at the hotel JW Marriott New Orleans, USA, during January 19–21, 2020.

Conference Description. VMCAI provides a forum for researchers from the communities of verification, model checking, and abstract interpretation, facilitating interaction, cross-fertilization, and advancement of hybrid methods that combine these and related areas. The topics of the conference include program verification, model checking, abstract interpretation, program synthesis, static analysis, type systems, deductive methods, decision procedures, theorem proving, program certification, debugging techniques, program transformation, optimization, and hybrid and cyber-physical systems.

Focus on Reproducibility of Research Results. VMCAI 2020 included, for the first time in this conference series, an optional artifact-evaluation (AE) process for submitted papers. Reproducibility of results is of the utmost importance to the VMCAI community. Therefore, we encouraged all authors to submit an artifact for evaluation. An artifact is any additional material (software, data sets, machine-checkable proofs, etc.) that substantiates the claims made in a paper and ideally makes them fully replicable. The evaluation and archival of artifacts improves replicability and traceability for the benefit of future research and the broader VMCAI community.

Paper Selection. VMCAI 2020 received a total of 44 paper submissions. After a rigorous review process, with each paper reviewed by at least 3 Program Committee (PC) members, followed by an online discussion, the PC accepted 21 full papers for publication in the proceedings and presentation at the conference. The main selection criteria were quality, relevance, and originality.

Invited Talks. The conference program includes three keynotes, by Rajeev Alur (University of Pennsylvania, USA) on "Model Checking for Safe Autonomy," Marta Kwiatkowska (University of Oxford, UK) on "Safety and Robustness for Deep Learning with Provable Guarantees," and Moshe Vardi (Rice University, USA) on "The Siren Song of Temporal Synthesis."

Winter School. The VMCAI Winter School is the second winter school on formal methods, associated with VMCAI 2020, New Orleans, USA, during January 16–18, 2020. In the vein of VMCAI, the school is meant to facilitate interaction, cross-fertilization, and advancement of hybrid methods that combine verification, model checking, and abstract interpretation. The school is aimed primarily at PhD students who intend to continue their study in the field of verification.

The VMCAI Winter School program features lectures and tutorials from both academia and industry experts in their respective fields. The school covers several fundamental aspects of formal methods and applications. The following speakers were invited to give lectures at the winter school: Dirk Beyer (Ludwig-Maximilians-Universität München, Germany), Igor Konnov (Interchain Foundation, Switzerland), Marta Kwiatkowska (University of Oxford, UK), Corina Pasareanu (NASA Ames and Carnegie Mellon University, USA), Andreas Podelski (University of Freiburg, Germany), Natasha Sharygina (University of Lugano, Switzerland), Helmut Seidl (TU Munich, Germany), Moshe Vardi (Rice University, USA), Mike Whalen (Amazon Web Services, USA), and Valentin Wüstholz (Consensys Diligence, Germany).

The venue of the second VMCAI Winter School is the New Orleans BioInnovation Center. The school location and schedule was chosen to integrate nicely with POPL and VMCAI, New Orleans, USA, during January 19–25, 2020. The registration for the winter school was free but mandatory. As part of the registration, the applicants could apply for travel and accommodation support, which we were able to provide thanks to the generous donations of the sponsors. Furthermore, we helped to find room mates to reduce the accommodation cost. Students with alternative sources of funding were also welcome.

Artifact-Evaluation Process. For the first time, VMCAI 2020 used an AE process. The goals of AE are: (1) getting more substantial evidence for the claims in the papers, (2) simplify the replication of results in the paper, and (3) reward authors who create artifacts. Artifacts are any additional material that substantiates the claims made in the paper. Examples for artifacts are software, tools, frameworks, data sets, test suites, and machine-checkable proofs.

Authors of submitted papers were encouraged to submit an artifact to the VMCAI 2020 Artifact-Evaluation Committee (AEC). We also encouraged the authors to make their artifacts publicly and permanently available. Artifacts had to be provided as `.zip` files and contain all necessary software for AE as well as a README file that describes the artifact and provides instructions on how to replicate the results. AE had to be possible in the VMCAI 2020 virtual machine, which runs an Ubuntu 19.04 with Linux 5.0.0-31 and was made publicly and permanently available on Zenodo[1].

All submitted artifacts were evaluated in parallel with the papers, and a meta-review of the AE was provided to the reviewers of the respective papers. We assigned three members of the AEC to each artifact and assessed it in two phases. First, the reviewers tested if the artifacts were working, e.g., no corrupted or missing files exist and the evaluation does not crash on simple examples. 5 of the 15 submitted artifacts passed the first phase without any problems and we skipped the author clarification phase for them. For the remaining 10 artifacts, we sent the issues of reviewers to the authors. The authors' answers to the reviewers were distributed among the reviewers, and the authors were allowed to submit an updated artifact to fix issues found during the test phase. In the second phase, the assessment phase, the reviewers aimed at replicating any experiments or activities and evaluated the artifact based on the following five questions:

1. Is the artifact consistent with the paper and the claims made by the paper?
2. Are the results of the paper replicable through the artifact?
3. Is the artifact complete, i.e., how many of the results of the paper are replicable?

---

[1] https://doi.org/10.5281/zenodo.3533104

4. Is the artifact well-documented?
5. Is the artifact easy to use?

10 of the 15 submitted artifacts passed this second phase and were rewarded with the 'Functional' VMCAI AE badge. Independently, artifacts that are permanently and publicly available were rewarded with the 'Available' VMCAI AE badge. 6 artifacts received this 'Available' badge.

The VMCAI 2020 AEC consisted of the two chairs, Daniel Dietsch and Marie-Christine Jakobs, and 20 committee members from 9 different countries.

Acknowledgments. We would like to thank, first of all, the authors for submitting their papers to VMCAI 2020. The PC and the AEC did a great job of reviewing: they contributed informed and detailed reports, and took part in the discussions during the virtual PC meeting. We warmly thank the keynote speakers for their participation and contributions. We also thank the general chair of the POPL 2020 week, Brigitte Pientka, and her team for the overall organization. We thank Alfred Hofmann and his publication team at Springer-Verlag for their support, and EasyChair for providing an excellent review system. Special thanks goes to the VMCAI Steering Committee, and in particular to Lenore Zuck, Ruzica Piskac, and Andreas Podelski, for their helpful advice, assistance, and support.

Last but not least, we thank the sponsors of the VMCAI winter school —Amazon Web Services, Moloch DAO/Consensys Diligence, Interchain, Cadence, and Springer— for their financial contributions to supporting the winter school for students.

December 2019

Dirk Beyer
Damien Zufferey
PC Chairs

Daniel Dietsch
Marie-Christine Jakobs
AEC Chairs

Organization

Program Committee

Dirk Beyer (PC Chair)	LMU Munich, Germany
Damien Zufferey (PC Chair)	MPI, Germany
Timos Antonopoulos	Yale University, USA
Nikolaj Bjorner	Microsoft, USA
Pavol Cerny	University of Colorado Boulder, USA
Rayna Dimitrova	University of Leicester, UK
Constantin Enea	IRIF and Université Paris Diderot, France
Pierre Ganty	IMDEA Software Institute, Spain
Alberto Griggio	Fondazione Bruno Kessler, Italy
Ashutosh Gupta	TIFR, India
Marie-Christine Jakobs	TU Darmstadt, Germany
Laura Kovacs	Vienna University of Technology, Austria
Jan Kretinsky	TU Munich, Germany
Markus Kusano	Google, USA
Ori Lahav	Tel Aviv University, Israel
David Monniaux	CNRS and VERIMAG, France
Kedar Namjoshi	Bell Labs, USA
Andreas Podelski	University of Freiburg, Germany
Nadia Polikarpova	UC San Diego, USA
Shaz Qadeer	Facebook, USA
Daniel Schwartz-Narbonne	Amazon Web Services, USA
Martina Seidl	Johannes Kepler University Linz, Austria
Natasha Sharygina	USI Lugano, Switzerland
Mihaela Sighireanu	IRIF, CNRS, and Université Paris Diderot, France
Jan Strejček	Masaryk University, Czechia
Alexander J. Summers	ETH Zurich, Switzerland
Michael Tautschnig	Queen Mary University of London and AWS, UK
Caterina Urban	Inria, France
Heike Wehrheim	University of Paderborn, Germany
Thomas Wies	New York University, USA
Lenore Zuck	University of Illinois in Chicago, USA

Artifact Evaluation Committee (AEC)

Daniel Dietsch (AEC Chair)	University of Freiburg, Germany
Marie-Christine Jakobs (AEC Chair)	TU Darmstadt, Germany
Aleš Bizjak	Aarhus University, Germany
Martin Bromberger	MPI-INF, Germany

Maryam Dabaghchian   University of Utah, USA
Simon Dierl   TU Dortmund, Germany
Rayna Dimitrova   University of Leicester, UK
Mathias Fleury   MPI-INF, Germany
Ákos Hajdu   Budapest University of Technology and Economics, Hungary
Marcel Hark   RWTH Aachen University, Germany
Ben Hermann   Paderborn University, Germany
Christian Herrera   fortiss GmbH, Germany
Martin Jonáš   Fondazione Bruno Kessler, Italy
Bishoksan Kafle   University of Melbourne, Australia
Martin Kellogg   University of Washington Seattle, USA
Sven Linker   University of Liverpool, UK
Alessio Mansutti   CNRS, LSV, and ENS Paris-Saclay, France
Marco Muñiz   Aalborg University, Denmark
Yannic Noller   Humboldt-Universität zu Berlin, Germany
Kostiantyn Potomkin   Australian National University, Australia
Christian Schilling   IST Austria, Austria
Martin Spießl   LMU Munich, Germany

Steering Committee

Andreas Podelski   University of Freiburg, Germany
  (SC Chair)
Tino Cortesi   Università Ca' Foscari Venezia, Italy
Patrick Cousot   New York University, USA
Ruzica Piskac   Yale University, USA
Lenore Zuck   UIC, USA

Additional Reviewers

Asadi, Sepideh
Ashok, Pranav
Basset, Nicolas
Beillahi, Sidi Mohamed
Blicha, Martin
Chalupa, Marek
Chatterjee, Krishnendu
Chen, Yu-Ting
Chevalier, Marc
Dohrau, Jérôme
Eilers, Marco
Eisentraut, Julia
Genaim, Samir
Guo, Zheng

Haltermann, Jan
Hyvärinen, Antti
Janota, Mikoláš
Kröger, Paul
König, Jürgen
Lewchenko, Nicholas
Magnago, Enrico
Marescotti, Matteo
Meggendorfer, Tobias
Mutluergil, Suha Orhun
Obdržálek, Jan
Oortwijn, Wytse
Rabe, Markus N.
Raskin, Jean-Francois

Reynolds, Andrew
Richter, Cedric
Roveri, Marco
Sallinger, Sarah
Schneidewind, Clara

Schwerhoff, Malte
Toews, Manuel
Unadkat, Divyesh
van Dijk, Tom

Contents

Witnessing Secure Compilation

Kedar S. Namjoshi[1](✉) and Lucas M. Tabajara[2]

[1] Nokia Bell Labs, Murray Hill, NJ, USA
kedar.namjoshi@nokia-bell-labs.com
[2] Rice University, Houston, TX, USA
lucasmt@rice.edu

Abstract. Compiler optimizations may break or weaken the security properties of a source program. This work develops a translation validation methodology for secure compilation. A security property is expressed as an automaton operating over a bundle of program traces. A refinement proof scheme derived from a property automaton guarantees that the associated security property is preserved by a program transformation. This generalizes known refinement methods that apply only to specific security properties. In practice, the refinement relations ("security witnesses") are generated during compilation and validated independently with a refinement checker. This process is illustrated for common optimizations. Crucially, it is not necessary to formally verify the compiler implementation, which is infeasible for production compilers.

1 Introduction

Optimizing compilers are used to improve the run time performance of software programs. An optimization is correct if it preserves input-output behavior. A number of approaches, including automated testing (cf. [13,28]), translation validation (cf. [22,25,31]), and full mathematical proof (cf. [14]) have been developed to gain confidence in the correctness of compilation.

Correctness does not, however, guarantee the preservation of security properties. It is known that common optimizations may weaken or break security properties that hold of a source program (cf. [10,12]). A *secure compiler* is one that, in addition to being correct, also preserves security properties. This work provides a methodology for formally establishing secure compilation.

```
int x := read_secret_key();        int x := read_secret_key();
use(x);                            use(x);
x := 0; // clear secret data       skip; // dead store removed
rest_of_program();                 rest_of_program();
```

Fig. 1. Information leakage through optimization. Source program on left, optimized program on right.

D. Beyer and D. Zufferey (Eds.): VMCAI 2020, LNCS 11990, pp. 1–22, 2020.
https://doi.org/10.1007/978-3-030-39322-9_1

Figure 1 shows an instance of the *dead store removal* optimization. This optimization eliminates stores (i.e., assignment statements) that have no effect on the input-output behavior of the source program. If variable x is not referenced in `rest_of_program`, the optimization correctly replaces x := 0 with skip. The replacement, however, exposes the secret key stored in x to the rest of the program, which may be vulnerable to an attack that leaks this secret, thus breaking a vital security property of the source program.

Compiler directives can be used to prevent this optimization from taking effect. Such fixes are unsatisfactory and brittle, however, as they assume that programmers are aware of the potential security issue and understand enough of a compiler's workings to choose and correctly place the directives. Moreover, the directives may not be portable across compilers [29].

It is far more robust to build security preservation into a compiler. The classical approach constructs a mathematical proof of secure compilation, applicable to all source programs. This is highly challenging for at least two reasons. The first is that of proof complexity. Past experience shows that such proofs can take man-years of effort, even for compact, formally designed compilers such as CompCert [4,14]. Constructing such proofs is entirely infeasible for production compilers such as GCC or LLVM, which have millions of lines of code written in hard-to-formalize languages such as C and C++. The second reason is that, unlike correctness, secure compilation is not defined by a single property: each source program may have its own notion of security. Even standard properties such as non-interference and constant-time have subtle variants.

This work addresses both issues. To tackle the issue of proof complexity, we turn to *Translation Validation* [25] (TV), where correctness is established at compile time only for the program being compiled. We use a form of TV that we call "witnessing" [21,26], where a compiler is *designed* to generate a proof (also called a "certificate" or a "witness") of property preservation. For correctness properties, this proof takes the form of a refinement relation relating single traces of source and target programs. For security preservation, it is necessary to have refinement relations that relate "bundles" of k traces ($k \geq 1$) from the source and target programs.

To address the second issue, we show how to construct property-specific refinement proof rules. A security property is defined as an automaton operating on trace bundles, a flexible formulation that encompasses standard security properties such as non-interference and constant-time. The shape of the induced refinement proof rule follows the structure of the property automaton.

Refinement rules are known for the important security properties of non-interference [3,8,17] and constant-time execution [4]. We show that these rules arise easily and directly from an automaton-based formulation. As automata can express a large class of security properties, including those in the HyperLTL logic [6], the ability to derive refinement proof rules from automata considerably expands the reach of the refinement method.

We now discuss these contributions in more detail. We use a logic akin to HyperLTL [6] to describe security hyperproperties [7,27], which are sets of sets of sequences. A security property φ is represented by a formula of the shape $Q_1\pi_1, \ldots, Q_k\pi_k : \kappa(\pi_1, \ldots, \pi_k)$, where the π_i's represent traces over an observation alphabet, the Q_i's stand for either existential or universal quantification, and κ is a set of bundles of k program traces, represented by a Büchi automaton A_κ whose language is the *complement* of κ. The structure of this automaton is reflected in the derived refinement proof rule for φ.

A transformation from program S to program T preserves a security property φ if every violation of φ by T has a matching violation of φ by S. Intuitively, matching violations have the same inputs and are of the same type.

The first refinement scheme applies to purely universal properties, those of the form $\forall \pi_1 \ldots \forall \pi_k : \kappa(\pi_1, \ldots, \pi_k)$. The witness is a refinement relation between the product transition systems $A_\kappa \times T^k$ and $A_\kappa \times S^k$. The second refinement scheme applies to arbitrary properties ($\forall\exists$ alternation is used to express limits on an attacker's knowledge). Here, the witness is a *pair* of relations: one being a refinement relation between $A_\kappa \times T^k$ and $A_\kappa \times S^k$, as before; the second component is an input-preserving bisimulation relation between T and S.

We define refinement relations for several common compiler optimizations. Those relations are logically simple, ensuring that their validity can be checked automatically with SMT solvers. Crucially, the witnessing methodology does not require one to verify either the compiler implementation or the proof generator, considerably reducing the size of the trusted code base and making the methodology applicable to production compilers.

2 Example

To illustrate the approach, consider the following source program, S.

```
L1:  int x := read_secret_input();
L2:  int y := 42;
L3:  int z := y - 41;
L4:  x := x * (z - 1);
L5:
```

In this program, x stores the value of a secret input. As will be described in Sect. 3.1, this program can be modeled as a transition system. The states of the system can be considered to be pairs (α, ℓ). The first component $\alpha : \mathcal{V} \rightarrow \text{INT}$ is a partial assignment mapping variables in $\mathcal{V} = \{x, y, z\}$ to values in INT, the set of values that a variable of type int can contain. The second component $\ell \in \text{LOC} = \{L1, L2, L3, L4, L5\}$ is a location in the program, indicating the next instruction to be executed. In the initial state, α is empty and ℓ points to location L1. Transitions of the system update α according to the variable assignment instructions, and ℓ according to the control flow of the program.

To specify a notion of security for this program, two elements are necessary: an attack model describing what an attacker is assumed to be capable of observing (Sect. 3.2) and a security property over a set of program executions (Sect. 4). Suppose that an attacker can see the state of the memory at the end of the program, represented by the final value of α, and the security property expresses that for every two possible executions of the program, the final state of the memory must be the same, regardless of the secret input, thus guaranteeing that the secret does not leak. Unlike correctness properties, this is a two-trace property, which can be written as a formula of the shape $\forall \pi_1, \pi_2 : \kappa(\pi_1, \pi_2)$, where $\kappa(\pi_1, \pi_2)$ expresses that the memory at the end of the program is the same for traces π_1 and π_2 (cf. Section 4). The negation of κ can then be translated into an automaton A that detects violations of this property.

It is not hard to see that the program satisfies the security property, since y and z have constant values and at the end of the program x is 0. However, it is important to make sure that this property is preserved after the compiler performs optimizations that modify the source code. This can be done if the compiler can provide a witness in the form of a *refinement relation* (Sect. 5). Consider, for example, a compiler which performs constant folding, which simplifies expressions that can be inferred to be constant at compile time. The optimized program T would be:

```
L1: int x := read_secret_input();
L2: int y := 42;
L3: int z := 1;
L4: x := 0;
L5:
```

By taking the product of the automaton A with two copies of S or T (one for each trace π_i considered by κ), we obtain automata $A \times S^2$ and $A \times T^2$ whose language is the set of pairs of traces in each program that violates the property. Since this set is empty for S, it should be empty for T as well, a fact which can be certified by providing a refinement relation R between the state spaces of $A \times T^2$ and $A \times S^2$.

As the transformation considered here is very simple, the refinement relation is simple as well: it relates configurations (q, t_0, t_1) and (p, s_0, s_1) of the two spaces if the automaton states p, q are identical, corresponding program states t_0, s_0 and t_1, s_1 are also identical (including program location), and the variables in s_0 and s_1 have the constant values derived at their location (see Sect. 6 for details). The inductiveness of this relation over transitions of $A \times T^2$ and $A \times S^2$ can be easily checked with an SMT solver by using symbolic representations.

3   Background

We propose an abstract program and attack model defined in terms of labeled transition systems. We also define Büchi automata over bundles of program traces, which will be used in the encoding of security properties, and describe a product operation between programs and automata that will assist in the verification of program transformations.

Notation. Let Σ be an *alphabet*, i.e., a set of symbols, and let Γ be a subset of Σ. An infinite sequence $u = u(0), u(1), \ldots$, where $u(i) \in \Sigma$ for all i, is said to be a "sequence over Σ". For variables x, y denoting elements of Σ, the notation $x =_\Gamma y$ (read as "x and y agree on Γ") denotes the predicate where either x and y are both not in Γ, or x and y are both in Γ and $x = y$. For a sequence u over Σ, the notation $u|_\Gamma$ (read as "u projected to Γ") denotes the sub-sequence of u formed by elements in Γ. The operator $\mathsf{compress}(v) = v|_\Sigma$, applied to a sequence v over $\Sigma \cup \{\varepsilon\}$, removes all ε symbols in v to form a sequence over Σ. For a bundle of traces $w = (w_1, \ldots, w_k)$ where each trace is an infinite sequence of Σ, the operator $\mathsf{zip}(w)$ defines an infinite sequence over Σ^k obtained by choosing successive elements from each trace. In other words, $u = \mathsf{zip}(w)$ is defined by $u(i) = (w_1(i), \ldots, w_k(i))$, for all i. The operator unzip is its inverse.

3.1 Programs as Transition Systems

A program is represented as a transition system $S = (C, \Sigma, \iota, \rightarrow)$:

- C is a set of program states, or configurations;
- Σ is a set of observables, partitioned into input, I, and output, O;
- $\iota \in C$ is the initial configuration;
- $(\rightarrow) \subseteq C \times (\Sigma \cup \{\varepsilon\}) \times C$ is the transition relation.

Transitions labeled by input symbols in I represent instructions in the program that read input values, while transitions labeled by output symbols in O represent instructions that produce observable outputs. Transitions labeled by ε represent internal transitions where the state of the program changes without any observable effect.

An *execution* is an infinite sequence of transitions $(c_0, w_0, c_1)(c_1, w_1, c_2) \ldots \in (\rightarrow)^\omega$ such that $c_0 = \iota$ and adjacent transitions are connected as shown. (We may write this as the alternating sequence $c_0, w_0, c_1, w_1, c_2, \ldots$.) To ensure that every execution is infinite, we assume that $(\rightarrow)$ is left-total. To model programs with finite executions, we assume that the alphabet has a special termination symbol $\perp$, and add a transition $(c, \perp, c)$ for every final state c. We also assume that there is no infinite execution where the transition labels are always ε from some point on.

An execution $x = (c_0, w_0, c_1)(c_1, w_1, c_2) \ldots$ has an associated *trace*, denoted $\mathsf{trace}(x)$, given by the sequence $w_0, w_1, \ldots$ over $\Sigma \cup \{\varepsilon\}$. The compressed trace of execution x, $\mathsf{compress}(\mathsf{trace}(x))$, is denoted $\mathsf{ctrace}(x)$. The final assumption above ensures that the compressed trace of an infinite execution is also infinite. The sequence of states on an execution x is denoted $\mathsf{states}(x)$.

3.2 Attack Models as Extended Transition Systems

The choice of how to model a program as a transition system depends on the properties one would like to verify. For correctness, it is enough to use the standard input-output semantics of the program. To represent security properties, however, it is usually necessary to extend this base semantics to bring out interesting features. Such an extension typically adds auxiliary state and new observations needed to model an attack. For example, if an attack is based on program location, that is added as an auxiliary state component in the extended program semantics. Other examples of such structures are modeling a program stack as an array with a stack pointer, explicitly tracking the addresses of memory reads and writes, and distinguishing between cache and main memory accesses. These extended semantics are roughly analogous to the *leakage models* of [4]. The base transition system is extended to one with a new state space, denoted C_e; new observations, denoted O_e; and a new alphabet, Σ_e, which is the union of Σ with O_e. The extensions do not alter input-output behavior; formally, the original and extended systems are bisimular with respect to Σ.

3.3 Büchi Automata over Trace Bundles

A Büchi automaton over a bundle of k infinite traces over Σ_e is specified as $A = (Q, \Sigma_e^k, \iota, \Delta, F)$, where:

- Q is the state space of the automaton;
- Σ_e^k is the alphabet of the automaton, each element is a k-vector over Σ_e;
- $\iota \in Q$ is the initial state;
- $\Delta \subseteq Q \times \Sigma_e^k \times Q$ is the transition relation;
- $F \subseteq Q$ is the set of accepting states.

A *run* of A over a bundle of traces $t = (t_1, \ldots, t_k) \in (\Sigma^\omega)^k$ is an alternating sequence of states and symbols, of the form $(q_0 = \iota), a_0, q_1, a_1, q_2, \ldots$ where for each i, $a_i = (t_1(i), \ldots, t_k(i))$—that is, $a_0, a_1, \ldots$ equals $\mathsf{zip}(t)$—and (q_i, a_i, q_{i+1}) is in the transition relation Δ. The run is accepting if a state in F occurs infinitely often along it. The *language* accepted by A, denoted $\mathcal{L}(A)$, is the set of all k-trace bundles that are accepted by A.

Automaton-Program Product. In verification, the set of traces of a program that violate a property can be represented by an automaton that is the product of the program with an automaton for the negation of that property. Security properties may require analyzing multiple traces of a program; therefore, we define the analogous automaton as a product between an automaton A for the negation of the security property and the k-fold composition P^k of a program P. For simplicity, assume for now that the program P contains no ε-transitions. Programs with ε-transitions can be handled by converting A over Σ_e^k into a new automaton $\hat{A}$ over $(\Sigma_e \cup \{\varepsilon\})^k$ (see full version [20] for details).

Let $A = (Q^A, \Sigma_e^k, \Delta^A, \iota^A, F^A)$ be a Büchi automaton (over a k-trace bundle) and $P = (C, \Sigma_e, \iota, \rightarrow)$ be a program. The product of A and P^k, written $A \times P^k$, is a Büchi automaton $B = (Q^B, \Sigma_e^k, \Delta^B, \iota^B, F^B)$, where:

- $Q^B = Q^A \times C^k$;
- $\iota^B = (\iota^A, (\iota, \ldots, \iota))$;

- $((q, s), u, (q', s'))$ is in Δ^B if, and only if, (q, u, q') is in Δ^A, and (s_i, u_i, s_i') is in $(\rightarrow)$ for all i;
- (q, s) is in F^B iff q is in F^A.

Lemma 1. *Trace* $\mathsf{zip}(t_1, \ldots, t_k)$ *is in* $\mathcal{L}(A \times P^k)$ *if, and only if,* $\mathsf{zip}(t_1, \ldots, t_k)$ *is in* $\mathcal{L}(A)$ *and, for all* i, $t_i = \mathsf{trace}(x_i)$ *for some execution* x_i *of* P.

Bisimulations. For programs $S = (C^S, \Sigma_e, \iota^S, \rightarrow^S)$ and $T = (C^T, \Sigma_e, \iota^T, \rightarrow^T)$, and a subset I of Σ_e, a relation $B \subseteq C^T \times C^S$ is a *bisimulation* for I if:

1. $(\iota^T, \iota^S) \in B$;
2. For every (t, s) in B and (t, v, t') in $(\rightarrow^T)$ there is u and s' such that (s, u, s') is in $(\rightarrow^S)$ and $(t', s') \in B$ and $u =_I v$.
3. For every (t, s) in B and (s, u, s') in $(\rightarrow^S)$ there is v and t' such that (t, v, t') is in $(\rightarrow^T)$ and $(t', s') \in B$ and $u =_I v$.

4   Formulating Security Preservation

A temporal correctness property is expressed as a set of infinite traces. Many security properties can only be described as properties of *pairs* or *tuples* of traces. A standard example is that of *noninterference*, which models potential leakage of secret inputs: if two program traces differ only in secret inputs, they should be indistinguishable to an observer that can only view non-secret inputs and outputs. The general notion is that of a *hyperproperty* [7, 27], which is a set containing sets of infinite traces; a program satisfies a hyperproperty H if the set of all compressed traces of the program is an element of H. Linear Temporal Logic (LTL) is commonly used to express correctness properties. Our formulation of security properties is an extension of the logic HyperLTL, which can express common security properties including several variants of noninterference [6].

A security property φ has the form $(Q_1 \pi_1, \ldots, Q_n \pi_k : \kappa(\pi_1, \ldots, \pi_k))$, where the Q_i's are first-order quantifiers over trace variables, and κ is set of k-trace bundles, described by a Büchi automaton whose language is the *complement* of κ. This formulation borrows the crucial notion of trace quantification from HyperLTL, while generalizing it, as automata are more expressive than LTL, and atomic propositions may hold of k-vectors rather than on a single trace.

The satisfaction of property φ by a program P is defined in terms of the following finite two-player game, denoted $\mathcal{G}(P, \varphi)$. The protagonist, Alice, chooses an execution of P for each existential quantifier position, while the antagonist, Bob, chooses an execution of P at each universal quantifier position. The choices are made in sequence, from the outermost to the innermost quantifier. A play of this game is a maximal sequence of choices. The outcome of a play is thus a "bundle" of program executions, say $\sigma = (\sigma_1, \ldots, \sigma_k)$. This induces a corresponding bundle of compressed traces, $t = (t_1, \ldots, t_k)$, where $t_i = \mathsf{ctrace}(\sigma_i)$ for each i. This play is a win for Alice if t satisfies κ and a win for Bob otherwise.

A *strategy* for Bob is a function, say ξ, that defines a non-empty set of executions for positions i where Q_i is a universal quantifier, in terms of the earlier choices $\sigma_1, \ldots, \sigma_{i-1}$; the choice of σ_i is from this set. A strategy for Alice is defined symmetrically. A strategy is *winning* for player X if every play following the strategy is a win for X. This game is determined, in that for any program P one of the players has a winning strategy. Satisfaction of a security property is defined by the following.

Definition 1. *Program P satisfies a security property φ, written $\models_P \varphi$, if the protagonist has a winning strategy in the game $\mathcal{G}(P, \varphi)$.*

4.1   Secure Program Transformation

Let $S = (C^S, \Sigma_e, \iota^S, \rightarrow^S)$ be the transition system representing the original *source* program and let $T = (C^T, \Sigma_e, \iota^T, \rightarrow^T)$ be the transition system for the transformed *target* program. Any notion of secure transformation must imply the preservation property that if S satisfies φ and the transformation from S to T is secure for φ then T also satisfies φ.

Preservation in itself is, however, too weak to serve as a definition of secure transformation. Consider the transformation shown in Fig. 1, with use(x) defined so that it terminates execution if the secret key x is invalid. As the source program violates non-interference by leaking the validity of the key, the transformation would be trivially secure if the preservation property is taken as the definition of secure transformation. But that conclusion is wrong: the leak introduced in the target program is clearly different and of a more serious nature, as the entire secret key is now vulnerable to attack.

This analysis prompts the formulation of a stronger principle for secure transformation. (Similar principles have been discussed in the literature, e.g., [11].) The intuition is that every instance and type of violation in T should have a matching instance and type of violation in S. To represent different types of violations, we suppose that the negated property is represented by a collection of automata, each checking for a specific type of violation.

Definition 2. *A strategy ξ^S for the antagonist in $\mathcal{G}(S, \varphi)$ (representing a violation in S) matches a strategy ξ^T for the antagonist in game $\mathcal{G}(T, \varphi)$ (representing a violation in T) if for every maximal play $u = u_1, \ldots, u_k$ following ξ^T, there is a maximal play $v = v_1, \ldots, v_k$ following ξ^S such that (1) the two plays are input-equivalent, i.e., $u_i|_I = v_i|_I$ for all i, and (2) if u is accepted by the m-th automaton for the negated property, then v is accepted by the same automaton.*

Definition 3. *A transformation from S to T preserves security property φ if for every winning strategy for the antagonist in the game $\mathcal{G}(T, \varphi)$, there is a matching winning strategy for the antagonist in the game $\mathcal{G}(S, \varphi)$.*

As an immediate consequence, we have the preservation property.

Theorem 1. *If a transformation from S to T preserves security property φ and if S satisfies φ, then T satisfies φ.*

In the important case where the security property is purely universal, of the form $\forall \pi_1, \ldots, \forall \pi_k : \kappa(\pi_1, \ldots, \pi_k)$, a winning strategy for the antagonist is simply a bundle of k traces, representing an assignment to $\pi_1, \ldots, \pi_k$ that falsifies κ.

In the rest of the paper, we consider φ to be specified by a single automaton rather than a collection, to avoid notational clutter.

5 Refinement for Preservation of Universal Properties

We define an automaton-based refinement scheme that is sound for purely-universal properties φ, of the form $(\forall \pi_1, \ldots, \forall \pi_k : \kappa(\pi_1, \ldots, \pi_k))$. In Sect. 8, this is generalized to properties with arbitrary quantifier prefixes. We assume for simplicity that programs S and T have no ε-transitions; we discuss how to remove this assumption at the end of the section. An automaton-based refinement scheme for preservation of φ is defined below.

Definition 4. *Let S, T be programs over the same alphabet, Σ_e, and A be a Büchi automaton over Σ_e^k. Let I be a subset of Σ_e. A relation $R \subseteq (Q^A \times (C^T)^k) \times (Q^A \times (C^S)^k)$ is a* refinement relation *from $A \times T^k$ to $A \times S^k$ for I if*

1. *Initial configurations are related, i.e., $((\iota^A, \iota^{T^k}), (\iota^A, \iota^{S^k}))$ is in R, and*
2. *Related states have matching transitions. That is, if $((q, t), (p, s)) \in R$ and $((q, t), v, (q', t')) \in \Delta^{A \times T^k}$, there are u, p', and s' such that the following hold:*
   (a) *$((p, s), u, (p', s'))$ is a transition in $\Delta^{A \times S^k}$;*
   (b) *u and v agree on I, that is, $u_i =_I v_i$ for all i;*
   (c) *the successor configurations are related, i.e., $((q', t'), (p', s')) \in R$; and*
   (d) *acceptance is preserved, i.e., if $q' \in F$ then $p' \in F$.*

Lemma 2. *If there exists a refinement from $A \times T^k$ to $A \times S^k$ then, for every sequence v in $\mathcal{L}(A \times T^k)$, there is a sequence u in $\mathcal{L}(A \times S^k)$ such that u and v are input-equivalent.*

Theorem 2 (Universal Refinement). *Let $\varphi = (\forall \pi_1, \ldots, \pi_k : \kappa(\pi_1, \ldots, \pi_k))$ be a universal security property; S and T be programs over a common alphabet $\Sigma_e = \Sigma \cup O_e$; $A = (Q, \Sigma_e^k, \iota, \Delta, F)$ be an automaton for the negation of κ; and $R \subseteq (Q \times (C^T)^k) \times (Q \times (C^S)^k)$ be a refinement relation from $A \times T^k$ to $A \times S^k$ for I. Then, the transformation from S to T preserves φ.*

Proof. A violation of φ by T is given by a bundle of executions of T that violates κ. We show that there is an input-equivalent bundle of executions of S that also violates κ. Let $x = (x_1, \ldots, x_k)$ be a bundle of executions of T that does not satisfy κ. By Lemma 1, $v = \mathsf{zip}(\mathsf{trace}(x_1), \ldots, \mathsf{trace}(x_k))$ is accepted by $A \times T^k$. By Lemma 2, there is a sequence u accepted by $A \times S^k$ that is input-equivalent to v. Again by Lemma 1, there is a bundle of executions $y = (y_1, \ldots, y_k)$ of S such that $u = \mathsf{zip}(\mathsf{trace}(y_1), \ldots, \mathsf{trace}(y_k))$ and y violates κ. As u and v are input equivalent, $\mathsf{trace}(x_i)$ and $\mathsf{trace}(y_i)$ are input-equivalent for all i, as required. $\square$

The refinement proof rule for universal properties is implicit: a witness is a relation R from $A \times T^k$ to $A \times S^k$; this is valid if it satisfies the conditions set out in Definition 4. The theorem establishes the soundness of this proof rule. Examples of witnesses for specific compiler transformations are given in Sect. 6, which also discusses SMT-based checking of the proof requirements.

To handle programs that include ε-transitions, we can convert the automaton A over Σ_e^k into a *buffering automaton* $\hat{A}$ over $(\Sigma_e \cup \{\varepsilon\})^k$, such that $\hat{A}$ accepts $\mathsf{zip}(v_1, \ldots, v_k)$ iff A accepts $\mathsf{zip}(\mathsf{compress}(v_1), \ldots, \mathsf{compress}(v_k))$. The refinement is then defined over $\hat{A} \times S^k$ and $\hat{A} \times T^k$. Details can be found in the full version [20]. Another useful extension is the addition of *stuttering*, which can be necessary for example when a transformation removes instructions. Stuttering relaxes Definition 4 to allow multiple transitions on the source to match a single transition on the target, or vice-versa. This is a standard technique for verification [5] and one-step formulations suitable for SMT solvers are known (cf. [14, 18]).

6 Checking Transformation Security

In this section, we formulate the general construction of an SMT formula for the correctness of a given refinement relation. We then show how to express a refinement relation for several common compiler optimizations.

6.1 Refinement Checking with SMT Solvers

Assume that the refinement relation R, the transition relations Δ, $(\rightarrow_T)$ and $(\rightarrow_S)$ and the set of accepting states F are described by SMT formulas over variables ranging over states and alphabet symbols.

To verify that the formula R is indeed a refinement, we perform an inductive check following Definition 4. To prove the base case, which says that the initial states of $A \times T^k$ and $A \times S^k$ are related by R, we simply evaluate the formula on the initial states. The proof of the inductive step requires establishing that R is closed under automaton transitions. This can be expressed by an SMT query of the shape $(\forall q^T, q^S, p^T, t, s, t', \sigma^T : (\exists \sigma^S, p^S, s' : \varphi_1 \rightarrow \varphi_2))$, where:

$$\varphi_1 \equiv R((q^T, t), (q^S, s)) \wedge \Delta(q^T, \sigma^T, p^T) \wedge \bigwedge_{i=1}^{k} (t_i \xrightarrow{\sigma_i^T}_T t_i')$$

$$\varphi_2 \equiv \Delta(q^S, \sigma^S, p^S) \wedge \bigwedge_{i=1}^{k} (s_i \xrightarrow{\sigma_i^S}_S s_i') \wedge \bigwedge_{i=1}^{k} (\sigma_i^T =_I \sigma_i^S)$$
$$\wedge R((p^T, t'), (p^S, s')) \wedge (F(p^T) \rightarrow F(p^S))$$

This formula has a quantifier alternation, which is difficult for SMT solvers to handle. It can be reduced to a quantifier-free form by providing Skolem functions from the universal to the existential variables. We expect the compiler to generate these functions as part of the witness generation mechanism.

As we will see in the examples below, in many cases the compiler can choose Skolem functions that are simple enough so that the validity of the formula can be verified using only equality reasoning, making it unnecessary to even expand the definitions of Δ and F. The general expectation is that a compiler writer must have a proof in mind for each optimization and should therefore be able to provide the Skolem functions necessary to establish refinement.

6.2   Refinement Relations for Compiler Optimizations

We consider three common optimizations below. In addition, further examples for *dead-branch elimination, expression flattening, loop peeling* and *register spilling* can be found in the full version [20]. All transformations are based on the examples in [4].

Example 1: Constant Folding. Section 2 presented an example of a program transformation by constant folding. We now proceed to show how a refinement relation can be defined to serve as a witness for the security of this transformation, so its validity can be checked using an SMT solver as described above.

Recall that states of S and T are of the form (α, ℓ), where $\alpha : \mathcal{V} \to \text{INT}$ and $\ell \in \text{LOC}$. Then, R can be expressed by the following formula over states q^T, q^S of the automaton A and states t of T^k and s of S^k, where $t_i = (\alpha_i^T, \ell_i^T)$:

$$(q^T = q^S) \wedge (t = s) \wedge \bigwedge_{i=1}^{k} (\ell_i^T = \text{L3} \to \alpha_i^T(\mathbf{y}) = 42)$$

$$\wedge \bigwedge_{i=1}^{k} (\ell_i^T = \text{L4} \to \alpha_i^T(\mathbf{z}) = 1) \wedge \bigwedge_{i=1}^{k} (\ell_i^T = \text{L5} \to \alpha_i^T(\mathbf{x}) = 0)$$

The final terms express known constant values, necessary to establish inductiveness. In general, if the transformation relies on the fact that at location ℓ variable v has constant value c, the constraint $\bigwedge_{i=1}^{k}(\ell_i^T = \ell \to \alpha_i^T(v) = c)$ is added to R. Since this is a simple transformation, equality between states is all that is needed to establish a refinement.

R can be checked using the SMT query described in Sect. 6.1. For this transformation, the compiler can choose Skolem functions that assign $\sigma^S = \sigma^T$ and $p^S = p^T$. In this case, from $(q^T = q^S)$ (given by the refinement relation) and $\Delta(q^T, \sigma^T, p^T)$ the solver can automatically infer $\Delta(q^S, \sigma^S, p^S)$, $(\sigma_i^T =_I \sigma_i^S)$ and $F(p^T) \to F(p^S)$ using only equality reasoning. Therefore, the refinement check is *independent* of the security property. This applies to several other optimizations as well, as the reasons for preserving security are usually simple.

Example 2: Common-Branch Factorization. Common-branch factorization is a program optimization applied to conditional blocks where the instructions at the beginning of the *then* and *else* blocks are the same. If the condition does not depend on a variable modified by the common instruction, this instruction can be moved outside of the conditional. Consider for example:

```
// Source program S              // Target program T
L1: if (j < arr_size) {          L1: a := arr[0];
L2:     a := arr[0];             L2: if (j < arr_size) {
L3:     b := arr[j];             L3:     b := arr[j];
L4: } else {                     L4: } else {
L5:     a := arr[0];             L5:
L6:     b := arr[arr_size-1];    L6:     b := arr[arr_size-1];
L7: }                            L7: }
```

Suppose that the attack model allows the attacker to observe memory accesses, represented by the index j of every array access arr[j]. We assume that other variables are stored in registers rather than memory (see full version [20] for a discussion on register spilling). Under this attack model the compressed traces produced by T are identical to the ones of S, therefore the transformation is secure regardless of the security property φ. However, because the order of instructions is different, a more complex refinement relation R is needed, compared to constant folding:

$$((t = s) \wedge (q^T = q^S)) \vee \bigwedge_{i=1}^{k} ((\ell_i^T = L2)$$
$$\wedge ((\alpha_i^S(j) < \alpha_i^S(\text{arr\_size})) ? (\ell_i^S = L2) : (\ell_i^S = L5))$$
$$\wedge (\alpha_i^T = \alpha_i^S[a := \text{arr}[0]]) \wedge \Delta(q^S, (0, \ldots, 0), q^T))$$

The refinement relation above expresses that the states of the programs and the automata are identical except when T has executed the factored-out instruction but S has not. At that point, T is at location $L2$ and S is either at location $L2$ or $L5$, depending on how the guard was evaluated. It is necessary for R to know that the location of S depends on the evaluation of the guard, so that it can verify that at the next step T will follow the same branch. The states of $\hat{A} \times S^k$ and $\hat{A} \times T^k$ are then related by saying that after updating a := arr[0] on every track of S the two states are identical. (The notation $\alpha[x := e]$ denotes the state α' that is identical to α except at x, where its value is given by $\alpha(e)$.) As this instruction produces an observation representing the index of the array access, the states of the automata are related by $\Delta(q^S, (0, \ldots, 0), q^T)$, indicating that the access has been observed by $\hat{A} \times T^k$ but not yet by $\hat{A} \times S^k$.

Example 3: Switching Instructions. This optimization switches two sequential instructions if the compiler can guarantee that the program's behavior will not change. For example, consider the following source and target programs:

```
// Source program S                    // Target program T
L1: int a[10], b[10], j;               L1: int a[10], b[10], j;
L2: a[0] := secret_input();            L2: a[0] := secret_input();
L3: b[0] := secret_input();            L3: b[0] := secret_input();
L4: for (j:=1; j<10; j++) {            L4: for (j:=1; j<10; j++) {
L5:     a[j] := b[j-1];                L5:     b[j] := a[j-1];
L6:     b[j] := a[j-1];                L6:     a[j] := b[j-1];
L7:     public_output(j);              L7:     public_output(j);
L8: }                                  L8: }
```

The traces produced by T and S have identical public outputs. Therefore, a refinement relation for this pair of programs can be given by the following formula, regardless of the security property under verification:

$$(q^S = q^T) \wedge \bigwedge_{i=1}^{k} ((\ell_i^S = \ell_i^T) \wedge (\ell_i^S \neq \text{L6} \rightarrow \alpha_i^S = \alpha_i^T)$$
$$\wedge \, (\ell_i^S = \text{L6} \rightarrow \alpha_i^S[\text{b[j]} := \text{a[j-1]}] = \alpha_i^T[\text{a[j]} := \text{b[j-1]}]))$$

The formula expresses that the state of the source and target programs is the same except between executing the two switched instructions. At that point, the state of the two programs is related by saying that after executing the second instruction in each of the programs they will again have the same state.

More generally, a similar refinement relation can be used for any source-target pair that satisfies the assumptions that (a) neither of the switched instructions produces an observable output, and (b) after both switched instructions are executed, the state of the two programs is always the same. All that is necessary in this case is to replace L6 by the appropriate location ℓ_{switch}^S where the switch happens and $\alpha_i^S[\text{b[j]} := \text{a[j-1]}] = \alpha_i^T[\text{a[j]} := \text{b[j-1]}]$ by an appropriate formula $\delta(\alpha_i^S, \alpha_i^T)$ describing the relationship between the states of the two programs at that location.

If the instructions being switched do produce observations, setting up the refinement relation becomes harder. This is due to the fact that the relationship $(q^S = q^T)$ might not hold in location ℓ_{switch}^S, but expressing the true relationship between q^S and q^T is complex and might require knowledge of the state of all copies of S and T at once. In general, reordering transformations require the addition of history variables to set up an inductive refinement relation. Details can be found in the full version [20].

7   Connections to Existing Proof Rules

We establish connections to known proof rules for preservation of the non-interference [3,8,17] and constant-time [4] properties. We show that under the assumptions of those rules, there is a simple and direct definition of a relation that meets the automaton-based refinement conditions for automata representing these properties. The automaton-based refinement method is thus general enough to serve as a uniform replacement for the specific proof methods.

7.1   Constant Time

We first consider the lockstep CT-simulation proof rule introduced in [4] to show preservation of the constant-time property. For lack of space, we refer the reader to the original paper for the precise definitions of observational non-interference (Definition 1), constant-time as observational non-interference (Definition 4), lockstep simulation (Definition 5, denoted $\approx$), and lockstep CT-simulation (Definition 6, denoted $(\equiv_S, \equiv_C)$).

We do make two minor adjustments to better fit the automaton notion, which is based on trace rather than state properties. First, we add a dummy initial source state $\hat{S}(i)$ with a transition with input label i to the actual initial state $S(i)$; and similarly for the target program, C. Secondly, we assume that a final state has a self-loop with a special transition label, $\perp$. Then the condition $(b \in S_f \leftrightarrow b' \in S_f)$ from Definition 1 in [4] is covered by the (existing) label equality $t = t'$. With these changes, the observational non-interference property can be represented in negated form by the automaton shown in Fig. 2, which simply looks for a sequence starting with an initial pair of input values satisfying ϕ and ending in unequal transition labels. The states are I (initial), S (sink), M (mid), and F (fail), which is also the accepting state.

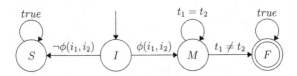

Fig. 2. A Büchi automaton for the negation of the constant-time property.

We now define the automaton-based relation, using the notation in Theorem 1 of [4]. Define relation R by $(q, \alpha, \alpha') R (p, a, a')$ if $a \approx \alpha$, $a' \approx \alpha'$, and

1. $p = F$, i.e., p is the fail state, or
2. $p = q = S$, or
3. $p = q = I$, and $\alpha = \hat{C}(i)$, $\alpha' = \hat{C}(i')$, $a = \hat{S}(i)$, $a = \hat{S}(i')$, for some i, i', or
4. $p = q = M$, and $\alpha \equiv_C \alpha'$, and $a \equiv_S a'$.

Theorem 3. *If $(\equiv_S, \equiv_C)$ is a lockstep CT-simulation with respect to the lockstep simulation $\approx$, the relation R is a valid refinement relation.*

Proof. Every initial state of $\mathcal{A} \times C^2$ has a related initial state in $\mathcal{A} \times S^2$. As related configurations are pairwise connected by $\approx$, which is a simulation, it follows that any pairwise transition from a C-configuration is matched by a pairwise transition from the related S-configuration, producing states b, b' and β, β' that are pointwise related by $\approx$. These transitions have identical input labels, as the only transitions with input labels are those from the dummy initial states.

The remaining question is whether the successor configurations are connected by R. We reason by cases.

First, if $p = F$, then the successor p' is also F. Hence, the successor configurations are related. This is also true of the second condition, where $p = q = S$, as the successor states are $p' = q' = S$.

If $p = q = I$ the successor states are $\beta = C(i), \beta' = C(i')$ and $b = S(i), b' = S(i')$, and the successor automaton state is either $p' = q' = S$, if $\phi(i, i')$ does not hold, or $p' = q' = M$, if it does. In the first possibility, the successor configurations are related by the second condition; in the second, they are related by the final condition, as $C(i) \equiv_C C(i')$ and $S(i) \equiv_S S(i')$ hold if $\phi(i, i')$ does [Definition 6 of [4]].

Finally, consider the interesting case where $p = q = M$. Let τ, τ' be the transition labels on the pairwise transition in C, and let t, t' be the labels on the corresponding pairwise transition in S. We consider two cases:

(1) Suppose $t \neq t'$. Then $p' = F$ and the successor configurations are related, regardless of q'.
(2) Otherwise, $t = t'$ and $p' = M$. By CT-simulation [Definition 6 of [4]: $a \equiv_S a'$ and $\alpha \equiv_C \alpha'$ by the relation R], it follows that $b \equiv_S b'$ and $\beta \equiv_C \beta'$ hold, and $\tau = \tau'$. Thus, the successor automaton state on the C-side is $q' = M$ and the successor configurations are related by the final condition.

This completes the case analysis. Finally, the definition of R implies that if $q = F$ then $p = F$, as required.

$\square$

7.2   Non-Interference

Refinement-based proof rules for preservation of non-interference have been introduced in [3,8,17]. The rules are not identical but are substantially similar in nature, providing conditions under which an ordinary simulation relation, $\prec$, between programs C and S implies preservation of non-interference. We choose the rule from [8], which requires, in addition to the requirement that $\prec$ is a simulation preserving input and output events, that (a) A final state of C is related by $\prec$ only to a final state of S (precisely, both are final or both non-final), and (b) If $t_0 \prec s_0$ and $t_1 \prec s_1$ hold, and all states are either initial or final, then the low variables of t_0 and t_1 are equal iff the low variables of s_0 and s_1 are equal.

We make two minor adjustments to better fit the automaton notion, which is based on trace rather than state properties. First, we add a dummy initial source state $\hat{S}(i)$ with a transition that exposes the value of local variables and moves to the actual initial state $S(i)$ (i is the secret input); and similarly for the target program, C. Secondly, we assume that a final state has a self-loop with a special transition label that exposes the value of local variables on termination. With these changes, the negated non-interference can be represented by the automaton shown in Fig. 3. It accepts an pair of execution traces if, and only if, initially the low-variables on the two traces have identical values, and either the corresponding outputs differ at some point, or final values of the low-variables are different. (The transition conditions are written as Boolean predicates which is a readable notation for describing a set of pairs of events; e.g., the $Low_1 \neq Low_2$ transition from state I represents the set of pairs (a, b) where a is the $init(Low = i)$ event, b is the $init(Low = j)$ event, and $i \neq j$.)

Define the automaton-based relation R by $(q, t_0, t_1) R(p, s_0, s_1)$ if $p = q$ and $t_0 \prec s_0$ and $t_1 \prec s_1$. We have the following theorem.

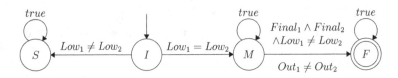

Fig. 3. A Büchi automaton for the negation of the non-interference property.

Theorem 4. *If the simulation relation $\prec$ between C and S satisfies the additional properties needed to preserve non-interference, then R is a refinement.*

Proof. Consider $(q, t_0, t_1)R(p, s_0, s_1)$. As $\prec$ is a simulation, for any joint transition from (t_0, t_1) to (t_0', t_1'), there is a joint transition from (s_0, s_1) to (s_0', s_1') such that $t_0' \prec s_0'$ and $t_1' \prec s_1'$ holds. This transition preserves input and output values, as $\prec$ is an input-output preserving simulation.

We have only to establish that the automaton transitions also match up. If the automaton state is either F or S, the resulting state is the same, so by the refinement relation, we have $p' = p = q = q'$.

Consider $q = I$. If $q' = S$ then the values of the low variables in t_0, t_1 differ; in which case, by condition (b), those values differ in s_0, s_1 as well, so p' is also S. Similarly, if $q' = M$, then $p' = M$.

Consider $q = M$. If $q' = F$ then either (1) t_0, t_1 are both final states and the values of the low variables differ, or (2) the outputs of the transitions from t_0, t_1 to t_0', t_1' differ. In case (1), by condition (a), s_0, s_1 are also final states, and therefore by condition (b) the values of the low variables differ in s_0, s_1 as well, so p' is also F. In case (2) the outputs of the transitions from t_0, t_1 to t_0', t_1' differ; in which case, as $\prec$ preserves outputs, this is true also of the transition from s_0, s_1 to s_0', s_1', so p' is also F. If $q' = M$ then, since $p = M$ and M has a self-loop on *true*, then p' can just be chosen to be M as well.

Finally, by the relation R, if $q = F$, the accepting state, then $p = F$ as well. This completes the case analysis and the proof.

$\square$

8   Witnessing General Security Properties

The notion of refinement presented in Sect. 5 suffices for universal hyperproperties, as in that case a violation corresponds to a bundle of traces rejected by the automaton. Although many important hyperproperties are universal in nature, some require quantifier alternation. One example is *generalized noninterference*, as formalized in [6], which says that for every two traces of a program, there is a third trace that has the same high inputs as the first but is indistinguishable from the second to a low-clearance individual. A violation for such hyperproperties, as defined in Sect. 4, is not simply a bundle of traces, but rather a winning strategy for the antagonist in the corresponding game. A refinement relation does not suffice to match winning strategies. Therefore, we introduce an additional input-equivalent bisimulation B from T to S, which is used in a back-and-forth manner to construct a matching winning strategy for the antagonist in $\mathcal{G}(S, \varphi)$ from any winning strategy for the antagonist in $\mathcal{G}(T, \varphi)$.

A bisimulation B ensures, by induction, that any infinite execution in T has an input-equivalent execution in S, and vice-versa. For an execution x of T, we use $B(x)$ to denote the non-empty set of input-equivalent executions in S induced by B. The symmetric notion, $B^{-1}(y)$, refers to input-equivalent executions in T induced by B for an execution y of S.

Definition 5. *Let ξ^T be a strategy for the antagonist in $\mathcal{G}(T, \varphi)$ and B be a bisimulation between T and S. Then, the strategy $\xi^S = \mathcal{S}(\xi^T, B)$ for the antagonist in $\mathcal{G}(S, \varphi)$ proceeds in the following way to produce a play $(y_1, \ldots, y_k)$:*

- *For every i such that π_i is existentially quantified, let y_i be chosen by the protagonist in $\mathcal{G}(S, \varphi)$. Choose an input-equivalent execution x_i from $B^{-1}(y_i)$;*
- *For every i such that π_i is universally quantified, choose x_i in T from $\xi^T(x_1, \ldots, x_{i-1})$ and choose y_i from $B(x_i)$.*

Thus, the bisimulation helps define a strategy ξ^S to match a winning antagonist strategy ξ^T in T. We can establish that this strategy is winning for the antagonist in S in two different ways. First, we do so under the assumption that S and T are *input-deterministic*, i.e., any two executions of the program with the same input sequence have the same observation sequence. This is a reasonable assumption, covering sequential programs with purely deterministic actions.

Theorem 5. *Let S and T be input-deterministic programs over the same input alphabet I. Let φ be a general security property with automaton A representing the negation of its kernel κ. If there exists (1) a bisimulation B from T to S, and (2) a refinement relation R from $A \times T^k$ to $A \times S^k$ for I, then T securely refines S for φ.*

Proof. We have to show, from Definition 3, that for any winning strategy ξ^T for the antagonist in $\mathcal{G}(T, \varphi)$, there is a matching winning strategy ξ^S in $\mathcal{G}(S, \varphi)$. Let $\xi^S = \mathcal{S}(\xi^T, B)$. Let $y = (y_1, \ldots, y_k)$ be the bundle of executions resulting from a play following the strategy ξ^S, and $x = (x_1, \ldots, x_k)$ the corresponding bundle resulting from ξ^T. By construction, y and x are input-equivalent.

Since ξ^T is a winning strategy, the trace of x is accepted by $A \times T^k$. Then, from the refinement R and Lemma 2, there is a bundle $z = (z_1, \ldots, z_k)$ accepted by $A \times S^k$ that is input-equivalent to x. Therefore, z is a win for the antagonist. Since z is input-equivalent to x, it is also input-equivalent to y. Input-determinism requires that z and y are identical, so y is also a win for the antagonist. Thus, ξ^S is a winning strategy for the antagonist in $\mathcal{G}(S, \varphi)$. □

If S and T are not input-deterministic, a new notion of refinement is defined that intertwines the automaton-based relation R with the bisimulation B. A relation $R \subseteq (Q^A \times (C^T)^k) \times (Q^A \times (C^S)^k)$ is a *refinement relation* from $A \times T^k$ to $A \times S^k$ for I *relative to* $B \subseteq C^T \times C^S$, if

1. $((\iota^A, \iota^{T^k}), (\iota^A, \iota^{S^k}))$ is in R and $(\iota_i^{T^k}, \iota_i^{S^k}) \in B$ for all i; and
2. If $((q, t), (p, s))$ is in R, (t_i, s_i) is in B for all i, $((q, t), v, (q', t'))$ is in $\Delta^{A \times T^k}$, (s, u, s') is in $(\to^{S^k})$, u and v agree on I, and $(t_i', s_i') \in B$, there is p' such that all of the following hold:
    (a) $((p, s), u, (p', s')) \in \Delta^{A \times S^k}$;
    (b) $((q', t'), (p', s')) \in R$;
    (c) if $q' \in F$ then $p' \in F$.

Refinement typically implies, as in Lemma 2, that a run in $A \times T^k$ is matched by some run in $A \times S^k$. The unusual refinement notion above instead considers already matching executions of T and S, and formulates an inductive condition under which a run of A on the T-execution is matched by a run on the S-execution. The result is the following theorem, establishing the new refinement rule, where the witness is the pair (R, B).

Theorem 6. *Let S and T be programs over the same input alphabet I. Let φ be a general security property with automaton A representing its kernel κ. If there exists (1) a bisimulation B from T to S, and (2) a relation R from $A \times T^k$ to $A \times S^k$ that is a refinement relative to B, then T securely refines S for φ.*

8.1   Checking General Refinement Relations

The main difference when checking security preservation of general hyperproperties, compared to the purely-universal properties handled in Sect. 5, is the necessity of the compiler to provide also the bisimulation B as part of the witness. The verifier must also check that B is a bisimulation, which can be performed inductively using SMT queries in a manner similar to the refinement check. If the language semantics guarantees input-determinism, then Theorem 5 holds and checking B and R separately is sufficient. Otherwise, the check for R described in Sect. 6.1 has to be modified to follow Theorem 6 to determine whether R is a refinement relative to B.

The optimizations discussed in Sect. 6 produce bisimular programs; the relation B in each case is defined as follows.

1. **Constant Folding:** $(t = s) \wedge (\ell^T = \text{L3} \to \alpha^T(\text{y}) = 42) \wedge (\ell^T = \text{L4} \to \alpha^T(\text{z}) = 1) \wedge (\ell^T = \text{L5} \to \alpha^T(\text{x}) = 0)$
2. **Common-Branch Factorization:** $(t = s) \vee ((\ell^T = \text{L2}) \wedge ((\alpha^S(\text{i}) < \alpha^S(\text{arr\_size}))\,?\,(\ell^S = \text{L2}) : (\ell^S = \text{L5})) \wedge (\alpha^T = \alpha^S[\text{a} := \text{arr[0]}]))$
3. **Switching Instructions:** $(\ell^S = \ell^T) \wedge (\ell^S \ne \text{L6} \to \alpha^S = \alpha^T) \wedge (\ell^S = \text{L6} \to \alpha^S[\text{b[j]} := \text{a[j-1]}] = \alpha^T[\text{a[j]} := \text{b[j-1]}])$

There are clear similarities between the bisimulations and the corresponding refinement relations defined in Sect. 6. When the transformation does not alter the observable behavior of a program, it is often the case that the refinement relation between $\hat{A} \times T^k$ and $\hat{A} \times S^k$ is essentially formed by the k-fold product of a bisimulation between T and S across the bundle of executions.

9   Discussion and Related Work

This work tackles the important problem of ensuring that the program transformations carried out by an optimizing compiler do not break vital security properties of the source program. We propose a methodology based on property-specific refinement rules, with the refinement relations (witnesses) being generated at compile time and validated independently by a generic refinement checker. This structure ensures that neither the code of the compiler nor the witness generator have to be formally verified in order to obtain a formally verifiable conclusion. It is thus eminently suited to production compilers, which are large and complex, and are written in hard-to-formalize languages such as C or C++.

The refinement rules are constructed from an automaton-theoretic definition of a security property. This construction applies to a broad range of security properties, including those specifiable in the HyperLTL logic [6]. When applied to automaton-based formulations of the non-interference and constant-time properties, the resulting proof rules are essentially identical to those developed in the literature in [3,8,17] for non-interference and in [4] for constant-time. Manna and Pnueli show in a beautiful paper [15] how to derive custom proof rules for deductive verification of an LTL property from an equivalent Büchi automaton; our constructions are inspired by this work.

Refinement witnesses are in a form that is composable: i.e., for a security property φ, if R is a refinement relation establishing a secure transformation from A to B, while R' witnesses a secure transformation from B to C, then the relational composition $R; R'$ witnesses a secure transformation from A to C. Thus, by composing witnesses for each compiler optimization, one obtains an end-to-end witness for the entire optimization pipeline.

Other approaches to secure compilation include full abstraction, proposed in [1] (cf. [23]), and trace-preserving compilation [24]. These are elegant formulations but difficult to check fully automatically, and are therefore not suitable for translation validation. The theory of hyperproperties [7] includes a definition of refinement in terms of language inclusion (i.e., T refines S if the language of T is a subset of the language of S), which implies that any subset-closed hyperproperty is preserved by this notion of refinement. Language inclusion is also not easily checkable and thus cannot be used for translation validation. The refinement theorem in this paper for universal properties (which are subset-closed) uses a tighter step-wise inductive check that is suitable for automated validation.

Translation validation through compiler-generated refinement relations was proposed in work on "Credible Compilation" by [16,26] and "Witnessing" by [21]. As the compiler and the witness generator do not require formal verification, the size of the trusted code base shrinks substantially. Witnessing also requires less effort than a full mathematical proof: as observed in [19], a mathematical correctness proof of SSA (Static Single Assignment) conversion in Coq is about 10,000 lines [30], while refinement checking can be implemented in around 1,500 lines of code; much of this code comprises a reusable witness validator.

Our work shows how to extend this concept, originally developed for correctness checking, to the preservation of a large class of security properties, with the following important distinction. Refinement relations for correctness preserve *all* linear-time properties defined over propositions common to both programs. This is necessary as a complete specification of correctness is usually not available in practice. On the other hand, security properties are likely to be known in advance (e.g., "do not leak secret keys"). This motivates our construction of property-specific refinement relations.

The refinement rules defined here implicitly require that a security specification apply equally well to the target and source programs. Thus, they are most applicable when the target and source languages and attack models are identical. That is the case in the optimization phase of a compiler, where a number of transformations are applied to code that remains within the same intermediate representation. To complete the picture, it is necessary to look more generally at transformations that convert a higher-level language (say LLVM bytecode) to a lower-level one (say x86 machine code). The so-called "attack surface" is then different, so it is necessary to incorporate a notion of *back-translation* of failures [9] in the refinement proof rules. How best to do so is an intriguing topic for future work.

Another question for future work is the completeness of the refinement rules. We have shown that a variety of common compiler transformations can be proved secure through logically simple refinement relations. The completeness question is whether *every* secure transformation has an associated stepwise refinement relation. In the case of correctness, this is a well-known theorem by Abadi and Lamport [2]. To the best of our knowledge, a corresponding theorem is not known for security hyperproperties.

A number of practical concerns must be addressed to implement this methodology. An important one is the development of a convenient notation for specifying the desired security properties at the source program level. It is also necessary to define how a security property is transformed through a program optimization. For instance, if a transformation introduces fresh variables, it is necessary to determine whether those variables are assigned a high or low security level for a non-interference property.

Acknowledgments. The authors were supported, in part, by NSF grant CCF-1563393 from the National Science Foundation. Any opinions, findings, and conclusions or recommendations expressed are those of the author(s) and do not necessarily reflect the views of the National Science Foundation. Kedar Namjoshi would like to acknowledge fruitful discussions during a Dagstuhl Seminar on Secure Compilation organized in May 2018.

References

1. Abadi, M.: Protection in programming-language translations. In: Vitek, J., Jensen, C.D. (eds.) Secure Internet Programming. LNCS, vol. 1603, pp. 19–34. Springer, Heidelberg (1999). https://doi.org/10.1007/3-540-48749-2_2

2. Abadi, M., Lamport, L.: The existence of refinement mappings. In: LICS 1988, pp. 165–175 (1988). https://doi.org/10.1109/LICS.1988.5115
3. de Amorim, A.A., et al.: A verified information-flow architecture. In: POPL 2014, pp. 165–178 (2014). https://doi.org/10.1145/2535838.2535839
4. Barthe, G., Grégoire, B., Laporte, V.: Secure compilation of side-channel counter-measures: the case of cryptographic "constant-time". In: CSF 2018, pp. 328–343 (2018). https://doi.org/10.1109/CSF.2018.00031
5. Browne, M.C., Clarke, E.M., Grumberg, O.: Characterizing finite Kripke structures in propositional temporal logic. Theor. Comput. Sci. **59**, 115–131 (1988). https://doi.org/10.1016/0304-3975(88)90098-9
6. Clarkson, M.R., Finkbeiner, B., Koleini, M., Micinski, K.K., Rabe, M.N., Sánchez, C.: Temporal logics for hyperproperties. In: Abadi, M., Kremer, S. (eds.) POST 2014. LNCS, vol. 8414, pp. 265–284. Springer, Heidelberg (2014). https://doi.org/10.1007/978-3-642-54792-8_15
7. Clarkson, M.R., Schneider, F.B.: Hyperproperties. In: CSF 2008, pp. 51–65 (2008). https://doi.org/10.1109/CSF.2008.7
8. Deng, C., Namjoshi, K.S.: Securing a compiler transformation. In: Rival, X. (ed.) SAS 2016. LNCS, vol. 9837, pp. 170–188. Springer, Heidelberg (2016). https://doi.org/10.1007/978-3-662-53413-7_9
9. Devriese, D., Patrignani, M., Piessens, F.: Fully-abstract compilation by approximate back-translation. In: POPL 2016, pp. 164–177 (2016). https://doi.org/10.1145/2837614.2837618
10. D'Silva, V., Payer, M., Song, D.X.: The correctness-security gap in compiler optimization. In: SPW 2015, pp. 73–87 (2015). https://doi.org/10.1109/SPW.2015.33
11. Fournet, C., Guernic, G.L., Rezk, T.: A security-preserving compiler for distributed programs: from information-flow policies to cryptographic mechanisms. In: CCS 2009, pp. 432–441 (2009). https://doi.org/10.1145/1653662.1653715
12. Howard, M.: When scrubbing secrets in memory doesn't work (2002). http://archive.cert.uni-stuttgart.de/bugtraq/2002/11/msg00046.html. Also https://cwe.mitre.org/data/definitions/14.html
13. Le, V., Afshari, M., Su, Z.: Compiler validation via equivalence modulo inputs. In: PLDI 2014, pp. 216–226 (2014). https://doi.org/10.1145/2594291.2594334
14. Leroy, X.: Formal certification of a compiler back-end or: programming a compiler with a proof assistant. In: POPL 2006, pp. 42–54 (2006). https://doi.org/10.1145/1111037.1111042
15. Manna, Z., Pnueli, A.: Specification and verification of concurrent programs by ∀-automata. In: Banieqbal, B., Barringer, H., Pnueli, A. (eds.) Temporal Logic in Specification. LNCS, vol. 398, pp. 124–164. Springer, Heidelberg (1989). https://doi.org/10.1007/3-540-51803-7_24
16. Marinov, D.: Credible compilation. Ph.D. thesis, Massachusetts Institute of Technology (2000)
17. Murray, T.C., Sison, R., Engelhardt, K.: COVERN: a logic for compositional verification of information flow control. In: EuroS&P 2018, pp. 16–30 (2018). https://doi.org/10.1109/EuroSP.2018.00010
18. Namjoshi, K.S.: A simple characterization of stuttering bisimulation. In: Ramesh, S., Sivakumar, G. (eds.) FSTTCS 1997. LNCS, vol. 1346, pp. 284–296. Springer, Heidelberg (1997). https://doi.org/10.1007/BFb0058037
19. Namjoshi, K.S.: Witnessing an SSA transformation. In: VeriSure Workshop, CAV (2014). https://kedar-namjoshi.github.io/papers/Namjoshi-VeriSure-CAV-2014.pdf

20. Namjoshi, K.S., Tabajara, L.M.: Witnessing Secure Compilation (2019). https://arxiv.org/abs/1911.05866
21. Namjoshi, K.S., Zuck, L.D.: Witnessing program transformations. In: Logozzo, F., Fähndrich, M. (eds.) SAS 2013. LNCS, vol. 7935, pp. 304–323. Springer, Heidelberg (2013). https://doi.org/10.1007/978-3-642-38856-9_17
22. Necula, G.: Translation validation of an optimizing compiler. In: (PLDI) 2000, pp. 83–95 (2000)
23. Patrignani, M., Ahmed, A., Clarke, D.: Formal approaches to secure compilation: a survey of fully abstract compilation and related work. ACM Comput. Surv. 51(6), 125:1–125:36 (2019). https://doi.org/10.1145/3280984
24. Patrignani, M., Garg, D.: Secure compilation and hyperproperty preservation. In: CSF 2017, pp. 392–404 (2017). https://doi.org/10.1109/CSF.2017.13
25. Pnueli, A., Shtrichman, O., Siegel, M.: The Code Validation Tool (CVT)- automatic verification of a compilation process. Softw. Tools Technol. Transf. 2(2), 192–201 (1998)
26. Rinard, M.: Credible compilation. Technical report. In: Proceedings of CC 2001: International Conference on Compiler Construction (1999)
27. Terauchi, T., Aiken, A.: Secure information flow as a safety problem. In: Hankin, C., Siveroni, I. (eds.) SAS 2005. LNCS, vol. 3672, pp. 352–367. Springer, Heidelberg (2005). https://doi.org/10.1007/11547662_24
28. Yang, X., Chen, Y., Eide, E., Regehr, J.: Finding and understanding bugs in C compilers. In: PLDI 2011, pp. 283–294 (2011). https://doi.org/10.1145/1993498.1993532
29. Yang, Z., Johannesmeyer, B., Olesen, A.T., Lerner, S., Levchenko, K.: Dead store elimination (still) considered harmful. In: USENIX Security 2017, pp. 1025–1040 (2017). https://www.usenix.org/conference/usenixsecurity17/technical-sessions/presentation/yang
30. Zhao, J., Nagarakatte, S., Martin, M.M.K., Zdancewic, S.: Formal verification of SSA-based optimizations for LLVM. In: PLDI 2013, pp. 175–186 (2013). https://doi.org/10.1145/2491956.2462164
31. Zuck, L.D., Pnueli, A., Goldberg, B.: VOC: a methodology for the translation validation of optimizing compilers. J. UCS 9(3), 223–247 (2003)

BackFlow: Backward Context-Sensitive Flow Reconstruction of Taint Analysis Results

Pietro Ferrara[1]([⊠]), Luca Olivieri[1,2], and Fausto Spoto[2]

[1] JuliaSoft SRL, Verona, Italy
pietro.ferrara@unive.it, luca.olivieri@juliasoft.com
[2] Università di Verona, Verona, Italy
fausto.spoto@univr.it

Abstract. Taint analysis detects if data coming from a source, such as user input, flows into a sink, such as an SQL query, unsanitized (not properly escaped). Both static and dynamic taint analyses have been widely applied to detect injection vulnerabilities in real world software. A main drawback of static analysis is that it could produce false alarms. In addition, it is extremely time-consuming to manually explain the flow of tainted data from the results of the analysis, to understand why a specific warning was raised. This paper formalizes BackFlow, a context-sensitive taint flow reconstructor that, starting from the results of a taint-analysis engine, reconstructs how tainted data flows inside the program and builds paths connecting sources to sinks. BackFlow has been implemented on Julia's static taint analysis. Experimental results on a set of standard benchmarks show that, when BackFlow produces a taint graph for an injection warning, then there is empirical evidence that such warning is a true alarm. Moreover BackFlow scales to real world programs.

1 Introduction

Software security vulnerabilities allow an attacker to perform unauthorized actions. In the last decade, hackers have widely exploited such vulnerabilities, in particular SQL injections and cross-site scripting (XSS), causing relevant damages. For instance, the Equifax data breach[1] relied on a command injection vulnerability. Hackers exploited this flaw to access data of hundreds of millions of Equifax customers, heavily impacting Equifax business and market value. Therefore, it is industrially relevant to *detect* and *prevent* such flaws and attacks.

Detection of cyber-attacks has been mostly based on run-time environments that monitor the system, in production, to discover anomalous situations. In this way, one discovers attacks based on the exploitation of software vulnerabilities, but also other types of attacks, such as denial-of-service through botnets.

---

[1] https://en.wikipedia.org/wiki/Equifax#May%E2%80%93July_2017_data_breach.

© Springer Nature Switzerland AG 2020
D. Beyer and D. Zufferey (Eds.): VMCAI 2020, LNCS 11990, pp. 23–43, 2020.
https://doi.org/10.1007/978-3-030-39322-9_2

```
                              var l, h
                              if h = true then          var l, h
    var l, h                      l := 3                if h = 1 then
    l := h                    else                          (* do some time−consuming work *)
                                  l := 42                   l := 0
       (a) Explicit flow
                                  (b) Implicit flow              (c) Side channel
```

Fig. 1. Different types of flows (from https://en.wikipedia.org/wiki/Information_flow_ (information_theory)).

For instance, the Mirai malware[2] exploited IoT devices with default credentials to gain administrative access to the device. The prevention of cyber-attacks has been also based on system safeguards, such as firewalls that block Internet traffic from and to malicious IP addresses; or on antivirus that detect and block malicious software running inside the system, that could be exploited by a hacker; or on the prevention of software vulnerabilities. In the latter case, two distinct approaches exist: *dynamic* analysis (notably, penetration testing [2]) runs the software as much pervasively as possible, in order to expose such vulnerabilities during the execution; *static* analysis, instead, builds a model of the program and detects patterns that might lead to security vulnerabilities.

Dynamic analysis does not produce false alarms: all reported vulnerabilities are real. However, it usually achieves limited coverage, since it cannot activate all possible run-time values. Static analysis, instead, can achieve high coverage, but at the price of precision. Namely, it might report false alarms that are not real flaws, since it must apply some forms of approximation to ensure the finiteness of the analysis. There exist two families of static analyzers: those based on *syntactic* reasoning, that operate locally on the abstract syntax tree of a code unit; and those based on *semantic* reasoning, that apply formal methods to approximate the overall structure of the code under analysis. The former might miss many real vulnerabilities and/or produce many false alarms, but typically scale to software of industrial size (between 100KLOCs and 1MLOCs); the latter can achieve full coverage, but are often slow or have limited precision.

Since security vulnerabilities, such as SQL injections and XSS, have heavy impact on a software system, semantic static analyzers attracted industrial attention. In particular, catching and fixing all possible software flaws before deployment is extremely valuable. Hence, the research community focused on these issues. In particular, information flow analyses [14,33] tackled the problem of tracking flows of information through a program. The problem was formalized as the detection of private information flowing into public channels. With the help of Fig. 1, where h and l represent secret and public variables, respectively, one can identify three main types of flows: (i) direct flows, when a secret variable is directly assigned to a public one (Fig. 1a); (ii) indirect flows, when the assignment of some public variable is performed in a branch of code whose execution is conditional on the value of a secret variable (Fig. 1b); and (iii) side channels,

---

[2] https://techcrunch.com/2016/10/10/hackers-release-source-code-for-a-powerful-ddos-app-called-mirai/.

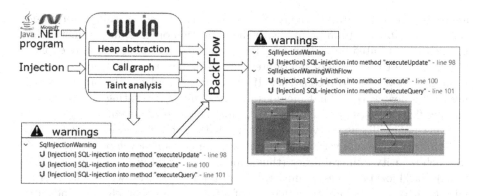

Fig. 2. The architecture of BackFlow.

where some observable property of the execution depends on the value of some secret variable (Fig. 1c).

All three types of flows are theoretically dangerous, since they could induce XSS, SQL injections (see for instance Fig. 7 of [7]) or leakages of sensitive data. However, in practice, hackers have rarely exploited implicit flows and side channels; moreover, their identification leads to very conservative results (too many false alarms). Therefore, *taint* analysis [3,8,28] focuses on explicit flows only, ignoring implicit flows and side channels. It has been applied to industrial software, both in dynamic and static flavor [36,41]. It checks if data coming from an untrusted source (such as user input or servlet parameters) flows, explicitly, into a trusted sink (such as the execution of an SQL query), unsanitized (that is, not correctly escaped). This analysis approximates values as Booleans (tainted/untainted), which helps scalability, since it does not require much memory and computational resources. However, it abstracts away precise information about the *exact source* of tainted data, and its *flow*.

1.1 Contribution

This paper introduces BackFlow, a new tool that reconstructs the flow of tainted data from sinks, backwards towards the sources, by building a complete *taint graph* from sources to sinks. BackFlow relies on a preliminary static taint analysis and on two standard semantic static analyses for heap abstraction and for callgraph construction. It builds a flow from a source of tainted data to a sink that receives such data. It does so in a *context-sensitive* way, that is, it considers under which circumstances the flow might exist, and discards unfeasible flows, under the information inferred by the semantic static analysis.

BackFlow has been implemented inside the Julia static analyzer [35], a semantic static analyzer for Java and C# programs, that already implements a static taint analysis [36], a call-graph construction and various heap abstractions. Figure 2 reports its overall architecture. Starting from a Java or .NET program, it first runs Julia's taint analysis. Such analysis requires to compute various heap abstractions (and in particular a creation point and a must aliasing analyses), and a call graph. The result is a set of (injection) warnings, for potentially vulnerable program points, with the indication of the sink parameter that is reached by tainted data. However, these warnings do not specify any explicative flow about the origin of the tainted data from a source. That flow is exactly what BackFlow tries to reconstruct. If successful, it replaces the original warning with a new warning that includes a *taint graph*, representing the previously missing flow. Otherwise, the original warning is left, unchanged.

This paper discusses two experiments with BackFlow. A first, *qualitative* experiment is the analysis of WebGoat, an application developed by OWASP to teach security vulnerabilities (thus containing several kinds of explicit injections). BackFlow produces a taint graph for all true positives, while it fails for all false positives. Therefore, the inference of a taint graph is an effective indicator of a true alarm[3]. A second, *quantitative* experiment is the analysis of a dozen standard benchmarks. BackFlow scales to these real world applications, by running in about a fifth of the time spent for the preliminary static taint analysis. The percentage of warnings for which BackFlow reconstructs a taint graph is smaller but comparable with that for WebGoat.

This paper is structured as follows. The rest of this section introduces a running example. Section 2 discusses related work and compares it to BackFlow. Section 3 formalizes BackFlow's approach. Section 4 describes the integration of BackFlow with Julia. Section 5 describes the implementation. Section 6 reports the experiments. Section 7 concludes.

1.2 Running Example

Figure 3 reports a minimal example that needs context-sensitive information in order to infer the correct flow of tainted data from a source to a sink. In this example, method source is assumed to yield tainted data that method sink should not receive. A sound static taint analyzer must issue a warning at line 11, since tainted data actually flows into sink there. A backward reconstructor then would look, from line 11, for assignments to w.f: it goes back to line 4 and then further backwards to the beginning of method set (line 3). It then queries the call graph to know where set might be called. This occurs at both lines 10 and 16, in both cases with

```
class Wrapper {                              1
  String f;                                  2
  void set(String f) {                       3
    this.f = f;                              4
  }                                          5
}                                            6
class Bugged {                               7
  void vulnerable() {                        8
    Wrapper w = new Wrapper();               9
    w.set(source());                        10
    sink(w.f);                              11
  }                                         12
}                                           13
class NotBugged {                           14
  void noise() {                            15
    new Wrapper().set(source());            16
  }                                         17
}                                           18
```

Fig. 3. Running example.

tainted data. However, a context-sensitive reconstructor should be able to discard the flow from line 16, since the receiver of the call to set, there, cannot be alias to w at line 11. Therefore, the only possible flow starts at line 10, goes to

---

[3] Note that this is an empirical result, since theoretically BackFlow might produce taint graphs for false alarms, and fail to produce taint graphs for true alarms.

the field assignment at line 4, continues with the field read at line 11, and ends with the sink call at the same line.

2   Related Work

Section 1 has already discussed different types of information flow analysis and taint analysis. This section discusses and compares to BackFlow the most representative static and dynamic analyses of programs, to detect security vulnerabilities and privacy leaks.

Information flow analysis has been widely applied to several programming languages. In the object-oriented context, JFlow [27] is possibly the most notable example. It is an extension of the Java programming language, that allows developers to add information flow annotations to the code, to classify variables into private or public. Then it statically checks such annotations, to discover if the value of a private variable can ever flow into a public variable. JFlow checks both implicit and explicit flows. SAILS [45] instead combines a generic information leakage analysis inside a generic static analyzer (Sample [10,17,18]) and applies this analysis to some Java benchmarks.

During the last decade, dynamic taint analysis has been widely exploited to detect, at run time, various types of security vulnerabilities and privacy leaks: the run-time environment gets augmented for tracking a Boolean mark for tainted variables, with low overhead. This augmentation can also be used to issue an alarm when a tainted value reaches a sink. Namely, TaintCheck [28] performs binary instrumentation to track tainted variables and detect vulnerabilities. Also Dytan [8] provides a generic framework for dynamic taint analysis and instantiates it to x86 executables. The dynamic taint analyzer Panorama [44] introduces the concept of *taint graphs*. For Panorama, these are very abstract, since they track how different executables propagate tainted data, but not through which exact statements. Comet [25] produces, instead, more concrete taint graphs, that represent how values in the heap or stack are affected by tainted data inside a single run-time state. BackFlow produces completely different taint graphs, that precisely represent how program statements propagate tainted data from a source to a sink.

Static taint analysis has been applied to different contexts and scenarios. During the last decade, web applications have been their most popular target, since security issues can have major impact on them. Pixy [24] applies a data flow analysis that detects XSS vulnerabilities in PHP code. Wasserman and Su [43] define a precise static taint analysis to detect SQL-injections, while JSA [39] uses dynamic information about the run-time context of a web application to reduce the rate of false alarms produced by static taint analysis. TAJ [41] applies an ad-hoc forward slicing technique to propagate tainted data. This tool produces a sort of taint graphs, but ignores dependencies through the heap, being based on the no-heap system dependence graph by Reps *et al.* [32].

There are also several tools that, starting from the results (that is, warnings) of a static analyzer, try to produce a witness through dynamic analysis or classify automatically true and false alarms. For instance, Check 'n' Crash [13] starts from the static checks performed by ESC/Java, builts a set of constraints that must hold to produce the error reported by a warning, and then produces concrete test cases to expose the error. Aletheia [40] instead applies statistical learning to discern between true and false alarms produced by a commercial static security analyzer for JavaScript.

More recently, static and dynamic taint analyses have been applied to Android applications. FlowDroid [3] is a precise static taint analysis that detects sensitive data leaks. TaintDroid [16] performs an efficient dynamic taint analysis. MorphDroid [20] specializes the analysis for specific categories of sensitive data, for more precise and detailed results. Other approaches [5,9] introduce various extensions of information flow and taint analysis to track which kind of sensitive data is managed and potentially disclosed by Android applications.

Some works combine dynamic and static taint analysis: Saner [4] detects faulty sanitization procedures in PHP programs, while Vogt *et al.* [42] detect XSS vulnerabilities in the client browser of a web application.

As far as we know, BackFlow is the first tool that, starting from a generic static taint analysis and exploiting some supporting heap analyses, builds a context-sensitive taint graph that provides evidence of the flows of tainted data from a source to a sink.

3 Formalization

This section formalizes our approach over a simple object-oriented language.

3.1 Language

Let Programs and Classes represent the set of all possible programs and classes, respectively. An object-oriented program is an element $p \in$ Programs $= \wp(\text{Classes})$. A class c is composed of a set of fields and methods: $c \in$ Classes $= \wp(\text{Fields}) \times \wp(\text{Methods})$, where Fields and Methods are the set of all possible fields and methods, respectively. A field f is a pair of its name and its type: $f \in$ Fields $=$ Names $\times$ Types, where Names and Types are the set of all names and types (including classes in Classes and native types such as int or double), respectively. A method m is a pair of a list of n parameters Parameters $=$ (Names $\times$ Types)^n and a body, represented as a control flow graph $\text{cfg} \in$ CFGs of basic statements: Methods $=$ Parameters $\times$ CFGs. Control flow graphs (CFGs) are directed graphs whose vertexes are statements (formally, graphs are elements of (Statements, Statements $\times$ Statements)). We assume that statements in Statements includes the label of the statement (thus we can have the same statement at different program points), but we omit it in the formalization for the sake of simplicity. The set VarAtStatement $=$ Statements $\times$ Names allows one to refer to a variable at a program point. Namely, $(s, v) \in$ VarAtStatement represents variable v at the exit state of s.

For the sake of simplicity, our formalization focuses on a minimal object-oriented programming language, whose statements Statements are either (i) the beginning of a method (start), (ii) a field read ($y = x.f$), (iii) a field write ($y.f = x$), (iv) a method call ($y = x.m(z_1, \cdots, z_n)$), or (v) a return (ret x). Function pred : Statements $\rightarrow \wp$(Statements) yields all predecessors of a given statement. Each statement belongs to a method. Therefore, function getMethod : Statements $\rightarrow$ Methods yields the method of each statement.

3.2 External Components

Before running BackFlow, a static analyzer must have already inferred some information: a taint analysis, a call graph and a heap abstraction.

A taint analysis specifies which variables, at which program points, have been inferred as tainted, since they might hold unsanitized user input or sensitive data. The taint analyzer must have received a specification of the set of sources and sinks: sources are values returned by specific methods (Sources $\subseteq$ Methods); sinks are values passed to method parameters (Sinks $\subseteq$ Methods $\times \mathbb{N}$, where the second element is the index of the parameter). The taint analysis is then a predicate taint : VarAtStatement $\rightarrow \{$true, false$\}$, that holds if a given variable, after a given statement, has been inferred as tainted. We assume it sound: if there is a feasible execution of the code where variable x actually contains a tainted value after a statement st, then taint(st, x) must hold.

A call graph is a function called : Statements $\rightarrow \wp$(Methods) that, given a call statement st, yields an over-approximation of the set of methods that might be called there. This is a standard component of a static analyzer [21,38]. It is handy, sometimes, to see the call graph as the inverse function caller : Methods $\rightarrow \wp$(Statements) that, given a method m, yields an over-approximation of the set of call statements that might call it.

There are many heap abstractions [15,22]. BackFlow is agnostic about the chosen one, as long as it provides a function writersVisible : Statements $\rightarrow \wp$(Statements) that, given a heap read $y = x.f$, yields an over-approximation of the set of heap writes $y.f = x$ where the read value might have been written, previously. The heap abstraction must also provide a must alias analysis, given as a predicate alias : Constraints $\rightarrow \{$true, false$\}$ over alias equality constraints between variables at some program points: Constraints = VarAtStatement $\times$ VarAtStatement. This predicate is extended to constraintsSatisfied : $\wp$(Constraints) $\rightarrow \{$true, false$\}$, by letting constraintsSatisfied(C) hold if and only if, for every $c \in C$, predicate alias(c) holds.

3.3 Flow Reconstruction

Once the supporting taint analysis has inferred a sink as potentially tainted, the backwards flow reconstructor tries to reconstruct a path of variables at statements, providing evidence about how tainted data flows, from a source, into that sink. The path is given as a *taint graph*, with vertexes in VarAtStatement. Taint graphs TG are then defined as (VarAtStatement, VarAtStatement $\times$ VarAtStatement), that is, a poset with upper bound operator $(v_1, e_1) \sqcup_{TG} (v_2, e_2) = (v_1 \cup v_2, e_1 \cup e_2)$.

(1) $\mathbb{S}[\![y_1 = x_1.f, y_1]\!] = \{((y_2.f = x_2, x_2), \{((y_1 = x_1.f, x_1), (y_2.f = x_2, y_2))\}) :$
$y_2.f = x_2 \in \text{writersVisible}(y_1 = x_1.f)\}$

(2) $\mathbb{S}[\![y_1 = x_1.m(\cdots), y_1]\!] = \{((\text{ret } x_2, x_2), \{((y_1 = x_1.m(\cdots), x_1), (\text{ret } x_2, \text{this}))\}) :$
$\exists(\text{pars}, \text{cfg}) \in \text{called}(y_1 = x_1.m(\cdots)) : \text{ret } x_2 \in \text{cfg}\}$

(3) $\mathbb{S}[\![\text{start}, p_i]\!] = \{((y = x.m(x_1, \cdots, x_n), x_i),$
$\{((\text{start}, \text{this}), (y = x.m(x_1, \cdots, x_n), x))\} \cup$
$\{((\text{start}, p_j), (y = x.m(x_1, \cdots, x_n), x_j)) : j \in [1..n]\}) :$
$((p_1, \cdots, p_n), \text{cfg}) = \text{getMethod}(\text{start}) \wedge$
$y = x.m(x_1, \cdots, x_n) \in \text{caller}((p_1, \cdots, p_n), \text{cfg})\}$

(4) $\mathbb{S}[\![\text{st}, x]\!] = \{((\text{st}', x), \emptyset) : \text{st}' \in \text{pred}(st)\}$ for any other statement.

Fig. 4. A single step of backwards propagation.

In order to be context-sensitive, the reconstructor, while proceeding backwards from a sink, collects a set of alias constraints in $\wp(\text{Constraints})$, that must hold if the path leading to the sink is feasible. Otherwise, the path is an artifact of the approximated taint analysis, not allowed by the heap abstraction. During this backwards procedure, the reconstructor builds the taint graph and attaches, to each of its newly discovered vertexes, the collected set of alias constraints that must hold there. Therefore, the reconstructor builds a function in $\text{CV} : \text{VarAtStatement} \to \wp(\text{Constraints})$. A larger set of alias constraints represents a smaller set of concrete states. Hence, the upper bound operator is $\hat{\cap}$, *i.e.*, the functional lifting of set intersection: $c_1 \sqcup_{\text{CV}} c_2 = c_1 \hat{\cap} c_2$. The poset of heap constraints is then $\langle \text{CV}, \sqcup_{\text{CV}} \rangle$.

The reconstructor keeps a state during its execution, consisting of the currently computed taint graph and of the function mapping each of its vertexes to the alias constraints that must hold there: $\Sigma^{\#} = \text{TG} \times \text{CV}$. These states form a poset with upper bound operator $(g_1, c_1) \sqcup_{\Sigma^{\#}} (g_2, c_2) = (g_1 \sqcup_{\text{TG}} g_2, c_1 \sqcup_{\text{CV}} c_2)$.

3.4   Backwards Propagation

This section formalizes how the flow reconstructor tracks, backwards, the value in a sink towards a source.

Figure 4 shows the rules for a single step of backwards propagation, for the language from Sect. 3.1, that will later be extended into a multi-steps propagation. It defines a function $\mathbb{S} : \text{VarAtStatement} \to \wp(\text{VarAtStatement} \times \wp(\text{Constraints}))$ that, given a variable $(\text{st}, n) \in \text{VarAtStatement}$, meaning that the reconstructor wants to follow, backwards, the value of v after statement st, computes a set of variables to track after the preceding statements and a set of alias constraints that must hold if that step is feasible. In particular, the three rules consider the following situations:

1. when tracking a field read statement, the reconstructor tracks the value assigned to the field by any possible writer, taking note of an alias constraint stating that the receiver of the field read and write must be aliased;
2. when tracking the value returned by a method call, the reconstructor tracks the value returned by any `ret` inside any method that might be called there, by using the call graph; moreover, it takes note of an alias constraint stating that the receiver of the method call and the `this` variable inside the callee must be aliased;
3. when tracking a method formal argument, once the beginning of the method has been reached, the reconstructor tracks the actual argument passed by any possible caller of the method, by using the call graph; moreover, it takes note of an alias constraint stating that `this` variable inside the method must be alias of the receiver of the method call, and that the corresponding formal and actual parameters must be aliased as well;
4. when tracking any other statement (assignments to other variables, not currently tracked, or field writes) the reconstructor simply propagates the tracked variable, backwards.

This single-step propagation does not check the feasibility of the step. Hence, the results of $\mathbb{S}$ are refined by dropping unfeasible states, through function

$$\mathsf{filter}(R) = \{(v, C) : (v, C) \in R \wedge \mathsf{taint}(v) \wedge \mathsf{constraintsSatisfied}(C)\}$$

used for the definition of the abstract state transformer:

$$
\begin{aligned}
\mathbb{S}_\sigma[\![(\mathsf{st}, \mathsf{x}), ((V, E), c)]\!] &= ((V', E'), c') \text{ where} \\
(1) &\quad \mathbb{S}[\![\mathsf{st}, \mathsf{x}]\!] = R \\
(2) &\quad R' = \mathsf{filter}(R) \\
(3) &\quad V' = V \cup_{(v', C) \in R'} \{v'\} \\
(4) &\quad E' = E \cup_{(v', C) \in R'} \{(v, v')\} \\
(5) &\quad c' = c[v' \mapsto (c(v') \cup C) : (v', C) \in R']
\end{aligned}
$$

In this way, filter drops all the flows that are unfeasible using the results of the taint analysis. For instance, if a sanitizer is used by the program, this would produce a not-tainted result, and even if the flow reconstructor backwardly reached the result of the method call, filter would drop it.

Intuitively, given the variable x at a statement st, whose value must be tracked backwards, and an abstract state (that is, a taint graph (V, E) and a function of constraints c), it (1) applies the single-step propagation, (2) drops all unfeasible values, (3) adds the new vertexes discovered by the single-step propagation, (4) the corresponding edges connecting the predecessor and the statements produced by the single-step propagation, and (5) updates the alias constraints tracked for the given statement and tracked variable.

Flow reconstruction is defined as a least fixpoint:

$$\mathsf{BackFlow}(v_0) = \mathit{lfp}\lambda_{\emptyset}^{\sqsubseteq^\#_\Sigma}((V, E), c).((\{v_0\}, \emptyset), \emptyset) \sqcup_{\Sigma^\#} \{\mathbb{S}_\sigma[\![v, ((V, E), c)]\!] : v \in V\}$$

This fixpoint requires an initial *seed* v_0, from where the backwards reconstruction starts. This is any sink where the taint analysis issues a warning, for which the flow reconstruction is performed. The fixpoint is reached in a final number of steps, since it works over a finite domain: there is only a finite set of statements and variables, hence a finite set of vertexes and edges of taint graphs, and a finite set of alias constraints.

4   Integration with Julia

We have implemented BackFlow inside the Julia static analyzer [35], an industrial tool that analyzes Java and C# bytecode. Julia is based on abstract interpretation [11,12], performs static analysis based on denotational or constraint-based semantics, and implements a taint analyzer, various heap abstractions and a call graph builder. This section presents the latter components and how BackFlow integrates inside Julia. For the sake of readability, the formalization from Sect. 3 deals with source code statements. However, Julia analyzes bytecode, hence this section refers to local variables and stack values instead of program variables.

BackFlow uses Julia's taint analysis to implement function taint (Sect. 3.2). Julia's taint analysis models explicit information flows through Boolean formulas. Boolean variables correspond to program variables and their models are a sound overapproximation of all taint behaviors for the variables in scope at a given program point. For instance, the abstraction of bytecode load k t, that pushes on the operand stack the value of local variable k, is the Boolean formula $(\check{l}_k \leftrightarrow \hat{s}_{top}) \wedge U$, stating that the taintedness of the topmost stack element after this instruction (denoted by hat ^) is equal to the taintedness of local variable k before the instruction (denoted by hat ˘); all other local variables and stack elements do not change (expressed by the formula U); taintedness before and after an instruction is distinguished by using distinct hats for the variables. There are such formulas for each bytecode instruction. Instructions that might have side-effects (field updates, array writes and method calls) need some approximation of the heap, to model the possible effects of the updates. The analysis of sequential instructions is merged through a sequential composition of formulas. Loops and recursion are saturated by fixpoint. The resulting analysis is a denotational, bottom-up taint analysis, that Julia implements through efficient binary decision diagrams [6]. Julia uses a dictionary of sources (for instance, servlets input and input methods) and sinks (such as SQL query methods, command execution routines, session manipulation methods) of tainted data, so that flows from sources to sinks can be established.

Julia contains several heap abstractions. In particular, a definite aliasing analysis between variables and expressions [29], that identifies local variables and stack elements that are definitely alias. A possible sharing analysis [34] and a possible reachability analysis [30] between pairs of variables allow one to reason about side-effects. In addition, a creation point analysis [1] infers the program points that might have created the objects flowing to a given local variable or stack element. BackFlow relies on the latter analysis to check if two reference values might be alias, and implement the alias function (Sect. 3.2). In addition, BackFlow uses the definite aliasing analysis to augment the set of alias constraints. Namely, if flow reconstruction requires variables x and y to be alias at some statement st, and definite aliasing analysis infers that y and z are definite alias at st, then BackFlow adds the constraint (x, z).

Julia approximates the dynamic targets of method calls through standard class analysis [31], widely adopted in practice [38]. BackFlow uses this information to implement functions caller and called (Sect. 3.2) and to determine the predecessors of statements start and $y = x.m(\cdots)$.

5   Implementation

Algorithm 1 reports the flow reconstruction algorithm. Its input is a program; its output is a set of warnings, possibly enriched with some taint graphs. The Julia analyzer is represented as a function JULIA that, given a program and a taint analysis (e.g., Injection) returns a set of warnings represented as potentially tainted sinks, that is, pairs of a statement and a local variable, from where flows should be reconstructed. The algorithm iterates on Julia's warnings (line 3). For each warning, it applies BackFlow, inferring a taint graph. For each statement in the taint graph, that is a source (line 6), it collects some paths that connect the source to the sink (line 7, where getPaths is a function that given a graph and two vertexes in the graph returns a set of paths in the given graph that connect the two vertexes). The collected taint graphs are then associated with the warning (line 8): since the taint graph returned by BackFlow might contain no calls to sources, f might well be empty here. At the end, the algorithm returns all warnings with the corresponding taint graphs (line 9).

Algorithm 1. Overall algorithm of flow reconstruction

```
1: procedure TAINTANALYSISWITHBackFlow(program, TaintAnalysis)
2:     res ← ∅
3:     for (st, x) ∈ JULIA(program, TaintAnalysis) do
4:         ((V, E), c) ← BackFlow((st, x))
5:         f ← ∅
6:         for (st', x') ∈ V : called(st) ∩ Sources ≠ ∅ do
7:             f ← f ∪ getPaths((V, E), (st, x), (st', x'))
8:         res ← res ∪ {(st, x), f}
9:     return res
```

Algorithm 1 reflects the formalization of Sect. 3. However, some implementation choices have been made to support scalability. Namely, keeping alias constraints can be expensive, in particular because the need of computing their closure, as well as the computation of function constraintsSatisfied. Hence, BackFlow caches the results of the evaluation of alias constraints, and their closure, to avoid recomputation. Moreover, closure of alias constraints, including the constraints inferred by the definite aliasing analysis (Sect. 4), leads easily to an unmanageable amount of constraints. Therefore, BackFlow drops the constraints that refer to variables not in scope (*i.e*, in another method). Finally, the backwards flow reconstruction has been limited to a maximal depth n, controlled by the user. This, however, reduces the number of taintness warnings for which the reconstructor succeeds in inferring a taint graph.

BackFlow uses library JGraphT 1.3.0[4] to implement the taint graphs. The latter have been represented as `graphml` files, in hierarchical structure: nodes are grouped by package, class, method and source line of the statement. BackFlow relies on the implementation of the Dijkstra shortest-path algorithm in class `DijkstraShortestPath`, to compute the final taint graphs (function `getPaths`).

BackFlow has been embedded inside Julia's `Injection` checker. Figure 5 shows the UI of BackFlow, as it appears in Julia's Eclipse plugin[5]. The following options have been added to the `Injection` checker:

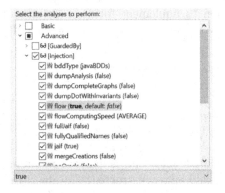

Fig. 5. BackFlow's UI in Eclipse.

1. flow (defaults to false): if true, BackFlow is used to infer the taint graphs for the warnings;
2. flowComputingSpeed (defaults to AVERAGE): specifies the maximal depth n of the inferred taint graphs: FASTEST ($n = 500$), FAST ($n = 1000$), AVERAGE ($n = 2000$), SLOW ($n = 4000$) or SLOWEST (no limit).
3. dumpCompleteGraphs (defaults to false): if true, dumps the complete backwards taint graph (that is, before the application of `getPaths`).

6   Experimental Results

This section presents the results of the application of BackFlow. It first analyzes the quality of these results on a specific application (how many alarms get a taint graph and which are true or false). Then it studies them quantitatively, on a well-known set of benchmarks used in previous works about taint analysis of Java programs. The experiments have been performed on a HP EliteBook 850 G4 laptop equipped with an Intel Core i7-7500 CPU at 2.7 GHz and 16 GB of RAM memory running Microsoft Windows 10 Pro and Oracle JDK version 1.8.0_141. During the analysis, 8 GB were allocated to Java.

---

[4] https://jgrapht.org/.

[5] The user manual can be retrieved at https://static.juliasoft.com/docs/latest/pdf/EclipsePluginUserGuide.pdf.

The raw experimental results have been published in Zenodo [19]. To reproduce the results:

1. register at https://portal.juliasoft.com,
2. install the Julia Eclipse plugin (https://static.juliasoft.com/docs/latest/pdf/EclipsePluginUserGuide.pdf),
3. contact JuliaSoft (info@juliasoft.com) asking enough credits to run the analyses,
4. import the projects in Eclipse (in some cases it might be easier to import them as "Julia projects" , check the Eclipse Plugin User Guide for details),
5. run the analyses with the configuration described in the previous section.

6.1 Qualitative Study: WebGoat

WebGoat is a "deliberately insecure web application maintained by OWASP and designed to teach web application security lessons"[6]. It is a good target to evaluate a taint analysis, since it contains a wide range of different injections (such as SQL injection or XSS) and it has been widely used as benchmark in the past.

Julia produces 78 warnings on WebGoat 6.0. BackFlow builds a taint graph for 64 (82%) of them. Table 1 reports our manual classification of the 78 warnings, where columns "# w. flow" and "# w/o flow" report the statistics of the 64

Table 1. Results on WebGoat 6.0.

Warning	# w. flow		# w/o flow	
	True	False	True	False
AddressInjection	1	0	0	0
CommandInjection	5	0	0	0
HttpResponseSplitting	3	0	0	3
LogForging	1	0	0	0
MessageInjection	0	0	0	1
PathInjection	6	0	0	3
ReflectionInjection	3	0	0	2
ResourceInjection	2	0	0	0
SessionInjection	2	0	0	2
SQLInjection	38	0	0	0
XPathInjection	1	0	0	0
XSSInjection	2	0	0	3
Total	64	0	0	14

warnings with a taint graph and of the 14 warnings without such graph, respectively. It shows that the 64 warnings for which BackFlow could reconstruct a taint graph are true alarms, while the remaining 14 are false alarms. Therefore, BackFlow's backwards flow reconstruction is an empirical evidence of a true alarm. This is an ideal result, since BackFlow was always able to discern between true and false alarms, but this is not always the case in general. In particular, BackFlow might produce a taint graph for a false alarm, for instance when dealing with code that stores tainted data into an array at some index, and then reads data from another index and passes it to a sink; and it might fail to produce a taint graph for a true alarm, because of limits of the static alias analysis engine.

---

[6] https://www.owasp.org/index.php/Category:OWASP_WebGoat_Project.

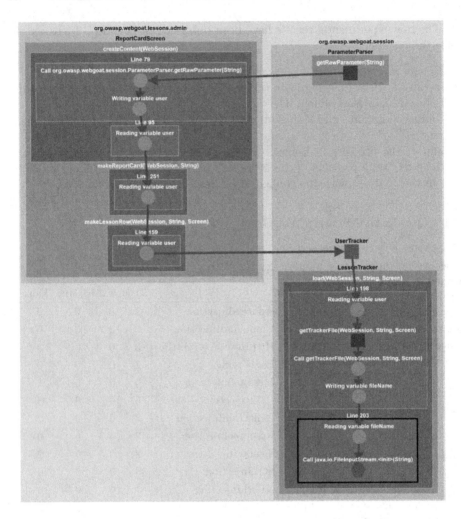

Fig. 6. The taint graph for a complex path injection warning.

6.2 True Alarms

BackFlow reconstructs taint graphs for two true alarms, allowing the user to immediately identify the source of tainted data. Manual inspection would have required relevant effort to identify these flows because of the complex structure of code.

Figure 6 shows the taint graph reconstructed for a complex path injection. Figure 7a shows the code where the flow occurs. Julia's taint analysis warns about a possible path injection at line 203 in class LessonTracker (corresponding to line 35 in Fig. 7a). Namely, the first parameter of the FileInputStream constructor receives a string fileName, returned by method getTrackerFile, that consumes the three parameters of method load. The taint analysis detects

```
1   class ReportCardScreen {
2     Element createContent(WebSession s) {
3       String user = s.getParser()
4         .getRawParameter(USERNAME);
5       ec.addElement(makeReportCard(s, user));
6     }
7     Element makeReportCard
8       (WebSession s, String u) {
9       t.addElement(makeLessonRow(s, u, screen));
10    }
11    private TR makeLessonRow
12      (WebSession s, String u, Screen screen) {
13      LessonTracker lessonTracker = UserTracker.
14        instance().getLessonTracker(s, u, screen);
15    }
16  }
17  class UserTracker{
18    public LessonTracker getLessonTracker
19      (WebSession s, String u, Screen screen) {
20      LessonTracker tracker =
21        LessonTracker.load(s, u, screen);
22    }
23  }
24  class LessonTracker{
25    static String getTrackerFile
26      (WebSession s, String user, Screen screen) {
27      return getUserDir(s) + user + "." +
28        screen.getClass().getName() + ".props";
29    }
30    LessonTracker load
31      (WebSession s, String user, Screen screen) {
32      String fileName =
33        getTrackerFile(s, user, screen);
34      FileInputStream in =
35        new FileInputStream(fileName);
36    }
37  }
```

(a) Snippet of the code for Figure 6.

```
1   class LessonAdapter extends AbstractLesson { ... }
2   class ThreadSafetyProblem extends LessonAdapter {
3     protected Element createContent(WebSession s) {
4       ElementContainer ec = new ElementContainer();
5       currentUser = s.getParser()
6         .getRawParameter(USER_NAME, "");
7       originalUser = currentUser;
8       ec.addElement("Account information for user: " +
9         originalUser + "<br><br>");
10      return ec;
11    }
12  class AbstractLesson extends Screen {
13    public void handleRequest(WebSession s) {
14      Form form = new Form(getFormAction(),
15      Form.POST).setName("form").setEncType("");
16      form.addElement(createContent(s));
17      setContent(form);
18    }
19  }
20  class Screen {
21    private Element content;
22    protected void setContent(Element content) {
23      this.content = content;
24    }
25    public String getContent() {
26      return content.toString();
27    }
28    public void output(PrintWriter out) {
29      out.print(getContent());
30    }
31  }
```

(b) Snippet of the code for Figure 8.

Fig. 7. Snippets of codes for two true alarms.

user as tainted, and then BackFlow tracks it backwards through UserTracker. getLessonTracker (line 21 of Fig. 7a), ReportCardScreen.makeLessonRow (line 14), ReportCardScreen.makeReportCard (line 9) and ReportCardScreen. createContent (line 5). There, user is assigned a raw servlet parameter, hence a source has been reached (line 3, where the parameter is returned by a method of WebGoat that calls the Java servlet API, but we omit this detail here). This example shows that BackFlow infers a taint graph that helps the programmer understand and hence fix the injection. Manual tracking of tainted data would be much harder. For instance, UserTracker.getLessonTracker is called five times in WebGoat: the programmer would have needed to check all of them to discover the one that taints user.

Figure 8 shows another taint graph produced by BackFlow, whose corresponding code is in Fig. 7b. Julia reports an XSS warning at line 201 of class Screen (line 29 in Fig. 7b), where field content is passed to PrintWriter.print, through a getter method. The setter method setContent for this field is called at 19 different places in WebGoat: manual inspection would be extremely difficult. Instead, the taint graph in Fig. 8, which is one of the eight different taint

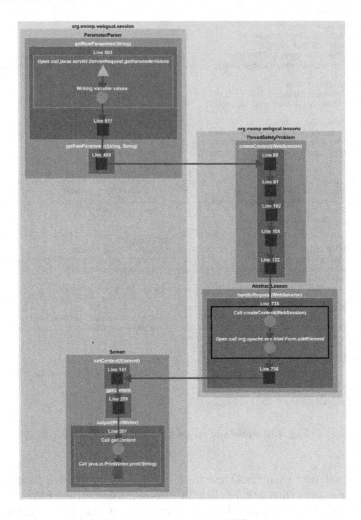

Fig. 8. The taint graph for an XSS warning.

graphs, each for a different source, reconstructed for this warning, shows that
the call from class `AbstractLesson` (that extends `Screen` and thus can call
the protected `setContent`) at line 736 (line 17 in Fig. 7b) passes tainted data
coming from `createContent`. The latter is an abstract method in class `Screen`,
implemented in 79 classes of WebGoat. The taint graph shows that an implementation passing tainted data is in class `ThreadSafetyProblem` (that extends
`LessonAdapter`, that in turn extends `AbstractLesson`). This accesses a servlet
parameter at line 80 (line 6 of Fig. 7b) and, after some computation, adds it at
line 122 to the element returned by the method.

```
1  class Encoding {
2    static String base64Encode(String str) {
3      byte[] b = str.getBytes();
4      return encoder.encode(b);
5    }
6  }
7  class Challenge2Screen {
8    private String user = "youaretheweakestlink";
9    protected Element doStage1(WebSession s) {
10     Cookie newCookie = new Cookie
11       (USER, Encoding.base64Encode(user));
12     s.getResponse().addCookie(newCookie);
13   }
14 }
```

(a) False HTTP response splitting.

```
1  class Course {
2    List <String> files = new LinkedList<>();
3    void loadFiles (ServletContext context, String path) {
4      Set resourcePaths = context.getResourcePaths(path);
5      Iterator itr = resourcePaths.iterator();
6      while ( itr.hasNext())
7        files.add( itr.next());
8    }
9    private void loadResources() {
10     for (String absoluteFile : files ) {
11       String fileName = getFileName(absoluteFile);
12       ...
13     }
14   }
15   private static String getFileName(String s) {
16     String fileName = new File(s).getName();
17     //Some computations on fileName
18     return fileName;
19   }
20 }
```

(b) False path injection.

Fig. 9. Snippets of code for the false alarms.

6.3 False Alarms

BackFlow fails to reconstruct a flow graph for two injection warnings reported by Julia's taint analysis. They turn out to be false alarms.

Julia warns about a potential HTTP response splitting at line 172 of class Challenge2Screen. Figure 9a reports the corresponding source code (see line 12). Julia's taint analysis infers that Encoding.base64Encode returns a tainted value, which taints variable newCookie. However, field user is not tainted and the code of Encoding.base64Encode is such that, if its parameter is not tainted, then also the returned value is not tainted. But Julia's taint analysis infers that the returned value could be tainted because encoder has class sun.misc.BASE64Encoder, not available to the analysis. Hence a worst-case assumption on missing code [36] is applied. BackFlow reconstructs the flow until the read of the static field encoder and stops there, since it does not find the origin of the tainted data.

Julia reports a possible path injection warning at line 83 of class Course. Figure 9b reports the corresponding source code (see line 16). Julia sees that method Course.loadResources might call getFileName with a tainted parameter (line 11), during the iteration over all file paths in the list files. This field is initialized to an empty list of strings (line 2) and only method loadFiles adds elements to it (line 7) from the parameters obtained from the resource paths of the servlet context. Julia taint analysis infers that elements of files might be tainted, but the only statement that adds elements to the list (line 7) does not deal with tainted data. BackFlow reconstructs the flow only until the beginning of the for each loop at line 10. The false alarm is due to the fact that Julia's taint analysis sees the receiver of the getfield files bytecode statement as tainted.

Table 2. Experimental results on standard benchmarks.

Program			Time (sec)		Other		Http		Log		Path		Refl		Sess		SQL		URL		XSS		Total	
Name	Ver.	LOC	Taint	Rec	w/o	w	w/o	w	w/o	w	w/o	w	w/o	w	w/o	w	w/o	w	w/o	w	w/o	w	w/o	w
blojsom	3.3b	17144	268	19	0	1	2	6			17	19			1	17			0	6	1	0	21	49
bluebog	0.9	1930	137	3							6	4											6	4
friki	1.3.0	7718	127	107							0	4	1	3	1	2							2	9
gestcv	1.0.0	3948	93	3							0	1									1	0	1	1
jboard	0.30	3397	143	3											0	1	11	1					11	2
jspwiki	2.11	30024	412	192	1	0	3	8	96	114	19	22	5	8	1	1			0	1	8	22	133	176
jugjobs		869	94	2	1	0					2	0	1	0			4	0					8	0
pebble	2.6.4	23124	581	55			1	6			69	29	13	0	0	3			1	1	3	12	87	51
personal	vel	3480	148	4			0	1			2	0	5	0			1	0	2	0			10	1
photov	2.1	9368	115	4					3	2					1	39	3	0					7	41
roller	0.9.6	11202	42	7			0	1	10	1	5	0			6	2					8	3	29	7
snipsnap	0.7	3736	96	2																			0	0
Total		115940	2256	401	2	1	6	22	109	117	120	79	25	11	10	65	19	1	3	8	21	37	315	341

6.4 Quantitative Study: Benchmarks

BackFlow has been run on a set of Java web applications used as benchmarks to evaluate similar tools, in previous work. In particular, this set is taken from [23], that collected these applications starting from other previous work [26,37,41]. The goal of this quantitative experiment is to study the scalability of BackFlow and see if it is as precise as on WebGoat.

Table 2 reports the results. For each application, it reports its version (column Vers.)[7], its number of lines of code (LOC, as estimated by Julia), the time for taint analysis and for BackFlow (in seconds), and the number of warnings with (column w) or without (column w/o) taint graph. This figure reports numbers only for the types of warnings that were actually raised by Julia: Http stands for Http response splitting, Log for log forging, Path for path injections, Refl for reflection injections, Sess for session injections, SQL for SQL injections, URL for URL injections, XSS for cross site scripting and Other for all remaining types of injection warnings - address injections for blojsom, DOS injections for jspkiwi and message injections for jugjobs.

All together, the analyzed applications consist in about 116KLOCs. Julia analysis and BackFlow took 37'26" and 6'41", respectively. Hence, BackFlow requires less than a fifth of the overall analysis time and it scales to real world applications.

Out of 656 injection warnings, BackFlow builds a taint graph for 341 (52%). While there are significant differences between different types of applications and warnings (for instance, BackFlow reconstructs 87% of session injection flows, but only 5% of SQL injection flows), the overall result shows that BackFlow is effective in building taint graphs for injection warnings in real world applications. The efficacy is smaller than on the qualitative study (where BackFlow reconstructs a taint graph for 82% of the warnings). This difference is possibly justified by the

---

[7] We were not able to find a distribution of jugjobs with a version number.

fact that WebGoat's didactic code is more regular than that of these benchmark applications.

7 Conclusion

BackFlow proves to be able to reconstruct the flow of tainted data, as taint graphs. Experimental results show that the fact that BackFlow provides (or not) a taint graph for a warning is a clear empirical indication that the alarm is true (respectively, false). Moreover BackFlow scales to real-world applications.

References

1. Andersen, L.: Program analysis and specialization for the C programming language. Ph.D. thesis, University of Copenhagen (1994)
2. Arkin, B., Stender, S., McGraw, G.: Software penetration testing. IEEE Secur. Priv. **3**(1), 84–87 (2005)
3. Arzt, S., et al.: FlowDroid: precise context, flow, field, object-sensitive and lifecycle-aware taint analysis for android apps. In: Proceedings of PLDI 2014. ACM (2014)
4. Balzarotti, D., et al.: Saner: composing static and dynamic analysis to validate sanitization in web applications. In: Proceedings of S&P 2008. IEEE (2008)
5. Barbon, G., Cortesi, A., Ferrara, P., Pistoia, M., Tripp, O.: Privacy analysis of android apps: implicit flows and quantitative analysis. In: Saeed, K., Homenda, W. (eds.) CISIM 2015. LNCS, vol. 9339, pp. 3–23. Springer, Cham (2015). https://doi.org/10.1007/978-3-319-24369-6_1
6. Bryant, R.: Symbolic Boolean manipulation with ordered binary-decision diagrams. ACM Comput. Surv. **24**(3), 293–318 (1992)
7. Buro, S., Mastroeni, I.: Abstract code injection. In: Dillig, I., Palsberg, J. (eds.) Verification, Model Checking, and Abstract Interpretation. LNCS, vol. 10747, pp. 116–137. Springer, Cham (2018). https://doi.org/10.1007/978-3-319-73721-8_6
8. Clause, J., Li, W., Orso, A.: Dytan: a generic dynamic taint analysis framework. In: Proceedings of ISSTA 2007. ACM (2007)
9. Cortesi, A., Ferrara, P., Pistoia, M., Tripp, O.: Datacentric semantics for verification of privacy policy compliance by mobile applications. In: D'Souza, D., Lal, A., Larsen, K.G. (eds.) VMCAI 2015. LNCS, vol. 8931, pp. 61–79. Springer, Heidelberg (2015). https://doi.org/10.1007/978-3-662-46081-8_4
10. Costantini, G., Ferrara, P., Cortesi, A.: A suite of abstract domains for static analysis of string values. Softw.: Pract. Exp. **45**(1), 245–287 (2015)
11. Cousot, P., Cousot, R.: Abstract interpretation: a unified lattice model for static analysis of programs by construction or approximation of fixpoints. In: Proceedings of POPL 1977. ACM (1977)
12. Cousot, P., Cousot, R.: Systematic design of program analysis frameworks. In: Proceedings of POPL 1979. ACM (1979)
13. Csallner, C., Smaragdakis, Y.: Check 'n' crash: combining static checking and testing. In: Proceedings of ICSE 2005. ACM (2005)
14. Denning, D.E.: A lattice model of secure information flow. Commun. ACM **19**(5), 236–243 (1976)
15. Deutsch, A.: Interprocedural may-alias analysis for pointers: beyond k-limiting. In: Proceedings of PLDI 1994. ACM (1994)

16. Enck, W., et al.: TaintDroid: an information-flow tracking system for realtime privacy monitoring on smartphones. ACM Trans. Comput. Syst. **32**(2), 5:1–5:29 (2014)

17. Ferrara, P.: Generic combination of heap and value analyses in abstract interpretation. In: McMillan, K.L., Rival, X. (eds.) VMCAI 2014. LNCS, vol. 8318, pp. 302–321. Springer, Heidelberg (2014). https://doi.org/10.1007/978-3-642-54013-4_17

18. Ferrara, P.: A generic framework for heap and value analyses of object-oriented programming languages. Theor. Comput. Sci. **631**, 43–72 (2016)

19. Ferrara, P., Olivieri, L., Spoto, F.: BackFlow: backward context-sensitive flow reconstruction of taint analysis results (2019). https://doi.org/10.5281/zenodo.3539240

20. Ferrara, P., Tripp, O., Pistoia, M.: MorphDroid: fine-grained privacy verification. In: Proceedings of ACSAC 2015. ACM (2015)

21. Grove, D., DeFouw, G., Dean, J., Chambers, C.: Call graph construction in object-oriented languages. In: Proceedings of OOPSLA 1997. ACM (1997)

22. Hind, M.: Pointer analysis: haven't we solved this problem yet? In: Proceedings of PASTE 2001. ACM (2001)

23. Huang, W., Dong, Y., Milanova, A.: Type-based taint analysis for Java web applications. In: Gnesi, S., Rensink, A. (eds.) FASE 2014. LNCS, vol. 8411, pp. 140–154. Springer, Heidelberg (2014). https://doi.org/10.1007/978-3-642-54804-8_10

24. Jovanovic, N., Kruegel, C., Kirda, E.: Pixy: a static analysis tool for detecting web application vulnerabilities. In: Proceeding of S&P 2006. IEEE (2006)

25. Leek, T.R., Brown, R.E., Zhivich, M.A., Leek, T.R., Brown, R.E.: Coverage maximization using dynamic taint tracing. Technical report, MIT Lincoln Laboratory (2007)

26. Livshits, V.B., Lam, M.S.: Finding security vulnerabilities in Java applications with static analysis. In: Proceedings of USENIX Security 2005. USENIX Association (2005)

27. Myers, A.C.: JFlow: practical mostly-static information flow control. In: Proceedings of POPL 1999. ACM (1999)

28. Newsome, J., Song, D.: Dynamic taint analysis for automatic detection, analysis, and signature generation of exploits on commodity software. In: Proceedings of NDSS 2005. The Internet Society (2005)

29. Nikolić, Đ., Spoto, F.: Definite expression aliasing analysis for Java bytecode. In: Roychoudhury, A., D'Souza, M. (eds.) ICTAC 2012. LNCS, vol. 7521, pp. 74–89. Springer, Heidelberg (2012). https://doi.org/10.1007/978-3-642-32943-2_6

30. Nikolic, D., Spoto, F.: Reachability analysis of program variables. ACM Trans. Program. Lang. Syst. **35**(4), 14:1–14:68 (2014)

31. Palsberg, J., Schwartzbach, M.I.: Object-oriented type inference. In: Proceedings of OOPSLA 1991. ACM (1991)

32. Reps, T., Horwitz, S., Sagiv, M.: Precise interprocedural dataflow analysis via graph reachability. In: Proceedings of POPL 1995. ACM (1995)

33. Sabelfeld, A., Myers, A.C.: Language-based information-flow security. IEEE J. Sel. A. Commun. **21**(1), 5–19 (2006)

34. Secci, S., Spoto, F.: Pair-sharing analysis of object-oriented programs. In: Hankin, C., Siveroni, I. (eds.) SAS 2005. LNCS, vol. 3672, pp. 320–335. Springer, Heidelberg (2005). https://doi.org/10.1007/11547662_22

35. Spoto, F.: The Julia static analyzer for Java. In: Rival, X. (ed.) SAS 2016. LNCS, vol. 9837, pp. 39–57. Springer, Heidelberg (2016). https://doi.org/10.1007/978-3-662-53413-7_3

36. Spoto, F., et al.: Static identification of injection attacks in Java. ACM Trans. Program. Lang. Syst. (TOPLAS) **41**, 18 (2019)
37. Sridharan, M., Artzi, S., Pistoia, M., Guarnieri, S., Tripp, O., Berg, R.: F4F: taint analysis of framework-based web applications. In: Proceedings of OOPSLA 2011. ACM (2011)
38. Tip, F., Palsberg, J.: Scalable propagation-based call graph construction algorithms. In: Proceedings of OOPSLA 2000. ACM (2000)
39. Tripp, O., Ferrara, P., Pistoia, M.: Hybrid security analysis of web JavaScript code via dynamic partial evaluation. In: Proceedings of ISSTA 2014. ACM (2014)
40. Tripp, O., Guarnieri, S., Pistoia, M., Aravkin, A.: ALETHEIA: improving the usability of static security analysis. In: Proceedings of CCS 2014. ACM (2014)
41. Tripp, O., Pistoia, M., Fink, S.J., Sridharan, M., Weisman, O.: TAJ: effective taint analysis of web applications. In: Proceedings of PLDI 2009. ACM (2009)
42. Vogt, P., Nentwich, F., Jovanovic, N., Kirda, E., Kruegel, C., Vigna, G.: Cross-site scripting prevention with dynamic data tainting and static analysis. In: Proceedings of NDSS 2005. The Internet Society (2007)
43. Wassermann, G., Su, Z.: Sound and precise analysis of web applications for injection vulnerabilities. In: Proceedings of PLDI 2007. ACM (2007)
44. Yin, H., Song, D., Egele, M., Kruegel, C., Kirda, E.: Panorama: capturing system-wide information flow for malware detection and analysis. In: Proceedings of CCS 2007. ACM (2007)
45. Zanioli, M., Ferrara, P., Cortesi, A.: SAILS: static analysis of information leakage with sample. In: Proceedings of SAC 2012. ACM (2012)

Fixing Code that Explodes Under Symbolic Evaluation

Sorawee Porncharoenwase[✉], James Bornholt, and Emina Torlak

University of Washington, Seattle, WA 98195, USA
{sorawee,bornholt,emina}@cs.washington.edu

Abstract. Effective symbolic evaluation is key to building scalable verification and synthesis tools based on SMT solving. These tools use symbolic evaluators to reduce the semantics of all paths through a finite program to logical constraints, discharged with an SMT solver. Using an evaluator effectively requires tool developers to be able to identify and repair performance bottlenecks in code under all-path evaluation, a difficult task, even for experts. This paper presents a new method for repairing such bottlenecks automatically. The key idea is to formulate the *symbolic performance repair* problem as combinatorial search through a space of semantics-preserving transformations, or *repairs*, to find an equivalent program with minimal cost under symbolic evaluation. The key to realizing this idea is (1) defining a small set of generic repairs that can be combined to fix common bottlenecks, and (2) searching for combinations of these repairs to find good solutions quickly and best ones eventually. Our technique, SymFix, contributes repairs based on deforestation and symbolic reflection, and an efficient algorithm that uses symbolic profiling to guide the search for fixes. To evaluate Sym-Fix, we implement it for the Rosette solver-aided language and symbolic evaluator. Applying SymFix to 18 published verification and synthesis tools built in Rosette, we find that it automatically improves the performance of 12 tools by a factor of $1.1\times–91.7\times$, and 4 of these fixes match or outperform expert-written repairs. SymFix also finds 5 fixes that were missed by experts.

Keywords: Symbolic evaluation · Performance optimization

1 Introduction

Tools based on SMT solving have automated vital programming tasks in many domains, from verifying safety-critical properties of medical software [33] to synthesizing fast computational kernels for cryptographic applications [35]. These tools employ *symbolic evaluation* [4,26] to reduce the semantics of all paths through a loop-free (i.e., *finite*) program to logical constraints. The resulting constraints are then used to express queries about program behavior as logical satisfiability queries, discharged with an SMT solver. Since the solvability of such

© Springer Nature Switzerland AG 2020
D. Beyer and D. Zufferey (Eds.): VMCAI 2020, LNCS 11990, pp. 44–67, 2020.
https://doi.org/10.1007/978-3-030-39322-9_3

queries hinges on the compactness and simplicity of the underlying constraints, effective symbolic evaluation is key to building effective solver-aided tools.

Building a tool used to require crafting a custom symbolic evaluator, a difficult task that can take years of expert work. Today, this burden is much lower thanks to reusable symbolic evaluators provided by *solver-aided host languages* [45, 47] and frameworks [9, 39]. To build a tool, developers simply write an interpreter for the tool's source language in the solver-aided host language. When this interpreter executes a source program, the host's symbolic evaluator reduces both the interpreter and the program to constraints. The interpreter can control its symbolic evaluation, and thus the encoding, through constructs [38, 44] exposed by the host language and through the structure of its implementation [7]. By exploiting these control mechanisms, developers can create, in weeks, state-of-the-art tools [29] that outperform a custom symbolic execution engine [30, 41].

But if an interpreter performs poorly on a host symbolic evaluator, finding and fixing the bottleneck can be daunting. Recent work on *symbolic profiling* [7] explains why: classic performance engineering techniques assume a single path of execution, and the all-path execution model of symbolic evaluation violates this assumption. As a result, standard profiling tools (e.g., time-based) fail to identify the code that needs to be optimized, and standard optimizations (e.g., breaking early out of a loop) can make performance asymptotically worse under symbolic evaluation. Symbolic profiling addresses the first problem, providing a new performance model for symbolic evaluation and an automatic technique for identifying performance bottlenecks in solver-aided code. The second problem, however, remains open, with developers relying on experience and ad-hoc experimentation to optimize their code.

To address this problem, we present a new method for automatic repair of common performance bottlenecks in solver-aided code. The key idea is to formulate the *symbolic performance repair* problem as combinatorial search in a space of semantics-preserving transformations, or *repairs*. Our technique, Sym-Fix, takes as input a solver-aided program and a workload, and it searches the repair space for a semantically equivalent program that minimizes the cost of symbolic evaluation [7] on the input workload. The choice of repairs and the search strategy are critical to the usefulness and completeness of SymFix. This paper contributes a small set of generic repairs that combine to fix common bottlenecks, and an effective algorithm for combining repairs into (optimal) fixes.

What makes a generic repair useful for code under symbolic evaluation? Intuitively, a repair is useful if its application reduces the cost of symbolic evaluation for a large class of programs. This cost depends on the program's control structure and the evaluator's strategy for splitting and merging states [7, 27, 46]. So useful repairs change the program's control structure or evaluation strategy.

Based on this insight, we develop a set of three repairs that employ *deforestation* [48] to simplify program structure and *symbolic reflection* [46] to simplify the evaluation strategy. Deforestation is a classic optimization for functional programming languages that eliminates intermediate lists. Under concrete evaluation, deforestation improves performance by a constant factor. Under symbolic evaluation, however, it can improve performance asymptotically when the intermediate lists are symbolic. We use deforestation based on build/foldr fusion [22] as one of our repairs. We also develop two repairs for host languages that support symbolic reflection—a set of language constructs that a program can use to inspect its symbolic state and control its symbolic evaluation (e.g., by forcing a split on a merged state). These two repairs work by creating more opportunities for concrete evaluation. As such, they can both improve performance asymptotically and, in some cases, fix divergence due to loss of concreteness.

The search space defined by our repairs is finite for every program, so it supports complete and optimal search. But it is also intractably large for real programs. We therefore formulate SymFix as an anytime algorithm, equipped with a pruning mechanism that exploits *precedence* of repairs and a prioritization heuristic that exploits symbolic profiling information. The pruning mechanism is inspired by partial order reduction [15]: if two repairs can always be reordered so that one is applied before the other without changing the result, SymFix explores only one of the orders. The prioritization heuristic uses ranking information computed by symbolic profiling to decide what parts of the program to repair first. In particular, symbolic profiling takes as input a program and a workload, and ranks the locations in the program from most to least likely bottlenecks. SymFix uses this ranking to quickly drive the search toward most promising solutions.

We implement SymFix for Rosette [43,45,46], a solver-aided host language that extends Racket [18,37] with support for symbolic evaluation, reflection, and profiling. To evaluate SymFix's effectiveness, we apply it to 15 solver-aided tools [2,5,6,8,10,12,14,25,33,36,46,50,51] studied in the paper on symbolic profiling [7], as well as 3 more recent tools [29,31,35]. SymFix improves the performance of 12 tools by a factor of $1.1\times$–$91.7\times$, and 4 of these fixes match or outperform those written by experts. SymFix also finds 5 fixes that were missed by experts. We further show that the improvements made by SymFix generalize to unseen workloads, and that its search strategy is essential for finding useful fixes.

In summary, this paper makes the following contributions:

1. A formulation of the symbolic performance repair problem as combinatorial search in a space of semantics-preserving transformations, or repairs.
2. SymFix, a new technique for solving this problem. SymFix contributes a set of repairs based on deforestation and symbolic reflection, and an effective anytime algorithm for combining these repairs into useful fixes.
3. An implementation of SymFix for the Rosette solver-aided language [43,46].
4. An evaluation of SymFix's effectiveness on 18 published solver-aided tools built in Rosette, showing that it can find repairs that outperform expert fixes and that generalize to unseen workloads.

The rest of the paper illustrates symbolic performance repair on a small example (Sect. 2); formulates the problem of repairing performance bottlenecks in solver-aided code (Sect. 3); presents the SymFix algorithm, repairs, and implementation for Rosette (Sect. 4); shows the effectiveness of SymFix at repairing bottlenecks in real solver-aided tools hosted by Rosette (Sect. 5); discusses related work (Sect. 6); and concludes with a summary of key points (Sect. 7).

2   Overview

This section illustrates symbolic performance repair on a small solver-aided program (Fig. 1). The program is adapted from Serval [29], a framework for verifying systems code at the instruction level. Serval is built in Rosette [43], and it supports creating scalable automated verifiers by writing interpreters. Serval's authors show how to profile this program with a symbolic profiler, and manually fix the bottleneck using a custom construct implemented as a Rosette macro. We first revisit this analysis to highlight the challenges of repairing bottlenecks in solver-aided code, and then show how SymFix repairs the problem automatically and generically, using a repair based on symbolic reflection [46].

```
1   ; cpu state: program counter and registers    33      (if (! (= (cpu-reg c rs) 0))
2   (struct cpu (pc regs) #:mutable)               34          (set-cpu-pc! c imm)           ; E
3                                                   35          (set-cpu-pc! c (+ 1 pc)))]  ; F
4   ; interpret a program from a cpu state         36    [(sgtz)
5   (define (interpret c program)       ; A        37      (set-cpu-pc! c (+ 1 pc))
6     (define i (fetch c program))      ; B        38      (if (> (cpu-reg c rs) 0)
7     (match i                                      39          (set-cpu-reg! c rd 1)        ; G
8       [(list opcode rd rs imm)                    40          (set-cpu-reg! c rd 0))]      ; H
9         (execute c opcode rd rs imm)              41    [(sltz)
10        (when (not (equal? opcode 'ret))          42      (set-cpu-pc! c (+ 1 pc))
11          (interpret c program))]))               43      (if (< (cpu-reg c rs) 0)
12                                                  44          (set-cpu-reg! c rd 1)        ; I
13  ; fetch an instruction at the current pc       45          (set-cpu-reg! c rd 0))]      ; J
14  (define (fetch c program)                       46    [(li)
15    (define pc (cpu-pc c))                        47      (set-cpu-pc! c (+ 1 pc))         ; K
16    (vector-ref program pc))          ; C         48      (set-cpu-reg! c rd imm)]))       ; L
17                                                  49
18  ; read register rs                             50  (define sgnt #( ; sign in ToyRISC
19  (define (cpu-reg c rs)                          51    (sltz 1 0 #f)   ; 0. r1 = r0<0 ? 1 : 0
20    (vector-ref (cpu-regs c) rs))                 52    (bnez #f 1 4)   ; 1. branch to 4 if r1!=0
21                                                  53    (sgtz 0 0 #f)   ; 2. r0 = r0>0 ? 1 : 0
22  ; write value v to register rd                 54    (ret #f #f #f)  ; 3. return
23  (define (set-cpu-reg! c rd v)                   55    (li 0 #f -1)    ; 4. r0 = -1
24    (vector-set! (cpu-regs c) rd v))              56    (ret #f #f #f)  ; 5. return
25                                                  57  ))
26  ; execute instruction (opcode rd rs imm)       58
27  (define (execute c opcode rd rs imm)            59  (define-symbolic X Y integer?)
28    (define pc (cpu-pc c))                        60  (define c (cpu 0 (vector X Y)))
29    (case opcode                                  61  (interpret c sgnt)
30      [(ret)                                      62  (verify
31        (set-cpu-pc! c 0)]           ; D          63    (assert (= (cpu-reg c 0) (sgn X))))
32      [(bnez)
```

Fig. 1. A ToyRISC interpreter and program in Rosette, adapted from Serval [29].

Solver-Aided Programming. Fig. 1 shows a small program [29] written in Rosette, a solver-aided host language that extends Racket [37] with support for symbolic evaluation. Rosette programs behave like Racket programs when executed on concrete values. But Rosette also *lifts* programs, via symbolic evaluation, to operate on *symbolic values*. These values are used to formulate *solver-aided queries*, such as verifying that a program satisfies its specification, expressed as assertions, on all inputs. The example verifies a program in ToyRISC, a small subset of RISC-V [1], by lifting its interpreter to work on symbolic values.

The ToyRISC interpreter (lines 1–48) implements a simple recursive procedure for executing a ToyRISC program from a given CPU state. The state consists of a program counter and vector of two registers, r_0 and r_1, both holding integers. A program is a sequence of instructions that manipulate the state. An instruction is a list of four values, (opcode rd rs imm), specifying the instruction's opcode, destination and source registers, and the immediate constant. Unused arguments are denoted by #f; for example, the return instruction takes no arguments, denoted by (ret #f #f #f). In addition to the return instruction, which halts the execution (line 10), the language also includes instructions for conditional branching (bnez), loading values into registers (li), and comparing register values to zero (sgtz and sltz). The example ToyRISC program, sgnt, uses these instructions to compute the sign of the value in register r_0, storing the result back into r_0 and using r_1 as a scratch register.

The sgnt program is correct if it produces the same result as the host sign procedure, sgn, for all valid CPU states. To verify sgnt, we first use Rosette's define-symbolic form to create two fresh symbolic integers, X and Y, and bind them to the variables X and Y (line 59). Next, we use these variables to create a CPU state c with the program counter set to 0 and registers set to X and Y (line 60). The symbolic state c represents all valid concrete CPU states. Finally, we interpret sgnt on c and use Rosette's verify query to search for a counterexample to the assertion that register r_0 holds the sign of X. A counterexample to this query would bind the symbolic values X and Y to concrete integers that trigger the assertion failure. But since sgnt is correct, the query returns (unsat) to indicate the absence of counterexamples.

Symbolic Evaluation and Profiling. When interpreting sgnt on the symbolic state c, Rosette evaluates all paths through the interpreter code and reduces their meaning to symbolic expressions over X and Y. For example, after the call to the interpreter (line 61), register r_0 of c holds the symbolic value $\text{ite}(X < 0, -1, \text{ite}(0 < X, 1, 0))$, which encodes the meaning of sgnt. This value is part of the *symbolic heap* that Rosette generates while exploring the interpreter's *symbolic evaluation graph* [7] (Fig. 2a). The heap consists of all symbolic values created during evaluation. The graph is a DAG over program states and guarded transitions between states, and its shape reflects the evaluator's strategy for path splitting and state merging. The symbolic heap and evaluation graph characterize the behavior of solver-aided code under every (forward) symbolic evaluation strategy, and controlling their complexity is key to good performance [7].

To help with this task, Rosette provides a *symbolic profiler*, SymPro, that monitors the heap and the graph to identify performance bottlenecks. SymPro computes summary statistics about the effect of each procedure call on these structures, such as the number of symbolic values added to the heap, and the number of path splits and state merges added to the graph. It then uses these statistics to rank the calls to suggest likely bottlenecks. When applied

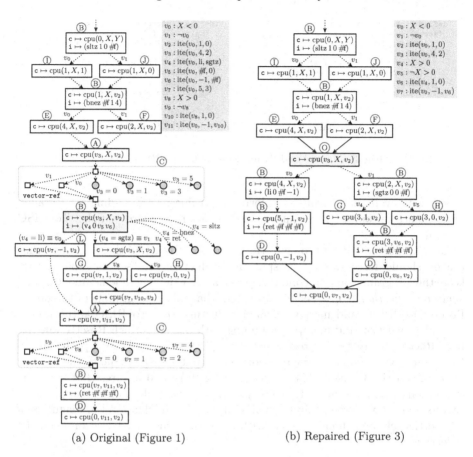

(a) Original (Figure 1)   (b) Repaired (Figure 3)

Fig. 2. Simplified symbolic evaluation heap and graph for the original (a) and repaired (b) ToyRISC code. Heaps are shown in gray boxes. Nodes in a symbolic evaluation graph are program states, and edges are guarded transitions between states, labeled with the condition that guards the transition. Edges ending at pink circles denote infeasible transitions. Dotted edges indicate elided parts of the graph. Circled letters are program locations, included for readability.

to ToyRISC, SymPro identifies the calls to execute at line 9 and vector-ref at line 16 as the likely bottlenecks. But how does one diagnose and fix these bottlenecks?

Manually Repairing Bottlenecks. The authors of ToyRISC reasoned [29] that the first location returned by SymPro "is not surprising since execute implements the core functionality, but vector-ref is a red flag." Examining the merging statistics for vector-ref, they concluded that vector-ref is being invoked with a symbolic program counter to produce a "merged symbolic instruction" (highlighted in Fig. 2a), which represents a set of concrete instructions, only some of which are feasible. Since execute consumes this symbolic instruction

```
(define (interpret c program)      ; A        (define (interpret c program)      ; A
  (serval:split-pc [cpu pc] c      ; 0          (split-all (c)                   ; 0
    (define i (fetch c program))   ; B            (define i (fetch c program))   ; B
    (match i                                      (match i
      [(list opcode rd rs imm)                      [(list opcode rd rs imm)
       (execute c opcode rd rs imm)                  (execute c opcode rd rs imm)
       (when (not (equal? opcode 'ret))              (when (not (equal? opcode 'ret))
         (interpret c program))]))))                   (interpret c program))]))))
```

(a) Manual repair [29]   (b) Generated repair

Fig. 3. Manual and SymFix repair for ToyRISC code.

(line 9), its evaluation involves exploring infeasible paths, leading to degraded performance on our example and non-termination on more complex ToyRISC programs.

Having diagnosed the problem, the authors of ToyRISC then reasoned that the fix should force Rosette to split the evaluation into separate paths that keep the program counter concrete. Such a fix can be implemented through *symbolic reflection* [46], a set of constructs that allow programmers to control Rosette's splitting and merging behavior. In this case, ToyRISC authors used symbolic reflection and metaprogramming with macros (which Rosette inherits from Racket) to create a custom construct, `split-pc`, that forces a path split on CPU states with symbolic program counters. Applying `split-pc` to the body of `interpret` (Fig. 3a) fixes this bottleneck (Fig. 2b)—and ensures that symbolic evaluation terminates on all ToyRISC programs. But while simple to implement, this fix is hard won, requiring manual analysis of symbolic profiles, diagnosis of the bottleneck, and, finally, repair with a custom construct based on symbolic reflection.

Repairing Bottlenecks with SymFix. SymFix lowers this burden by automatically repairing common performance bottlenecks in solver-aided code. The core idea is to view the repair problem (Sect. 3) as search for a sequence of semantics-preserving repairs that transform an input program into an equivalent program with minimal symbolic cost—a value computed from the program's symbolic profiling metrics. To realize this approach, SymFix solves two core technical challenges (Sect. 4): (1) developing a small set of generic repairs that can be combined into useful and general repair sequences for common bottlenecks, and (2) developing a search strategy that discovers good fixes quickly and best fixes eventually.

SymFix can repair complex bottlenecks in real code as well as or better than experts (Sect. 5). It can also repair ToyRISC, finding the fix in Fig. 3b. This fix has the same effect as the expert `split-pc` fix but uses a generic `split-all` construct. The construct forces a split on the value stored in a variable depending on its type: if the value is a `struct`, the split is performed on all of its fields that hold symbolic values. The `split-all` construct can be soundly applied to any bound occurrence of a local variable in a program, leading to intractable search spaces even for small programs. For example, there are 55 bound local variables in ToyRISC, so the `split-all` repair alone can be used to transform ToyRISC into 2^{55} syntactically distinct programs. SymFix is able to navigate this large search space effectively, matching the expert fix in a few seconds.

3   Symbolic Performance Repair

As Sect. 2 illustrates, performance bottlenecks in solver-aided code are difficult to repair manually. This section presents a new formulation of this problem that enables automatic solving. Our formulation is based on two core concepts: repairs and fixes. A *repair* is a semantics-preserving transformation on programs. A *fix* combines a sequence of repair steps, with the goal of reducing the *cost* of a program under symbolic evaluation. The *symbolic performance repair problem* is to find a fix, drawn from a finite set of repairs, that minimizes this cost. We describe repairs and fixes first, present the symbolic performance repair problem next, and end with a discussion of key properties of repairs that are sufficient for solving the repair problem in principle and helpful for solving it in practice.

3.1   Repairs, Fixes, and Symbolic Cost

Repairs. A *repair* transforms a program to a set of programs that are syntactically different but semantically equivalent (Definitions 1 and 2). A repair operates on programs represented as abstract syntax trees (ASTs). It takes as input an AST and a node in this AST, and produces an ordered set of ASTs that transform the input program at the given node or one of its ancestors. This interface generalizes classic program transformations by allowing repairs to produce multiple ASTs. The classic interface is often implemented by heuristically choosing one of many possible outputs that an underlying rewrite rule can generate. Our interface externalizes this choice, while still letting repairs provide heuristic knowledge in the order of the generated ASTs, as illustrated in Example 1. This enables an external algorithm to drive the search for fixes, with advice from the repairs.

Definition 1 (Program). *A* program *is an abstract syntax tree (AST) in a language $\mathcal{P}$, consisting of labeled nodes and edges. A program $P \in \mathcal{P}$ denotes a function $[\![P]\!] : \Sigma \to \Sigma$ on program states, which map program variables to values. Programs P and P' are syntactically equivalent if their trees consist of identically labeled nodes, connected by identically labeled edges. They are semantically equivalent iff $[\![P]\!]^{\mathcal{P}} \sigma \equiv [\![P']\!]^{\mathcal{P}} \sigma$ for all program states $\sigma \in \Sigma$, where $[\![\cdot]\!]^{\mathcal{P}} : \mathcal{P} \to \Sigma \to \Sigma$ denotes the concrete semantics of $\mathcal{P}$.*

Definition 2 (Repair). *A* repair $R : \mathcal{P} \to \mathcal{L} \to 2^{\mathcal{P}}$ *is a function that maps a program and a location to an ordered finite set of programs. A location $l \in \mathcal{L}$ identifies a node in an AST. The set $R(P, l)$ is empty if the repair R is not applicable to P at the location l. Otherwise, each program $P_i \in R(P, l)$ satisfies two properties. First, P and P_i differ in a single subtree rooted at l or an ancestor of l in P. Second, P and P_i are semantically equivalent.*

Example 1. Consider a repair R_1 that performs the rewrite $e * 2 \rightarrow e \mathbin{<\!\!<} 1$ on integer expressions. There are three ways to apply this rewrite to the program $P = 1 + (a * 2) * 2$ at the node a or its ancestors, and R_1 orders them as follows:

```
1 + (a << 1) << 1  ; 0: Apply the rewrite exhaustively.
1 + (a << 1) * 2   ; 1: Apply the rewrite just to a's parent.
1 + (a * 2) << 1   ; 2: Apply the rewrite just to a's grandparent.
```

The order of the generated ASTs suggests that applying the rewrite exhaustively is most useful, followed by applying it from the inside out.

Fixes. A *fix* composes a sequence of *repair steps* into a function from programs to programs (Definitions 3 and 4). A repair step $\langle R, l, i \rangle$ specifies the repair R to apply to a program, the location l at which to apply it, and the index i of the program to select from the resulting ordered set of programs. In essence, a repair step turns a repair into a classic program transformation by choosing one of the repair's outputs, and fixes can compose these steps to create new transformations, as illustrated in Example 2.

Definition 3 (Repair step). *A repair step $\langle R, l, i \rangle$ consists of a repair R, program location l, and non-negative integer i. A step denotes the function $[\![\langle R, l, i \rangle]\!] : \mathcal{P} \cup \{\bot\} \rightarrow \mathcal{P} \cup \{\bot\}$ as follows: $[\![\langle R, l, i \rangle]\!]P = R(P, l)[i]$ if $P \neq \bot$ and $|R(P, l)| > i$; otherwise the result is $\bot$. We write $R(P, l)[i]$ to mean the ith program in the ordered set $R(P, l)$.*

Definition 4 (Fix). *A fix $F = [\langle R_1, l_1, i_1 \rangle, \ldots, \langle R_n, l_n, i_n \rangle]$ is a finite sequence of one or more repair steps. A fix F denotes the function that composes the repair steps of F, i.e., $[\![F]\!] = [\![\langle R_n, l_n, i_n \rangle]\!] \circ \ldots \circ [\![\langle R_1, l_1, i_1 \rangle]\!]$. We say that fix is successful for a program P if $[\![F]\!]P \neq \bot$.*

Example 2. Consider the fix $F = [\langle R_1, a, 0 \rangle, \langle R_2, a, 0 \rangle]$, where R_1 is the repair from Example 1 and R_2 performs the rewrite $(e \mathbin{<\!\!<} 1) \mathbin{<\!\!<} 1 \rightarrow e \mathbin{<\!\!<} 2$. Applying F to the program P from Example 1 produces the program $1 + (a \mathbin{<\!\!<} 2)$: $[\![\langle R_2, a, 0 \rangle]\!]([\![\langle R_1, a, 0 \rangle]\!]P) = [\![\langle R_2, a, 0 \rangle]\!](1 + (a \mathbin{<\!\!<} 1) \mathbin{<\!\!<} 1) = 1 + (a \mathbin{<\!\!<} 2)$. In other words, the fix F composes its repair steps to rewrite the second subexpression of P using the rule $(e * 2) * 2 \rightarrow e \mathbin{<\!\!<} 2$.

Cost. There are many ways to combine repairs into fixes for a given program, even when the program is small and repairs are few (Example 3). To choose a fix that is *useful* for improving the performance of a program under *symbolic evaluation*, we need a way to measure the *cost* of symbolic evaluation (Definition 5). We address this challenge by building on the observation that the behavior of symbolic evaluators is characterized by two structures: the symbolic heap and the symbolic evaluation graph. Our framework defines symbolic evaluation as a function from programs and program states to these structures (Definition 6), and the cost of symbolic evaluation as a function from these structures to (natural) numbers (Definition 7). The details of the cost function are not important for the framework, although they are important in practice: the symbolic cost should correlate with concrete metrics that are meaningful to developers (e.g., end-to-end running time), and SymFix uses a cost function (Sect. 4) that is simple but effective (Sect. 5). What matters, however, is that the symbolic evaluator is a total function, which means that we consider only finite computations. In particular, we make the standard assumption that programs $P \in \mathcal{P}$ are free of input-dependent loops, and are therefore guaranteed to terminate under symbolic evaluation, ensuring that we can compute the cost for every fix.

Definition 5 (Useful fix). *A fix F is* useful *for a program $P \in \mathcal{P}$, program state $\sigma \in \Sigma$, symbolic evaluator $S : \mathcal{P} \to \Sigma \to \mathcal{G}$, and cost $c : \mathcal{G} \times \mathcal{H} \to \mathbb{N}$, if $\llbracket F \rrbracket P \neq \bot$ and $c(S(\llbracket F \rrbracket P, \sigma)) < c(S(P, \sigma))$.*

Definition 6 (Symbolic evaluator). *A symbolic evaluator $S : \mathcal{P} \to \Sigma \to \mathcal{G} \times \mathcal{H}$ is a function that takes as input a program $P \in \mathcal{P}$ and program state $\sigma \in \Sigma$, and outputs a pair $\langle G, H \rangle$, where $G \in \mathcal{G}$ is a symbolic evaluation graph and $H \in \mathcal{H}$ is a symbolic heap [7]. A symbolic heap $H = (V_H, E_H)$ is a directed acyclic graph (DAG) with labeled nodes and edges. Heap nodes are symbolic values, and heap edges connect compound symbolic values to the symbolic or concrete values from which they are built. A symbolic evaluation graph $G = (V_G, E_G)$ is a DAG where nodes $V_G \subseteq \Sigma$ are program states and edges are transitions between states, each labeled with a (symbolic or concrete) boolean value that guards the transition and a program location in P that caused the transition. The graph G has $\sigma \in V_G$ as its sole source node. The heap H contains all symbolic values that appear in G as part of a program state or as an edge label. If $H = (\emptyset, \emptyset)$ is empty, then G consists of a single path from σ to $\llbracket P \rrbracket^{\mathcal{P}} \sigma$, where all edges are labeled with $\top$.*

Definition 7 (Symbolic cost). *A symbolic cost function $c : \mathcal{G} \times \mathcal{H} \to \mathbb{N}$ assigns a cost, expressed as a natural number, to the results of symbolic evaluation.*

Example 3. Consider again the fix F, repairs R_1 and R_2, and program P from Examples 1 and 2. In addition to F, there are seven different ways to compose repair steps over R_1 and R_2 into fixes for P; two are equivalent to F and five to the outputs of R_1 on P. Intuitively, F produces the best program for all workloads, and in this case, the intuition is captured by a simple cost function that measures the size of the symbolic heap, i.e., $c(\langle G, H \rangle) = |V_H|$. For example, letting $\sigma = \{a \mapsto A\}$, where A is a symbolic integer, we can compute the cost of P, the output of the fix $[\langle R_1, a, 0 \rangle]$, and the output of the fix F as follows:

$$c(S(1 + (a * 2) * 2, \sigma)) = |\{v_0 : A * 2, v_1 : v_0 * 2, v_2 : 1 + v_1\}| \quad = 3$$
$$c(S(1 + (a << 1) << 1, \sigma)) = |\{v_0 : A << 1, v_1 : v_0 << 1, v_2 : 1 + v_1\}| = 3$$
$$c(S(1 + (a << 1) << 2, \sigma)) = |\{v_0 : A << 2, v_1 : 1 + v_0\}| \quad = 2$$

As expected, the program produced by F has the lowest cost.

3.2   The Symbolic Performance Repair Problem

The *symbolic performance repair problem* is to find a fix, drawn from a finite set of repairs, that minimizes the symbolic cost of a program on a given workload

(Definition 8). To make this problem solvable in principle, it is sufficient to ensure that the set of repairs is *terminating* [17], preventing the repairs from being indefinitely applicable to any program (Definition 9). To help solve the repair problem in practice, we can use a general property of repairs, *precedence*, to prune fixes during search without missing any programs (Definition 10). A partial order $\preceq_R$ is a precedence relation on a set of repairs R if every successful fix over R can be turned into an equivalent fix by permuting its repair steps to respect $\preceq_R$. To search for a fix over R with $\preceq_R$, it is sufficient to explore successful fixes that order all repair steps according to $\preceq_R$. Example 4 illustrates these definitions, and we use them in the next section to develop the SymFix algorithm for solving the repair problem.

Definition 8 (Symbolic performance repair). *Let $P \in \mathcal{P}$ be a program, $\sigma \in \Sigma$ a program state, R a finite set of repairs for $\mathcal{P}$, S a symbolic evaluator for $\mathcal{P}$, and c a symbolic cost function for S. The* symbolic performance repair problem *is to find a useful fix F over R that minimizes the cost of evaluating P on σ; i.e., for all useful fixes $F' \neq F$ over R, $c(S(\llbracket F \rrbracket P, \sigma)) \leq c(S(\llbracket F' \rrbracket P, \sigma))$.*

Definition 9 (Terminating repair set). *Let R be a finite set of repairs for the language $\mathcal{P}$. We say this set is* terminating *if for every program $P \in \mathcal{P}$, there is an upper bound on the length of every successful fix for P drawn from R.*

Definition 10 (Repair precedence). *Let R be a finite set of repairs and $\preceq_R$ a partial order on R. Let* spine *be a function that projects out the repairs from a fix, i.e., $\mathrm{spine}(F) = [R_1, \ldots, R_n]$ for $F = [\langle R_1, l_1, i_1 \rangle, \ldots, \langle R_n, l_n, i_n \rangle]$. We say that $\preceq_R$ is a* precedence *on R if for every program P and every successful fix F for P drawn from R, there is a fix F' such that $\llbracket F \rrbracket P = \llbracket F' \rrbracket P$ and $\mathrm{spine}(F')$ permutes $\mathrm{spine}(F)$ to respect $\preceq_R$, i.e., $\forall i, j.\, \mathrm{spine}(F')[i] \preceq_R \mathrm{spine}(F')[j] \implies i \leq j$.*

Example 4. Recall the program P, repairs R_1 and R_2, fix F, and cost c from Examples 1–3. The repair set $R = \{R_1, R_2\}$ is terminating; $R_1 \preceq_R R_2$; and F is a solution to the symbolic performance repair problem for P, R, and c.

4   The SymFix Algorithm and Repairs

This section presents the SymFix system for solving the symbolic performance repair problem. SymFix consists of two components: an anytime algorithm for searching the space of fixes drawn from a terminating set of repairs, and a set of three generic repairs for functional solver-aided languages with symbolic reflection. We present the algorithm first and prove its correctness and optimality (Sect. 4.1). We then describe the repairs and a total precedence relation on them, and argue that they form a terminating set (Sect. 4.2). We end by highlighting the key details of our implementation of SymFix for the Rosette language (Sect. 4.3).

```
 1  function SymFix(P_in, σ, S, M, R, ⪯_R)
 2      function Info(P, F)                         ▷ Symbolic profile sorts P's locations from most to least
 3          ⟨L_P, m_P⟩ ← M(S(P, σ))                 ▷ likely bottlenecks & collects k profiling metrics.
 4          c_P ← Σ_{0≤i<k} m_i                     ▷ P's cost is the sum of its profiling metrics.
 5          return {P ↦ {cost ↦ c_P, locs ↦ L_P, fix ↦ F}}
 6      function Next(P, info)                      ▷ Picks a successor of P, if any, with an extra repair.
 7          F ← info[P][fix]                        ▷ Get the fix that generated P.
 8          for R in R do                           ▷ Iterate over the repairs in R that do not precede
 9              if ⋀_{R_i ∈ spine(F)} R_i = R ∨ R ⪯̸_R R_i then          ▷ any repairs in P's fix,
10                  for l in info[P][locs] do       ▷ then over the ranked locations in P,
11                      for P_j ∈ R(P, l) do        ▷ and then over the ordered results
12                          if info[P_j] = ⊥ then   ▷ to find a new program P_j.
13                              return ⟨P_j, append(F, ⟨R, l, j⟩)⟩     ▷ Return P_j and its fix.
14          return ⟨⊥, ⊥⟩                           ▷ No new programs can be obtained from P.
15      function Search(P_in)
16          W, info ← {P_in}, Info(P_in, [])        ▷ Initialize the work set and info map.
17          minCost ← info[P_in][cost]              ▷ Set P's cost as current best cost.
18          while W ≠ ∅ do
19              P ← min(W, λP.info[P][cost])        ▷ Choose the cheapest P ∈ W to work on.
20              ⟨P', F'⟩ ← Next(P, info)            ▷ Get a successor P' of P and its fix.
21              if ⟨P', F'⟩ ≠ ⟨⊥, ⊥⟩ then           ▷ If P' exists,
22                  W, info ← W ∪ {P'}, info ∪ Info(P', F')            ▷ add P' to W and info;
23                  if info[P'][cost] < minCost then ▷ and if P' is best so far,
24                      minCost ← info[P'][cost]     ▷ update minCost and
25                      print P'                     ▷ output P'.
26              else
27                  W ← W \ {P}                      ▷ No new programs can be obtained from P.
28      Search(P_in)
```

Fig. 4. The SymFix search algorithm takes as input a program P_{in} in a language $\mathcal{P}$, a workload σ, a symbolic evaluator S for $\mathcal{P}$, a symbolic profiler M for S, a terminating set of repairs R for $\mathcal{P}$, and a precedence relation $\preceq_R$ on R. It searches the space of fixes drawn from R to find a program that is equivalent to P_{in} and minimizes the cost of symbolic evaluation on σ according to the profiler M.

4.1 Profile-Guided Search for Fixes

The SymFix algorithm (Fig. 4) solves the symbolic performance repair problem for a cost function based on symbolic profiling. As shown in prior work [7], the metrics computed by a symbolic profiler closely reflect the overall running time of solver-aided code (i.e., symbolic evaluation together with solving time), and reducing these metrics is key to improving performance. In addition to computing these metrics, which measure the size and shape of the symbolic heap and evaluation graph, a symbolic profiler M also ranks all locations in a program from most to least expensive to evaluate. The SymFix algorithm uses both of these outputs: it searches for a fix that minimizes the sum of the profiling metrics for a given program and workload, and the search is guided by the profiling ranks.

The algorithm relies on the SEARCH procedure to explore the space of fixes for a program P_{in} and a terminating set of repairs R. SEARCH performs exhaustive (rather than greedy) best-first search over this space. It starts by initializing the work set W with the input program P_{in}; the *info* map with a binding from P_{in} to its profiling metrics, cost, and the empty fix; and the minimum cost *minCost* with the cost of P_{in}. The main search loop then picks a program P from the work set, applies one repair step to P to get a new program P' (corresponding to a fix F' that extends P's fix by one step), and adds P' to both W and *info*. If the new program P' has lower cost than *minCost*, SEARCH prints it and updates *minCost* accordingly. But if no new programs can be obtained from P by applying a repair from R, then P has no more children in the underlying search graph, and SEARCH removes it from the work set W. The search continues as long as there are programs in W, so the entire search graph is eventually explored.

To make the algorithm practically useful, SEARCH employs the procedure NEXT to explore the most promising fixes first and to prune the search space without losing completeness. SEARCH selects the cheapest fix F to extend (line 19), and NEXT constructs the repair step $\langle R, l, j \rangle$ to add to F. To construct $\langle R, l, j \rangle$, NEXT first choses a repair R that does not strictly precede any of the repairs in F, according to the precedence relation $\preceq_R$. Then, it uses profiling rankings and the repair's ordering heuristics to select the location l and the result index j. This ensures that SEARCH explores only fixes that respect $\preceq_R$, and that it tries to repair most likely bottlenecks first.

The SymFix algorithm is sound, complete, and optimal (Theorem 1). It produces correct fixes that are semantically equivalent to the input program (soundness). It always finds a useful fix if one exists in the space defined by the given set of repairs (completeness). And it eventually finds the best such fix that minimizes the symbolic profiling cost on the given workload (optimality).

Theorem 1. *Let P_{in} be a program, σ a workload, R a terminating set of repairs, and $\preceq_R$ a precedence relation on R. Then $\text{SYMFIX}(P_{in}, \sigma, S, M, R, \preceq_R)$ terminates and satisfies the following conditions. (1) If SEARCH produces a program at line 25, then every such program P' is semantically equivalent to P_{in} (soundness). (2) For every cost $C < info[P_{in}][cost]$, if there is a fix over R with cost C, then line 25 will produce a program P' with $info[P'][cost] \leq C$ (completeness and optimality).*

Proof (sketch). First, note that SymFix explores a search graph where nodes are programs; two nodes are related by a repair step drawn from R; and a path in the graph corresponds to a fix over R that respects $\preceq_R$. All paths through this graph are finite because R is terminating (Definition 9). There are also finitely many such paths because each node has finitely many outgoing edges (repair steps), which follows from the finite number of repairs, locations in a program, and repair outputs. So, (1) the underlying search graph is finite, and (2) by definition of $\preceq_R$ (Definition 10), it contains the same programs (nodes) as the search graph that includes all fixes (paths) over R. Next, note that (3) SymFix adds each program in this graph to the work set W exactly once, and (4) each added program is removed after all of its children have been visited, i.e., added to the *info* map. These facts (1–4) imply that the algorithm terminates after visiting each program in the space defined by R. Completeness and optimality then follow from lines 17, 23–25, and soundness follows from the definition of repairs (Definition 2).

4.2 Effective Repairs for Functional Hosts with Symbolic Reflection

The effectiveness of SymFix hinges on the choice of the repair set R. An ideal repair set includes a few key repairs that can be combined into useful fixes for most common performance bottlenecks. This section presents three such repairs for solver-aided languages with functional programming primitives and symbolic reflection. We use Rosette to illustrate these repairs, but they are applicable to any solver-aided language or framework with similar features (e.g., [13,39,47]).

Deforestation. Higher-order combinators (e.g., `map`, `fold`, and `filter`) are commonly used to operate on lists. Using these combinators generates intermediate lists that are immediately consumed and discarded, slowing down concrete evaluation by a constant factor. Under symbolic evaluation, however, the resulting slow down is asymptotically worse, as the following example demonstrates.

```
(define (sum-slow xs)            ; Sums the positive numbers in xs using an
   (foldr + 0 (filter positive? xs)))  ; intermediate list (the result of filter).

(define (sum-fast xs)            ; Sums the positive numbers in xs without
   (foldr (lambda (e acc)        ; creating any intermediate lists.
            (if (positive? e)
                (+ e acc)
                acc))
          0 xs))

> (define-symbolic xs integer? [100])  ; xs is a list of 100 symbolic integers.

> (time (sum-slow xs))                 ; Adds 520,000 values to the symbolic heap.
cpu time: 5119 real time: 4954 gc time: 2194

> (time (sum-fast xs))                 ; Adds 100 values to the symbolic heap.
cpu time: 3 real time: 3 gc time: 0    ; Times are given in milliseconds.
```

Deforestation [48] is a classic program transformation that eliminates intermediate lists produced by list combinators. As such, it makes a powerful repair for performance bottlenecks in solver-aided code. In the above example, it automatically transforms `sum-slow` into `sum-fast`, avoiding the expensive call to `filter` that creates a symbolic intermediate list when the input `xs` is symbolic. Many variants of deforestation exist for different functional languages; for Rosette, SymFix uses a repair based on build/foldr fusion [22]. This repair applies deforestation exhaustively at a given location and outputs at most one program.

Path Splitting. Deforestation changes the behavior of a program under symbolic evaluation by restructuring its implementation. But if the host language supports symbolic reflection [46], we can control the evaluation more directly, by using dedicated constructs to force path splitting [44] (or state merging [38]) at specific program locations. We have seen an example of this in Sect. 2, where SymFix used a path splitting construct to fix the ToyRISC interpreter. In Rosette, this construct takes the form (`split-all` (x) E), where x is an identifier and E an expression over x. If x is bound to a symbolic value that ranges over a small finite set of concrete values, $\{v_1, \ldots, v_n\}$, then `split-all` splits the evaluation of E into n paths, one for each value that x can take, i.e., $x = v_i \vdash$ (`let` (`[`x v_i`]`) E) for $1 \leq i \leq n$. Otherwise, `split-all` acts as the identity transformation on E. Because path splitting increases the number of paths that are evaluated, it must be applied carefully to avoid path explosion—a task we delegate to automated search.

The SymFix path splitting repair works as follows. Given a program location l in a procedure body P, it outputs all valid ways to insert (split-all (x) E) into P, so that E contains the location l, x is bound in E's context, and there is no other split on x in E or its context. So, nested splits on the same identifier, (split-all (x) $(\ldots$(split-all (x) $\ldots)$), are disallowed. The resulting set of transformed programs is finite but large, and the repair heuristically prefers splits with broadest scope (i.e., where E is the highest ancestor of l in P).

Value Splitting. Path splitting allows programs to exert local control on the symbolic evaluation strategy, by concretizing a specific symbolic value at a specific program location. In principle, it is possible to combine many path splitting repairs to implement a global change in the evaluation strategy, such as concretizing every operation on a given user-defined type. In practice, however, this would require prohibitively long and complex fixes. We therefore develop a global value splitting repair that assumes the host language provides a mechanism for controlling how all values of a given type are merged and split. In Rosette, this is done with a *transparency* annotation, illustrated in the following example.

```
(require rosette/lib/match)                    (require rosette/lib/match)

(struct Cell (v) #:transparent)                (struct Cell (v))      ; Opaque struct.

; Return a new Cell that doubles             ; Return a new Cell that doubles
; the value v of c.                          ; the value v of c.
(define (twice c)                            (define (twice c)
  (match c                                     (match c
    [(Cell v) (Cell (+ v v))]))                  [(Cell v) (Cell (+ v v))]))

; Create a symbolic Cell.                    ; Create a symbolic Cell.
(define-symbolic b boolean?)                 (define-symbolic b boolean?)
(define c (if b (Cell 1) (Cell 0)))          (define c (if b (Cell 1) (Cell 0)))

; Fields of transparent structs are merged,  ; Fields of opaque structs are not merged,
; so 'twice' works on symbolic values.       ; so 'twice' works on concrete values.
> c                                          > c
(Cell (ite b 1 0))                           {[b ⊢ (Cell 1)] [(! b) ⊢ (Cell 0)]}
> (twice c)                                  > (twice c)
(Cell (+ (ite b 1 0) (ite b 1 0)))           {[b ⊢ (Cell 2)] [(! b) ⊢ (Cell 0)]}

; The symbolic heap now contains 4 values:   ; The symbolic heap now contains 2 values,
; b, ¬b, ite(b, 1, 0), ite(b, 1, 0) + ite(b, 1, 0).   ; b, ¬b, but the graph has more paths.
```

The SymFix value splitting repair toggles the transparency annotation on user-defined structures in a way that preserves soundness. Under Rosette semantics, it is sound to make structs less transparent (i.e., the transparency annotation can be removed) but not more. So given a location within a struct declaration, the value splitting repair produces at most one program. Like path splitting, this repair creates more opportunities for concrete evaluation, at the cost of adding more paths to the symbolic evaluation graph.

Termination and Precedence. The SymFix repairs form a terminating set with a total precedence relation $R_V \preceq_R R_D \preceq_R R_P$ that orders value splitting first, deforestation second, and path splitting last. To see this, first note that value splitting applies to structs, while neither of the other repairs does, so R_V can be freely reordered with R_D and R_P. Next, observe that if deforestation R_D follows path splitting R_P, then either they were applied to disjoint locations, or R_P was applied to an expression that is moved but not transformed by deforestation (e.g., xs in the sum-slow example). In either case, the same effect can be achieved by applying R_P after R_D (though not vice versa). Finally, note that R_V and R_D can be applied to the same location at most once, and R_P can be applied at most N times, where N is the number of bound identifiers in the enclosing context. Hence, the set $\{R_V, R_D, R_P\}$ is terminating.

4.3   Implementation

We implemented the SymFix algorithm and repairs for Rosette. All three repairs require side effect analysis to preserve soundness, and we implement a simple conservative analysis that allows repairs only on expressions built out of procedures and constructs known to be safe. Because the repairs are totally ordered, we apply them in stages so that all of our fixes are of the form $R_V^* R_D^* R_P^*$. While our repair framework assumes that programs have no unbounded loops, Rosette places no bounds on loops by design [46], so it is possible to write a Rosette program that does not terminate under symbolic evaluation. Our implementation deals with diverging and slow executions with timeouts.

5   Evaluation

To evaluate the effectiveness of SymFix, we address three research questions:

RQ1: Can SymFix repair the performance of state-of-the-art solver-aided tools, and how do its fixes compare to those written by experts?

RQ2: Do the fixes found by SymFix generalize to different workloads?

RQ3: How important is SymFix's search strategy for finding useful fixes?

All results in this section were collected using an Intel Core i7-7700K at 4.20 GHz with 16 GB of RAM, running Racket v7.4. Each timing result is the average of 10 executions of the corresponding experiment.

5.1   Can SymFix Repair the Performance of State-of-the-Art Solver-Aided Tools, and How Do Its Fixes Compare to Experts'?

To demonstrate that SymFix is effective on state-of-the-art solver-aided tools, we collected a suite of 15 tools [2,5,6,8,10,12,14,25,33,36,46,50,51] built in Rosette from a prior literature survey [7], together with 3 more recent tools [29,31,35]. For each of these Rosette programs, we applied SymFix to identify and repair performance bottlenecks.

Figure 5 shows the results. For each program, we report the original running time in seconds, and the cost of the original program as estimated by SymFix. We report three sources of repairs: fixes found by SymFix, fixes found by a baseline greedy algorithm discussed in Sect. 5.3, and manual fixes from prior work [7,29]. We used a one-hour timeout for all experiments. For each fix, we

Program	LoC	Original Time	Original Cost	SymFix Time	SymFix Cost	$|F|$	#	Greedy Time	Greedy Cost	Manual Time	Manual Cost
Bagpipe	3317	17 s	6.0e4	1.0×	1.0×	1	6	–	–	–	–
Bonsai[†]	641	27 s	1.5e6	1.3×	1.3×	2	21	1.1×	1.1×	1.0×	0.9×
Cosette[§]	2709	–	–	21 s	6.8e5	3	33	–	–	15 s	7.4e5
Ferrite	350	13 s	9.8e5	2.8×	3.8×	4	11	–	–	1.6×	1.1×
Fluidics	145	10 s	6.5e5	1.9×	1.7×	1	1	1.9×	1.7×	2.1×	1.8×
FRPSynth	304	3 s	2.3e4	3.1×	1.6×	4	93	1.4×	1.3×	–	–
GreenThumb	934	1179 s	2.0e5	1.3×	1.1×	1	1	1.3×	1.1×	–	–
IFCL	574	53 s	6.2e5	–	–	–	–	–	–	–	–
Memsynth	3362	15 s	2.0e6	1.1×	1.1×	1	2	1.0×	1.1×	–	–
Neutrons	37317	29 s	5.6e6	2.0×	2.3×	3	5	2.0×	2.3×	193.7×	869.9×
Nonograms	6693	8 s	1.5e5	1.1×	1.4×	7	46	–	–	–	–
Quivela	5946	47 s	2.9e6	91.7×	218.4×	6	7	90.1×	187.3×	86.1×	218.5×
RTR	2007	282 s	1.6e7	–	–	–	–	–	–	7.2×	4.1×
Serval[‡]	8641	116 s	7.3e6	6.2×	80.7×	1	1	–	–	6.2×	80.7×
Swizzle	1240	7 s	3.1e5	1.8×	1.3×	2	18	–	–	–	–
SynthCL	3732	16 s	7.5e5	–	–	–	–	–	–	–	–
Wallingford	3866	2 s	8.5e3	1.0×	1.0×	1	2	–	–	–	–
WebSynth	2057	7 s	1.0e6	–	–	–	–	–	–	–	–

† The manual repair was made unnecessary by a subsequent Rosette improvement.
§ The repair by SymFix involves independent changes from users.
‡ The repair by SymFix uses user-supplied repairs.

Fig. 5. Summary of fixes found by SymFix, a baseline greedy search, and experts. "LoC" is the number of lines of code in a given benchmark; "Cost" is SymFix's cost function for search; "$|F|$" is the number of repair steps in the fix found by SYMFIX; and "#" is the number of fixes explored in one hour before the reported best one is found.

report the relative speedup and cost decrease compared to the original run time and cost. A dash "–" indicates the absence of data due to timeouts or the lack of known manual fixes. One original program (Cosette) does not terminate within an hour, so we report only its repaired running times and costs.

SymFix finds fixes that improve the performance of 12 programs, with the improvements ranging from 1.1× to 91.7×. SymFix also finds 2 fixes that lower the symbolic cost and runtime only slightly, marked as 1.0× in Fig. 5. The "#" column reports the number of iterations of SymFix's search procedure needed to find the fix, and "$|F|$" reports the number of repair steps in the fix. Most fixes are found in fewer than 10 iterations, and most have up to 2 repair steps.

Of the 15 benchmarks from prior work, 7 were manually fixed by the authors of that paper. For two of these benchmarks (Neutrons and RTR), the expert finds a significantly better fix than SymFix or finds some fix while SymFix finds none. Overall, SymFix matches or outperforms experts on 4 benchmarks, and it finds fixes for 5 benchmarks with no expert fix. We inspected all the fixes manually, and discuss interesting cases below.

For **Bonsai** (a synthesis tool for checking type-system soundness [12]), **Neutrons** (a verifier for safety-critical systems [33]), and **RTR** (a refinement type checker for Ruby), the manual fixes were sound but not semantics-preserving, so SymFix cannot discover them. For Bonsai, the manual fix was made unnecessary by a subsequent Rosette improvement, but SymFix still discovers a new repair

Program	Input	Original		SymFix	
		Time (s)	Cost	Time	Cost
Bonsai	nanodot	17 s	7.8e5	1.2×	1.1×
Cosette	q2	1 s	4.6e4	2.2×	9.8×
Cosette	q3	–	–	33 s	1.3e6
Ferrite	chrome	99 s	2.1e7	16.2×	15.6×
FRPSynth	program0	2 s	1.9e4	0.8×	0.8×
Quivela	test-etm-10	19 s	6.7e5	1.8×	1.8×
Serval	enosys	105 s	8.0e5	1.8×	11.3×
Swizzle	stencil	6 s	2.1e5	1.1×	1.1×
Swizzle	aos-sum	5 s	5.4e4	1.1×	1.0×

Fig. 6. Effectiveness of SymFix's repairs from Fig. 5 on alternative workloads.

that improves the performance further. For Neutrons, SymFix cannot recover the manual fix but does find a concretization opportunity offering a 2.0× speedup. For RTR, SymFix does not find a useful fix, suggesting future opportunities to exploit *conditional* repairs that are only sound under certain preconditions [40].

For **Cosette**, an automated prover for deciding the equivalence of two SQL queries [14], the original implementation did not terminate within one hour. The expert fix allowed Cosette to terminate in 15 s. Because SymFix needs to execute the original program during the search for repairs, we imposed a timeout of 60 s per execution. SymFix finds a fix that reduces Cosette's run time to 21 s, comparable to the manual fix. This new fix combines path splitting and deforestation of the map–reduce pattern Cosette uses to filter SQL tables. Finding the deforestation repair required converting Cosette's recursive implementation of this pattern into a higher-order version, but the Cosette developers made this change independently to implement the manual fix; SymFix exploited this new structure to find another fix that allows Cosette to terminate in seconds.

For **Fluidics**, a tool for synthesizing programs that control a digital microfluidics array [51], the expert-written fix involves a change to the core data structure the tool uses to represent the array. This change is outside the scope of SymFix's search space. However, SymFix instead discovers a different fix that uses path splitting and requires no changes to the data structure. This fix offers a 1.9× speedup instead of 2.1× for the manual one, but it is made automatically and allows the tool's developers to retain their preferred data structure.

For **Ferrite**, a tool for checking file-system crash consistency [5], SymFix improves upon the expert-written fix by finding additional opportunities for concretization through path and value splitting. These changes make Ferrite close to 2× faster than the expert-repaired version.

For **GreenThumb**, a tool for developing superoptimizers [36], SymFix finds a concretization opportunity that the expert did not. The concretization both improves symbolic evaluation and alters the shape of the SMT formula so that SMT solving is 1.1× faster. SymFix also finds previously unknown concretization opportunities for **FRPSynth**, a tool for synthesizing functional reactive programs [31], and **Swizzle**, a tool for synthesizing GPU kernels [35], leading to a 3.1× and 1.8× speed-up, respectively.

For **Serval**, a toolset for automatic verification of systems software [29], Sym-
Fix does not discover a significant fix using its built-in repairs. But Serval comes
with its own set of *symbolic optimizations*, which were originally designed for
manual application [29]. Using these optimizations as repairs, SymFix discovers
the manual fix, showing that its algorithm works well with a variety of repairs.

5.2 Do the Fixes Found by SymFix Generalize to Different Workloads?

SymFix generates each of the fixes in Fig. 5 using a single input to the respective
program. To determine whether discovered repairs generalize to *different* program inputs, we identified the programs in Fig. 5 that have alternative inputs
available and executed the repaired versions on them.

Figure 6 shows the performance of each program on alternative inputs, both
before and after the fix that SymFix discovered in Fig. 5. In all but one case, the
fix generalizes to the new input and improves the program's performance. The
relative performance improvement varies from Fig. 5 due to different problem
sizes; for example, the new Ferrite input is much larger than the original and so
spends comparatively less time in the fixed procedure. The one exception is the
"program0" input to FRPSynth, which is 20% slower than the original version.
Manual inspection of this fix shows that the last of its 4 repair steps overfits to
the initial input, and the first 3 steps improve the performance on both inputs.

5.3 How Important Is SymFix's Search Strategy for Finding Fixes?

SymFix employs a complete form of best-first search, guided by symbolic profiling ranks. To evaluate the importance of these design choices, we consider two
alternative algorithms without them:

Random implements a complete best-first search that is not guided by profiling
  ranks, and instead chooses a location randomly at line 10 in Fig. 4; and
Greedy implements the standard greedy best-first search, which applies only the
  first repair produced by NEXT at line 20 and never backtracks (by removing
  P from W unconditionally at line 27).

The **Random** algorithm discovers no useful fix for any benchmark within a
one hour timeout. This is not surprising since the space of fixes is exponential
in the number of potential repair locations, and there are thousands of such
locations in each benchmark. The results for the **Greedy** algorithm are reported
in the last two columns of Fig. 5. **Greedy** finds a useful fix for only half (7) of the
benchmarks repaired by SymFix, and none of its fixes are better than those found
by SymFix. These results show that the key features of the SymFix algorithm
are vital for fixing performance bottlenecks in real solver-aided tools.

6 Related Work

Profile-Guided Optimization. Compilers often support *profile-guided* optimization, in which the compiler uses profile data to guide its optimization phases (see Gupta et al. [23] for a survey). For example, the efficacy of inlining depends on factors including cache size and access patterns that are best determined by executing the program in the intended environment. Pettis and Hansen [34] introduce a profile-guided code layout algorithm that tries to position commonly used code together in memory to improve spatial locality. As another example, many JIT compilers for both static and dynamic languages will *specialize* methods based on type information observed at run time [20,32] (e.g., specializing virtual calls for a particular concrete receiver). SymFix takes inspiration from these approaches, using profile data to guide the application of semantics-preserving repairs. But unlike them, SymFix focuses on optimizing a program's symbolic evaluation strategy rather than its utilization of machine resources.

Not all profile-guided optimization techniques are automated. Optimization coaching [42] is an interactive tool that gives programmers feedback about the optimizations a compiler applied to their program, and optimizations that it tried unsuccessfully. SymFix does not provide interactivity, but because its repairs are high level, it can follow the optimization coach approach of reporting them to the programmer as syntactic changes to their input program.

Symbolic Profiling. Because SymFix uses profile data to guide the search for fixes, its effectiveness depends on high quality profiles. SymFix builds on *symbolic profiling* [7], a technique for profiling the behavior of symbolic evaluation engines. Symbolic profiling generalizes across a spectrum of symbolic evaluation techniques, and so SymFix's approach could generalize to other engines that support symbolic profiling (e.g., Crucible [21]). Other profiling techniques measure different aspects of automated tools. The Z3 Axiom Profiler [3] measures axiom instantiations in the Z3 [16] SMT solver's quantifier theory module. It can be used to detect optimization opportunities at the SMT level. Using such profilers to extend SymFix to the SMT level is an interesting direction for future work.

Optimizing Symbolic Evaluation. A number of approaches exist for interactively improving the performance of tools based on symbolic evaluation. Wagner et al. [49] introduce a configuration for optimizing compilers to prioritize generating code that is amenable to symbolic execution. Cadar [11] develops a suite of compiler optimizations that make code easier to evaluate symbolically. Nelson et al. [29] develop a set of custom symbolic optimizations that can be manually applied to build scalable verifiers for low-level languages (e.g., RISC-V [1], LLVM [28], x86 [24], and eBPF [19]) on top of a generic verification framework. SymFix is complimentary to these approaches: it can automatically apply custom optimizations to verifiers for low-level code, and these verifiers can further benefit from the custom compiler optimizations applied to their input programs.

7 Conclusion

This paper presented a new approach to repairing performance bottlenecks in code under symbolic evaluation. Our approach rests on three technical contributions. We formulate the symbolic performance repair problem as combinatorial search for a fix that applies a sequence of semantics-preserving repairs to a program and a workload; the resulting fixed program is guaranteed to be equivalent to the input program, and to have minimal symbolic evaluation cost on the input workload. To solve this repair problem, we develop SymFix, a system with two key components: (1) a small set of generic repairs based on deforestation and symbolic reflection, and (2) an anytime search algorithm that uses symbolic profiling to guide the exploration of this space. Our evaluation shows that SymFix can discover useful fixes for state-of-the-art verification and synthesis tools, matching or outperforming experts, and that the fixed programs continue to work well across different workloads. As more programmers employ symbolic evaluation to automate verification and synthesis tasks for new domains, SymFix can help them build better tools more easily.

References

1. The RISC-V Instruction Set Manual, Volume II: Privileged Architecture. RISC-V Foundation, June 2019
2. Amazon Web Services: Quivela (2018). https://github.com/awslabs/quivela
3. Becker, N., Müller, P., Summers, A.J.: The axiom profiler: understanding and debugging SMT quantifier instantiations. In: Vojnar, T., Zhang, L. (eds.) TACAS 2019. LNCS, vol. 11427, pp. 99–116. Springer, Cham (2019). https://doi.org/10.1007/978-3-030-17462-0_6
4. Biere, A., Cimatti, A., Clarke, E., Zhu, Y.: Symbolic model checking without BDDs. In: Cleaveland, W.R. (ed.) TACAS 1999. LNCS, vol. 1579, pp. 193–207. Springer, Heidelberg (1999). https://doi.org/10.1007/3-540-49059-0_14
5. Bornholt, J., Kaufmann, A., Li, J., Krishnamurthy, A., Torlak, E., Wang, X.: Specifying and checking file system crash-consistency models. In: Proceedings of the 21st International Conference on Architectural Support for Programming Languages and Operating Systems (ASPLOS), Atlanta, GA, USA, pp. 83–98, April 2016
6. Bornholt, J., Torlak, E.: Synthesizing memory models from framework sketches and litmus tests. In: Proceedings of the 38th ACM SIGPLAN Conference on Programming Language Design and Implementation (PLDI), Barcelona, Spain, pp. 467–481, June 2017
7. Bornholt, J., Torlak, E.: Finding code that explodes under symbolic evaluation. Proc. ACM Program. Lang. (OOPSLA) **2**, 149:1–149:26 (2018)
8. Borning, A.: Wallingford: toward a constraint reactive programming language. In: Proceedings of the Constrained and Reactive Objects Workshop (CROW), Málaga, Spain, March 2016
9. Bucur, S., Kinder, J., Candea, G.: Prototyping symbolic execution engines for interpreted languages. In: Proceedings of the 19th International Conference on Architectural Support for Programming Languages and Operating Systems (ASPLOS), Salt Lake City, UT, USA , pp. 239–254, March 2014

10. Butler, E., Torlak, E., Popović, Z.: Synthesizing interpretable strategies for solving puzzle games. In: Proceedings of the 12th International Conference on the Foundations of Digital Games (FDG), No. 10, Hyannis, MA, USA, August 2017
11. Cadar, C.: Targeted program transformations for symbolic execution. In: Proceedings of the 10th Joint Meeting of the European Software Engineering Conference and the ACM SIGSOFT Symposium on the Foundations of Software Engineering (ESEC/FSE), Bergamo, Italy, pp. 906–909, August 2015
12. Chandra, K., Bodik, R.: Bonsai: synthesis-based reasoning for type systems. Proc. ACM Program. Lang. 2(POPL), 62:1–62:34 (2018)
13. Chipounov, V., Kuznetsov, V., Candea, G.: S2E: a platform for in-vivo multi-path analysis of software systems. In: Proceedings of the 16th International Conference on Architectural Support for Programming Languages and Operating Systems (ASPLOS), pp. 265–278 (2011)
14. Chu, S., Wang, C., Weitz, K., Cheung, A.: Cosette: an automated prover for SQL. In: Proceedings of the 8th Biennial Conference on Innovative Data Systems (CIDR), Chaminade, CA, USA, January 2017
15. Clarke Jr., E.M., Grumberg, O., Peled, D.A.: Model Checking. MIT Press, Cambridge (1999)
16. de Moura, L., Bjørner, N.: Z3: an efficient SMT solver. In: Ramakrishnan, C.R., Rehof, J. (eds.) TACAS 2008. LNCS, vol. 4963, pp. 337–340. Springer, Heidelberg (2008). https://doi.org/10.1007/978-3-540-78800-3_24
17. Dershowitz, N., Jouannaud, J.: Rewrite systems. In: Handbook of Theoretical Computer Science, Volume B: Formal Models and Semantics, pp. 243–320 (1990)
18. Flatt, M.: PLT: Reference: Racket. Technical report, PLT-TR-2010-1, PLT Design Inc. (2010)
19. Fleming, M.: A thorough introduction to eBPF, December 2017. https://lwn.net/Articles/740157/
20. Gal, A., et al.: Trace-based just-in-time type specialization for dynamic languages. In: Proceedings of the 30th ACM SIGPLAN Conference on Programming Language Design and Implementation (PLDI), pp. 465–478, June 2009
21. Galois Inc: Crucible (2018). https://github.com/GaloisInc/crucible
22. Gill, A.J., Jones, S.L.P.: Cheap deforestation in practice: an optimizer for Haskell. In: IFIP Congress (1994)
23. Gupta, R., Mehofer, E., Zhang, Y.: Profile guided compiler optimizations (chap. 4). In: The Compiler Design Handbook: Optimizations and Machine Code Generation. CRC Press, September 2002
24. Intel Corporation: Intel 64 and IA-32 Architectures Software Developer's Manual. Intel Corporation (2015). Revision 53
25. Kazerounian, M., Vazou, N., Bourgerie, A., Foster, J.S., Torlak, E.: Refinement types for ruby. In: Dillig, I., Palsberg, J., et al. (eds.) Verification, Model Checking, and Abstract Interpretation. LNCS, vol. 10747, pp. 269–290. Springer, Cham (2018). https://doi.org/10.1007/978-3-319-73721-8_13
26. King, J.C.: Symbolic execution and program testing. Commun. ACM 19(7), 385–394 (1976)
27. Kuznetsov, V., Kinder, J., Bucur, S., Candea, G.: Efficient state merging in symbolic execution. In: Proceedings of the 33rd ACM SIGPLAN Conference on Programming Language Design and Implementation (PLDI), Beijing, China, pp. 89–98, June 2012
28. Lattner, C., Adve, V.: LLVM: a compilation framework for lifelong program analysis & transformation. In: Proceedings of the 2004 International Symposium on Code Generation and Optimization (CGO), Palo Alto, California, March 2004

29. Nelson, L., Bornholt, J., Gu, R., Baumann, A., Torlak, E., Wang, X.: Scaling symbolic evaluation for automated verification of systems code with Serval. In: Proceedings of the 27th ACM Symposium on Operating Systems Principles (SOSP), pp. 225–242 (2019)
30. Nelson, L., et al.: Hyperkernel: push-button verification of an OS kernel. In: Proceedings of the 26th ACM Symposium on Operating Systems Principles (SOSP), pp. 252–269 (2017)
31. Newcomb, J.L., Bodik, R.: Using human-in-the-loop synthesis to author functional reactive programs (2019)
32. Paleczny, M., Vick, C., Click, C.: The Java HotSpot server compiler. In: Proceedings of the 2001 Symposium on Java Virtual Machine Research and Technology (JVM), Monterey, CA, USA, April 2001
33. Pernsteiner, S., Loncaric, C., Torlak, E., Tatlock, Z., Wang, X., Ernst, M.D., Jacky, J.: Investigating safety of a radiotherapy machine using system models with pluggable checkers. In: Chaudhuri, S., Farzan, A. (eds.) CAV 2016. LNCS, vol. 9780, pp. 23–41. Springer, Cham (2016). https://doi.org/10.1007/978-3-319-41540-6_2
34. Pettis, K., Hansen, R.C.: Profile guided code positioning. In: Proceedings of the 11th ACM SIGPLAN Conference on Programming Language Design and Implementation (PLDI), White Plains, NY, USA, pp. 16–27, June 1990
35. Phothilimthana, P.M., et al.: Swizzle inventor: data movement synthesis for GPU kernels. In: Proceedings of the 24th International Conference on Architectural Support for Programming Languages and Operating Systems (ASPLOS), pp. 65–78 (2019)
36. Phothilimthana, P.M., Thakur, A., Bodik, R., Dhurjati, D.: Scaling up superoptimization. In: Proceedings of the 21st International Conference on Architectural Support for Programming Languages and Operating Systems (ASPLOS), Atlanta, GA, USA, pp. 297–310, April 2016
37. Racket: The Racket Programming Language (2017). https://racket-lang.org
38. S2E: S2E: exponential analysis speedup with state merging (2019). http://s2e.systems/docs/StateMerging.html
39. Sen, K., Kalasapur, S., Brutch, T., Gibbs, S.: Jalangi: a selective record-replay and dynamic analysis framework for JavaScript. In: Proceedings of the 9th Joint Meeting of the European Software Engineering Conference and the ACM SIGSOFT Symposium on the Foundations of Software Engineering (ESEC/FSE), Saint Petersburg, Russian Federation, pp. 488–498, August 2013
40. Sharma, R., Schkufza, E., Churchill, B., Aiken, A.: Conditionally correct superoptimization. In: Proceedings of the 30th ACM SIGPLAN International Conference on Object-Oriented Programming, Systems, Languages, and Applications (OOPSLA), Pittsburgh, PA, USA, pp. 147–162, October 2015
41. Sigurbjarnarson, H., Nelson, L., Castro-Karney, B., Bornholt, J., Torlak, E., Wang, X.: Nickel: a framework for design and verification of information flow control systems. In: Proceedings of the 12th Symposium on Operating Systems Design and Implementation (OSDI), pp. 287–305 (2018)
42. St-Amour, V., Tobin-Hochstadt, S., Felleisen, M.: Optimization coaching: optimizers learn to communicate with programmers. In: Proceedings of the 27th ACM SIGPLAN International Conference on Object-Oriented Programming, Systems, Languages, and Applications (OOPSLA), Tuscon, AZ, USA, pp. 163–178, October 2012
43. Torlak, E.: Rosette (2018). http://github.com/emina/rosette
44. Torlak, E.: The Rosette guide: symbolic reflection (2019). https://docs.racket-lang.org/rosette-guide/ch_symbolic-reflection.html

45. Torlak, E., Bodik, R.: Growing solver-aided languages with Rosette. In: Proceedings of the 2013 ACM Symposium on New Ideas in Programming and Reflections on Software (Onward!), Indianapolis, IN, USA, pp. 135–152, October 2013
46. Torlak, E., Bodik, R.: A lightweight symbolic virtual machine for solver-aided host languages. In: Proceedings of the 35th ACM SIGPLAN Conference on Programming Language Design and Implementation (PLDI), Edinburgh, United Kingdom, pp. 530–541, June 2014
47. Uhler, R., Dave, N.: Smten with satisfiability-based search. In: Proceedings of the 29th ACM SIGPLAN International Conference on Object-Oriented Programming, Systems, Languages, and Applications (OOPSLA), Portland, OR, USA, pp. 157–176, October 2014
48. Wadler, P.: Deforestation: transforming programs to eliminate trees. In: Ganzinger, H. (ed.) ESOP 1988. LNCS, vol. 300, pp. 344–358. Springer, Heidelberg (1988). https://doi.org/10.1007/3-540-19027-9_23
49. Wagner, J., Kuznetsov, V., Candea, G.: -OVERIFY: optimizing programs for fast verification. In: Proceedings of the 14th Workshop on Hot Topics in Operating Systems (HotOS), Santa Ana Pueblo, NM, USA, May 2013
50. Weitz, K., Woos, D., Torlak, E., Ernst, M.D., Krishnamurthy, A., Tatlock, Z.: Scalable verification of border gateway protocol configurations with an SMT solver. In: Proceedings of the 31st ACM SIGPLAN International Conference on Object-Oriented Programming, Systems, Languages, and Applications (OOPSLA), Amsterdam, The Netherlands, pp. 765–780, October 2016
51. Willsey, M., Ceze, L., Strauss, K.: Puddle: an operating system for reliable, high-level programming of digital microfluidic devices. In: Proceedings of the 23rd International Conference on Architectural Support for Programming Languages and Operating Systems (ASPLOS), Wild and Crazy Ideas Session, Williamsburg, VA, USA, March 2018

The Correctness of a Code Generator for a Functional Language

Nathanaël Courant[1], Antoine Séré[2], and Natarajan Shankar[3(✉)]

[1] Inria Paris and Université Paris Diderot, Paris, France
[2] École Polytechnique, Palaiseau, France
[3] Computer Science Laboratory, SRI International, Menlo Park, CA 94025, USA
shankar@csl.sri.com

Abstract. Code generation is gaining popularity as a technique to bridge the gap between high-level models and executable code. We describe the theory underlying the PVS2C code generator that translates functional programs written using the PVS specification language to standalone, efficiently executable C code. We outline a correctness argument for the code generator. The techniques used are quite generic and can be applied to transform programs written in functional languages into imperative code. We use a formal model of reference counting to capture memory management and safe destructive updates for a simple first-order functional language with arrays. We exhibit a bisimulation between the functional execution and the imperative execution. This bisimulation shows that the generated imperative program returns the same result as the functional program.

1 Introduction

Functional languages offer a convenient and expressive notation for defining programs in a form that is referentially transparent and amenable to mathematical proof. One way of implementing a functional language on a machine is to transform a given program into a corresponding program in an imperative programming language. There are two key challenges in defining such a transformation. One, the evaluation of expressions in a functional language is pure, so that updating an array creates a fresh copy of the array being updated. Replacing such an update with a destructive, in-place update is not always sound. Two, allocated structures like arrays have to be garbage collected when they are no longer referenced in the evaluation.

We are interested in proving the correctness of a transformation from a functional program to a self-contained imperative program that executes efficiently and performs its own memory management. To this end, we use a transformation that employs reference counting for managing memory as well as for identifying opportunities for safe destructive updates during execution. The transformation is enabled by a light static analysis on the input functional program. This analysis helps release references as soon as possible in order to maximize the opportunities for destructive updates. We present a proof method for demonstrating

© Springer Nature Switzerland AG 2020
D. Beyer and D. Zufferey (Eds.): VMCAI 2020, LNCS 11990, pp. 68–89, 2020.
https://doi.org/10.1007/978-3-030-39322-9_4

the correctness of the transformation and a formalization of the correctness of a transformation from a small functional language to a C-like imperative language. The transformation from functional to self-contained imperative code forms the core of the PVS2C code generator [10,23]. Such transformations and the intermediate languages used in them are of foundational interest and practical utility for the generation of efficient code from executable fragments of specification and modelling languages.

Since code generators are becoming increasingly popular, it is important to ensure that they can be backed with simple, easily verifiable correctness proofs. The correctness of the transformation from a functional to an imperative language is carried out in multiple steps. The source language *FL* for our code generator is an idealized first-order functional language where programs are written in A-normal form [11]. This language is lightly typed and can serve as an intermediate language for multiple source languages. The operational semantics is presented in terms of reductions within an evaluation context [9]. This semantics is pure: each array update allocates a new array and copies the contents of the old array and performs the update on the copy.

We next define the operational semantics of an annotated variant *RL* of *FL* that exploits reference counting and destructive updates. We exhibit a bisimilarity between the *FL* and *RL* operational semantics so that these two forms of evaluation always yield the same value, when either evaluation terminates. The correspondence between *FL* and *RL* has been already been verified in PVS.

Next, we define a translation from annotated *FL* to an imperative language *KL*. The latter language is inspired by the operational semantics given by Appel and Blazy [1]. The language *KL* uses explicit assignments and the operational semantics employs continuations so that there is a significant semantic gap between *RL* executions and their *KL* counterparts. Even so, we exhibit a bisimulation between the operational semantics for the reference counting execution of *RL* and that of the imperative language *KL*.[1]

We give a brief overview of languages, the code generator, and the correctness arguments. Consider the *FL* program *swap* which swaps two elements of an array.

$$\texttt{swap}(u, i, j) = \texttt{let } a = u[i]$$
$$\texttt{in let } b = u[j]$$
$$\texttt{in let } u' = u[i \mapsto b]$$
$$\texttt{in } u'[j \mapsto a]$$

The body of the definition is in A-normal form [11]. The array access and update operations are applied to arguments that are variables. Our A-normal form is

---

[1] We had initially used a different semantics for the imperative language based on call stacks and program counters that is closer to the machine execution, but this led to a fairly cumbersome definition of the bisimulation. We found the mechanization (https://github.com/SRI-CSL/PVSCodegen) of the correspondence quite challenging. The correspondence given here between *RL* and *KL* executions has not yet been formalized using a proof assistant, but we expect it to be a significantly easier exercise.

unflattened so that the expressions e_1 and e_2 in a let-expression $\texttt{let } x = e_1 \texttt{ in } e_2$ are both recursively in A-normal form.

Given a body of definitions Δ of the above form, we would like to evaluate an expression given in A-normal form. The evaluation of an expression e can be carried out with respect to a stack S which binds variables to values (integers or references) and a store which maps references to arrays. For example if the expression e is $\texttt{let } x = y[i \mapsto k] \texttt{ in } x[i]$, where the subexpression $y[i \mapsto k]$ denotes the result of updating the array y at i with k. Let us assume that we are evaluating e with a stack S of the form $\langle y \mapsto r_0, i \mapsto 2, k \mapsto 5 \rangle$ and a store $\mathcal{M}$ given by the map $\{r_0 \mapsto \mathbf{A}\}$, where $\mathbf{A}$ is the array $\langle 1, 2, 3 \rangle$. The expression e can be viewed as an evaluation context $\texttt{let } x = \square \texttt{ in } x[i]$ with a single hole $\square$, and a redex $y[i \mapsto k]$ filling the hole. The operational semantics is given as a set of rewrite rules on the triple $(d, S, \mathcal{M})$ for redex d, stack S, and store $\mathcal{M}$. In this case, the reduction yields a reference r_1 and a new store $\mathcal{M}'$ that extends $\mathcal{M}$ with the map $\{r_1 \mapsto \langle 1, 2, 5 \rangle\}$. The new state now has the expression $\texttt{let } x = r_1 \texttt{ in } x[i]$, which contains an explicit reference, namely, the reference resulting from the prior reduction. This expression is a redex by itself. Reducing this redex with stack S and store $\mathcal{M}'$ yields the expression $\mathbf{pop}(x[i])$, the new stack $\langle x \mapsto r_1, y \mapsto r_0, i \mapsto 2, k \mapsto 5 \rangle$, and the same store $\mathcal{M}$. The operation $\mathbf{pop}$ is a book-keeping operation used to pop the stack at the end of the evaluation of the body of the let-expression. The subexpression $x[i]$ is a redex and reduces to 5, and finally the redex $\mathbf{pop}(5)$ is reduced by popping the binding for x off the stack to yield the value 5 and the resulting stack S and store $\mathcal{M}'$.

The reference counting semantics maintains a count for each reference in the domain of the store $\mathcal{M}$. The RL expression being evaluated is annotated so that the last lexical occurrence of a variable along any evaluation path is marked (i.e., underlined). For example, the expression e above would be annotated as $\texttt{let } x = \underline{y}[i \mapsto \underline{k}] \texttt{ in } \underline{x}[\underline{i}]$. If we evaluate this expression with a stack S as above, and a store $\mathcal{M}$ of the form $\{r_0 \mapsto [1, 2, 3]\}$, and a reference count C of the form $\{r_0 \mapsto 0\}$. With this, the redex $\underline{y}[i \mapsto \underline{k}]$ is reduced to r_0, the new stack S' is of the form $\langle y \mapsto \mathbf{nil}, i \mapsto 2, k \mapsto 5 \rangle$, the new store $\mathcal{M}'$ is just $\{r_0 \mapsto \langle 1, 2, 5 \rangle\}$, and the new reference count C' is $\{r_0 \mapsto 1\}$. In other words, we can perform the update in place since the variable y is marked and its reference count is 1, indicating that there are no further uses of the reference r_0 in the evaluation nor for the stack binding of the variable y in the stack. If the variable y is unmarked or the corresponding reference r_0 has a count greater than 1, then we need to create a (shallow) copy of the array before updating it. The next step of evaluation binds x to r_0 in the stack and continues executing as above. When the redex $\underline{x}[\underline{i}]$ is evaluated, the reference count for r_0 becomes 0, and the array is freed. Here, the array contains integers, but if the array being freed contains references, these references need to have their reference counts decremented. The bisimulation between the pure evaluation and the reference counting destructive evaluation shows that the reference count is tracked accurately. It also shows that there is a map from the references in the destructive evaluation to those in the pure evaluation such that the corresponding expressions, stacks, and stores match.

The next step in our proof transforms the annotated language RL to an imperative language KL. The imperative language, by design, looks quite similar to the functional language but employs assignments. The translation of the expression $\texttt{let } x = y[i \mapsto \underline{k}] \texttt{ in } \underline{x}[\underline{i}]$ into KL is done in the context of a result variable $\texttt{return}$. In $\overline{IL}$, we get a program $\{\texttt{int } x; x := y[i \mapsto \underline{k}]; \texttt{return} := \underline{x}[\underline{i}]\}$.

Like RL, the execution of the imperative language $\overline{KL}$ tracks reference counts and uses the marking to release references. A reference is released by decrementing its reference count and freeing memory when the reference count drops to 0, but only after recursively releasing the references in the contents of the array. In addition to the stack $\mathcal{S}$, the store $\mathcal{M}$, and the reference count $\mathcal{C}$, the operational semantics for KL maintains a continuation $\mathcal{K}$ that is just a program representing the rest of the computation. Let the initial continuation $\mathcal{K}_0$ be $\{\texttt{int } x; x := y[i \mapsto \underline{k}]; \texttt{return} := \underline{x}[\underline{i}]\}$, the initial stack $\mathcal{S}_0$ be $\langle \texttt{return} \mapsto \texttt{undef}, i \mapsto 2, k \mapsto 5, y \mapsto r \rangle$, the initial store $\mathcal{M}_0$ be $\{r_0 \mapsto \langle 1, 2, 3 \rangle\}$, and the initial reference count table $\mathcal{C}_0$ be $\{r_0 \mapsto 1\}$. The declaration $\texttt{int } x$ is evaluated by extending the stack with the binding $x \mapsto \texttt{undef}$ so that $\mathcal{S}_1$ is $\langle x \mapsto \texttt{undef}, \texttt{return} \mapsto \texttt{undef}, i \mapsto 2, k \mapsto 5, y \mapsto r_0 \rangle$, while appending a $\texttt{pop}$ instruction to the right of the continuation corresponding to the binding for x to yield $\mathcal{K}_1 = x := y[i \mapsto \underline{k}]; \texttt{return} := \underline{x}[\underline{i}]; \texttt{pop}$. The store and reference count tables are left unchanged in $\mathcal{M}_1$ and $\mathcal{C}_1$. The assignment $x := y[i \mapsto \underline{k}]$ is executed by evaluating the right-hand side by updating the array bound to r_0 in the store, binding x in the stack to the reference r_0, and releasing the binding to y. Now, $\mathcal{K}_2$ is $\texttt{return} := \underline{x}[\underline{i}]; \texttt{pop}$, $\mathcal{S}_2$ is $\langle x \mapsto r_0, \texttt{return} \mapsto \texttt{undef}, i \mapsto 2, k \mapsto 5, y \mapsto \texttt{nil} \rangle$, $\mathcal{M}_1$ is $\{r_0 \mapsto \langle 1, 2, 5 \rangle\}$, and $\mathcal{C}_1$ is $\{r_0 \mapsto 1\}$. The assignment to $\texttt{return}$ is then executed and the remaining $\texttt{pop}$ instructions are executed to yield the final state where $\mathcal{K}_4$ is empty, the $\mathcal{S}_4$ is set to $\langle \texttt{return} \mapsto 5, i \mapsto 2, k \mapsto 5, y \mapsto \texttt{nil} \rangle$, and $\mathcal{M}_4$ and $\mathcal{C}_4$ are both empty. The bisimulation between the evaluation of an RL expression and the execution of its translation in KL is quite challenging since there are subtle semantic differences between the executions of these two languages.

The goal of our proof exercise is to construct a simple and elegant formalization of the correctness of the correspondence between the evaluations of the source and target of a code generator that is amenable to easy mechanical verification. We have defined intermediate representations that simplify the proofs while retaining the flexibility to support multiple source languages and target multiple imperative languages. The proofs have been designed so that the language can be extended with new features with minimal impact on the invariants and bisimulations. The formally defined code generator presented here is an idealization of a practical code generator from a functional language to C. This code generator produces readable, self-contained C code with a modest overhead for reference counting.

Related Work. Reference counting was introduced by Collins [5] in 1960. It was shown to fail in the presence of cyclic structures by McBeth [18] in 1963. Reference cycles cannot appear in the execution of PVS or in any of the languages FL, RL, or KL so that our use of reference counting is sound. There are several proofs of the correctness of reference counting implementations and reference counting garbage collectors [8,19]. Hudak [13] presents an abstract interpretation in terms reference counts as a way of optimizing program execution. Several papers present static analyses for safe destructive updates in functional languages [2,7,12,14,22,26]. Chirimar, Gunter, and Riecke [4] define a reference counting abstract machine for a computational interpretation of linear logic. The work that is closest to our own is Schulte's code generator [21] for the specification language Opal [6] that translates a first-order functional fragment of the language into a reference counted implementation in C in which execution interacts with the garbage collector to reuse storage (see also de Moura and Ullrich [25]). The analysis and transformations used here are similar though the intermediate languages and proof techniques are quite different. We are using a formal model of reference counting to dynamically manage memory for a source language with object updates that can be executed destructively when safe. The presentation here is the basis for a practical implementation of a code generator that covers a full functional language with arrays, records, tuples, algebraic datatypes, and closures, as well as the outline for a machine-verified proof for its correctness.

Formal verification of compilers is a well-studied topic [3,15–17,20,24]. This paper presents the theory underlying a simple code generator. Based on our prior experience, we estimate that the mechanization of the proofs here would require fewer than ten person-weeks, whereas the correctness of the full PVS2C code generator would involve a substantial months-long effort. In contrast, proving the correctness of a compiler is a much larger undertaking.

2   A Small Functional Language

The source functional language *FL* features recursive functions, let-bindings and immutable arrays, and is in A-normal form. Internally we always use de Bruijn indices everywhere for the variables for simplicity; however, in the paper we will use identifiers when giving examples to make the example more readable. The syntax of *FL* is defined in Fig. 1a. The functions f can be primitive functions like $+$, $*$, and $-$, or defined functions. The sequence of variables $x_1, \ldots, x_n$ in a function application $f(x_1, \ldots, x_n)$ may contain duplicates.

The variables and operations have types associated with them in order to simplify the definition of various memory management operations. The expression $vars(e)$ is defined as the set of free variables in e. A type t is either the integer type int or is an n-element array $t[n]$ with element type t. The constant nil is seen as a valid constant for any array type of the form $t[n]$.

$$t:: = \texttt{int} \mid t[n]$$

Each function symbol has a type $t_1 \times \ldots \times t_n \to t$, where the i'th argument has type t_i, and the range type is t. Given the types of the variables and function symbols, the type of a well-formed expression e can be computed as $\tau(e)$.

$$e ::= \mid n \qquad\qquad\qquad \text{redex} ::= \mid x$$

$$\mid x \qquad\qquad\qquad\qquad \mid f(x_1, \ldots, x_n)$$

$$\mid \texttt{nil} \qquad\qquad\qquad\quad\; \mid x[y]$$

$$\mid f(x_1, \ldots, x_n) \qquad\quad \mid x[y \mapsto z]$$

$$\mid \texttt{let } (x : t) = e_1 \texttt{ in } e_2 \quad \mid \texttt{newint}(n)$$

$$\mid \texttt{ifnz } x \texttt{ then } e_1 \texttt{ else } e_2 \quad \mid \texttt{newref}(n)$$

$$\mid x[y] \qquad\qquad\qquad \mid \texttt{ifnz } x \texttt{ then } e_1 \texttt{ else } e_2$$

$$\mid x[y \mapsto z] \qquad\qquad\; \mid \texttt{let } x = v \texttt{ in } e$$

$$\mid \texttt{newint}(n) \mid \texttt{newref}(n) \quad \mid \texttt{pop}(v)$$

$$\mid \texttt{pop}(e_1) \mid \texttt{ref}(k) \qquad\quad \text{, where } v \text{ is a value.}$$

(a) Syntax of *FL*   (b) Definition of a redex

Fig. 1. Expression and Redex Syntax of *FL*

The type system does not rule out errors due to null dereferencing and out-of-bounds array access. Given the types for variables and operations, each well-typed expression has a unique type. The type rules are straightforward and are left as an exercise for the reader. For the sake of simplicity, we will often omit the type annotations on the **let** constructors. Note that the **pop** and **ref** constructors are not allowed in programs and are used only during reduction. We also restrict the primitive functions to operate solely over the integers.

We also define an evaluation context with a hole $\square$ marking the location where evaluation occurs, as below.

$$K ::= \square \mid \texttt{let } (x : t) = K_1 \texttt{ in } e_1 \mid \texttt{pop}(K_1)$$

The composition $K[e]$ of a context K and an expression e consists in replacing the hole $\square$ in K by the expression e. A *value* is a reference, a constant or **nil**. A *redex* is defined in Fig. 1b.

Theorem 1. *Every expression that is not a value can be uniquely decomposed as the composition of a context and a redex.*

The state is defined as a triplet $(e, S, \mathcal{M})$, where e is an expression, S is the stack, which maps variables to values, and $\mathcal{M}$ the state of the memory, which maps a finite number of references to finite sequences of values. The empty stack is written as *empty*. Entries A are pushed on to the stack by the operation $\textbf{push}(A, S)$. When S is a stack of variable bindings, a binding $x \mapsto v$ is pushed on to the stack by the operation $\textbf{push}(x \mapsto v, S)$. For a sequence of variables $x_1, \ldots, x_n$ (abbreviated as $\overline{x}$) and values $v_1, \ldots, v_n$ (abbreviated as $\overline{v}$), we abbreviate $\textbf{push}(x_n \mapsto v_n, \ldots, \textbf{push}(x_1 \mapsto v_1, S) \ldots)$ as $\textbf{push}(\overline{x} \mapsto \overline{v}, S)$. The lookup operation $S(x)$ retrieves the topmost binding for x. This operation is only invoked when there is a binding for x in S. We also use the operation $S[x \mapsto v]$

$$(x, S, \mathcal{M}) \rightarrow (S(x), S, \mathcal{M})$$
$$(x[y], S, \mathcal{M}) \rightarrow (\mathcal{M}(S(x))(S(y)), S, \mathcal{M})$$
$$(x[y \mapsto z], S, \mathcal{M}) \rightarrow (r, S, \mathcal{M}[r \mapsto \mathcal{M}(S(x))[S(y) \mapsto S(z)]]),$$
$$\text{where } r = \mathbf{new}(\mathcal{M})$$
$$(\mathtt{newint}(n), S, \mathcal{M}) \rightarrow (\mathbf{new}(\mathcal{M}), S, \mathcal{M}[\mathbf{new}(\mathcal{M}) \mapsto \langle 0, \ldots, 0 \rangle])$$
$$(\mathtt{newref}(n), S, \mathcal{M}) \rightarrow (\mathbf{new}(\mathcal{M}), S, \mathcal{M}[\mathbf{new}(\mathcal{M}) \mapsto \langle \mathtt{nil}, \ldots, \mathtt{nil} \rangle])$$
$$(\mathtt{let}\ x = v\ \mathtt{in}\ e, S, \mathcal{M}) \rightarrow (\mathbf{pop}(e), \mathbf{push}(x \mapsto v, S), \mathcal{M})$$
$$(\mathbf{pop}(v), S, \mathcal{M}) \rightarrow (v, \mathbf{pop}(S), \mathcal{M})$$
$$(\mathtt{ifnz}\ x\ \mathtt{then}\ e_1\ \mathtt{else}\ e_2, S, \mathcal{M}) \rightarrow \begin{cases} (e_1, S, \mathcal{M}), & \text{if } S(x) \neq 0 \\ (e_2, S, \mathcal{M}), & \text{otherwise} \end{cases}$$
$$(f(x_1, \ldots, x_n), S, \mathcal{M}) \rightarrow (v, S, \mathcal{M}) \text{ for primitive } f,$$
$$\text{where } f(S(x_1), \ldots, S(x_n)) \xrightarrow{\delta} v$$
$$(f(x_1, \ldots, x_n), S, \mathcal{M}) \rightarrow (\mathbf{pop}^n(e), \mathbf{push}(\overline{y} \mapsto S(\overline{x}), S), \mathcal{M})$$
$$\text{where } f(y_1, \ldots, y_n) = e\ \text{in } \Delta.$$

Fig. 2. Operational semantics of *FL*

to update the topmost binding for x in the stack. This operation is also applied only when there is a binding for x in S. We denote by $\mathbf{new}(\mathcal{M})$, a reference that is not yet defined in $\mathcal{M}$. We use $f(v_1, \ldots, v_n) \xrightarrow{\delta} v$ for the reduction relation capturing the evaluation of primitive functions such as $+$. The non-primitive functions are defined in the program Δ which maps the function symbol f to its definition of the form $f(y_1, \ldots, y_n) = e$ where $vars(e) = \{y_1, \ldots, y_n\}$, and $y_i \neq y_j$ for $1 \leq i < j \leq n$.

The small-step semantics are defined as the unique context-preserving relation $\rightarrow$ that is defined on redexes as in Fig. 2. It is easy to see that the reductions are deterministic. An evaluation step has the form $(E[e], S, \mathcal{M}) \longrightarrow (E[e'], S', \mathcal{M}')$ iff $(e, S, \mathcal{M}) \rightarrow (e', S', \mathcal{M}')$.

It is an error to access or modify outside the bounds given by the store, to call a non-existent function, to call a function with an incorrect number of arguments, or to use primitive operations with unsupported arguments. The state obtained after such erroneous reductions is $\bot$.

Let $\mathtt{swap}(u, i, j)$ be defined as

$$\mathtt{let}\ a = u[i]\ \mathtt{in}\ \mathtt{let}\ b = u[j]\ \mathtt{in}\ \mathtt{let}\ u' = u[i \mapsto b]\ \mathtt{in}\ u'[j \mapsto a].$$

Given $e = \mathtt{let}\ z = +(y, 1)\ \mathtt{in}\ \mathtt{swap}(x, y, z)$ with $S = (y \mapsto 0, x \mapsto r)$ and $\mathcal{M} = (r \mapsto \langle 0, 1 \rangle)$, we show the steps in the reduction of $(e, S, \mathcal{M})$ in Fig. 3.

$$\begin{pmatrix} \texttt{let } z = +(y,1) \texttt{ in swap}(x,y,z), \\ (y \mapsto 0, x \mapsto r), (r \mapsto \langle 0,1 \rangle) \end{pmatrix} \tag{1}$$

$$\longrightarrow (\texttt{let } z = 1 \texttt{ in swap}(x,y,z), (y \mapsto 0, x \mapsto r), (r \mapsto \langle 0,1 \rangle)) \tag{2}$$

$$\longrightarrow (\texttt{pop}(\texttt{swap}(x,y,z)), (z \mapsto 1, y \mapsto 0, x \mapsto r), (r \mapsto \langle 0,1 \rangle)) \tag{3}$$

$$\longrightarrow \begin{pmatrix} \dots \texttt{let } a = u[i] \texttt{ in } \dots, \\ (j \mapsto 1, i \mapsto 0, u \mapsto r, \dots), \\ (r \mapsto \langle 0,1 \rangle) \end{pmatrix} \tag{4}$$

$$\longrightarrow \begin{pmatrix} \dots \texttt{let } a = 0 \texttt{ in } \dots, \\ (j \mapsto 1, i \mapsto 0, t \mapsto r, \dots), (r \mapsto \langle 0,1 \rangle) \end{pmatrix} \tag{5}$$

$$\longrightarrow \dots \texttt{let } b = u[j] \texttt{ in } \dots, (a \mapsto 0, j \mapsto 1, \dots), (r \mapsto \langle 0,1 \rangle)) \tag{6}$$

$$\longrightarrow (\dots \texttt{let } b = 1 \texttt{ in } \dots, (a \mapsto 0, j \mapsto 1, \dots), (r \mapsto \langle 0,1 \rangle)) \tag{7}$$

$$\longrightarrow \begin{pmatrix} \dots \texttt{let } u' = u[i \mapsto b] \texttt{ in } \dots, \\ (b \mapsto 1, a \mapsto 0, \dots), \\ (r \mapsto \langle 0,1 \rangle) \end{pmatrix} \tag{8}$$

$$\longrightarrow \begin{pmatrix} \dots \texttt{let } u' = r' \texttt{ in } \dots, \\ (b \mapsto 1, a \mapsto 0, \dots), \\ (r' \mapsto \langle 1,1 \rangle, r \mapsto \langle 0,1 \rangle) \end{pmatrix} \tag{9}$$

$$\longrightarrow (\dots u'[j \mapsto a] \dots, (u' \mapsto r', b \mapsto 1, \dots), (r' \mapsto \langle 1,1 \rangle, \dots)) \tag{10}$$

$$\longrightarrow (\texttt{pop}^7(r''), (u' \mapsto r', b \mapsto 1, \dots), (r'' \mapsto \langle 1,0 \rangle, \dots)) \tag{11}$$

$$\stackrel{+}{\longrightarrow} (r'', (y \mapsto 0, x \mapsto r), (r'' \mapsto \langle 1,0 \rangle, r' \mapsto \langle 1,1 \rangle, r \mapsto \langle 0,1 \rangle)) \tag{12}$$

Fig. 3. An example FL reduction

3   Evaluation with Reference Counting

The reference-counting language RL extends FL with an additional constructor, $\texttt{release}(x, e)$, which is also a redex. In addition, a variable occurrence in RL can be *marked* to indicate that this is the last occurrence of the variable along an evaluation path. The evaluation state is extended with $\mathcal{C}$ which maps each reference to its reference count.

Define $\#(S, r)$ as the number of times the reference r occurs as a binding in stack S, $\#(a, r)$ as the number of occurrences of r as an element of the array a, and $\mathbb{1}_{r \in e}$ as 1 if r occurs as a value in e, and 0, otherwise. The key invariant that is maintained is that the value of $\mathcal{C}(\texttt{ref}(k))$ is exactly the reference count of $\texttt{ref}(k)$ in e, S, and $\mathcal{M}$.

$$\mathcal{C}(\texttt{ref}(k)) = \mathbb{1}_{\texttt{ref}(k) \in e} + \#(S, \texttt{ref}(k)) + \sum_{\texttt{ref}(j) \in \mathcal{M}} \#(\mathcal{M}(\texttt{ref}(j)), \texttt{ref}(k)) \tag{13}$$

The advantage of defining and maintaining this reference count is to be able to free memory as soon as it is no longer needed, and to be able to perform more efficient destructive updates on the arrays.

The evaluation also preserves three key invariants:

early-release. Each variable in S that is no longer live in e is not bound to a reference.

correct-marking. The expression e is correctly marked (deleting all the markings in e and re-marking the result (using the **mark** algorithm shown below) returns an expression identical to e).

release-marked. All subterms of e of the form $\mathtt{release}(x, e')$ have the occurrence of x in the first argument marked.

We use the following helper functions:

$$\mathbf{incr}(\mathtt{ref}(k), \mathcal{C}) = \mathcal{C}[\mathtt{ref}(k) \mapsto \mathcal{C}(v) + 1]$$
$$\mathbf{incr}(v, \mathcal{C}) = \mathcal{C} \qquad\qquad \text{otherwise}$$
$$\mathbf{decr}(\mathtt{ref}(k), \mathcal{C}) = \mathcal{C}[\mathtt{ref}(k) \mapsto \mathcal{C}(v) - 1]$$
$$\mathbf{decr}(v, \mathcal{C}) = \mathcal{C} \qquad\qquad \text{otherwise}$$

The function **decref** takes a value, the state of memory and a count, and if the value is a reference, decreases its count. In case the count is 1, it recursively (using **decref⋆**) decreases the count of all the non-nil references pointed by that one and replaces them by **nil** before freeing the memory allocated to a reference r by setting $\mathcal{M}(r)$ to $\bot$. The termination of the mutually recursive definitions of **decref** and **decref⋆** is given by a lexicographic measure on the size of the type t and the array index m.[2]

$$\mathbf{decref}(t[n])(\mathtt{ref}(k), (\mathcal{M}, \mathcal{C})) = (\mathcal{M}, \mathbf{decr}(\mathtt{ref}(k), \mathcal{C})), \text{ if } \mathcal{C}(\mathtt{ref}(k)) > 1$$
$$\mathbf{decref}(t[n])(\mathtt{ref}(k), (\mathcal{M}, \mathcal{C})) = (\mathcal{M}'[\mathtt{ref}(k) \mapsto \bot], \mathbf{decr}(\mathtt{ref}(k), \mathcal{C}')),$$
$$\text{if } \mathcal{C}(\mathtt{ref}(k)) = 1$$
$$\text{where } (\mathcal{M}', \mathcal{C}') = \mathbf{decref}\star(t)(v, (\mathcal{M}, \mathcal{C}), n)$$
$$\mathbf{decref}(t)(v, (\mathcal{M}, \mathcal{C})) = (\mathcal{M}, \mathcal{C}), \text{ otherwise}$$
$$\mathbf{decref}\star(t[n])(\mathtt{ref}(k), (\mathcal{M}, \mathcal{C}), m+1) = \mathbf{decref}(t)(\mathcal{M}(\mathtt{ref}(k))[m], (\mathcal{M}'', \mathcal{C}')),$$
$$\text{where } (\mathcal{M}', \mathcal{C}') = \mathbf{decref}\star(t[n])(r, (\mathcal{M}, \mathcal{C}), m)$$
$$\mathcal{M}'' = \mathcal{M}'[r \mapsto \mathcal{M}'(r)[m \mapsto \mathtt{nil}]]$$
$$r = \mathtt{ref}(k)$$
$$\mathbf{decref}\star(t[n])(\mathtt{ref}(k), (\mathcal{M}, \mathcal{C}), 0) = (\mathcal{M}, \mathcal{C})$$
$$\mathbf{decref}\star(t)(v, (\mathcal{M}, \mathcal{C}), m) = (\mathcal{M}, \mathcal{C}), \text{ otherwise}$$

---

[2] Note that due to the recursion on type structure, the termination proofs do not need to assume that the store is non-cyclic. In our mechanization, we use a slightly different definition and exploit Invariant 13 and the invariant (also implicit in **decref**) that $\mathcal{M}$ contains no (dangling) references that are not in the domain of $\mathcal{M}$ so that the total reference count in $\mathcal{M}$ decreases with each call to **decref**.

Expressions being evaluated are analyzed in order to mark the last occurrence of a variable along any evaluation path. This marking helps to identify the lifetime of the variable by indicating the point at which the variable is no longer used in a computation. The operation $\mathbf{mark}(X, e)$, a few cases of which are defined below, marks each variable in e that is not in X. In the remaining cases, $\mathbf{mark}(X, e)$ marks the last (non-binding) occurrence in e of any variable in $vars(e) - X$. We overload $\mathtt{release}$ so that $\mathtt{release}(\{x_1, \ldots, x_n\}, e)$ is shorthand for $\mathtt{release}(x_n, \ldots \mathtt{release}(x_1, e) \ldots)$.

$\mathbf{mark}(X, x) =$

$$\begin{cases} x & \text{if } x \in X \\ \underline{x} & \text{otherwise} \end{cases}$$

$\mathbf{mark}(X, \mathtt{let}\ x = e_1\ \mathtt{in}\ e_2) =$

$$\begin{cases} \mathtt{let}\ x = \mathbf{mark}(X \cup \mathbf{vars}(e_2), e_1) \\ \quad \mathtt{in}\ \mathbf{mark}(X, e_2) & \text{if } x \in \mathbf{vars}(e_2) \\ \mathtt{let}\ x = \mathbf{mark}(X \cup \mathbf{vars}(e_2), e_1) \\ \quad \mathtt{in}\ \mathtt{release}(\underline{x}, \mathbf{mark}(X, e_2)) & \text{otherwise} \end{cases}$$

$\mathbf{mark}(X, \mathtt{ifnz}\ x\ \mathtt{then}\ e_1\ \mathtt{else}\ e_2) =$

$$\begin{cases} \mathtt{ifnz}\ \mathbf{mark}(\mathbf{vars}(e_1) \cup \mathbf{vars}(e_2) \cup X, x) \\ \quad \mathtt{then}\ \mathtt{release}(\mathbf{vars}(e_2) - (X \cup \mathbf{vars}(e_1)), \mathbf{mark}(X, e_1)) \\ \quad \mathtt{else}\ \mathtt{release}(\mathbf{vars}(e_1) - (X \cup \mathbf{vars}(e_2)), \mathbf{mark}(X, e_2)) \end{cases}$$

For example, $\mathbf{mark}(\emptyset, \mathtt{let}\ x = f(y)\ \mathtt{in}\ \mathtt{ifnz}\ z\ \mathtt{then}\ g(x, y)\ \mathtt{else}\ f(x))$ is

$$\mathtt{let}\ x = f(y)\ \mathtt{in}\ \mathtt{ifnz}\ \underline{z}\ \mathtt{then}\ g(\underline{x}, \underline{y})\ \mathtt{else}\ \mathtt{release}(y, f(\underline{x}))$$

We translate FL programs into marked RL programs by replacing each definition of the form $f(\overline{y}) = e$ in Δ by $f(\overline{y}) = \mathbf{mark}(\emptyset, e)$ in the RL program $\Delta^{\#}$.

Given a sequence $x_1, \ldots, x_n$ (abbreviated as $\overline{x}$) of (possibly marked) variables. Let $\mathbf{incvars}(\overline{x}, S, \mathcal{C})$ represent the result of incrementing the count of $S(y)$ by one for each unmarked variable y in $\overline{x}$.

$$\mathbf{incvars}(\langle\rangle, S, \mathcal{C}) = \mathcal{C}$$
$$\mathbf{incvars}((x_1, x_2, \ldots, x_n), S, \mathcal{C}) = \mathbf{incvars}((x_2, \ldots, x_n), S, \mathcal{C}'), \text{ where}$$
$$\mathcal{C}' = \begin{cases} \mathbf{incr}(S(x), \mathcal{C}), & \text{if } x \text{ is unmarked} \\ \mathcal{C}, & \text{otherwise .} \end{cases}$$

Figure 4 shows a few cases of the definition of reduction for RL redexes.

The reduction of *update* redexes is by far the most complicated of all; but it is also the main reason why we perform this step of reference counting.

$$(x, S, (\mathcal{M}, \mathcal{C})) \rightarrow^{\#} (S(x), S[x \mapsto \texttt{nil}], (\mathcal{M}, \mathcal{C}))$$
$$\text{if } x \text{ is marked and } S(x) \text{ is a reference}$$
$$(x, S, (\mathcal{M}, \mathcal{C})) \rightarrow^{\#} (S(x), S, (\mathcal{M}, \mathbf{incvars}(x, \mathcal{M}, \mathcal{C}))) \text{ otherwise}$$
$$(f(\overline{x}), S, (\mathcal{M}, \mathcal{C})) \rightarrow^{\#} (e, S_n, (\mathcal{M}, \mathcal{C}')), \text{ where}$$
$$\mathcal{C}' = \mathbf{incvars}(\overline{x}, S, \mathcal{C})$$
$$S_0 = \mathbf{push}(\overline{y} \mapsto S(\overline{x}), S)$$
$$S_{i+1} = \begin{cases} S_i[x_i \mapsto \texttt{nil}], \\ \quad \text{if } x_i \text{ is a marked and } S(x) \text{ is a reference} \\ S_i, \text{ otherwise} \end{cases}$$
$$(x[y \mapsto z], S, (\mathcal{M}, \mathcal{C})) \rightarrow^{\#} (S(x), S'[x \mapsto \texttt{nil}], (\mathcal{M}'', \mathcal{C}'')),$$
$$\text{if } \mathcal{C}(S(x)) = 1 \text{ and } x \text{ is marked}$$
$$\text{where } \tau(x) = t[n], \text{ for some } n,$$
$$\mathcal{M}' = \mathcal{M}[S(x) \mapsto \mathcal{M}(S(x))[S(y) \mapsto S(z)]],$$
$$\mathcal{C}' = \mathbf{incvars}(z, S, \mathcal{C})$$
$$(\mathcal{M}'', \mathcal{C}'') = \mathbf{decref}(t)(\mathcal{M}(S(x))[S(y)], (\mathcal{M}', \mathcal{C}'))$$
$$(x[y \mapsto z], S, (\mathcal{M}, \mathcal{C})) \rightarrow^{\#} (r, S'', (\mathcal{M}', \mathcal{C}''')), \text{ otherwise}$$
$$\text{where } r = \mathbf{new}(\mathcal{M}),$$
$$\mathcal{M}' = \mathcal{M}[r \mapsto \mathcal{M}(S(x))[S(y) \mapsto S(z)]],$$

$$(\mathcal{C}', S') = \begin{cases} (\mathbf{decr}(S(z), \mathcal{C}), S[z \mapsto \texttt{nil}]) \\ \quad \text{if } z \text{ is marked} \\ (\mathcal{C}, S), \text{ otherwise,} \end{cases}$$
$$(\mathcal{C}'', S'') = \begin{cases} (\mathbf{decr}(S(x), \mathcal{C}', S[x \mapsto \texttt{nil}])) \\ \quad \text{if } x \text{ is marked} \\ (\mathcal{C}', S'), \text{ otherwise} \end{cases}$$
$$\mathcal{C}''' = (\#(\mathcal{M}'(r)) + \mathcal{C}'')[r \mapsto 1],$$
$$(\texttt{release}(\underline{x}, e), S, (\mathcal{M}, \mathcal{C})) \rightarrow^{\#} (e, S[x \mapsto \texttt{nil}], \mathbf{decref}(\tau(x))(S(x), (\mathcal{M}, \mathcal{C})))$$
$$\text{if } S(x) \text{ is a reference}$$
$$(\texttt{release}(\underline{x}, e), S, (\mathcal{M}, \mathcal{C})) \rightarrow^{\#} (e, S, (\mathcal{M}, \mathcal{C})), \text{ otherwise}$$

Fig. 4. Operational semantics of some reductions in RL

For instance, let $\texttt{swap}(u, i, j)$ be defined as

$$\texttt{let } a = u[i] \texttt{ in let } b = u[j] \texttt{ in let } u' = \underline{u}[\underline{i} \mapsto \underline{b}] \texttt{ in } \underline{u}'[\underline{j} \mapsto \underline{a}].$$

Suppose that $e = \texttt{let } z = +(y, 1) \texttt{ in swap}(\underline{x}, \underline{y}, \underline{z})$, with $S = (y \mapsto 0, x \mapsto r)$, $\mathcal{M} = (r \mapsto \langle 0, 1 \rangle)$ and $\mathcal{C} = (r \mapsto 2)$. Steps of the reduction are detailed in Fig. 5.

Notice how even though the reference count of r was 2 initially, we still saved a copy compared to Fig. 3 and performed a destructive update instead. Indeed, the reference count of the result of an array update is *always* 1: either it is the

$$\begin{pmatrix} \texttt{let } z = +(y,1) \texttt{ in swap}(\underline{x},\underline{y},\underline{z}), (y \mapsto 0, x \mapsto r), \\ (r \mapsto \langle 0,1 \rangle), (r \mapsto 2) \end{pmatrix} \tag{1}$$

$$\longrightarrow^{\#} \begin{pmatrix} \texttt{let } z = 1 \texttt{ in swap}(\underline{x},\underline{y},z), (y \mapsto 0, x \mapsto r), \\ (r \mapsto \langle 0,1 \rangle), (r \mapsto 2) \end{pmatrix} \tag{2}$$

$$\longrightarrow^{\#} \begin{pmatrix} \texttt{pop}(\texttt{swap}(\underline{x},\underline{y},\underline{z})), (z \mapsto 1, y \mapsto 0, x \mapsto r), \\ (r \mapsto \langle 0,1 \rangle), (r \mapsto 2) \end{pmatrix} \tag{3}$$

$$\longrightarrow^{\#} \begin{pmatrix} \dots \texttt{let } a = u[i] \texttt{ in } \dots, \\ (j \mapsto 1, i \mapsto 0, u \mapsto r, \dots, x \mapsto \texttt{nil}), \\ (r \mapsto \langle 0,1 \rangle), (r \mapsto 2) \end{pmatrix} \tag{4}$$

$$\longrightarrow^{\#} \begin{pmatrix} \dots \texttt{let } a = 0 \texttt{ in } \dots, (j \mapsto 1, i \mapsto 0, u \mapsto r, \dots), \\ (r \mapsto \langle 0,1 \rangle), (r \mapsto 2) \end{pmatrix} \tag{5}$$

$$\longrightarrow^{\#} \begin{pmatrix} \dots \texttt{let } b = u[j] \texttt{ in } \dots, (a \mapsto 0, j \mapsto 1, \dots), \\ (r \mapsto \langle 0,1 \rangle), (r \mapsto 2) \end{pmatrix} \tag{6}$$

$$\longrightarrow^{\#} \begin{pmatrix} \dots \texttt{let } b = 1 \texttt{ in } \dots, (a \mapsto 0, j \mapsto 1, \dots), \\ (r \mapsto \langle 0,1 \rangle), (r \mapsto 2) \end{pmatrix} \tag{7}$$

$$\longrightarrow^{\#} \begin{pmatrix} \dots \texttt{let } u' = \underline{u}[\underline{i} \mapsto \underline{b}] \texttt{ in } \dots, (b \mapsto 1, a \mapsto 0, \dots), \\ (r \mapsto \langle 0,1 \rangle), (r \mapsto 2) \end{pmatrix} \tag{8}$$

$$\longrightarrow^{\#} \begin{pmatrix} \dots \texttt{let } u' = r' \texttt{ in } \dots, \\ (b \mapsto 1, a \mapsto 0, \dots, u \mapsto \texttt{nil}, \dots), \\ (r' \mapsto \langle 1,1 \rangle, r \mapsto \langle 0,1 \rangle), (r' \mapsto 1, r \mapsto 1) \end{pmatrix} \tag{9}$$

$$\longrightarrow^{\#} (\dots \underline{u'}[\underline{j} \mapsto \underline{a}] \dots, (u' \mapsto r', b \mapsto 1, \dots), (r' \mapsto \langle 1,1 \rangle, \dots)) \tag{10}$$

$$\longrightarrow^{\#} \begin{pmatrix} \texttt{pop}^7(r'), (u' \mapsto \texttt{nil}, b \mapsto 1, \dots), \\ (r' \mapsto \langle 1,0 \rangle, \dots), (r' \mapsto 1, \dots) \end{pmatrix} \tag{11}$$

$$\longrightarrow^{\#}_{\star} \begin{pmatrix} r', (y \mapsto 0, x \mapsto \texttt{nil}), \\ (r' \mapsto \langle 1,0 \rangle, r \mapsto \langle 0,1 \rangle), (r' \mapsto 1, r \mapsto 1) \end{pmatrix} \tag{12}$$

Fig. 5. An example reduction in RL

result of a destructive update, in which case the reference count has to be 1, or it is a fresh copy, in which case the count is 1 as well.

Theorem 2. *With the reductions in Fig. 4, it is an invariant that the count is accurate, that is, Eq. 13 holds, and the other invariants (**early-release**, **correct-marking**, and **release-marked**), are preserved as well.*

To establish a bisimulation between the RL state $(e', S', (\mathcal{M}', \mathcal{C}'))$ and the FL one $(e, S, \mathcal{M})$, we say these two states match if there exists a translation function ρ from the elements of the domain of $\mathcal{M}'$ with a count greater than zero to those of the domain of $\mathcal{M}$ such that:

- The expression e is the result of translating the references (applying ρ to each of the references) when unmarking all the variables and removing all `release` constructors in e',
- For each variable x in $vars(e')$, $S(x) = \rho(S'(x))$,
- For each reference r in the domain of $\mathcal{M}'$ with a count greater than zero, $\mathcal{M}(\rho(r))$ is the result of translating the references of $\mathcal{M}'(r)$.

The mapping ρ is not fixed across the two executions but depends on the pairs of states being matched. For example, the bisimulation between the *FL* execution in Fig. 3 and the *RL* execution in Fig. 5 lines up the twelve states in each execution exactly. The mapping $\{r \mapsto r\}$ is used for matching states 1 through 8, and $\{r \mapsto r, r' \mapsto r'\}$ for states 9 and 10, and $\{r \mapsto r, r' \mapsto r''\}$ for states 11 and 12. Note that although it is not required for the mapping between references to be injective, it happens to be an invariant (that is not needed for proving the bisimulation result). We also do not need to assume that the store does not contain any cycles, though this too is an invariant that is preserved by both *FL* and *RL* executions.

Theorem 3. *If the state $S = (e, S, \mathcal{M})$ matches the state $S' = (e', S', (\mathcal{M}', \mathcal{C}'))$, we have:*

- *if the current redex of e' is a `release` redex, then the state obtained when reducing S' after one step still matches the state S,*
- *if it is not a `release` redex, then the state obtained when reducing S and the one obtained when reducing S' for a step each still match each other.*

Theorem 4. *The reduction relations $\longrightarrow$ in FL and $\longrightarrow^{\#}$ in RL are in bisimulation.*

As a step toward an imperative translation of *RL*, we extend *RL* by adding a construct of the form `return(e)` to mark the return from a function call. Since the `return` label will be used as a variable in the imperative translation, it cannot be used as a variable identifier in *RL*. In the expanded language, `return(□)` is an evaluation context. We also have a redex of the form

$$(\texttt{return}(v), S, (\mathcal{M}, \mathcal{C})) \rightarrow^{\#} (v, S, (\mathcal{M}, \mathcal{C})).$$

The evaluation rule for function calls is modified as below.

$$(f(\overline{x}), S, (\mathcal{M}, \mathcal{C})) \rightarrow^{\#} (\texttt{return}(\texttt{pop}^n(e)), S_n, (\mathcal{M}, \mathcal{C})), \text{ where}$$
$$\mathcal{C}' = \textbf{incvars}(\overline{x}, S, \mathcal{C})$$
$$S_0 = \textbf{push}(\overline{y} \mapsto S(\overline{x}), S)$$
$$S_{i+1} = \begin{cases} S_i[x_i \mapsto \texttt{nil}], \\ \quad \text{if } x_i \text{ is a marked and } S(x) \text{ is a reference} \\ S_i, \text{ otherwise} \end{cases}$$

We also label the `pop` operations with the variable being popped so that it has the form $\texttt{pop}_x$ when the stack entry to be popped binds x. Neither of these extensions affects any of the claims about RL since the **return** operation essentially functions as a skip operation, and labeling the occurrences of **pop** has no impact on the evaluation. Both these constructs together with let-binding are used to define the stack employed in the imperative evaluation in terms of the RL stack.

The operation $\mathbf{stack}(x)(E)$ on an evaluation context E collects the stack of variables introduced by **return**, **pop**, and pending let-bindings on the path to the hole in the RL expression being evaluated. This operation fuses consecutive return variables so that the return value from the evaluation of a function is passed directly to the outermost return point. The stack used in the imperative evaluation binds variables in a somewhat different order than the operational semantics for RL. The **stack** operation is used to capture the sequence of variables that appear at the top of the stack during the evaluation of the imperative counterpart of an RL expression. It is used in defining the bisimulation between RL executions and the imperative semantics presented in the next section.

$$\mathbf{stack}(x)(\square, st) = st$$
$$\mathbf{stack}(x)(\mathtt{let}\ y = a\ \mathtt{in}\ b, st) = \mathbf{stack}(y)(a, \mathbf{push}(y, st))$$
$$\mathbf{stack}(x)(\mathbf{pop}_y(a), st) = \mathbf{stack}(x)(a, \mathbf{push}(y, st))$$
$$\mathbf{stack}(x)(\mathbf{return}(a), st) = \begin{cases} \mathbf{stack}(x)(a, st), & \text{if } x = \mathbf{return} \\ \mathbf{stack}(\mathbf{return})(a), \mathbf{push}(\mathbf{return}, st)), & \text{otherwise} \end{cases}$$

4   A Small Imperative Language

Mapping RL expressions to imperative code poses significant semantic challenges. In RL, we evaluate expressions, whereas in an imperative language, the statements are executed sequentially. RL evaluation returns a value, whereas the execution in an imperative language returns a state mapping variables to values. This changes the signalling mechanism used to identify the redexes. In FL and RL, a let-redex is triggered when the binding expression becomes a value. There is no such signalling mechanism in an imperative program since statements are executed successively. There is no handy equivalent of let-expressions $\mathtt{let}\ x = a\ \mathtt{in}\ b$ in imperative languages since this expression is mapped to two statement blocks: s_a for computing a and assigning the value to x, and s_b for evaluating b. Since x is assigned in s_a and used in s_b, it has to be declared ahead of the block s_a, but this has the unfortunate side-effect of including s_a in its scope. Such issues of scope can be handled in a formalization based on the de Bruijn representation (as we do in our mechanized proofs), but require some care when using a named representation.

The target of our code generation is an imperative language KL which looks quite similar to RL. From KL, we can target a lower-level imperative language such as C that does not keep track of reference counts automatically. A program KL is defined as a sequence of functions, whose body is a statement, with the definitions in Fig. 6.

$$e ::= \mid n$$
$$\mid x$$
$$\mid \texttt{nil}$$
$$\mid f(x_1, \ldots, x_n)$$
$$\mid x[y]$$
$$\mid x[y \mapsto z]$$
$$\mid \texttt{newint}(n)$$
$$\mid \texttt{newref}(n)$$

$$s ::= \mid x := e$$
$$\mid \texttt{ifnz } x \texttt{ then } s_1 \texttt{ else } s_2$$
$$\mid \texttt{skip}$$
$$\mid s_1; s_2$$
$$\mid \{t\ x; s\}$$
$$\mid \texttt{release } x$$
$$\mid \texttt{pop}$$

$$\text{decl} ::= t\ x$$
$$\text{function} ::= (\text{name}, \text{decl}^*, s)$$
$$\text{program} ::= \text{function}^*$$

Fig. 6. Syntax of *KL*

As in *KL*, variables can be marked. A *value* is now either `nil`, an integer, a reference, or `undef`. It is an error to use the value `undef` within a program since it is there only for evaluation purposes. There is a special variable named `return` that is used as the return value of a function and is never used as a regular variable in a program.

Once a program with definitions Π is fixed, the evaluation state for *KL* is a triplet $(\mathcal{K}, S, (\mathcal{M}, \mathcal{C}))$, where as previously, S is the stack, which maps variables to values, $\mathcal{M}$ and $\mathcal{C}$ are the store and the reference counts, respectively. $\mathcal{K}$ is the (possibly empty) statement (or continuation) being evaluated. The evaluation rules for *KL* are given in Fig. 9 (for non-assignment statements), Fig. 10 (for non-array assignment statements), and Fig. 11 (for assignment statements).

Next, we illustrate the translation of *RL* expressions into *KL* code. To translate a function with body e from *RL* to *KL*, we use **translate**$(e, \texttt{return})$, where **translate** is defined in Fig. 7. The operation assumes that in any *RL* subexpression of the form `let` $x = a$ `in` b, the variable x does not occur free in a.

To translate the *RL* program $\Delta^{\#}$ into a *KL* program Π, we translate each function definition $f(\overline{x}) = e$ in $\Delta^{\#}$ as $f(x_1, \ldots, x_d) = s_f$, where

$$s_f = \textbf{translate}(\text{pop}^d(e), \texttt{return}).$$

For the example of the $swap(u, i, j)$ program, the body

$$\texttt{let } a = u[i] \texttt{ in let } b = u[j] \texttt{ in let } u' = \underline{u[i \mapsto b]} \texttt{ in } \underline{u'[j \mapsto a]}$$

is translated as

$$\{\texttt{int } a; a := u[i]; \{\texttt{int } b; b := u[j]; \{\texttt{int[2] } u'; u' := \underline{u[i \mapsto b]}; \texttt{return} := \underline{u'[j \mapsto a]}\}\}\}$$

$$\textbf{translate}(n, x) = x := n$$

$$\textbf{translate}(y, x) = x := y$$

$$\textbf{translate}(\texttt{nil}, x) = x := \texttt{nil}$$

$$\textbf{translate}(f(x_1, \ldots, x_n), x) = x := f(x_1, \ldots, x_n)$$

$$\textbf{translate}(\texttt{let } (y : t) = e_1 \texttt{ in } e_2, x) = \{t\ y; \textbf{translate}(e_1, y); \textbf{translate}(e_2, x)\}$$

$$\textbf{translate}(\texttt{ifnz } y \texttt{ then } e_1 \texttt{ else } e_2, x) = \texttt{ifnz } y \texttt{ then } s_1 \texttt{ else } s_2,$$

$$s_1 = \textbf{translate}(e_1, x),$$

$$s_2 = \textbf{translate}(e_2, x)$$

$$\textbf{translate}(y[z], x) = x := y[z]$$

$$\textbf{translate}(y[z \mapsto w], x) = x := y[z \mapsto w]$$

$$\textbf{translate}(\texttt{newint}(n), x) = x := \texttt{newint}(n)$$

$$\textbf{translate}(\texttt{newref}(n), x) = x := \texttt{newref}(n)$$

$$\textbf{translate}(\texttt{release}(y, e), x) = \texttt{release } y; \textbf{translate}(e, x)$$

$$\textbf{translate}(\texttt{pop}_y(e), x) = \textbf{translate}(e, x); \texttt{pop}_y$$

$$\textbf{translate}(\texttt{return}(e), x) = \begin{cases} \textbf{translate}(e, x), & \text{if } x = \texttt{return} \\ \{t \texttt{ return}; s_e; x := \texttt{return}\}, & \text{otherwise,} \\ \quad \textit{where} \\ \quad s_e = \textbf{translate}(e, \texttt{return}), \\ \quad t = \tau(e) \end{cases}$$

Fig. 7. Translation from RL to KL

Next, we demonstrate a bisimulation between the evaluation of an RL expression and the execution of its translated program.

We define $\textbf{lvars}(S)$ to represent the stack of variables bound in the stack.

$$\textbf{lvars}(\textbf{push}(x \mapsto v, S)) = \textbf{push}(x, \textbf{lvars}(S))$$

$$\textbf{lvars}(\textbf{push}(x \mapsto \texttt{undef}, S)) = \textbf{lvars}(S)$$

$$\textbf{lvars}(empty) = empty$$

The operation $\textbf{defined}(S)$ extracts the defined bindings in the stack S:

$$\textbf{defined}(\textbf{push}(x \mapsto v, S)) = \textbf{push}(x \mapsto v, \textbf{lvars}(S))$$

$$\textbf{defined}(\textbf{push}(\texttt{return} \mapsto v, S)) = \textbf{defined}(S)$$

$$\textbf{defined}(\textbf{push}(x \mapsto \texttt{undef}, S)) = \textbf{defined}(S)$$

$$\textbf{defined}(empty) = empty$$

For KL program s, let $\textbf{body}(s)$ be defined as below.

$$\textbf{body}(\{t\ x; s\}) = \textbf{body}(s); \texttt{pop}$$

$$\textbf{body}(s_1; s_2) = \textbf{body}(s_1); s_2$$

$$\begin{pmatrix} \{\text{int } z; z := +(y,1); \text{return} := \text{swap}(\underline{x}, \underline{y}, \underline{z})\}; \mathcal{K}, \\ (\text{return} \mapsto \textbf{undef}, y \mapsto 0, x \mapsto r), \\ ((r \mapsto \langle 0,1 \rangle), (r \mapsto 2)) \end{pmatrix} \tag{1}$$

$$\longrightarrow^! \begin{pmatrix} z := +(y,1); \text{return} := \text{swap}(\underline{x}, \underline{y}, \underline{z}); \text{pop}; \mathcal{K}, \\ (z \mapsto \textbf{undef}; \text{return} \mapsto \textbf{undef}, y \mapsto 0, x \mapsto r), \\ ((r \mapsto \langle 0,1 \rangle), (r \mapsto 2)) \end{pmatrix} \tag{2}$$

$$\longrightarrow^! \begin{pmatrix} \text{return} := \text{swap}(\underline{x}, \underline{y}, \underline{z}); \text{pop}; \mathcal{K}, \\ (z \mapsto 1, \text{return} \mapsto \textbf{undef}, y \mapsto 0, x \mapsto r), \\ ((r \mapsto \langle 0,1 \rangle), (r \mapsto 2)) \end{pmatrix} \tag{3}$$

$$\longrightarrow^! \begin{pmatrix} s_{swap}; \text{pop};^3 \text{pop}; \mathcal{K}, \\ (j \mapsto 1, i \mapsto 0, u \mapsto r, z \mapsto 1, \text{return} \mapsto \textbf{undef}, y \mapsto 0, x \mapsto \textbf{nil}), \\ ((r \mapsto \langle 0,1 \rangle), (r \mapsto 2)) \end{pmatrix} \tag{4}$$

$$\longrightarrow^! \begin{pmatrix} a := u[i]; \dots; \text{pop};^5 \mathcal{K}, \\ (a \mapsto \textbf{undef}, j \mapsto 1, i \mapsto 0, u \mapsto r, z \mapsto 1, \text{return} \mapsto \textbf{undef}, \dots), \\ ((r \mapsto \langle 0,1 \rangle), (r \mapsto 2)) \end{pmatrix} \tag{5}$$

$$\xrightarrow{\;\;\;}^{\star\;!} \begin{pmatrix} b := u[j]; \dots; \text{pop};^6 \mathcal{K}, \\ (b \mapsto \textbf{undef}, a \mapsto 0, j \mapsto 1, \dots), \\ ((r \mapsto \langle 0,1 \rangle), (r \mapsto 2)) \end{pmatrix} \tag{6}$$

$$\xrightarrow{\;\;\;}^{\star\;!} \begin{pmatrix} u' := \underline{u}[\underline{i} \mapsto \underline{b}]; \dots; \dots; \text{pop};^7 \mathcal{K}, \\ (u' \mapsto \textbf{undef}, b \mapsto 1, a \mapsto 0, j \mapsto 1, \dots), \\ ((r \mapsto \langle 0,1 \rangle), (r \mapsto 2)) \end{pmatrix} \tag{7}$$

$$\xrightarrow{\;\;\;}^{\star\;!} \begin{pmatrix} \text{return} := \underline{u}'[\underline{j} \mapsto \underline{a}]; \dots; \mathcal{K}, \\ (u' \mapsto r; b \mapsto 1, a \mapsto 0, u \mapsto \textbf{nil}, \dots), \\ ((r' \mapsto \langle 1,1 \rangle, r \mapsto \langle 0,1 \rangle), (r' \mapsto 1, r \mapsto 1)) \end{pmatrix} \tag{8}$$

$$\xrightarrow{\;\;\;}^{\star\;!} (\mathcal{K}, (\text{return} \mapsto r', \dots), ((r' \mapsto \langle 1,0 \rangle, \dots), (r' \mapsto 1, r \mapsto 1))) \tag{9}$$

Fig. 8. An example reduction in *KL*

A rough point of correspondence between an *RL* state $(e, S_1, (\mathcal{M}, \mathcal{C}))$ and *KL* state $(s_e, S_2, (\mathcal{M}_2, \mathcal{C}_2))$ is:

1. The *KL* program s_e corresponding to e is the empty program when e is a value, and is **body**(**translate**(e, return)), otherwise.
2. The correspondence between the *RL* stack S_1 and *KL* stack S_2 is that **lvars**(S_2) = **stack**(return)(e, **push**(return, *empty*)) ∘ **lvars**(S) for some S, and **defined**(S_2) = **push**(return $\mapsto v, S_1$), when e is the value v, and otherwise S_1 = **defined**(S_2).
3. $(\mathcal{M}_1, \mathcal{C}_1) = (\mathcal{M}_2, \mathcal{C}_2)$.

The idea is that we initiate both evaluations with a stack S_0 but the *KL* state stack is of the form **push**(return $\mapsto$ **undef**, S_0) to capture the return value.

$$(\texttt{skip}; \mathcal{K}, S, (\mathcal{M}, \mathcal{C})) \longrightarrow^! (\mathcal{K}, S, (\mathcal{M}, \mathcal{C}))$$

$$(\{t\ x; s\}; \mathcal{K}, S, (\mathcal{M}, \mathcal{C})) \longrightarrow^! \begin{pmatrix} s; \texttt{pop}; \mathcal{K}, \mathbf{push}(x \mapsto \texttt{undef}, S) \\ (\mathcal{M}, \mathcal{C}) \end{pmatrix}$$

$$(\texttt{ifnz}\ x\ \texttt{then}\ s_1\ \texttt{else}\ s_2; \mathcal{K}, S, (\mathcal{M}, \mathcal{C})) \longrightarrow^! (s_i; \mathcal{K}, S, (\mathcal{M}, \mathcal{C})), \text{ where}$$

$$i = \begin{cases} 2, & \text{if } S(x) = 0 \\ 1, & \text{otherwise} \end{cases}$$

$$(\texttt{release}\ x; \mathcal{K}, S, (\mathcal{M}, \mathcal{C})) \longrightarrow^! (\mathcal{K}, S[x \mapsto \texttt{nil}], (\mathcal{M}', \mathcal{C}')), \text{ where}$$

$$(\mathcal{M}', \mathcal{C}') = \mathbf{decref}(S(x), (\mathcal{M}, \mathcal{C}))$$

$$(\texttt{pop}; \mathcal{K}, S, (\mathcal{M}, \mathcal{C})) \longrightarrow^! (\mathcal{K}, \mathbf{pop}(S), (\mathcal{M}, \mathcal{C}))$$

Fig. 9. Operational semantics of KL: non-assignment statements

$$(x := \underline{y}; \mathcal{K}, S, (\mathcal{M}, \mathcal{C})) \longrightarrow^! (\mathcal{K}, S[x \mapsto S(y)], (\mathcal{M}, \mathcal{C}))$$

$$(x := y; \mathcal{K}, S, (\mathcal{M}, \mathcal{C})) \longrightarrow^! (\mathcal{K}, S[x \mapsto S(y)], (\mathcal{M}, \mathcal{C}')),$$

$$\text{where } y \text{ is unmarked,}$$

$$\mathcal{C}' = \mathbf{incr}(S(y), \mathcal{C})$$

$$(x := n; \mathcal{K}, S, (\mathcal{M}, \mathcal{C})) \longrightarrow^! (\mathcal{K}, S[x \mapsto n], (\mathcal{M}, \mathcal{C}))$$

$$(y := f(x_1, \ldots, x_n); \mathcal{K}, S, (\mathcal{M}, \mathcal{C}')) \longrightarrow^! (\mathcal{K}', S_n, (\mathcal{M}, \mathcal{C}')), \text{ where}$$

$$\mathcal{K}' = \begin{cases} s_f; \texttt{pop}^n; \mathcal{K}, & \text{if } y = \texttt{return} \\ s_f; \texttt{pop};^n y := \underline{\texttt{return}}; \texttt{pop}; \mathcal{K}, \\ & \text{otherwise} \end{cases}$$

$$S' = \begin{cases} \mathbf{push}(\overline{y} \mapsto S(\overline{x}), \\ \qquad \mathbf{push}(\texttt{return} \mapsto \texttt{undef}, S)), \\ \qquad \text{if } y \neq \texttt{return} \\ \mathbf{push}(\overline{y} \mapsto S(\overline{x}), S), \text{ otherwise} \end{cases}$$

$$S_0 = S'$$

$$S_{i+1} = \begin{cases} S_i[x_i \mapsto \texttt{nil}], & \text{if} \\ \qquad x_i \text{ is a marked and} \\ \qquad S(x) \text{ is a reference} \\ S_i, & \text{otherwise} \end{cases}$$

$$\mathcal{C}' = \mathbf{incvars}(\overline{x}, S, \mathcal{C})$$

Fig. 10. Operational semantics of KL: non-array assignment statements

Furthermore, the S_2 stack contains bindings, defined and undefined, for the variables in $\mathbf{stack}(\texttt{return})(e)$, whereas all the bindings in S_1 are defined.

However, the first bullet holds only for canonical states, as defined below. For example, in RL, e can have the form $\texttt{let}\ x = r\ \texttt{in}\ e'$ for some reference r but the syntax of KL does not allow explicit references in expressions. The fourth state in Fig. 8 has a program of the form $\{\texttt{int}\ a; a := u[i]; \ldots\}$, which is not the body of

$$(x := y[z]; \mathcal{K}, S, (\mathcal{M}, \mathcal{C})) \longrightarrow^! (\mathcal{K}, S[x \mapsto v], (\mathcal{M}, \mathcal{C}')), \text{ where}$$
$$v = \mathcal{M}(S(y))[S(z)], \mathcal{C}' = \mathbf{incr}(v, \mathcal{C})$$
$$(x := y[z \mapsto w]; \mathcal{K}, S, (\mathcal{M}, \mathcal{C})) \longrightarrow^! (\mathcal{K}, S[x \mapsto v], (\mathcal{M}'', \mathcal{C}'')), \text{ where}$$
$$v = S(y), \mathcal{C}(v) = 1, v \text{ is a reference,}$$
$$\mathcal{M}' = \mathcal{M}(v)[S(z) := S(w)],$$
$$\mathcal{C}' = \mathbf{incvars}(w, S, \mathcal{C}),$$
$$(\mathcal{M}'', \mathcal{C}'') = \mathbf{decref}(t)(\mathcal{M}(v)[S(z)], (\mathcal{M}', \mathcal{C}'))$$
$$(x := y[z \mapsto w]; \mathcal{K}, S, (\mathcal{M}, \mathcal{C})) \longrightarrow^! (\mathcal{K}, S[x \mapsto v], (\mathcal{M}', \mathcal{C}'')), \text{ where}$$
$$v = S(y), v \text{ is a reference,}$$
$$y \text{ is unmarked or } \mathcal{C}(v) > 1,$$
$$r = \mathbf{new}(\mathcal{M}),$$
$$\mathcal{M}' = \mathcal{M}[r \mapsto \mathcal{M}(S(y))[S(z) := S(w)],$$
$$\mathcal{C}' = (\#\mathcal{M}'(r) + \mathcal{C})[r \mapsto 1],$$
$$\mathcal{C}'' = \mathbf{decr}(\mathcal{M}(v)(S(z)), \mathcal{C}')$$

Fig. 11. Operational semantics of KL: assignment statements

let $z = +(y,1)$ in swap($\underline{x}, y, \underline{z}$)	$z := +(y,1); \mathtt{return} := \mathtt{swap}(\underline{x}, y, \underline{z}); \mathtt{pop};$
swap($\underline{x}, y, \underline{z}$)	$\mathtt{return} := \mathtt{swap}(\underline{x}, y, \underline{z}); \mathtt{pop};$
return(let $a = u[i]$ in ...)	$a := \underline{u[i]}; \ldots; \mathtt{pop};^5$
return(let $b = u[j]$ in ...)	$b := \underline{u[j]}; \ldots; \mathtt{pop};^6$
return(let $u' = \underline{u[i \mapsto b]}$ in ...)	$u' := \underline{u[i \mapsto b]}; \ldots; \mathtt{pop};^7$
return($\underline{u'[j \mapsto a]}$)	$\mathtt{return} := \underline{u'[j \mapsto a]}; \ldots; \mathtt{pop};^7$
r'	

Fig. 12. Correspondence between RL and KL evaluation

the program. To get around these discrepancies, we restrict the correspondence to states in canonical form obtained by applying certain reductions. In RL, in any state $(e, S_1, (\mathcal{M}_1, \mathcal{C}_2))$, redexes e' of the form let $x = v$ in e'', return(v), and pop(v), where $e = E[e']$, must be silently reduced. Similarly, in any KL state $(s; S_2, (\mathcal{M}_2, \mathcal{C}_2))$ any of the following redexes must be silently reduced:

1. $\{t\ x; s\}; \mathcal{K}$
2. $x := v; \mathcal{K}$
3. $x := \mathtt{return}; \mathcal{K}$
4. pop; $\mathcal{K}$

With these reductions, the above correspondence yields a bisimulation between RL and KL execution steps. For example, in the derivation in Fig. 8 (assuming that continuation $\mathcal{K}$ is empty) the canonical states are 2, 3, 5, 6, 7, 8, and 9, which correspond to the RL evaluation states 1, 3, 4, 6, 8, 10, and 12 in

Fig. 5. The correspondence between the canonical *RL* expressions in evaluation in Fig. 5 and their translations in the *KL* evaluation in Fig. 8 is shown in Fig. 12.

Theorem 5. *The reduction relations* $\longrightarrow^{\#}$ *in* RL *and* $\longrightarrow^{!}$ *in* KL *are in bisimulation.*

5 Conclusions

Functional languages offer significant advantages in terms of expressiveness and verifiability, but they require fairly extensive runtime support. Our goal here is to generate efficient, standalone code from an executable fragment of a logic in which we can unify specification, modeling, and execution. The PVS2C code generator translates an applicative fragment of PVS into C code. The generated C code is self-contained and does not rely on a run time. The generated code preserves the type safety of the typechecked PVS. It can only crash by exhausting resource bounds. The generated C code is comparable in efficiency to the corresponding hand-crafted C, and is typically a lot faster than the Common Lisp code generated from PVS.

The intermediate languages presented here: *FL, RL,* and *KL* form the core of the translation from the applicative subset of PVS to executable C code. The translations between these languages and the bisimulation proofs presented here form a step toward the mechanized verification of the code generator. We believe that the proof outlined in the paper can be easily mechanized, and can also be used as a foundation for similar proofs involving more sophisticated language features.

Acknowledgment. This work was supported by the National Institute of Aerospace Award C18-201097-SRI, NSF Grant SHF-1817204, and DARPA under agreement number HR001119C0075. The views and conclusions contained herein are those of the authors and should not be interpreted as necessarily representing the official policies or endorsements, either expressed or implied, of NASA, NSF, DARPA, or the U.S. Government. We thank the anonymous referees for their constructive feedback.

References

1. Appel, A.W., Blazy, S.: Separation logic for small-step CMINOR. In: Schneider, K., Brandt, J. (eds.) TPHOLs 2007. LNCS, vol. 4732, pp. 5–21. Springer, Heidelberg (2007). https://doi.org/10.1007/978-3-540-74591-4_3
2. Aspinall, D., Hofmann, M.: Another type system for in-place update. In: Le Métayer, D. (ed.) ESOP 2002. LNCS, vol. 2305, pp. 36–52. Springer, Heidelberg (2002). https://doi.org/10.1007/3-540-45927-8_4
3. Bevier, W.R., Hunt, W.A., Moore Jr., J.S., Young, W.D.: An approach to systems verification. J. Autom. Reason. **5**(4), 411–428 (1989)
4. Chirimar, J., Gunter, C.A., Riecke, J.G.: Reference counting as a computational interpretation of linear logic. J. Funct. Program. **6**(2), 195–244 (1996)
5. Collins, G.E.: A method for overlapping and erasure of lists. Commun. ACM **3**(12), 655–657 (1960)

6. Didrich, K., Fett, A., Gerke, C., Grieskamp, W., Pepper, P.: OPAL: design and implementation of an algebraic programming language. In: Gutknecht, J. (ed.) Programming Languages and System Architectures. LNCS, vol. 782, pp. 228–244. Springer, Heidelberg (1994). https://doi.org/10.1007/3-540-57840-4_34

7. Draghicescu, M., Purushothaman, S.: A uniform treatment of order of evaluation and aggregate update. Theor. Comput. Sci. **118**(2), 231–262 (1993)

8. Emmi, M., Jhala, R., Kohler, E., Majumdar, R.: Verifying reference counting implementations. In: Kowalewski, S., Philippou, A. (eds.) TACAS 2009. LNCS, vol. 5505, pp. 352–367. Springer, Heidelberg (2009). https://doi.org/10.1007/978-3-642-00768-2_30

9. Felleisen, M.: On the expressive power of programming languages. In: Jones, N. (ed.) ESOP 1990. LNCS, vol. 432, pp. 134–151. Springer, Heidelberg (1990). https://doi.org/10.1007/3-540-52592-0_60

10. Férey, G., Shankar, N.: Code Generation using a formal model of reference counting. In: Rayadurgam, S., Tkachuk, O. (eds.) NFM 2016. LNCS, vol. 9690, pp. 150–165. Springer, Cham (2016). https://doi.org/10.1007/978-3-319-40648-0_12

11. Flanagan, C., Sabry, A., Duba, B.F., Felleisen, M.: The essence of compiling with continuations (with retrospective). In: McKinley, K.S. (ed.) Best of PLDI, pp. 502–514. ACM (1993)

12. Gopinath, K., Hennessy, J.L.: Copy elimination in functional languages. In: 16th ACM Symposium on Principles of Programming Languages. Association for Computing Machinery, January 1989

13. Hudak, P.: A semantic model of reference counting and its abstraction (detailed summary). In: Proceedings 1986 ACM Conference on LISP and Functional Programming, pp. 351–363. ACM, August 1986

14. Hudak, P., Bloss, A.: The aggregate update problem in functional programming systems. In: Proceedings of the 12th ACM SIGACT-SIGPLAN Symposium on Principles of Programming Languages, POPL 1985, pp. 300–314. ACM, New York (1985)

15. Kanade, A., Sanyal, A., Khedker, U.: A PVS based framework for validating compiler optimizations. In: Fourth IEEE International Conference on Software Engineering and Formal Methods (SEFM 2006) (2006)

16. Kumar, R., Myreen, M.O., Norrish, M., Owens, S.: CakeML: a verified implementation of ML. In: Proceedings of the 41st ACM SIGPLAN-SIGACT Symposium on Principles of Programming Languages, POPL 2014, pp. 179–191. ACM, New York (2014)

17. Leroy, X.: Formal verification of a realistic compiler. Commun. ACM **52**(7), 107–115 (2009)

18. Harold McBeth, J.: On the reference counter method. Commun. ACM **6**(9), 575 (1963)

19. Moreau, L., Duprat, J.: A construction of distributed reference counting. Acta Inf. **37**(8), 563–595 (2001)

20. Polak, W.: Compiler Specification and Verification. Springer, Berlin (1981)

21. Schulte, W.: Deriving residual reference count garbage collectors. In: Hermenegildo, M., Penjam, J. (eds.) PLILP 1994. LNCS, vol. 844, pp. 102–116. Springer, Heidelberg (1994). https://doi.org/10.1007/3-540-58402-1_9

22. Shankar, N.: Static analysis for safe destructive updates in a functional language. In: Pettorossi, A. (ed.) LOPSTR 2001. LNCS, vol. 2372, pp. 1–24. Springer, Heidelberg (2002). https://doi.org/10.1007/3-540-45607-4_1

23. Shankar, N.: A brief introduction to the PVS2C code generator. In: Dutertre, B., Shankar, N. (eds.) AFM@NFM, EasyChair, vol. 5, pp. 109–116. Kalpa Publications in Computing (2017)
24. David W.J.: Stringer-Calvert. Mechanical Verification of Compiler Correctness. Ph.D. thesis, University of York, Department of Computer Science, York, England, March 1998
25. Ullrich, S., de Moura, L.: Counting immutable beans: Reference counting optimized for purely functional programming. CoRR, abs/1908.05647, 2019. Appears in pre-conference proceedings of IFL2019: http://2019.iflconference.org/pre-conference-proceedings.pdf
26. Wand, M., Clinger, W.D.: Set constraints for destructive array update optimization. In: Proceedings of the IEEE Conference on Computer Languages 1998, pp. 184–193. IEEE, April 1998

Leveraging Compiler Intermediate Representation for Multi- and Cross-Language Verification

Jack J. Garzella, Marek Baranowski, Shaobo He[(✉)], and Zvonimir Rakamarić

School of Computing, University of Utah,
Salt Lake City, UT, USA
jjgarzella@gmail.com,
{baranows,shaobo,zvonimir}@cs.utah.edu

Abstract. Developers nowadays regularly use numerous programming languages with different characteristics and trade-offs. Unfortunately, implementing a software verifier for a new language from scratch is a large and tedious undertaking, requiring expert knowledge in multiple domains, such as compilers, verification, and constraint solving. Hence, only a tiny fraction of the used languages has readily available software verifiers to aid in the development of correct programs. In the past decade, there has been a trend of leveraging popular compiler intermediate representations (IRs), such as LLVM IR, when implementing software verifiers. Processing IR promises out-of-the-box multi- and cross-language verification since, at least in theory, a verifier ought to be able to handle a program in any programming language (and their combination) that can be compiled into the IR. In practice though, to the best of our knowledge, nobody has explored the feasibility and ease of such integration of new languages. In this paper, we provide a procedure for adding support for a new language into an IR-based verification toolflow. Using our procedure, we extend the SMACK verifier with prototypical support for 6 additional languages. We assess the quality of our extensions through several case studies, and we describe our experience in detail to guide future efforts in this area.

Keywords: Verification · Multi-language · Cross-language · Compiler intermediate representation

1 Introduction

The evolution of software systems motivates the need for new programming languages with novel features to better adapt to new programming goals, such

This work was supported by funding from the Undergraduate Research Opportunities Program at the University of Utah awarded to Jack J. Garzella, the National Science Foundation awards CNS 1527526 and CCF 1837051, and a gift from the VMware's University Research Fund.

D. Beyer and D. Zufferey (Eds.): VMCAI 2020, LNCS 11990, pp. 90–111, 2020.
https://doi.org/10.1007/978-3-030-39322-9_5

as improving program safety or easing programming. For example, Rust [45] is a novel performant systems programming language with guaranteed memory safety and safer parallel programming. The D programming language also aims to provide memory safety and high-level programming primitives, while maintaining performance and low-level programming capabilities. Swift and Kotlin employ modern programming language concepts to reduce language verbosity and allow for easier programming. On the other hand, there are legacy languages that are still widely used in certain domains. For example, Fortran dominates as a programming language of choice among domain scientists, such as physicists and chemists. To further complicate matters, developers typically build real-world software systems using a combination of several programming languages by implementing various components in different languages depending on the requirements and trade-offs.

Software verification is integral to improving software quality. Among software verification techniques, the ones based on *satisfiability modulo theories* (SMT) have become increasingly popular due to its rigor, automation, and tremendous scalability improvements of the past two decades. There are numerous SMT-based tools available with various capabilities, features, and trade-offs (e.g., [1–3, 5–8, 10–15, 23, 30, 37, 39, 41, 47, 51]). However, the traditional way to prototype a program verifier, by implementing all of its components (e.g., front-end, SMT formula generator) from scratch, is extremely time-consuming and heavily coupled with target language details. Hence, despite widespread usage of many programming languages and their combinations, automatic software verifiers still predominantly target the C programming language, thereby denying many developers a valuable tool for ensuring safety and reliability of their programs. It would be ideal if program verifiers can keep pace with the development of emerging programming languages such that users can benefit from this rigorous software analysis technique.

LLVM [34, 35] is a popular, open source compiler infrastructure, which features an assembly-like intermediate compiler representation, known as the LLVM intermediate representation (IR). LLVM IR has been leveraged to build program verifiers [26, 37, 41], since LLVM IR frees the verifier designer from the error prone tasks of modeling the semantics and parsing of the source language [41]. In theory, a well-designed verifier targeting LLVM IR should be able to support any programming language that has a compiler front-end capable of emitting LLVM IR, as well as their combinations. However, to the best of our knowledge, verifiers built upon LLVM IR only support C/C++, and there has been no systematic study exploring how well such verifiers extend to support other programming languages. This is despite the fact that compilers for other programming languages can produce LLVM IR, such as the Rust compiler and the Flang compiler [24] for Fortran.

The goal of this paper is to investigate the feasibility of multi- and cross-language verification that leverages an intermediate compiler representation (e.g., LLVM IR). We chose to use SMACK [41, 48] as an exemplar mature verification toolchain based on LLVM IR. As our first step, we prescribe a procedure for adding a new language to such a tool chain, consisting of interoperating with language models, compiling into IR, and adding models for missing language features. Then, we evaluate our procedure by prototyping in SMACK support for 6 additional programming languages with compilers capable of emitting LLVM IR. Since SMACK is an LLVM IR-based verifier with extensive, preexisting support for the C programming language, it is a good basis for building a verifier for a new language. Additionally, the modular design of SMACK is a desirable feature due to its decoupling of source language details from the verification task through LLVM IR.

We performed several empirical case studies based around multi- and cross-language verification. To this end, we created a microbenchmark suite that tests support for key language features such as dynamic dispatch. We also explore cross-language verification using an example that exercises the interaction between Rust, Fortran, and C code. This is an important task as many new programming languages include a facility to invoke C functions natively to support legacy code. We summarize our experience and lessons learned. We observe that depending on features present in a programming language, SMACK may not always work out-of-the-box. This is due to either SMACK not supporting certain LLVM IR patterns or lack of suitable models for the standard libraries and runtime. We discuss the process of improving SMACK's support for various LLVM IR patterns, which involves modeling additional IR instructions. We also describe how we provide basic models for standard libraries and runtimes for several languages we added.

To summarize, our main contributions are as follows:

- We prescribe a procedure by which support for new programming languages can be added to an IR-based software verifier.
- By following our procedure, we added basic multi-language support to the SMACK software verifier for 6 additional programming languages: C++, Objective-C, D, Fortran, Swift, and Kotlin. We also made the preexisting support for Rust more robust, and hence we include it in our evaluation.
- We developed a suite of microbenchmarks for testing the robustness of multi-language verification, which implements key language features across all of the additional languages.
- We performed several multi- and cross-language case studies using SMACK, and we report on our experience and lessons learned in the process to guide future efforts in this area.

2   Related Work

In the past decade, numerous software verifiers have been developed on top of the LLVM compiler infrastructure (e.g., [5,6,20,26,37,41]), while others leverage GCC in a similar fashion (e.g., [21,27]). The authors of these tools have realized the benefits LLVM offers for the development of verifiers, such as a canonical intermediate representation and readily available analysis and optimization passes. In particular, verifiers such as SAW [20], LLBMC [37], SeaHorn [26], and SMACK [41] all take as input LLVM bitcode produced by the clang compiler, which is then handled differently by each verifier. SAW (Software Analysis Workbench) uses symbolic execution with path merging to produce formal models from LLVM IR in a dependently-typed intermediate verification language; it reasons about the resulting models using rewriting or external satisfiability solvers. LLBMC generates its own intermediate logical representation (ILR) based on the input LLVM IR program, and leverages SMT solvers to check the formula derived from ILR. SeaHorn encodes an input LLVM IR program into Horn clauses, which are further solved using different techniques. SMACK translates LLVM IR into an intermediate verification language called Boogie, which is then verified using different back-end verification engines. Both LLBMC and SeaHorn support both C and C++ (to some extent), while SMACK has mature support only for C. Unlike the aforementioned tools, ESBMC [14] leverages clang just as a parser to obtain ASTs, and it does not use LLVM IR; it supports both C and C++. Despite the popularity of LLVM IR in building software verifiers, to the best of our knowledge, we are the first to study the feasibility of leveraging an intermediate representation to perform multi- and cross-language verification.

Some of the languages we considered in this paper have standalone verifiers. For instance, CRUST [50] verifies unsafe Rust code by translating a Rust program into a C program, and then using an off-the-shelf C verifier. Rust2Viper [28] and its successor Prusti [4] are modular verifiers for Rust programs that include a design-by-contract specification language. As input they take an annotated program in the Rust's high-level intermediate representation, which simplifies and canonicalizes complex language constructs. Then, such a program is encoded into the Viper intermediate verification language [38] for verification. These approaches would require substantial effort to support verification of other programming languages. To the best of our knowledge, there are no verifiers available targeting Swift, Kotlin, D, or Fortran.

There are software verifiers that process the input languages directly as opposed to delegating to a compiler IR. For example, CPAchecker [7], Ultimate Automizer [30], CBMC [12], SAW [20], and CIVL [47] all leverage off-the-shelf or custom parsers to generate abstract syntax trees (ASTs), and then process these ASTs in various ways to carry out verification. (Note that CPAchecker, CBMC, and SAW support LLVM IR as well.) The verifiers in this category can potentially perform multi-language verification, but often at the expense of having to perform some language-specific work. For example, SAW's work-in-progress support for Rust involves implementing a designated symbolic simulator. While taking compiler IR as input has its drawbacks over directly handling input languages, such as losing type information and precise debugging data, it also demonstrates an advantage in the context of multi-language verification — only the details of one language (namely compiler IR) need to be addressed. This implies that supporting a new programming language does not require supporting all the new constructs that it brings to the table. For example, C++ templates are completely compiled away at the LLVM IR level. Instead, only the new program constructs in the IR that are not yet supported, but are used by the new language, need to be modeled.

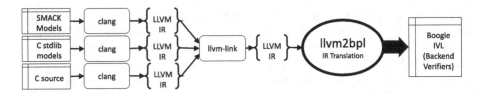

Fig. 1. Toolflow of SMACK.

3   SMACK Software Verification Toolchain

SMACK [9,41,48] is an open source, modular software verification toolchain. The core component of SMACK converts LLVM IR code into Boogie intermediate verification language [18]. The remainder of the SMACK toolchain handles details such as compiling the source program into LLVM IR and invoking a Boogie verifier. Its modular nature decouples source language details from verification by leveraging compiler front-ends to translate programs into the Boogie intermediate verification language through LLVM IR. Before we implemented the multi-language extensions described in this paper, SMACK had been predominantly used to verify LLVM IR programs produced by the clang C compiler.

Figure 1 shows the current toolflow of SMACK, which proceeds as follows:

1. SMACK first invokes clang, the LLVM's C compiler, to compile the input program, SMACK models, and C standard library models (e.g., strings, pthreads, math). SMACK models contain various verification primitives (e.g., for generating nondeterministic values) and the encoding of the memory model for handling of dynamically allocated memory. All of the models are written in C since SMACK provides a convenient mechanism for interoperating with the underlying Boogie code, which we describe below.
2. SMACK links together all of the generated LLVM IR files into one LLVM IR program.
3. The core LLVM2BPL component of SMACK transforms an LLVM IR program produced by the previous step into a semantically equivalent Boogie program.
4. Finally, a back-end verifier, such as Corral [33], verifies the generated Boogie program using an SMT solver, such as Z3 [17].

In this work, we use Corral in its bounded verification mode, meaning that it unrolls loops and recursion up to a certain user-provided bound.

SMACK models verifier primitives and memory models through the use of __SMACK_code function. This C routine takes a formatted string as a parameter, and is declared in the SMACK header files, but not implemented in any models. When LLVM2BPL comes across a call to this function, instead of translating the function call, it simply inserts the parameters into the Boogie code snippet passed as string; this functionality is akin to C's inline assembly. This allows for Boogie code or ghost variables to be injected into the translation, giving an easy way to encapsulate routines like **assume** which are not normally available in C. It also provides an abstraction that can be used for any primitive or model.

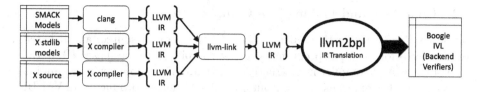

Fig. 2. Toolflow for adding support for programming language X to SMACK.

4 Procedure for Adding a Language

In this section, we introduce our prescribed procedure for adding support for a
new programming language into an LLVM-based software verifier. The procedure
is based on our study of adding languages to SMACK, but the lessons we learned
generalize to other verifiers that have similar architecture. By showing how the
procedure of adding a new language to SMACK is relatively straightforward,
we also motivate the adoption of a SMACK-like verifier architecture. Note that
while our procedure is focused on LLVM, we expect that a similar process could
be adopted for any IR-based verifier. We structure our procedure into three
tasks: interoperating with language models, compiling into compiler intermediate
representation (IR), and adding models for missing language features.

4.1 Interoperating with Language Models

A software verifier has to encode the desired semantics of an input programming
language in order to perform verification. In the case of an LLVM-based software
verifier, that typically amounts to providing a memory model in addition to
models for LLVM IR statements generated by the chosen compiler. A memory
model encodes dynamic memory allocation, pointer dereferencing, and memory
accesses. Adding a new programming language necessitates for the verification
to be able to interoperate with the mentioned models.

The architecture of SMACK allows for a new programming language to easily interoperate with SMACK models, as Fig. 2 shows. First, SMACK's models for LLVM IR instructions are general and internal to SMACK, and hence
they can be shared across all languages that are compiled into LLVM IR. Second, SMACK's memory model [42] is encoded as a regular C language header
and its accompanying implementation. This is achieved using the convenient
__SMACK_code mechanism described in the previous section, which allows for the
low-level model encoding to be done at the level of C. We must be able to link an
input program with this header in order to interoperate with the memory model.
According to our experience, most languages have interoperability with the C
language as a feature. Hence, linking against the SMACK's memory model in a
new programming language is an easy task. It is worth emphasizing that since
the code in the new language is linking with the C code of the memory model,
every verification in a new language is already a cross-language verification.

4.2 Compiling and Linking into Compiler IR

As opposed to verifiers that operate directly on program source, an IR-based verifier needs for the input program to be first compiled into the chosen IR. In the case of the LLVM compiler infrastructure, there are many popular programming languages with front-ends that output LLVM IR. Hence, producing LLVM IR for the programming language of choice is typically straightforward. Once the input program is compiled into IR, it gets linked with the SMACK models, which are written in either C (common ones) or the target language (language-specific ones) and automatically compiled by SMACK. The resulting linked IR file is in turn handed over to the SMACK verifier for processing (see Fig. 2). A verifier needs a program entry point, such as function `main` in C, to know from where to start the verification process. The LLVM IR specification does not prescribe a well-defined entry point, and hence language developers are free to choose how to define the entry point for a program in their language—most languages define entry points other than `main`. Thus, we either implement a simple post-processing step to mark the program's entry point, or manually specify it in SMACK's command line, which is in turn passed to the SMACK verifier.

4.3 Adding Models for Missing Language Features

When adding a new language, we typically observe three categories of models that might be missing in a verifier: unsupported LLVM IR instructions, runtime features, and standard libraries.

LLVM IR is an extensive format comprised of more than one hundred instructions and intrinsics [36], many of which are not commonly used. Hence, when adding a new language, its compiler can potentially generate IR instructions or intrinsics that a verifier has not encountered before, and hence are potentially not supported. This necessitates updating the verifier to account for the semantics of such instructions. Our experience shows that in the case of a mature LLVM-based verifier such as SMACK, we rarely encountered a new compiler generating instructions/intrinsics that it did not already support.

Most languages require the use of a standard library to achieve almost anything of practical value. SMACK provides extensive models for the C standard library, such as pthreads, strings, and math. However, every programming language comes with its own standard libraries that it relies on, with different specifications. A language may rely heavily on its standard libraries, even if it has little or no runtime. For example, unlike C, D, and Fortran, languages such as Rust and Swift implement arrays as a compound type in the standard library. Hence, models for the standard libraries of a new programming language have to be written manually mostly from scratch. This is the most tedious and time consuming aspect of adding support for a new language. To somewhat alleviate the burden of developing models, SMACK architecture enables for a user to write models for standard library functions as header files that are linked with input programs. This is a convenient mechanism for writing such models since it requires no updates to be made to the actual SMACK verifier source code.

Some languages are also heavily dependent on runtime functionality, such as Objective-C, Swift, and Kotlin. For example, Objective-C relies heavily on its runtime for method dispatch, memory management, and other basic features. Code from the runtime is not included in the LLVM IR which is generated by the compiler. Therefore, runtime functions must be modeled before any nontrivial verification. Languages like C, Fortran, and D have very few runtime models, and as a result these are much easier languages to verify out-of-the-box.

5 Case Studies

We perform three case studies to assess the feasibility and ease of adding support for an additional input programming language into an IR-based software verification toolchain such as SMACK. Before we describe each case study in detail, we provide our strategy for selecting input programming languages we attempted to support.

5.1 Choice of Input Programming Languages

There are numerous programming languages in existence today, and clearly it would be infeasible for us to handle all of them. Hence, for our case studies, we used the following criteria for choosing which languages to add support for in SMACK. First, we selected popular languages from the Stack Overflow Developer Survey [19] that can be compiled down into LLVM IR. Second, we performed a thorough search for other languages that can be compiled into LLVM IR, and are important in certain domains but less popular overall (i.e., domain specific). Then, we prune this list based on our requirements on the front-end, which are as follows:

1. Compile input programs into LLVM IR *Ahead-of-Time*
2. Target the same version of LLVM as SMACK
3. Be stable and under active development

Table 1 lists the languages we considered and their relevant properties.

As SMACK directly translates an entire program from LLVM to Boogie, it requires all related definitions to be available at translation time. A *Just-in-Time* compiler does not have a whole program readily available in the LLVM IR format for SMACK to process. Therefore, *Ahead-of-Time* compilers are the only ones that can currently be used with SMACK. LLVM does not preserve backwards compatibility of the LLVM IR format. Hence, the LLVM version supported by SMACK and the chosen language front-end have to match. The used version of SMACK supports LLVM 3.9, and hence our requirement is for a language front-end to support the same LLVM version. We sometimes had to revert to an older front-end version to satisfy this requirement. For example, Swift 4.2 does not target the required LLVM 3.9, but Swift 3.0 does. Of course, as SMACK gets updated to newer LLVM versions, this requirement will change as well. In

Table 1. List of programming languages we considered and their properties. Column **Ahead-of-Time** shows whether an Ahead-of-Time compiler is available for the language; column **LLVM 3.9** indicates whether the needed LLVM version is supported; column **Active** indicates whether the compiler is under active development, while column **Stable** indicates if there is a stable release; finally, column **Used it?** shows whether we used the language in our evaluation.

Language	Compiler	Ahead-of-Time	LLVM 3.9	Active	Stable	Used it?
C	clang	✓	✓	✓	✓	✓
C++	clang	✓	✓	✓	✓	✓
Fortran [24]	flang	✓	✓	✓	✓	✓
D [16]	ldc	✓	✓	✓	✓	✓
Rust [45]	rustc	✓	✓	✓	✓	✓
Objective-C	clang	✓	✓	✓	✓	✓
Swift [49]	swiftc	✓	✓	✓	✓	✓
Kotlin [32]	kotlinc	✓	✓	✓	✓	✓
Scala [46]	scala-native	✓	✓	✓	✓	✗
C# [52]	llilc	✓	?	✓	✓	✗
Haskell [29]	ghc	✓	✓	✓	✓	✗
Julia [31]	julia	✗	✓	✓	✗	✗
Go [25]	llgo	✓	✓	✗	✗	✗
Python [40]	pyston	✓	?	✗	✗	✗
Ruby [43]	ruby-llvm	✓	✗	✗	✗	✗
Java [22]	falcon (Azul)	✗	✗	✓	✗	✗

order to limit our focus to compilers of practical value, we ignore the ones that are not stable and under active development.

Of the LLVM-IR-based languages in the developer survey, there are 4 that satisfy our criteria: C, C++, Objective-C, and Swift. Kotlin, Scala [46], and C# [52]) have compilers that are not yet fully mature, but are stable and under active development. We chose Kotlin as the representative of this "managed language into LLVM IR" category. In addition to the popular languages listed on Stack Overflow, there are other notable, stable languages that target LLVM. Most of these are tailored for domain-specific coding. The Rust programming language [45] is a performant systems language with an emphasis on safety and concurrency. The D programming language [16] is a mature language which offers low-level control combined with high-level abstractions. Both Rust and D target the systems programming community. Fortran is primarily used in the scientific programming community, since it provides support for parallel processing and compatibility with legacy code for projects that span multiple decades. The only language we do not use which satisfies our criteria is Haskell. Its LLVM back-end

```
int cap(int x) {
  int y = x;
  if (10 < x) { y = 10; }
  return y;
}

int main(void) {
  assert(cap(2) == 2);
  assert(cap(15) == 10);
  int x = nondet_int();
  assert(cap(x) <= 10);
}
```

```
func cap(_ x: Int) -> Int {
  var y = x
  if 10 < x {
    y = 10
  }
  return y
}

assert(cap(2) == 2)
assert(cap(15) == 10)
let x = Int(nondet_int())
assert(cap(x) <= 10)
```

```
fn cap(x: usize) -> usize {
  let mut y = x;
  if 10 < x {
    y = 10;
  }
  return y;
}

fn main() {
  let two = cap(2);
  let ten = cap(15);
  assert!(two == 2);
  assert!(ten == 10);
  let x = nondet_int();
  assert!(x <= 10);
}
```

```
pure function cap(x)
  integer, intent(in) :: x
  integer :: cap, y
  y = x
  if (10 < y) then
    y = 10
  end if
  cap = y
end function

program main
  integer :: cap, x
  call assert(cap(2) == 2)
  call assert(cap(15) == 10)
  x = nondet_int()
  call assert(cap(x) <= 10)
end program main
```

Fig. 3. Microbenchmark with program versions in C, Swift, Rust, and Fortran.

is not compatible with SMACK, mainly because the entry point for the code is not included in a standalone bitcode file.

5.2 Case Study 1: Microbenchmarks

We developed a microbenchmark suite to evaluate the quality of the support for different languages we implemented in SMACK. We crafted each benchmark to exercise across all languages (8 languages total, see Table 1) a specific language feature we deem important, meaning that a benchmark consists of a number of programs, each implementing the chosen feature in a different language. In addition, we injected a property to be verified into each benchmark using assertions. Hence, there are several (at least two) program versions per each benchmark-language pair: a passing version (i.e., no failing assertions) and a failing version (i.e., a failing assertion) for each assertion. Figure 3 shows

Table 2. Characteristics of our microbenchmark suite. Column **LOC** is the average number of lines of code per benchmark across supporting languages; column **#Lang** is the number of languages supporting the features tested.

Benchmark	Features tested	LOC	#Lang
basic	basic assertions	8	8
compute	integer arithmetic	12	8
function	functions, if-then-else, nondet values	19	8
forloop	for loops	14	8
fib	recursion	20	8
compound	objects and structures, fields	18	8
array	array creation, array access	10	8
pointer	dynamic memory allocation, references	14	6
inout	updates via side effects	17	7
method	single type dispatch	26	6
dynamic	polymorphic dispatch	29	6

several variations of one of our microbenchmarks. Table 2 gives basic characteristics of our microbenchmark suite.[1]

We designed the microbenchmarks to be as small as possible, and yet still test a particular language feature. Hence, a failing benchmark is a good indicator of which feature is not properly supported by a verifier. While our microbenchmarks are not based on real-world programs, since they focus on common and widely-used language features, being able to handle them is a prerequisite to verifying real-world code. One can think of our microbenchmarks as being *litmus tests* for various key language features.

Not all benchmarks have a program version for every language since not all language features are supported across the board. For example, languages without support for object-oriented programming (e.g., C, Fortran) do not have versions of the corresponding benchmark (i.e., method). Then, Swift and Kotlin do not have syntactic support for pointers, and so we could not implement versions of the pointer benchmark for these languages. We also sometimes had to implement benchmark versions differently across languages. For example, we implemented the dynamic dispatch benchmark in Rust using *traits* instead of inheritance. As another example, we implemented the inout benchmark in Swift and Fortran using a specific mutable-parameter syntax, while in most other languages we replicate this feature using pointers. We did not implement this benchmark in Kotlin since it has no support for pointers, nor for mutable-parameter syntax.

---

[1] We made our microbenchmark suite publicly available at https://github.com/soarlab/gandalv.

Table 3. Results of running SMACK on our microbenchmarks. Symbol ✓ marks passing, symbol ✗ failing, and N/A marks benchmarks that do not have a version for the corresponding language.

Benchmark	C	C++	Objective-C	Rust	Fortran	D	Swift	Kotlin
basic	✓	✓	✓	✓	✓	✓	✓	✓
compute	✓	✓	✓	✓	✓	✓	✓	✓
function	✓	✓	✓	✓	✓	✓	✓	✓
forloop	✓	✓	✓	✓	✓	✓	✗	✓
fib	✓	✓	✓	✓	✓	✓	✓	✓
compound	✓	✓	✗	✓	✓	✓	✓	✗
array	✓	✓	✗	✓	✓	✓	✗	✗
pointer	✓	✓	✓	✓	✓	✓	N/A	N/A
inout	✓	✓	✓	✓	✓	✓	✓	N/A
method	N/A	✓	✗	✓	N/A	✓	✗	✓
dynamic	N/A	✗	✗	✓	N/A	✗	✗	✗

Table 3 summarizes the results of running SMACK with our extensions on the microbenchmarks. Overall, SMACK successfully discharges all available program versions of benchmarks in C, Fortran, and Rust. For C++ and D, the main missing language feature that we still have to add support for is dynamic dispatch. Swift, Objective-C, and Kotlin need more work before SMACK could support language features beyond just the very basic ones. The primary cause for the failing benchmarks is SMACK lacking models of standard libraries and runtime.

Swift, Objective-C, Kotlin, and Rust are all very library- and runtime-dependent. Hence, there are many basic language features that SMACK does not capture precisely (i.e., that are not modeled in SMACK), which causes even some small benchmarks to fail. As we note in Sect. 6.2, developing such models for a verifier is typically a tedious manual process, and is an exercise we could not perform for all languages in the limited amount of time we had for our case study. However, the version of SMACK we used already contained models of several popular Rust standard library functions. Hence, in our experiments, the other three languages have more failing benchmarks than Rust, which are caused by the following unmodeled functionality:

Swift range structures (forloop), array subscripts (array), dispatching functions via function pointers (method)
Obj-C objc-msg-send for dispatching methods via function pointers (compound, method), NSArray class (array)
Kotlin dynamic object instantiation (compound, array)

Table 4. Time commitment summary for adding a new language.

Procedure step	Person-Hours
Write code to interoperate with SMACK models	8
Compile and link at the LLVM IR level, test	3
Add and model missing functionality	4
Total:	15

5.3   Case Study 2: Adding a Language

In order to get a rough estimate of the time commitment required to add support for a new language to an IR-based verifier, we conducted an informal timed exercise where an undergraduate student working on this project (Jack J. Garzella, one of the coauthors) added support for one additional language, the D programming language, to SMACK. During the exercise, the student followed the steps we prescribe in our procedure from Sect. 4, and we measured elapsed time (in hours) it took him to accomplish each of the steps. Table 4 summarizes our measurements.

The student had no experience with D beyond implementing the microbenchmarks; he was also not familiar with the SMACK internals, which ended up not being important for this exercise since no changes to SMACK were needed. However, as D was the sixth programming language the student added, he had ample experience adding support for new languages, which contributed to this exercise proceeding smoothly. Furthermore, D was an easy language to add since the LLVM IR it generates is close to the one generated by the C clang compiler, and hence heavily tested with SMACK. In addition, basic code in D does not heavily depend on its standard library and runtime. Hence, the student spent very little time modeling missing functions for D. For languages with extensive usage of standard libraries and runtime (e.g., Swift, Kotlin), we expect that modeling the runtime and standard library functionality to dominate the total time.

5.4   Case Study 3: Cross-Language Verification

One of the major advantages to the IR-based approach to verification is the ease of cross-language verification. In fact, with the approach that SMACK takes, every verification (of a non-C language) is a cross-language verification, as SMACK's models that have to be linked against the input program are written in C. With this in mind, non-trivial cross-language verification efforts are typically as simple as any regular single-language verification. As a proof of this concept, we took a simple algorithm, namely a classic triangle classifier, and implemented it in C, Rust, and Fortran. Our triangle classifier takes 3 integers as input, which represent the sides of a triangle, and it determines and returns the type of the triangle defined by the input sides. We wrote a harness program that invokes triangle classifiers from each language in turn, feeds equal nondeterministic inputs to all of them, and asserts that they return the same result.

Table 5. Equivalence checking of half-precision floating-point implementations in C and Rust. Column **Equal?** shows whether the two implementations are equivalent; column **Time** gives the verification runtime in seconds; column **LOC** gives the number of lines of code in the checked Rust function.

Function	Equal?	Time (s)	LOC
eq	✓	13	8
lt	✓	22	13
le	✓	18	13
gt	✓	17	13
ge	✓	18	13
to_f32	✓	8	41
to_f64	✓	8	41
from_f32	✗	5	68
from_f64	✗	4	70
is_nan	✓	4	3

Hence, we performed cross-language verification to verify the equivalence of our implementations in all three languages. SMACK was able to verify the equivalence (i.e., the harness program) in around 19 s. We expect such cross-language equivalence checking to be a valuable tool for developers when rewriting legacy applications in, for example Fortran or C, into more modern languages, such as C++ or Rust.

We further push our cross-language verification case study to a real-world Rust application—the *half* crate [44] that implements the half-precision floating-point type f16. We chose the *half* crate because its implementation is compact in terms of code size (functions range from only a few to around 70 LOC, see Table 5), but difficult to reason about because it frequently performs low-level bit manipulations. Furthermore, the equivalence of functions implementing the half-precision floating-point type can be easily expressed. This makes the *half* crate a suitable target for our cross-language verification case study.

For the purpose of this case study, we developed a simple C reference implementation of the half-precision floating-point type that leverages the available _f16 type. Then, we verify that several important representative methods of the *half* crate, such as lt, gt, and to_f32, are equivalent to the respective C implementations. We leverage the Rust's *Foreign Function Interface* to write harness programs that assert the equivalence between Rust and C functions. (Note that if such a mechanism for interoperating between languages does not exist, we could implement the equivalence check at the LLVM IR level; however, working directly with the low-level LLVM IR would be more tedious.) Thanks to Rust's high interoperability with C, we are able to trivially express equivalence using the equality operator. For example, relational operators in C evaluate to 1 if the relation is true and otherwise they evaluate to 0. In Rust, casting a value of type `bool` into an integer has the same behavior. Therefore, comparing a predicate function such as `eq` in C and Rust reduces to checking if the return value of the C version is equal to the return value of the Rust version cast to type `u8`.

Table 5 summarizes the results of this case study. SMACK is able to verify that most of the chosen functions of the `f16` type are equivalent to their reference C implementations. The only exceptions are functions from_f32 and from_f64, for which SMACK discovered inconsistencies between the two implementations: conversions from larger bit-width floating-point types to `f16` are rounded differently. We reported this issue to the *half* crate developers, and they confirmed and fixed it. The verification runtimes range between 4–22 s on a 3.5 GHz Intel 3770k machine.

6   Experience

In this section, we describe our experience of applying the procedure introduced in Sect. 4 to add support for new languages into SMACK as well as perform cross-language verification. First, we discuss why our approach and procedure allow us to trivially support many language constructs of the added programming languages (Sect. 6.1). Second, we describe key challenges that we encountered in the process of adding support for new languages and propose solutions for them (Sect. 6.2). Third, we present our experience with leveraging the cross-language verification capability to perform equivalence checking (Sect. 6.3).

6.1   Trivially Supported Features

SMACK is a mature C verifier that has been successfully applied on numerous C programs, including large-scale real-world C projects such as OpenSSH, SQLite, and Linux device drivers. Hence, SMACK already fully supports an extensive subset of LLVM IR that gets generated by the clang C compiler. For example, the key language constructs of LLVM IR such as functions, control flow, arithmetic, and derived types are completely modeled. As a result, SMACK readily supports new languages of which compilers emit LLVM IR code that is akin to what clang generates. We find that these languages are typically also procedural C-like languages, such as Fortran and D.

As it turns out, to our surprise, SMACK was often able to out-of-the-box support even language features that are not found in C. For example, without any modifications SMACK could handle the vectorized addition of arrays in Fortran, which we show in Fig. 4. After inspecting the IR code generated by the Fortran compiler, we observe that the vectorized addition operation compiles into an element-wise array addition, which is a common IR operation and hence was already supported by SMACK.

Having an extensive subset of LLVM IR supported also saved us from modeling a lot of key program constructs in non-C-like languages such as Rust and Swift. For example, even though function calls and control flow constructs are different from those found in C (e.g., closures and match expressions), they are

```
program main
  use smack
  implicit none
  integer, dimension(2) :: A = (/ 2, 3 /)
  integer, dimension(2) :: B = (/ 3, 4 /)
  integer, dimension(2) :: S
  S = A + B
  call assert(S(1) == 5)
  call assert(S(2) == 7)
end program main
```

Fig. 4. Fortran program that utilizes vectorized addition.

compiled to the subset of LLVM IR that was already understood by SMACK. Therefore, our approach enables us to evade cumbersome modeling of advanced language features such as closures. In this regard, our experience demonstrates the advantages of our IR-based approach for multi-language verification.

6.2 Adding New Languages: Challenges and Solutions

As expected, supporting even a small subset of a new language in a verifier is often challenging. For example, a major challenge is the need to model previously unsupported LLVM IR constructs. Our experience shows that the compilers of non-C-like languages, such as Rust and Swift, indeed produce LLVM IR that was not supported by SMACK. Moreover, another important challenge is that we have to model a language runtime and its standard libraries to enable for practically usable verification. In the rest of this section, we describe in detail these challenges as well as our efforts to solve them.

Unsupported LLVM Constructs. SMACK is a mature verifier that has been thoroughly tested on C programs, including thousands of SVCOMP benchmarks as well as large real-world applications such as OpenSSH. Despite SMACK's maturity, we found that compilers for the emerging languages, such as Rust and Swift, readily generate LLVM IR constructs we do not observe in LLVM IR generated from C code by clang. Hence, we had to extend SMACK with support for such constructs, and we describe some of these next.

Both the Rust and Swift compilers heavily rely on the use of LLVM structure types, often emitting different instructions involving structures than what clang would generate. We solved this problem by modeling LLVM IR structure types using uninterpreted functions that recursively constrain each field. For example, we represent value {v,1} of structure type {T,i1} using an integer s with constraint f(s,0)==v && f(s,1)==1, where f is an uninterpreted function with the second argument being the index of a structure field. This encoding allows us to model two basic LLVM IR structure instructions **extractvalue** and insertvalue that read and write structure fields, respectively. Loads and stores of structures into memory are recursively translated into a sequence of instructions that generate load/store for each field of primitive type, in conjunction with the two aforementioned instructions.

Another previously unsupported but frequently used LLVM IR construct is intrinsics. For example, both the Rust and Swift compilers default to using LLVM IR's overflow arithmetic intrinsics, such as llvm.add.with.overflow.i32. The leading_zeros methods of unsigned integer types in Rust are compiled to llvm.ctlz.* intrinsics. Such intrinsics can be easily modeled. For example, we model these intrinsics in SMACK by first performing the requested operation in the double-bit-width precision, to avoid potential overflows. Then, we inspect the result to detect if it overflowed, in which case we either report an overflow error or we block the overflowing path.

In addition to supporting more LLVM IR instructions, we also extended SMACK to support instruction sequences that are not regularly generated by clang. For example, the Rust compiler performs a *packing* optimization where structures with a size less than 8 bytes are packed into 8 byte integers (e.g., a load of a structure of type {i32,i32} gets encoded as a load of i64). This breaks the completeness of SMACK's memory model [42], which is not precise enough to capture such low-level operations, thereby leading to false alarms. We added an analysis pass to SMACK that detects load/store instruction patterns with pointer operands of integer element type that refer to structures. We translate such patterns to load from or store into structure fields (following the encoding described earlier), thereby avoiding packing.

Although we had to model these additional constructs, our approach still demonstrates the advantages discussed in Sect. 6.1: modeling one LLVM IR construct benefits the support of multiple languages, and this process becomes progressively easier as adding a new language benefits from previous modeling efforts.

Languages with Large Runtimes. Getting a verifier to translate LLVM IR generated from a language with a large runtime is not any more difficult than for languages with smaller runtimes. However, performing a nontrivial verification task for such a language is much harder, because even rudimentary language features are sometimes under the hood implemented using complex runtime constructs and standard libraries. Moreover, the source code implementing such features is not readily accessible to the verifier as IR code linked with the program source. We found this to be the most challenging problem when adding a new language to a verifier. Note that this problem persists even if the verification is done directly on program source (as opposed to IR) since the source code of the underlying runtime is typically not available, written in a different programming language, or too large to be efficiently handled by a verifier.

As an example of such a language feature, consider the for-in loop over an iterable structure. All of the languages with substantial runtime we considered provide such a feature. In fact, in Swift, Kotlin, and Rust, the C-style for loop is

Table 6. Sizes of models we developed for each language. Column **Model LOC** gives the size of each model in terms of lines of code.

Language	Model LOC
C	2566
C++	13
Fortran	38
D	0
Rust	480
Objective-C	0
Swift	2
Kotlin	17

not even supported, and range structures are used to emulate the same behavior. Consider this simple example in Swift: **for** i **in** 0..<10 {x += 5}. The compiler translates the code 0..<10 using a Range<**Int**> structure/class, whose member methods are then called in the compiled loop code. The code of such member methods is not readily available to the verifier, but is a part of the runtime. On the other hand, both Kotlin and Rust compile such loops into basic LLVM IR instructions that do not contain method calls into runtime, despite the high-level concept of a range being similar to Swift. Many features of large-runtime languages are implemented like this, and they vary wildly between languages. Examples of other basic language features the heavily depend on runtime include method dispatch (Swift, Objective-C), arrays (Swift, Objective-C, Rust, Kotlin), and object instantiation (Kotlin). As a more extreme example, even basic arithmetic in Kotlin is abstracted into invoking methods belonging to its runtime, instead of generating the appropriate LLVM IR instructions directly. We relied on two solutions to overcome such problems, with different trade-offs, as we describe next.

We compile and link an existing implementation of the runtime/standard library with the input program. For example, to support basic integer operations in Kotlin, we used the existing implementation of these operations from the Kotlin runtime and linked it with the input program. The main advantage of this approach is that it requires no manual effort. It also avoids the user potentially introducing errors while modeling the runtime. The main drawback is that the standard libraries and runtime are generally very large, and this may cause verification to blow up even on small input programs. For example, the implementation of the array structure in Swift is thousands of lines of code. Such code is also heavily optimized, and often relies on low-level bit vector operations and compiler builtins, which further complicate its verification.

We model the standard libraries and runtime by writing stubs for the relevant methods. Table 6 gives the sizes of the models we developed for each language we support. SMACK already came with extensive models for the C standard library and a part of the Rust standard library, which is why these two models are by far the largest. The main advantage of this approach is that the manually written models make the verification much more tractable, and hence most verifiers, no matter whether they are IR-based or not, require it to achieve scalable verification. The main drawback is that writing them is a tedious manual effort that requires detailed understanding of the language specifications. Hence, we did not do that for other languages. In principle, the standard libraries and runtime of Kotlin, Objective-C, and Swift could each be modeled in a similar way to Rust. Note that this solution is contradictory to the general principle of our approach since it requires per-language modeling.

6.3   Cross-Language Verification

Although our experience with cross-language verification is limited to equivalence checking of programs written in different languages, it captures an important pattern in cross-language development: a program written in one language uses external libraries written in another language. Furthermore, equivalence checking is a useful application of cross-language verification, giving confidence to developers that a new, native implementation of a library retains the behaviors of the previous non-native implementation. This is especially true when large rewriting efforts are under way, such as replacing legacy libraries implemented using Fortran with C/C++ implementations in the context of high-performance computing, or libraries implemented using C with their Rust counterparts.

We find that once the languages involved in the cross-language verification process are well-supported and there are available mechanisms for these languages to interoperate, cross-language verification is feasible, highly automated, and comes almost for free. This is expected since our approach casts the problem of cross-language verification into the problem of verifying a single language, namely LLVM IR. Therefore, the main impediments we encountered while verifying cross-language programs were related to SMACK's incomplete support for LLVM IR, similarly to our efforts to add support for new languages. For example, while performing the case study, the only issue we encountered was that SMACK did not model the LLVM count-leading-zeros intrinsics. We quickly added support for this instruction and were able to complete the verification process smoothly.

7   Conclusions

In this paper, we proposed a procedure for extending an IR-based verifier with multi- and cross-language verification capabilities. By relying on the proposed procedure, we extended the LLVM-IR-based SMACK software verification toolchain with basic prototypical support for 6 additional languages. We performed several case studies to assess the quality of our extensions and the feasibility of leveraging the IR-based verifier architecture in the context of multi- and cross-language verification. Our evaluation is encouraging and indicates that the IR-based architecture indeed lowers the bar for adding support for a new language into an existing verifier—languages with small runtimes could be reliably added with only a modest effort. It also allows for straightforward cross-language verification. As we anticipated, supporting languages with large runtimes that heavily rely on standard libraries is possible, but mature support would require a large manual effort to model the runtime and libraries.

References

1. Albarghouthi, A., Li, Y., Gurfinkel, A., Chechik, M.: UFO: a framework for abstraction- and interpolation-based software verification. In: Madhusudan, P., Seshia, S.A. (eds.) CAV 2012. LNCS, vol. 7358, pp. 672–678. Springer, Heidelberg (2012). https://doi.org/10.1007/978-3-642-31424-7_48
2. Arlt, S., Rubio-González, C., Rümmer, P., Schäf, M., Shankar, N.: The gradual verifier. In: Badger, J.M., Rozier, K.Y. (eds.) NFM 2014. LNCS, vol. 8430, pp. 313–327. Springer, Cham (2014). https://doi.org/10.1007/978-3-319-06200-6_27
3. Arlt, S., Rümmer, P., Schäf, M.: Joogie: from java through jimple to boogie. In: ACM SIGPLAN International Workshop on State of the Art in Java Program Analysis (SOAP), pp. 3–8 (2013). https://doi.org/10.1145/2487568.2487570
4. Astrauskas, V., Müller, P., Poli, F., Summers, A.J.: Leveraging rust types for modular specification and verification. Proc. ACM Program. Lang. 3(OOPSLA), 147:1–147:30 (2019). https://doi.org/10.1145/3360573
5. Babić, D., Hu, A.J.: Calysto: scalable and precise extended static checking. In: International Conference on Software Engineering (ICSE), pp. 211–220 (2008). https://doi.org/10.1145/1368088.1368118
6. Baranová, Z., et al.: Model checking of C and C++ with DIVINE 4. In: D'Souza, D., Narayan Kumar, K. (eds.) ATVA 2017. LNCS, vol. 10482, pp. 201–207. Springer, Cham (2017). https://doi.org/10.1007/978-3-319-68167-2_14
7. Beyer, D., Keremoglu, M.E.: CPACHECKER: a tool for configurable software verification. In: Gopalakrishnan, G., Qadeer, S. (eds.) CAV 2011. LNCS, vol. 6806, pp. 184–190. Springer, Heidelberg (2011). https://doi.org/10.1007/978-3-642-22110-1_16
8. Cadar, C., Dunbar, D., Engler, D.: KLEE: unassisted and automatic generation of high-coverage tests for complex systems programs. In: USENIX Conference on Operating Systems Design and Implementation (OSDI), pp. 209–224 (2008)
9. Carter, M., He, S., Whitaker, J., Rakamarić, Z., Emmi, M.: SMACK software verification toolchain. In: International Conference on Software Engineering (ICSE), pp. 589–592 (2016). https://doi.org/10.1145/2889160.2889163
10. Chatterjee, S., Lahiri, S.K., Qadeer, S., Rakamarić, Z.: A reachability predicate for analyzing low-level software. In: Grumberg, O., Huth, M. (eds.) TACAS 2007. LNCS, vol. 4424, pp. 19–33. Springer, Heidelberg (2007). https://doi.org/10.1007/978-3-540-71209-1_4
11. Clarke, E., Kroening, D., Sharygina, N., Yorav, K.: SATABS: SAT-based predicate abstraction for ANSI-C. In: Halbwachs, N., Zuck, L.D. (eds.) TACAS 2005. LNCS, vol. 3440, pp. 570–574. Springer, Heidelberg (2005). https://doi.org/10.1007/978-3-540-31980-1_40
12. Clarke, E., Kroening, D., Lerda, F.: A tool for checking ANSI-C programs. In: Jensen, K., Podelski, A. (eds.) TACAS 2004. LNCS, vol. 2988, pp. 168–176. Springer, Heidelberg (2004). https://doi.org/10.1007/978-3-540-24730-2_15

13. Cohen, E., et al.: VCC: a practical system for verifying concurrent C. In: Berghofer, S., Nipkow, T., Urban, C., Wenzel, M. (eds.) TPHOLs 2009. LNCS, vol. 5674, pp. 23–42. Springer, Heidelberg (2009). https://doi.org/10.1007/978-3-642-03359-9_2

14. Cordeiro, L., Fischer, B., Marques-Silva, J.: SMT-based bounded model checking for embedded ANSI-C software. In: IEEE/ACM International Conference on Automated Software Engineering (ASE), pp. 137–148 (2009). https://doi.org/10.1109/TSE.2011.59

15. Cuoq, P., Kirchner, F., Kosmatov, N., Prevosto, V., Signoles, J., Yakobowski, B.: Frama-C. In: Eleftherakis, G., Hinchey, M., Holcombe, M. (eds.) SEFM 2012. LNCS, vol. 7504, pp. 233–247. Springer, Heidelberg (2012). https://doi.org/10.1007/978-3-642-33826-7_16

16. The D programming language. https://dlang.org/

17. de Moura, L., Bjørner, N.: Z3: an efficient SMT solver. In: Ramakrishnan, C.R., Rehof, J. (eds.) TACAS 2008. LNCS, vol. 4963, pp. 337–340. Springer, Heidelberg (2008). https://doi.org/10.1007/978-3-540-78800-3_24

18. DeLine, R., Leino, K.R.M.: BoogiePL: A typed procedural language for checking object-oriented programs. Technical Report MSR-TR-2005-70, Microsoft Research (2005). 10.1.1.212.7449

19. Stack overflow developer survey (2018). https://insights.stackoverflow.com/survey/2018

20. Dockins, R., Foltzer, A., Hendrix, J., Huffman, B., McNamee, D., Tomb, A.: Constructing Semantic models of programs with the software analysis workbench. In: Blazy, S., Chechik, M. (eds.) VSTTE 2016. LNCS, vol. 9971, pp. 56–72. Springer, Cham (2016). https://doi.org/10.1007/978-3-319-48869-1_5

21. Dudka, K., Peringer, P., Vojnar, T.: Predator: a practical tool for checking manipulation of dynamic data structures using separation logic. In: Gopalakrishnan, G., Qadeer, S. (eds.) CAV 2011. LNCS, vol. 6806, pp. 372–378. Springer, Heidelberg (2011). https://doi.org/10.1007/978-3-642-22110-1_29

22. Azul Falcon. https://www.azul.com/called-new-jit-compiler-falcon/

23. Filliâtre, J.-C., Marché, C.: Multi-prover verification of C programs. In: Davies, J., Schulte, W., Barnett, M. (eds.) ICFEM 2004. LNCS, vol. 3308, pp. 15–29. Springer, Heidelberg (2004). https://doi.org/10.1007/978-3-540-30482-1_10

24. The Flang Fortran compiler. https://github.com/flang-compiler/flang

25. The Go programming language. https://golang.org/

26. Gurfinkel, A., Kahsai, T., Komuravelli, A., Navas, J.A.: The seahorn verification framework. In: Kroening, D., Păsăreanu, C.S. (eds.) CAV 2015. LNCS, vol. 9206, pp. 343–361. Springer, Cham (2015). https://doi.org/10.1007/978-3-319-21690-4_20

27. Habermehl, P., Holík, L., Rogalewicz, A., Šimáček, J., Vojnar, T.: Forest automata for verification of heap manipulation. In: Gopalakrishnan, G., Qadeer, S. (eds.) CAV 2011. LNCS, vol. 6806, pp. 424–440. Springer, Heidelberg (2011). https://doi.org/10.1007/978-3-642-22110-1_34

28. Hahn, F.: Rust2Viper: Building a Static Verifier for Rust. Master's thesis, ETH (2016)

29. The Haskell programming language. https://www.haskell.org/

30. Heizmann, M., et al.: Ultimate automizer with SMTInterpol. In: Piterman, N., Smolka, S.A. (eds.) TACAS 2013. LNCS, vol. 7795, pp. 641–643. Springer, Heidelberg (2013). https://doi.org/10.1007/978-3-642-36742-7_53

31. Bezanson, J., Edelman, A., Karpinski, S., Shah, V.B.: Julia: a fresh approach to numerical computing. SIAM Rev. **59**, 65–98 (2017). https://doi.org/10.1137/141000671

32. Kotlin/Native for native. https://kotlinlang.org/docs/reference/native-overview. html
33. Lal, A., Qadeer, S., Lahiri, S.K.: A solver for reachability modulo theories. In: Madhusudan, P., Seshia, S.A. (eds.) CAV 2012. LNCS, vol. 7358, pp. 427–443. Springer, Heidelberg (2012). https://doi.org/10.1007/978-3-642-31424-7_32
34. Lattner, C., Adve, V.: LLVM: A compilation framework for lifelong program analysis & transformation. In: International Symposium on Code Generation and Optimization (CGO), pp. 75–86 (2004)
35. The LLVM compiler infrastructure. http://llvm.org
36. LLVM language reference manual. https://llvm.org/docs/LangRef.html
37. Merz, F., Falke, S., Sinz, C.: Bounded model checking of C and C++ programs using a compiler IR. In: Joshi, R., Müller, P., Podelski, A. (eds.) VSTTE 2012. LNCS, vol. 7152, pp. 146–161. Springer, Heidelberg (2012). https://doi.org/10. 1007/978-3-642-27705-4_12
38. Müller, P., Schwerhoff, M., Summers, A.J.: Viper: a verification infrastructure for permission-based reasoning. In: Jobstmann, B., Leino, K.R.M. (eds.) VMCAI 2016. LNCS, vol. 9583, pp. 41–62. Springer, Heidelberg (2016). https://doi.org/10.1007/ 978-3-662-49122-5_2
39. Păsăreanu, C.S., et al.: Combining unit-level symbolic execution and system-level concrete execution for testing NASA software. In: International Symposium on Software Testing and Analysis (ISSTA), pp. 15–26 (2008). https://doi.org/10.1145/ 1390630.1390635
40. Pyston. https://blog.pyston.org/about/
41. Rakamarić, Z., Emmi, M.: SMACK: Decoupling source language details from verifier implementations. In: Biere, A., Bloem, R. (eds.) CAV 2014. LNCS, vol. 8559, pp. 106–113. Springer, Cham (2014). https://doi.org/10.1007/978-3-319-08867-9_7
42. Rakamarić, Z., Hu, A.J.: A scalable memory model for low-level code. In: Jones, N.D., Müller-Olm, M. (eds.) VMCAI 2009. LNCS, vol. 5403, pp. 290–304. Springer, Heidelberg (2008). https://doi.org/10.1007/978-3-540-93900-9_24
43. Ruby-LLVM. https://github.com/ruby-llvm/ruby-llvm
44. half: f16 type for Rust. https://github.com/starkat99/half-rs
45. The Rust programming language. https://www.rust-lang.org
46. Scala Native. http://www.scala-native.org/en/v0.3.8/
47. Siegel, S.F., et al.: CIVL: the concurrency intermediate verification language. In: International Conference for High Performance Computing, Networking, Storage and Analysis (SC), pp. 61:1–61:12 (2015). https://doi.org/10.1145/2807591. 2807635
48. SMACK software verifier and verification toolchain. http://smackers.github.io
49. The Swift programming language. https://swift.org/
50. Toman, J., Pernsteiner, S., Torlak, E.: CRUST: a bounded verifier for rust. In: IEEE/ACM International Conference on Automated Software Engineering (ASE), pp. 75–80 (2015). https://doi.org/10.1109/ASE.2015.77
51. Wang, W., Barrett, C., Wies, T.: Cascade 2.0. In: McMillan, K.L., Rival, X. (eds.) VMCAI 2014. LNCS, vol. 8318, pp. 142–160. Springer, Heidelberg (2014). https:// doi.org/10.1007/978-3-642-54013-4_9
52. Woodward, M.: Announcing LLILC – a new LLVM-based compiler for.NET (2015). https://www.dotnetfoundation.org/blog/2015/04/14/announcing-llilc-llvm-for-dotnet

Putting the Squeeze on Array Programs: Loop Verification via Inductive Rank Reduction

Oren Ish-Shalom[1]([✉]), Shachar Itzhaky[2]([✉]), Noam Rinetzky[1]([✉]), and Sharon Shoham[1]([✉])

[1] Tel Aviv University, Tel Aviv, Israel
tuna.is.good.for.you@gmail.com, noam.rinetzky@gmail.com,
sharon.shoham@gmail.com
[2] Technion, Haifa, Israel
shachari@cs.technion.ac.il

Abstract. Automatic verification of array manipulating programs is a challenging problem because it often amounts to the inference of inductive quantified loop invariants which, in some cases, may not even be first-order expressible. In this paper, we suggest a novel verification technique that is based on induction on user-defined *rank* of program states as an alternative to loop-invariants. Our technique, dubbed *inductive rank reduction*, works in two steps. Firstly, we simplify the verification problem and prove that the program is correct when the input state contains an input array of length ℓ_B or less, using the length of the array as the rank of the state. Secondly, we employ a *squeezing function* Υ which converts a program state σ with an array of length $\ell > \ell_B$ to a state $\Upsilon(\sigma)$ containing an array of length $\ell - 1$ or less. We prove that when Υ satisfies certain natural conditions then if the program violates its specification on σ then it does so also on $\Upsilon(\sigma)$. The correctness of the program on inputs with arrays of arbitrary lengths follows by induction.

We make our technique automatic for array programs whose length of execution is proportional to the length of the input arrays by (i) performing the first step using symbolic execution, (ii) verifying the conditions required of Υ using Z3, and (iii) providing a heuristic procedure for synthesizing Υ. We implemented our technique and applied it successfully to several interesting array-manipulating programs, including a bidirectional summation program whose loop invariant cannot be expressed in first-order logic while its specification is quantifier-free.

1 Introduction

Automatic verification of array manipulating programs is a challenging problem because it often amounts to the inference of inductive quantified loop invariants. These invariants are frequently quite hard to come up with, even for seemingly simple and innocuous program, both automatically and manually. The purpose of this paper is to suggest an alternative kind of correctness witness, which is

© Springer Nature Switzerland AG 2020
D. Beyer and D. Zufferey (Eds.): VMCAI 2020, LNCS 11990, pp. 112–135, 2020.
https://doi.org/10.1007/978-3-030-39322-9_6

often simpler than inductive invariants and hence more amenable to automated search.

Loop invariants, the basis of traditional verification approaches, offer an induction scheme based on the time axis, *i.e.*, on the number of loop iterations. We suggest an alternative approach in which induction is carried out on the space axis, i.e. on a (user-defined notion of the) *rank* (e.g., size) of the program state. This is particularly useful in the setting of infinite-state systems, where the size of the state may be unbounded. In this induction scheme, establishing the induction step relies on a *squeezing function* $\Upsilon : \Sigma \rightarrow \Sigma$ (read Υ as *squeeze*) that maps program states to lower-ranked program states (up to a given minima). Roughly speaking, the squeezing function should satisfy the following conditions, described here intuitively and formalized in Definition 3:

- **Initial anchor.** Υ maps initial states to initial states.
- **Simulation inducing.** Υ induces a certain form of simulation between the program states and their squeezed counterparts.
- **Fault preservation.** Υ maps unsafe states to unsafe states.

Our main theorem (Theorem 1) shows that if these conditions are satisfied then P is correct, provided it is correct on its *base*, i.e., on the states with minimal rank. The crux of the proof is that as a consequence of the aforementioned conditions, if P violates its specification on a state σ then it also violates it on $\Upsilon(\sigma)$. Hence, if P satisfies the specification on the base states, by induction it satisfies it on any state.

The function Υ itself can be given by the user or, as we show in Sect. 4, automatically obtained for a class of array programs which iterate over their input arrays looking for a particular element (e.g., `strchr`) or aggregating their elements (e.g., `max`). In our experiments, we utilized automatically synthesized squeezing functions to verify natural specifications of several interesting array-manipulating programs, some of which are beyond the capabilities of existing automatic techniques. Arguably, the key benefit of the our approach is that the squeezing functions are often rather simple, and thus finding them and establishing that they satisfy the required properties is an easier task than the inference of loop invariants. For example, in the next section we show a program whose loop invariant cannot be expressed in first order logic but can be proven correct using a squeezing function which is first-order expressible, in fact, the reasoning about the automatically synthesized squeezing function is quantifier free.

The last point to discuss is the verification of the program on states in the base of Υ. Here, we apply standard verification techniques but to a simpler problem: we need to establish correctness only on the base, a rather small subset of the entire state space. For example, for the programs in our experiments it is possible to utilize symbolic execution to verify the correctness of the programs on all arrays of length three or less. This approach is effective because on the programs in our benchmarks, the bound on the length of the input arrays also determines a bound on the length of the execution. As this aspect of our technique is rather standard we do not discuss it any further.

```
void sum_bidi(int a[], int n) {
    int l = 0, r = 0;
    for (int i = 0; i < n; i++) {
        l += a[i];
        r += a[n - i - 1];
    }
    assert(l == r);
}
```

$$I \triangleq \left(l + \mathrm{sum}(a[i:n]) = \\ r + \mathrm{sum}(a[0:n-i]) \right)$$

$$\mathrm{sum}(a[j:k]) \triangleq$$
$$\textbf{if } j < k$$
$$\textbf{then } a[j] + sum(a[j+1:k])$$
$$\textbf{else } 0$$

Fig. 1. A bidirectional sum example and a loop invariant for it.

Outline. The rest of the paper is structured as follows: We first give an informal overview of our approach (Sect. 2) which is followed by a formal definition of our technique and a proof of its soundness (Sect. 3). We continue with a description of our heuristic procedure for synthesizing squeezing functions (Sect. 4) and a discussion about our implementation and experimental results (Sect. 5). We then review closely related work (Sect. 6) and conclude (Sect. 7).

2 Overview

In this section, we give a high-level view of our technique.

Running Example. Program sum_bidi, shown in Fig. 1, computes the sum of the input array a in two ways: One computation accumulates elements from left to right, and the other—from right to left (assuming that indexes grow to the right). Ignoring its dubious usefulness, sum_bidi possesses an intricate property: the variables l and r are both computed to be the sum of the input array a. A natural property one expect to hold when the program terminates is that $l = r$.

The Challenge. To verify the aforementioned postcondition when the length of the array is not known and *unbounded*, a loop invariant is often employed. It is important to remember, that a loop invariant must hold on all intermediate loop states—every time execution hits the loop header. For this reason, the loop invariant needed in this case is more involved than the mere assertion $l = r$ that follows the loop. The right side of Fig. 1 shows a possible loop invariant for this scenario. Intuitively, the invariant says that l and r differ by the sum of the elements that they have not yet, respectively, accumulated. Notice that the invariant's formulation relies on a function sum($\cdot$) for arrays (and array slices), the definition of which is also included in the figure. This definition is recursive; indeed, any definition of sum will require some form of recursion or loop due to the unbounded sizes of arrays in program memory. This kind of "logical escalation" (from quantifier-free $l = r$ to a fixed-point logic) makes such verification tasks challenging, since modern solvers are not particularly effective in the presence of quantifiers and recursive definitions.

Moreover, a system attempting to automate discovery of such loop invariants is prone to serious scalability issues since it has to discover the definition of sum($\cdot$)

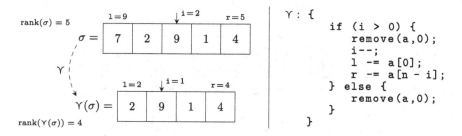

Fig. 2. A bidirectional sum example and its squeezing function.

along the way. The subject program `sum_bidi` effectively computes a sum, so this auxiliary definition is at the same scale of complexity as the program itself.

Our Approach. We suggest to leverage the semantics already present in the subject program for a more compact proof of safety. Instead of having to summarize partial executions of the program via a loop invariant, we show that the program is correct for all arrays of size $0...r$ for some *base rank* r (the size of the array serves as the rank of the program state), and further show how to derive the correctness of the program for arrays of size $n > r$, from its correctness for arrays of size $n - 1$. To achieve the latter, we rely on a function that "squeezes" states in which the array length is n to states in which the array length is $n - 1$, as we illustrate next.

Continuing with the example `sum_bidi` described above, we use the function $\Upsilon : \Sigma \to \Sigma$, defined as a code block on the right side of Fig. 2, to "squeeze" program states. In this case, the state consists of the variables $\langle a, n, i, l, r \rangle$, and it is squeezed by removing the first element of a and adjusting the indices and sums accordingly. The base rank here is $r = 0$, since any non-empty array can be squeezed in this manner. The bottom part of Fig. 3 shows the effect of applying Υ to each of the states in the execution trace of `sum_bidi` on the example input `[7,2,9,1,4]`. The first property that is demonstrated by the diagram is the "initial anchor" property, stating that initial states are "squeezed" into initial states. As is obvious from the diagram, the execution on the squeezed array `[2,9,1,4]` is accordingly shorter, so Υ cannot be injective—in this case, $\Upsilon(\sigma_0) = \Upsilon(\sigma_1) = \sigma_0'$. Still, the sequence $\sigma_0' \to \sigma_1' \to \sigma_2' \to \sigma_3' \to \sigma_4'$ constitutes a valid trace of `sum_bidi`. This is the second property required of Υ, which we refer to as *simulation inducing* and define it formally in the next section.

Now, draw attention to *fault preservation*, the third property required of Υ: whenever a state σ falsifies the safety property φ, denoted $\sigma \not\models \varphi$, it is also the case that $\Upsilon(\sigma)$ falsifies the safety property, i.e. $\Upsilon(\sigma) \not\models \varphi$. In our example, the safety property can be formalized as $\varphi \triangleq (i = n \to l = r)$. The reasoning establishing fault preservation is not immediate but still quite simple: if $\sigma \not\models \varphi$, it means that $i = n$ but $l \neq r$ (at σ). In that case, $a[n - i] = a[0]$; so

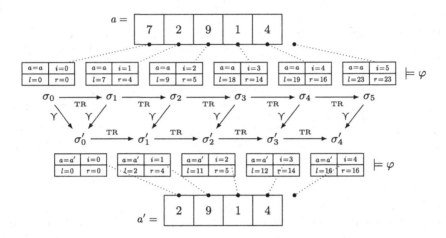

Fig. 3. Example trace of `sum_bidi`, and the corresponding shrunken image.

$l' = l - a[0] \neq r - a[n-i] = r'$, where l', r' are the values of l and r, respectively, at state $\Upsilon(\sigma)$. Since i and n are both decremented[1] we get $\Upsilon(\sigma) \not\models \varphi$.

In this manner, from *the assumption that $\Upsilon(\sigma_j)$, for $j = 0..5$, induces a safe trace*, we conclude that σ_j is safe as well. This lends the notion of constructing a proof by induction on the size of the initial state σ_0, provided that Υ cannot "squeeze forever" and that we can verify all the minimal cases more easily, *e.g.* with bounded verification. This is definitely true for `sum_bidi`, since the minimal case would be an empty array, in which the loop is never entered. In some situations the minima contains states with small but not empty arrays. In general, if one can verify that the program is correct when started with a minimal initial state, thus establishing the base case of the induction, our technique would lift this proof to hold for unbounded initial states. In particular, if the length of the program's execution trace can be bounded based on the size of the initial state then bounded model checking and symbolic execution can be lifted to obtain unbounded correctness guarantee.

It is worth mentioning at this point that Υ is in no sense "aware" that it is, in fact, reasoning about sums. It only has to handle scalar operations, in this case subtraction (as the counterpart of addition that occurs in `sum_bidi`; the same will be true for any other commutative, invertible operation.) The folding semantics arises spontaneously from the induction over the size of the array.

Recap. We suggest a novel verification technique that is based on induction on the size of the input states as an alternative to loop-invariants. The technique is based on utilizing a squeezing function which converts high-ranked states into low-ranked ones, and then applying a standard verification technique to establish the correctness of the program on the minimally-ranked states. In a manner

---

[1] Notice that we assume a positive size ($n > 0$), otherwise the array cannot be squeezed in the first place.

analogous to that which is carried out with "normal" verification using loop invariants, the squeezer has to uphold the three properties described in Sect. 1, namely *initial anchor, simulation inducing*, and *fault preservation*. (See Sect. 3 for a formal definition.) These properties ensure that the mapping induces a valid reduction between the safety of any trace and that of its squeezed counterpart.

Why Bother. The attentive readers may ask themselves, given that both loop invariants and squeezers incur some proof obligations for them to be employed for verification, what benefit may come of favoring the latter over the former. While the verification condition scheme proposed here is not inherently simpler (and arguably less so) than its Floyd-Hoare counterpart, we would like to point out that the *squeezer itself*, at least in the case of sum_bidi, *is indeed simpler* than the loop invariant that was needed to verify the same specification. It is simpler in a sense that it resides in a *weaker logical fragment*: while the invariant relies on having a definition of (partial) sums, itself a recursive definition, the squeezer Υ can be axiomatized in a quantified-free formula using a theory of strings (sequences) [8] and linear arithmetic. In Sect. 4 we take advantage of the simplicity if the squeezing function, and show that it is feasible to *generate it automatically* using a simple enumerative synthesis procedure.

On top of that, it is quite immediate to see that the induction scheme outlined above is still sound even if the properties of Υ (initial anchor, simulation, and fault preservation) only hold for *reachable* states. Obviously, the set of reachable states cannot be expressed directly—otherwise we would have just used its axiomatization together with the desired safety property, making any use of induction superfluous. Even so, if we can acquire any known property of reachable states, *e.g.* through a preliminary phase of abstract interpretation [16], then this property can be added as an assumption, simplifying Υ itself. A keen reader may have noticed that the specification of sum_bidi has been written down as $\varphi \mathrel{\hat{=}} (i = n \rightarrow l = r)$, while a completely honest translation of the assertion would in fact produce a slightly stronger form, $\varphi' \mathrel{\hat{=}} (i \geq n \rightarrow l = r)$. This was done for presentation purposes; in an actual scenario the "proper" specification φ' is used, and a premise $0 \leq i \leq n$ is assumed. Such range properties are prevalent in programs with arrays and indexes, and can be discovered easily using static analysis, e.g., using the Octagon domain [36].

This final point is encouraging because it gives rise to a hybrid approach, where a *partial* loop invariant is used as a baseline—verified via standard techniques—and is then *stengthened* to the desired safety property via squeezer-based verification. Or, the order could be reversed. There can even be alternating strengthening phases each using a different method. These extended scenarios are potentialities only and are matter for future work.

3   Verification by Induction over State Size

In this section we formalize our approach for verifying programs that operate over states (inputs) with an unbounded size. The approach mimics induction over the state size. The base case of the induction is discharged by verifying the program for executions over "small" low-ranked states (to be formalized later). For the induction step, we need to deduce correctness of executions over "larger" higher-ranked states from the correctness of executions over "smaller" states. This is facilitated by the use of a *simulation-inducing squeezing function* Υ. Intuitively, the function transforms a state σ into a corresponding "smaller" state $\Upsilon(\sigma)$ such that executions starting from the latter simulate executions starting from the former. The simulation ensures that correctness of the executions starting from the smaller state, $\Upsilon(\sigma)$, implies correctness of the executions starting from the larger one, σ.

Transition Systems and Safety Properties. To formalize our technique, we first define the semantics of programs using *transition systems*. The is quite standard.

Definition 1 (Transition Systems). *A transition system $TS = (\Sigma, Init, Tr, P)$ is a quadruple comprised of a* universe *(a set of states)* Σ, *a set of* initial states $Init \subseteq \Sigma$, *a transition relation* $Tr \subseteq \Sigma \times \Sigma$, *and a set of* good states $P \subseteq \Sigma$.

A *trace* of TS is a (finite or infinite) sequence of states $\tau = \sigma_0, \sigma_1, \ldots$ such that for every $0 \le i < |\tau|$, $(\sigma_i, \sigma_{i+1}) \in Tr$. In the following, we write Tr^k, for $k \ge 0$ to denote k self compositions of Tr, where $Tr^0 = Id$ denotes the identity relation. That is, $(\sigma, \sigma') \in Tr^k$ if and only if σ' is reachable from σ by a trace of length k (where the length of a trace is defined to be the number of transitions along the trace).

A transition system $TS = (\Sigma, Init, Tr, P)$ is *safe* if all its *reachable states* are good (or "safe"), where the set of reachable states is defined, as usual, to be the set of all states that reside on traces that start from the initial states. A *counterexample trace* is a trace that starts from an initial state and includes a "bad" state, i.e., a state that is not in P. The transition system is safe if and only if it has no counterexample traces.

Simulation-Inducing Squeezer. To present our technique, we start by formalizing the notion of a simulation-inducing squeezing function (*squeezer* for short).

Definition 2 (Squeezing function). *Let X be a set and $\preceq$ a well-founded partial order over X. Let $B \supseteq \min(X)$ be a base for X, where $\min(X)$ is the set of all the minimal elements of X w.r.t. $\preceq$, and let $\rho : \Sigma \to X$ be a rank on the program states. A function $\Upsilon : \Sigma \to \Sigma$ is a squeezing function, or squeezer for short, with base B if for every state $\sigma \in \Sigma$ such that $\rho(\sigma) \in X \setminus B$, it holds that $\rho(\Upsilon(\sigma)) \prec \rho(\sigma)$.*

That is, Υ must strictly decrease the rank of any state unless its rank is in the base, B. We refer to states whose size is in B as *base states*, and denote them $\Sigma_B = \{\sigma \in \Sigma \mid \rho(\sigma) \in B\}$. We denote by $\Sigma_{\overline{B}} = \Sigma \setminus \Sigma_B$ the remaining states. Since $\preceq$ is well-founded and all the minimal elements of X w.r.t. $\preceq$ must be in B (additional elements may be included as well), any maximal strictly decreasing sequence of elements from X will reach B (i.e., will include at least one element from B). Hence, the requirement of a squeezer ensures that any state will be transformed into a base state by a *finite* number of Υ applications.

Example 1. In our examples, we use $(\mathbb{N}, \leq)$ as a well-founded set, and define the base as an interval $[0, k]$ for some (small) $k \geq 0$. While it suffices to define $B = \min(\mathbb{N}) = \{0\}$, it is sometimes beneficial to extend the base to an interval since it excludes additional states from the squeezing requirement of Υ (see Sect. 5). For array-manipulating programs, the rank used is often (but not necessarily) the size of the underlying array, in which case, the "squeezing" requirement is that whenever the array size is greater than k, the squeezer must remove at least one element from the array. For example, for `sum_bidi` (Fig. 2), we consider $k = 0$, i.e., the base consists of arrays of size 0, and, indeed, whenever the array size is greater than 0, it is decremented by Υ. For arrays of size 0, Υ behaves as the identity function (this case is omitted from the figure). In addition, whenever the state contains more than one array, we will use the sum of lengths of all arrays as a rank.

Definition 3 (Simulation-inducing squeezer). *Given a transition system* $TS = (\Sigma, \mathit{Init}, \mathit{Tr}, P)$, *a squeezer* $\Upsilon : \Sigma \to \Sigma$ *is* simulation-inducing *if the following three conditions hold for every* $\sigma \in \Sigma$:

- **Initial anchor:** *if* $\sigma \in \mathit{Init}$ *then* $\Upsilon(\sigma) \in \mathit{Init}$ *as well.*
- **Simulation inducing:** *there exist* $n_\sigma \geq 1$ *and* $m_\sigma \geq 0$ *such that if* $(\sigma, \sigma') \in \mathit{Tr}^{n_\sigma}$ *then* $(\Upsilon(\sigma), \Upsilon(\sigma')) \in \mathit{Tr}^{m_\sigma}$, *i.e., if* σ *reaches* σ' *in* n_σ *steps, then the same holds for their* Υ-*images, except that the number of steps may be different.*
- **Fault preservation:** *if* $\sigma \notin P$ *then* $\Upsilon(\sigma) \notin P$ *as well.*

The definition implies that $\{(\sigma, \Upsilon(\sigma)) \mid \sigma \in \Sigma\}$ is a form of a "skipping" simulation relation, where steps taken both from the simulated state, σ, and from the simulating state, $\Upsilon(\sigma)$, may skip over some states. This allows the simulated and the simulating execution to proceed in a different pace, but still remain synchronized. In fact, to ensure that we obtain a "skipping" simulation, it suffices to consider a weaker simulation inducing requirement where the parameter m_σ that determines the number of steps in the simulating trace depends not only on σ but also on σ' and may be different for each σ'. Note that for deterministic programs (as we use in our experiments) these requirements are equivalent. Another possible, yet stronger, relaxation is to weaken the requirement that $(\Upsilon(\sigma), \Upsilon(\sigma')) \in \mathit{Tr}^{m_\sigma}$ into $(\Upsilon(\sigma), \Upsilon(\sigma')) \in \mathit{Tr}^i$ for some $0 \leq i \leq m_\sigma$.

Example 2. To illustrate the simulation inducing requirement, recall the program `sum_bidi` from Example 1. For the base states ($n = 0$), Υ behaves as the identity function. Hence, for such states the skipping parameters n_σ and m_σ are both 1 (letting each step be simulated by itself). For non-base states, n_σ, the "skipping" parameter of σ, is still 1, while m_σ, the "skipping" parameter of $\Upsilon(\sigma)$, is 0 if σ is an initial state, and 1 otherwise. This accounts for the fact

```
bool is_sorted(int a[], int n) {        Y: if (a[n-3] <= a[n-2] &&
    for (int i = 1; i < n; i++)                   a[n-2] <= a[n-1])
        if (a[i] < a[i-1])                      remove(a,n-1);
            return false;                    else remove(a,n-4);
    return true;
}
```

Fig. 4. Another program with Υ demonstrating a scenario where $n_\sigma < m_\sigma$.

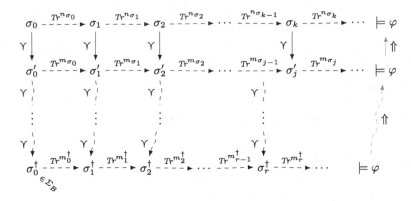

Fig. 5. Soundness proof sketch; an arbitrary trace can be reduced to a low-ranked trace by countable applications of Υ. Since ranks form a well-founded set, a base element is encountered after finitely many such reductions. Arrows with vertical ellipses indicate alternating applications of Υ and Tr^*, except for initial states where Definition 3(1) ensures straight applications of Υ alone.

that Υ truncates the head of the array; hence, the first step in an execution is skipped in the corresponding "squeezed" execution, while the rest of the steps are synchronized in both executions (see Fig. 3 for an illustration).

Intuitively, one may conjecture that given a loop that iterates over an array, it will essentially perform fewer iterations when run on $\Upsilon(\sigma)$ than it does on σ, always resulting in $m_\sigma \le n_\sigma$. The following example shows that this is not necessarily the case (Fig. 5).

Example 3. The program is_sorted (Fig. 4) checks whether the input array elements are ascending by comparing all consecutive pairs. Our squeezer (for $n > 3$) checks whether the last three elements form an ascending sequence; if so, removes the last element, otherwise it removes the forth element from the right. Consider the input $a = 1, 0, 2, 3, 1$ and the squeezed $a' = 1, 2, 3, 1$. is_sorted(a) terminates after one iteration, but is_sorted(a') after three iterations. Let $\sigma = [a, i \mapsto 1]$. The simulation inducing requirement can only be satisfied with $n_\sigma = 1$ and $m_\sigma = 3$. Since $Tr^{n_\sigma}(\sigma) = [a, ret = \text{false}]$, no smaller value of m_σ can satisfy the requirement that $Tr^{m_\sigma}(\Upsilon(\sigma)) = \Upsilon(Tr^{n_\sigma}(\sigma))$.

Checking If a Squeezer is Simulation-Inducing. The initial anchor and fault preservation requirements are simple to check. To facilitate checking the simulation inducing requirement, we do not allow arbitrarily large numbers n_σ, m_σ but, rather, determine a bound N on the value of n_σ and a bound M on the value of m_σ. This makes the simulation inducing requirement stronger than required for soundness, but avoids the need to reason about pairs of states that are reachable by traces of unbounded lengths (n_σ and m_σ).

Using Simulation-Inducing Squeezer for Safety Verification. Roughly, the existence of a simulation-inducing squeezer ensures that any counterexample to safety, i.e., an execution starting from an initial state and ending in a *bad* state (a state that falsifies the safety property), can be "squeezed" into a counterexample that starts from a "smaller" initial state. In this sense, the squeezer establishes the induction step for proving safety by induction over the state rank. To ensure the correctness of this argument, we need to require that a "bad" state may not be "skipped" by the simulation induced by the squeezer.

Formally, this is captured by the following definition.

Definition 4. *A transition system $TS = (\Sigma, \mathit{Init}, \mathit{Tr}, P)$ is recidivist if no "bad" state is a dead-end, i.e., $\sigma \notin P \implies \exists \sigma'. (\sigma, \sigma') \in \mathit{Tr}$, and that transitions leaving "bad" states lead to "bad" states, i.e., $\sigma \notin P \land (\sigma, \sigma') \in \mathit{Tr} \implies \sigma' \notin P$.*

Recidivism can be obtained by removing any outgoing transition of a bad state and adding a self loop instead. Importantly, this transformation does not affect the safety of the underlying program. In our examples, terminal states of the program are treated as self loops, thus ensuring recidivism.

Lemma 1. *Let $\Upsilon : \Sigma \to \Sigma$ be a simulation-inducing squeezer for a recidivist transition system $TS = (\Sigma, \mathit{Init}, \mathit{Tr}, P)$. For every $\sigma_0 \in \Sigma$, if there exists a counterexample that starts from σ_0, then there also exists a counterexample that starts from $\Upsilon(\sigma_0)$.*

The proof is constructive: given a counterexample trace from σ_0, we use the simulation-inducing parameters n_σ of the states σ along the trace to divide it into segments such that the first and last state of each segment are the ones used as synchronization points for the simulation and the inner ones are the ones "skipped" over. We then match each segment (σ, σ') with the corresponding trace of length m_σ from $\Upsilon(\sigma)$ to $\Upsilon(\sigma')$, whose existence is guaranteed by the simulation inducing requirement. The concatenation of these traces forms a counterexample trace from $\Upsilon(\sigma_0)$. Formally:

Proof. Let $\tau = \sigma_0, \sigma_1, \ldots, \sigma_n$ be a counterexample trace starting from an initial state $\sigma_0 \in \mathit{Init}$. If the counterexample is of length 0, then $\Upsilon(\sigma_0)$ is also a counterexample of length 0 (by the initial anchor and fault preservation requirements). Consider a counterexample of length $n > 0$. We show how to construct a corresponding counterexample from $\Upsilon(\sigma_0)$. We first split the indices $0, \ldots, n$ into (overlapping) intervals $I_0, \ldots, I_k$, where $I_0 = 0, \ldots, n_\sigma$, and for every $i \geq 1$, if the last index in I_{i-1} is j for $j < n$, then $I_i = j, \ldots, j + n_{\sigma_j}$. If $j + n_{\sigma_j} \geq n$, then $k := i$. Since TS is recidivist, we may assume, without loss of generality, that $j + n_{\sigma_j} = n$ (otherwise, because TS is recidivist and $\sigma_n \notin P$, we can exploit one of the transitions leaving σ_n, which necessarily exists and leads to a bad state, to extend the counterexample trace as needed.) We denote by $first(I_i)$, respectively $last(I_i)$, the smallest, respectively largest, index in I_i. By the definition of the intervals, for every $0 \leq i \leq k$, we have that $last(I_i) = first(I_i) + n_{\sigma_{first(I_i)}}$. Hence, the simulation inducing requirement for $\sigma_{first(I_i)}$ ensures that there exists a trace of $m_{\sigma_{first(I_i)}}$ steps from $\Upsilon(\sigma_{first(I_i)})$ to $\Upsilon(\sigma_{last(I_i)})$. Since $\sigma_{first(I_0)} = \sigma_0$ and for every $0 < i \leq k$, $\sigma_{first(I_i)} = \sigma_{last(I_{i-1})}$, we can glue these traces together to obtain a trace from $\Upsilon(\sigma_0)$ to $\Upsilon(\sigma_{last(I_i)})$. Finally, it remains to show that $\Upsilon(\sigma_{last(I_k)}) \notin P$. This follows from the fault preservation requirement, since $last(I_k) = n$, hence $\sigma_{last(I_k)} = \sigma_n \notin P$. $\qquad\square$

Ultimately, the existence of a simulation-inducing squeezer implies that a counterexample can be "squeezed" to one that starts from a base initial state. Hence, to establish that the transition system is safe, it suffices to check that it is safe when the initial states are restricted to the base states, i.e., to $Init \cap \Sigma_B$.

Theorem 1 (Soundness). *Let $\Upsilon : \Sigma \to \Sigma$ be a simulation-inducing squeezer with base B for a recidivist transition system $TS = (\Sigma, Init, Tr, P)$. If $TS_B = (\Sigma, Init \cap \Sigma_B, Tr, P)$ is safe then TS is safe.*

Proof. Suppose for the sake of contradiction, that $\{\sigma_i\}_{i=0}^{d}$ is a counterexample trace with minimal rank for σ_0 (such a state with a minimal rank exists since $\preceq$ is well-founded). Since TS_B is safe, it must be that $\sigma_0 \in \Sigma_{\overline{B}}$ (since $\sigma_0 \in Init$, while safety of TS_B ensures that no counterexample trace can start from $Init \cap \Sigma_B$). By Lemma 1, we have that $\Upsilon(\sigma_0)$ also has an outgoing counterexample trace. However, since $\sigma_0 \in \Sigma_{\overline{B}}$, we get that $\rho(\Upsilon(\sigma_0)) \prec \rho(\sigma_0)$, in contradiction to the minimality of σ_0. $\qquad\square$

In all of our examples, the transitions of TS do not increase the rank of the state. In such cases, we can also restrict the state space of TS_B (and accordingly Tr) to the base states in Σ_B. Furthermore, in these examples, the size of the state (array) also determines the length of the executions up to a terminal state. Hence, bounded model checking suffices to determine (unbounded) safety of TS_B, and together with Υ, also of TS.

Remark 1. As evident from the proof of Theorem 1, it suffices to require that Υ decreases the rank of the *initial* non-base states, and not of all the non-base states.

4 Synthesizing Squeezing Functions

So far we have assumed that the squeezer Υ is readily available, in much the same way that loop invariants are available—typically, as user annotations—in standard unbounded loop verification. As demonstrated by the examples in

body	::=	**if** (cond)
		remove(arr, expr_{index}) $\left[\text{var}_{int} = \text{expr}_{int}\right]^*$
		else
		remove(arr, expr_{index}) $\left[\text{var}_{int} = \text{expr}_{int}\right]^*$
cond	::=	$\text{elem}_\tau \diamond (\text{elem}_\tau \mid \text{const}_\tau)$
		$\mid \text{var}_{index} \diamond (\text{var}_{index} \mid \text{const}_{index})$ $\diamond ::=$ **==** $\mid$ **!=** $\mid$ **<=** $\mid$ **>=**
		$\mid$ cond **&&** cond $\mid$ cond $\mid\mid$ cond
expr_{index}	::=	$\text{const}_{index} \mid \text{var}_{index} \mid \text{len}(\text{arr}) - (\text{const}_{index} \mid \text{var}_{index})$
expr_{int}	::=	var_{int} (**+** $\mid$ **-**) elem_{int}
elem_τ	::=	arr [expr_{index}]
const_{index}	::=	0 $\mid$ 1 $\mid$ 2
const_τ	::=	0 $\mid$ other constants occurring in the program
arr, var_{index}, var_{int}, var_{char} — identifiers occurring in the program

Fig. 6. Program space for syntax-guided synthesis of Υ. Expressions are split into three categories: *index*, *int*, and *char* as described in Sect. 4. $\tau \in \{int, char\}$.

Sects. 2 and 3, Υ is specific to a given program and safety property. Thus, it might be tedious to provide a different squeezer every time we wish to check a different safety property. In this section we show how to lighten the burden on the user by automating the process of obtaining squeezing functions for a class of typical programs that loop over arrays.

The solution for the *squeezer-inference* problem we take in this paper is to utilize a rather standard enumerative synthesis technique of multi-phase generate-and-test: We take advantage of the relative simplicity of Υ and provide a synthesis loop where we generate grammatically-correct squeezing functions and test whether they induce simulation.

4.1 Generate

First we note that while Υ is applied to arbitrary states in Definition 3, it is only required to reduce the rank of non-base states $\sigma \in B$. For states $\sigma \in B$ it is trivial to satisfy all the requirements by defining $\Upsilon(\sigma) = \sigma$. In the sequel, we therefore only consider squeezing functions whose restriction to B is the identity, and synthesize code for squeezing non-base states.

A central insight is that squeezing functions Υ for different programs still have some structure in common: for programs with arrays, squeezing amounts to removing an element from the array, and adjusting the index variables accordingly. Some more detailed treatment may be needed for general purpose variables, such as the accumulators l and r of sum_bidi (recall Fig. 1), but the resulting expressions are still small.

We have found that, for the set of programs used in our experiments, Υ can be characterised by the grammar in Fig. 6. The grammar allows for functions comprised of a single if statement, where in each branch an array is squeezed using the `remove` function, and several integer variables are set. Conditions are generating by composing array elements, local variables and a fixed set of constants based on the given program, with standard comparison operators and boolean connectives. The semantics of `remove(arr, position)` are such that a single element is removed from the array at the specified position, and all index variables are adjusted by decrementing them if they are larger from the index of the element being removed. This behavior is hard-coded and is specific to array-based loops. Our experience has shown that a single conditional statement is indeed sufficient to cover many different cases (see Sect. 5).

To bound the search space, expressions and conditions have bounded sizes (in terms of AST height) imposed by the generator and the user selects the set of basic predicates from which the condition of the `if` statement is constructed. The resulting space, however, is still often too large to be explored efficiently. To reduce it, some type-directed pruning is carried out so that only valid functions are passed to the checker. Moreover, our synthesis procedure distinguishes between variables that are used as indices to the array (var_{index}) and regular integer variables (var_{int}), and does not mix between them. We further assume that we can determine, from analyzing the program's source code, which index variable is used with which array(s). So when generating expressions of the form `arr[ i ]` *etc.*, only relevant index variables are used. Also, we note that generated squeezers preserve in bounds access by construction.

4.2 Test

The *test* step checks whether a candidate squeezer that is generated by the synthesizer satisfies the requirements of Definition 3. For the simulation-inducing requirement, we restrict $n_\sigma = 1..2$ and $m_\sigma = 0..1$. The step is divided into three phases. In the first phase, candidates are checked against a bank of concrete program states (both reachable and unreachable). In the second phase, candidates are verified for a bounded array size, but with no restrictions on the values of the elements. Those that pass bounded verification enter the third phase where full, unbounded verification is performed.

The second and third phases of the test step require the use of an SMT solver. The second phase is useful since incorrect candidates may cause the solver to diverge when queried for arbitrary array sizes. Limiting the array size to a small number (we used 6) enables to rule out these candidates in under a second. To simplify the satisfiability checks, we found it beneficial to decompose the verification task. To do so, we take advantage of the structure of the squeezer, and split each satisfiability query (that corresponds to one of the requirements in Definition 3) into two queries, where in each query we make a different assumption regarding the branch the squeezer function takes. We note in this context that the capabilities of the underlying solver direct (or limit in some sense) the expressive power of the squeezer. In this aspect, it is also worth mentioning that sequence theory support for element removal helped to define squeezers format.

For the simulation inducing check, we further exploit the property that for the kind of programs and squeezers we consider, the transitions of the program usually do not change the truth value of the condition of the if statement in the definition of the squeezer. Namely, if σ makes a transition to σ' then either both of them satisfy the condition or both of them falsify it; either way, their definition of Υ follows the same branch. This form of preservation can be checked automatically using additional queries. When it holds, we can consider the same branch of the squeezer program in both the pre- and post-states, thus simplifying the query for checking simulation. Similarly, we can opportunistically split the transition relation of the program into branches (e.g., one that executes an iteration of the loop and one that exits the loop). In most cases, the same branch that was taken for σ is also the one that needs to be taken from $\Upsilon(\sigma)$ to establish simulation. This leads to another simplification of the queries, which is sound (i.e., never concludes that the simulation-inducing requirement holds when it does not), but potentially incomplete. We can therefore use it as a "cheaper" check and resort to the full check if it fails.

4.3 Filtering Out Unreachable States

For soundness, a squeezer needs to satisfy Definition 3 only on the reachable states. As we do not have a description of this set, for otherwise the verification task would be essentially voided, we need to ensure that the requirements of simulation-inducement on a safe over-approximation of this set. A simple over-approximation would be the set of all states. However, this over-approximation might be too coarse, indeed we noticed in our experiments that in some cases, unreachable states have caused phases 1, 2 and 3 to produce false negatives,*i.e.*, disqualify squeezers which can be used safely to verify the program. Therefore we used an over-approximation of reachable states using

1. Bound constraints on the index variables: the index is expected to be within bounds of the traversed array. This property can be easily verified using other verifiers or by applying our verifier in stages, first proving this property and then proving the actual specification of the verified procedure under the assumption that the property hold.
2. 2-step bounded reachability: We found out that for our examples, looking only at states that are reachable from another state in at most two steps is a general enough inclusion criterion. Note that we do not require 2-step reachability from an initial state, but rather from *any* state, hence this set over-approximates the set of reachable states.

5   Implementation and Experimental Results

We implemented an automatic verifier for array programs based on our approach, and applied it successfully to verify natural properties of a few interesting array-manipulating programs.

Base Case. We discharged the base case of the induction (the verification on the base states) using KLEE [12]—a state-of-the-art symbolic execution [13] engine. It took KLEE less than one tenth of a second to verify the correctness of each program in our benchmarks on the states in its base. This part of our verification approach is standard, and we discuss it no further; in the rest of this section we focus on the generation of the squeezing functions.

5.1 Implementation

The generate step and phase 1 of the test step of the squeezer synthesizer were implemented using a standalone C++ application that generates all Υ candidates with an AST of depth three. Each squeezer was tested on a pre-prepared state bank and every time a squeezer passed the tests it was immediately passed on to phase 2. The state bank contained states with arrays of length five or less. For each benchmark, we used up to 24,386 states with randomly selected array contents. The number of states was determined as follows: Suppose the program state is comprised of k variables and an array of size n. We randomly selected p elements that can populate the array: $p = \{'a','b',0\}$ for string manipulating procedures and $p = \{-4,-2,9,100,200\}$ for programs that manipulate integer arrays. We determined the number test states according to the following formula: $d^k \cdot |p|^n/df$, where df is an arbitrary dilution factor used to reduce the number of states from thousands to hundreds. (In our experiments, $df = 17$.)

The second and third phases were implemented using Z3 [17], a state of the art SMT solver. We chose to use the theory of sequences, since its API allows for a straightforward definition of the operation remove(arr,i) (see Fig. 6). In practice, the sequence solver proved to be overall more effective than a corresponding encoding using the more mature array solver. In that aspect, it is worth mentioning that verifying fault preservation on its own *is* faster with the theory of arrays. We conjecture that this is because the specification has quantifiers while the other requirements can be verified using quantifier-free reasoning.

The transition relation was manually encoded in SMT-LIB2 format. However, it should be straightforward to automate this step.

5.2 Experimental Evaluation

We evaluated our technique by verifying a few array-manipulating programs against their expected specifications. The experiments were executed on a laptop with Intel i7-8565 CPU (4 cores) with 16 GB of RAM running Ubuntu 18.04.

Benchmarks. We ran our experiments on seven array-manipulating programs: strnchr looks for the first appearance of a given character in the first n characters of a string buffer. strncmp compares whether two strings are identical up to their first n characters or the first zero character. max_ind (resp. min_ind) looks for the index of the maximal (resp. minimal) element in an integer array. sum_bidi is our running example. is_sorted checks if the elements of an array are sorted in an increasing order. long_pref is looking for the longest prefix

Table 1. Experimental results (end-to-end). Time in seconds. G&T is a shorthand for Generate&Test

Program	B	# Cand	Phase 1			Phase 2		Phase 3	Total time G&T + KLEE	QUIC3 time
			|Bank|	Test	Time	BMC	Time	Time		
strnchr	2	80	356	29	0.004	1	0.12	0.16	0.28 + 0.07	0.32
strncmp	2	980	76	196	0.02	1	7.2	154.48	161.70 + 0.05	0.19
max_ind	2	8000	368	10	0.18	2	1.86	4.44	4.73 + 0.05	0.11
min_ind	2	8000	257	9	0.26	2	2.1	16.86	17.21 + 0.05	0.09
sum_bidi	2	6328125	4602	1200	2.18	1	0.57	0.61	3.36 + 0.05	t.o.
is_sorted	4	900	25736	764	4.37	1	0.59	0.67	5.63 + 0.06	0.15
long_pref	3	6480	24386	4696	22.93	1	1.25	0.89	25.07 + 0.05	t.o.

of an array comprised of either a monotonically increasing or a monotonically decreasing sequence.

The user supplies predicates that are used when synthesizing each squeezer. These were selected based on understanding what the program does and the operations it uses internally. *E.g.*, for strncmp equality comparisons between same-index elements of the two input arrays are used (s1[0]==s2[0] etc.), as well as comparison with constant 0; for long_pref, order comparisons (s1[1]<=s1[2] etc.) between different elements of the same array are used instead.

Results. Table 1 describes the end-to-end running times of our verifier, i.e., the time it took our tool to establish the correctness of each example. In this experiment, every candidate squeezer was tested before the next squeezer was generated. The table shows the time it took the synthesizer to find the first simulation-inducing squeezer plus the time it took to establish the correctness of the programs on the states in the base using KLEE (Total Time). The table also compares our verifier to QUIC3 [28], an automatic synthesizer of loop invariants. In general, when both tools where able to prove that the analyzed procedure is correct, QUIC3 was somewhat faster, and in the case of strncmp much faster. However, on two of our benchmarks QUIC3 timed out (1 h) whereas our tool was able to prove them correct in less than 30 s.

Table 1 also provides more detailed statistics regarding the experiments: The rank of the base states (B), the total number of possible candidates based on the supplied predicates and the bound on the depth of the AST (# Cand), and a more detailed view of each phase in the testing step. For phase 1, it reports the number of states in the pre-prepared state bank (|Bank|), the number of squeezers tested until a simulation-inducing one was found (Test), and the total time spent to test these squeezers (Time). For phase 2, it reports the number of candidates which passed phase 1 and survived bounded verification (BMC) and the time spent in this phase (Time). For phase 3, we report how many simulation-inducing squeezers were found the time it took to apply full verification.

Table 2. Experimental results. Time in seconds. $\epsilon \leq 0.0001$

Program	Phase 1				Phase 2			Phase 3		
	|Pos.|	Time	|Neg.|	Time	|Pos.|	Time	Time$_{\|\text{Neg.}\|}$	|Pos.|	Time	Time$_{\|\text{Neg.}\|}$
strnchr	1	ϵ	9	ϵ	1	0.94	–	1	0.98	–
strncmp	3	ϵ	36	ϵ	3	14.29	–	3	154.48	–
max_ind	11	ϵ	3	ϵ	2	0.78	1.08	1	31.00	0.41
min_ind	11	ϵ	7	ϵ	2	0.91	1.19	1	16.00	0.43
sum_bidi	12	ϵ	1	0.05	1	0.56	0.69	1	0.61	–
is_sorted	1	ϵ	18	ϵ	1	0.59	–	1	0.67	–
long_pref	2	ϵ	74	ϵ	1	1.03	1.22	1	0.89	–

Table 3. Synthesized squeezers. n is the size of the input array

Program	Squeezer
strchr(c)	if (s[0] == c || s[0]==0) remove(s,1) else remove(s,0)
strncmp	(1) if (s1[0] == s2[0] && s1[0] != 0) remove(s1,0); remove(s2,0)
	else remove(s1,1); remove(s2,1)
	(2) if (s1[0] == s2[0] && s2[0] != 0) remove(s1,0); remove(s2,0)
	else remove(s1,1); remove(s2,1)
	(3) if (s1[0] != s2[0]) || (s1[0] == 0 && s2[0] == 0))
	remove(s1,1); remove(s2,1)
	else remove(s1,0); remove(s2,0)
max_ind	if (s[n-2] <= s[n-1]) remove(s,n-2) else remove(s,n-1)
is_sorted	if (s[n-3]<=s[n-2]<=s[n-1]) remove(s,n-1) else remove(s,n-4)
long_pref	if ((s[0]<=s[1]<= s[2]) || (s[0]>s[1]>s[2])) remove(s,0)
	else remove(s,n-1)

In all our experiments except of max/min_ind only the simulation-inducing squeezers passed bounded verification. In the latter case, a squeezer passed BMC due to the use of arrays of size at most five where the cells $a[2]$ and $a[n-2]$ are adjacent. Had we increased the array bound to six, these false positives would have been eliminated by the bounded verification.

Table 2 provides average times required to pass all the generated squeezers through the testing pipeline. For phase 1, it reports the number of squeezers which passed (Pos) resp. failed (Neg) testing against the randomly generated states and the average time it took to test the squeezers in each category (Time). The table reports the statistics pertaining to phase 2 and 3 in a similar manner, except that it omits the number of squeezers which failed the phase as this number can be read off the number of squeezers which reached this phase.

Table 3 shows some of the automatically generated squeezers. We obtained a single simulation-inducing squeezer in all of our tests except for strncmp where three squeezers were synthesized. The three differ only syntactically by the condition of the if statements. However, semantically, the three conditions are equivalent. Thus, improving the symmetry-detection optimizations to include equivalence up-to-de morgan rules would have filtered out two of the three squeezers.

6 Related Work

Automatic verification of infinite-state systems, *i.e.*, systems where the size of an individual state is unbounded such as numerical programs (where data is considered unbounded), array manipulating programs (where both the length of the array and the data it contains may be unbounded), programs with dynamic memory allocation (with unbounded number of dynamically-allocatable memory objects), and parameterized systems (where, in most cases, there is an unbounded number of instances of finite subsystems) is a long standing challenge in the realm of formal methods.

Well Structured Transition Systems. Well structured transition systems (WSTS) [1,2,22] are a class of infinite-state transition systems for which safety verification is decidable, with a backward reachability analysis being a decision procedure. In these transitions systems, the set of states is accompanied by a well-quasi order that induces a simulation relation: a state is simulated by those that are "larger" than it. As a result, the set of backward-reachable states is upward closed. The simulation-inducing well-quasi order used in WSTS resembles our condition of a simulation-inducing squeezer. However, there are several fundamental differences: (i) The order underlying our technique is required to be well-founded, which is a strictly weaker requirement than that of a well-quasi order; (ii) The simulation-inducing requirement requires each state to be simulated by its squeezed version, which has a *lower* rank rather than greater; further, a state need not be simulated by *every* state with a lower rank; accordingly, the set of backward-reachable states need not be upward (nor downward) closed. (iii) Our procedure is not based on backward (or any other form of) reachability analysis.

Reductions. Cutoff-based techniques, e.g., [18], reduce model checking of unbounded parameterized systems to model checking for systems of size (up to) a small predetermined cutoff size. Verification based on dynamic cut-offs [3,31] also considers parameterized systems but employs a verification procedure which can dynamically detect cut-off points beyond which the search of the state space need not continue. Invisible invariants [39,48] are used to verify unbounded parameterized systems in a bounded way. The idea is to use the standard deductive invariance rule for proving invariance properties but consider only bounded systems for discharging the verification conditions, while ensuring that they hold for the unbounded system. The approach provides (i) a heuristic to generate a candidate inductive invariant for the proof rule, and (ii) a method to validate the premises of the proof rule once a candidate is generated [48].

Similar reductions were applied to array programs–a particular form of parameterized systems but with unbounded data–as we consider in this work. For example, in [33], *shrinkable* loops are identified as loops that traverse large or unbounded arrays but may be soundly replaced by a bounded number of nondeterministically chosen iterations; and in [37], abstraction is used to replace reasoning about unbounded arrays and quantified properties by reasoning about a bounded number of array cells.

A fundamental difference between our approach and these works is that we do not reduce the problem to a bounded verification problem. Instead, we generate verification conditions which amount to a proof by induction on the size of the system. In fact, from the perspective of deductive verification, our work can be seen as introducing a new induction scheme.

Loop Invariant Inference. Arguably, inference of loop invariants is the ubiquitous approach for automatic verification of infinite-size systems. Recent research efforts in the area have concentrated around inference of quantified invariants, in particular, the search for universal loop invariants is a central issue.

Classical predicate abstraction [7,25] has been adapted to quantified invariants by extending predicates with *skolem* (fresh) variables [23,34]. This is sufficient for discovering complex loop invariants of array manipulating programs similar to the simpler programs used in our experiments.

A research avenue that has received ongoing popularity is the use of constrained Horn clauses (CHCs) to model properties of transition systems which have been used for inference of universally quantified invariants [9,27,37] by limiting the quantifier nesting in the loop invariant being sought. In [20], universally quantified solutions (inductive invariants) to CHCs are inferred via syntax-guided synthesis.

Another active research area is Model-Checking Modulo Theories (MCMT) [24] which extends model checking to array manipulating programs and has been used for verifying heap manipulating programs and parameterized systems (e.g., [15]) using quantifier elimination techniques. For example, in SAFARI [4] (and later BOOSTER [5]), the theory of arrays [11] is used to construct a QF proof of bounded safety which is generalized by universally quantifying out some terms.

IC3 [10] extends predicate abstraction into a framework in which the predicate discovery is directed by the verification goal and heuristics are used to generalize proofs of bounded depth execution to inductive invariants. UPDR [32] and QUIC3 [28] extend IC3 to quantified invariants. UPDR focuses on programs specified using the Effectively PRopositional (EPR) fragment of *uninterpreted* first order logic (e.g., without arithmetic) for which quantified satisfiability is decidable. As such, UPDR does not deal with quantifier instantiation. QUIC3 uses model based projection and generalizations based on bounded exploration.

Like these techniques we also use heuristics to overcome the unavoidable undecidability barrier. In our case, this amounts to the selection of the squeezing function. In contrast to all the aforementioned approaches, our technique does not rely on the inference of loop invariant but rather proves programs correct by induction on the size (rank) of their states.

We note that we do not position our technique as a replacement to automatic inference of loop invariants but rather as a complementary approach. Indeed, while some tricky properties can be easily verified by our approach, e.g., the postcondition of sum_bidi, a property which we believe no other automatic technique can deduce, other properties which are simple to establish using loop invariants, e.g., that variable i is always in the range $0..n-1$, are surprisingly challenging for our technique to establish.

Recurrences. Other approaches represent the behavior of loops in array-programs via recurrences defined over an explicit loop counter, and use these recurrences to directly verify post-conditions with universal quantification over the array indices. In [40] this is done by customized instantiation schemes and explicit induction when necessary. In [14], verification is done by identifying a relation between loop iterations (characterized by the loop counter) and the array indices that are affected by them, and verifying that the post-condition holds for these indices. Similarly to our approach, these works do not rely on loop invariants, but they do not allow to verify global properties over the arrays, such as the postcondition of sum_bidi.

Program Synthesis. The inference we use for ϒ is indeed a form of program synthesis, as was alluded to in Sect. 2 by representing ϒ via pseudo-code. In particular, *syntax-guided synthesis* (SyGuS) [6] is the domain of program synthesis where the target program is derived from a programming language according to its syntax rules. [19, 30, 45, 46] all fall within this scope.

Sketching is a common feature of SyGuS. The term is inspired by Sketch [42], referring to the practice of giving synthesizers a program skeleton with a missing piece or pieces. This uses domain knowledge to reduce the size of the candidate space. It is quite common to use a domain-specific language (DSL) for this purpose [29, 41, 43, 44, 47]. [38] restricts programs by typing rules in addition to just syntax. [26] develops it further by restricting how operators may be composed. Our synthesis procedure (Sect. 4) follows the same guidelines: the domain of array-scanning programs dictates the constructed space of squeezer functions, and moreover, inspecting the analyzed program allows for more pruning by (i) matching index variables to array variables and (ii) focusing on operators and literal values occurring in the program. This early pruning is responsible for the feasibility of our synthesis procedure, which apart from that is rather naive and does not facilitate clever optimizations such as equivalence reduction [21, 38].

7   Conclusions

At the current state of affairs in automatic software verification of infinite state systems, the scene is dominated by various approaches with a common aim: computing over-approximations of unbounded executions by means of inferring loop invariants. Indeed, *abstract interpretation* [16], *property-directed reachability* [10], unbounded model checking [35], or template-based verification [44] can be seen as different techniques for computing such approximations by finding inductive loop invariants which are tight enough not to intersect with the set of bad behaviors. Experience has shown that these invariants are frequently quite hard to come by, even for seemingly simple and innocuous program, both automatically and manually. The purpose of this paper is to suggest an alternative kind of correctness witness, which may be more amenable to automated search. We successfully applied our novel verification technique to array programs and managed to prove programs and properties which are beyond the ability of existing automatic verifiers. We believe that our approach can be combined with standard techniques to give rise to a new kind of hybrid techniques, where, e.g., a *partial* loop invariant is used as a baseline—verified via standard techniques—and is then *strengthened* to the desired safety property via squeezer-based verification.

Acknowledgements. The research leading to these results has received funding from the European Research Council under the European Union's Horizon 2020 research and innovation programme (grant agreement No. [759102-SVIS]), the Lev Blavatnik and the Blavatnik Family foundation, Blavatnik Interdisciplinary Cyber Research Center at Tel Aviv University, Pazy Foundation, Israel Science Foundation (ISF) grants No. 1996/18 and 1810/18, and the Binational Science Foundation (NSF-BSF) grant 2018675.

References

1. Abdulla, P.A., Cerans, K., Jonsson, B., Tsay, Y.: General decidability theorems for infinite-state systems. In: Proceedings, 11th Annual IEEE Symposium on Logic in Computer Science, New Brunswick, New Jersey, USA, 27–30 July 1996, pp. 313–321 (1996). https://doi.org/10.1109/LICS.1996.561359
2. Abdulla, P.A., Cerans, K., Jonsson, B., Tsay, Y.: Algorithmic analysis of programs with well quasi-ordered domains. Inf. Comput. **160**(1–2), 109–127 (2000). https://doi.org/10.1006/inco.1999.2843
3. Abdulla, P.A., Haziza, F., Holík, L.: All for the price of few. In: Giacobazzi, R., Berdine, J., Mastroeni, I. (eds.) VMCAI 2013. LNCS, vol. 7737, pp. 476–495. Springer, Heidelberg (2013). https://doi.org/10.1007/978-3-642-35873-9_28
4. Alberti, F., Bruttomesso, R., Ghilardi, S., Ranise, S., Sharygina, N.: SAFARI: SMT-based abstraction for arrays with interpolants. In: Madhusudan, P., Seshia, S.A. (eds.) CAV 2012. LNCS, vol. 7358, pp. 679–685. Springer, Heidelberg (2012). https://doi.org/10.1007/978-3-642-31424-7_49
5. Alberti, F., Ghilardi, S., Sharygina, N.: Booster: an acceleration-based verification framework for array programs. In: Cassez, F., Raskin, J.-F. (eds.) ATVA 2014. LNCS, vol. 8837, pp. 18–23. Springer, Cham (2014). https://doi.org/10.1007/978-3-319-11936-6_2
6. Alur, R., et al.: Syntax-guided synthesis. In: Dependable Software. Systems Engineering, vol. 40, pp. 1–25 (2015)
7. Ball, T., Podelski, A., Rajamani, S.K.: Boolean and Cartesian abstraction for model checking C programs. In: Margaria, T., Yi, W. (eds.) TACAS 2001. LNCS, vol. 2031, pp. 268–283. Springer, Heidelberg (2001). https://doi.org/10.1007/3-540-45319-9_19
8. Bjørner, N., Ganesh, V., Michel, R., Veanes, M.: SMT-LIB sequences and regular expressions. In: 10th International Workshop on Satisfiability Modulo Theories, SMT 2012, Manchester, UK, 30 June–1 July 2012, pp. 77–87 (2012)
9. Bjørner, N., McMillan, K., Rybalchenko, A.: On solving universally quantified horn clauses. In: Logozzo, F., Fähndrich, M. (eds.) SAS 2013. LNCS, vol. 7935, pp. 105–125. Springer, Heidelberg (2013). https://doi.org/10.1007/978-3-642-38856-9_8

10. Bradley, A.R.: SAT-based model checking without unrolling. In: Jhala, R., Schmidt, D. (eds.) VMCAI 2011. LNCS, vol. 6538, pp. 70–87. Springer, Heidelberg (2011). https://doi.org/10.1007/978-3-642-18275-4_7

11. Bruttomesso, R., Ghilardi, S., Ranise, S.: Quantifier-free interpolation of a theory of arrays. Log. Methods Comput. Sci. **8**(2) (2012). https://doi.org/10.2168/LMCS-8(2:4)2012

12. Cadar, C., Dunbar, D., Engler, D.: Klee: unassisted and automatic generation of high-coverage tests for complex systems programs. In: Proceedings of the 8th USENIX Conference on Operating Systems Design and Implementation, OSDI 2008, pp. 209–224. USENIX Association, Berkeley (2008). http://dl.acm.org/citation.cfm?id=1855741.1855756

13. Cadar, C., Sen, K.: Symbolic execution for software testing: three decades later. Commun. ACM **56**(2), 82–90 (2013). https://doi.org/10.1145/2408776.2408795

14. Chakraborty, S., Gupta, A., Unadkat, D.: Verifying array manipulating programs by tiling. In: Ranzato, F. (ed.) SAS 2017. LNCS, vol. 10422, pp. 428–449. Springer, Cham (2017). https://doi.org/10.1007/978-3-319-66706-5_21

15. Conchon, S., Goel, A., Krstic, S., Mebsout, A., Zaïdi, F.: Invariants for finite instances and beyond. In: Formal Methods in Computer-Aided Design, FMCAD 2013, Portland, OR, USA, 20–23 October 2013, pp. 61–68 (2013). http://ieeexplore.ieee.org/document/6679392/

16. Cousot, P., Cousot, R.: Abstract interpretation: a unified lattice model for static analysis of programs by construction or approximation of fixpoints. In: Conference Record of the Fourth Annual ACM SIGPLAN-SIGACT Symposium on Principles of Programming Languages, pp. 238–252. ACM Press, New York, Los Angeles (1977)

17. de Moura, L., Bjørner, N.: Z3: an efficient SMT solver. In: Ramakrishnan, C.R., Rehof, J. (eds.) TACAS 2008. LNCS, vol. 4963, pp. 337–340. Springer, Heidelberg (2008). https://doi.org/10.1007/978-3-540-78800-3_24

18. Emerson, E.A., Kahlon, V.: Reducing model checking of the many to the few. In: McAllester, D. (ed.) CADE 2000. LNCS (LNAI), vol. 1831, pp. 236–254. Springer, Heidelberg (2000). https://doi.org/10.1007/10721959_19

19. Farzan, A., Nicolet, V.: Modular divide-and-conquer parallelization of nested loops. In: Proceedings of the 40th ACM SIGPLAN Conference on Programming Language Design and Implementation, PLDI 2019, pp. 610–624. ACM, New York (2019). https://doi.org/10.1145/3314221.3314612

20. Fedyukovich, G., Prabhu, S., Madhukar, K., Gupta, A.: Quantified invariants via syntax-guided synthesis. In: Computer Aided Verification - Proceedings of the 31st International Conference, CAV 2019, New York City, NY, USA, 15–18 July 2019, Part I, pp. 259–277 (2019). https://doi.org/10.1007/978-3-030-25540-4_14

21. Feser, J.K., Chaudhuri, S., Dillig, I.: Synthesizing data structure transformations from input-output examples. In: ACM SIGPLAN Notices. vol. 50, pp. 229–239. ACM (2015)

22. Finkel, A., Schnoebelen, P.: Well-structured transition systems everywhere!. Theor. Comput. Sci. **256**(1–2), 63–92 (2001). https://doi.org/10.1016/S0304-3975(00)00102-X

23. Flanagan, C., Qadeer, S.: Predicate abstraction for software verification. In: Conference Record of POPL 2002: The 29th SIGPLAN-SIGACT Symposium on Principles of Programming Languages, Portland, OR, USA, 16–18 January 2002, pp. 191–202 (2002). https://doi.org/10.1145/503272.503291

24. Ghilardi, S., Ranise, S.: MCMT: a model checker modulo theories. In: Giesl, J., Hähnle, R. (eds.) IJCAR 2010. LNCS (LNAI), vol. 6173, pp. 22–29. Springer, Heidelberg (2010). https://doi.org/10.1007/978-3-642-14203-1_3

25. Graf, S., Saidi, H.: Construction of abstract state graphs with PVS. In: Grumberg, O. (ed.) CAV 1997. LNCS, vol. 1254, pp. 72–83. Springer, Heidelberg (1997). https://doi.org/10.1007/3-540-63166-6_10

26. Gulwani, S.: Programming by examples (and its applications in data wrangling). In: Esparza, J., Grumberg, O., Sickert, S. (eds.) Verification and Synthesis of Correct and Secure Systems. IOS Press (2016)

27. Gurfinkel, A., Shoham, S., Meshman, Y.: SMT-based verification of parameterized systems. In: Proceedings of the 24th ACM SIGSOFT International Symposium on Foundations of Software Engineering, FSE 2016, Seattle, WA, USA, 13–18 November 2016, pp. 338–348 (2016). https://doi.org/10.1145/2950290.2950330

28. Gurfinkel, A., Shoham, S., Vizel, Y.: Quantifiers on demand. In: Lahiri, S.K., Wang, C. (eds.) ATVA 2018. LNCS, vol. 11138, pp. 248–266. Springer, Cham (2018). https://doi.org/10.1007/978-3-030-01090-4_15

29. Hua, J., Khurshid, S.: EdSketch: execution-driven sketching for Java. In: Proceedings of the 24th ACM SIGSOFT International SPIN Symposium on Model Checking of Software, pp. 162–171. ACM (2017)

30. Itzhaky, S., et al.: Deriving divide-and-conquer dynamic programming algorithms using solver-aided transformations. In: Proceedings of the 2016 ACM SIGPLAN International Conference on Object-Oriented Programming, Systems, Languages, and Applications, pp. 145–164. ACM (2016)

31. Kaiser, A., Kroening, D., Wahl, T.: Dynamic cutoff detection in parameterized concurrent programs. In: Touili, T., Cook, B., Jackson, P. (eds.) CAV 2010. LNCS, vol. 6174, pp. 645–659. Springer, Heidelberg (2010). https://doi.org/10.1007/978-3-642-14295-6_55

32. Karbyshev, A., Bjørner, N., Itzhaky, S., Rinetzky, N., Shoham, S.: Property-directed inference of universal invariants or proving their absence. In: Kroening, D., Păsăreanu, C.S. (eds.) CAV 2015. LNCS, vol. 9206, pp. 583–602. Springer, Cham (2015). https://doi.org/10.1007/978-3-319-21690-4_40

33. Kumar, S., Sanyal, A., Venkatesh, R., Shah, P.: Property checking array programs using loop shrinking. In: Beyer, D., Huisman, M. (eds.) TACAS 2018. LNCS, vol. 10805, pp. 213–231. Springer, Cham (2018). https://doi.org/10.1007/978-3-319-89960-2_12

34. Lahiri, S.K., Bryant, R.E.: Constructing quantified invariants via predicate abstraction. In: Steffen, B., Levi, G. (eds.) VMCAI 2004. LNCS, vol. 2937, pp. 267–281. Springer, Heidelberg (2004). https://doi.org/10.1007/978-3-540-24622-0_22

35. McMillan, K.L.: Lazy abstraction with interpolants. In: Ball, T., Jones, R.B. (eds.) CAV 2006. LNCS, vol. 4144, pp. 123–136. Springer, Heidelberg (2006). https://doi.org/10.1007/11817963_14

36. Miné, A.: The octagon abstract domain. High.-Order Symb. Comput. **19**(1), 31–100 (2006)

37. Monniaux, D., Gonnord, L.: Cell morphing: from array programs to array-free horn clauses. In: Rival, X. (ed.) SAS 2016. LNCS, vol. 9837, pp. 361–382. Springer, Heidelberg (2016). https://doi.org/10.1007/978-3-662-53413-7_18

38. Osera, P.M., Zdancewic, S.: Type-and-example-directed program synthesis. In: ACM SIGPLAN Notices. vol. 50, pp. 619–630. ACM (2015)

39. Pnueli, A., Ruah, S., Zuck, L.: Automatic deductive verification with invisible invariants. In: Margaria, T., Yi, W. (eds.) TACAS 2001. LNCS, vol. 2031, pp. 82–97. Springer, Heidelberg (2001). https://doi.org/10.1007/3-540-45319-9_7

40. Rajkhowa, P., Lin, F.: Extending VIAP to handle array programs. In: Piskac, R., Rümmer, P. (eds.) VSTTE 2018. LNCS, vol. 11294, pp. 38–49. Springer, Cham (2018). https://doi.org/10.1007/978-3-030-03592-1_3

41. Smith, C., Albarghouthi, A.: Mapreduce program synthesis. In: Proceedings of the 37th ACM SIGPLAN Conference on Programming Language Design and Implementation, pp. 326–340. ACM (2016)

42. Solar-Lezama, A., Tancau, L., Bodik, R., Seshia, S., Saraswat, V.: Combinatorial sketching for finite programs. ACM SIGOPS Oper. Syst. Rev. **40**(5), 404–415 (2006)

43. Srivastava, S., Gulwani, S., Foster, J.S.: From program verification to program synthesis. In: ACM Sigplan Notices, vol. 45, pp. 313–326. ACM (2010)

44. Srivastava, S., Gulwani, S., Foster, J.S.: Template-based program verification and program synthesis. Int. J. Softw. Tools Technol. Transfer **15**(5–6), 497–518 (2013)

45. Udupa, A., Raghavan, A., Deshmukh, J.V., Mador-Haim, S., Martin, M.M., Alur, R.: TRANSIT: specifying protocols with concolic snippets. ACM SIGPLAN Not. **48**(6), 287–296 (2013)

46. Wang, C., Cheung, A., Bodik, R.: Synthesizing highly expressive SQL queries from input-output examples. In: Proceedings of the 38th ACM SIGPLAN Conference on Programming Language Design and Implementation, pp. 452–466. ACM (2017)

47. Wang, K., Sullivan, A., Marinov, D., Khurshid, S.: Solver-based sketching of alloy models using test valuations. In: Butler, M., Raschke, A., Hoang, T.S., Reichl, K. (eds.) ABZ 2018. LNCS, vol. 10817, pp. 121–136. Springer, Cham (2018). https://doi.org/10.1007/978-3-319-91271-4_9

48. Zuck, L.D., McMillan, K.L.: Invisible invariants are neither. In: Bartocci, E., Cleaveland, R., Grosu, R., Sokolsky, O. (eds.) From Reactive Systems to Cyber-Physical Systems. LNCS, vol. 11500, pp. 57–72. Springer, Cham (2019). https://doi.org/10.1007/978-3-030-31514-6_5

A Systematic Approach to Abstract Interpretation of Program Transformations

Sven Keidel$^{(\boxtimes)}$ and Sebastian Erdweg

JGU Mainz, Mainz, Germany
{keidel,erdweg}@uni-mainz.de

Abstract. Abstract interpretation is a technique to define sound static analyses. While abstract interpretation is generally well-understood, the analysis of program transformations has not seen much attention. The main challenge in developing an abstract interpreter for program transformations is designing good abstractions that capture relevant information about the generated code. However, a complete abstract interpreter must handle many other aspects of the transformation language, such as backtracking and generic traversals, as well as analysis-specific concerns, such as interprocedurality and fixpoints. This deflects attention.

We propose a systematic approach to design and implement abstract interpreters for program transformations that isolates the abstraction for generated code from other analysis aspects. Using our approach, analysis developers can focus on the design of abstractions for generated code, while the rest of the analysis definition can be reused. We show that our approach is feasible and useful by developing three novel interprocedural analyses for the Stratego transformation language: a singleton analysis for constant propagation, a sort analysis for type checking, and a locally-illsorted sort analysis that can additionally validate type changing generic traversals.

1 Introduction

Abstract interpretation is a technique to define sound static analyses [6]. Static analyses have proved useful in providing feedback to developers (e.g., dead code [4], type information), in finding bugs (e.g., uninitialized read [25], type errors [20]), and in enabling compiler optimizations (e.g., constant propagation [3], purity analysis [21]). It is therefore no surprise that the field of abstract interpretation and static analysis has seen significant attention both in academia and industry.

Unfortunately, the analysis of program transformations has not seen much attention so far. Program transformations are a central tool in language engineering and modern software development. For example, they are used for code desugaring, macro expansion, compiler optimization, refactoring, migration scripting, or model-driven development. The development of such program

© Springer Nature Switzerland AG 2020
D. Beyer and D. Zufferey (Eds.): VMCAI 2020, LNCS 11990, pp. 136–157, 2020.
https://doi.org/10.1007/978-3-030-39322-9_7

transformations tends to be difficult because they act at the metalevel and should work for a large class of potential input programs. Yet, there are hardly any static analyses for program transformation languages available, and it appears to be difficult to develop such analyses. To this end, we identified the following challenges:

Domain-Specific Features Program transformation languages such as Stratego [24], Rascal [14], and Maude [5] aim to simplify the development of program transformations. Therefore, they provide domain-specific language features such as rich pattern-matching, backtracking, and generic traversals. These domain-specific language features usually cannot be found in other general-purpose languages and the literature on static analysis provides only little guidance on how to tackle them.

Term Abstraction Programs are first-class in program transformations and are represented as terms (e.g., abstract syntax trees). Therefore, analysis developers need to find a good abstraction for terms, such as syntactic sorts or grammars [8]. This term abstraction heavily influences the precision and usefulness of the analysis and most of the analysis development effort should be spent on the design of this abstraction. We expect analysis developers to experiment with alternative term abstractions: The design of good abstract domains is inherent to the development of any abstract interpreter and cannot be avoided.

Soundness Developing an abstract interpreter that soundly predicts the generated code of program transformations is difficult. This is because real-world transformation languages have many edge cases and an abstract interpreter has to account for all of these edge cases to be sound. Furthermore, transformation languages often do not have a formal semantics, which makes it hard to verify that the abstract interpreter covered all cases.

In this paper we present a systematic approach to develop abstract interpreters for program transformation languages that addresses these challenges. It is based on the well-founded theory of *compositional soundness proofs* [13] and *reusable analysis components* [12]. In particular, our approach captures the core semantics of a transformation language with a *generic interpreter* [13] that does not refer to any analysis-specific details. This simplifies the analysis of the domain-specific language features. Furthermore, our approach decouples the term abstraction from the remainder of the analysis through an interface. This means that any term abstraction that implements this interface gives rise to a complete abstract interpreter. Thus, analysis developers can fully focus on developing good term abstractions. Lastly, our approach reuses language-independent functionality, such as abstractions for environments, exceptions and fixpoints, from the Sturdy standard library. This not only reduces the analysis development effort, but also simplifies its soundness proof as we can rely on the soundness proofs of the Sturdy library [12].

We demonstrate the feasibility and usefulness of our approach by developing abstract interpreters for Stratego [24]. Stratego is a complex dynamic program transformation language featuring rich pattern matching, backtracking, generic traversals, higher-order transformations, and an untyped program representation. Despite these difficulties, based on our approach we developed three novel abstract interpreters for Stratego: We developed a constant propagation analysis, a sort analysis, which checks that transformations are well-typed, and an advanced sort analysis, which can even validate type-changing generic traversals which produce ill-sorted intermediate terms. Our systematic approach was crucial in allowing us to focus on each of these abstract domains without being concerned with other aspects of the Stratego language. We implemented the analyses in Haskell in the *Sturdy* analysis framework and the code of the analyses is open-source.[1]

In summary, we make the following contributions:

- We propose a systematic approach to the development of abstract interpreters for program transformations, that lets analysis developers focus on designing the term abstraction.
- We show that many features of program transformation languages can be implemented on top of existing analysis functionality and do not require specific analysis code.
- We demonstrate the feasibility and usefulness of our approach by applying it to Stratego, for which we develop three novel abstract interpreters.

2   Illustrating Example: Singleton Analysis

The static analysis of program transformations can have significant merit helping developers to understand and debug their code and helping compilers to optimize the code. For example, we would like to support the following analyses: *Singleton analysis* to enable constant propagation, *purity analysis* to enable function inlining, *dead code* analysis to discover irrelevant code, *sort analysis* to prevent ill-sorted terms. While these and many other analyses would be useful, their development is complicated. In this section, we illustrate our approach by developing a singleton analysis for Stratego [24].

2.1   Abstract Interpreter for Program Transformations = Generic Interpreter + Term Abstraction

The development of analyses for program transformations is complicated for two reasons. First, each analysis requires a different term abstraction, with which it represents the generated code. The choice of term abstraction is crucial since it directly influences the precision, soundness, and termination of the analysis. Second, program transformation languages provide domain-specific language features such as rich pattern matching, backtracking, and generic traversals. Soundly approximating these features in an analysis is not easy, and resolving this challenge for each analysis anew is impractical.

---

[1] https://gitlab.rlp.net/plmz/sturdy/tree/master/stratego.

```
data Pat = Var String | As String Pat | Cons String [Pat]
  | StringLit String | NumLit Int | Explode Pat Pat
match :: (IsTerm term c, ArrowEnv String term c,
            ArrowExcept () c, ...) ⇒ c (Pat,term) term
match = proc (pat,t) → case pat of
  Var "_" → returnA ≺ t
  Var x → lookup
    (proc (t',(x,t)) → do t'' ← equal ≺ (t,t');
      insert ≺ (x,t''); returnA ≺ t'')
    (proc (x,t) → insert ≺ (x,t); returnA ≺ t) ≺ (x,(x,t))
  As v p → do t' ← match ≺ (Var v,t); match ≺ (p,t')
  StringLit s → matchStringLit ≺ (s,t)
  NumLit n → matchNumLit ≺ (n,t)
  Cons c ps → matchCons (zipWith match) ≺ (c,ps,t)
  Explode c ts → matchExplode
    (proc c' →  match ≺ (c,c'))
    (proc ts' → match ≺ (ts,ts')) ≪ t
```

Listing 1. Generic abstract pattern matching for Stratego.

In this paper, we propose a more systematic approach to developing static analyses for program transformations. To support static analyses for a given transformation language, we first develop a generic interpreter that implements the abstract semantics of the domain-specific language features in terms of standard language features whose abstract semantics is well-understood already. The generic interpreter is parametric in the term abstraction, such that we can derive different static analyses in a second step by providing different term abstractions. This architecture enables analysis developers to separately tackle the challenge of designing a good term abstraction.

We have developed a generic interpreter for Stratego based on the Sturdy analysis framework [12,13] in Haskell. We explain the full details of generic interpreters and background about Sturdy in Sect. 3. Here, we only illustrate a small part of the generic interpreter, namely pattern matching.

Listing 1 shows the generic analysis code for pattern matching. We parameterized the pattern-matching function **match** using a type class IsTerm as an interface. Pattern matching interacts with the term abstraction to deconstruct terms but implements other aspects generically. In Listing 1, we have highlighted all calls to operations of IsTerm; the remaining code is generic. We provide a short notational introduction before delving deeper into the analysis code.

Our approach is based on Sturdy, which requires analysis code to be written in *arrow style* [11]. Like monads, arrows (c x y) generalize pure functions (x → y) to support side-effects in a principled fashion. For users of our approach, this mostly means that they have to use Haskell's built-in syntax for arrows, as shown in Listing 1. Expression (proc x → e) introduces an arrow computation similar to the pure (λx → e). Do notation (do cmd∗)

denotes a sequence of arrow commands, where each command takes the form (y ← f ≺ x) or (f ≺ x) [18]. Command (y ← f ≺ x) calls f on x and stores the result in y; (f ≺ x) ignores the resulting value but not the potential side-effect of f. For a more in-depth introduction to arrows, we refer to Hughes's original paper [11] and online resources such as https://www.haskell.org/arrows.

The generic analysis code for pattern matching in Listing 1 describes a computation (c (Pat, t) t) that is parametric in c and t, but restricts these types through type-class constraints. Type t must implement the term abstraction interface IsTerm. Type c is an arrow that encapsulates the side-effects of the computation and must at least support environments and exception handling. We use these side-effects to implement pattern variables and backtracking in match.

Computation match takes a pattern and the matchee (the term to match) as input and yields the possibly refined term as output. For a wildcard pattern, we yield the matchee unchanged. For pattern variables, we look up the variable in the environment and distinguish two cases. If the variable is already bound to t', we require the matchee t to be equal to t'. If the variable is not bound yet, we insert a binding into the environment. For named subpatterns (As v p), we invoke the code for pattern variables recursively. The remaining four cases delegate to the term abstraction, passing the function for matching subterms as needed. When a pattern match fails, it throws an exception to reset all bound pattern variables.

The generic analysis code for pattern matching captures the essence of pattern matching in Stratego and closely follows Stratego's concrete semantics. In fact, the generic code can be instantiated to retrieve a fully functional concrete interpreter for Stratego. This makes the generic interpreter relatively easy to develop: no analysis-specific code is required. All analysis-specific code resides in instances of interfaces like ArrowExcept and IsTerm. Sturdy further exploits this to support compositional soundness proofs of analyses [13].

2.2 A Singleton Term Abstraction

We can derive complete Stratego analyses from the generic interpreter by instantiation. Specifically, we need to provide implementations for the type classes it is parameterized over. For standard interfaces like ArrowExcept and ArrowEnv, we provide reusable abstract semantics. However, the term abstraction IsTerm is language-specific and analysis-specific. Thus, this interface needs to be implemented by the analysis developer.

To illustrate the definition of term abstractions, here we develop a singleton analysis for Stratego. The analysis determines if (part of) a program transformation yields a constant output, such that the transformation can be optimized by constant propagation. Note that in this paper we are only concerned with the definition of analyses; the implementation of subsequent optimizations is outside the scope of the paper.

```
instance (ArrowExcept () c, ArrowJoin c, ...) ⇒ IsTerm Term̂ c where
  matchString = proc (s,t) → case t of
    Single ct → liftConcrete matchString ≺ (s,ct)
    Any → (returnA ≺ t) ⊔ (throw ≺ ())

  matchNum = proc (i,t) → case t of
    Single ct → liftConcrete matchNum ≺ (i,ct)
    Any → (returnA ≺ t) ⊔ (throw ≺ ())

  matchCons matchSub = proc (c,ps,t) → case t of
    Single (Cons d ts) | c ≡ d && eqLen ps ts → do
      ts' ← matchSub ≺ (ps,map Single ts)
      case allSingle ts' of
        Nothing → returnA ≺ Any
        Just cts → returnA ≺ Single (Cons c cts)
    Single _ → throw ≺ ()
    Any → do matchSub ≺ (ps,replicate (length ps) Any)
             (returnA ≺ t) ⊔ (throw ≺ ())
```

Listing 2. Parts of a singleton term abstraction for Stratego.

Each term abstraction needs to choose a term representation. For the singleton analysis, we use a simple data type $\widehat{\text{Term}}$ with two constructors:

```
data Term̂ = Single Term | Any
```

A term `Single ct` means that the transformation produces a single concrete Stratego term `ct` of type `Term`. In contrast, `Any` means that the transformation cannot be shown to produce a single concrete term.

Based on such term representation, a term abstraction for Stratego must implement the 10 functions from the IsTerm interface. We show the implementation of four of these functions in Listing 2 that also appeared in Listing 1.

Function matchString in Listing 2 defines a computation that takes a string value `s` and a matchee `t` of type `Term` as input. If `t` denotes a single concrete term, matchString delegates to the concrete string matching semantics using `liftConcrete`. However, if the matchee is `Any`, we cannot statically determine if the pattern match should succeed or fail. Thus, we join ⊔ the two potential outcomes: Either pattern matching succeeds and we return `t` unchanged, or pattern matching fails and we abort the matching by throwing an exception. Function matchNum is analogous to matchString.

Function matchCons distinguishes three cases. The first case checks if matchee `t` denotes a single concrete term with constructor `c` and right number of subterms. If so, we recursively match the subpatterns against the subterms, converted to singletons. Then, if all submatches yielded singleton terms again, we refine the matchee accordingly. The second case occurs when `t` denotes a singleton term but does not match the constructor pattern. In this case, we simply abort. Finally, if `t` is `Any`, we combine the two cases using a list of `Any` terms as subterms. Note that the recursive match on the subpatterns ps is necessary to bind pattern variables that may occur.

2.3 Soundness

Our approach drastically simplifies the soundness proof of the abstract interpreter. In particular, by factoring the concrete and abstract interpreter into a generic interpreter, we do not have to worry about soundness of the generic interpreter. Instead, its soundness proof follows by composing the proof of smaller soundness lemmas about its instances [13]. Furthermore, because we instantiate the generic interpreter with sound analysis components for environments, stores and exceptions, we do not have to worry about soundness of these analysis concerns either [12]. All that is left to prove, is the soundness of the term operations.

2.4 Summary

Our approach to developing static analyses for program transformations consists of two steps. First, develop a generic interpreter based on standard semantic components and a parametric term abstraction. Second, define a term abstraction and instantiate the generic interpreter. While the term abstraction is language-specific and analysis-specific, the generic interpreter can be reused across analyses and only needs to be implemented once per transformation language. In the subsequent section, we explain how to develop and instantiate generic interpreters for transformation languages using standard semantic components. Sections 4 and 5.1 demonstrate the development of sophisticated term abstractions.

3   Generic Interpreters for Program Transformations

Creating sound static analyses is a laborious and error-prone process. While there is a rich body of literature on analyzing functional and imperative programming languages, static analysis of program transformation languages is under-explored. Most work in the area of program transformations so far focused on type checking, which considers each rewriting separately and is limited to intra-procedural analysis.

The key enabler of our approach are generic interpreters that can be instantiated with different term abstractions to obtain different analyses. In this section, we demonstrate our approach at the example of Stratego and show how to develop generic interpreters for Stratego. In particular, we show that the features of program transformation languages do *not* require specific analysis code but can be mapped to existing language concepts whose analysis is already well-understood.

```
desugar-type:  PairType(t1,t2)  →  ⟦Pair<~t1,~t2>⟧
desugar-expr:  PairExpr(e1,e2)  →  ⟦new Pair<>(~e1,~e2)⟧

topdown(s) = s; all(topdown(s))          try(s) = s <+ id
main = topdown(try(desugar-type + desugar-expr))
```

Listing 3. A generic traversal for desugaring pair notation.

3.1   The Program Transformation Language Stratego

Stratego is a program transformation language featuring rich pattern matching, backtracking, and generic traversals [24]. For example, consider the following desugaring of Java extended with pairs [9] in Listing 3. The two rewrite rules of the form above use pattern matching to select pair types and expressions, respectively. They then generate representations of pair types and expressions using the `Pair` class. The `main` rewriting strategy traverses the input AST top-down and tries to apply both rewrite rules at every node, leaving a node unchanged if neither rule applies. We also added the definitions of the higher-order functions `topdown` and `try` from the standard library. The built-in primitive `all` takes a transformation and applies it to each direct subterm of the current term. Function `topdown` uses `all` to realize a generic top-down traversal over a term, applying `s` to every node. Function `try` uses left-biased choice `<+` to catch any failure in `s` and to resume with the identity function `id` instead. Furthermore, the Stratego compiler translates the rewrite rules of the form `r : p → t` to transformations `r = ?p; !t`:

```
desugar-type = ?PairType(t1,t2); !ClassType("Pair",[t1,t2])
desugar-expr = ?PairExpr(e1,e2); !NewInstance("Pair",[e1,e2])
```

The translated rule first matches the pattern `p`, binding all pattern variables to the respective subterms and then builds the term `t` using the abstract syntax of Java.

3.2   A Generic Interpreter for Stratego

We demonstrate how to map these language features to standard language concepts and how this enables static analysis of program transformations. To this end, we developed a generic interpreter for Stratego.[2] The generic interpreter is based on a previous Sturdy case study [13] that was never described in detail.

We consider fully desugared Stratego code in our interpreter, ignoring Stratego's dynamic rules. This core Stratego language [23] only contains 12 constructs as defined by the data type `Strat` in Listing 4. We explain these constructs together with their generic semantics, shown in the same listing. The semantics is defined by a function `eval` that accepts a Stratego program and yields

---

[2] https://gitlab.rlp.net/plmz/sturdy/blob/master/stratego/src/GenericInterpreter. hs.

```
data Strat = Match Pat | Build Pat | Id | Seq Strat Strat
    | Fail | GuardedChoice Strat Strat Strat | Scope [String] Strat
    | Call String [Strat] [String] | Let [(String,Strategy)] Strat
    | One Strat | Some Strat | All Strat

eval :: (IsTerm term c, ArrowEnv String term c, ArrowExcept () c,
           ArrowFix c, ...) ⇒ Strat → c term term
eval = fix $ λev strat → case strat of
  Match pat → proc t → match ≺ (pat,t)
  Build pat → proc _ → build ≺ pat

  Id → proc x → returnA ≺ x
  Seq s1 s2 → proc t1 →
      do t2 ← ev s1 ≺ t1; t3 ← ev s2 ≺ t2; returnA ≺ t3
  Fail → proc _ → throw ≺ ()
  GuardedChoice s1 s2 s3 → try (ev s1) (ev s2) (ev s3)

  Scope vars s → scoped vars (ev s)
  Call f ss ts → proc t → do
    senv ← readStratEnv ≺ ()
    case Map.lookup f senv of
      Just (Closure s@(Strat _ ps _) senv') → do
        args ← mapA lookupOrFail ≺ ts
        scoped ps (invoke ev) -≪ (s, senv', ss, args, t)
      Nothing → failString ≺ "Cannot␣find␣strat"
  Let bnds body → let_ bnds body eval'

  One s → mapSubterms (one (ev s))
  Some s → mapSubterms (some (ev s))
  All s → mapSubterms (all (ev s))

scoped vars f = proc t → do
  oldEnv ← getEnv ≺ ()
  deleteEnvVars ≺ vars
  finally (proc (t,_) → f ≺ t)
          (proc (_,oldE) → restoreEnvVars vars ≺ oldE)
    ≺ (t, oldEnv)
```

Listing 4. Generic interpreter for Stratego.

a computation of type (c term term), meaning that a Stratego program takes a term as input and yields another term as output. That is, Stratego programs are term transformations as expected. The arrow c captures the side-effects of the computation, as explained in Sect. 2.1.

The first two core Stratego constructs deconstruct and construct terms. A (Match pat) transformation is based on a term pattern pat, which it matches against the input term t. Function match from Listing 1 implements the actual pattern matching, as we have discussed in Sect. 2. Recall that match binds pattern variables in the environment as a side-effect and throws an exception if the pattern match fails. We will see shortly how these side-effects are supported by the generic interpreter. A (Build pat) transformation is the dual of match: it constructs a new term according to the pattern, filling in information from the environment in place of pattern variables.

The next four core Stratego constructs handle control-flow. The identity transformation Id returns the input term unchanged. A sequence (Seq s1 s2) of transformations s1 and s2 pipes the output of s1 into s2. The Fail transformation never succeeds and always throws an exception using throw, which we also used to indicate failed pattern matches. To catch such exceptions, core Stratego programs can use guarded choice, written (s1 < s2 + s3) in Stratego notation. Guarded choice runs s3 if s1 fails (throws an exception) and s2 otherwise. We implemented guarded choice using the try function. Like throw, try is declared in the ArrowExcept interface and allows us to catch exceptions triggered by throw. There are two things to note here:

- The implementation of throw and try are not specific to Stratego and are provided as sound reusable analysis components [12] by the standard library of Sturdy. We are effectively mapping Stratego features to these pre-defined features of Sturdy.
- We can choose how exceptions affect the variables bound during pattern matching. For Stratego, we need exceptions to undo variable bindings in order to correctly implement backtracking. However, in other languages we may want to retain the state of a computation even after an exception was thrown.

The next three constructs handle scoping, strategy calls, and local strategy definitions. We discuss the first two of these in some detail. Stratego's scoping is somewhat unconventional, because Stratego has explicit scope declarations and environments follow store-passing style. Variables listed in a scope declaration are lexically scoped as usual, but other variables can occur in the environment and must be preserved. We use function scoped (at the bottom of Listing 4) to implement this scoping. First, we unbind the scoped variables from the current environment to allow pattern matching to bind them afresh. Second, after the scoped code finishes, we restore the bindings of scoped variables from the old environment while retaining other bindings from the current environment unchanged. Scoping also occurs when calling a strategy. To evaluate a call, we first find the strategy definition, then lookup the term arguments ts in the current environment, and then invoke the strategy using scoped for the term parameters ps.

The final three constructs are generic traversals that use mapSubterms to call one, some, or all on the subterms of the current input term. Function mapSubterms is part of the IsTerm interface and thus analysis-specific because depends on the term representation. Functions one, some, or all are part of the generic interpreter and ensure that, respectively, exactly one, at least one, or all of subterms are transformed by the given strategy s. This way our generic interpreter separates term-specific operations from operations that can be defined generically.

```
class Arrow c ⇒ IsTerm term c where
  matchString    :: c (String ,term) term
  matchNum       :: c (Int ,term) term
  matchCons      :: c ([p] ,[term]) [term] →
                    c (String ,[p] ,term) term
  matchExplode   :: c term term → c term term → c term term

  buildString    :: c String term
  buildNum       :: c Int term
  buildCons      :: c (String ,[term]) term
  buildExplode   :: c (term ,term) term

  equal          :: c (term ,term) term
  mapSubterms    :: c [term] [term] → c term term
```

Listing 5. An interface for operations on terms.

3.3   The Term Abstraction

At this point, all that it takes to define a Stratego analysis is to implement the IsTerm interface for a new term abstraction. The rest of the analysis is given by the generic interpreter and reusable functionality from the Sturdy library.

The generic interpreter described in the previous section crucially relies on the term abstraction. In particular, pattern matching, term construction, and generic traversals must inspect or manipulate terms. In Sect. 2 we have seen how match used term operations and how we could implement these for the singleton term abstraction. Here we show the complete interface for term abstractions.

Stratego terms are strings, numbers, or constructor terms:

```
data Term = Cons String [Term] | StringLit String | NumLit Int
```

Our interface must at least provide operations to match and construct such terms. In addition, we must support Stratego's generic traversals and explode patterns. Note that Stratego represents lists using constructors Cons and Nil:

```
Cons "Cons" [NumLit 1, Cons "Cons" [NumLit 2, Cons "Nil" []]]
```

We designed an interface for term abstractions of Stratego terms that requires only 10 operations. Listing 5 shows the corresponding type class. The interface contains four functions for pattern matching, four functions for term construction, one equality function, and one function to map subterms.

We have discussed the functions for pattern matching Sect. 2 already. Function matchCons takes a function for matching subterms against subpatterns. Function matchExplode takes functions for matching the constructor name and the subterms. The functions for term construction are straightforward. While function buildCons takes a String and a list of terms, function buildExplode takes two terms. The first of these terms must be a string term, the second one must represent a list of terms. Finally, we require functions for checking the equality of two terms and for mapping a function over a term's subterms. This last function enables generic traversals as shown in Listing 4.

Our interface for term abstractions can be instantiated in various ways by defining instances of the type class. We have shown an instance for the singleton term abstraction in Listing 2 and will describe further term abstractions in the upcoming sections. But it is worth noting that the interface can also be instantiated for concrete Stratego terms:

```
instance ... ⇒ IsTerm Term c where ...
```

This concrete term instance allows us to run the generic interpreter as a concrete Stratego semantics. This is not only great for testing the generic interpreter against a reference implementation of Stratego, but also crucial for proving the soundness of term abstractions against the concrete semantics.

To summarize, we implemented the Stratego language semantics as a generic interpreter based on a few term operations only. The generic interpreter maps many aspects of Stratego language to standard language concepts such as environments and exceptions. For these language concepts, we reuse the abstract semantics found in the Sturdy standard library. In the end, to design and implement a new analysis for Stratego, all it takes is a new term abstraction. We exploit this reduction of effort in the next two sections, where we develop two novel static analyses for Stratego by defining term abstractions.

4   Sort Analysis

In this section, we define an inter-procedural sort analysis for Stratego. The analysis checks if a program transformation generates well-formed programs and to which sort the program belongs. That is, we implement a term abstraction where we choose to represent terms through their sort.

4.1   Sorts and Sort Contexts

We describe the sorts of Stratego terms by the following Haskell datatype:

```
data Sort = Lexical | Numerical | Sort String | List Sort
  | Tuple [Sort] | Option Sort | Bottom | Top
```

Sort Lexical represents string values, Numerical represents numeric values. We use (Sort s) to represent named sorts such as (Sort "Exp"). We further include sorts for representing Stratego's lists, tuples, and option terms. Finally, Bottom represents the empty set of terms and Top represents all terms (also ill-formed ones). This means, we can guarantee a term is well-formed if its sort is not Top.

To associate terms to sorts, we parse the declaration of constructor signatures that are part of any Stratego program. Typically, these declarations are automatically derived from the grammar of the source and target language.

```
Num : Int → ArithExp
Add : ArithExp * ArithExp → ArithExp
    : ArithExp → PythonExp
```

Each line declares a constructor, the sorts of its arguments and the generated sort. We allow overloaded constructor signatures as long as they generate terms of the same sort. That is, if $c : s_1 \ldots s_m \to s \in \Gamma$ and $c : s_1' \ldots s_n' \to s' \in \Gamma$, then $s = s'$.

The third signature declares that any term of sort `ArithExp` should also be considered a term of sort `PythonExp`. This is the result of injection production in the grammar and effectively declares a subtype relation `ArithExp <: PythonExp`. Dealing with subtyping correctly is one of the major challenges of developing a sort analysis. Thanks to our separation of concerns, we can fully focus on that challenge here.

We collect all constructor signatures and the subtyping relation in a sort context:

```
type Sig = ([Sort], Sort)
data Context = Context { sorts :: Map Sort [(String,Sig)],
                         subtypes :: SubtypeRelation }
```

Since we require the context when operating on sorts, we actually represent terms abstractly as a pair `(Sort,Context)`. However, all terms refer to the same context and the context never changes. To simplify the presentation in this paper, we assume the context is globally known and terms are represented by `Sort` alone.

4.2   Abstract Term Operations

In the remainder of this section, we explain how to implement the term abstraction for our sort analysis. To this end, we have to provide an instance of type class `IsTerm` as shown in Listing 6. We only show the code for lists and user-defined constructor and omit the other cases for tuples and optionals for brevity.

As a warm-up, consider operation `buildString` that yields sort `Lexical` independent of the string literal. When matching a string against sort `s` in `matchString`, the match can only succeed if `Lexical` terms may be part of `s` terms. Otherwise the match must fail.

Arguably the most interesting part of the term abstraction is building and matching constructor terms. Let's start with operation `buildCons`, which obtains the constructor name `c` and the list of subsorts `ss`. In Stratego, list, tuple, and optional terms use reserved constructor names. We include one case for each reserved constructor to generate the appropriate sort. For example, constructor `Nil` can be applied to an empty argument list to generate an empty list. This list has sort `(List Bottom)`. Constructor `Cons` generates a compound term that has sort list if the second argument was a list. The sort of the resulting list is the least super-sort ($\sqcup$) of the new head list and the tail. The empty constructor `""` generates tuples; `None` and `Some` generate optional terms.

```
instance (ArrowExcept () c, ArrowJoin c, ...) ⇒ IsTerm Sort c where
   buildString = proc _ → returnA ≺ Lexical

   matchString = proc (_,s) → if subtype Lexical s
      then (returnA ≺ s) ⊔ (throw ≺ ()) else throw ≺ ()

   buildCons = proc (c, ss) → returnA ≺ case (c, ss) of
      ("Nil",[]) → List Bottom
      ("Cons",[a,s]) | subtype (List Bottom) s → List a ⊔ s
      _ → ⊓ (Top : [t | (ss',t) ← constrSigs c, ss ⊑ ss'])

   matchCons matchSubs = proc (c,ps,s)→ case (c,ps)
      ("Nil",[]) → if subtype (List Bottom) s
         then (buildCons≺("Nil",[])) ⊔ (throw≺()) else throw≺()
      ("Cons",[hd,tl]) → if subtype (List Bottom) s
         then do let subterms = [getListElem s, s]
                 ss ← matchSubs ≺ ([hd,tl],subterms)
                 (buildCons ≺ ("Cons",ss)) ⊔ (throw ≺ ())
         else throw ≺ ()
      _ → ⊔ (proc (c',ss) → if c ≡ c' && length ss ≡ length ps
         then do ss' ← matchSubs ≺ (ps,ss); cons ≺ (c,ss')
         else throw ≺ ()) ≪ constructorsOfSort s

   mapSubterms f = proc s → do ⊔ (proc (c,ts) →
      do ts' ← f ≺ ts buildCons ≺ (c,ts'))
         ≺ constructorsOfSort s
```

Listing 6. Abstract term operations for the sort analysis.

The last case of buildCons handles user-defined constructor symbols c. We use (constrSigs c) to look up the signatures (ss',t) of c from the sort context. We only retain those signatures that can accept the constructor arguments ss. Finally, we collect all result sorts t and compute their greatest lower bound. If none of the signatures matches, we return sort Top. For example, consider the call:

buildCons ≺ ("While",[Sort "Exp",Sort "Block"])

If the signature of While is (Exp ∗ Block → Stmt), we obtain Sort "Stmt''" as result. If the signature is instead declared as (Exp ∗ Exp → Stmt), we obtain Top because the constructed term is ill-formed (unless Block is a sub-sort of Exp).

Operation matchCons is quite complex, although all cases for reserved constructors follow the same pattern:

1. We check if the sort of the current term s is compatible with the matched constructor. For example, a match against Nil can only succeed if the sort is a list.

```
desugar-type: PairType(t1,t2) → [Pair<~t1,~t2>]
desugar-expr: PairExpr(e1,e2) → [new Pair<>(~e1,~e2)]

topdown(s) = s; all(topdown(s))      try(s) = s <+ id
main = topdown(try(desugar-type + desugar-expr))
```

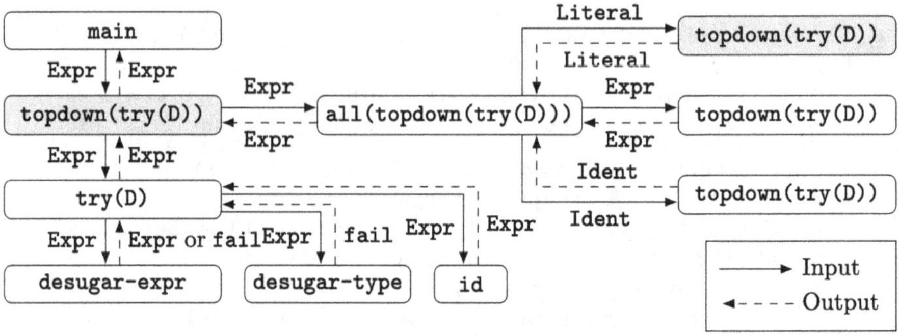

Fig. 1. A simplified trace of the sort analysis of the pair desugaring, where we abbreviate desugar-type + desugar-expr with D.

2. We retrieve the subterm sorts if any. For example, for Cons we have two subterms: the head element and the tail list. Auxiliary function getListElem carefully finds all possible list elements, taking subtyping into account.
3. We match the subterms against the subpatterns, yielding refined subterms ss.
4. We refine the current term by calling buildCons on the refined subterms and the matched constructor. Since matching may always fail, we join the result with a call to throw.

The last case of matchCons again handles user-defined constructor symbols c. We use constructorsOfsort s to obtain all constructors c' and their argument types ss. If the constructor has the required name and the right number of arguments, then the corresponding match might succeed. We match the subterms and refine the current term as in the other cases, but the we compute the least upper bound over all possible results. For example, when we match a constructor Add against sort Exp, we would lookup all constructors that generate sort Exp. For (Add : Exp * Exp → Exp) the match can succeed, but for (Var : Lexical → Exp) the match must fail. The join operator merges the results to compute a sound approximation.

Lastly, we show the code of mapSubterms, which needs to retrieve the current subterms as a list and pass them to f. However, sorts do not directly point out their subterms. Again we use constructorsOfsort s to retrieve the sorts of subterms indirectly by finding all constructors of the current sort and taking their parameter lists. For example, if we call mapSubterms with sort "Exp", then computation f will be called on [Sort "Exp", Sort "Exp"] for constructor Add and on [Lexical] for constructor Var.

To summarize, in this section we defined a sort analysis for Stratego, simply by designing a sort term abstraction which implements the IsTerm interface. The rest of the analysis we get for free from the generic interpreter and reusable analysis code. As the reader probably noticed, the term abstraction for sorts is fairly complex in its own right. Being able to focus on the term abstraction without considering other analysis aspects was crucial.

4.3   Sort Analysis and Generic Traversals

In this subsection, we showcase the inter-procedurality of our sort analysis by analyzing generic traversals. A generic traversal traverses a syntax tree independent of its shape and transforms the visited nodes. Statically assigning types to a generic traversal is notoriously difficult, because the type needs to summarize all changes the traversal does to the entire tree. In this subsection, we will illustrate how our inter-procedural sort analysis can support some generic traversals, before refining our analysis further in the subsequent section.

Consider the trace of the sort analysis (Fig. 1) of the pair desugaring from Sect. 3.1. The trace starts in the main function with an input term of sort Expr. The main function calls topdown, which calls try(D), which calls the desugaring rules desugar-type + desugar-expr. The rule desugar-expr either yields a term of sort Expr or fails because the pattern PairExpr(...) matches some but not all terms of sort Expr. Furthermore, the rule desugar-type definitely fails because no terms of sort Expr match the pattern PairType(...). Even though one of the rules failed, the call try(D) produces a successful result by applying the input term to the identity transformation. The function topdown then passes the resulting term of sort Expr to the generic traversal all(...). Since we know the sort of the current term, we enumerate all relevant constructors and the sorts of their direct subterms and recursively analyze the desugaring for them. In the example trace of Fig. 1, we consider three subterm sorts of Expr. The second and third recursive call to topdown(try(D)) resolve easily, whereas the first recursive call would end up in a cycle (shaded nodes in Fig. 1). To this end, we use a fixpoint algorithm with widening to ensure that the analysis terminates.

The example shows why it is hard to analyze the type of a generic traversal: For different input sorts, a generic traversal might produce different output sorts. Therefore, our sort analysis reanalyzes a generic traversal for each input sort, instead of assigning a fixed type like a type checker would do.

The example we considered here is a special case of generic traversals, known as type-preserving. A generic traversal is type-preserving if the sort of the input and output term are the same at every node. However, some generic traversals change the sort of the input term. The sort analysis of this section is not capable of analyzing such type-changing generic traversals. To this end, we require a more precise analysis, which we develop in the following section.

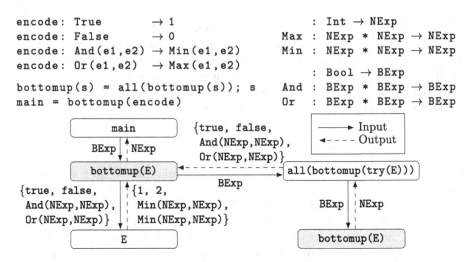

Fig. 2. The top of the figure contains a type-changing generic traversal that translates boolean to numeric expressions. The bottom contains the analysis trace of the transformation, where we abbreviate `encode` with **E**.

5   Locally Ill-Sorted Sort Analysis

Many program transformations, like a compiler, translate terms from one sort to terms of another sort. When these program transformations use generic traversals, they produce mixed intermediate terms, which contain subterms of the input sort *and* subterms of the output sort. Because mixed intermediate terms are not well-sorted, these program transformations are challenging to type check.

For example, consider the traversal in Fig. 2 that translates Boolean expressions into numeric expressions in a bottom-up fashion. The boolean expression `And(True(),False())` is transformed in two steps:

`And(True(),False())` ⤳ `And(1,0)` ⤳ `Min(1,0)`

Even though the input term `And(True(),False())` is a valid boolean expression and the output term `Min(1,0)` a valid numeric expression, the transformation creates an intermediate term `And(1,0)`, which is ill-sorted. The sort analysis of the previous section is only able to check transformations which produce well-sorted terms and therefore cannot handle this example. To analyze this example, we need a more precise sort analysis that can represent ill-sorted terms, which we develop in the remainder of this section

5.1   Term Abstraction for Ill-Sorted Terms

The key idea is to use a term abstraction which can represent terms with well-sorted leafs and an possible ill-sorted prefix, such as `And(NumExp,NumExp)`. This abstract term represents all terms with `"And"` as top-level constructor and two

```
matchCons matchSub = proc (c,ps,t) → case t of
   MaybeSorted cs → matchCons' ≺(c,ps,cs)
   Sorted s → Sort.matchCons matchSub≺(c,ps,lookupSort' ctx s)
   where
   matchCons' = proc (c,ps,cs) → ⨆(proc (c',ss) →
      if c == c' && length ss == length ps
         then do ss' ← mapSub ≺ (ps,ss); cons ≺ (c,ss')
         else throw ≺ ()) -≪ cs
buildCons = proc (c,ts) → returnA ≺ MaybeSorted [(c,ts)]
widening :: Context → Int → Term → Term → Term
widening ctx k cs1 cs2
   | k == 0 = Sorted (typecheck ctx (cs1 ⊔ cs2))
   | otherwise =
      MaybeSorted (zipSubterms (termWidening ctx (k-1)) cs1
      cs2)
   where typecheck :: Context → Term → Sort
```

Listing 7. Abstract term operations for the locally ill-sorted sort analysis.

numeric expressions as subterms. We implement this term abstraction with the following Haskell type:

```
data Term = Sorted Sort | MaybeSorted (Set (String,[Term]))
```

The case `Sorted` s represents well-sorted terms that belong to sort s, and the case `MaybeSorted` represents terms with an possibly ill-sorted prefix. For example, this datatype allows us to represent the ill-sorted term `And(1,0)` with the abstract term

```
MaybeSorted [("And",[Sorted "NExp",Sorted "NExp"])].
```

5.2   Abstract Term Operations

We develop an analysis for Stratego by implementing the term operations with the term abstraction from above. We only discuss the `matchCons` and `buildCons` operations (Listing 7), because the remaining functions are similar to the operations of the sort analysis.

The `matchCons` operation first matches on the term representation and in both cases calls the `matchCons'` helper function, which compares the constructors, arity and subterms. The `lookupSort'` function, similar to Listing 6, looks up all constructor signature for a sort, but additionally converts the signatures to abstract terms. This `matchCons` operation is more than the `matchCons` of the sort analysis, because we may know the top-level constructor of the term. This improved precision results in more pattern matches which *unconditionally* succeed or fail.

In contrast to the sort analysis, the `buildCons` operation in Listing 7 does not check if the constructor and its subterms belong to a valid sort. Instead, it constructs a new abstract term, which may or may not be well-sorted. The type checking of this term is then delayed until a later point.

With these definitions, the analysis would be able to check some type-changing generic traversals, however, it might not terminate because the abstract terms might grow arbitrarily large. To avoid this problem, we reduce the size of abstract terms by type checking their subterms. For example, we can type check the immediate subterms of `Or(And(1,0),1)` to obtain the abstract term `Or(⊤,NumExp)`. In the new term, the sort ⊤ indicates the type checking of `And(1,0)` failed and the term is ill-sorted. We use this technique in a widening operator [7] that ensures that the analysis terminates. The operator simply type checks all subterms deeper than a certain limit k, such that the resulting terms are not deeper than k.

5.3   Analyzing Type-Changing Generic Traversals

In the remainder of this section, we discuss how the analysis of this section checks type-changing generic traversals. To this end, we discuss an analysis trace of the example at the beginning of this of this section (Fig. 2).

The trace in Fig. 2 shows only the final fixpoint iteration (earlier iterations produce subsets of the sets shown in the trace). It starts with the analysis of the `main` function with the boolean expression sort `BExp`, which is then passed to `bottomup(E)`. In contrast to the top-down traversal, the bottom-up traversal first traverses with `all(bottomup(E))` over the subterms of boolean expressions and replaces them by numeric expressions, e.g., `And(NExp,NExp)`. The resulting set of ill-sorted terms is then passed to the rewrite rule `E`. The rule `E` then replaces each top-level boolean constructor with a numeric constructor without touching the subterms. All terms in the resulting set are now well-typed and `bottomup(E)` applies the widening operator to reduce this set to `NExp`.

In summary, we defined an advanced sort analysis, which can represent ill-sorted terms. This analysis is able to check type-changing generic traversals, which produces ill-sorted intermediate terms.

6   Related Work

Transformation languages like Stratego [10] and PLT Redex [17] have a dynamic type checker for syntactic well-formedness. While dynamic type checking supports generic traversals, it does not help developers of transformations to understand the code. In contrast, we developed a static analysis such that program transformations can be checked before running them.

Other program transformation languages like Ott [22], Maude [5], Tom [2] and Rascal [14] use static type checking to ensure syntactic well-formedness. However, these languages do not support or struggle to statically check arbitrary generic traversals. Ott is a language for specifying rewrite systems and exporting them to proof assistants such as Coq or Isabelle. However, it does not support generic traversals. Maude is a language for specifying rewrite systems in membership equational logic. However, it implements generic traversals with reflection and hence cannot statically check their type. Tom and Rascal are statically typed transformation languages with support for type-preserving generic traversals. However, they do not support type-changing generic traversals. We explained in Sect. 5 why conventional static type checkers cannot analyze type-changing generic traversals: these traversals produce intermediate terms which are ill-sorted. In this work, we aim to analyze type-preserving as well as type-changing generic traversals. We solve this problem by defining a static analysis which can represent terms with a finite ill-sorted prefix. In contrast to a conventional type checking, this term abstraction is more precise than regular types, but requires computing a fixed point.

Lämmel distinguishes "type-preserving" from "type-unifying" generic traversals [15], as realized in Scrap-Your-Boilerplate [19]. A unifying generic traversal is a fold over the term that yields a value of the same "unified" type at each node. These kinds of generic traversals are easier to type statically, however, not all generic traversals fit in one of these two typing schemes. For example, a generic traversal that translates code from one language to another is neither type-preserving nor type-unifying. Rather than developing additional specialized traversal styles, our paper aims to support static analysis for arbitrary generic traversals.

Most closely related to our work, Al-Sibahi et al. present an abstract interpreter of a subset of Rascal, including generic traversals [1]. Al-Sibahi et al. use inductive refinement types as abstract domain. The main difference of our work is that we separated analysis-independent concerns (the generic interpreter) from analysis-specific concerns (the instances). This way we can develop different analyses for program transformations with relatively little effort. Furthermore, it also simplifies the analysis definition, because most of the language complexity is captured in the generic interpreter. Lastly, our work is based on the well-founded theory of compositional soundness proofs [13] provided by the Sturdy framework. This allows us to verify that soundness of analyses more easily, as we only need to prove that the instances are sound.

CompCert [16] is a formally verified C compiler. The compiler guarantees that the compiled program has the same semantics as the input program. To this end, each program transformation in the compiler passes has to preserve the semantics of the transformed program. While CompCert focuses on the semantics of the transformed program, the static analyses for program transformations in this work have to satisfy a different correctness property. Soundness of these static analyses guarantees that the analyses results overapproximate which programs can be generated by a program transformation. However, soundness does not give any guarantees about the semantics of the transformed program. In the future, we aim to develop more precise analyses for program transformation languages that allow us to draw conclusion about the semantics of transformed programs.

7   Conclusion

To summarize, in this work, we presented a systematic approach to designing static analyses for program transformations. Key of our approach is to capture the core semantics of the program transformations with a *generic interpreter* that does not refer to any analysis-specific details. This lets the analysis developer focus on designing a good abstraction for programs. We demonstrated the usefulness of our approach by designing three analyses for the program transformation language Stratego. Our sort analyses are able to check the well-sortedness of type-preserving and even type-changing generic traversals.

Acknowledgements. This research was supported by DFG grant "Evolute". We thank André Pacak and Tamás Szabó who provided helpful feedback on the introduction.

References

1. Al-Sibahi, A.S., Jensen, T.P., Dimovski, A.S., Wasowski, A.: Verification of high-level transformations with inductive refinement types. CoRR (2018)
2. Balland, E., Brauner, P., Kopetz, R., Moreau, P.-E., Reilles, A.: Tom: piggybacking rewriting on Java. In: Baader, F. (ed.) RTA 2007. LNCS, vol. 4533, pp. 36–47. Springer, Heidelberg (2007). https://doi.org/10.1007/978-3-540-73449-9_5
3. Callahan, D., Cooper, K.D., Kennedy, K., Torczon, L.: Interprocedural constant propagation. In: Proceedings of the 1986 SIGPLAN Symposium on Compiler Construction, Palo Alto, California, USA, 25–27 June 1986, pp. 152–161 (1986)
4. Chen, Y.-F.R., Gansner, E.R., Koutsofios, E.: A C++ data model supporting reachability analysis and dead code detection. In: Jazayeri, M., Schauer, H. (eds.) ESEC/SIGSOFT FSE-1997. LNCS, vol. 1301, pp. 414–431. Springer, Heidelberg (1997). https://doi.org/10.1007/3-540-63531-9_28
5. Clavel, M., et al.: Maude: specification and programming in rewriting logic. Theor. Comput. Sci. **285**(2), 187–243 (2002)
6. Cousot, P., Cousot, R.: Abstract interpretation: a unified lattice model for static analysis of programs by construction or approximation of fixpoints. In: Conference Record of the Fourth ACM Symposium on Principles of Programming Languages, Los Angeles, California, USA, January 1977, pp. 238–252 (1977)
7. Cousot, P., Cousot, R.: Comparing the Galois connection and widening/narrowing approaches to abstract interpretation. In: Bruynooghe, M., Wirsing, M. (eds.) PLILP 1992. LNCS, vol. 631, pp. 269–295. Springer, Heidelberg (1992). https://doi.org/10.1007/3-540-55844-6_142
8. Cousot, P., Cousot, R.: Formal language, grammar and set-constraint-based program analysis by abstract interpretation. In: Proceedings of the Seventh International Conference on Functional Programming Languages and Computer Architecture, FPCA 1995, La Jolla, California, USA, 25–28 June 1995, pp. 170–181 (1995)
9. Erdweg, S., Rendel, T., Kästner, C., Ostermann, K.: SugarJ: library-based syntactic language extensibility. In: Proceedings of the 26th Annual ACM SIGPLAN Conference on Object-Oriented Programming, Systems, Languages, and Applications, OOPSLA 2011, part of SPLASH 2011, Portland, OR, USA, 22–27 October 2011, pp. 391–406 (2011)

10. Erdweg, S., Vergu, V., Mezini, M., Visser, E.: Modular specification and dynamic enforcement of syntactic language constraints. In: Proceedings of International Conference on Modularity (AOSD), pp. 241–252. ACM (2014)
11. Hughes, J.: Generalising monads to arrows. Sci. Comput. Program. **37**(1–3), 67–111 (2000)
12. Keidel, S., Erdweg, S.: Compositional soundness proofs of abstract interpreters. PACMPL **3**(OOPSLA), 176:1–176:28 (2019). https://dblp.uni-trier.de/rec/bibtex/journals/pacmpl/KeidelE19
13. Keidel, S., Poulsen, C.B., Erdweg, S.: Compositional soundness proofs of abstract interpreters. PACMPL **2**(ICFP), 72:1–72:26 (2018)
14. Klint, P., van der Storm, T., Vinju, J.J.: RASCAL: a domain specific language for source code analysis and manipulation. In: Ninth IEEE International Working Conference on Source Code Analysis and Manipulation, SCAM 2009, Edmonton, Alberta, Canada, 20–21 September 2009, pp. 168–177 (2009)
15. Lämmel, R.: Typed generic traversal with term rewriting strategies. Log. Algebr. Program. **54**(1–2), 1–64 (2003)
16. Leroy, X., et al.: The CompCert C verified compiler. Documentation and user's manual. INRIA Paris-Rocquencourt 53 (2012)
17. Matthews, J., Findler, R.B., Flatt, M., Felleisen, M.: A visual environment for developing context-sensitive term rewriting systems. In: van Oostrom, V. (ed.) RTA 2004. LNCS, vol. 3091, pp. 301–311. Springer, Heidelberg (2004). https://doi.org/10.1007/978-3-540-25979-4_21
18. Paterson, R.: A new notation for arrows. In: Proceedings of the Sixth ACM SIGPLAN International Conference on Functional Programming (ICFP 2001), Firenze, Florence, Italy, 3–5 September 2001, pp. 229–240 (2001)
19. Jones, S.P., Lämmel, R.: Scrap your boilerplate. In: Ohori, A. (ed.) APLAS 2003. LNCS, vol. 2895, pp. 357–357. Springer, Heidelberg (2003). https://doi.org/10.1007/978-3-540-40018-9_23
20. Pierce, B.C.: Types and Programming Languages. MIT Press, Cambridge (2002)
21. Sălcianu, A., Rinard, M.: Purity and side effect analysis for Java programs. In: Cousot, R. (ed.) VMCAI 2005. LNCS, vol. 3385, pp. 199–215. Springer, Heidelberg (2005). https://doi.org/10.1007/978-3-540-30579-8_14
22. Sewell, P., et al.: Ott: effective tool support for the working semanticist. Funct. Program. **20**(1), 71–122 (2010)
23. Visser, E., Benaissa, Z.: A core language for rewriting. Electr. Notes Theor. Comput. Sci. **15**, 422–441 (1998)
24. Visser, E., Benaissa, Z., Tolmach, A.P.: Building program optimizers with rewriting strategies. In: Proceedings of the Third ACM SIGPLAN International Conference on Functional Programming (ICFP 1998), Baltimore, Maryland, USA, 27–29 September 1998, pp. 13–26 (1998)
25. Xie, Y., Chou, A., Engler, D.R.: ARCHER: using symbolic, path-sensitive analysis to detect memory access errors. In: Proceedings of the 11th ACM SIGSOFT Symposium on Foundations of Software Engineering 2003 held jointly with 9th European Software Engineering Conference, ESEC/FSE 2003, Helsinki, Finland, 1–5 September 2003, pp. 327–336 (2003)

Sharing Ghost Variables in a Collection of Abstract Domains

Marc Chevalier[1,2(✉)] and Jérôme Feret[1,2]

[1] Inria, Paris, France
[2] Département d'informatique de l'ENS, ENS, CNRS, PSL University, Paris, France
{marc.chevalier,feret}@ens.fr

Abstract. We propose a framework in which we share ghost variables across a collection of abstract domains allowing precise proofs of complex properties.

In abstract interpretation, it is often necessary to be able to express complex properties while doing a precise analysis. A way to achieve that is to combine a collection of domains, each handling some kind of properties, using a reduced product. Separating domains allows an easier and more modular implementation, and eases soundness and termination proofs. This way, we can add a domain for any kind of property that is interesting. The reduced product, or an approximation of it, is in charge of refining abstract states, making the analysis precise.

In program verification, ghost variables can be used to ease proofs of properties by storing intermediate values that do not appear directly in the execution.

We propose a reduced product of abstract domains that allows domains to use ghost variables to ease the representation of their internal state. Domains must be totally agnostic with respect to other existing domains. In particular the handling of ghost variables must be entirely decentralized while still ensuring soundness and termination of the analysis.

1   Introduction

Ghost variables can help to proof complex properties on programs: they store intermediate values that do not appear in the program but help to express complex values or allow better expressivity, like in [16]. We would like to reason on these variables as well as we do on real variables. We propose here a flexible way to make abstract interpretation and ghost variables to work together.

Abstract interpretation [7] is a framework of semantics approximation that allow to prove semantic properties on programs such as the absence of runtime errors. Analyses using abstract interpretation are usually made to be sound and terminating and consequently are not complete. False alarms are unavoidable in theory, but we can strive to make them as rare as possible.

This work was partially supported by ANR project AnaStaSec ANR-14-CE28-0014.

D. Beyer and D. Zufferey (Eds.): VMCAI 2020, LNCS 11990, pp. 158–179, 2020.
https://doi.org/10.1007/978-3-030-39322-9_8

Running an analysis using several domains without communication is no better than running separate analyses. Each domain handles some kind of properties but independently, they are usually not precise enough to prove the properties we are interested in. Yet there are good sides to use separate domains. From a mathematical point of view, it makes the proofs of soundness and termination easier and compositional. From a software engineering point of view, it makes the implementation more modular. Usually, we use a reduced product [8] that preserves soundness and termination while improving internal states of the domains: each domain communicates what it knows to all other domains so that they can use this information to improve their own internal state and thus avoiding some false alarms. In this framework, we benefit from mutual induction (where each domain can refine its state thanks to any other domain's information) which is better than cascading analyses, where domains can only get information from previous domain, with respect to a linear ordering. We want to keep the power of mutual induction. A classical method in program verification to express complex properties is to refer to ghost variables. They are variables that are useful for the proof but do not appear in the program. A standard (but not the only) usage of ghost variables is to remember former values of real variables.

Though, ghost variables are difficult to use in a reduced product. The constraints are plenty, since each domain shall not make any assumption on other existing domains. Whatever the chosen combination of domains, the result should always be correct. This has several implications. Firstly, a ghost variable can need another ghost variable to represent its state, thus the set of ghost variables must be handled dynamically. The management of ghost variables (creation, deletion and all operations) is totally distributed. Consequently, we must be sure that these concurrent operations still guarantee a sound abstraction, with very little knowledge on evaluation order. Indeed, deciding an evaluation order would require to know all involved domains. Moreover, the analysis should always terminate even for non-terminating programs.

An example that illustrates the need for ghost variables is to abstract precisely Global Descriptor Table (GDT) entries. In the x86 architecture, GDT is an array in which each entry describes a memory segment or some kind of enriched function pointer (e.g. call gate). Along with various flags controlling permissions and miscellaneous settings, these entries need to store an address: the base address of the memory segment or the bare function pointer. But these addresses are not stored contiguously in memory: they are chopped into several pieces with bitwise operations. Though, remembering precise information is necessary to be able to get a precise pointer when reconstructing it (e.g. to call the function pointed by the call gate). A quite realistic case is the following:

```
1   /* Given int limit, *base; char access, flags; short t[4]; */
2   t[0]=limit&0xffff
3   t[1]=base&0xffff;
4   t[2]=((base>>16)&0xff)|((access&0xff)<<8);
5   t[3]=((base>>24)<<8)|((limit>>16)&0xf)|((flags&0xf)<<4);
```

We assume that we have some hypotheses on the architecture and on the compiler that go beyond the C standard but are usual in the context of embedded systems. We want to know that `t[1] | ((t[2]&0xff)<<16) | ((t[3]&0xff00)<<16)` has the same value as `base`. It may be a variable or an arbitrary expression, and evaluates to an integer or a pointer. Typically, it may be `fn_ptr_array[index]` or `&some_function`. More generally, low level programming uses extensively bitwise operations, e.g. for pointer alignment or to change the endianness when communicating on a network.

It might be tempting to simply stack domains: each domain has one underlying domain and acts on it as it decides. However, this has several limitations. Firstly, properties of the overlaying domain can use the ones of the underlying domain, but not in the other way or with recursive nesting. For instance, we might want to represent simultaneously slices of linear combinations of pointers, and linear combinations of slices of pointers (this is not a fantasy, it happens in real world low-level source code). Moreover, from an implementation point of view, adding a domain is very costly as it requires to implement all the primitives to translate and forward instructions to the underlying level and to compute inductive invariant from increasing iterations.

2   Related Work

Our work stands in the ancient tradition of abstract interpretation which goes back to Cousot and Cousot [7]. Analysis precision can be improved through several strategies, like disjunction of states depending on their contents [4], or the context [2]. Non-standard semantics can also enhance analyses by adding information that does not directly appear in the semantics, for instance in [11, 18,19] where objects are enriched with information about their history. In [5] ghost variables are used to represent expressions with external symbols. Here, ghost variables are statically allocated. [1,12,15] are examples of works where ghost variables have a more dynamic semantics, but they are local to the domain and are not shared with outside domains.

Another way to improve precision is to make several abstract domains work together, typically, with a reduced product [6,8]. Our work is motivated by pragmatic constraints: allowing easy proofs and implementation by delegation to the domains. In particular our work is an extension of [9]. Our product was introduced to add some new specific domains, that will be discussed in the following, that get their power from shared ghost variables. Nevertheless, some existing abstract domains were adjusted to this new framework such as Miné's pointer abstraction [14]. There are other works on domain cooperation with dynamic support, like cofibered domains [17]. Those have some limitations we try to overcome. The product we propose does not enforce a hierarchy between domains and the current support is known by every domain to improve precision.

[13] also uses transformation of statements but based on expression rewriting. In this approach, several abstraction levels use rewriting rules to gradually simplify expressions. This strategy is well-fitted for function resolution in a context where there are function overloading and dynamic typing, which is crucial

to analyze Python source code. Given our application, we have other priorities. This is why we choose to promote a more flexible framework where statement transformation may depend on the history (see Subsect. 5.2 for an example). It allows domains to declare new ghost variables without knowing *a priori* when they will be used; their value will be updated during the following computation steps, and used when useful without knowing precisely when they have been declared. Another requirement is to allow arbitrary predicate nesting (cf. Sect. 1): domains are free to use ghost variables to represent any available property, even if it means that some kinds of transformations are not so straightforward.

We implemented all the following in a development version of Astrée. Astrée is a static analyzer designed to analyze critical C source code coming from automotive application, avionics, astronautics, etc. [3]. This development version goes beyond safety and aims to prove security properties that are crucial in critical contexts. It has been successfully used to analyze the source code of a proprietary host platform.

3   The Setup

Let us define the framework in which to work. We remain very general at this point and simply define the concrete semantics as the composition of primitives.

We denote by $\mathbb{V}$ the set of variables, and by $\mathbb{E}$ the set of expressions. We consider any usual operation except dereferencing. Nevertheless, we do not forbid the use of "address of" (& in C), so variables may store pointers. Variables are assumed to not alias. For instance, they may represent memory blocks in C and each C statement is transformed to multiple statements to simulate the effect of the C statements on overlapping memory blocks. This is because in Astrée, pointer resolution is performed before (and thanks to) pointer abstraction.

To stay very general, we describe the (non-deterministic) semantics with variable allocation and killing, comparison, assignment and union. Since we have variable allocation and killing, the support (set of living variables) is dynamic. Formally, let $S = \mathbb{V} \rightharpoonup \mathbb{I}$ be the set of states: they are partial maps from variables to values where $\mathbb{I}$ is an arbitrary set. The support of such a state s is denoted $\mathrm{supp}\,(s)$.

We assume we are given a primitive to assign a variable, one to guard by an arbitrary comparison and one to allocate and kill a variable. The two former shall not change the support, while the two latter respectively add and remove a variable to the support. So, even though the semantics is non-deterministic, each step leads to a set of states with the same support. We denote the poset $D \doteq (\{S \in \mathcal{P}(S) \mid \forall (s, s') \in S^2, \mathrm{supp}\,(s) = \mathrm{supp}\,(s')\}, \subseteq)$. The unique support of all states in a $d \in D$ is also denoted $\mathrm{supp}\,(d)$. We denote $\mathbb{O} = \{<, >, =, \neq, \leqslant, \geqslant\}$, $\mathbb{C} = \mathbb{E} \times \mathbb{O} \times \mathbb{E}$ the type of comparisons and $\mathbb{A} = \mathbb{V} \times \mathbb{E}$ the type of assignments. The directives aforementioned have types $Assign : \mathbb{A} \times S \to D$, $Comp : \mathbb{C} \times S \to D$, $Alloc : \mathbb{V} \times S \to D$ and $Kill : \mathbb{V} \times S \to D$, with the assumptions:

- $\forall (a, s) \in \mathbb{A} \times S, \mathrm{supp}\,(Assign(a, s)) = \mathrm{supp}\,(s)$
- $\forall (c, s) \in \mathbb{C} \times S, \mathrm{supp}\,(Comp(c, s)) = \mathrm{supp}\,(s)$

- $\forall s \in S, \forall v \notin \mathrm{supp}\,(s), Alloc(v, s) = \mathrm{supp}\,(s) \cup \{v\}$
- $\forall s \in S, \forall v \in \mathrm{supp}\,(s), Kill(v, s) = \mathrm{supp}\,(s) \setminus \{v\}$

We identify these functions with their lift to D, ie., they respectively are $Assign$: $\mathbb{A} \times D \to D$, $Comp : \mathbb{C} \times D \to D$, $Alloc : \mathbb{V} \times D \to D$ and $Kill : \mathbb{V} \times D \to D$.

Let us add some requirements inspired by the C language. First, even if the support is dynamic (due to local variables, scopes, ...), we assume that non existing variables do not appear in expressions, and that binary flow operations (such as union) are performed with the same support in both operands. We also assume there is no allocating an existing variable or killing of a dead variable. Allocations of variables are done by $Alloc$ and killings by $Kill$; all other primitives keep the same support. We add a few assumptions:

- In assignments, the left-hand side variable does not appear in the right-hand side expression.
- $\forall a \in D, \forall (c, d) \in \mathbb{C}^2, \forall (e, f, g) \in \mathbb{E}^3, \forall (v, w) \in \mathbb{V}^2, \forall o \in \mathbb{O}, v \neq w$
    - $\{v, w\} \cap (\mathrm{Var}\,(e) \cup \mathrm{Var}\,(f)) = \emptyset \Rightarrow Assign((v, e), Assign((w, f), a)) = Assign((w, f), Assign((v, e), a))$ where $\mathrm{Var}\,(e)$ is the set of variables in e (independent assignments commute)
    - $Comp(c, Comp(d, a)) = Comp(d, Comp(c, a))$ (comparisons commute)
    - $v \notin \mathrm{Var}\,(e) \cup \mathrm{Var}\,(f) \Rightarrow Comp((e, o, f), Assign((v, g), a)) = Assign((v, g), Comp((e, o, f), a))$ (independent comparison and assignment commute)
    - $Comp(c, a) \subseteq a$

These assumptions are quite reasonable and allow to commute statements as long as they are independent enough. It will come in handy to run a set of statements in a distributed way without guarantees on the execution order.

We write $[\![c]\!]$ the function $D \to D$ that runs the statement c. We naturally extend this notation to any sequence of instructions and control flow graphs (using least fix-point operator to stabilize loops).

4   An Abstract Domain with Dynamic Support

4.1   The Difficulties

Using a single abstract domain to analyze programs may result in poor precision. To overcome this issue, we use the reduced product [8]. This is a compound abstract domain that runs a collection of domains and make them cooperate to improve their internal states. Formally, the internal state of each domain is the best abstraction of the intersection of the concretization of all internal states. This structure allows easier (because separate) implementation and correctness proofs. The reduced product ensures the best possible precision given the set of available domains, however, this is not realistic. But we can use an over-approximation of the reduced product: internal states may be improved, but they are not supposed to be the best possible.

We want a product that allows each domain to add new ghost variables to the current state, reduce them and kill them. All domains must store ghost variables of all domains: they must communicate their policy for ghost variables management, i.e. what to do on ghost variables while we operate on real variables. Recursively, reduction of ghost variables may trigger new reductions.

There are several problems that the proposed framework is solving: – one cannot order meaningfully constraints coming from different domains. So concurrent constraints must be safely reorderable; – we need to recursively collect all constraints on ghost variables while ensuring termination; – when performing binary operations, we have assumed that the support of real variables is the same, but there is no such guarantee about ghost variables. So, before performing a binary operation, supports shall be unified.

Let us take a look at a simpler code that sublimates the difficulties of the real-world case and that will be used all along the paper to illustrate the framework:

```
1   int* x = &t[idx]; /* given int t[]; and int idx; */
2   int low = x & 0xffff;
3   int high = x >> 16;
4   int* y = low | (high << 16);
```

In this example, mask and bit shift are used to split a pointer and recombine it.

4.2   Ghost Variables and Constraints

Let us define ghost variables, their structure and their relation to abstract domains. Ghost variables are built recursively from normal or ghost variables using unary constructors. These constructors specify the semantics of the ghost variable, for this reason, these constructors are called "roles". Each role must be associated to the domain in charge of managing this kind of ghost variables. To define all the component of the signatures of abstract domains, we need to reference them, although we still are not able to define them entirely.

Notation 1 (Domain name). *Let us denote $\mathcal{N}$ a set of domain names.*

To analyze properly the running example we will use 3 domains: bitwise properties, pointers as a memory block and an offset [14] and equality. These domains are respectively named 𝔖𝔩𝔦𝔠𝔢, 𝔒𝔣𝔣𝔰𝔢𝔱 and 𝔈𝔮𝔲𝔞𝔩𝔦𝔱𝔶. In the examples, we can choose $\mathcal{N}$ to contain only these three names.

Each role is associated to the domain that decides what to do with ghost variables that have this role as outermost one.

Definition 1 (Roles). *Let $\mathcal{R}$ be a set of unary constructors. These constructors are called "roles". Let $\mathrm{o} : \mathcal{R} \to \mathcal{N}$. When $\mathrm{o}(\mathcal{R}) = d$, we say that d is the owner of a role $\mathcal{R}$, or that $\mathcal{R}$ belongs to d, and we denote $\mathcal{R} \Subset d$.*

For instance, after the second line of the simplified example, we would like to remember that the 16 upper bits of `low` are 0 and the 16 lower bits are the 16 lower bits of a ghost variable named $\mathscr{S}lice_{[0,15]\to[0,15]}(\texttt{low})$. We can write this property $\mathtt{low} = [_0 \mathscr{S}lice_{[0,15]\to[0,15]}(\mathtt{low})[0,15]\ _{15}|_{16}\ 0\ _{31}]$, where $v[a,b]$ designates the bits a to b of the variable v, and $\mathscr{S}lice_{[0,15]\to[0,15]}(\mathtt{low})$ stores the value of x. This way, even if x falls out of scope or is modified, the ghost variable is safe.

From now on, everything written in this Round Hand style (like $\mathscr{R}$) is about ghost variables.

Notation 2 (All variables). *We denote by $\mathscr{V}$ the inductively defined set of all variables, starting with real variables (in $\mathbb{V}$).*

Formally $\mathscr{V} := \bigcup\limits_{i\in\mathbb{N}} \mathscr{V}_i$ *where* $\mathscr{V}_i := \begin{cases} \mathbb{V} & \text{if } i = 0 \\ \{\mathscr{R}(v) \mid \mathscr{R} \in \mathcal{R}, v \in \mathscr{V}_{i-1}\} & \text{otherwise} \end{cases}$

$\mathscr{E}$ denotes the set of expressions whose variables are $\mathscr{V}$.

It is worth noticing that $\mathbb{V} \subseteq \mathscr{V}$ and $\mathbb{E} \subseteq \mathscr{E}$. We assume we can naturally extend concrete primitives to $\mathscr{V}$ and $\mathscr{E}$.

Though the handling of ghost variables is decentralized, there are restrictions on which variables a domain can create or delete. For instance, only the domain $\mathfrak{Slice}$ should be able to decide what to do with $\mathscr{S}lice_{[0,15]\to[0,15]}(\mathtt{low})$. So, we need a belonging relation between ghost variables and domain names.

Definition 2. *We extend the $\Subset$ to $\mathscr{V} \times \mathcal{N}$ by $\forall v \in \mathscr{V}, \forall \mathscr{R} \in \mathcal{R}, \mathscr{R}(v) \Subset \mathfrak{o}(\mathscr{R})$.*

The ownership is purely syntactic: the topmost role is enough to decide the owner of a ghost variable. Real variables (in $\mathbb{V}$) are not owned.

A role defines the semantics of the ghost variable. This is usually a relation between the value of the ghost variable and the variable immediately above. For instance, $\mathscr{O}ffset(p)$ should be the offset of p.

Notation 3. *Let $(\!|\_|\!) : \mathscr{V} \to \mathcal{P}(S)$ be the semantics of ghost variables.*

For instance, $(\!|\mathscr{O}ffset(p)|\!)$ is the set of states where $\mathscr{O}ffset(p)$ is indeed the offset part of the pointer p. The codomain of $(\!|\_|\!)$ is not D since legal states do not have necessarily the same support.

Definition 3 (Ghostly ordering). *Let $\vartriangleleft$ be the smallest transitive relation on $\mathscr{V}^2$ such that $\forall v \in \mathscr{V}, \forall \mathscr{R} \in \mathcal{R}, \mathscr{R}(v) \vartriangleleft v$. Let $\trianglelefteq$ be the reflexive closure of $\vartriangleleft$. If $x \vartriangleleft y$, we say that x is less real (or ghostlier) than y. We extend this relation to $\mathscr{E}^2$ by $\forall(e,e') \in \mathscr{E}^2, (\forall v' \in Var(e'), \exists v \in Var(e) : v' \trianglelefteq v) \Leftrightarrow e' \trianglelefteq e$ where $Var(e)$ is the set of variables of the expression e. That is every variable in e' is ghostlier than a variable in e.*

$\trianglelefteq$ is clearly an order on $\mathscr{V}$ and a preorder on $\mathscr{E}$. Now that we have all variables, we want to operate on them. In addition to variable creation/deletion that are handled separately, domains can exchange information about ghost variables in the form of comparisons and directed reduction.

Definition 4 (Ghost constraints). *We let $\mathcal{O} := \{\leqslant, <, \geqslant, >, =, \neq\}$, $\mathscr{C} := \mathscr{E} \times \mathcal{O} \times \mathscr{E}$ (comparison), $\mathscr{A} := \mathscr{V} \times \mathscr{E}$ (directed constraint) and $\mathscr{U} := \mathscr{C} \uplus \mathscr{A}$.*

These are the types of constraints about ghost variables. $\mathscr{C}$ is the set of comparisons of two arbitrary expressions. $\mathscr{A}$ are equality between a variable and an expression, but with a restriction: they are used to point out the variable is unknown (it is $\top$) and that reduction may only occur in one direction. This reduction can be implemented very efficiently as an assignment. These constraints are written in the form $v \leftarrow e$. This may look like a mere implementation concern, but it relies on fundamental assumptions.

First constraints are generated from the executed statement (in A or C), then each constraint may trigger the generation of several other constraints. Let us see on a simple example why atomic constraints are not expressive enough. We consider two variables a and b that have been built with bitwise instructions, like in the example. Let us say they are both made of two parts of 16 bits:

$$\mathsf{a} = [_0 \quad \mathscr{S}lice_{[0,15]\rightarrow[0,15]}(a)[0,15] \quad _{15}|_{16} \quad \mathscr{S}lice_{[16,32]\rightarrow[16,32]}(a)[16,31] \quad _{31}]$$
$$\mathsf{b} = [_0 \quad \mathscr{S}lice_{[0,15]\rightarrow[0,15]}(b)[0,15] \quad _{15}|_{16} \quad \mathscr{S}lice_{[16,32]\rightarrow[16,32]}(b)[16,31] \quad _{31}]$$

A way to run the comparison $a = b$ in a state s is to compute $f \circ g(s)$ where

- $f = [\![\mathscr{S}lice_{[0,15]\rightarrow[0,15]}(a)[0,15] = \mathscr{S}lice_{[0,15]\rightarrow[0,15]}(b)[0,15]]\!]$
- $g = [\![\mathscr{S}lice_{[16,31]\rightarrow[16,31]}(a)[16,31] = \mathscr{S}lice_{[16,31]\rightarrow[16,31]}(b)[16,31]]\!]$

So we need to be able to sequence constraints. If we want the result of $a \neq b$, we need to compute $f(s) \cup g(s)$ where

- $f = [\![\mathscr{S}lice_{[0,15]\rightarrow[0,15]}(a)[0,15] \neq \mathscr{S}lice_{[0,15]\rightarrow[0,15]}(b)[0,15]]\!]$
- $g = [\![\mathscr{S}lice_{[16,31]\rightarrow[16,31]}(a)[16,31] \neq \mathscr{S}lice_{[16,31]\rightarrow[16,31]}(b)[16,31]]\!]$

To combine both branching and sequencing, and still have obvious termination, the compound constraints communicated across domains are DAGs. More precisely the internal language to communicate constraints is made of DAGs with one source and one sink and whose edges wear sequence of constraints in $\mathscr{U}$. Edges converging to a node mean that a join must be performed before guarding by the constraints on the node. It allows conditional branching and avoids loops and thus non-termination. For instance, the graph corresponding to the test $a \neq b$ is given in Fig. 1.

This kind of compound constraints is quite powerful. The graph in Fig. 2 computes $\kappa(\theta(\zeta(i) \sqcup \eta(i)) \sqcup \iota(\eta(i)))$ where $i \in D^\sharp$ is the input. We notice that

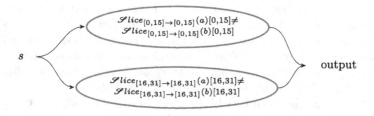

Fig. 1. An example of a constraint DAG

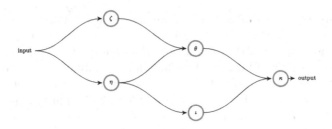

Fig. 2. A more complicated constraint DAG

$\eta(i)$ appears several times in the one-line expression, but the graph form allows easy sharing of intermediate computations.

Notation 4 (Constraint graph). $\mathscr{G}$ *is the set of 3-tuples* (V, E, n) *where* (V, E) *is a DAG with exactly one source and one sink and* $n : V \to \mathscr{U}^*$ *maps nodes to finite sequences of elements of* $\mathscr{U}$. *Given* $g \in \mathscr{G}$ *and* $u \in \mathscr{U}$, *we write* $u \in g$ *when* $\exists v \in V : u \in n(v)$.

In fact, the exact form of the intermediate language does not matter. If needed, it could include other terminating constructs like constant-bounded for-style loops. We choose this language made of DAGs because it is both simple and expressive enough.

Given a support V, the semantics of such graph is defined inductively on the nodes and is an element of D denoted $[\![G]\!]_V$. The semantics of the source is $\{s \in S \mid \mathrm{supp}\,(s) = V\}$ and the semantics of each node is the union of the semantics of the parent nodes guarded by the constraints of the node. The semantics of the graph is the semantics of the sink. This is well-founded thanks to acyclicity.

A graph expresses constraints about ghost variables, so to be a sound constraint, its semantics shall be bigger than the intersection of the semantics of ghost variables. In other words, it can do no more than enforcing the semantics of ghost variables.

Definition 5 (Constraint-DAG soundness). *A graph* G *is said to be sound in the support* $V \subseteq \mathscr{V}$ *if* $\left\{ s \in \bigcap_{v \in V \setminus \mathbb{V}} (\![v]\!) \,\middle|\, \mathrm{supp}\,(s) = V \right\} \subseteq [\![G]\!]_V$.

Though any sound graph can be used, there are several ways to build them systematically. Here is a non-exhaustive list that covers most common cases.

- If we test equality between variables x and y in a context where both $\mathscr{R}(x)$ and $\mathscr{R}(y)$ exist, for a given role $\mathscr{R}$, and the implication $x = y \Rightarrow \mathscr{R}(x) = \mathscr{R}(y)$ is true in all states, we can generate the one-node graph containing the unique constraint $\mathscr{R}(x) = \mathscr{R}(y)$. If several such implications hold, we may simply sequence all graphs in an arbitrary order (since these conditions do not interfere). This is the general case of the example $\mathtt{a} = \mathtt{b}$.
- To test difference between variables x and y in a context where $(\mathscr{R}_i(x))_{i \in [\![1,n]\!]}$ and $(\mathscr{R}_i(y))_{i \in [\![1,n]\!]}$ exist, for a given family of roles $(\mathscr{R}_i)_{i \in [\![1,n]\!]}$ and the implication $x \neq y \Rightarrow \bigvee_{i \in [\![1,n]\!]} \mathscr{R}_i(x) \neq \mathscr{R}_i(y)$ holds in any state, we can generate

the graph that joins the results of these n conditions taken separately (like Fig. 1). This is like the comparison a $\neq$ b in the last example.
– Some constraints come from the language semantics but can be reinterpreted with ghost variables. E.g. since the ghost variable offset must coincide with the C standard offset, the latter can be substituted by the former.

Directed constraints $(v \leftarrow e)$ enforce that the left-hand side is $\top$, to be able to run it efficiently as an assignment. The way to ensure this property stands in two arguments: – a directed constraint about a variable can only be issued by the domain that owns the variable; – after a variable assignment, all consequent assignments can only modify ghostlier variables.

Of course, the condition cannot be totally local. Here, the hidden global hypothesis is that the roles of different domains are disjoint. To help the proof that the restriction on directed constraints holds, we introduce the following relation. If any generated constraint is smaller than the previous with respect to this relation, then only variables set to $\top$ will appear in the left-hand side of a directed constraint, and at most once.

Definition 6. *Let $n \in \mathcal{N}$. Let $\succ_n$ the smallest relation on $(\mathbb{A} \uplus \mathbb{C} \uplus \mathcal{U}) \times \mathcal{U}$ satisfying:*

– $\forall v \in \mathcal{V}, \forall \mathcal{R} \in \mathcal{R}, \forall (e, e') \in \mathcal{E}^2, \mathcal{R} \Subset n \wedge e' \lhd e \Rightarrow (v, e) \succ_n (\mathcal{R}(v), e')$
– $\forall (a, b, c, d) \in \mathcal{E}^4, \forall (o, p) \in \mathcal{O}^2, a \lhd c \wedge b \lhd d \Rightarrow (c, o, d) \succ_n (a, p, b)$
– $\forall (a, b, c) \in \mathcal{E}^3, \forall v \in \mathcal{V}, \forall o \in \mathcal{O}, b \lhd a \wedge c \lhd a \Rightarrow (v, a) \succ_n (b, o, c)$

The type of the left-hand side is $\mathbb{A} \uplus \mathbb{C} \uplus \mathcal{U}$, this is because a ghost constraint can be generated from a real assignment ($\mathbb{A}$), a real comparison ($\mathbb{C}$), or another ghost constraint ($\mathcal{U}$). At the first step, the left-hand side is in $\mathbb{A} \uplus \mathbb{C}$; after, only elements of $\mathcal{U}$ appear. Let us reword the three cases: – a directed reduction (resp. assignment) can trigger a directed reduction about a variable immediately ghostlier with a ghostlier right-hand side; – a (real or ghost) comparison can trigger a comparison that involves ghostlier expression; – a directed reduction (resp. assignment) can trigger a comparison whose expressions are ghostlier than the right-hand side of the directed reduction (resp. assignment).

4.3 Generic Abstract Domain

Before describing the structure of an abstract domain, let us see how the running example behaves. We assume we use the 3 domains we introduced before: one to express bitwise properties (named $\mathfrak{Slice}$), one that represents pointers as a block and an offset [14] ($\mathfrak{Offset}$) and one about equality ($\mathfrak{Equality}$). The $\mathfrak{Offset}$ domain uses a single role $\mathcal{O}$ffset that means the ghost variable is the offset of the base variable as a pointer. The equality domain does not have any role.

At the end of the third line, we have:

$$\text{low} = [_0 \; \mathscr{S}lice_{[0,15]\to[0,15]}(\text{low})[0,15] \;_{15}|_{16} \; 0 \;_{31}]$$
$$\text{high} = [_0 \; \mathscr{S}lice_{[16,31]\to[0,15]}(\text{high})[16,31] \;_{15}|_{16} \; 0 \;_{31}]$$

$\left.\right\}$ $\mathfrak{Slices}$

$$\text{x} = \text{t} + \mathcal{O}\text{ffset}(\text{x})$$
$$\mathscr{S}lice_{[0,15]\to[0,15]}(\text{low}) = \text{t} + \mathcal{O}\text{ffset}(\mathscr{S}lice_{[0,15]\to[0,15]}(\text{low}))$$
$$\mathscr{S}lice_{[16,31]\to[0,15]}(\text{high}) = \text{t} + \mathcal{O}\text{ffset}(\mathscr{S}lice_{[16,31]\to[0,15]}(\text{high}))$$

$\left.\right\}$ $\mathfrak{Offset}$

$$\mathcal{O}\text{ffset}(\mathscr{S}lice_{[0,15]\to[0,15]}(\text{low})) = \mathcal{O}\text{ffset}(\text{x})$$
$$\mathcal{O}\text{ffset}(\mathscr{S}lice_{[16,31]\to[0,15]}(\text{high})) = \mathcal{O}\text{ffset}(\text{x})$$

$\left.\right\}$ $\mathfrak{Equality}$

The support consists in the following trees of variables:

```
                low                              high
                 |                                |
   x    Slice[0,15]→[0,15](low)       Slice[16,31]→[0,15](high)
   |                 |                            |
Offset(x)  Offset(Slice[0,15]→[0,15](low))  Offset(Slice[16,31]→[0,15](high))
```

Now, let us run the last statement. $\mathfrak{Offset}$ and $\mathfrak{Equality}$ domains get nothing interesting from that. However, the $\mathfrak{Slice}$ domain is more clever. It can deduce

$$\text{y} = [_0 \quad \mathscr{S}lice_{[0,15]\to[0,15]}(\text{y})[0,15] \quad_{15}|_{16} \quad \mathscr{S}lice_{[0,15]\to[16,31]}(\text{y})[0,15] \quad_{31}]$$

but requires the creation of two ghost variables (initialized to $\top$) and yields two directed reductions: $\mathscr{S}lice_{[0,15]\to[0,15]}(\text{y}) \leftarrow \mathscr{S}lice_{[0,15]\to[0,15]}(\text{low})$ and $\mathscr{S}lice_{[0,15]\to[16,31]}(\text{y}) \leftarrow \mathscr{S}lice_{[16,31]\to[0,15]}(\text{high})$.

One can remark that the restriction on directed constraints is satisfied: both left-hand sides are $\top$ since they are freshly allocated. After this reduction, we know that:

$$\mathscr{S}lice_{[0,15]\to[0,15]}(\text{y}) = \text{t} + \mathcal{O}\text{ffset}(\mathscr{S}lice_{[0,15]\to[0,15]}(\text{y}))$$
$$\mathscr{S}lice_{[0,15]\to[16,31]}(\text{y}) = \text{t} + \mathcal{O}\text{ffset}(\mathscr{S}lice_{[0,15]\to[16,31]}(\text{y}))$$

$\left.\right\}$ $\mathfrak{Offset}$

$$\mathcal{O}\text{ffset}(\mathscr{S}lice_{[0,15]\to[0,15]}(\text{y})) \leftarrow \mathcal{O}\text{ffset}(\mathscr{S}lice_{[0,15]\to[0,15]}(\text{low}))$$
$$\mathcal{O}\text{ffset}(\mathscr{S}lice_{[0,15]\to[16,31]}(\text{y})) \leftarrow \mathcal{O}\text{ffset}(\mathscr{S}lice_{[16,31]\to[0,15]}(\text{high}))$$

Again, left hand-sides of constraints are unknown before reduction. Finally, we get:

$$\mathcal{O}\text{ffset}(\mathscr{S}lice_{[0,15]\to[0,15]}(\text{y})) = \mathcal{O}\text{ffset}(\text{x})$$
$$\mathcal{O}\text{ffset}(\mathscr{S}lice_{[16,31]\to[16,31]}(\text{y})) = \mathcal{O}\text{ffset}(\text{x})$$

$\left.\right\}$ $\mathfrak{Equality}$

and we use this additional tree of ghost variables:

```
                            y
                  ╱                  ╲
   Slice[0,15]→[0,15](y)        Slice[0,15]→[16,31](y)
             |                            |
 Offset(Slice[0,15]→[0,15](y))   Offset(Slice[0,15]→[16,31](y))
```

This illustrates why we need distributed handling of ghost variables and that they should be known by other domains. In fact, when we use a ghost variable, it is likely that another domain can do better about it, otherwise we wouldn't need a ghost variable. For instance, parts of low, high and y are pointers: it is more suitable to ask the pointer domain to represent them. Likewise, the offset is a numeric value so, while the pointer domain associates it to the pointer of which it is the offset, it is worth to let a numeric domain represent the offset value. But, if we know for offset, in general we don't *a priori* know the kind of value the ghost variable store, for instance, in the case of bitwise slices that can be pointers, numeric values or anything else. Furthermore, we do not know in advance the list of available domains, so we cannot decide which domain is the best to represent a ghost variable. Thus, every ghost variable must be known by all domains. This prevents the simple use of stacked domains, each being controlled by the overlaying one. Indeed, a domain won't be able to make one of its ghost variable represented by a domain higher in the hierarchy.

Let us discuss the problems that we have highlighted. The termination is satisfied: directed reductions of offsets do not trigger new constraints. We can observe that each constraint is more elementary than the previous, and there is nothing simpler than copying a numeric variable. The decreasing complexity is a good approach to ensures termination. The other problem was the execution order. Here, we can see that the assignments are disjoint: we assign variables under y from variables under low and high. So, an assigned variable is never in the right-hand side of an assignment and since we always go deeper in ghost variables, each variable is assigned only once, making directed reductions legal. Both these points will be detailed and generalized later.

This result is correct but not interesting in this form. With domain cooperation, we can infer $\mathscr{S}lice_{[0,15]\to[0,15]}(\mathtt{y}) = \mathtt{x}$ and $\mathscr{S}lice_{[0,15]\to[16,31]}(\mathtt{y}) = \mathtt{x}$, hence $\mathtt{y} = \mathtt{x}$ which is the expected result.

We can be very general on the form of the abstract domains. Classically, a domain needs a set of abstract states and their meaning in the concrete world, fixpoint approximation and abstract counterparts of concrete primitives. In addition, we add two other kinds of function.

First, there are two maps to decide what to do with ghost variables: one to react to the execution of a unary statement or a ghost constraint, and one to unify supports before performing a binary operation (typically, the join).

Moreover, domains include primitives to communicate information about their abstract state *á la* [9]. This allows domains to refine themselves (as a reduced product is meant to) but also to communicate their policy on ghost variables management: since all domains must care about the ghost variables of the other domains, they need to communicate what to do.

We are given a lattice $IO^\sharp$ with a concretization $\gamma_{IO} : IO^\sharp \to D$. This is a lattice common to all domains that will be the middleman for all communication.

Definition 7 (Generic abstract domain). *A generic abstract domain with dynamic support is a tuple* $(n, D^\sharp, \gamma, \sqcup, \mathrm{lfp}^\sharp, \textsc{Assign}, \textsc{Comp}, \textsc{Alloc}, \textsc{Kill}, \textsc{Extract}, \textsc{Refine}, \mathcal{U}, \mathcal{B})$ *where:*

- $n \in \mathcal{N}$
- $D^\sharp$ is a set of abstract properties,
- $\gamma : D^\sharp \rightarrow D$ is the concretization, for any $a \in D^\sharp$ we denote $\operatorname{supp}(a) :=$ $\operatorname{supp}(\gamma(a))$,
- $\sqcup : D^\sharp \rightarrow D^\sharp \rightarrow D^\sharp$ such that $\forall (a,b) \in D^{\sharp 2}, \operatorname{supp}(a) = \operatorname{supp}(b) \Rightarrow \gamma(a) \cup \gamma(b) \subseteq \gamma(a \sqcup b)$
- $\operatorname{lfp}^\sharp : (D^\sharp \rightarrow D^\sharp) \rightarrow D^\sharp \rightarrow D^\sharp$ such that $\forall f : D \rightarrow D, \forall f^\sharp : D^\sharp \rightarrow D^\sharp, f \circ \gamma \subseteq \gamma \circ f^\sharp \Rightarrow \operatorname{lfp}(f) \subseteq \gamma \circ \operatorname{lfp}^\sharp(f^\sharp)$
- ASSIGN : $(\mathcal{V} \times \mathcal{E}) \times D^\sharp \rightarrow D^\sharp$ such that
    - $\forall (v,e,a) \in \mathcal{V} \times \mathcal{E} \times D^\sharp, Assign((v,e), \gamma(a)) \subseteq \gamma(\text{ASSIGN}((v,e), a))$
    - $\forall ((v,e), a) \in \mathscr{A} \times D^\sharp$, **let** $d = \gamma(\text{ASSIGN}(v,e,a))$ **in** $\forall (w,s,x) \in \{v\}^\lhd \times d \times \mathbb{I}, s[w \mapsto x] \in d$ where $S^\mathcal{R} := \{x \mid \exists y \in S : x \mathcal{R} y\}$.
- COMP : $\mathscr{C} \times D^\sharp \rightarrow D^\sharp$ such that $\forall (c,a) \in \mathscr{C} \times D^\sharp, Compare(c, \gamma(a)) \subseteq \gamma(\text{COMP}(c, a))$
- ALLOC : $\mathcal{V} \times D^\sharp \rightarrow D^\sharp$ such that $\forall (v,a) \in \mathcal{V} \times D^\sharp, Allocate(v, \gamma(a)) \subseteq \gamma(\text{ALLOC}(v, a))$
- KILL : $\mathcal{V} \times D^\sharp \rightarrow D^\sharp$ such that $\forall (v,a) \in \mathcal{V} \times D^\sharp, Kill(v, \gamma(a)) \subseteq \gamma(\text{KILL}(v, a))$
- EXTRACT : $D^\sharp \times IO^\sharp \rightarrow IO^\sharp$ such that $\forall a \in D^\sharp, \forall io \in IO^\sharp, \gamma(a) \cap \gamma_{IO}(io) \subseteq \gamma_{IO}(\text{EXTRACT}(a, io))$
- REFINE : $D^\sharp \times IO^\sharp \rightarrow D^\sharp$ such that $\forall a \in D^\sharp, \forall io \in IO^\sharp, \gamma(a) \cap \gamma_{IO}(io) \subseteq \gamma(\text{REFINE}(a, io))$
- $\mathcal{U} : D^\sharp \rightarrow (\mathbb{A} \uplus \mathbb{C} \uplus \mathscr{U}) \rightarrow \mathcal{P}(\mathcal{V}) \times \mathcal{P}(\mathcal{V}) \times \mathscr{G}$ such that for all $(a, u) \in D^\sharp \times (\mathbb{A} \uplus \mathbb{C} \uplus \mathscr{U})$, letting $(new, old, G) := \mathcal{U}(a)(u)$
    - $new \cap \operatorname{supp}(a) = \emptyset$ and $old \subseteq \operatorname{supp}(a)$
    - variables that occur in G belong to $new \cup \operatorname{supp}(a)$.
    - G is sound in support $(\operatorname{supp}(a) \cup new) \setminus old$
    - $\forall (u', u'') \in G^2, u \succ_n u' \wedge ((u', u'') \in \mathscr{A}^2 \wedge \pi_1(u') = \pi_1(u'') \Rightarrow u' = u'')$ where π_i is the ith projection.
- $\mathcal{B} : D^\sharp \times D^\sharp \rightarrow \mathbb{N} \rightarrow (\mathcal{P}(\mathcal{V}) \times \mathcal{P}(\mathcal{V}) \times \mathscr{G})^2$ such that $\forall (a,b) \in D^{\sharp 2}, \forall i \in \mathbb{N}$
    - $\gamma(a) \subseteq \gamma(a') \wedge \gamma(b) \subseteq \gamma(b')$
    - $((\forall j \in [\![0, i-1]\!], \operatorname{supp}(a) \cap \mathcal{V}_j = \operatorname{supp}(b) \cap \mathcal{V}_j) \Rightarrow (\forall j \in [\![0, i]\!], \operatorname{supp}(a') \cap \mathcal{V}_j = \operatorname{supp}(b') \cap \mathcal{V}_j))$

where $a' = [\![(new_1, old_1, g_1)]\!]^\sharp(a)$, $b' = [\![(new_2, old_2, g_2)]\!]^\sharp(b)$, $((new_1, old_1, g_1), (new_2, old_2, g_2)) = \mathcal{B}(a, b)(i)$ and $[\![(new, old, g)]\!]^\sharp$ denote allocating variables in new guarding by g, and killing variables in old.

The ASSIGN directive makes all ghost variables under the assigned variable unknown, since their previous value is not *a priori* valid anymore.

Let us take a look at the types of ghost variables management maps. Given a state $a \in D^\sharp$ and an unary statement or a constraint $u \in (\mathbb{A} \uplus \mathbb{C} \uplus \mathscr{U})$, $\mathcal{U}(a)(u)$ yields a 3-tuple: the sets of ghost variables to add, the set of ghost variables to kill and a constraint-DAG. This result must be shared across all domains, and we must proceed recursively for each constraint in the DAG.

Of course there are more hypotheses for the domain to be always terminating during recursive exploration of constraints. They will be detailed in the following since it isn't an intrinsic property of domains.

The $\mathcal{B}$ map is slightly more tricky. It is used to unify supports of ghost variables layer by layer: the first call care about ghost variables that have only one role around a real variable, the second call is for variable with two nested roles, and so on. Similarly to $\mathcal{U}$ it returns the actions to perform on each branch.

4.4 Running Ghost Constraints

To get more precision, functions $\mathcal{U}$ of all domains must be called recursively to get as many constraints about ghost variables as possible. In the state a, $\mathcal{U}(a) : (\mathbb{A} \uplus \mathbb{C} \uplus \mathscr{U}) \to \mathcal{P}(\mathscr{V}) \times \mathcal{P}(\mathscr{V}) \times \mathscr{G}$ is the function that returns sub-constraints that are implied by the constraint in argument. We denote this map by $\mathcal{U}_a$. Every domain shall receive the partial application $\mathcal{U}_a$ of all domains, making them able to know what other domains know. Transmitting these partial applications can be done using EXTRACT and REDUCE via the channel $IO^\sharp$ which must be performed before each real statement.

We combine them using the function

$$ C = (f_n)_{n \in N} \mapsto \left(u \mapsto \bigcup_{n \in N} \pi_1(f_n(u)), \bigcup_{n \in N} \pi_2(f_n(u)), \bigcup_{n \in N} \{\pi_3(f_n(u))\} \right) $$

Overall, in the state a we get from all domains a single function $\mathcal{U}_a = C((\mathcal{U}_n(a_n))_{n \in N})$ where all returned sets are finite. Especially, the third component has the same cardinal as N.

When executing a constraint, all these functions are called, and they return constraint-DAGs to run. The domain executes these constraints (using the abstract primitives) by taking care of recursively asking other domains for ghostlier constraints. Eventually, each constraint generates a tree of constraint-DAGs. The recursive exploration terminates when the graph returned is empty.

Definition 8. *Given* $\mathcal{U}_a : (\mathbb{A} \uplus \mathbb{C} \uplus \mathscr{U}) \to \mathcal{P}(\mathscr{V}) \times \mathcal{P}(\mathscr{V}) \times \mathcal{P}(\mathscr{G})$ *we define*

$$ \mathcal{U}_a^* : (\mathbb{A} \uplus \mathbb{C} \uplus \mathscr{U}) \to \mathcal{P}(\mathscr{V}) \times \mathcal{P}(\mathscr{V}) \times \mathcal{P}(\mathscr{G}) $$

$$ u \mapsto \begin{array}{l} \textbf{let } new, old, g = \mathcal{U}_a(u) \textbf{ in} \\ \text{lfp} \left(\begin{array}{l} (N, O, G) \mapsto \textbf{let } R = \{\mathcal{U}_a(u') \mid g' \in G, u' \in g'\} \textbf{ in} \\ new \cup \{\pi_1(r) \mid r \in R\}, old \cup \{\pi_2(r) \mid r \in R\}, g \cup \{\pi_3(r) \mid r \in R\} \end{array} \right) \end{array} $$

$\mathcal{U}_a^*$ *is the analog of a transitive closure, hence the notation.*

Communications are performed between a recursive ghost reduction and the next real statement (in $\mathbb{A}$ or $\mathbb{C}$) to improve precision and exchange new $\mathcal{U}_n(a_n)$.

4.5 Non-interference

As previously mentioned, directed constraints ensure that their left-hand side is $\top$ so as to be able to implement them as assignments. Clearly, such assignments cannot interfere with each other or with other comparisons, since they are semantically equivalent to a comparison (and we assumed comparisons commute). We just have to ensure that the hypothesis holds: the left-hand side of directed constraints must be $\top$. In the example, we see that it was achieved by increasing the ghostliness of the involved variables. We would like to guarantee non-interference with a local condition, i.e. a hypothesis that must be verified in each domain independently and that makes any combination of domains correct.

Theorem 1 (Non-interference). *Let $n \in \mathbb{N}$ and $(\mathfrak{D}_i)_{i \in [\![1,n]\!]}$ a collection of domains with distinct names. Let $(a_i \in D_i^\sharp)_{i \in [\![1,n]\!]}$. Let $\mathcal{U}_a := C\left((\mathcal{U}_i(a_i))_{n \in [\![1,n]\!]}\right)$. Let $u \in \mathbb{A} \uplus \mathbb{C} \uplus \mathcal{U}$ and $G := \pi_3(\mathcal{U}_a^*(u))$.*

- *If $u \in \mathbb{A} \uplus \mathscr{A}$, $\forall(u', u'') \in G^2, ((u', u'') \in \mathscr{A}^2 \wedge \pi_1(u') = \pi_1(u'')) \Rightarrow (u' = u'' \wedge \pi_1(u') \in \pi_1(u)^\triangleleft)$*
- *If $u \in \mathbb{C} \uplus \mathscr{C}$, $\forall u' \in G, u' \in \mathscr{C}$*

That is, there is at most one directed reduction for each variable under the left-hand side of an assignment and none for other variables.

Rewording the hypothesis hidden in the definition of abstract domains, there is a family of $\mathcal{U}_a$ functions such that: – they only allocate and kill variables belonging to the domain they are part of; – constraint triggering process satisfies the relation $\succ_n$ (increasing ghostliness); – a constraint-DAG does not involve twice the same variable in a directed constraint.

Let us draw a proof sketch. We made the assumption that real assignments never use their left-hand side in their right-hand side. Thus, the tree of variables that are ghostlier than the left-hand side and the forest of variables ghostlier than variables in the right hand-side are disjoint. This has a crucial consequence: all left-hand sides of assignments may never appear in the right-hand side of a directed constraint or in a comparison. Indeed, in the example, the last directed constraint assign variables under y using variables under low and high.

We now have to check that an assigned variable can only be written once. Let $v \in \mathcal{V}$. We distinguish two cases:

- $v \in \mathbb{V}$. A directed constraint can only assign a ghost variable (thank to $\succ_n$). So v is only assigned by the real assignment. So, only once.
- $v \notin \mathbb{V}$. There is a variable v', a role $\mathscr{R}$ and an integer i such that $v = \mathscr{R}(v')$ and $v \in \mathscr{V}_i$. Since each directed constraint triggered by another directed constraint writes in a variable exactly one level more ghostly, an assignment to a variable in $\mathscr{V}_i$ can only be generated at the ith step of recursion. Moreover, it can only come from the domain that owns the role $\mathscr{R}$. Consequently, there is only one constraint-DAG that may contain an assignment to v. As we assumed that constraint-DAGs may only assign each variable once, there is only one assignment to v.

So, variables under the left-hand side of an assignment appear at most once and only as the left-hand side of a directed constraint, and these variables were previously set to $\top$ by ASSIGN. Hence the hypothesis on directed constraints holds.

4.6   Termination

Generally, $\mathcal{U}_a^*(u)$ is an infinite set. But it can be made finite, which is necessary to actually execute ghost constraints, under some conditions. The example shows that ghostlier and ghostlier variables are assigned from simpler and simpler expressions. The idea behind is to use a well-founded order: if ghost constraints keep being simpler, within the meaning of a well-founded notion of "simplicity", recursive exploration of constraints eventually terminates.

Let us take a look to the tree of ghost constraints. From y = low | (high << 16), at the first step of recursion we got

- $\mathscr{S}lice_{[0,15]\to[0,15]}(\text{y}) \leftarrow \mathscr{S}lice_{[0,15]\to[0,15]}(\text{low})$
- $\mathscr{S}lice_{[0,15]\to[16,31]}(\text{y}) \leftarrow \mathscr{S}lice_{[16,31]\to[0,15]}(\text{high})$

and at the second step

- $\mathscr{O}\text{ffset}(\mathscr{S}lice_{[0,15]\to[0,15]}(\text{y})) \leftarrow \mathscr{O}\text{ffset}(\mathscr{S}lice_{[0,15]\to[0,15]}(\text{low}))$
- $\mathscr{O}\text{ffset}(\mathscr{S}lice_{[0,15]\to[16,31]}(\text{y})) \leftarrow \mathscr{O}\text{ffset}(\mathscr{S}lice_{[16,31]\to[0,15]}(\text{high}))$

It's clear that the left-hand side of assignment decreases (like prescribed by the non-interference condition). Sadly, it is not enough to ensure termination: since we can add ghost variables, we may end up into adding an infinitely deep tree of ghost variables. It is also worth noticing that all new ghost variables are under the left-hand side of an assignment, which is pretty natural.

The relation we are going to define has no fundamental importance, unlike non-interference condition. Here, any well-founded relation is acceptable and the relation might be fine-tuned depending on the domains. Here, the hypothesis is global to all involved domains. Indeed, the union of well-founded relations is not necessarily well-founded, so if each domain has its own relation, it does not guarantee termination. When implementing, there are two philosophies. One can choose a reasonable relation and dictate itself to stick with it. Or, conversely, one can try to adapt the relation according to the domains. In practice, a hybrid approach should be favored since the first method can lack flexibility and the second may result in trying to use a non-terminating set of domains.

The following relation is a real-world one that covers most of the cases while still being simple. As said before, the main idea is to increase the ghostliness of assigned variables, but, to avoid allocation of an infinitely deep tree of ghost variables, we consume "complexity" of expressions (right-hand side of assignments or operand in comparisons) on allocation.

First let us define the complexity order on expressions.

Notation 5. *Let us denote $\preccurlyeq$ the order relation on $\mathscr{E}$ defined by $a \preccurlyeq b :\Leftrightarrow$ VarM $(a) \lhd_{\mathcal{M}}$ VarM $(b) \lor ($VarM $(a) \trianglelefteq_{\mathcal{M}}$ VarM $(b) \land a \subseteq b)$ where $\subseteq$ is the structural inclusion, VarM (e) is the multiset of variables in e and $\trianglelefteq_{\mathcal{M}}$ is the multiset order induced by $\lhd$ [10]. $\prec$ denotes the corresponding strict order.*

Lemma 1. *Let V be a finite subset of $\mathcal{V}$ and $E := \{e \in \mathscr{E} \mid \text{Var}(e) \subseteq V\}$. The restriction to E of $\trianglelefteq_{\mathcal{M}}$ is well-founded.*

It is a well-known result [10], since $\trianglelefteq$ is well-founded on such a set.

Lemma 2. *Let V be a finite subset of $\mathcal{V}$ and $E := \{e \in \mathcal{E} \mid \mathrm{Var}\,(e) \subseteq V\}$. The restriction to E of $\preccurlyeq$ is well-founded.*

It is a lexicographic order induced by two well-founded orders.

Notation 6. *Let us denote $\twoheadrightarrow$ the smallest relation on $\mathcal{U}$ that satisfies*

- $\forall(v,e) \in \mathbb{A} \uplus \mathscr{A}, \forall(l,op,r) \in \mathscr{C}, \mathrm{Var}\,(l) \cup \mathrm{Var}\,(r) \subseteq \mathrm{Var}\,(e)^{\trianglelefteq} \Rightarrow (v,e) \twoheadrightarrow (l,op,r)$
- $\forall((l,op,r),(l',op',r')) \in (\mathbb{C} \uplus \mathscr{C}) \times \mathscr{C}, l' \prec l \wedge r' \prec r \Rightarrow (l,op,r) \twoheadrightarrow (l',op',r')$
- $\forall((v,e),(v',e')) \in (\mathbb{A} \uplus \mathscr{A}) \times \mathscr{A}, v' \triangleleft v \wedge \begin{cases} e' \prec e \text{ if } v \text{ is freshly allocated} \\ e' \preccurlyeq e \text{ otherwise} \end{cases} \Rightarrow$
$(v,e) \twoheadrightarrow (v',e')$

Theorem 2. *Let V be a finite subset of $\mathcal{V}$, $E := \{e \in \mathcal{E} \mid \mathrm{Var}\,(e) \subseteq V\}$ and $U := (E \times \mathcal{O} \times E) \uplus \{(v,e) \mid v \in \mathcal{V}, e \in E\}$. $\twoheadrightarrow$ is well-founded on U.*

This is not enough to ensures termination in all cases. We add a last constraint that has been already observed in the example: new variables are under the left-hand side of an assignment:

- $\forall c \in \mathbb{C} \uplus \mathscr{C}, \pi_1(\mathcal{U}_a(c)) = \emptyset$ (comparisons don't allocate ghost variables)
- $\forall(v,e) \in \mathbb{A} \uplus \mathscr{A}, \forall w \in \pi_1(\mathcal{U}_a((v,e))), w \triangleleft v$ (assignments allocate only under their left-hand side)

Finally, we need to recall an intermediate result of non-interference: the tree of ghost variables under the left-hand side of an assignment has no intersection with the trees under other involved variables. Consequently, any new variable cannot appear in a comparison or the right-hand side of an assignment. Thus, the hypotheses of Theorem 2 are indeed satisfied, ensuring termination.

4.7   Support Unification

A last big part is the problem of support unification prior to binary operation. Unifying the support implies adding, killing and assigning variables so as to ensure consistency of both states. But, when a variable is allocated and reduced, it can lead to the allocation of new ghostlier variables that may be not unified. Thus, the way to proceed is to unify the support layer by layer. First, there are real variables: they are already unified since it is guaranteed by the language. The first step is to unify the ghost variables in $\mathcal{V}_1$. This may add new ghost variables in deeper layers. Then, variables in $\mathcal{V}_2$ can be unified. At this round, domains can allocate and reduce variables only in $\mathcal{V}_2$ and lower layers, but, they cannot constrain (or kill) any variable of $\mathcal{V}_1$ and higher. Thus, at the end of this step, both $\mathcal{V}_1$ and $\mathcal{V}_2$ are unified. We continue this way until all variables are unified. We simply iterate calls to $\mathcal{B}$ to unify layer $\mathcal{V}_i$ with i increasing.

Ensuring termination of this process is quite tricky. Since each round consists in applying unary operations on the two abstract states, they will all clearly terminate. But, we should still have a finite number of rounds.

Unlike regular assignments that can lead to a finite but arbitrarily high number of new ghost variables depending on the right-hand side expression, unification assignments are meant to make both states similar. The form of the forest of ghost variables can change, but its depth must stay the same. It is a reasonable constraint since adding a variable where there weren't any means guessing some information from nothing, which seems dubious.

Thus, to ensure termination, we dictate that the depth of the ghost variable tree should not increase. The depth is the maximum number of roles nested around a living variable. In other words, the depth for an abstract state a is $\text{depth}(a) = \max\{i \in \mathbb{N} \mid \text{supp}(a) \in \mathcal{V}_i \neq \emptyset\}$. At the end, the depth should not be bigger than $\max(\text{depth}(a), \text{depth}(b)) + 1$. It is not a natural property but a political one. It is ensured by assigning $\top$ in all variables that exceed the maximum depth. We need each domain to be able to represent the $\top$ value for a variable without using ghost variables. Actually, with reasonable domains, especially domains given in example, unification never allocate variables beyond the limit and this forced-termination protocol is never triggered.

Some unification examples will be detailed in the following.

5 Some Abstract Domains

Here are some abstract domains that benefit from this framework, or simply, that tolerate it well.

5.1 Pointers as Base + Offset

The domain described in [14] represents each pointer as a set of blocks (typically, structures or arrays) it can point to and a numeric offset inside these blocks. This domain has been reimplemented in this framework.

```
1   int t[3];
2   int u[3];
3   int* p;
4   if (?)
5     p = &t;
6   else
7     p = &u;
8   if (?)
9     p++;
```

The old implementation use an underlying numeric domain to handle offsets. In the new implementation, the offset is a ghost variable. More precisely, the domain defines a single role $\mathcal{O}$ffset such that the offset of the variable v is stored in the ghost variable $\mathcal{O}$ffset(v). Pointer arithmetic is translated on arithmetic computation on the offset.

For instance, at the end of the program beside, we have $p = \{t, u\} + \mathcal{O}\text{ffset}(p)$ and $\mathcal{O}\text{ffset}(p) = \{0, 4\}$ (in a possible numeric domain).

If we look closer at the p++; statement. In expanded form, it is p = p + 1;. This violates the hypothesis that the left-hand side is not part of the right-hand side. So, internally, this statement is rewritten as q = p + 1; p = q; where q is a fresh variable. The second generated statement is a mere copy, so not very interesting. Let examine the first one.

Before this assignment we have $p = \{t, u\} + \mathscr{O}\text{ffset}(p)$. The pointer domain can check that this computation is correct and has two effects: setting the base of q to $\{t, u\}$ and modifying the offset of q as $\mathscr{O}\text{ffset}(q) \leftarrow \mathscr{O}\text{ffset}(p) + \texttt{sizeof(int)} \times 1$.

5.2 Slices

In low-level system management, bitwise operations on pointers are sometimes mandatory. A natural example is the initialization of Global Descriptor Table (GDT) in x86 architecture. It is a structure that describes memory spaces with their base address, their size, and some miscellaneous flags. The base address is not stored contiguously in memory: each part is computed using bitwise operations (typically, shifts and bitwise and). The GDT can be used to describe the main memory, but also special structures like call gates: these are mechanisms by which a non privileged application can perform system calls. In this case, the base address is a pointer to the function to call. And so, while accessing a call gate, we must be able to reconstruct the pointer to check the call is valid and continue the analysis. This need a domain that smartly handle bitwise computations. It should be able to keep a precise representation of variables that are cut and rebuilt with bitwise operators.

The main idea is to remember that bit slices of different variables are equal. A slice may also be 0, 1 or $\top$ (unknown). Remembering the 0 and 1 parts is necessary to handle nicely bitmasks.

For instance, with the instruction $z = x$ & $\texttt{0xff}$ | (y & $\texttt{0xff}$ << 16) using the notation defined in Sect. 4.2, the slices domain will remember that

$$z = [_0 \; \mathscr{S}lice_{[0,7] \to [0,7]}(z)[0,7] \; _7|_8 \; 0 \; _{15}|_{16} \; \mathscr{S}lice_{[0,7] \to [16,23]}(z)[0,7] \; _{23}|_{24} \; 0 \; _{31}]$$

It requires two ghost variables to store the same value. With more expressive roles, we could use only one ghost to mean "this variable represents slices $[0,7]$ and $[16,23]$ of y". This solution may be appealing but was rejected due to the complexity it adds into algorithms while being very rarely useful. Indeed, it is uncommon to select two non-consecutive slices of the same variable (here x).

```
1   int x, y;
2   if (?)
3       y=x&0xffff
4   else
5       y=x&0xff
```

Let us also look at support unification. The code above a non-trivial join. At the end of the "if" branch, the 16 lower bits of y are those of x, while at the end of the "else", only the 8 lower bits are those of x. To compute the state after the last line, we need to join these states. But the supports are different. We have to unify the subdivisions. The first branch becomes

$$y = [_0 \; \mathscr{S}lice_{[0,7] \to [0,7]}(y)[0,7] \; _7|_8 \; \mathscr{S}lice_{[8,16] \to [8,15]}(y)[8,15] \; _{15}|_{16} \; 0 \; _{31}]$$

while in the "else" branch, we add a useless $\mathscr{S}lice_{[8,15] \to [8,15]}(y)$ variable equal to x. We can now proceed to the join. The first slice is the same, we keep it. The second slice join "0" and $\mathscr{S}lice_{[8,15]\to[8,15]}(y)[8,15]$ which becomes $\top$. The third slice is just "0" so we keep it. Overall

$$y = [_0 \quad \mathscr{S}lice_{[0,7]\to[0,7]}(y)[0,7] \quad _7|_8 \quad \top \quad _{15}|_{16} \quad 0 \quad _{31}]$$
$$x = \mathscr{S}lice_{[0,7]\to[0,7]}(y) = \mathscr{S}lice_{[8,15]\to[8,15]}(y)(\text{unused})$$

Some ghost variables haven't been deleted but are not used anymore. They may be garbage collected after reduction.

5.3 Numeric Domains: A Singular Case

We can adapt vanilla numeric domains in this framework as a domain without role. All the ghost variables management functions are consequently trivial. This allows straightforward integration of existing numeric abstract domains to this framework.

The converse is not true: there are numerical domains that may take advantage of ghost variables. For instance, it is a way to implement signedness-agnostic domains that need to remember the unsigned value that have the same bit-representation of a signed variable, and conversely. This domain was already part of Astrée but used an ad hoc implementation trick that cannot be generalized. This domain was naturally adapted to the new framework.

5.4 Linear Combinations

In assembly, there are several kinds of jumps. Among near jumps (the simple family of jumps), there are two ways of specifying the destination: either by giving the explicit address of the target instruction, or the offset relative to the address of the current instruction. During system initialization, it might be necessary (for technical reasons) to write dynamically in the code to set such an offset computed as the difference between the destination function pointer and the address of the jump instruction (pinned with a label). Both these addresses are unknown, thus the difference must be remembered symbolically. Later, when the jump is executed and the destination computed, the current address is added to the previously computed difference. We can symbolically simplify this result, and we get the expected function pointer.

The ghost variables are the terms of the linear combination. Just like the slices domain, this domain uses ghost variables to remember values of expressions that may be rvalues, may change or whose variables might fall out of scope.

6   Conclusion

We have proposed a new product of abstract domains that handles ghost variables. It allows decentralized allocation and deletion of ghost variables, while still being shared by all domains. Moreover, it supports communication of arbitrary constraints to allow reduction of internal states, thus to improve precision.

This framework has been implemented in the Astrée static analyzer along with the base-offset domain [14], slices domain and an adapter from old framework to new one to reuse all the numerical domains. This development version of Astrée has been successfully used to analyze real-world critical source code where the old framework is not expressive enough.

Some domains can be added to the current implementation, like linear combinations domain. Beyond that, though we designed this product with dynamic support to ease pointer abstraction, there is no *a priori* limitation on the abstraction level at which it can work. For instance, one can adapt this domain to make reduced product of shape abstraction domains. A product with dynamic support can indeed be a nice and modular way to implement cofibered domains. Thereby, a list-abstraction domain can seamlessly use integers as the content of the list, or any other available domain, such as another kind of data-structure.

References

1. Alur, R., Černý, P., Weinstein, S.: Algorithmic analysis of array-accessing programs. In: Grädel, E., Kahle, R. (eds.) CSL 2009. LNCS, vol. 5771, pp. 86–101. Springer, Heidelberg (2009). https://doi.org/10.1007/978-3-642-04027-6_9

2. Amato, G., Scozzari, F., Seidl, H., Apinis, K., Vojdani, V.: Efficiently intertwining widening and narrowing. Sci. Comput. Program. **120**, 1–24 (2016). https://doi.org/10.1016/j.scico.2015.12.005

3. Blanchet, B., et al.: A static analyzer for large safety-critical software. In: Proceedings of the ACM SIGPLAN 2003 Conference on Programming Language Design and Implementation (PLDI 2003), pp. 196–207. ACM Press, San Diego (2003)

4. Bourdoncle, F.: Abstract interpretation by dynamic partitioning. J. Funct. Program. **2**(4), 407–423 (1992). https://doi.org/10.1017/S0956796800000496

5. Chang, B.-Y.E., Leino, K.R.M.: Abstract interpretation with alien expressions and heap structures. In: Cousot, R. (ed.) VMCAI 2005. LNCS, vol. 3385, pp. 147–163. Springer, Heidelberg (2005). https://doi.org/10.1007/978-3-540-30579-8_11

6. Cortesi, A., Costantini, G., Ferrara, P.: A survey on product operators in abstract interpretation. In: Semantics, Abstract Interpretation, and Reasoning about Programs: Essays Dedicated to David A. Schmidt on the Occasion of his Sixtieth Birthday, Manhattan, Kansas, USA, 19–20 September 2013, pp. 325–336 (2013). https://doi.org/10.4204/EPTCS.129.19

7. Cousot, P., Cousot, R.: Abstract interpretation: a unified lattice model for static analysis of programs by construction or approximation of fixpoints. In: Conference Record of the Fourth Annual ACM SIGPLAN-SIGACT Symposium on Principles of Programming Languages, pp. 238–252. ACM Press, New York, Los Angeles (1977)

8. Cousot, P., Cousot, R.: Systematic design of program analysis frameworks. In: Conference Record of the Sixth Annual ACM Symposium on Principles of Programming Languages, San Antonio, Texas, USA, January 1979, pp. 269–282 (1979). https://doi.org/10.1145/567752.567778

9. Cousot, P., et al.: Combination of abstractions in the ASTRÉE static analyzer. In: Okada, M., Satoh, I. (eds.) ASIAN 2006. LNCS, vol. 4435, pp. 272–300. Springer, Heidelberg (2007). https://doi.org/10.1007/978-3-540-77505-8_23

10. Dershowitz, N., Manna, Z.: Proving termination with multiset orderings. Commun. ACM **22**(8), 465–476 (1979). https://doi.org/10.1145/359138.359142
11. Feret, J.: Confidentiality analysis of mobile systems. In: Palsberg, J. (ed.) SAS 2000. LNCS, vol. 1824, pp. 135–154. Springer, Heidelberg (2000). https://doi.org/10.1007/978-3-540-45099-3_8
12. Halbwachs, N., Péron, M.: Discovering properties about arrays in simple programs. In: Proceedings of the ACM SIGPLAN 2008 Conference on Programming Language Design and Implementation, Tucson, AZ, USA, 7–13 June 2008, pp. 339–348 (2008). https://doi.org/10.1145/1375581.1375623
13. Journault, M., Miné, A., Monat, M., Ouadjaout, A.: Combinations of reusable abstract domains for a multilingual static analyzer. In: Proceedings of the 11th Working Conference on Verified Software: Theories, Tools, and Experiments (VSTTE19), New York, USA, pp. 1–17 (2019, to appear). http://www-apr.lip6.fr/~mine/publi/article-mine-al-vstte19.pdf
14. Miné, A.: Field-sensitive value analysis of embedded C programs with union types and pointer arithmetics. In: Proceedings of the 2006 ACM SIGPLAN/SIGBED Conference on Language, Compilers, and Tool Support for Embedded Systems, LCTES 2006, pp. 54–63. ACM, Ottawa (2006). https://doi.org/10.1145/1134650.1134659
15. Péron, M.: Contributions à l'analyse statique de programmes manipulant des tableaux. (Contributions to the Static Analysis of Programs Handling Arrays). Grenoble Alpes University, France (2010)
16. Platzer, A., Tan, Y.K.: Differential equation axiomatization: the impressive power of differential ghosts. In: Proceedings of the 33rd Annual ACM/IEEE Symposium on Logic in Computer Science, LICS 2018, Oxford, UK, 09–12 July 2018, pp. 819–828 (2018). https://doi.org/10.1145/3209108.3209147
17. Venet, A.: Abstract cofibered domains: application to the alias analysis of untyped programs. In: Cousot, R., Schmidt, D.A. (eds.) SAS 1996. LNCS, vol. 1145, pp. 366–382. Springer, Heidelberg (1996). https://doi.org/10.1007/3-540-61739-6_53
18. Venet, A.: Automatic analysis of pointer aliasing for untyped programs. Sci. Comput. Program. **35**(2), 223–248 (1999)
19. Venet, A.: Automatic determination of communication topologies in mobile systems. In: Levi, G. (ed.) SAS 1998. LNCS, vol. 1503, pp. 152–167. Springer, Heidelberg (1998). https://doi.org/10.1007/3-540-49727-7_9

Harnessing Static Analysis to Help Learn Pseudo-Inverses of String Manipulating Procedures for Automatic Test Generation

Oren Ish-Shalom[1(✉)], Shachar Itzhaky[2(✉)], Roman Manevich[3(✉)], and Noam Rinetzky[1(✉)]

[1] Tel Aviv University, Tel Aviv, Israel
tuna.is.good.for.you@gmail.com, noam.rinetzky@gmail.com
[2] Technion, Haifa, Israel
shachari@cs.technion.ac.il
[3] Ben-Gurion University of the Negev, Beersheba, Israel
rumster@gmail.com

Abstract. We present a novel approach based on supervised machine-learning for inverting String Manipulating Procedures (SMPs), i.e., given an SMP $p : \bar{\Sigma} \to \bar{\Sigma}$, we compute a partial pseudo-inverse function p^{-1} such that given a target string $t \in \bar{\Sigma}$, if $p^{-1}(t) \neq \bot$ then $p(p^{-1}(t)) = t$. The motivation for addressing this problem is the difficulties faced by modern symbolic execution tools, e.g., KLEE, to find ways to execute loops inside SMPs in a way which produces specific outputs required to enter a specific branch. Thus, we find ourselves in a pleasant situation where program analysis assists machine learning to help program analysis.

Our basic attack on the problem is to train a machine learning algorithm using (output, input) pairs generated by executing p on random inputs. Unfortunately, naively applying this technique is extremely expensive due to the size of the alphabet. To remedy this situation, we present a specialized static analysis algorithm that can drastically reduce the size of the alphabet Σ from which examples are drawn without sacrificing the ability to cover all the behaviors of the analyzed procedure. Our key observation is that often a procedure treats many characters in a particular uniform way: it only copies them from the input to the output in an order-preserving fashion. Our static analysis finds these *good* characters so that our learning algorithm may consider examples coming from a reduced alphabet containing a single representative good character, thus allowing to produce smaller models while using fewer examples than had the full alphabet been used. We then utilize the learned pseudo-inverse function to invert specific desired outputs by translating a given query to and from the reduced alphabet.

We implemented our approach using two machine learning algorithms and show that indeed our string inverters can find inputs that can drive a selection of procedures taken from real-life software to produce desired outputs, whereas KLEE, a state-of-the-art symbolic execution engine, fails to find such inputs.

© Springer Nature Switzerland AG 2020
D. Beyer and D. Zufferey (Eds.): VMCAI 2020, LNCS 11990, pp. 180–201, 2020.
https://doi.org/10.1007/978-3-030-39322-9_9

1 Introduction

Recently, there has been a growing interest in applying machine learning techniques to challenging program analysis problems [9,22,23,25,27,28,32]. In this paper, we address the dual question: Can program analysis techniques help machine learning? We perform a preliminary case study in which machine learning algorithms are used to invert *string manipulating procedures* (SMPs), and show that in this domain the answer is reassuringly positive. Interestingly, the models generated by the machine learning algorithms can themselves be of help to other program analysis tools. Specifically, they can help improve the coverage of symbolic execution tools such as KLEE [2]. Thus, we find ourselves in a pleasant situation where program analysis assists machine learning to help program analysis.

Research Problem. Let Σ be a (possibly infinite) set of *characters* ranged over by a meta-character σ. A *string* $s \in \overline{\Sigma}$ is a finite sequence of *characters*. Given a deterministic SMP $p()$ which transforms input strings $s \in \overline{\Sigma}$ to output strings $p(s) \in \overline{\Sigma}$, where $p(s)$ denotes the output $p()$ returns when invoked on s, our goal is to find a *partial right pseudo-inverse* of a (possibly non-injective) p, i.e., a function $p^{-1} : \overline{\Sigma} \hookrightarrow \overline{\Sigma}$ such that

$$\forall s' \in \overline{\Sigma}.\, p^{-1}(s') \neq \bot \implies p(p^{-1}(s')) = s'.$$

Clearly, the problem is decidable as we can always have $p^{-1} = \bot$. Another trivial solution is to define p^{-1} to be the identity function wherever it coincides with the inverse of p, i.e., have

$$p^{-1}(s') = \begin{cases} s' & p(s') = s' \\ \bot & \text{otherwise.} \end{cases}$$

Thus, the challenge is to come up with a function p^{-1} with non-trivial domain of definition. Ideally, p^{-1} should be able to help automatic test generation, as we discuss now.

Motivation. The ability to invert string-manipulating procedures (SMPs) is useful, for example, in the context of tools for automatic test generation, e.g., KLEE [2]—a state-of-the-art symbolic execution engine. These tools automatically generate test cases, aiming to exercise as much of the program's code as possible. For example, KLEE uses various heuristics to explore the program's code: it continuously selects code paths that lead to not-yet-explored statements, applying a satisfiability-modulo theory solver (SMT) [4,6] to determine whether a path is feasible, i.e., that there is an input which causes the selected path to be executed. As the exploration is path-sensitive, the tool may inspect an exponential number of code paths when exploring a loop containing a conditional, while generating formulae whose size is proportional to the length the inspected path. As a result, it can be challenging to cover a statement following a call to an SMP p which can be reached only if p returns a specific output s'. Ideally, when the engine reaches such a difficult-to-handle branch condition, one would want the symbolic execution engine to abandon the execution path it followed within $p()$, and instead, try to execute it "backward" to produce s'. Our technique equips the engine with such an ability by generating an "inverse shortcut"—a function that inverts the behavior of $p()$ without the cost of a path-by-path exploration.

Learning Pseudo-Inverses. Our goal is to help tools such as KLEE to find inputs which drive SMPs to produce desired outputs. We suggest to do it using machine learning: Given an SMP $p()$ mapping input strings s to output strings $p(s)$, we apply a supervised machine learning algorithm to learn a *model* of a pseudo inverse of p. The model should be capable of *translating* strings, i.e., given a string s' the model should be able to find a string s which it predicts to be an inverse of s under p.

Roughly speaking, producing the model entails generating a set of arbitrary inputs $\{s_i\}_{i=1}^n$, executing p on each input, thus producing a training set $T = \{(p(s_i), s_i)\}_{i=1}^n$, and finally training the algorithm on T. Note that T is comprised of pairs of strings mapping the *output* of $p()$ to the input which produced it. Thus, by training the algorithm using T, we in fact learn a model which approximates the behavior of a pseudo-inverse of $p()$.

The Challenge. Unfortunately, a naive generation of the training set can be extremely inefficient in the sense that many output/input pairs effectively expose the same behavior. For example, consider an SMP which adds an escape character before tab and new-line characters in its input. If we use randomly generated training sets, $p()$ will act as the identity function on most of the examples, and it might require a very large training set to expose other, more "interesting", behaviors: A randomly constructed string with 10 resp. 88 characters has a 92% resp. 50%, chance not to include a tab or a newline character. As a result, the machine learning algorithm might find it difficult to generalize the interesting cases (or outright ignore them, considering them to be noise), and end up learning a bad approximation of the inverse.

Our Solution: Learning with Reduced Alphabets. To remedy the above situation, we propose a static analysis which allows to reduce the alphabet from which the training set examples are drawn, without scarifying the ability to encode any "interesting" behaviors. In fact, our approach increases the chances of generating "interesting" examples by reducing the part of the alphabet from which "non-interesting" examples are drawn. Intuitively, we identify a *set of good characters* (Definition 2) whose only effect on the analyzed procedure is to be copied in an order-preserving manner from the input to the output. Our *key insight* is that given such a set, it is possible to expose all the interesting behaviors of a procedure using an alphabet containing a single representative good character, and deduce the effect of an SMP on a string containing characters which were not found in the reduced alphabet from its effect on a *similar* string (Definition 1) whose characters do.

Alphabet Reduction via Static Analysis. To automate the selection of good characters, we designed a static analysis that can find the set of good characters for a given string manipulating procedure. Our analysis handles a restricted class of procedures. In this class, a procedure takes a string input and returns a string output. The procedure can read its input from left-to-right, from right-to-left, or in both directions, however each input character is read only once. The procedure is allowed to use variables that can hold character values and employ conditionals and loops, where condition can only test whether a character variable is equal or not to another variable or to a constant. While simple, we found that our restricted programming model is still expressive enough to handle a variety of procedures.

Technically, the static analysis maintains an order between the variables according to the position of the input character that they got their value from. Essentially, whenever a variable x containing an input character is written to the output out of turn, i.e., before any other variable y holding an input value σ which was read off the input x was set, the analysis determines that the σ cannot be good. Similarly, writing a constant character const to the output leads the analysis to dictate that const is not good either.

Implementation and Experimental Evaluation. We implemented our analysis in a tool called STRINVER. We applied it to invert a small selection of procedures written in C and taken from real-life software. (The tool operates on LLVM bitcode.) We then ran KLEE on a simple program containing a call to the SMP followed by an erroneous command whose execution is predicated on the SMP returning a particular output. Our analysis succeeded to find useful pseudo-inverses of the particular outputs in a few seconds, whereas KLEE, a state-of-the-art symbolic execution tool, failed to find an input which lead to the bug.

Main Contributions. The main conceptual contribution of our work is the observation that when a machine learning algorithm is used to discover properties of programs, it might be possible to use program analysis to help direct the choice of the training set towards examples that expose interesting behaviors. The main technical contribution of our work is the concretization of this observation by developing a static analysis algorithm which allows to reduce the size of the alphabet from which examples are drawn when learning pseudo inverses of a restricted class of string manipulating procedures. The main practical contribution of our work is the implementation of the analysis and an empirical evaluation where we applied our technique to a small selection of procedures taken from real-life software. Also, to the best of our knowledge, the idea of using machine learning to invert string-manipulating procedures is novel.

2   Overview

In this section, we motivate our research problem and give a high-level overview of our approach by walking the reader through a series of examples.

Example 1. *Figure 1 shows procedure* escapeWS(), *an SMP which returns a copy of its input string with a $ character before every 5 and 8 character it contains.[1] For example, given the input string "Ali5BaBa8", escapeWS() outputs "Ali$5BaBa$8".*

To motivate the need for computing inverses of SMPs, assume that we wish to symbolically execute a program which aborts in an error state only if escapeWS() produces a particular output, e.g.,

---

[1] The procedure is based on a GCC procedure which adds an escape character before tab and newline characters. For clarity, we replaced the whitespace characters with more visible characters. For simplicity, we removed code concerning array bound checking.

```
ret = escapeWS(input);
if (strcmp(ret, "Ali$5BaBa$8") == 0) abort();
...
```

Note that `escapeWS()` produces "Ali$5BaBa$8" only if it is given "Ali5BaBa8" as input. To find this input, symbolic execution engines such as KLEE would have to follow a very particular code path, namely the one in which the loop body is executed nine times and the true branches of the first and second `if` statements are taken after reading the fourth and ninth input characters, respectively.

Our goal is to help tools such as KLEE to find inputs which drive SMPs to produce specific desired outputs. We would like to use an off-the-shelf supervised machine learning algorithm and train it to generate a model of the inverse function. While it is quite easy to generate random inputs, most of them will be non-representative of the function's actual semantics, necessitating large training sets, as we noticed in our experiments. Consider again procedure `escapeWS()` shown in Fig. 1. It is easy to see that the procedure acts rather uniformly on most of the input characters: all the characters are copied from the input string to the output string in an order-preserving fashion, only characters 5 and 8 trigger an insertion of the '$' character. Thus, if the input string does not contain characters 5 and 8 then the procedure acts as the identity function. Thus, intuitively, all the "interesting" behaviors of the procedure should be detected by considering string comprised of four characters: 5, 8, $, and an arbitrary character M representing all other characters.

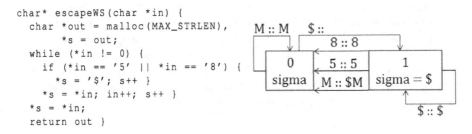

Fig. 1. A simple SMP[4] and a transducer approximating its pseudo-inverse under the reduced alphabet

Inverting SMPs with Reduced Alphabets. To remedy the above situation, we propose a static analysis which allows to reduce the alphabet from which the training set examples are drawn, without scarifying the ability to encode any "interesting" behaviors. Our *key insight* is that if we can identify that the SMP does not distinguish between several characters then it might be possible to expose all the interesting behaviors of a procedure using an alphabet containing a single representative character of the set, and deduce the effect of an SMP on a string containing characters which were not found in the reduced alphabet from its effect on a *similar* string whose characters do. In this paper, we focus on a particular class of indistinguishable characters, those which the procedure act on as, essentially, the identity function, and refer to these characters *good* characters.

Definition 1 (Similar strings). *Let $S \subseteq \Sigma$ be a set of characters. Strings $s_1 \in \overline{\Sigma}$ and $s_2 \in \overline{\Sigma}$ are* similar up to S, *denoted by $s_1 \sim_S s_2$, if $|s_1| = |s_2|$, where $|s|$ denotes the length of a string s, and for every $i = 1..|s_1|$, it holds that either $s_1(i) = s_2(i)$ or $\{s_1(i), s_2(i)\} \subseteq S$.*

Definition 2 (Good characters). *Given a procedure $p()$ and a string s, a set of characters $G(s) \subseteq \Sigma$ is* good *for s and $p()$ if $s|_{G(s)} = p(s|_{G(s)})$, where $s|_{G(s)}$ denotes the maximal subsequence of s comprised of characters in $G(s)$. A set of characters G is* good *for $p()$ if it is good for $p()$ and any input string s.*

Lemma 1. *Let $G \subseteq \Sigma$ be a set of good characters for $p()$. For any two strings s_1 and s_2, if $s_1 \sim_G s_2$ then $p(s_1) \sim_S p(s_2)$.*

Given a procedure $p()$, our static analyzer, discussed next, finds a set of good characters for $p()$ by way of elimination. For example, our analyzer finds that the set $\{\$,5,8\}$ is bad for procedure escapeWS(). We use this result to construct a *reduced alphabet* $\Gamma = \{\$,5,8,M\}$, where $M \in \Sigma$ is the single representative of the good characters, which we refer to as a *metacharacter*. Given Γ, we apply the aforementioned learning process; this time, however, we generate the training set by only drawing examples from Γ. Our static analysis is independent of the machine learning algorithm used to find the inverse. In our experiments, we use two such algorithms: OSTIA [14], which learns a *transducer*, and the other is a non deterministic model for character insertion/replacement/deletion based on the Needleman Wunsch alignment algorithm [20]. (See Sect. 6.) A transducer is a finite state machine that, instead of accepting or rejecting an input string, outputs characters upon transition. Figure 1 depicts a transducer approximating the pseudo inverse of escapeWS() which OSTIA has learned using a training set comprised of 100 strings, randomly generated over Γ. (We explain the graphical notations in Sect. 6.1.) In our example, the transducer has two states, where state 0 is the initial one. An edge labeled $\overset{x::s}{\rightarrow}$ is traversed when reading an input character x and it outputs the string s. (For further details, see Sect. 6.) For example, when applied to the string $s' = MM\$5\$5MM\$8$, the transducer outputs the string $s = MM55MM8$. Note that executing escapeWS() on s results in s', i.e.,

$$escapeWS^{-1}(MM\$5\$5MM\$8) = MM55MM8.$$

In fact, if we only consider strings comprised of characters coming from Γ then the transducer in Fig. 1 can invert any string in the image of escapeWS().

Static Analysis for a Restricted Class of SMPs. One of the key technical contributions of this paper is the design of a static analysis that can find a set of good characters for a given string manipulating procedure. Our analysis handles a restricted class of procedures. In this class, a procedure takes a string input and returns a string output. The procedure can read its input from left to right or from right to left, however each input character is read only once. The procedure is allowed to use variables that can hold character values and employ loops and conditions where a variable is compared with a constant character or another variable. While simple, we found that our restricted programming model is still expressive enough to handle a variety of procedures.

The analysis abstracts the execution trace of the procedure by maintaining an ordering over program variables according to the position of the input character that they got their value from. Essentially, whenever a variable containing an input character is written out of order, the analysis determines that the values of all the unwritten variables that may have been read before it are *not* good. Writing a constant character to the output also leads the analysis to decide that this character is not good either.

String Inversion. Given the machine learning model approximating a pseudo inverse of $p()$ and an output string s', we first replace every good character in s' with the meta character. For example,

$$s' = Ab\$5\$5T@\$8 \xrightarrow{\text{translates to}} s'_0 = MM\$5\$5MM\$8.$$

We then execute the transducer using s'_0, which returns s_0. Recall that $escapeWS^{-1}(s'_0) = s_0$. Our main theorem (see Sect. 5) ensures that the static analysis indeed finds a set of good characters for the analyzed procedure. Thus, using Definition 2, we can get an input s which would lead to the desired output s' by replacing the meta character M back to the good character it came from in s'. For example,

$$s_0 = MM55MM \xrightarrow{\text{translates back to}} s = Ab55T@8.$$

Indeed, $escapeWS(Ab55T@8) = Ab\$5\$5T@\$8$.

Disclaimer. We note that our technique is not guaranteed to always find an input s which leads $p()$ to produce a particular output string s'. This can be because $p()$ is not surjective and $p^{-1}(s')$ is undefined, or because the translation model produced by the machine learning algorithm is not accurate enough. (To isolate any client application from this kind of inaccuracy, and as we have $p()$ at our disposal, we can execute $p()$ on s and validate that indeed it returns s'). Furthermore, in case $p()$ is not injective, and there might be multiple inputs leading to a specific output, the model we learn may return an arbitrary string, which, untested by a forward execution, might not even be in the preimage of p. However, as our technique involves generating a random training set, re-executing the learning phase may create a different model which would possibly find a different input.

3   Programming Language

We formalize our results for a simple imperative programming language specialized for string processing: Every program receives a string as input and produces a string as output. The design of the language is inspired by real life examples of string manipulating procedures which often process their inputs character by character.[2]

---

[2] We remind the reader that our tool operates directly on LLVM bitcode.

Computation Model. Roughly speaking, programs have at their disposal two *read heads* and two *write heads*. The input resides in the *read buffer*. The *first read head* is used to read the input from left to right, and the *last read head* allows to read the input from right to left. Once a read head inspects a character, it advances to the next position. A special built-in expression done() allows the programmer to determine whether all the input characters have been read. Trying to read a character after all the input has been read blocks the program.[3] The program produces its output using the write heads. The *first write head* writes characters to the program's *first write buffer*, and the *last write head* writes to the program's *last write buffer*. The first write buffer is written from left to tight and the last write buffer is written from right to left. When the program terminates, it returns a concatenation of the first and last write buffers. This model allows us to handle programs which process their input string in a character by character fashion and read every character at most once in a sequential manner going from the beginning of the string to it end, the other way around, or even alternating between the two directions.

$$
\begin{aligned}
&stmt \ ::= \ cmd \ | \ stmt \ stmt \ | \\
&\quad | \ \texttt{if} \ (bexp) \ \{ \ stmt \ \} \ \texttt{else} \ \{ \ stmt \ \} \\
&\quad | \ \texttt{while} \ (bexp) \ \{ \ stmt \ \} \\
&cmd \ ::= \ x = \texttt{read-first()} \ | \ x = \texttt{read-last()} \\
&\quad | \ \texttt{write-first}(x) \ | \ \texttt{write-last}(x) \\
&\quad | \ x := exp \ | \ \texttt{return} \\
&exp \ ::= \ \texttt{const} \ | \ y \\
&bexp \ ::= \ x \bowtie exp \ | \ \texttt{done()} \ | \ \texttt{!done()}
\end{aligned}
$$

```
d = $
while(!done()) {
    x = read-first()
    if (x = 5) {
            write-first(d) }
    if (x = 8) {
            write-first(d) }
    write-first(x) }
return
```

Fig. 2. Syntax of the programming language and a version of procedure escapeWS() written in our programming language. $\bowtie \in \{=, \neq\}$

3.1 Syntax

Figure 2 defines the syntax of our programming language and, as an example, shows a possible encoding of procedure escapeWS() in our language.

A program is a statement *stmt*, which can be either a primitive command *cmd*, a sequential composition of statements, denoted by juxtaposition, a conditional statement, or a while loop.

Primitive commands allow to read input characters, write output characters, and assign the values of *expressions* to variables: The command $x = \texttt{read-first()}$ reads a character from the input using the first reading head, and assigns it to variable x. The command $x = \texttt{read-last()}$ does the same using the last read head. The commands $\texttt{write-first}(x)$ and $\texttt{write-last}(x)$ write the contents of x to the first and last output buffers, respectively. We allow for assignments of the form expression $x = exp$ where an

---

[3] The choice to block the program was done in the sake of simplicity. Alternatively, we could have designed the language to signal an error.

expression *exp* is either a character variable or a constant character. The return command terminates the execution of the program and produces the output by concatenating the write buffers.

Conditional statements and while loops use boolean expressions *bexp* which allow to check whether the value of a given variable is equal to a given expression or not. Two additional boolean expressions are the special built in operators done() and !done(), which allow the program to determine whether all its input has, respectively, has not, been read.

$$(\sigma in, out_F, out_L, env) \xrightarrow{v=read-first()} (in, out_F, out_L, env[v \mapsto \sigma])$$

$$(in, out_F, out_L, env) \xrightarrow{write-first(v)} (in, out_F\, env(v), out_L, env)$$

$$(in\sigma, out_F, out_L, env) \xrightarrow{v=read-last()} (in, out_F, out_L, env[v \mapsto \sigma])$$

$$(in, out_F, out_L, env) \xrightarrow{write-last(v)} (in, out_F, env(v) out_L, env)$$

$$(in, out_F, out_L, env) \xrightarrow{v:=const} (in, out_F, out_L, env[v \mapsto const])$$

$$(in, out_F, out_L, env) \xrightarrow{v:=x} (in, out_F, out_L, env[v \mapsto env(x)])$$

$$(in, out_F, out_L, env) \xrightarrow{assume(x \bowtie const)} (in, out_F, out_L, env) \qquad env(x) \bowtie const$$

$$(in, out_F, out_L, env) \xrightarrow{assume(x \bowtie y)} (in, out_F, out_L, env) \qquad env(x) \bowtie env(y)$$

$$(in, out_F, out_L, env) \xrightarrow{assume(done())} (in, out_F, out_L, env) \qquad in = \varepsilon$$

$$(in, out_F, out_L, env) \xrightarrow{assume(!done())} (in, out_F, out_L, env) \qquad in \neq \varepsilon$$

$$(in, out_F, out_L, env) \xrightarrow{return} out_F\, out_L$$

Fig. 3. Concrete meaning of commands. $\bowtie \in \{=, \neq\}$

3.2 Concrete Semantics

Before defining the meaning of programs in our language, we introduce some notation.

Notation. We assume a (possibly infinite) domain (alphabet) of characters Σ ranged over by the meta variable σ, and a syntactic domain *VAR* of variable names, ranged over by $v, x, \ldots$, which we also use as a semantic domain. A *string* $s \in \overline{\Sigma}$ is a sequence of characters, i.e., a function from $1..n$, for some $n \in \mathbb{N}^0$, to Σ. In the following, we denote string concatenation by juxtaposition and the empty string by ε. Given a function *env*, we write $env[x \mapsto y]$ to denote a function which acts like *env* anywhere except at x, where its value is y.

Concrete Memory States. A *concrete memory state*

$$m = (in, out_F, out_L, env) \in \mathcal{M} = \overline{\Sigma} \times \overline{\Sigma} \times \overline{\Sigma} \times E$$

is a quadruple. The first three components, namely *in*, out_F, and out_L, are strings which store the contents of the program's read buffer, first write buffer, and last write buffer, respectively. $env \in E = VAR \rightarrow \Sigma$ is an *environment* which records the values of variables. We assume that variables are initialized to some fixed *zero* character. By abuse of notation, we let $env(\text{const}) = \text{const}$ for any constant character const.

Operational Semantics. Figure 3 defines the meaning of programs using a small step operational semantics. The latter is defined by translating the program into a control-flow graph form, and encoding conditional using assume commands in the standard way: executing an assume (bexp) command blocks the execution on state where bext does not hold, and does not change the state otherwise. The meaning of commands is rather self explanatory. We only direct the reader's attention to the fact that a write-first() command adds a character at the *end* of the first write buffer whereas the write-last() command adds a character at the *beginning* of the last write buffer and that the program gets stuck if it tries to read an input character when the read buffer is empty.

4   Instrumented Semantics

The purpose of our static analyzer is to help reduce the size of the input alphabet used by the machine learning algorithm when computing the pseudo-inverse of the analyzed SMP. To do so, it detects characters on which the SMP act as the identity function: It turns out that rather often a string-manipulating procedure treats many characters in a particularly uniform way; it only copies them once from the input to the output in an order-preserving fashion. The static analyzer conservatively finds these *good* characters, and enables the use of a single good representative character in the alphabet during learning. This reduction in the size of the alphabet translates to a huge benefit for the learning algorithms, as we discovered in our experiments.

The instrumented semantics extends the concrete one with properties which are of matter to the analysis. The main tracked property is the set $BAD \subseteq \Sigma$ of *bad* characters for the execution. We explain the role of BAD by describing its complement $GOOD = \Sigma - BAD$. A set of characters $G \subseteq \Sigma$ is *good* if every time a character $\in G$ is read off the input, it is copied as-is to the output. In particular, the subsequences of the input and output strings comprised of the good characters are identical. (see Definition 2.)

The goal of our static analysis is to determine a set of good characters for an SMP. The role of the instrumented semantics is to explicate which properties of the execution are tracked to facilitate this task. Thus, when the instrumented semantics terminates, it returns, in addition to the output string, the set of bad characters it computed. Let $\hat{p}(s) = (s', BAD)$ denote the output $p()$ produces if it executes according to the instrumented semantics on input string s. The usefulness of the instrumented semantics as a basis for analysis stems from the following lemma.

Lemma 2. *Let $p()$ be an SMP and s, s' strings. If $\hat{p}(s) = (s', BAD)$ then $\Sigma \setminus BAD$ is a good set of characters for $p()$ and s.*

```
        x = read-first()
        y = read-first()
    3:  z = y
        if (y = $) { write-first(y); write-first(x) }
        else { write-first(x); write-first(z) }
        while (!done()) { x = read-first(); write-first(x) }
```

Fig. 4. SMP showDough()

4.1 Instrumented States

Instrumented states record properties pertaining to the flow of information from the input string through variables to the output string. Specifically, every instrumented state augments a concrete state with four binary relations $E_F, E_L, R_F, R_L \subseteq \Sigma \times \Sigma$ and the set of possibly-not-good characters $BAD \subseteq \Sigma$. We refer to the quintuple $\iota = (E_F, E_L, R_F, R_L, BAD)$ as an *instrumentation*. We assume the components of the instrumentation are initialized to $\emptyset$.

$$\hat{m} = (m, \iota) \in \hat{\mathcal{M}} = \mathcal{M} \times \hat{I}$$

$$\text{where } \iota = (R_F, R_L, E_F, E_L, BAD) \in \hat{I} = (2^{VAR \times VAR})^4 \times 2^{\Sigma}.$$

The m component of an instrumented state is the concrete state it augments.

E_F and E_L are equivalence relations over variable names. Recall that in our language, a variable can be assigned a value either by reading into it a character from the input, assigning into it a constant value, or assigning into it the value of another variable. E_F equates variables whose values originated from the same read-first() operation, either directly, or through a sequence of copy assignments. For example, in the instrumented state which arises at program point 3 in Fig. 4, $E_F = \{(x,x), (y,y), (y,z), (z,y), (z,z)\}$. E_L does the same for variables whose value was originated from a read-last() command. In Fig. 4, there are no read-last() commands. Thus, $E_L = \emptyset$ at any state which arises during the execution.

R_F and R_L are preorders over variable names. R_F represents the order in which variables were read using the first reading head, and R_F represents the order in which variables were read using the last reading head. Both orders take variable copy-assignments into account. For instance, at the instrumented state in program point 3, $R_F = \{(x,x), (y,y), (z,z), (y,z), (z,y), (x,y), (x,z)\}$. $R_L = \emptyset$ because there are no read-last() commands.

BAD over approximates the set of bad characters for the input string on which the SMP executes to produce the state. The over approximation is based on the flow of characters from the input string to output string, as we discuss in Sect. 4.2.

Healthiness Conditions. The instrumentation in instrumented states respects certain natural *healthiness* conditions: A variable may appear in R_F only if it appears in E_F, as in a concrete execution the order in which input characters is read is total and every input character may be read at most once. In fact, R_F can be seen as a total order over the equivalence classes of E_F. A similar relation exists between R_L and E_L. Finally, a variable cannot appear in both E_F and E_L as an input character may be read either by the first read head or by the last read head.

4.2 Instrumented Small-Step Operational Semantics

The instrumentation is manipulated by the instrumented transformers presented in Fig. 5 which defines a deterministic transition relation over $\hat{I} \times \hat{I}$.[4] The transition rules of the instrumented semantics extends the ones of the concrete semantics to track *must* value-flow information:

$$\frac{m \xrightarrow{cmd} m' \quad \iota \xrightarrow{cmd}_m \iota'}{(m,\iota) \xrightarrow{cmd} (m',\iota')} \; cmd \neq \texttt{return} \qquad \frac{m \xrightarrow{return} s \quad \iota \xrightarrow{return}_m BAD}{(m,\iota) \xrightarrow{return} (s,BAD)}$$

The transition relation of the instrumented part of the state is parameterized with the source concrete state of the transition because it requires access to the environment.

We define the rules in Fig. 5, which we explain next, using the following shorthand: Let R resp. E be a binary resp. equivalence relation over variable names and X a set of variable names. We use the following as shorthand $R|_{\neg X} \equiv \{(a,b) \in R \mid (a \notin X) \wedge (b \notin X)\}$ removes from R any pair coming from $X \times X$, $[\![v]\!]_E \equiv \{x \mid (x,v) \in E\}$ denotes the equivalence class of v in E, and $\text{Add}(R,v,x) \equiv R \cup \{(a,v) \mid (a,x) \in R\} \cup \{(v,a) \mid (x,a) \in R\}$ adds v to R in the same positions as x.

The instrumented semantics of a $v = \texttt{read-first}()$ command removes any mention of v from all the relations in the instrumentation—it might be there because its value could have come from a previous read command. It then places it in its own equivalence class in E_F and as the minimal element in R_F: v is the only variable that got its value from that $\texttt{read-first}()$ operation, which is the last command executed so far. If before the assignment v relates only to itself in either E_F or E_L then its value is about to be overridden and lost before having a chance to get written to the output. Hence, in this case the value of $env(v)$ is considered a bad character.

The instrumented meaning of $\texttt{write-first}(v)$ removes any mention of v or any of the variables in its equivalence class according to E_F from any relation it belongs to. This is because a *read* good character should not be written more than one time to the output. If v got its value from a constant assignment or from the opposite read head, or if its value has already been written then $env(v)$ becomes a bad character. If v did get its value from the *first-head* but it is not written in the right order, i.e., it is not a maximal element in R_F then the contents of all the larger variables in R_F becomes bad.[5]

The instrumented meaning of a $v := exp$ removes v from its current place in the instrumentation and, if exp is a variable, places v in the same relations and at the same positions as exp. If v was the only variable to contain a value coming from a read command then $env(v)$ becomes a bad character.

The instrumented meaning of a $\texttt{return}$ command ends the execution with the accumulated *BAD* set.

---

[4] The transformers pertaining to $\texttt{read-last}()$ and $\texttt{write-last}()$ operations are similar to those of $\texttt{read-first}()$ and $\texttt{write-first}()$, respectively, and are thus omitted.

[5] An equally plausible alternative would be to make $env(v)$ bad.

$$(R_F, R_L, E_F, E_L, BAD) \xrightarrow{v=read-first()}_m (R_F^r, R_L|_{\neg v}, E_F|_{\neg v} \cup \{(v,v)\}, E_L|_{\neg v}, BAD \cup BAD^r)$$

$$R_F^r = R_F|_{\neg v} \cup \{(x,v) \mid (x,x) \in E_F\} \cup \{(v,v)\}$$

$$BAD^r = \begin{cases} \{env(v)\} & [\![v]\!]_{E_F} = \{v\} \vee [\![v]\!]_{E_L} = \{v\} \\ \emptyset & otherwise \end{cases}$$

$$(R_F, R_L, E_F, E_L, BAD) \xrightarrow{write-first(v)}_m \left(R_F^w, R_L|_{\neg v}, E_F|_{\neg([\![v]\!]_{E_F})}, E_L|_{\neg([\![v]\!]_{E_L})}, BAD \cup BAD^w\right)$$

$$R_F^w = \begin{cases} \{(z,y) \in R_F \mid z \notin [\![v]\!]_{E_F}\} & (v,v) \in E_F \\ R_F & otherwise \end{cases}$$

$$BAD^w = \begin{cases} \{env(v)\} & (v,v) \notin E_F \vee (v,v) \in E_L \vee exp = const \\ \{\sigma \in \{env(y)\} \mid (y,y) \in E_F \wedge y \neq v \wedge (v,y) \notin R_F\} & (v,v) \in E_F \wedge exp = v \end{cases}$$

$$(R_F, R_L, E_F, E_L, BAD) \xrightarrow{v:=const}_m (R_F|_{\neg v}, R_L|_{\neg v}, E_F|_{\neg v}, E_L|_{\neg v}, BAD \cup BAD_v)$$

$$(R_F, R_L, E_F, E_L, BAD) \xrightarrow{v:=x}_m (R_F|_{\neg v}, R_L|_{\neg v}, E_F|_{\neg v}, E_L|_{\neg v}, BAD \cup BAD_v) \qquad (x,x) \notin E_F \cup E_L$$

$$(R_F, R_L, E_F, E_L, BAD) \xrightarrow{v:=x}_m (Add(R_F|_{\neg v}, v, x), R_L, Add(E_F|_{\neg v}, v, x), E_L, BAD \cup BAD_v) \qquad (x,x) \in E_F$$

$$(R_F, R_L, E_F, E_L, BAD) \xrightarrow{v:=x}_m (R_F, Add(R_L|_{\neg v}, v, x), E_F, Add(E_L|_{\neg v}, v, x), BAD \cup BAD_v) \qquad (x,x) \in E_L$$

$$\text{where } BAD_v = \begin{cases} \{env(v)\} & [\![v]\!]_{E_F} = \{v\} \vee [\![v]\!]_{E_L} = \{v\} \\ \emptyset & otherwise \end{cases}$$

$$(R_F, R_L, E_F, E_L, BAD) \xrightarrow{return}_m BAD$$

Fig. 5. Instrumented semantics. The transformers pertaining to assume commands act like the identity function. $m = (\_,\_,\_,env)$. We assume $v \neq x$

The rules in Fig. 5 never interfere with neither the values nor the control of the underlying concrete semantics. They also preserve healthiness.

Lemma 3. *Let (m, ι) and (m', ι') be instrumented states and cmd a command such that $(m, \iota) \xrightarrow{cmd} (m', \iota')$. If ι is a healthy instrumentation then ι' is healthy too.*

5   Static Analysis

Our abstract interpretation algorithm over-approximates the instrumented semantics described in Sect. 4 by replacing the concrete memory state component of instrumented states with an abstract one.

Abstract States. Our static analysis algorithm computes an *abstract instrumented state*

$$A = (m^\sharp, \iota) \in \mathcal{A} = \mathcal{M}^\sharp \times \hat{I} \qquad \text{where } m^\sharp = (Done, env^\sharp) \in \mathcal{M}^\sharp.$$

at every program point. An abstract instrumented state is comprised of an *abstract state* $m^\sharp = (Done, env^\sharp)$ and an instrumentation $\iota \in \hat{I}$ (see Sect. 4.1). The *Done* component of the abstract state abstracts the number of unread characters, i.e., whether the two read-heads passed each other or not: $\{T\}$ means that all the input characters have been read, $\{F\}$ means the opposite, and $\{T, F\}$ means that the situation is unknown. $env^\sharp : VAR \rightarrow 2^\Sigma$ is an abstract environment mapping variable names to the sets of their possible values. The instrumentation component ι is utilized for the same purpose and in the same way as in the instrumented semantics.

Notice that while $env^{\#}(x) \in 2^{\Sigma}$ may be infinite, the only changes to it are additions and removals of values that occur as literal constants in the program. Therefore the number of such distinct values is at most 2^k, where k is the number of such constants. This provides a termination guarantee of the analysis even with an infinite alphabet.

Join. The least upper bound (join) operator is defined as follows:

$$(m_1^{\#}, \iota_1) \sqcup (m_2^{\#}, \iota_2) = (m_1^{\#} \sqcup m_2^{\#}, \iota_1 \sqcup \iota_2), \qquad \text{where}$$

$$(Done_1, env_1^{\#}) \sqcup (Done_1, env_1^{\#}) = (Done_1 \cup Done_1, \lambda x. env_1^{\#}(x) \cup env_2^{\#}(x))$$

$$(R_F^1, R_L^1, E_F^1, E_L^1, C^1, BAD^1) \sqcup (R_F^2, R_L^2, E_F^2, E_L^2, C^2, BAD^2) =$$
$$(R_F^1 \cap R_F^2, R_L^1 \cap R_L^2, E_F^1 \cap E_F^2, E_L^1 \cap E_L^2, BAD^3)$$

where $BAD^3 = BAD^1 \cup \{\sigma \in \rho_1(x) \mid x \in E_F^1 - E_F^2 \cup E_L^1 - E_L^2\} \cup$
$$BAD^2 \cup \{\sigma \in \rho_2(x) \mid x \in E_F^2 - E_F^1 \cup E_L^2 - E_L^1\}$$

With the exception of the *BAD* component, it is easy to see that the resulting state is indeed the least upper bound of the two abstract instrumented states. The reason we chose in to intersect most of the component of joined instrumentations is rather clear— we track must information. To understand the reason why defining $BAD^3 = BAD^1 \cup BAD^2$ would not suffice to ensure a sound analysis consider a scenario when $(x,x) \in E_F^1 - E_F^2$. Had we kept $(x,x) \in E_F^3$, then a future write-first(x) possibly violates the goodness of the character set $\rho_3(x)$ as it may be written without ever being read. On the other hand, as we discarded (x,x) from E_F^3, we opened the door for a future x = read-first$()$ to possibly violate the goodness of the character set $\rho_3(x)$, as some characters may have been read without ever being written. So whenever $(x,x) \in E_F^i - E_F^j$ ($\{i,j\} = \{1,2\}$) we include $\rho_i(x)$ in BAD^3. The same line of reasoning applies to E_L too. Thus, we add to BAD^3 the characters associated with the variables found in the symmetrical difference of the relevant equivalence relations.

5.1 Concretization

The concrete domain which we use to justify the soundness of our analysis is the powerset of instrumented states. The concretization function γ maps an abstract state to a set of instrumented ones. Let $\iota = (R_F, R_L, E_F, E_L, BAD)$, then

$$\gamma(((Done, env^{\#}), \iota)) = \{((in, out_F, out_L, env), (R_F^c, R_L^c, E_F^c, E_L^c, BAD^c)) \mid$$
$$in = \varepsilon \to T \in Done \wedge in \neq \varepsilon \to F \in Done \wedge$$
$$\forall x. env(x) \in env^{\#}(x) \wedge$$
$$R_F^c \supseteq R_F \wedge R_L^c \supseteq R_L \wedge E_F^c \supseteq E_F \wedge E_L^c \supseteq E_L \wedge BAD^c \subseteq BAD$$

When an abstract instrumented state $\iota^{\#} = (A, \iota)$ represents an instrumented state $((in, out_F, out_L, env), \iota^c)$, A's *Done* component conservatively tracks whether all the input characters in *in* have been read and that the values *env* gives to variables agree with the ones provided by the abstract environment. The instrumentation ι^c of the concrete state should track no less information regarding the information flow of characters from the input string to the output string as does the instrumentation ι. The latter should also consider as bad any bad character in ι^c.

$$(env^\sharp, Done) \xrightarrow{v=read-first() \;/\; v=read-last()} (env^\sharp[x \mapsto \Sigma], Done \cup \{T\}) \qquad\qquad Done \neq \{T\}$$

$$(env^\sharp, Done) \xrightarrow{write-first(v) \;/\; write-first(v)} (env^\sharp, Done)$$

$$(env^\sharp, Done) \xrightarrow{v:=const} (env^\sharp[v \mapsto \{const\}], Done)$$

$$(env^\sharp, Done) \xrightarrow{v:=x} (env^\sharp[v \mapsto env^\sharp(x)], Done)$$

$$(env^\sharp, Done) \xrightarrow{assume(v=const)} (env^\sharp[v' \mapsto \{const\} \mid \varphi(v)], Done) \qquad\qquad const \in env^\sharp(x)$$

$$(env^\sharp, Done) \xrightarrow{assume(v!=const)} (env^\sharp[v' \mapsto env^\sharp(x) \setminus \{const\} \mid \varphi(v)], Done) \qquad\qquad \{const\} \neq env^\sharp(x)$$

$$(env^\sharp, Done) \xrightarrow{assume(v=x)} (env^\sharp[v', x' \mapsto env^\sharp(v) \cap env^\sharp(x) \mid \varphi(v) \wedge \varphi(x)], Done) \qquad env^\sharp(v) \cap env^\sharp(x) \neq \emptyset$$

$$(env^\sharp, Done) \xrightarrow{assume(v!=x)} (env^\sharp[v \mapsto V, x \mapsto X \mid \varphi(v) \wedge \varphi(x)], Done) \qquad env^\sharp(v) = env^\sharp(x)$$
$$V = \text{if } (|env^\sharp(x)| = 1) \text{ then } env^\sharp(v) \setminus env^\sharp(x) \text{ else } env^\sharp(v) \qquad\qquad \implies |env^\sharp(v)| > 1$$
$$X = \text{if } (|env^\sharp(v)| = 1) \text{ then } env^\sharp(x) \setminus env^\sharp(v) \text{ else } env^\sharp(x)$$

$$(env^\sharp, Done) \xrightarrow{assume(done())} (env^\sharp, \{T\}) \qquad\qquad \{F\} \neq Done$$

$$(env^\sharp, Done) \xrightarrow{assume(!done())} (env^\sharp, \{F\}) \qquad\qquad \{T\} \neq Done$$

$$(env^\sharp, Done) \xrightarrow{return} (env^\sharp, Done))$$

Fig. 6. Abstract semantics. $\varphi(z) = z' = z \vee z' \in [\![z]\!]_{E_F} \vee [\![z]\!]_{E_L}$

5.2   Abstract Transformers

The abstract transformers are defined by replacing the concrete component in the transition rules of the instrumented semantics with the rules pertaining to abstract states defined in Fig. 6 and adapting the rules in Fig. 5 to utilize an abstract environment instead of a concrete one as explained below

$$\frac{m^\sharp \xrightarrow{cmd} m^{\sharp'} \qquad \iota \xrightarrow{cmd}_{m^\sharp} \iota'}{(m^\sharp, \iota) \xrightarrow{cmd} (m^{\sharp'}, \iota')}$$

Again, the transition relation of the instrumented part of the state is parameterized with the source abstract state of the transition because it requires access to the abstract environment. The required adaptation of Fig. 5 is rather direct: where ever an expression of the form $\{env(x)\}$ appears in a rule, we replace it with $env(x)$.

The rules are quite simple; the tricky ones pertain to assume statements regarding inequalities, which we now explain.

The abstract transformer of command assume(v!=const) blocks the execution if the only possible value of v is const. Otherwise, it merely records that const is not in fact a possible value of v. Note that not only $env^\sharp(v)$ may be adapted, but in case v got its value from the input string, any variable who got its value from the same read operation, i.e., in the same equivalence class as v in either E_F or E_L, may have the set of its possible values refined.

```c
char* ReplaceSpaces(char *in) {
  char *out = malloc(MAX_STRLEN),
       *s = out, c = 0, skip_next_lf = 0;
  while (*in != 0) {
    c = *in; in++;
    if (skip_next_lf) {
      skip_next_lf = 0;
      if (c == '#') {
        c = *in; in++;
        if (!c) break; }}
    if (*c == '$') {
      skip_next_lf = 1;
      c = '#'; }
    *s = c; s++;}}
  *s = *in;
  return out; }
```

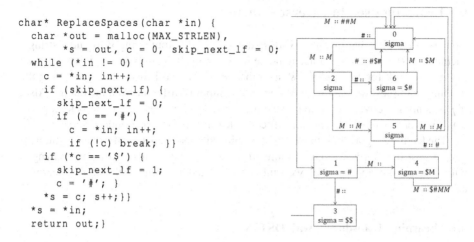

Fig. 7. An SMP written in C and its pseudo-inverse as learned by OSTIA.

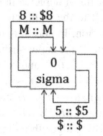

Fig. 8. A transducer implementing the SMP in Fig. 2

The abstract transformer of command assume($v! =$const) blocks the execution if the only possible value of v is const. Otherwise, it merely records that const is not in fact a possible value of v. The abstract transformer of command assume($v! =y$) blocks the execution if the abstract environment associates both variables with the same single character. Otherwise it attempts to refine the set of possible values of one variable if the other one is associated with a singleton set.

Main Theorem. The static analysis algorithm computes at every program point an abstract state which over-approximates any instrumented state which can arise at this point for some input string. We denote by $BAD(p)$ the union of the BAD sets at $p()$'s exit points, i.e., right after $p()$ executes a return command. Our main theorem, whose proof follows directly from Lemma 2 and the soundness of the analysis, states that the analyzer computes a set of good characters $p()$.

Theorem 1. *Let $p()$ be an SMP. $\Sigma \setminus BAD(p)$ is a* good *set of characters for $p()$.*

6   Learning Pseudo-Inverse Functions

Our overall goal is that given an SMP p and a desired output string s' to find a string s such that $p(s) = s'$. One natural candidate for s is s' itself. Thus, when trying to learn an inverse we look for an input $s \neq s'$ such that $p(s) = s'$ and hence when generating the training examples, we only use ones where the input is different from the output. Also, if $p()$ is not injective, then it may have many pseudo-inverses, and there is no a priori way to favor any of them. Thus, it suffices to learn an *arbitrary* pseudo-inverse of $p()$.

The learning algorithms chosen to be employed in this paper are the ones we thought handle best the SMPs we have examined. However, they can be easily interchanged with others—our approach, as we said before, is independent of the chosen learning algorithm.

6.1   Learning Transducers with OSTIA

Transducers are deterministic finite state machines that are used to translate strings. We explain them using the example transducer depicted in Fig. 7. Just like DFAs, transducer read their input strings from the left to the right, character by character, and traverse edges according to a transition function. In addition, as edges are traversed, the transducer prints characters to the output. If the input string *MMMM##* is fed to the transducer, it will go through states $0, 2, 5, 0, 2, 6, 0$, and print the output string *MMMM#$#*. Any states of the transducer can hold inner strings. If some state q is a final state for the transduction, and it holds an inner string *sigma*, then it is appended at the end of the output. For example, the transduction of *MMMM#* equals *MMMM$#*.

OSTIA [14] is a supervised learning algorithm that is capable of learning transducers. Assuming the training set is without noise, like in our case, OSTIA is guaranteed to converge to the real transducer as the size of the training set increases. The SMP from Fig. 2 and its inverse are both transducers, and we depict them in Figs. 1 and 8, respectively. Every state of the transducer is depicted as a square containing a unique identifier, with state 0 being the initial state, and the string *sigma* which is appended to the output if the transduction end at that state. Transitions between states are depicted as edges annotated with $\sigma :: s$ denoting the character σ which triggers the transition and the string s appended to the output due to taking the transition.

OSTIA succeeds in learning the exact inverse at the right hand side of the figure. In its essence, OSTIA is an iterative state merging algorithm. At each step the algorithm considers pairs of states as candidates for a possible merge, and if the resulting merged transducer is consistent with the training set, it accepts the merge and proceeds to the next iteration. The transducer in Fig. 7 is the pseudo inverse OSTIA learns for the SMP shown in the same figure. The character # in an output string could have originated from either #, $ or $# in the input string. While randomizing our input for the training set, all three possibilities introduce themselves. This is evident in the transducer, as the edges $(5, 0), (2, 6), (6, 0)$ choose a different source for the # character each. Thus neither # nor $ can be good characters.

6.2   Needleman Wunsch Alignment Algorithm

To show the versatility of our approach, we also used the alignment algorithm of Needleman-Wunsch [20] to learn procedure inverses. The algorithm is designed to align input and output strings, where the latter comes from the former by performing a sequence of steps. In each step a character is either deleted, inserted or replaced by another character. Naturally, as the number of steps is smaller, and the input and output are close in terms of edit distance, the results of the alignment are better. Our application uses a random set of inputs $\{s_i\}_{i=1}^n$ just as before, and apply p on each element of the set to end up with a training set $\{(s_i, p(s_i))\}_{i=1}^n$. Note, the order of the training set has changed, as we now want to learn the effect of the *original* SMP p. Each (input,output) pair is then aligned, and three probability tables are accumulated for the original SMP p: (1) A two dimensional table $T_r(p)$ for character replacements, in which $T_r(p)[\$][\#] = 0.45$ means that there is an estimated probability that a $\$$ in the input string will be replaced by a $\#$. (2) A one dimensional table $T_d(p)$, in which $T_d(p)[*] = 0.95$ means there is a probability of 0.95 that $*$ will be deleted from the input string. (3) A one dimensional table $T_i(p)$, in which $T_i(p)[@] = 0.55$, means there is a 0.55 probability of inserting $@$ *somewhere* in the output. Once these tables have been learned for the original SMP p, they can be used to deduce pseudo inverses p^{-1}: If $T_r(p)[\$][\#] = 0.45$ then clearly $T_r(p^{-1})[\#][\$] = 0.45$. Deducing $T_i(p^{-1})[*]$ based on $T_d(p)[*]$ is a little more subtle, and should also take into account the prevalence of the character $*$ in the input strings of the training set. Note that for more accurate results, $T_i(p^{-1})[*]$ depends on the length of the string y it wishes to invert. Finally, computing $T_d(p^{-1})[@]$ from $T_i(p)[@]$ depends on the prevalence of the character $@$ in the output strings of training set, the prevalence of $@$ in y, and the length of y too. It is important to stress out that the resulting pseudo inverse p^{-1} is *not* deterministic, and could return different outputs when invoked multiple times. This can be seen as an advantage, because of $p^{-1}(y)$ failed to find a relevant x, we do not have to perform the learning process again, but simply call $p^{-1}(y)$ again.

7   Implementation and Experimental Evaluation

We have implemented our ideas in a tool called STRINVER. The tool gets as input an SMP $p()$ written in LLVM [18] intermediate representation language, and a concrete query string y. (In our experiments, we used procedures written in C, compiled using Visual C 2010.) The tools checks whether the procedure falls within the class of restricted SMPs we handle (see Sect. 3) by expecting it to follow certain syntactic conventions, and if so it looks for a string s such that $s \neq s'$ and $p(s) = s'$. If the learning algorithm failed to find a model that returns a non-identity inverse for the given string s', it is retried with a new randomized training set. The algorithms were trained using a training set comprised of 64–100 examples, with a bias towards choosing shorter strings.

Table 1 summarizes our experimental results. We considered four string manipulating procedures coming from real-life software. DPSTrim() removes prefixes and suffixes comprised of character #. It is taken from *DataparkSearch* [1] open source search

Table 1. Experimental evaluation of selected SMPs. The table shows the size of the reduced alphabet and the machine learning algorithm used to model the pseudo inverse.

Procedure	Reduced alphabet	ML. Alg.
DPSTrim()	$\{M,\#\}$	Needleman Wunsch
escapeWS()	$\{\$,5,8,M\}$	OSTIA
ReplaceSpaces()	$\{\$,\#,M\}$	OSTIA
DosNames()	$\{.,\_,M\}$	OSTIA

engine and is used to help parse configuration files. escapeWS() is our running example shown in Fig. 1 and ReplaceSpaces() is shown in Fig. 7. Both come from GCC. DosNames() is a python library function which replaces all the dots in a file name with underscores, except for the last one.

In our experiments, we randomly chose output strings using uniform distribution and with average length of 32 characters. We applied our technique to invert 100 strings for and each procedure. Table 1 shows the reduced alphabet our analysis discovered and the machine learning algorithm which we used. We ran our experiments in a laptop equipped with an $i5$ 2.3 Ghz CPU with 6 GB memory running Windows 7. In all our experiments, it took our analysis to invert each string less than 10 s, whereas KLEE [2], a state of the art symbolic executor, failed to invert any string after running for one hour. (KLEE was able to invert short strings containing around 5 characters in a few seconds.) Similarly, a machine learning algorithm trained with randomly selected strings chosen using the full alphabet failed to invert the given output strings. It might be the case that using a larger training set would make the naive machine learning more successful, however, this process might lead to expensive analyses as the space of possible strings grows exponentially with the length of the string.

8   Related Work, Conclusion and Future Work

Automatic inversion of programs was first studied by Dijkstra who manually inverted simple array-manipulating programs [5]. Follow up works looked at inverting (i) simple programs whose semantics is given as logic programs [26], (ii) tree-traversal programs using relational calculus and deductive methods [3,29], (iii) array transformers using techniques based on LR-parsing [8,16] or testing [15], and (iv) bijective string-manipulating procedures [13,19]. To the best of our knowledge, we are the first to apply machine learning tools to invert programs. We also note that the programs we invert are not necessarily injective.

Recent advances in machine learning lead researchers to explore its capabilities in helping challenging program analysis tasks, e.g., specification inference [25,28], speed up abstraction refinement [9], invariant generation [7,22,27], setting up parameters for parametrized static analyses [24], and infer clustering of variables in partially relational static analyses [12]. In our work, we address a dual question–how can machine learning technique help program analyses. To the best of our knowledge the question has not been widely addressed, with the notable exception of [21] which also argues that a combination of machine learning and program analysis can be a win-win situation.

Another active research area is the use of input/output examples to learn computer programs. Often, this is done in the context of synthesis, where examples guide a search-based synthesis process [11]. For example, in [10], a learning procedure is used to synthesize string manipulating procedures which appears in the context of spreadsheets based on syntactic manipulation. Another attack on this problem was taken in [30], where the procedures where synthesized using database-like lookup operations. In these works, the focus is on designing a language in which programs can be synthesized and an efficient search heuristics. In this work we too focus on string manipulating procedures (SMPs), which are abundant in almost all software packages. However, instead of asking the user for input/output examples, we analyze the code of one procedure and its behavior, as expressed by input-output pairs, to synthesize another procedure.

In [33], the authors suggest to learn the behavior of a procedure by inspecting its code and input-output examples. Their technique applies to a class of procedures which accepts their input character by character, e.g., multi-digit addition. They use recurrent neural network models with long short-term memory to accurately learn a model of the procedure behavior as a sequence-to-sequence transformer [31]. It can be interesting to see if a preliminary phase of program analysis, as we do in this work, can help improve the accuracy of their technique.

String solvers, e.g., [17, 34], can reason about constraints involving operations on strings. For example, HAMPI [17], can reason about constraints expressing membership in regular languages and fixed-size context-free languages. In contrast, we provide a technique based on a combination of machine learning and static analysis that can help invert string manipulating procedures written in a restricted programming language.

Conclusion and Future Work. We present a machine learning-based approach for inverting string manipulating procedures (SMPs). To the best of our knowledge, the use of machine learning for program inversion is novel. We make the approach feasible by developing a static analysis which reduces the size of the alphabet of the examples used during training. While the idea of reducing the input domain size is a known idea, we believe that we are the first to design a static analysis specific for enabling such a reduction. We evaluated our technique using a small selection of procedures taken from real-life software. Our approach does not require that the inverted SMP be bijective. However, our analysis is beneficial when the SMP acts as the identity on a large part of its alphabet, which we refer to as the "good" characters.

Acknowledgments. This research was sponsored by the Len Blavatnik and the Blavatnik Family foundation, Blavatnik Interdisciplinary Cyber Research Center at Tel Aviv University, the Pazy Foundation, and the Israel Science Foundation (ISF) grant No. 1996/18.

References

1. http://www.dataparksearch.org/
2. Cadar, C., Dunbar, D., Engler, D.: Klee: unassisted and automatic generation of high-coverage tests for complex systems programs. In: Proceedings of the 8th USENIX Conference on Operating Systems Design and Implementation, OSDI 2008, pp. 209–224. USENIX Association, Berkeley (2008)

3. Checn, W., Duding, J.T.: Program inversion: More than fun! Sci. Comput. Program. **15**(1), 1–13 (1990)
4. de Moura, L., Bjørner, N.: Z3: an efficient SMT solver. In: Ramakrishnan, C.R., Rehof, J. (eds.) TACAS 2008. LNCS, vol. 4963, pp. 337–340. Springer, Heidelberg (2008). https://doi.org/10.1007/978-3-540-78800-3_24
5. Dijkstra, E.W.: Program inversion. In: Bauer, F.L., et al. (eds.) Program Construction. LNCS, vol. 69, pp. 54–57. Springer, Heidelberg (1979). https://doi.org/10.1007/BFb0014657. http://dl.acm.org/citation.cfm?id=647639.733360
6. Ganesh, V.: Decision procedures for bit-vectors, arrays and integers. Ph.D. thesis, Stanford, CA, USA (2007). aAI3281841
7. Garg, P., Neider, D., Madhusudan, P., Roth, D.: Learning invariants using decision trees and implication counterexamples. In: Proceedings of the 43rd Annual ACM SIGPLAN-SIGACT Symposium on Principles of Programming Languages, POPL 2016, St. Petersburg, FL, USA, 20–22 January 2016, pp. 499–512 (2016)
8. Glück, R., Kawabe, M.: A method for automatic program inversion based on LR(0) parsing. Fundam. Inform. **66**, 367–395 (2005)
9. Grigore, R., Yang, H.: Abstraction refinement guided by a learnt probabilistic model. SIG-PLAN Not. **51**(1), 485–498 (2016). https://doi.org/10.1145/2914770.2837663
10. Gulwani, S.: Automating string processing in spreadsheets using input-output examples. SIGPLAN Not. **46**(1), 317–330 (2011)
11. Gulwani, S.: Programming by examples: applications, algorithms, and ambiguity resolution. In: Olivetti, N., Tiwari, A. (eds.) IJCAR 2016. LNCS (LNAI), vol. 9706, pp. 9–14. Springer, Cham (2016). https://doi.org/10.1007/978-3-319-40229-1_2
12. Heo, K., Oh, H., Yang, H.: Learning a variable-clustering strategy for octagon from labeled data generated by a static analysis. In: Rival, X. (ed.) SAS 2016. LNCS, vol. 9837, pp. 237–256. Springer, Heidelberg (2016). https://doi.org/10.1007/978-3-662-53413-7_12
13. Hu, Q., D'Antoni, L.: Automatic program inversion using symbolic transducers. In: Proceedings of the 38th ACM SIGPLAN Conference on Programming Language Design and Implementation, PLDI 2017, pp. 376–389. ACM, New York (2017). https://doi.org/10.1145/3062341.3062345
14. Jose Oncina, P.G., Vidal, E.: Learning subsequential transducers for pattern recognition interpretation tasks. IEEE Trans. Pattern Anal. Mach. Intell. **15**(5), 448–458 (1993)
15. Kanade, A., Alur, R., Rajamani, S., Ramanlingam, G.: Representation dependence testing using program inversion. In: Proceedings of the Eighteenth ACM SIGSOFT International Symposium on Foundations of Software Engineering, FSE 2010, pp. 277–286. ACM, New York (2010). https://doi.org/10.1145/1882291.1882332
16. Kawabe, M., Glück, R.: The program inverter LRinv and its structure. In: Hermenegildo, M.V., Cabeza, D. (eds.) PADL 2005. LNCS, vol. 3350, pp. 219–234. Springer, Heidelberg (2005). https://doi.org/10.1007/978-3-540-30557-6_17
17. Kiezun, A., Ganesh, V., Guo, P.J., Hooimeijer, P., Ernst, M.D.: HAMPI: a solver for string constraints. In: Proceedings of the Eighteenth International Symposium on Software Testing and Analysis, ISSTA 2009, pp. 105–116. ACM, New York (2009). https://doi.org/10.1145/1572272.1572286
18. Lattner, C., Adve, V.: LLVM: a compilation framework for lifelong program analysis & transformation. In: Proceedings of the International Symposium on Code Generation and Optimization: Feedback-directed and Runtime Optimization, CGO 2004, p. 75. IEEE Computer Society, Washington, DC (2004)
19. Miltner, A., Fisher, K., Pierce, B.C., Walker, D., Zdancewic, S.: Synthesizing bijective lenses. Proc. ACM Program. Lang. **2**(POPL), 1:1–1:30 (2017). https://doi.org/10.1145/3158089
20. Needleman, S.B., Wunsch, C.D.: A general method applicable to the search for similarities in the amino acid sequence of two proteins. J. Mol. Biol. **48**(3), 443–453 (1970)

21. Nori, A.V., Rajamani, S.K.: Program analysis and machine learning: a win-win deal. In: Yahav, E. (ed.) SAS 2011. LNCS, vol. 6887, pp. 2–3. Springer, Heidelberg (2011). https://doi.org/10.1007/978-3-642-23702-7_2

22. Nori, A.V., Sharma, R.: Termination proofs from tests. In: Proceedings of the 2013 9th Joint Meeting on Foundations of Software Engineering, ESEC/FSE 2013, pp. 246–256. ACM, New York (2013). https://doi.org/10.1145/2491411.2491413

23. Octeau, D., et al.: Combining static analysis with probabilistic models to enable market-scale android inter-component analysis. In: Proceedings of the 43rd Annual ACM SIGPLAN-SIGACT Symposium on Principles of Programming Languages, POPL 2016, pp. 469–484. ACM, New York (2016). https://doi.org/10.1145/2837614.2837661

24. Oh, H., Yang, H., Yi, K.: Learning a strategy for adapting a program analysis via Bayesian optimisation. In: Proceedings of the 2015 ACM SIGPLAN International Conference on Object-Oriented Programming, Systems, Languages, and Applications, OOPSLA 2015, pp. 572–588. ACM, New York (2015). https://doi.org/10.1145/2814270.2814309

25. Raychev, V., Bielik, P., Vechev, M., Krause, A.: Learning programs from noisy data. In: Proceedings of the 43rd Annual ACM SIGPLAN-SIGACT Symposium on Principles of Programming Languages, POPL 2016, pp. 761–774. ACM, New York (2016). https://doi.org/10.1145/2837614.2837671

26. Ross, B.J.: Running programs backwards: the logical inversion of imperative computation. Formal Aspects Comput. 9(3), 331–348 (1997)

27. Sankaranarayanan, S., Chaudhuri, S., Ivančić, F., Gupta, A.: Dynamic inference of likely data preconditions over predicates by tree learning. In: Proceedings of the 2008 International Symposium on Software Testing and Analysis, ISSTA 2008, pp. 295–306. ACM, New York (2008). https://doi.org/10.1145/1390630.1390666

28. Sankaranarayanan, S., Ivančić, F., Gupta, A.: Mining library specifications using inductive logic programming. In: Proceedings of the 30th International Conference on Software Engineering, ICSE 2008, pp. 131–140. ACM, New York (2008). https://doi.org/10.1145/1368088.1368107

29. Schoenmakers, B.: Inorder traversal of a binary heap and its inversion in optimal time and space. In: Bird, R.S., Morgan, C.C., Woodcock, J.C.P. (eds.) MPC 1992. LNCS, vol. 669, pp. 291–301. Springer, Heidelberg (1993). https://doi.org/10.1007/3-540-56625-2_19

30. Singh, R., Gulwani, S.: Learning semantic string transformations from examples. Proc. VLDB Endow. 5(8), 740–751 (2012). https://doi.org/10.14778/2212351.2212356

31. Sutskever, I., Vinyals, O., Le, Q.V.: Sequence to sequence learning with neural networks. In: Advances in Neural Information Processing Systems 27: Annual Conference on Neural Information Processing Systems 2014, Montreal, Quebec, Canada, 8–13 December 2014, pp. 3104–3112 (2014)

32. Yi, K., Choi, H., Kim, J., Kim, Y.: An empirical study on classification methods for alarms from a bug-finding static C analyzer. Inf. Process. Lett. 102(2–3), 118–123 (2007). https://doi.org/10.1016/j.ipl.2006.11.004

33. Zaremba, W., Sutskever, I.: Learning to execute. CoRR abs/1410.4615 (2014)

34. Zheng, Y., Ganesh, V., Subramanian, S., Tripp, O., Dolby, J., Zhang, X.: Effective search-space pruning for solvers of string equations, regular expressions and length constraints. In: Kroening, D., Păsăreanu, C.S. (eds.) CAV 2015. LNCS, vol. 9206, pp. 235–254. Springer, Cham (2015). https://doi.org/10.1007/978-3-319-21690-4_14

Synthesizing Environment Invariants
for Modular Hardware Verification

Hongce Zhang[1]([✉]), Weikun Yang[1], Grigory Fedyukovich[2], Aarti Gupta[1],
and Sharad Malik[1]

[1] Princeton University, Princeton, NJ 08544, USA
{hongcez,weikuny,aartig,sharad}@princeton.edu
[2] Florida State University, Tallahassee, FL 32306, USA
grigory@cs.fsu.edu

Abstract. We automate synthesis of environment invariants for modular hardware verification in processors and application-specific accelerators, where functional equivalence is proved between a high-level specification and a low-level implementation. Invariants are generated and iteratively strengthened by reachability queries in a counterexample-guided abstraction refinement (CEGAR) loop. Within each iteration, we use a syntax-guided synthesis (SyGuS) technique for generating invariants, where we use novel grammars to capture high-level design insights and provide guidance in the search over candidate invariants. Our grammars explicitly capture the separation between control-related and data-related state variables in hardware designs to improve scalability of the enumerative search. We have implemented our SyGuS-based technique on top of an existing Constrained Horn Clause (CHC) solver and have developed a framework for hardware functional equivalence checking that can leverage other available tools and techniques for invariant generation. Our experiments show that our proposed SyGuS-based technique complements or outperforms existing property-directed reachability (PDR) techniques for invariant generation on practical hardware designs, including an AES block encryption accelerator, a Gaussian-Blur image processing accelerator and the PicoRV32 processor.

1 Introduction

This paper addresses hardware verification of processing cores in modern complex Systems-on-Chip (SoCs). These comprise general purpose processors and also application-specific hardware accelerators. Despite advances in automated verification, scalability with increasing design complexity remains elusive. For general-purpose processors, where the instruction set architecture (ISA) serves as a specification, a natural approach is to take advantage of the modular per-instruction specification and perform equivalence checking against a microarchitectural implementation on a per-instruction basis [9,36,41,44]. However, increasingly, domain-specific hardware accelerators are being used in SoCs to meet power-performance requirements. Traditionally these accelerators do not

© Springer Nature Switzerland AG 2020
D. Beyer and D. Zufferey (Eds.): VMCAI 2020, LNCS 11990, pp. 202–225, 2020.
https://doi.org/10.1007/978-3-030-39322-9_10

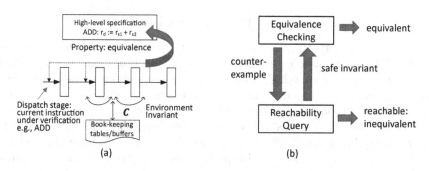

Fig. 1. (a) An example of environment invariants when verifying an ADD instruction in a pipelined processor. (b) Counterexample-guided environment invariant synthesis.

have an ISA or a high-level specification. Recent work has addressed this gap and proposed a generalization of the ISA referred to as an instruction-level abstraction (ILA) [33,54,55]. Similar to the ISA, an ILA provides a high-level modular specification that can be used for modular verification of accelerator implementations. Thus, per-instruction modular verification is applicable on general-purpose processors using ISA [37,49,50], as well as on accelerators using ILA [33].

Although per-instruction equivalence checking[1] helps improve scalability due to modularity, it has its own challenges. Each sub-task in verification checks whether a well-founded equivalence bisimulation (WEB) relation [41] holds between an ISA/ILA model and a low-level model (e.g., the register-transfer-level, or RTL implementation) when the same instruction is executed. The correspondence between states in the two models is specified by a refinement map, typically provided by the user. However, in each check, the given instruction starts to execute from an *arbitrary state* that is left by some previous (sequence of) instructions. For example, when a specified ADD instruction is in the dispatch stage in a processor, as shown in Fig. 1(a), the state of the other pipeline stages (and other microarchitecture variables) constitutes the *environment*. If this environment is not in some consistent or reachable state, the equivalence check on the instruction may generate (spurious) counterexamples even when an implementation is correct. Thus, as in any modular verification method, one needs to model the environment adequately for the per-instruction equivalence checks to be successful.

Past efforts in processor verification have used a *flushing* abstraction [9] as a workaround to this problem. However, in general, modeling the environment constraints usually requires manual work [37,41,50]. Furthermore, a flushing abstraction is not readily available, and may not even be applicable, in the context of accelerator cores. Prior work on ILA-based verification of accelerators [33] also used manually-constructed environment invariants (after automatically checking their validity).

---

[1] Hereafter, we will use "equivalence checking" to refer to instruction-level functional equivalence checking.

1.1 Automatic Discovery of Environment Invariants

Our goal is to *automate* the process of discovering adequate environment abstractions for instruction-based equivalence checking. This would significantly reduce the human burden in applying verification (in other settings as well, described later in Sect. 6). One approach is to view this problem as relational program verification, and to automatically derive both environment and relational invariants (described in Sect. 2). We tried this approach and found that existing tools (e.g., Spacer [25,38], FreqHorn [19,20]) fail to solve these problems, likely due to large sizes of the hardware models and bit-precise reasoning required for equivalence checking (Sect. 5).

Instead, we adopt a counterexample-guided abstraction refinement (CEGAR) approach [12], where the environment is refined iteratively by blocking spurious counterexamples that are found during equivalence checking. Since counterexamples are often due to inconsistent (unreachable) states in the low-level implementations, we pose a reachability query to check whether the starting state of the counterexample is reachable in the implementation. If it is unreachable, we add invariants[2] generated during the reachability query, to provide generalizations that can potentially block a larger set of unreachable states.

Our top-level method using an equivalence checker and a reachability query engine is shown in Fig. 1(b). While CEGAR-based approaches for refining environments have been used in other verification settings (e.g., in angelic [14] or depth-bounded [34] program verification, and also in hardware verification [40]), these have not been targeted at per-instruction equivalence checking in processors and accelerators, or customized for this purpose.

For invariant generation within each reachability query, we explored several existing techniques including Property Directed Reachability (PDR) [15], originally proposed by Bradley as IC3 [6]. PDR has been used successfully with Constrained Horn Clause (CHC) solvers on programs [25,27], and with bit-level and word-level abstraction techniques in ABC [7,28,45] on hardware designs. Interestingly, we found in our experiments (Sect. 5) that accelerators are more challenging than processors for existing PDR-based tools. We conjecture this is due to two reasons: (1) accelerators tend to have wide bit-vectors (e.g., 128-bits), and word-level operations on wide bit-vectors are not handled well at the bit-level; and (2) control flow in accelerators is often more complex and software-like, in comparison to processors. These reasons make it harder for bit-level PDR and CHC-solvers (that support bit-vectors by bit-blasting) to converge with CEGAR.

1.2 SyGuS-Based Invariant Generation

To overcome these additional challenges in our setting, we adopt syntax-guided synthesis (SyGuS) [1] for invariant generation. SyGuS has been applied very

---

[2] Our tool implementation can utilize general constraints in an environment abstraction, not necessarily invariants; however, we focus on invariant generation in this paper – hence we will use abstractions/constraints/invariants interchangeably when discussing the environment hereafter.

successfully in many applications, e.g., invariant generation in programs [22, 47] and program synthesis [2,53]. In our method, candidates for invariants are generated by an *enumerative search* over a space of formulas restricted by a *grammar* (similar to prior work [20,21]). When the grammar covers a small space of expressive formulas, then candidates can be enumerated efficiently and checked for invariance and safety using an off-the-shelf SMT solver.

The main novelty in our SyGuS-based method is the grammar used for generating candidates, and the filtering and prioritizing heuristics to prune the search space of candidates. Specifically, our grammar exploits the separation between data-related and control-related state variables that naturally exists in hardware designs for processing cores. Such "control-or-data" difference often affects how variables appear in invariants. For example, concrete values of data-related variables appear less frequently in environment invariants, whereas concrete values of control-related variables are more significant. Our SyGuS-based method generates small candidates (in term of formula size) and iteratively strengthens the learned invariant with relatively inductive candidates (those becoming inductive after assuming the learned candidates) until it is safe for a given query. This shows better scalability in comparison to searching for a single monolithic candidate that satisfies all the constraints, which is often used in a generic SyGuS procedure (e.g., in CVC4SY [3,51]).

We have implemented our SyGuS-based method in a tool called GRAIN (**Gra**mmar-based **in**variant generator), developed on top of an existing CHC solver [20,21]. To the best of our knowledge, this is the first SyGuS-based tool for synthesizing invariants on large hardware designs. We also provide a detailed experimental comparison with existing PDR-based and SyGuS-based tools for invariant generation. Our results show that GRAIN often complements or outperforms existing tools on practical hardware designs. Our overall approach is especially beneficial in enabling *automated* modular verification for accelerators, such as the AES block encryption accelerator and the Gaussian-Blur image processing accelerator reported in this paper.

In summary, the contributions of this paper are:

- We *automate* the generation of environment invariants for modular hardware equivalence checking to reduce human effort in relation to prior work. Our CEGAR-based approach leverages available techniques and tools for invariant generation.
- We propose a syntax-guided method for synthesizing environment invariants, with a novel grammar that leverages insights about hardware designs and uses pruning techniques to reduce the search space.
- We implement our SyGuS-based method as a prototype tool GRAIN on top of an existing CHC solver, and demonstrate its usefulness on a range of hardware designs that include accelerators and processors. To the best of our knowledge, this is the first SyGuS-based tool that has been applied for invariant generation on large hardware designs.
- We provide a detailed experimental comparison against existing PDR-based and SyGuS-based tools for generating invariants. This has identified their

key weaknesses in our application setting – inadequate handling of word-level operations (in bit-level PDR techniques), and poor scalability in the enumeration of complex candidates on large hardware designs (in existing SyGuS-based techniques).

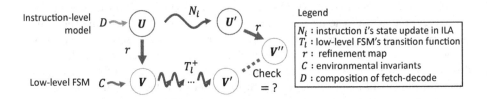

Fig. 2. The verification task in instruction-level modular verification.

We start by introducing instruction-level equivalence checking, and then present our top-level CEGAR-based method. In Sect. 4, we present our novel grammar and SyGuS-based method for generating invariants. We describe our tool GRAIN and present detailed evaluation results in Sect. 5, followed by a discussion of related work and conclusions.

2   Background and Preliminaries

2.1   Instruction-Level Modular Verification

We consider checking equivalence of a low-level implementation, e.g., an RTL design in Verilog, against a formal instruction-level (ILA) specification [33]. The implementation is represented as a finite state machine (FSM): $\langle V, T_l, Init_l \rangle$, where V is a set of states, T_l is a transition relation representing the next-state function, and $Init_l$ is an initial state.

The ILA specification has program-visible (architectural) state variables S and input variables W (on its interface). Instructions to update S are modeled using a standard *fetch-decode-execution* style. In the following, $bvec_w$ denotes a bit-vector of width w, and $\mathbb{B} = \{true, false\}$. To simplify the presentation, we omit W in formulas hereafter, since inputs can be treated as free state variables.

- *fetch* function $F : S \rightarrow bvec_w$, maps states to an instruction word,
- *decode* predicate $\delta_i : bvec_w \rightarrow \mathbb{B}$, identifies if an instruction word corresponds to instruction i,
- *state update* function $N_i : S \rightarrow S$, specifies the effect of executing instruction i on the state.

We use predicate $D_i(\cdot) \stackrel{\text{def}}{=} \delta_i(F(\cdot))$ to denote the composition of *fetch* and *decode*. Thus, an instruction i is triggered only when D_i evaluates to true. (When clear from the context, we drop the subscript i.)

The equivalence verification task is shown in Fig. 2: an instruction i in the ILA model updates the architectural state from U to U', and correspondingly the implementation transitions from state V to V'. A *refinement map* [41] r (could be one-to-many) maps the ILA states to the implementation states.

Informally, the verification task checks that the diagram commutes, i.e., starting from states that are matched by r, and updating both models by executing instruction i, the ending states U' and V' should also be matched by r.

The following details are needed to describe the starting and ending states in the models.

- We use predicate $D_i(U)$ to ensure that only one ILA instruction i executes.
- Although an ILA updates the state in a single transition N_i, the implementation could use multiple transitions T_l^+ to perform the same operation. Therefore, we use a *completion* predicate $E(V)$ (provided by a user) on the implementation state V to denote its ending state. (It is a common design practice to have an instruction commit signal in the low-level FSM).
- Predicate $C(V)$ on the starting state of the implementation represents the environment invariant that we seek to discover. Without such invariants, the implementation is free to start from inconsistent or unreachable states, those that no past instructions can reach. This often results in spurious counterexamples-to-equivalence, even when an implementation is correct.

More formally, the verification task for each instruction is the following:

Definition 1. *The two transition systems ILA and FSM start from arbitrary states U, V respectively, where $r(U, V) \wedge D_i(U) \wedge C(V)$ holds. After applying an instruction i, if their ending states U',V', (defined as $U' = N_i(U)$, $V' = T_l^+(V) \wedge E(V')$) are related by r, then they are equivalent for instruction i.*

To use off-the-shelf property verification tools, we can rephrase the task using a *product* transition system $\langle U \times V, T_p, Init_p \rangle$, where: $Init_p(U, V) = r(U, V) \wedge D(U) \wedge C(V)$, and $T_p((U, V), (U', V')) = T_h(U, U') \wedge T_l(V, V')$. Here, T_l is the transition relation of the low-level FSM, and T_h is a stuttering version of the ILA transition relation N whose first transition corresponds to state update of instruction i, after which the state remains unchanged. The equivalence check is represented as a property $\phi(U', V') \stackrel{\text{def}}{=} E(V') \implies r(U', V')$.

2.2   Checking Equivalence via Relational Program Verification

The ILA vs. FSM equivalence checking problem can be solved using techniques for relational program verification, where relational invariants are automatically derived. In the product state transition system, there are two invariants to find—the environment invariant $C(V)$, and an invariant $I(U, V)$ that can prove equivalence. Using the notations defined in the previous section, the equivalence checking problem can be formulated using constrained horn clauses (CHCs)[3]:

$$Init_l(V) \implies C(V) \tag{1}$$

---

[3] All CHC rules are considered to be universally quantified over the variables.

$$C(V) \wedge T_l(V, V') \implies C(V') \qquad (2)$$
$$r(U, V) \wedge D(U) \wedge C(V) \implies I(U, V) \qquad (3)$$
$$I(U, V) \wedge T_p(U \cup V, U' \cup V') \implies I(U', V') \qquad (4)$$
$$I(U, V) \wedge \neg\phi(U, V) \implies \bot \qquad (5)$$

The first two Horn rules define C to be closed in the transition relation of the low-level FSM. C is then used as an environment invariant in (3) to constrain arbitrary starting states in the product FSM to avoid infeasible states. Another relational invariant $I(U, V)$ is needed to prove safety with respect to the equivalence property ϕ.

The above formulation allows the use of existing CHC tools (e.g., Spacer [25, 38]) for simultaneously finding environment invariants C and checking equivalence property ϕ. However, this monolithic approach shows poor scalability as the CHC instances grow in size, as shown in our experiments (Sect. 5). This motivates our CEGAR-based approach for finding environment invariants, described in the next section.

3   Counterexample-Guided Invariant Synthesis

To improve scalability of the overall procedure, we propose finding environment invariants iteratively by using counterexample-guided abstraction refinement (CEGAR) [12]. Our CEGAR-based method to discover an environment invariant C (in the form of a conjunction of multiple invariants) is presented in Algorithm 1.

Algorithm 1. EQCHECK-INV-SYN(i, FSM, r): Equivalence Checking with Counterexample-Guided Abstraction Refinement for the Environment

---

Input: i: an instruction in ILA with its associated predicate and function,
        FSM: the low-level model, r: the refinement map.
Output: C: the environmental invariant; $res \in$ {Equivalent, Not-Equivalent}.
1 $C \leftarrow \top$;
2 **while** *true* **do**
3      $cex \leftarrow$ EQCHECK(i, FSM, r, C);
4   **if** $cex = \varnothing$ **then return** Equivalent, C;
5      $V_{start} \leftarrow$ GETASSIGNMENT(cex);
6      $result, Inv \leftarrow$ REACHABILITY(FSM, V_{start});
7   **if** $result = reachable$ **then return** Not-Equivalent;
8      $C \leftarrow C \wedge Inv$;

It starts by initializing C to $\top$ (line 1). Then it iteratively checks equivalence (line 3) of the ILA and the low-level FSM (where they start from states that satisfy $r(U, V) \wedge D(U) \wedge C(V)$, as described earlier). If these models are not equivalent, a counterexample cex is returned, and the environment abstraction needs to be refined. From the counterexample trace cex, an assignment to the variables in the starting state V_{start} of the FSM is extracted (line 5), and the algorithm checks whether V_{start} is reachable in the FSM (line 6).

If the state V_{start} is unreachable, i.e., the safety property holds, then a formula that blocks V_{start} could be used to refine the environment invariant C. However, blocking each such counterexample individually could be expensive, and require many iterations for the algorithm to converge. Instead, our algorithm discovers a *safe inductive invariant Inv* as a proof of unreachability of V_{start} (in the REACHABILITY procedure on line 6).

Formally, for an FSM $\langle V, T_l, Init_l \rangle$ and a set of error states Bad, a safe inductive invariant is defined as a formula Inv such that the followings are valid:

$$Init_l(V) \implies Inv(V) \tag{6}$$

$$Inv(V) \land T_l(V, V') \implies Inv(V') \tag{7}$$

$$Inv(V) \land Bad(V) \implies \bot \tag{8}$$

In our case, $Bad \stackrel{\text{def}}{=} (V = V_{start})$. Thus, when $Bad(V)$ is unreachable, an invariant Inv is a strengthened constraint from $V \neq V_{start}$ (because $Inv(V) \implies V \neq V_{start}$ from (8)) This potentially blocks additional unreachable states, thereby requiring fewer iterations of the CEGAR loop to converge.

Note that the CEGAR approach decouples equivalence checking from environment invariant synthesis. This allows freely applying other tools and techniques in equivalence checking. In case the CEGAR-loop does not terminate due to time or resource limits, one can still get some useful invariants from the iterations that have completed.

Furthermore, we can leverage any existing technique or tool to discover safe inductive invariants during the reachability query. As we show in our detailed evaluations (Sect. 5), many CHC-based and SyGuS-based tools can be applied here. We found that existing reachability solvers based on bit-blasting tend to perform poorly on accelerators that require word-level reasoning on wide bit-vectors. In the next section, we present our novel SyGuS-based method for *word-level* invariant synthesis that is designed to overcome these limitations.

4   SyGuS for Word-Level Invariant Synthesis

While SyGuS-based techniques have been successfully applied to synthesize loop invariants in software programs [22,47], to the best of our knowledge, they have not been applied to generate invariants in large hardware designs before. In general, to use grammar-based enumeration of invariant candidates, one has to balance between the expressiveness of a grammar (to find adequate invariants) and the size of the related search space (for achieving tractability in practice). In addition, one needs to use pruning where possible during enumeration, to quickly eliminate non-promising candidates. In this section, we describe the design of our grammar, pruning techniques, and enumeration-based method targeted toward synthesis of word-level environment invariants for RTL hardware designs.

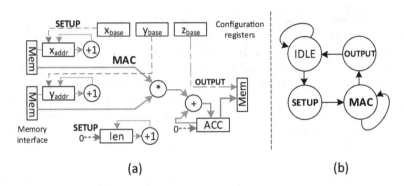

(a)   **(b)**

Fig. 3. Example of a HLSM model for a vector dot-product accelerator: (a) datapath, (b) control FSM. Paths in (a) are activated according to the state in (b).

4.1   Designing a Grammar for Environment Invariant Synthesis

One common design pattern in RTL processing cores is a separation between control and data. In particular, hardware accelerators often implement some high-level algorithm. It is typical to use a high-level state machine (HLSM) model [39], which is comprised of two interacting parts: a control finite state machine (FSM) and the datapath. The control FSM often tracks status signals (predicates) from the datapath, and triggers various datapath operations depending on the control state.

Example 1. Figure 3 shows a simplified view of an HLSM model for a vector dot-product accelerator that computes $z = x \cdot y$. The datapath is shown on the left and the control FSM on the right. The input vectors are fetched from starting addresses in the configuration registers x_{base} and y_{base}, and the dot-product result is stored in the address pointed by z_{base}. The datapath may perform: (a) a multiplication-accumulation (MAC) operation, (b) set up the counters and

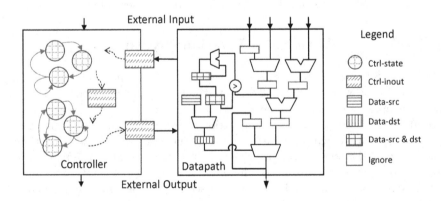

Fig. 4. Tags for state variables in the control FSM and datapath of a processing unit.

Table 1. Tags of variables, invariants, and grammar for Example 1

Tags	ctrl-state	state
	ctrl-inout	<none>
	data-src	x_{base}, y_{base}, z_{base}, len
	data-dst	x_{addr}, y_{addr}, len
	ignore	ACC
Invariants (automatically generated)		state $\neq IDLE \implies x_{addr} = x_{base} + $ len
		state $\neq IDLE \implies y_{addr} = y_{base} + $ len
Grammar		$\langle$Cand$\rangle$ ::= $\langle$CSpred$\rangle \implies \langle$Dpred$\rangle$
		$\langle$CSpred$\rangle$ ::= $\langle$CSvar$\rangle = \langle$Const$_C\rangle$ | $\langle$CSvar$\rangle \neq \langle$Const$_C\rangle$
		$\langle$Dpred$\rangle$ ::= $\langle$DDvar$\rangle = \langle$DSvar$\rangle + \langle$DSvar$\rangle$
		$\langle$Const$_C\rangle$ ::= 00 | 01 | 10 | 11

the accumulator, (c) send the output, or (d) do nothing, when the control FSM is in MAC, SETUP, OUTPUT, or IDLE state, respectively. In the SETUP state, address counters are initialized to the base address, and length counter will be set to zero. When the control FSM is in the MAC state, the address counter x_{addr} will be incremented, and so will the vector length counter len. But their increments are the same, namely $x_{addr} = x_{base} + $ len. Note this relation holds in all control states except IDLE. When the control FSM is in the IDLE state, there is no update of x_{addr}, but the x_{base} register can be programmed to an arbitrary address. Similar relations can be found among y_{addr}, y_{base} and len. We aim to find such relations in certain control states as environment invariants.

Our grammar builds on top of *tags* that are assigned to all state variables in an RTL design description (e.g., registers in Verilog). These tags are based on their role, shown pictorially in a generic HLSM model in Fig. 4.

- ctrl-state (CS): state of a control FSM (there could be multiple FSMs)
- ctrl-inout (CIO): signals between control FSM and datapath, or between control FSMs
- data-src (DS): source in datapath operation
- data-dst (DD): destination in datapath operation
- ignore: none of the above, typically internal/temporary state variables.

In our experiments, we currently tag all variables manually, based on our knowledge of the designs (details described in Sect. 5.3). It does not seem too difficult to implement a simple analysis (over Verilog or an intermediate representation) for tagging variables automatically.

The main idea is to construct a grammar for formula expressions where these tags are used as "types" of the variables, to allow limited operators over certain types and to restrict the sets of variables during enumeration of expressions. In particular, state variables with the tag "ignore" are not considered in expressions at all. (Some variables could have multiple tags, e.g., DS and DD.) Incorrect tags may result in either an unnecessary enumeration overhead (e.g., DS tagged as CS) or missing candidates (e.g., variables incorrectly tagged as "ignore"). As a preview of the full grammar (described in detail in the next section), the tags, invariants, and relevant grammar snippets for Example 1 are shown in Table 1.

4.2 SyGuS Grammar

Our full grammar for generating invariant candidates is shown in Fig. 5. The terminals of this grammar represent tagged variables, where CSvar represents a ctrl-state variable, CIOvar represents a ctrl-inout variable, and DSvar and DDvar represent a source and destination (data-src/-dst) in the datapath, respectively. (Recall that a variable can have multiple tags.)

$$\langle\texttt{Cand}\rangle ::= \langle\texttt{Ante}\rangle \implies \langle\texttt{Conseq}\rangle$$
$$\langle\texttt{Ante}\rangle ::= \langle\texttt{CSpred}\rangle \wedge \langle\texttt{Ante}\rangle \mid true$$
$$\langle\texttt{CSpred}\rangle ::= \langle\texttt{CSvar}\rangle = \langle\texttt{Const}_C\rangle \mid \langle\texttt{CSvar}\rangle \neq \langle\texttt{Const}_C\rangle$$
$$\langle\texttt{Conseq}\rangle ::= \langle\texttt{Disj}\rangle \mid \langle\texttt{Disj}\rangle \vee \langle\texttt{Conseq}\rangle$$
$$\langle\texttt{Disj}\rangle ::= \langle\texttt{CIOpred}\rangle \mid \langle\texttt{Dpred}\rangle$$
$$\langle\texttt{CIOpred}\rangle ::= \langle\texttt{CIOvar}\rangle = \langle\texttt{Const}_C\rangle \mid \langle\texttt{CIOvar}\rangle \neq \langle\texttt{Const}_C\rangle$$
$$\langle\texttt{Dpred}\rangle ::= \langle\texttt{DDvar}\rangle = \langle\texttt{Const}_D\rangle \mid \langle\texttt{DDvar}\rangle \neq \langle\texttt{Const}_D\rangle$$
$$\mid \langle\texttt{DDvar}\rangle = op \ \langle\texttt{DSvar}\rangle \mid \langle\texttt{DDvar}\rangle = \langle\texttt{DSvar}\rangle \ op \ \langle\texttt{DSvar}\rangle$$

Fig. 5. The grammar for environment invariants.

The first (top-level) production rule of our grammar defines the shape of a candidate invariant to be an implication between an antecedent (Ante) and a consequent (Conseq). The antecedent is typically a condition on states of the control FSM(s). Thus, it is expressed as a conjunction of predicates that allow comparison of CSvar against constants (that define the control states). The consequent is a disjunction over predicates that allow comparison of CIOvar and DDvar against constants, or express datapath operations on DSvar. Since our invariant synthesis algorithm (to be outlined in Sect. 4.4) can discover conjunctive invariants, our grammar does not need to enumerate a top-level conjunction of implications. Furthermore, this also avoids a need to have disjunctions in the antecedent or conjunctions in the consequent.

Note that our grammar allows operators on only word-level variables that are data-related. We identified a small set of operators (negation, truncation, addition, subtraction) that is sufficient for our benchmarks. Intuitively, environment invariants are generally *independent* of the actual computation in the datapath. Although the datapath may be capable of using a rich set of operators, those needed for environment invariants tend to be fairly simple.

The sets of constants $Const_C$ and $Const_D$ (used with control and data variables, respectively) need not be the same. The set $Const_C$ can be derived from the Verilog descriptions—it is common practice for designers to define such constants using macros or parameters in Verilog. The concrete values of data variables are less important, and $Const_D$ can be populated with a few concrete values. In our implementation, we use all 0's and all 1's (of appropriate bit-widths that match the variables). One can also extend this set with data constants that appear in Verilog descriptions.

The grammar shown in Fig. 5 is recursively defined to allow an arbitrary number of conjuncts (in `Ante`) and disjuncts (in `Conseq`). In practice, we instantiate it with a bound on each, and our experiments (in Sect. 5) show that a small bound of 2 is sufficient in our benchmark examples.

4.3   Candidate Enumeration

We enumerate over all allowed variables in the tagged sets for invariant candidates using the grammar. In addition, we use the following *meta*-production rules and heuristics to prune the set of enumerated candidates.

Grouping (Meta-rule). For verifying processor designs, we place additional restrictions during enumeration by using *grouping* over variables, whereby predicates on only the grouped variables are allowed to appear in the same clause in the antecedent or the consequent. For pipeline designs, the variables are grouped together if they are read in the same stage or written by the same stage. In a sense, combinations of grouped variables are likely to be more significant than combinations of unrelated variables. Enumerating clauses by choosing combinations of grouped variables can dramatically reduce the total number of invariant candidates to be checked.

Cone-of-Influence (Meta-rule). Not all variables that are tagged need to appear in the invariants. For example, some datapath variables may not affect control-flow, i.e., they are outside the cone-of-influence (COI) of control states. Such variables can be dropped during enumeration. For a specific counterexample-to-equivalence, all variables might not appear in the COI of the equivalence property. The equivalence checker can identify the set of variables in the COI, so we enumerate only these variables and drop the rest.

Ordering the Candidates (Heuristic). The ordering of enumeration is important: if Inv_1 is inductive relative to Inv_2, then it is useful to first learn Inv_2 and then try Inv_1. Thus, we want to carefully choose an enumeration ordering that is efficient. Our heuristic is to respect the ordering of data-flow/control-flow in Verilog. For example, if there is a flow pattern like $a \rightarrow b$, $a \rightarrow c$, and $b \rightarrow c$, then relations between (a, b) and (a, c) are enumerated before (b, c). This allows the first two relations to set up some relation between b and c, thus making it more likely to be learned as a relative inductive invariant later in the ordering.

4.4 Enumerative SyGuS Solver

Our enumerative SyGuS solver method is shown in Algorithm 2. It takes as inputs the low-level FSM, grammar G, and an error state Bad (V_{start} from Sect. 3); and either successfully finds a safe inductive invariant Inv or fails (with result UNKNOWN).

We follow a standard *guess-and-check* paradigm for generating safe invariants (e.g., [19,22]). The set of candidates, $CandSet$, is initialized with expressions enumerated from the given grammar G and pruning heuristics (line 1). The algorithm continues until either the error state is proved to be unreachable (line 3), or there are no more candidates to process (line 4). A candidate must be implied by the initial state of the FSM (line 7), and it should be inductive relative to the already learned invariants (line 8), in order to be added to the *Learned* set. A candidate is not totally discarded if the inductiveness check fails, but is placed in the *2ndChance* set (line 10). We re-evaluate the inductiveness of such candidates by adding them back to the *CandSet* if their corresponding counterexample-to-induction (CTI, not to be confused with the counterexample-to-equivalence in Sect. 3) can be blocked by newly learned invariants (line 11).

Algorithm 2. INV-SYN(FSM, Bad, G): Synthesize invariant to block Bad

---

Input: $FSM = \langle V \cup V', Init, t_l \rangle$: the low-level (FSM) model, Bad, and G:
　　　　SyGuS grammar
Output: Safe inductive invariant Inv or UNKNOWN

1　$CandSet \leftarrow$ ENUMERATE(G);
2　$Learned, 2ndChance \leftarrow \varnothing$;
3　**while** $Bad \wedge \bigwedge_{\ell \in Learned} \ell(V) \not\Longrightarrow \bot$ **do**
4　　　**if** $CandSet = \varnothing$ **then return** UNKNOWN;
5　　　**for each** $cand \in CandSet$ **do**
6　　　　$CandSet \leftarrow CandSet \setminus \{cand\}$;
7　　　　**if** $Init(V) \not\Longrightarrow cand(V)$ **then Continue**;
8　　　　**if** $cand(V) \wedge \bigwedge_{\ell \in Learned} \ell(V) \wedge t_l(V, V') \Longrightarrow cand(V')$ **then**
9　　　　　$Learned \leftarrow Learned \cup \{cand\}$;
10　　　　**else** $2ndChance \leftarrow 2ndChance \cup \{cand\}$;
11　　　**for** $cand \in 2ndChance$ **where** CTI($cand$) $\not\models \bigwedge_{\ell \in Learned} \ell(V)$ **do**
12　　　　$2ndChance \leftarrow 2ndChance \setminus \{cand\}$;
13　　　　$CandSet \leftarrow CandSet \cup \{cand\}$;
14　**return** $Learned$;

5　Experimental Evaluation and Comparison

We have developed GRAIN, a prototype implementation of our SyGuS-based method for invariant synthesis, on top of an existing CHC solver [19]. We have also developed a flexible CEGAR-based framework for equivalence checking, where we use GRAIN for synthesis of environment invariants. In this section, we describe an evaluation of these methods on benchmark examples, along with a comparison against other tools for invariant synthesis.

5.1 Methods Evaluated

For the purpose of detailed comparison, we consider the following five methods:

RELCHC encodes the equivalence checking and environment invariant synthesis as a single CHC problem (Sect. 2.2), which is solved by Spacer [38]. Since this does not use CEGAR explicitly in an outer loop, it serves as a top-level comparison for our CEGAR-based method.

PDRABC uses our CEGAR-based approach with PDR-based techniques in the ABC tool [15] for solving the reachability query and generating safe invariants. We used Yosys [56] to parse Verilog descriptions and generated AIGER format [35] as input to ABC (since ABC's Verilog parser did not support all Verilog features in our designs). Due to this translation, we were unable to use word-level abstraction techniques in ABC [28].

PDRCHC uses our CEGAR-based approach with the Spacer tool [38], a CHC-solver that uses PDR techniques to generate safe invariants. Again, we used Yosys [56] to parse Verilog descriptions and generate SMT-LIB2 [4] instances.

CVC4SY uses our CEGAR-based approach with the SyGuS procedure in CVC4 [51] to synthesize a function that satisfies the constraints (6)–(8). We use the same grammar and variable tagging as in GRAIN. The difference from GRAIN is that CVC4SY searches for a single expression that satisfies all three constraints at the same time, whereas GRAIN iteratively strengthens a candidate with more lemmas that are found inductive.

GRAIN uses our CEGAR-based approach with our SyGuS-based method for generating invariants.

5.2 Benchmark Examples

We applied all methods on five hardware designs (two synthetic and three from real-world) including processors and accelerators. The ILA specifications for some designs were developed in prior work [33,55], where manually constructed environment invariants were used to prove equivalence against RTL designs.

Redundant Counters (RC). This example is a synthetic test case that implements a high-level specification of a 4-bit counter. The RTL implementation uses an extra counter for redundancy, storing it as 1's-complement. The RTL output is computed as $BitwiseAnd(c_1, 15 - c_2)$, which can be simplified as c_1. This relation between c_1 and c_2 is not visible at the high level, and is the environment invariant that needs to be discovered by the synthesis process. This design is used as a small sanity check for our synthesis algorithm.

Simple Pipeline (SP). This design mimics the back-end of a simple pipelined processor. It has three stages (dispatch, execute, and write-back), and four 8-bit wide architectural registers. The instruction set has four instructions (ADD,

NOT, AND, and NOP). The pipelined implementation has a scoreboard to track latest register values for data forwarding. The environment invariants need to capture the relation between the scoreboard and the intermediate stage registers among the three stages. The human-provided invariant contains 16 implications in conjunction, where each implication is not inductive by itself.

AES Block Encryption Accelerator (AES). The AES block encryption accelerator is a publicly available design from OpenCores.org [31]. An ILA specification was constructed in prior work [55], where a START_ENCRYPT command triggers a "load-compute-store" loop that works block-by-block. Although AES is not the largest design we checked, it poses the most challenges: (a) it needs wide 128-bit state variables in the invariants, (b) the accelerator operation is like software, with a large maximum loop bound (4096), and (c) one of the (human-provided) invariants required a large number of conjunctions.

PicoRV32 Processor (Pico). The PicoRV32 processor [13] is a size-optimized RISC-V processor that implements the RISC-V RV32IMC instruction set. The processor is basically a multi-cycle implementation with an average CPI (cycle-per-instruction) of 4, but it also has some pipelining features, for example, instruction fetch can take place while another instruction is still executing.

Gaussian Blur Accelerator (GB). The Gaussian Blur image processing accelerator is a design generated by high-level synthesis (HLS) in Halide [48], for computing the convolution of an image with a Gaussian kernel. The accelerator streams in and out an image pixel-by-pixel, and buffers the pixels with internal memories (about 32Kb), while multiplication-accumulation (MAC) units are used for convolution. For environment invariant synthesis, we over-approximate the internal memories and MACs by replacing their outputs with free variables (since it is reasonable to expect that their values do not affect the environment invariants). However, we do not over-approximate them for equivalence checking, which is performed using Cadence JasperGold [10] that has built-in abstraction models for memory and computation units. Although the design size of this accelerator is the largest (in number of state bits), the environment invariants required are relatively simple.

5.3   Grammars Used for SyGuS

The RTL designs and the instantiations of grammar we used for each benchmark example can be found in our Github repository [57], and our tools will be released as part of the ILAng verification framework [32]. Statistics for the benchmarks and grammars are reported in Table 2, where the last row reports the total number of candidates generated. We used a maximum bound of 2 for number of conjuncts/disjuncts (as shown). We used grouping in SP and PicoRV32 to prune the number of candidates – the number without grouping is 6137 and 255410, i.e., grouping reduced the number of candidates to 34% and 25%, respectively. We briefly summarize key points about tagging variables.

- Redundant Counters (RC): has only two variables, both are `data-src/-dst`.
- Simple Pipeline (SP): the scoreboard is tagged as `ctrl-state`, write-enable signals are `ctrl-inout`, and destination signals are `data-dst`. Grouping is used to group together the signals in the same stage of the pipeline.
- AES accelerator: computation in the datapath is ignored (plaintexts, ciphertexts, and keys), control FSM is kept, index and block counters are tagged as `ctrl-inout`, address and length registers are tagged as `data-src/-dst`.
- PicoRV32 processor: The ALU, register files, memory input/output data, and performance counters are ignored for environment invariants, while flags and control FSMs are kept. Flags are tagged as `ctrl-inout`, and grouped by the stage where they are set (decode/execute units, interrupts).
- Gaussian Blur accelerator (GB): Since this design is generated by HLS, the naming of state variables follows some conventions. Control FSMs with names `ap_CS_fsm` are tagged as `ctrl-state`. Flag bits, tagged as `ctrl-inout`, have names like `xxx_full_n`, `xxx_empty_n`, or `exitcond_xxx`. Address pointers (with name `mOutPtr`), column or row counters (with names `col_reg_xxx` or `row_reg_xxx`) are tagged as `data-dst`.

Table 2. Statistics of benchmarks and SyGuS grammars

Benchmarks	RC	SP	AES	PicoRV32	Gaussian Blur
#. state-bits	8	72	963[†]	1817	4840[†]
#. word-level state-vars	2	16	14[†]	149	176[†]
#. ctrl-state	–	4	3	30	4
#. ctrl-inout	–	2	2	34	8
#. data-src	2	–	2	–	–
#. data-dst	2	2	3	–	11
#. groups	–	2	–	3	–
Max. antecedent size	1	1	2	2	2
Max. consequent size	1	2	1	1	1
#. candidates	2	2112	22048	63663	19195

[†] For AES, this model abstracts the round-level computation; for Gaussian Blur, this model abstracts internal block RAMs and MACs.

5.4   Results of Experiments

The experiments were conducted on a laptop with 4-core i5-8300H processor and 32 GB memory, except for Gaussian Blur which needs Cadence JasperGold (available on a server with 56 cores and 256 GB memory). All other benchmarks used CoSA [42] for equivalence checking. Counterexamples are extracted by parsing the waveform generated by JasperGold or CoSA. We set the time-out limit for the CEGAR-loop to be 10 h, which includes time for both equivalence checking and environment invariant synthesis.

The results are reported in Table 3 for the five methods (along columns) on the benchmark examples (along rows). We also report additional details (number of iterations for CEGAR-based methods and times for synthesis and equivalence checking). Note that our proposed method GRAIN successfully finds environment invariants in all benchmarks, and outperforms the other four methods on the three real-world designs (AES, Pico, GB).

5.5   Detailed Comparison and Discussion

CEGAR-Loop vs. Monolithic CHC Query. As PDRCHC uses the same CHC solver as RELCHC, we use the results of the two as a comparison between CEGAR-loop and using a monolithic CHC query. RELCHC succeeds on only the first two examples, both under 100 state bits. We looked at the invariants produced by the two methods and saw that RELCHC generated invariants that were easier to understand. For example, for RC, it generated $\bigwedge_i c_1[i] \oplus c_2[i], i \in \{1, .., 4\}$ (where $\oplus$ is the XOR operator), which is more succinct than those generated by PDRCHC. However, the overall results clearly show that CEGAR-based approaches are more scalable.

PDR-Based Methods: Spacer vs. ABC. Although Spacer and ABC both use PDR, their performance varies. For benchmarks where both succeeded, PDRABC requires less synthesis time and fewer CEGAR iterations. However, ABC seems to have bigger memory requirements – two of the five benchmarks failed due to out-of-memory error. For GB, using PDRABC results in CEGAR-loop time-out. For the failing query of AES, we also tested gate-level abstraction techniques in ABC [28,45], but these did not succeed (due to either timeout or too coarse abstraction). As mentioned earlier, due to our translation to AIGER, we were not able to test the word-level abstraction technique in ABC.

SyGuS-Based Methods: Grain vs. cvc4sy. One main difference between our method GRAIN and cvc4sy is how they construct the required invariant. Since cvc4sy is a generic SyGuS solver, its verifier requires a term enumerator to propose a candidate that satisfies all constraints (i.e., all three conditions for a safe inductive invariant) at the same time. In contrast, GRAIN is specialized for finding safe invariants for transition systems by incrementally conjoining relatively inductive candidates (inspired by PDR).

To study this further, we tested cvc4sy in more detail on the SP example. We instantiated the grammar with a fixed number of implications (based on known invariants) and asked cvc4sy to fill in the antecedent and consequent of each implication. This significantly shrinks the search space for cvc4sy. However, this still resulted in out-of-memory errors. This is likely due to a large number of syntactic constraints that the CVC4 term generator learns from failing candidates.

For AES, cvc4sy finished the first four iterations of the CEGAR-loop fairly fast, where the invariants contain at most one implication. In the fifth round, an invariant with many conjoined implications is needed, but it failed. cvc4sy

Table 3. Results of experiments

		RelChc	PdrAbc	PdrChc	cvc4sy	Grain
				CEGAR		
Solver		Z3	ABC	Z3	CVC4	Z3
RC	# iter	–	4	6	1	1
	$t_{syn}(s)$	–	30.2	11.5	0.2	1.2
	$t_{eq}(s)$	–	2.1	4.7	0.8	0.8
	$t_{total}(s)$	1.6	32.3	16.2	**1.0**	2.0
SP	# iter	–	21	36	1	4
	$t_{syn}(s)$	–	1.9	2.9	O.O.M	134.4
	$t_{eq}(s)$	–	27.8	37.5	1.2	10.7
	$t_{total}(s)$	1035.2	**29.7**	40.4	O.O.M	145.1
AES	# iter	–	2	2	4	5
	$t_{syn}(s)$	–	O.O.M	T.O	O.O.M	912.3
	$t_{eq}(s)$	-	6.4	6.5	17.5	35.5
	$t_{total}(s)$	T.O	O.O.M	T.O	O.O.M	**947.8**
Pico	# iter	–	3	149	1	9
	$t_{syn}(s)$	–	O.O.M	3771.7	O.O.M	4345.9
	$t_{eq}(s)$	–	87.2	4493.1	6.8	83.5
	$t_{total}(s)$	T.O	O.O.M	7864.8	O.O.M	**4429.4**
GB	# iter	–	176	7	8	3
	$t_{syn}(s)$	–	63.1	1292.4	161.9	414.5
	$t_{eq}(s)$	–	T.O	1491.3	1653.2	631.5
	$t_{total}(s)$	T.O	T.O	2783.7	1815.1	**1046.0**

RC, SP, AES, Pico, GB denote the five benchmarks: Redundant Counters, Simple Pipeline, AES block encryption accelerator, PicoRV32 processor, and Gaussian Blur accelerator.

O.O.M indicates out-of-memory (>32 GB) and T.O. indicates time-out (>10 h). "# iter." reports the number of CEGAR iterations. For methods that did not converge within the time/memory limit, we report the last iteration it finished before it terminates.

RelChc does not use CEGAR, we only report total solving time. For all CEGAR methods, the total time (t_{total}) is the sum of time for synthesis (t_{syn}) and time for equivalence checking (t_{eq}).

is also successful on GB, where no invariant requires more than one implication. It seems that a large number of top-level conjunctions is an obstacle for cvc4sy, whereas Grain can handle this by candidate strengthening techniques.

Another difference is that Grain collects inductive candidates along the search for safe inductive invariants. These inductive invariants can block other infeasible counterexamples. Therefore, Grain requires fewer CEGAR iterations.

SyGuS-Based vs. PDR-Based Techniques. When well-guided by grammars, GRAIN can deliver comparable performance to PDR-based approaches, and it outperforms them on large real-world designs. We believe this is mainly due to our emphasis on word-level invariants, which seem more difficult to derive in PDRABC and PDRCHC. For example, in AES, the failing query for PDRABC and PDRCHC needs an invariant: $\mathtt{STATUS} \neq 0 \implies \mathtt{IV} + \mathtt{BLK\_CNT} = \mathtt{AES\_CNT}$. This says that when the accelerator is operating, the current operation counter is the sum of a block counter and the initial value (IV), where the three variables in the consequent are all 128-bit. This relation is simple on the word-level but complex on the bit-level. Another challenge in accelerators is they contain loop structures similar to software. For example, the "load-compute-store" loop in AES can iterate as many as 4096 times. With a large number of variables after bit-blasting, it becomes harder for PDR to reach a fixpoint when computing forward reachability.

An interesting difference we noticed is that both PDRABC and PDRCHC sometimes produce invariants that refer to datapath variables. For example, instead of a generalized invariant Inv, one may get $(D = v \implies Inv)$, where D is a datapath variable and v is some concrete value. The antecedent here is usually unnecessary, as in many processing units, the datapath variable can have an arbitrary value, and the consequent is a valid fact regardless of the value of D. These invariants could result in more CEGAR iterations and longer synthesis time in total. On the other hand, our grammars used in GRAIN target word-level expressions, place restrictions on variable sets, and do not enumerate concrete values on data-related variables. Therefore, they generate candidates that can produce a more general invariant.

For GRAIN, PicoRV32 is the hardest example due to a large number of state variables, which results in a large search space for enumeration. In this case, it would be beneficial for a human designer to provide additional insights to shrink the search space.

Lessons Learned and Potential Improvements. The above experiments show that PDR-based techniques sometimes suffer from an explosion of state bits due to bit-blasting, and sometimes generate invariants that are too specific to a query (thereby requiring more CEGAR iterations). By working on the word-level and using guidance on state variables to consider in candidate invariants, GRAIN can outperform PDR-based techniques under such situations. It would be interesting to investigate in future work whether the generalization step in PDR can benefit from guidance using grammars.

6   Related Work

Invariant Synthesis. Automatic generation of invariants has been studied extensively in verification. Among symbolic model checking techniques, IC3/PDR [6,15] has demonstrated success for both hardware and software verification. It incrementally constructs an inductive invariant by iteratively removing counterexamples to induction. In software verification, several application of PDR [5,11,25,29,38] for linear arithmetic and arrays have been proposed. PDR engines that support bit-vectors often use bit-blasting and find fixpoints on the bit-level. As the data-width increases, the same word-level formula becomes larger on the bit-level. For hardware, PDR has been combined with various abstraction techniques [18,45], including the use of word-level information to construct abstractions [28,40]. In GRAIN, we continue this trend of leveraging word-level information to help with scalability, and extend it by considering roles of the variables (e.g., control or data) in the design.

Other work also targets bit-precise invariants for software [8,26,30] by lazily encoding the program in parts by using bit-vectors, along with light-weight theories (such as equality with uninterpreted functions, Presburger arithmetic, and linear rational arithmetic). These techniques, however, have not been evaluated on large hardware designs so far, and we expect they would require many refinement iterations before converging.

Syntax-Guided Synthesis [1] has also been used successfully for invariant generation, although not for large hardware designs so far. LOOPINVGEN [47] takes a data-driven approach and learns features for loop invariance inference, whereas GRAIN relies more on the structure of hardware designs to provide guidance and enumeration heuristics. The cvc4sy solver [51] employs various advanced enumeration techniques from user-provided grammars, but attempts to generate a whole invariant *at once*, which has significant scalability implications. Liquid Fixpoint [52] has been used in IODINE [24] to generate invariants for constant-time property checking for hardware. It uses candidates from predicate abstraction rather than a grammar. The approach closest to ours is FREQHORN [19–21] that also generates individual lemmas first and then conjoins them together to derive an invariant. However it relies on various heuristics to automatically construct grammars (e.g., from the syntax and bounded semantics of the program). In contrast, our grammars leverage domain-specific knowledge of hardware designs.

Modular Hardware Verification. Our focus is on using instruction-level modularity in hardware equivalence checking, which has also been embraced in industrial practice [37,50]. For modular verification of systems, in general, the specification and implementation are partitioned component-wise and assume-guarantee rules are used to reason about a component and its interaction with the environment [23,41,43]. Our environment invariants are also a form of environment assumptions, which we aim to discover automatically.

Other instruction-level verification efforts can also benefit from automatic generation of environment invariants. For example, Symbolic Quick-Error-Detection (S-QED) [17], unbounded protocol compliance verification [46], hardware information flow tracking [16] – all used some form of symbolic initial state constraints to avoid spurious counterexamples, where these constraints are manually constructed. Our methods for automated discovery of environment invariants can potentially benefit these applications by reducing human effort.

7   Conclusions

In this paper, we described techniques for automating the discovery of environment invariants for per-instruction modular hardware verification. We used an equivalence checker coupled with a CEGAR-based method to iteratively construct such invariants. We proposed a SyGuS-based method for invariant synthesis in each iteration, where we use a novel grammar to guide the search for invariant candidates. The grammar leverages domain-specific features in hardware designs, and can be tuned by a user. Our invariant synthesis approach is inspired by existing PDR-based and SyGuS-based techniques. It targets word-level invariants, to avoid dealing with complex relations at the bit-level, and constructs conjunctive invariants incrementally. Our detailed experiments demonstrate the effectiveness of our proposed CEGAR-based and SyGuS-based methods on several hardware designs including processors and accelerators.

Acknowledgements. This work was supported in part by the Applications Driving Architectures (ADA) Research Center, a JUMP Center co-sponsored by SRC and DARPA; by the DARPA POSH and DARPA SSITH programs; and by NSF Grants 1525936 and 1628926.

References

1. Alur, R., et al.: Syntax-guided synthesis. In: FMCAD, pp. 1–8 (2013)
2. Alur, R., Singh, R., Fisman, D., Solar-Lezama, A.: Search-based program synthesis. Commun. ACM **61**(12), 84–93 (2018)
3. Barrett, C., et al.: CVC4. In: Gopalakrishnan, G., Qadeer, S. (eds.) CAV 2011. LNCS, vol. 6806, pp. 171–177. Springer, Heidelberg (2011). https://doi.org/10.1007/978-3-642-22110-1_14
4. Barrett, C.W., Sebastiani, R., Seshia, S.A., Tinelli, C.: Satisfiability modulo theories. In: Handbook of Satisfiability, pp. 825–885 (2009)
5. Bjørner, N., Gurfinkel, A.: Property directed polyhedral abstraction. In: D'Souza, D., Lal, A., Larsen, K.G. (eds.) VMCAI 2015. LNCS, vol. 8931, pp. 263–281. Springer, Heidelberg (2015). https://doi.org/10.1007/978-3-662-46081-8_15
6. Bradley, A.R.: SAT-based model checking without unrolling. In: Jhala, R., Schmidt, D. (eds.) VMCAI 2011. LNCS, vol. 6538, pp. 70–87. Springer, Heidelberg (2011). https://doi.org/10.1007/978-3-642-18275-4_7
7. Brayton, R., Mishchenko, A.: ABC: an academic industrial-strength verification tool. In: Touili, T., Cook, B., Jackson, P. (eds.) CAV 2010. LNCS, vol. 6174, pp. 24–40. Springer, Heidelberg (2010). https://doi.org/10.1007/978-3-642-14295-6_5
8. Bueno, D., Sakallah, K.A.: EUFORIA: complete software model checking with uninterpreted functions. In: Enea, C., Piskac, R. (eds.) VMCAI 2019. LNCS, vol. 11388, pp. 363–385. Springer, Cham (2019). https://doi.org/10.1007/978-3-030-11245-5_17
9. Burch, J.R., Dill, D.L.: Automatic verification of pipelined microprocessor control. In: Dill, D.L. (ed.) CAV 1994. LNCS, vol. 818, pp. 68–80. Springer, Heidelberg (1994). https://doi.org/10.1007/3-540-58179-0_44
10. Cadence Design Systems Inc: Jaspergold: Formal property verification app (2019). http://www.jasper-da.com/products/jaspergold-apps/. Accessed 20 Sept 2019

11. Cimatti, A., Griggio, A.: Software model checking via IC3. In: Madhusudan, P., Seshia, S.A. (eds.) CAV 2012. LNCS, vol. 7358, pp. 277–293. Springer, Heidelberg (2012). https://doi.org/10.1007/978-3-642-31424-7_23

12. Clarke, E., Grumberg, O., Jha, S., Lu, Y., Veith, H.: Counterexample-guided abstraction refinement. In: Emerson, E.A., Sistla, A.P. (eds.) CAV 2000. LNCS, vol. 1855, pp. 154–169. Springer, Heidelberg (2000). https://doi.org/10.1007/10722167_15

13. Clifford Wolf: Picorv32 - a size-optimized RISC-V cpu (2019). https://github.com/cliffordwolf/picorv32. Accessed 20 Sept 2019

14. Das, A., Lahiri, S.K., Lal, A., Li, Y.: Angelic verification: precise verification modulo unknowns. In: Kroening, D., Păsăreanu, C.S. (eds.) CAV 2015. LNCS, vol. 9206, pp. 324–342. Springer, Cham (2015). https://doi.org/10.1007/978-3-319-21690-4_19

15. Een, N., Mishchenko, A., Brayton, R.: Efficient implementation of property directed reachability. In: FMCAD, pp. 125–134 (2011)

16. Fadiheh, M.R., Stoffel, D., Barrett, C., Mitra, S., Kunz, W.: Processor hardware security vulnerabilities and their detection by unique program execution checking. In: DATE, pp. 994–999 (2019)

17. Fadiheh, M.R., et al.: Symbolic quick error detection using symbolic initial state for pre-silicon verification. In: DATE, pp. 55–60 (2018)

18. Fan, K., Yang, M.J., Huang, C.Y.: Automatic abstraction refinement of TR for PDR. In: Asia and South Pacific Design Automation Conference, pp. 121–126 (2016)

19. Fedyukovich, G., Bodík, R.: Accelerating syntax-guided invariant synthesis. In: Beyer, D., Huisman, M. (eds.) TACAS 2018. LNCS, vol. 10805, pp. 251–269. Springer, Cham (2018). https://doi.org/10.1007/978-3-319-89960-2_14

20. Fedyukovich, G., Kaufman, S., Bodík, R.: Sampling invariants from frequency distributions. In: FMCAD, pp. 100–107 (2017)

21. Fedyukovich, G., Prabhu, S., Madhukar, K., Gupta, A.: Solving constrained horn clauses using syntax and data. In: FMCAD, pp. 170–178 (2018)

22. Garg, P., Löding, C., Madhusudan, P., Neider, D.: ICE: a robust framework for learning invariants. In: Biere, A., Bloem, R. (eds.) CAV 2014. LNCS, vol. 8559, pp. 69–87. Springer, Cham (2014). https://doi.org/10.1007/978-3-319-08867-9_5

23. Giannakopoulou, D., Namjoshi, K.S., Păsăreanu, C.S.: Compositional reasoning. Handbook of Model Checking, pp. 345–383. Springer, Cham (2018). https://doi.org/10.1007/978-3-319-10575-8_12

24. Gleissenthall, K., Kıcı, R.G., Stefan, D., Jhala, R.: IODINE: verifying constant-time execution of hardware. In: USENIX Security Symposium, pp. 1411–1428 (2019)

25. Gurfinkel, A.: IC3, PDR, and Friends. Summer School on Formal Techniques (2015)

26. Gurfinkel, A., Belov, A., Marques-Silva, J.: Synthesizing safe bit-precise invariants. In: Ábrahám, E., Havelund, K. (eds.) TACAS 2014. LNCS, vol. 8413, pp. 93–108. Springer, Heidelberg (2014). https://doi.org/10.1007/978-3-642-54862-8_7

27. Gurfinkel, A., Kahsai, T., Komuravelli, A., Navas, J.A.: The seahorn verification framework. In: Kroening, D., Păsăreanu, C.S. (eds.) CAV 2015. LNCS, vol. 9206, pp. 343–361. Springer, Cham (2015). https://doi.org/10.1007/978-3-319-21690-4_20

28. Ho, Y.S., Mishchenko, A., Brayton, R.: Property directed reachability with word-level abstraction. In: FMCAD, pp. 132–139 (2017)

29. Hoder, K., Bjørner, N.: Generalized property directed reachability. In: Cimatti, A., Sebastiani, R. (eds.) SAT 2012. LNCS, vol. 7317, pp. 157–171. Springer, Heidelberg (2012). https://doi.org/10.1007/978-3-642-31612-8_13

30. Hojjat, H., Rümmer, P.: The ELDARICA horn solver. In: FMCAD, pp. 158–164. IEEE (2018)

31. Hsing, H.: Opencores.org tiny_aes project page. https://opencores.org/projects/tiny_aes (2014). Accessed 20 Sept 2019

32. Huang, B.-Y., Zhang, H., Gupta, A., Malik, S.: ILAng: a modeling and verification platform for SoCs using instruction-level abstractions. In: Vojnar, T., Zhang, L. (eds.) TACAS 2019. LNCS, vol. 11427, pp. 351–357. Springer, Cham (2019). https://doi.org/10.1007/978-3-030-17462-0_21

33. Huang, B., Zhang, H., Subramanyan, P., Vizel, Y., Gupta, A., Malik, S.: Instruction-level abstraction (ILA): a uniform specification for system-on-chip (SoC) verification. ACM Trans. Design Autom. Electr. Syst. 24(1), 10:1–10:24 (2019)

34. Ivancic, F., et al.: Scalable and scope-bounded software verification in varvel. Autom. Softw. Eng. 22(4), 517–559 (2015)

35. Jacobs, S.: Extended AIGER format for synthesis. arXiv preprint:1405.5793 (2014)

36. Jhala, R., McMillan, K.L.: Microarchitecture verification by compositional model checking. In: Berry, G., Comon, H., Finkel, A. (eds.) CAV 2001. LNCS, vol. 2102, pp. 396–410. Springer, Heidelberg (2001). https://doi.org/10.1007/3-540-44585-4_40

37. Kaivola, R., et al.: Replacing testing with formal verification in Intel Core^{TM}i7 processor execution engine validation. In: CAV, pp. 414–429 (2009)

38. Komuravelli, A., Gurfinkel, A., Chaki, S.: SMT-based model checking for recursive programs. FMSD 48(3), 175–205 (2016)

39. Kuehlmann, A., Bergamaschi, R.A.: High-level state machine specification and synthesis. In: ICCD, pp. 536–539 (1992)

40. Lee, S., Sakallah, K.A.: Unbounded scalable verification based on approximate property-directed reachability and datapath abstraction. In: Biere, A., Bloem, R. (eds.) CAV 2014. LNCS, vol. 8559, pp. 849–865. Springer, Cham (2014). https://doi.org/10.1007/978-3-319-08867-9_56

41. Manolios, P., Srinivasan, S.K.: A refinement-based compositional reasoning framework for pipelined machine verification. IEEE Trans. VLSI Syst. 16(4), 353–364 (2008)

42. Mattarei, C., Mann, M., Barrett, C., Daly, R.G., Huff, D., Hanrahan, P.: CoSA: integrated verification for agile hardware design. In: FMCAD. IEEE (2018)

43. McMillan, K.L.: Verification of an implementation of Tomasulo's algorithm by compositional model checking. In: Hu, A.J., Vardi, M.Y. (eds.) CAV 1998. LNCS, vol. 1427, pp. 110–121. Springer, Heidelberg (1998). https://doi.org/10.1007/BFb0028738

44. McMillan, K.L.: Modular specification and verification of a cache-coherent interface. In: FMCAD, pp. 109–116 (2016)

45. Mishchenko, A., Een, N., Brayton, R., Baumgartner, J., Mony, H., Nalla, P.: Gla: gate-level abstraction revisited. In: DATE, pp. 1399–1404 (2013)

46. Nguyen, M.D., Thalmaier, M., Wedler, M., Bormann, J., Stoffel, D., Kunz, W.: Unbounded protocol compliance verification using interval property checking with invariants. IEEE Trans. CAD Integr. Circ. Syst. 27(11), 2068–2082 (2008)

47. Padhi, S., Sharma, R., Millstein, T.D.: Data-driven precondition inference with learned features. In: PLDI, pp. 42–56. ACM (2016)

48. Ragan-Kelley, J., Adams, A., Paris, S., Durand, F., Barnes, C., Amarasinghe, S.: Halide: a language and compiler for optimizing parallelism, locality, and recomputation in image processing pipelines. In: PLDI, pp. 519–530 (2013)

49. Reid, A.: Trustworthy specifications of ARM® v8-A and v8-M system level architecture. In: FMCAD, pp. 161–168 (2017)

50. Reid, A., et al.: End-to-end verification of ARM *textregistred* processors with ISA-formal. In: Chaudhuri, S., Farzan, A. (eds.) CAV 2016. LNCS, vol. 9780, pp. 42–58. Springer, Cham (2016). https://doi.org/10.1007/978-3-319-41540-6_3

51. Reynolds, A., Barbosa, H., Nötzli, A., Barrett, C., Tinelli, C.: CVC4SY: smart and fast term enumeration for syntax-guided synthesis. In: Dillig, I., Tasiran, S. (eds.) CAV 2019. LNCS, vol. 11562, pp. 74–83. Springer, Cham (2019). https://doi.org/10.1007/978-3-030-25543-5_5

52. Rondon, P.M., Kawaguci, M., Jhala, R.: Liquid types. In: PLDI, pp. 159–169 (2008)

53. Si, X., Yang, Y., Dai, H., Naik, M., Song, L.: Learning a meta-solver for syntax-guided program synthesis. In: International Conference on Learning Representations (2019)

54. Subramanyan, P., Huang, B.Y., Vizel, Y., Gupta, A., Malik, S.: Template-based parameterized synthesis of uniform instruction-level abstractions for SoC verification. IEEE Trans. Comput.-Aided Des. Integr. Circ. Syst. **37**(8), 1692–1705 (2018)

55. Subramanyan, P., Vizel, Y., Ray, S., Malik, S.: Template-based synthesis of instruction-level abstractions for SoC verification. In: FMCAD, pp. 160–167 (2017)

56. Wolf, C.: Yosys open synthesis suite. http://www.clifford.at/yosys/. Accessed 20 Sept 2019

57. Zhang, H., Yang, W., Fedyukovich, G.: Benchmark examples for environment invariant synthesis. https://github.com/zhanghongce/vmcai2020-inv-syn-benchmarks. Accessed 3 Oct 2019

Systematic Classification of Attackers via Bounded Model Checking

Eric Rothstein-Morris[1]([⊠]), Jun Sun[2], and Sudipta Chattopadhyay[1]

[1] Singapore University of Technology and Design, Singapore, Singapore
{eric_rothstein,sudipta_chattopadhyay}@sutd.edu.sg
[2] Singapore Management University, Singapore, Singapore
junsun@smu.edu.sg

VMCAI
Artifact
Evaluation
★ ★
Functional

Abstract. In this work, we study the problem of verification of systems in the presence of attackers using bounded model checking. Given a system and a set of security requirements, we present a methodology to generate and classify attackers, mapping them to the set of requirements that they can break. A naive approach suffers from the same shortcomings of any large model checking problem, i.e., memory shortage and exponential time. To cope with these shortcomings, we describe two sound heuristics based on cone-of-influence reduction and on learning, which we demonstrate empirically by applying our methodology to a set of hardware benchmark systems.

1 Introduction

Problem Context. Some systems are designed to provide security guarantees in the presence of attackers. For example, the Diffie-Hellman key agreement protocol guarantees perfect forward secrecy [21,27] (PFS), i.e., that the session key remains secret even if the long-term keys are compromised. These security guarantees are only valid in the context of the attacker models for which they were proven; more precisely, those guarantees only hold for attackers that fit those or weaker attacker models. For instance, PFS describes an attacker model (i.e., an attacker that can compromise the long-term keys, *and only those*), and a property that is guaranteed in the presence of an attacker that fits the model (i.e., confidentiality of the session keys). However, if we consider an attacker model that is stronger (e.g., an attacker that can directly compromise the session key), then Diffie-Hellman can no longer guarantee the confidentiality of the session keys. Clearly, it is difficult to provide any guarantees against an attacker model that is too capable, so it is in the interest of the system designer to choose an adequate attacker model that puts the security guarantees of the system in the context of realistic and relevant attackers.

Consider the following research question: **(RQ1)** given a system and a list of security requirements, how do we systematically generate attackers that can potentially break these requirements, and how do we verify if they are successful? We approach this question at a high level for a system S with a set C of n

© Springer Nature Switzerland AG 2020
D. Beyer and D. Zufferey (Eds.): VMCAI 2020, LNCS 11990, pp. 226–247, 2020.
https://doi.org/10.1007/978-3-030-39322-9_11

components, and a set of security requirements R as follows. Let A be a subset of C; the set A models an attacker that can interact with S by means of each component c in it. More precisely, for every component c in A, the attacker can change the value of c at any time and any number of times during execution, possibly following an attack strategy. Considering the exponential size of the set of attackers (i.e., 2^n), a brute-force approach to checking whether each of those attackers breaks each requirement in R is inefficient for two reasons: (1) an attacker A may only affect an isolated part of the system, so requirements that refer to other parts of the system should not be affected by the presence of A, and (2) if some attacker B affects the system in a similar way to A (e.g., if they control a similar set of components), then the knowledge we obtain while verifying the system in the presence of A may be useful when verifying the system in the presence of B. These two reasons motivate a second research question: **(RQ2)** which techniques can help us to *classify* attackers, i.e., to map each attacker to the set of requirements that it breaks?

To answer these two research questions in a more concrete and practical context, we study systems modelled by *And-inverter Graphs (AIGs)* (see [23, 25]). AIGs describe hardware models at the bit-level [10], and have attracted the attention of industry partners including IBM and Intel [16]. Due to being systems described at bit-level, AIGs present a convenient system model to study the problem of attacker classification, because the range of actions that attackers have over components is greatly restricted: either the attacker leaves the value of the component as it is, or the attacker negates its current value. However, this approach can be generalised to other systems by considering non-binary ranges for components, and by allowing attackers to choose any value in those ranges.

Contributions. In this paper, we provide:

- a formalisation of attackers of AIGs and how they interact with systems,
- a methodology to perform bounded model checking while considering the presence of attackers,
- a set of heuristics that characterise attacker frontiers for invariant properties using bounded model checking,
- experimental evidence of the effectiveness of the proposed methodology and heuristics.

2   Preliminaries

In this section, we provide the foundation necessary to formally present the problem of model checking And-inverter Graph (AIGs) in the presence of attackers. Let $\mathbb{B} = \{\,0,1\,\}$ be the set of booleans/bits. An *And-inverter Graph* models a system of equations that has m boolean inputs, n boolean state variables and o boolean gates. The elements in the set $W = \{\,w_1, \ldots, w_m\,\}$ represent the *inputs*, the elements in $V = \{\,v_1, \ldots, v_n\,\}$ represent the *latches*, and the elements in $G = \{\,g_1, \ldots, g_o\,\}$ represent the *and-gates*. We assume that W, V and G are pairwise disjoint, and we define the set of *components* C by $C \triangleq W \cup V \cup G$.

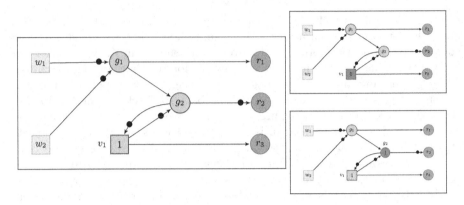

Fig. 1. Left: And-inverter graph describing a system with two inputs w_1 and w_2 (green boxes), one latch v_1 with initial value 1 (grey box), two gates $g1$ and $g2$ (gray circles), and three invariant requirements $r_1 = \Box g_1$, $r_2 = \Box \neg g_2$ and $r_3 = \Box v_1$ (red circles). Arrows represent logical dependencies, and bullets in the arrows imply negation. **Right above:** an attacker that controls latch v_1 can set its initial value to 0 to break r_2 and r_3 in 0 steps. **Right below:** an attacker that controls gate g_2 can set its value to 1 at time 0 to break r_2 in 0 steps and r_3 in 1 step, because the value of v_1 at time 1 is 0. (Color figure online)

An *expression* e is described by the grammar $e ::= 0 \mid 1 \mid c \mid \neg c$, where $c \in C$. The set of all expressions is E. We use discrete time steps $t = 0, 1, ..$ to describe the system of equations. To each latch $v \in V$ we associate a transition equation of the form $v(t+1) = e(t)$ and an initial equation of the form $v(0) = b$, where $e \in E$ and $b \in \mathbb{B}$. To each gate $g \in G$ we associate an equation of the form $g(t) = e_1(t) \wedge e_2(t)$, where $e_1, e_2 \in E$.

Example 1. Figure 1 shows an example AIG with $W = \{w_1, w_2\}$, $V = \{v_1\}$ and $G = \{g_1, g_2\}$. The corresponding system of equations is

$$v_1(0) = 1, \qquad\qquad v_1(t+1) = \neg g_2(t),$$
$$g_1(t) = \neg w_1(t) \wedge \neg w_2(t), \qquad\qquad g_2(t) = g_1(t) \wedge \neg v_1(t).$$

The states of a system are all the different valuations of the variables in V; formally, a state $\overrightarrow{v} : V \to \mathbb{B}$ is a map from V to bits. Similarly, the valuations of the variables in W are all the inputs to the systems; again, an input $\overrightarrow{w} : W \to \mathbb{B}$ is a map from W to bits. We refer to the set of all states by $\overrightarrow{V}$, and to the set of all inputs by $\overrightarrow{W}$. For $t = 0, 1, ...$, we denote the state of the system at time t by $\overrightarrow{v}(t)$, with $\overrightarrow{v}(t) \triangleq \langle v_1(t), ..., v_n(t) \rangle$. The initial state is $\overrightarrow{v}(0)$, defined by the initial equations for the latches. Similarly, we denote the input of the system at time t by $\overrightarrow{w}(t)$, with $\overrightarrow{w}(t) \triangleq \langle w_1(t), ..., w_n(t) \rangle$. There are no restrictions or assumptions over $\overrightarrow{w}(t)$, so it can take any value in $\overrightarrow{W}$.

In Example 1, the states are $\vec{V} = \{ \langle (v_1, 0) \rangle, \langle (v_1, 1) \rangle \}$, the inputs are $\vec{W} = \{ \langle (w_1, 0), (w_2, 0) \rangle, \langle (w_1, 0), (w_2, 1) \rangle, \langle (w_1, 1), (w_2, 0) \rangle, \langle (w_1, 1), (w_2, 1) \rangle \}$, and the initial state is $\vec{v}(0) = \langle (v_1, 1) \rangle$.

Given an expression $e \in E$, the invariant $\Box e$ is the property that requires $e(t)$ to be true for all $t \geq 0$. The system S *fails* the invariant $\Box e$ iff there exists a finite sequence of inputs $\langle \vec{w}_0, \ldots, \vec{w}_t \rangle$ such that, if we assume $\vec{w}(t) = \vec{w}_t$, then $e(t)$ is false. The system *satisfies* the invariant $\Box e$ if no such sequence of inputs exists. Every expression e represents a boolean predicate over the state of the latches of the system, and can be used to characterise states that are (un)safe. These expressions are particularly useful in safety-critical hardware, as they can signal the approach of a critical state.

In Example 1, we define three requirements: $r_1 \triangleq \Box g_1$, $r_2 \triangleq \Box \neg g_2$, and $r_3 \triangleq \Box v_1$. This system satisfies r_2 and r_3, but it fails r_1 because $w_1 = 1$ and $w_2 = 0$ results in $g_1(0)$ being 0.

The *Cone-of-Influence* (COI) is a mapping from an expression to the components that can potentially influence its value. We obtain the COI of an expression $e \in E$, denoted $\blacktriangledown(e)$, by transitively tracing its dependencies to inputs, latches and gates. More precisely,

- $\blacktriangledown(0) = \emptyset$ and $\blacktriangledown(1) = \emptyset$;
- if $e = \neg c$ for $c \in C$, then $\blacktriangledown(e) = \blacktriangledown(c)$;
- if $e = w$ and w is an input, then $\blacktriangledown(e) = \{ w \}$;
- if $e = v$ and v is a latch whose transition equation is $l(t+1) = e'(t)$, then $\blacktriangledown(e) = \{ v \} \cup \blacktriangledown(e')$;
- if $e = g$ and g is a gate whose equation is $g(t) = e_1(t) \wedge e_2(t)$ then $\blacktriangledown(e) = \{ g \} \cup \blacktriangledown(e_1) \cup \blacktriangledown(e_2)$.

The COI of a requirement $r = \Box e$ is $\blacktriangledown(r) \triangleq \blacktriangledown(e)$.

In Example 1, the COI for the requirements are $\blacktriangledown(\Box g_1) = \{ g_1, w_1, w_2 \}$, and $\blacktriangledown(\Box g_2) = \blacktriangledown(\Box g_3) = \{ g_1, g_2, v_1, w_1, w_2 \}$.

The set of *sources* of an expression $e \in E$, denoted $\mathtt{src}(e)$ is the set of latches and inputs in the COI of e; formally, $\mathtt{src}(e) \triangleq \blacktriangledown(e) \cap (V \cup W)$. The *Jaccard index* of two expressions e_1 and e_2 is equal to $\frac{|\mathtt{src}(e_1) \cap \mathtt{src}(e_2)|}{|\mathtt{src}(e_1) \cup \mathtt{src}(e_2)|}$. This index provides a measure of how similar the sources of e_1 and e_2 are.

The *dual cone-of-influence* (IOC) of a component $c \in C$, denoted $\blacktriangle(c)$, is the set of components influenced by c; more precisely $\blacktriangle(c) \triangleq \{ c' \in C \mid c \in \blacktriangledown(c') \}$.

3 Motivational Example

In this section, we provide a motivational example of the problem of model checking compromised systems, and we illustrate how to classify attackers given a list of security requirements. Consider a scenario where an attacker A controls

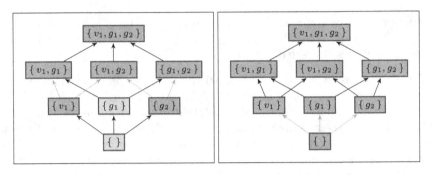

Fig. 2. Left: classification of attackers for requirements r_2 and r_3. Right: classification of attackers for requirement r_1. A green attacker cannot break the requirement, while a red attacker can. (Color figure online)

the gate g_2 of Example 1. By controlling g_2, we mean that A can set the value of $g_2(t)$ at will for all $t \geq 0$. Since $r_2 = \Box \neg g_2$, it is possible for A to break r_2 by setting $g_2(0)$ to 1. We note that the same strategy works to break both requirements, but it need not be in the general case; i.e., an attacker may have one strategy to break one requirement, and a different strategy to break another. A can also break $r_3 = \Box v_1$, because, if A sets $g_2(0)$ to 1, then $v_1(1)$ is equal to 0. Since the original system fails to enforce r_1, we say that A has the *power to break the requirements* r_1, r_2 and r_3. Now, consider a different attacker B which only controls the gate g_1. No matter what value B chooses for $g_1(t)$ for all t, it is impossible for B to break r_2 or r_3, so we say that B only has the power to break r_1.

If we allow attackers to control any number of components, then there are 8 different attackers, described by the subsets of $\{v_1, g_1, g_2\}$. We do not consider attackers that control inputs, because the model checking of invariant properties requires the property to hold for all inputs, so giving control of inputs to an attacker does not make it more powerful (i.e. the attacker cannot break more requirements than it already could without the inputs). Figure 2 illustrates the classification of attackers depending on whether they can break a given requirement or not. Based on it, we can provide the following security guarantees: (1) the system cannot enforce r_1, and (2) that the system can only enforce r_2 and r_3 in the presence of attackers that are as capable to interact with the system as $\{g_1\}$ (i.e. they only control g_1 or nothing).

According to the classification, attacker $\{g_2\}$ is as powerful as the attacker $\{v_1, g_1, g_2\}$, since both attackers can break the same requirements r_1, r_2 and r_3. This information may be useful to the designer of the system, because it may prioritise attackers that control less components but are as powerful as attackers that control more when deploying defensive mechanisms.

4   Bounded Model Checking of Compromised Systems

We recall the research questions that motivate this work: **(RQ1)** given a system and a list of security requirements, how do we systematically generate attackers that can potentially break these requirements, and how do we verify if they are successful? and **(RQ2)** which techniques can help us *classify* attackers, i.e., to map each attacker to the set of requirements that it breaks? In this section, we aim to answer these research questions on a theoretical level by formalising the problem of attacker classification via bounded model checking AIGs in the presence of attackers. More precisely, to answer **RQ1**, we formalise attackers and their interactions with systems, and we show how to systematically generate bounded model checking problems that solve whether some given attackers can break some given requirements. We then propose two methods for the classification of attackers: (1) a brute-force method that creates a model checking problem for each attacker-requirement pair, and (2) a method that incrementally empowers attackers to find "minimal attackers," since minimal attackers represent large portions of the universe of attackers thanks to a monotonicity relation between the set of components controlled by the attacker and the set of requirements that the attacker can break. The latter method is a theoretical approach to answer **RQ2**, while its practical usefulness is evaluated in Sect. 5.

4.1   Attackers and Compromised Systems

Since an AIG describes a system of equations, to incorporate the actions of an attacker A into the system, we modify the equations that are associated to the components controlled by A. Let $S = (W, V, G)$ be a system described by an AIG, let $R = \{r_1, \ldots, r_n\}$ be a set of invariant requirements for S, and let $C = W \cup V \cup G$ be the set of components of S. By definition, an *attacker* A is any subset of C. If a component c belongs to an attacker A, then A has the *capability to interact with S through* c. We modify the equations of every latch $v \in V$ to be parametrised by an attacker A as follows: the original transition equation $v(t + 1) = e(t)$ and the initial equation $v(0) = b$ changes to

$$v(t+1) = \begin{cases} e(t), & \text{if } v \notin A; \\ A_v(t+1), & \text{otherwise,} \end{cases} \qquad v(0) = \begin{cases} b, & \text{if } v \notin A; \\ A_v(0), & \text{otherwise.} \end{cases} \tag{1}$$

where $A_v(t)$ is a value chosen by the attacker A at time t. Similarly, we modify the equation of gate $g \in G$ as follows: the original equation $g(t) = e_1(t) \wedge e_2(t)$ changes to

$$g(t) = \begin{cases} e_1(t) \wedge e_2(t), & \text{if } g \notin A; \\ A_g(t), & \text{otherwise,} \end{cases} \tag{2}$$

where $A_g(t)$ is, again, a value chosen by the attacker A at time t. We use $A[S]$ to denote the system S under the influence of attacker A; i.e., $A[S]$ is the modified system of equations.

An *attack* $\vec{a} : A \to \mathbb{B}$ is a map of components in A to booleans. An *attack strategy* is a finite sequence of attacks $(\vec{a}_0, \vec{a}_1, \ldots, \vec{a}_t)$ that fixes the values of all $A_c(k)$ (used in the equations above) by $A_c(k) = \vec{a}_k(c)$, with $c \in A$ and $0 \le k \le t$.

Definition 1 (Broken Requirement). *Given a requirement $r \in R$ with $r = \Box e$, we say that A breaks the requirement r if and only if there exists a sequence of inputs of length k and an attack strategy of length k such that $e(k)$ is false. We denote the set of requirements that A breaks by $A[R]$.*

Finally, we define two partial orders for attackers: (**1**) an attacker A_i is strictly less *capable* (to interact with the system) than an attacker A_j in the context of S iff $A_i \subseteq A_j$ and $A_i \neq A_j$. The attacker A_i is equally capable to attacker A_j iff $A_i = A_j$; and (**2**) an attacker A_i is strictly less *powerful* than an attacker A_j in the context of S and R iff $A_i[R] \subseteq A_j[R]$ and $A_i[R] \neq A_j[R]$. Similarly, attacker A_i is equally powerful to attacker A_j iff $A_i[R] = A_j[R]$. We simply state that A_i is less capable than A_j if S is clear from the context. Similarly, we simply say that A_i is less powerful than A_j if S and R are clear from the context.

We can now properly present the problem of *attacker classification*.

Definition 2 (Attacker Classification via Model Checking). *Given a system S, a set of requirements R, and a set of h attackers $\{A_1, \ldots, A_h\}$, for every attacker A, we compute the set $A[R]$ of requirements that A can break by performing model checking of each requirement in R on the compromised system $A[S]$.*

Definition 2 assumes that exhaustive model checking is possible for S and the compromised versions $A[S]$ for all attackers A. However, if exhaustive model checking is not possible (e.g., due to time limitations or memory restrictions), we consider an alternative formulation for *Bounded Model Checking* (BMC):

Definition 3 (Attacker Classification via Bounded Model Checking). *Let S be a system, R be a set of requirements, and t be a natural number. Given a set of attackers $\{A_1, \ldots, A_h\}$, for each attacker A, we compute the set $A[R]$ of requirements that A can break using a strategy of length up to t on the compromised system $A[S]$.*

In the following, we show how to construct a SAT formula that describes the attacker classification problem via bounded model checking.

4.2   A SAT Formula for BMC up to t Steps

For a requirement $r = \Box e$ and a time step $t \ge 0$, we are interested in finding an assignment of sources and attacker actions (i.e., an attack strategy) such that, for $0 \le k \le t$, the value of $e(k)$ is false. We define the proposition $\texttt{goal}(r, t)$ by

$$\texttt{goal}(\Box e, t) \triangleq \bigvee_{k=0}^{t} \neg e(k), \tag{3}$$

We must inform the SAT solver of the equalities and dependencies between expressions given by the definition of the AIG (e.g., that $e(k) \Leftrightarrow \neg v_1(k)$). Inspired by the work of Biere *et al.* [8], we transform the equations into a Conjunctive Normal Form formula (CNF) that the SAT solver can work with using *Tseitin encoding* [31]. Each equation of the form

$$v(0) = \begin{cases} b, & \text{if } v \notin A; \\ A_v(0), & \text{otherwise,} \end{cases}$$

becomes $\left(v^\downarrow \vee (v(0) \Leftrightarrow b)\right) \wedge \left(\neg v^\downarrow \vee (v(0) \Leftrightarrow A_v(0))\right)$

where $v^\downarrow$ is a literal that marks whether the latch v is an element of the attacker A currently being checked; i.e., we assume that $v^\downarrow$ is true if $v \in A$, and we assume that $v^\downarrow$ is false if $v \notin A$. Consequently, if $v \notin A$, then $v(0) \Leftrightarrow b$ must be true, and if $v \in A$, then $v(0) \Leftrightarrow A_v(0)$ must be true. We denote this new proposition by $\texttt{encode}(v, 0)$, and it characterises the initial state of v.

Similarly, for $0 \leq k < t$, each equation of the form

$$v(k+1) = \begin{cases} e(k), & \text{if } v \notin A; \\ A_v(k+1), & \text{otherwise,} \end{cases}$$

becomes $\left(v^\downarrow \vee (v(k+1) \Leftrightarrow e(k))\right) \wedge \left(\neg v^\downarrow \vee (v(k+1) \Leftrightarrow A_v(k+1))\right).$

We denote this new proposition by $\texttt{encode}(v, k)$. Finally, for $0 \leq k \leq t$, each equation of the form

$$g(k) = \begin{cases} e_1(k) \wedge e_2(k), & \text{if } g \notin A; \\ A_g(k), & \text{otherwise,} \end{cases}$$

becomes $\left(g^\downarrow \vee (g(k) \Leftrightarrow e_1(k) \wedge e_2(k))\right) \wedge \left(\neg g^\downarrow \vee (g(k) \Leftrightarrow A_g(k))\right),$

where $g^\downarrow$ is a literal that marks whether the gate g is an element of the attacker A currently being checked in a similar way that the literal $v^\downarrow$ works for the latch v. We denote this new proposition by $\texttt{encode}(g, k)$.

To perform SAT solving, we need to find an assignment of inputs in W and attacker actions for each component c in A over t steps; thus, we need to assign at least $|W \times A| \times t$ literals. The SAT problem for checking whether requirement r is safe up to t steps, denoted $\texttt{check}(r, t)$, is defined by

$$\texttt{check}(r, t) \triangleq \texttt{goal}(r, t) \wedge \bigwedge_{c \in (V \cup G)} \left(\bigwedge_{k=0}^{t} \texttt{encode}(c, k) \right). \tag{4}$$

Proposition 1. *For a given attacker A and a requirement $r = \Box e$, if we assume the literal $c^\downarrow$ for all $c \in A$ and we assume $\neg x^\downarrow$ for all $x \notin A$ (i.e., $x \in (V \cup G) - A$), then A can break the requirement r in t steps (or less) if and only if $\texttt{check}(r, t)$ is satisfiable.*

Proof. We first show that if A can break the requirement in t steps or less, then check(r, t) is satisfiable. Since A breaks $r = \Box e$ in t steps or less, then, by Definition 1, there exists an assignment of inputs $(\vec{w}_0, \dots, \vec{w}_k)$ and an attacker strategy $(\vec{a}_0, \dots, \vec{a}_k)$ which causes $e(k)$ to be false for some $k \leq t$; this means that goal(r, t) is satisfiable, which, in turn, makes check(r, t) satisfiable.

Data: system $S = (W, V, G)$, a time step $t \geq 0$, a set of requirements R.

Result: A map that maps the attacker A to $A[R]$.

1 Map $\mathcal{H}$;
2 for*each* $r \in R$ do
3   for*each* A such that $A \subseteq (V \cup G)$ do
4   if check(r, t) is satisfiable while assuming $c^{\downarrow}$ for all $c \in A$ then
5 | insert r in $\mathcal{H}(A)$;
6   end
7   end
8 end
9 return $\mathcal{H}$;

Algorithm 1. Naive attacker classification algorithm.

We now show that if check(r, t) is satisfiable, then A can break the requirement. If check(r, t) is satisfiable then goal(r, t) is satisfiable, and $e(k)$ is false for some $k \leq t$. Consequently, there is an assignment of inputs $\vec{w}(k)$ and attacker actions $A_c(k)$, such that the encode(c, k) propositions are satisfied for all $c \in A$. With $\vec{a}_k(c) = A_c(k)$ and $\vec{w}_k = \vec{w}(k)$, we obtain a witness input sequence and a witness attack strategy which proves that A can break r in k steps (i.e., in t steps or less since $k \leq t$).   □

Algorithm 1 describes a naive strategy to compute the sets $A[R]$ for each attacker A; i.e. the set of requirements that A breaks in t steps (or less). Algorithm 1 works by solving, for each of the $2^{|V \cup G|}$ different attackers, a set of $|R|$ SAT problems, each of which has a size of at least $\mathcal{O}(|C| \times t)$ on the worst case.

In the rest of the section, we propose two sound heuristics in an attempt to improve Algorithm 1: the first technique aims to reduce the size of the SAT formula, while the other aims to record and propagate the results of verifications among the set of attackers so that some calls to the SAT solver can be avoided.

4.3 Isolation and Monotonicity

The first strategy involves relying on *isolation* to prove that it is impossible for a given attacker to break some requirements. To formally capture this notion, we first extend the notion of IOC to attackers. The IOC of an attacker A, denoted $\blacktriangle(A)$, is defined by the union of IOCs of the components in A; more precisely, $\blacktriangle(A) \triangleq \bigcup \{ \blacktriangle(c) \mid c \in A \}$.

Informally, isolation happens whenever the IOC of A is disjoint from the COI of r, implying that A cannot interact with r.

Proposition 2 (Isolation). *Let A be an attacker and r be a requirement that is satisfied in the absence of A. If $\blacktriangle(A) \cap \blacktriangledown(r) = \emptyset$, then A cannot break r.*

Proof. For the attacker A to break the requirement r, there must be a component $c \in \blacktriangledown(r)$ whose behaviour was affected by the presence of A, and whose change of behaviour caused r to fail. However, for A to affect the behaviour of c, there must be a dependency between the variables directly controlled by A and c, since A only chooses actions over the components it controls; implying that $c \in \blacktriangle(A)$. This contradicts the premise that the IOC of A and the COI of r are disjoint, so the component c cannot exist. $\square$

Isolation reduces the SAT formula by dismissing attackers that are outside the COI of the requirement to be verified. Isolation works similarly to *COI reduction* (see [7,13–15,18]), and it transforms Eq. 4 into

$$\texttt{check}(r,t) \triangleq \texttt{goal}(r,t) \wedge \bigwedge_{c \in (\blacktriangledown(r) - W)} \left(\bigwedge_{k=0}^{t} \texttt{encode}(c,k) \right) \tag{5}$$

The second strategy uses *monotonicity* relation between capabilities and power of attackers.

Proposition 3 (Monotonicity). *For attackers A and B and a set of requirements R, if $A \subseteq B$, then $A[R] \subseteq B[R]$.*

Proof. If A is a subset of B, then attacker B can always choose the same attack strategies that A used to break the requirements in $A[R]$; thus, $A[R]$ must be a subset of $B[R]$. $\square$

Monotonicity allows us to define the notion of minimal (successful) attackers for a requirement r: attacker A is a *minimal attacker* for requirement r if and only if A breaks r, and there is no attacker $B \subset A$ such that B also breaks r. In the remainder of this section, we expand on this notion, and we describe a methodology for attacker classification that focuses on the identification of these minimal attackers.

4.4   Minimal (Successful) Attackers

The set of minimal attackers for a requirement r partitions the set of attackers into those that break r and those who do not. Any attacker that is more capable than a minimal attacker is guaranteed to break r by monotonicity (cf. Proposition 3), and any attacker that is less capable than a minimal attacker cannot break r; otherwise, this less capable attacker would be a minimal attacker. Consequently, we can reduce the problem of attacker classification to the problem of finding the minimal attackers for all requirements.

Existence of a Minimal Attacker. Thanks to isolation (cf. Proposition 2) we can guarantee that a requirement r that is safe in the absence of an attacker A remains safe in the presence of A if $\blacktriangledown(r) \cap \blacktriangle(A)$ is empty. Thus, for each requirement $r \in R$, the set of attackers that could break r is $\mathscr{P}(\blacktriangledown(r) - W)$. Out of all the attackers of r, the most capable attacker is $\blacktriangledown(r) - W$, so we can test whether there *exists* any attacker that can break r in t steps by solving $\mathrm{check}(r, t)$ against attacker $\blacktriangledown(r) - W$. For succinctness, we henceforth denote the attacker $\blacktriangledown(r) - W$ by r^{max}.

Corollary 1. *From monotonicity and isolation (cf. Propositions 3 and 2), if attacker r^{max} cannot break the requirement r, then there are no minimal attackers for r. Equivalently, if r^{max} cannot break r, then r does not belong to any set of broken requirements $A[R]$.*

Data: system S, a requirement r, and a time step $t \geq 0$.
Result: set M of *minimal* attackers for r, bounded by t.
1 **if** $check(r, t)$ *is* **not** *satisfiable while assuming* $c^{\downarrow}$ *for all* $c \in r^{max}$
   then
2 | **return** $\emptyset$;
3 **end**
4 Set: $P = \{\emptyset\}$, $M = \emptyset$; $//(P$ contains the empty attacker $\emptyset)$
5 **while** P *is not empty* **do**
6 | extract A from P such that the size of A is minimal;
7 | **if** *not (exists* $B \in M$ *such that* $B \subseteq A)$ **then**
8 | | **if** $check(r, t)$ *is satisfiable when assuming* $c^{\downarrow}$ *for all* $c \in A$
          then
9 | | | insert A in M;
10 | | **else**
11 | | | **for***each* $c \in (r^{max} - A)$ **do**
12 | | | | insert $A \cup \{c\}$ in P;
13 | | | **end**
14 | | **end**
15 | **end**
16 **end**
17 **return** M;

Algorithm 2. The MinimalAttackers algorithm.

Finding Minimal Attackers. After having confirmed that at least one minimal attacker for r exists, we can focus on finding them. Our strategy consist of systematically increasing the capabilities of attackers that fail to break the requirement r until they do. Algorithm 2 describes this empowering procedure to computes the set of minimal attackers for a requirement r, which we call

MinimalAttackers. As mentioned, we first check to see if a minimal attacker exists (Lines 1–3); then we start evaluating attackers in an orderly fashion by always choosing the smallest attackers in the set of pending attackers P (Lines 5–16). Line 7 uses monotonicity to discard the attacker A if there is a successful attacker B with $B \subseteq A$. Line 8 checks if the attacker A can break r in t steps (or less); if so, then A is a minimal attacker for r and is included in M (Line 9); otherwise, we empower A with a new component c, and we add these new attackers to P (Lines 11–13). We note that Line 11 relies on isolation, since we only add components that belong to the COI of r.

Data: system S, a time step $t \geq 0$, and a set of requirements R.
Result: Set of all minimal attackers $\mathcal{M}$ and an initial classification
map $\mathcal{H}$.

1 Set: $\mathcal{M} = \emptyset$;
2 Map: $\mathcal{H}$;
3 **for** *each* $r \in R$ **do**
4   **for** *each* $A \in$ MinimalAttackers(S, t, r) **do**
5   insert r in $\mathcal{H}(A)$;
6   insert A in $\mathcal{M}$;
7   **end**
8 **end**
9 **return** $(\mathcal{M}, \mathcal{H})$;

Algorithm 3. The AllMinimalAttackers algorithm.

We recall the motivational example from Sect. 3. Consider the computation of MinimalAttackers for requirement r_2. In this case, r_2^{max} is $\{ g1, g2, v_1 \}$, which is able to break r_2, confirming the existence of (at least) a minimal attacker (Lines 1–3). We start to look for minimal attackers by checking the attacker $\emptyset$ (Lines 5–8); after we see that it fails to break r_2, we conclude that $\emptyset$ is not a minimal attacker and that we need to increase its capabilities. We then derive the attackers $\{ g_1 \}, \{ g_2 \}$ and $\{ v_1 \}$ by adding one non-isolated component to $\emptyset$, and we put them into the set of pending attackers (Lines 11–13). For attackers $\{ v_1 \}$ and $\{ g_2 \}$, we know that they can break the requirement r_2, so they get added to the set of minimal attackers, and are not empowered (Line 9); however, for attacker $\{ g_1 \}$, since it fails to break r_2, we increase its capabilities and we generate attackers $\{ v_1, g_1 \}$ and $\{ g_1, g_2 \}$. Finally, for these two latter attackers, since the minimal attackers $\{ v_1 \}$ and $\{ g_2 \}$ have already been identified, the check in Line 7 fails, and they are dismissed from the set of pending attackers, since they cannot be minimal. The algorithm finishes with $M = \{ \{ v_1 \}, \{ g_2 \} \}$.

Algorithms 3 applies Algorithm 2 to each requirement; it collects all minimal attackers in the set $\mathcal{M}$ and initialises the attacker classification map $\mathcal{H}$. Finally,

Algorithm 4 exploits monotonicity to compute the classification of each attacker A by aggregating the requirements broken by the minimal attackers that are subsets of A.

For the motivational example in Sect. 3, Algorithm 3 returns $\mathcal{M} = \{\emptyset, \{v_1\}, \{g_2\}\}$ and $\mathcal{H} = \{(\emptyset, \{r_1\}), (\{v_1\}, \{r_2, r_3\}), (\{g_2\}, \{r_2, r_3\})\}$. From there, Algorithm 4 completes the map $\mathcal{H}$, and returns

$$\mathcal{H} = \{(\emptyset, \{r_1\}), (\{v_1\}, \{r_1, r_2, r_3\}), (\{g_1\}, \{r_1\}), (\{g_2\}, \{r_1, r_2, r_3\}),$$
$$(\{v_1, g_2\}, \{r_1, r_2, r_3\}), (\{v_1, g_2\}, \{r_1, r_2, r_3\}),$$
$$(\{g_1, g_2\}, \{r_1, r_2, r_3\}), (\{v_1, g_1, g_2\}, \{r_1, r_2, r_3\})\}$$

Data: system $S = (W, V, G)$, a time step $t \geq 0$, a set of requirements R.

Result: A map $\mathcal{H}$ that maps the attacker A to $A[R]$.

1   $(\mathcal{M}, \mathcal{H}) = \texttt{AllMinimalAttackers}(S, t, R)$;

2   for*each* $A \subseteq (V \cup G)$ do

3   for*each* $A' \in \mathcal{M}$ do

4   if $A' \subseteq A$ then

5   insert all elements of $\mathcal{H}(A')$ in $\mathcal{H}(A)$;

6   end

7   end

8   end

9   return $\mathcal{H}$;

Algorithm 4. Improved classification algorithm. We assume that $\mathcal{H}$ initially maps every A to the empty set.

4.5   On Soundness and Completeness

Just like any bounded model checking problem, if the time parameter t is below the *completeness threshold* (see [24]), the resulting attacker classification up to t steps could be *incomplete*. More precisely, an attacker classification up to t steps may prove that an attacker A cannot break some requirement r with a strategy up to t steps, while in reality A can break r by using a strategy whose length is strictly greater than t. There are practical reasons that justify the use of a time parameter that is lower than the completeness threshold: (1) computing the exact completeness threshold is often as hard as solving the model-checking problem [18], so an approximation is taken instead; and (2), the complexity of the classification problem growths exponentially with t in the worst case, since the size of the SAT formulae grow with t, and there is an exponential number of attackers that need to be classified by making calls to the SAT solver.

A classification that uses a t below the completeness threshold, while possibly incomplete, is *sound*, i.e., it does not falsely report that an attacker can break a requirement when in reality it cannot. In Sect. 6 we discuss possible alternatives to overcome incompleteness, but we leave a definite solution as future work.

We also consider the possibility of limiting the maximum size of minimal attackers to approximate the problem of attacker classification. The result of a classification whose minimal sets are limited to have up to z elements is also sound but incomplete, since does not identify minimal attackers that have more than z elements. We show in Sect. 5 that, even with restricted minimal attackers, it is possible to obtain a high coverage of the universe of attackers.

4.6   Requirement Clustering

Property clustering [7,13,14] is a state-of-the-art technique for the model checking of multiple properties. Clustering allows the SAT solver to reuse information when solving a similar instance of the same problem, but under different assumptions. To create clusters for attacker classification, we combine the SAT problems whose COI is similar (i.e., requirements that have a Jaccard index close to 1), and incrementally enable and disable properties during verification. More precisely, to use clustering, instead of computing $\mathtt{goal}(r, t)$ for a single requirement, we compute $\mathtt{goal}(Y, t)$ for a cluster Y of requirements, defined by

$$\mathtt{goal}(Y, t) \triangleq \bigwedge_{r \in Y} (\neg r^{\downarrow} \vee \mathtt{goal}(r, t)). \tag{6}$$

where $r^{\downarrow}$ is a new literal that plays a similar role to the ones used for gates and latches; i.e., we assume $r^{\downarrow}$ when we want to find the minimal attackers for r, and we assume $\neg y^{\downarrow}$ for all other requirements $y \in Y$.

The SAT problem for checking whether the cluster of requirements Y is safe up to t steps is

$$\mathtt{check}(Y, t) \triangleq \mathtt{goal}(Y, t) \wedge \bigwedge_{c \in (\blacktriangledown(Y) - W)} \left(\bigwedge_{k=0}^{t} \mathtt{encode}(c, k) \right), \tag{7}$$

where $\blacktriangledown(Y) = \bigcup \{ \blacktriangledown(r) \mid r \in Y \}$.

5   Evaluation

In this section, we perform experiments to evaluate how effective is the use of isolation and monotonicity for the classification of attackers, and we evaluate the completeness of partial classifications for different time steps.

For evaluation, we use a sample of AIG benchmarks from past Hardware Model-Checking Competitions (see [1,2]), from their multiple-property verification track. Each benchmark has an associated list of invariants to be verified which, for the purposes of this evaluation, we interpret as the set of security requirements. As of 2014, the benchmark set was composed of 230 different instances, coming from both academia and industrial settings [16]. We quote from [16]:

> "Among industrial entries, 145 instances belong to the SixthSense family (6s*, provided by IBM), 24 are Intel benchmarks (intel*), and 24 are Oski benchmarks. Among the academic related benchmarks, the set includes 13 instances provided by Robert (Bob) Brayton (bob*), 4 benchmarks coming from Politecnico di Torino (pdt*) and 15 Beem (beem*). Additionally, 5 more circuits, already present in previous competitions, complete the set."

All experiments are performed on a quad core MacBook with 2.9 GHz Intel Core i7 and 16GB RAM, and we use the SAT solver CaDiCaL version 1.0.3 [3]. The source code of the artefact is available at [4].

We separate our evaluation in two parts: (1) a comparative study where we evaluate the effectiveness of using of monotonicity and isolation for attacker classification in several benchmarks, and (2) a case study, where we apply our classification methodology to a single benchmark –pdtvsarmultip– and we study the results of varying the time parameters for partial classification.

5.1 Evaluating Methodologies

Given a set of competing classification methodologies $\mathcal{M}_1, \ldots, \mathcal{M}_n$ (e.g., Algorithms 1 and 4), each methodology is given the same set of benchmarks $S_1, \ldots, S_m$, each with its respective set of requirements $R_1, \ldots, R_m$. To evaluate a methodology $\mathcal{M}$ on a benchmark $S = (W, V, G)$ with a set of requirements R, we allow $\mathcal{M}$ to "learn" for about 10 min per requirement by making calls to the SAT solver, and produce a (partial) attacker classification $\mathcal{H}$. Afterwards, we compute the coverage metric obtained by $\mathcal{M}$, defined as follows.

Definition 4 (Coverage). *Let $\mathscr{P}(V)$ be the set of all attackers, and let $\mathcal{H}$ be the attacker classification produced by the methodology $\mathcal{M}$. We recall that $\mathcal{H}$ is a map that maps each attacker A to a set of requirements, and in the ideal case, $\mathcal{H}(A) = A[R]$, for each attacker A. The attacker coverage obtained by methodology $\mathcal{M}$ for a requirement r is the percentage of attackers $A \in \mathscr{P}(V)$ for which we can correctly determine whether A breaks r by computing $r \in \mathcal{H}(A)$ (i.e., we do not allow guessing and we do not allow making new calls to the SAT solver).*

We also measure the execution time of the classification per requirement. More precisely, the time it takes for the methodology to find minimal attackers, capped at about 10 min per requirement. We force stop the classification for each requirement if a timeout occurs, but not while the SAT solver is running (i.e., we do not interrupt the SAT solver), which is why sometimes the reported time exceeds 10 min.

5.2   Effectiveness of Isolation and Monotonicity

To test the effectiveness of isolation and monotonicity, we selected a small sample of seven benchmarks. For each benchmark, we test four variations of our methodology:

1. $(+IS, +MO)$: Algorithm 4, which uses both isolation and monotonicity
2. $(+IS, -MO)$: Algorithm 4 but removing the check for monotonicity on Algorithm 2, Line 7;
3. $(-IS, +MO)$: Algorithm 4 but using Eq. 5 instead of Eq. 7 to remove isolation while preserving monotonicity; and
4. $(+IS, +MO)$ Algorithm 1, which does not use isolation nor monotonicity.

The benchmarks we selected have an average of 173 inputs, 8306 gates, 517 latches, and 80 requirements. Under our formulation of attackers, these benchmarks have on average 2^{8823} attackers . However, since an attacker that controls a gate g can be emulated by an attacker that controls all latches in the sources of g, we restrict attackers to be comprised of only latches; reducing the size of the set of attackers from 2^{8823} to 2^{517} on average per benchmark. Furthermore, we arbitrarily restrict the number of components that minimal attackers may control to a maximum of 3, which implies that, on a worst case scenario, we need to make a maximum of $80 \times \sum_{k=0}^{3} \binom{517}{k}$ calls to the SAT solver per benchmark. We also arbitrarily define the time step parameter t to be 10.

Figure 3 illustrates the average coverage for the four different methodologies, for each of the seven benchmarks. The exact coverage values are reported in the Appendix of [29] (an extended version of this article). We see that our methodology consistently obtains the best coverage of all the other methodologies, with the exception of benchmark 6s155, where the methodology that removes isolation triumphs over ours. We attribute this exception to the way the SAT solver reuses knowledge when working incrementally; it seems that, for $(-IS, +MO)$, the SAT solver can reuse more knowledge than for $(+IS, +MO)$, which is why $(-IS, +MO)$ can discover more minimal attackers in average than $(+IS, +MO)$.

We observe that the most significant element in play to obtain a high coverage is the use of monotonicity. Methodologies that use monotonicity always obtain better results than their counterparts without monotonicity. Isolation does not show a trend for increasing coverage, but has an impact in terms of classification time. Figure 4 presents the average classification time per requirement for the benchmarks under the different methodologies. We note that removing isolation often increases the average classification time of classification methodologies; the only exception –benchmark 6s325– reports a smaller time because the SAT solver ran out of memory during SAT solving about 50% of the time, which caused an early termination of the classification procedure. This early termination also reflects on the comparatively low coverage for the method $(-IS, +MO)$ in this benchmark, reported on Fig. 3.

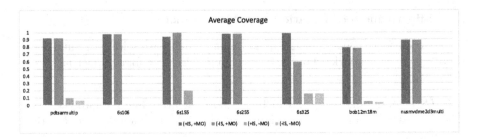

Fig. 3. Average requirement coverage per benchmark. A missing bar indicates a value that is approximately 0.

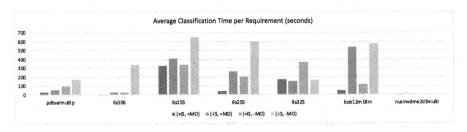

Fig. 4. Average classification time per requirement per benchmark. A missing bar indicates a value that is approximately 0.

5.3 Partial Classification of the pdtvsarmultip Benchmark

The benchmark pdtvsarmultip has 17 inputs, 130 latches, 2743 gates, and has an associated list of 33 invariant properties, out of which 31 are unique and we interpret as the list of security requirements. Since we are only considering attackers that control latches, there are a total of 2^{130} attackers that need to be classified for the 31 security requirements.

We consider 6 scenarios for partial classification up to t, with t taking values in $\{0, 1, 5, 10, 20, 30\}$. For each requirement, we obtain the execution time of classification (ms), the size of the set of source latches for the requirement (#C), the number of minimal attackers found (#Min.), the total number of calls to the SAT solver (#SAT), the average number of components per minimal attacker (#C./Min) and the coverage for the requirement (Cov.). We present the average of these measures in Table 1.

Normally, the attacker classification behaves in a similar way to what is reported for requirement $\Box\neg g_{2177}$, shown in Table 2. More precisely, coverage steadily increases and stabilises as we increase t. However, we like to highlight two interesting phenomena that may occur: (1) coverage may *decrease* as we increase the time step (e.g., as shown in Table 3) and (2) the number of minimal attackers decreases while the coverage increases, as shown in Tables 2 and 3.

Case (1) occurs because the set of attackers that can effectively interact with the system at time 0 is rather small, i.e., 2^6, while the set of attackers that can affect the system at times 0 and 1 has size 2^{26}. The size of this set increases

Table 1. Average measures for all requirements per time steps.

Steps	ms	#C.	#Min.	#SAT	#C./Min.	Cov.
0	683.1290323	34.96774194	2.451612903	16328.77419	1.4	0.527277594
1	2387.548387	46.22580645	6.387096774	24420	1.650232484	0.572533254
5	5229.935484	58.93548387	44.90322581	28355.29032	1.639645689	0.84956949
10	24967.12903	58.93548387	151.1935484	25566.54839	1.460869285	0.918973269
20	13632.51613	58.93548387	17.67741935	20849.70968	1.176272506	0.979354259
30	12208.25806	58.93548387	15.93548387	20798.16129	1.104563895	0.979354274

Table 2. Coverage for $\Box \neg g_{2177}$.

$\Box \neg g_{2177}$						
Steps	ms	#C	#Min.	#SAT	#C./Min.	Cov.
0	895	59	0	34281	–	5.94E-14
1	2187	66	10	47378	2	0.499511
5	1735	66	205	12476	1.912195	0.999997
10	968	66	27	9948	1	0.999999
20	1275	66	27	9948	1	0.999999
30	1819	66	27	9948	1	0.999999

Table 3. Coverage for $\Box \neg g_{2220}$.

$\Box \neg g_{2220}$						
Steps	ms	#C.	#Min	#SAT	#C./Min.	Cov.
0	1	6	1	28	1	0.90625
1	86	26	1	2628	1	0.500039
5	4511	67	17	47664	2.588235	0.852539
10	3226	67	6	37889	1	0.984375
20	3355	67	6	37889	1	0.984375
30	3562	67	6	37889	1	0.984375

with time until it stabilises at 2^{66}, which is the size of the set of attackers that cannot be dismissed by isolation.

Case (2) occurs because the minimal attackers that are found for smaller time steps represent a small percentage of the set of attackers that can affect the system, so there is very little we can learn by using monotonicity. More precisely, those minimal attackers control a relatively large set of components, which they need to be successful in breaking requirements, as shown in Step 5, column #C./Min in Tables 2 and 3. By considering more time steps, we are allowing attackers that control less components to further propagate their actions through the system, which enables attack strategies that were unsuccessful for smaller choices of time steps.

By taking an average over all requirements, we observe that coverage seems to steadily increase as we increase the number of steps for the classification, as reported in Table 1, column Cov. The low coverage for small t is due to the restriction on the size of minimal attackers. More precisely, for small t, attackers can only use short strategies, which limits their interaction with the system; we expect attackers to control a large number of components if they want to successfully influence a requirement in this single time step, and since we restricted our search to attackers of size 3 maximum, these larger minimal attackers are not found (e.g., as reported in Table 2 for Step 0).

We conclude that experimental evidence favours the use of both monotonicity and isolation for the classification of attackers, although some exceptions may occur for the use of isolation. Nevertheless, these two techniques help our classification methodology $(+IS, +MO)$ consistently obtain significantly better coverage when compared to the naive methodology $(-IS, -MO)$.

6   Related Work

On Defining Attackers. Describing an adequate attacker model to contextualise the security guarantees of a system is not a trivial task. Some attacker models may be adequate to provide guarantees over one property (e.g. confidentiality), but not for a different one (e.g., integrity). Additionally, depending on the nature of the system and the security properties being studied, it is sensible to describe attackers at different levels of abstraction. For instance, in the case of security protocols, Basin and Cremers define attackers in [6] as combinations of compromise rules that span over three dimensions: *whose* data is compromised, *which* kind of data it is, and *when* the compromise occurs. In the case of Cyber-physical Systems (CPS), works like [19,30] model attackers as sets of components (e.g., some sensors or actuators), while other works like [17,32,33] model attackers that can arbitrarily manipulate any control inputs and any sensor measurements at will, as long as they avoid detection. In the same context of CPS, Rocchetto and Tippenhauer [28] model attackers more abstractly as combinations of quantifiable traits (e.g., insider knowledge, access to tools, and financial support), which, when provided a compatible system model, ideally fully define how the attacker can interact with the system.

Our methodology for the definition of attackers combines aspects from [6,19] and [30]. The authors of [6] define symbolic attackers and a set of rules that describe how the attackers affect the system, which is sensible since many cryptographic protocols are described symbolically. Our methodology describes attackers as sets of components (staying closer to the definitions of attackers in [19] and [30]), and has a lower level of abstraction since we describe the semantics of attacker actions in terms of how they change the functional behaviour of the AIG, and not in terms of what they ultimately represent. This lower level of abstraction lets us systematically and exhaustively generate attackers by simply having a benchmark description, but it limits the results of the analysis to the benchmark; Basin and Cremers can compare among different protocol implementations, because attackers have the same semantics even amongst different protocols. If we had an abstraction function from sets of gates and latches to symbolic notions (e.g., "components in charge of encryption", or "components in charge of redundancy"), then it could be possible to compare results amongst different AIGs.

On Efficient Classification. The works by Cabodi, Camurati and Quer [15], Cabodi et al. [13], and Cabodi and Nocco [14] present several useful techniques that can be used to improve the performance of model checking when verifying multiple properties, including COI reduction and property clustering. We also mention the work by Goldberg et al. [20] where they consider the problem of efficiently checking a set of safety properties P_1 to P_k by individually checking each property while assuming that all other properties are valid. Ultimately, all these works inspired us to incrementally check requirements in the same cluster, helping us transform Eqs. 4 into 7. Nevertheless, we note that all these techniques are described for model checking systems in the absence of attackers, which is why we needed to introduce the notions of isolation and monotonicity to account for them. Additionally, it may be possible to use or incorporate other techniques that improve the efficiency of BMC in general (e.g., interpolation [26]).

On Completeness. As mentioned in Sect. 4.5, if the time parameter for the classification is below the completeness threshold, the resulting attacker classification is most likely incomplete. To guarantee completeness, it may be possible to adapt existing termination methods (see [5]) to consider attackers. Alternatively, methods that compute a good approximation of the completeness threshold (see [24]) which guarantee the precision of resulting the coverage should help improve the completeness of attacker classifications. If we consider alternative verification techniques, then IC3 [11,12] and PDR [11], which have seen some success in hardware model checking, may address the limitation of boundedness. Finally, interpolation [26] could also help finding a guarantee of completeness.

On Verifying Non-safety Properties. In this work, we focused our analysis exclusively on safety properties of the form $\Box e$. However, we believe that it is possible to extend this methodology to other types of properties, it is possible to efficiently encode Linear Temporal Logic formulae for bounded model checking [8,9]. The formulations of the SAT problem change for the different nature of the formulae, but both isolation and monotonicity should remain valid heuristics, since they ultimately refer to how strategies of attackers can be inferred, not how they are constructed.

7   Conclusion and Future Work

In this work, we present a methodology to model check systems in the presence of attackers with the objective of mapping each attacker to the list of security requirements that it breaks. This mapping of attackers creates a classification for them, defining equivalence classes of attackers by the set of requirements that they can break. The system can then be considered safe in the presence of attackers that cannot break any requirement. While it is possible to perform a classification of attackers by exhaustively performing model checking, the exponential size of the set of attackers renders this naive approach impractical. Thus, we rely on ordering relations between attackers to efficiently classify a large percentage of them, and we demonstrate empirically by applying our methodology to a set of benchmarks that describe hardware systems at a bit level.

In our view, ensuring the completeness of the attacker classification is the most relevant direction for future work. Unlike complete classifications, incomplete classifications cannot provide guarantees that work in the general case if minimal attackers are not found. We also note that the effectiveness of monotonicity for classification is directly related to finding minimal attackers. Consequently, our methodology may benefit from any other method that helps in the identification of those minimal attackers. In particular, we are interested in checking the effectiveness of an approach where, instead of empowering attackers, we try to reduce successful attackers into minimal attackers by removing unnecessary capabilities. This, formally, is an *actual causality analysis* [22] of successful attackers.

References

1. November 2011. http://fmv.jku.at/hwmcc11/index.html
2. October 2013. http://fmv.jku.at/hwmcc13/index.html
3. September 2019. http://fmv.jku.at/cadical/
4. November 2020. https://gitlab.com/asset-sutd/public/aig-ac
5. Awedh, M., Somenzi, F.: Proving more properties with bounded model checking. In: Alur, R., Peled, D.A. (eds.) CAV 2004. LNCS, vol. 3114, pp. 96–108. Springer, Heidelberg (2004). https://doi.org/10.1007/978-3-540-27813-9_8
6. Basin, D., Cremers, C.: Know your enemy: compromising adversaries in protocol analysis. ACM Trans. Inf. Syst. Secur. **17**(2), 7:1–7:31 (2014). https://doi.org/10.1145/2658996
7. Biere, A., Heule, M., van Maaren, H., Walsh, T.: Handbook of Satisfiability: Volume 185 Frontiers in Artificial Intelligence and Applications. IOS Press, Amsterdam (2009)
8. Biere, A., Cimatti, A., Clarke, E., Zhu, Y.: Symbolic model checking without BDDs. In: Cleaveland, W.R. (ed.) TACAS 1999. LNCS, vol. 1579, pp. 193–207. Springer, Heidelberg (1999). https://doi.org/10.1007/3-540-49059-0_14
9. Biere, A., Heljanko, K., Junttila, T., Latvala, T., Schuppan, V.: Linear encodings of bounded LTL model checking. Log. Methods Comput. Sci. **2**(5), 1–64 (2006)
10. Biere, A., Heljanko, K., Wieringa, S.: AIGER 1.9 and beyond. Technical report, FMV Reports Series, Institute for Formal Models and Verification, Johannes Kepler University, Altenbergerstr, Linz, Austria (2011)
11. Bradley, A.R.: SAT-based model checking without unrolling. In: Jhala, R., Schmidt, D. (eds.) VMCAI 2011. LNCS, vol. 6538, pp. 70–87. Springer, Heidelberg (2011). https://doi.org/10.1007/978-3-642-18275-4_7
12. Bradley, A.R.: Understanding IC3. In: Cimatti, A., Sebastiani, R. (eds.) SAT 2012. LNCS, vol. 7317, pp. 1–14. Springer, Heidelberg (2012). https://doi.org/10.1007/978-3-642-31612-8_1
13. Cabodi, G., et al.: To split or to group: from divide-and-conquer to sub-task sharing for verifying multiple properties in model checking. Int. J. Softw. Tools Technol. Transf. **20**(3), 313–325 (2018). https://doi.org/10.1007/s10009-017-0451-8
14. Cabodi, G., Nocco, S.: Optimized model checking of multiple properties. In: 2011 Design, Automation Test in Europe, pp. 1–4, March 2011
15. Cabodi, G., Camurati, P., Quer, S.: A graph-labeling approach for efficient cone-of-influence computation in model-checking problems with multiple properties. Softw.: Pract. Exp. **46**(4), 493–511 (2016). https://doi.org/10.1002/spe.2321
16. Cabodi, G., et al.: Hardware model checking competition 2014: an analysis and comparison of model checkers and benchmarks. J. Satisf. Boolean Model. Comput. **9**, 135–172 (2015)
17. Cárdenas, A.A., Amin, S., Lin, Z.S., Huang, Y.L., Huang, C.Y., Sastry, S.: Attacks against process control systems: risk assessment, detection, and response. In: Proceedings of the 6th ACM Symposium on Information, Computer and Communications Security. ASIACCS 2011, pp. 355–366. ACM, New York (2011), https://doi.org/10.1145/1966913.1966959

18. Clarke, E.M., Henzinger, T.A., Veith, H., Bloem, R. (eds.): Handbook of Model Checking. Springer (2018). https://doi.org/10.1007/978-3-319-10575-8
19. Giraldo, J., et al.: A survey of physics-based attack detection in cyber-physical systems. ACM Comput. Surv. **51**(4), 76:1–76:36 (2018). https://doi.org/10.1145/3203245
20. Goldberg, E., Güdemann, M., Kroening, D., Mukherjee, R.: Efficient verification of multi-property designs (the benefit of wrong assumptions). In: 2018 Design, Automation Test in Europe Conference Exhibition (DATE), pp. 43–48, March 2018
21. Günther, C.G.: An identity-based key-exchange protocol. In: Quisquater, J.-J., Vandewalle, J. (eds.) EUROCRYPT 1989. LNCS, vol. 434, pp. 29–37. Springer, Heidelberg (1990). https://doi.org/10.1007/3-540-46885-4_5
22. Halpern, J.Y.: Actual Causality. MIT Press (2016). http://www.jstor.org/stable/j.ctt1f5g5p9
23. Hellerman, L.: A catalog of three-variable or-invert and and-invert logical circuits. IEEE Trans. Electron. Comput. EC **12**(3), 198–223 (1963)
24. Kroening, D., Strichman, O.: Efficient computation of recurrence diameters. In: Zuck, L.D., Attie, P.C., Cortesi, A., Mukhopadhyay, S. (eds.) VMCAI 2003. LNCS, vol. 2575, pp. 298–309. Springer, Heidelberg (2003). https://doi.org/10.1007/3-540-36384-X_24
25. Kuehlmann, A., Paruthi, V., Krohm, F., Ganai, M.K.: Robust boolean reasoning for equivalence checking and functional property verification. IEEE Trans. Comput. Aided Des. Integr. Circuits Syst. **21**(12), 1377–1394 (2002)
26. McMillan, K.L.: Interpolation and SAT-based model checking. In: Hunt, W.A., Somenzi, F. (eds.) CAV 2003. LNCS, vol. 2725, pp. 1–13. Springer, Heidelberg (2003). https://doi.org/10.1007/978-3-540-45069-6_1
27. Menezes, A.J., Vanstone, S.A., Oorschot, P.C.V.: Handbook of Applied Cryptography, 1st edn. CRC Press Inc., Boca Raton (1996)
28. Rocchetto, M., Tippenhauer, N.O.: On attacker models and profiles for cyber-physical systems. In: Askoxylakis, I., Ioannidis, S., Katsikas, S., Meadows, C. (eds.) ESORICS 2016. LNCS, vol. 9879, pp. 427–449. Springer, Cham (2016). https://doi.org/10.1007/978-3-319-45741-3_22
29. Rothstein-Morris, E., Sun, J., Chattopadhyay, S.: Systematic Classification of Attackers via Bounded Model Checking (Extended Version). arXiv:1911.05808 (2019). http://arxiv.org/abs/1911.05808
30. Rothstein, E., Murguia, C.G., Ochoa, M.: Design-time quantification of integrity in cyber-physical systems. In: Proceedings of the 2017 Workshop on Programming Languages and Analysis for Security, PLAS 2017, pp. 63–74. ACM, New York (2017). https://doi.org/10.1145/3139337.3139347
31. Tseitin, G. S.: On the complexity of derivation in propositional calculus. In: Automation of Reasoning: 2: Classical Papers on Computational Logic (1967–1970)
32. Urbina, D.I., et al.: Limiting the impact of stealthy attacks on industrial control systems. In: Proceedings of the 2016 ACM SIGSAC Conference on Computer and Communications Security. CCS 2016, pp. 1092–1105. ACM, New York (2016), https://doi.org/10.1145/2976749.2978388
33. Weerakkody, S., Sinopoli, B., Kar, S., Datta, A.: Information flow for security in control systems. In: 2016 IEEE 55th Conference on Decision and Control (CDC), pp. 5065–5072, December 2016

Cheap CTL Compassion in NuSMV

Daniel Hausmann[(✉)], Tadeusz Litak[(✉)],
Christoph Rauch[(✉)], and Matthias Zinner[(✉)]

Chair of Theoretical Computer Science,
Friedrich-Alexander-Universität Erlangen-Nürnberg,
Martensstraße 3, 91058 Erlangen, Germany
{daniel.hausmann,tadeusz.litak,
christoph.rauch,matthias.zinner}@fau.de

Abstract. We discuss expansions of CTL with connectives able to express Streett fairness objectives for single paths. We focus on (E)SFCTL: (*Extended*) *Streett-Fair* CTL inspired by a seminal paper of Emerson and Lei. Unlike several other fair extensions of CTL, our entire formalism (not just a subclass of formulas in some canonical form) allows a succinct embedding into the μ-calculus, while being able to express concisely all relevant types of path-based fairness objectives. We implement our syntax in the well-known symbolic model checker NuSMV, consequently also implementing CTL model checking with "compassion" objectives. Since the μ-calculus embedding requires only alternation depth two, the resulting specifications correspond to parity games with two priorities. This allows a comparison of the performance of our NuSMV^{sf} with existing parity game solvers (both explicit and symbolic). The advantages of the symbolic approach seem to extend to fair model checking.

Keywords: Model checking · Fairness and compassion · CTL · μ-calculus · NuSMV · Parity games

1 Introduction

Computation tree logic (CTL) [12] enjoys linear complexity of model checking (unlike LTL), but is unable to express fairness objectives. Since the 1980's, this has led to numerous proposals for extensions of CTL which overcome this limitation while (sometimes) preserving low complexity of the model checking problem:

- CTL^f [22] extends ordinary CTL with a binary version of EG,
- FCTL [18] allows restricting path quantifiers with *fairness constraints* (written using LTL operators), whereas
- both ECTL$^+$ and the most powerful CTL* [15,16][1] involve full-blown mutually recursive grammars of state and path formulas, although a formalism equivalent to ECTL$^+$ can be defined using one connective EM of unrestricted arity (*i.e.*, an infinite family of fixed-arity connectives $\{EM_n\}_{n\in\mathbb{N}}$) [31].

---

[1] The name "ECTL$^+$" was used in the conference version [15].

© Springer Nature Switzerland AG 2020
D. Beyer and D. Zufferey (Eds.): VMCAI 2020, LNCS 11990, pp. 248–269, 2020.
https://doi.org/10.1007/978-3-030-39322-9_12

Details are given in Sect. 2. Furthermore, various notions of path-based fairness have been proposed [19,21] to specify the manner in which (a combination of) certain events happen(s) along infinite sequences of transitions within some graph:

- The most basic of these notions, *unconditional fairness* (or just *fairness*), requires that a certain event *p* happens infinitely often but allows for arbitrarily long breaks between any two occurrences of this event.
- *Conditional fairness* (also referred to as *weak fairness* or *justice*) requires that if some event *q* does not happen from some state on, then some event *p* happens infinitely often.
- *Strong fairness* (also called *compassion* or *Streett fairness*) requires that if an event *q* happens infinitely often, then some event *p* holds infinitely often.

Strong fairness appears to be the most expressive notion of fairness considered in classical literature within the context of temporal logic [19] and indeed it has been argued that every ω-regular fairness objective can be expressed by a Streett objective [9]. Initially, the use of such fairness objectives in model checking appears to have mostly been restricted to fairness constraints in the style of FCTL, which one can think of as global path quantifiers $\forall(fair \rightarrow \varphi)$ and $\exists(fair \wedge \varphi)$, where *fair* expresses some fairness condition on the path level and φ does not contain further fairness properties [1, Sect. 6.5]. However, some fair extensions of CTL mentioned above allow, *e.g.*, for checking whether all paths in a given model are fair, which cannot be done using just fairness constraints.

A well-known example of a tool supporting model checking under fairness constraints is the *symbolic* model checker NuSMV ([10], sources available at http://nusmv.fbk.eu), in which input models are internally represented as binary decision diagrams (BDDs); CTL (or LTL) formulas are then evaluated by fixpoint computations over BDDs. The practical viability of this symbolic approach has been demonstrated repeatedly, both for the model checking approach that is used in NuSMV [5] and, more recently, for BDD-based solving of parity games [32]. In NuSMV, the user can annotate a CTL specification with JUSTICE constraints, which in NuSMV express *unconditional* fairness constraints contrary to the use of the term in the literature, restricting the evaluation of formulas to paths that satisfy the constraint (this is redundant for LTL specifications, where fairness is directly expressible). However, this strategy can be awkward to work with: NuSMV, for example, has never implemented the COMPASSION keyword (enabling the specification of strong fairness constraints) for CTL, which seems the most natural and useful extension of fairness discussed in classical references [18].

The excellent computational properties of CTL model checking can be easily explained by the existence of a direct translation into a well-behaved fragment of the modal μ-calculus (alternation depth 1). Nevertheless, this perspective makes inexpressibility of fairness constraints even more inexplicable, calling the choice of original CTL primitives into question: such properties require only (succinct!) μ-calculus formulas of alternation depth at most 2.

1.1   Our Contributions

Inspired by the above considerations, we propose a new Streett-fair temporal formalism ESFCTL, investigate its model-checking properties, implement it in NuSMV and use a collection of benchmarks and examples to compare our extension of NuSMV with parity game solvers.

We begin by revisiting Emerson and Lei's paper [17] and as our first contribution in Sect. 2 we extend CTL with primitives directly corresponding to fixpoint formulas used by them. One primitive $\mathsf{E}(\varphi_1 \blacktriangleright \psi_1, \ldots, \varphi_n \blacktriangleright \psi_n)\mathsf{G}\chi$, expressing the existence of a compassionate path, leads to a language we call SFCTL (standing for *Streett-Fair* CTL or *Strongly Fair* CTL) which succinctly encodes unconditional, weak and strong fairness operators and is a fragment of ECTL$^+$ [15, 16, 29] and hence CTL*. The second language ESFCTL (*Extended* SFCTL) is based on a more powerful primitive $\langle \varphi_1 \triangleright \psi_1, \ldots, \varphi_n \triangleright \psi_n \rangle$, which is central to our implementation and implicitly used already in [17], where its nontrivial semantics has not been clarified. The latter logic does not appear to be a CTL* fragment, yet enjoys efficient model checking: linear in the formula size when the arity of the main connective is bounded, and quadratic in the formula size otherwise, *cf.* Sect. 3. The unrestricted fair connective EM [31] and the binary EG [22] can be encoded already in the weaker logic SFCTL, but the reverse translation is altogether impossible for binary EG and apparently incurs exponential blowup for n-ary EM. Furthermore, fairness operators can occur at any point in formulas of our logics so that we can express fairness constraints without automatically restricting all path quantifiers in the formula to conforming paths.

As our second contribution we implement model checking for the connectives of ESFCTL within the (open source) current version of NuSMV (v2.6.0, see Sect. 4), using the fixpoint characterizations that allow us to give the linear translation into the μ-calculus in Sect. 3. In this paper, we refer to the proposed extension[2] of NuSMV as NuSMV^{sf}. It adds a new ESFCTLSPEC keyword, which one can use to write ESFCTL specifications, disabling and making redundant the JUSTICE and COMPASSION keywords. Thus, we repair the longstanding problem that model checking under COMPASSION constraints for CTL was not supported in NuSMV. Furthermore, our syntax allows the user to, *e.g.*, verify whether all paths in some input model are fair. There is also another sense in which we are completing the NuSMV implementation of the model checking procedure for CTL under fairness: the NuSMV implementation was not covering all canonical form FCTL formulas as given by Emerson and Lei [18]. In fact, NuSMV seems to have been implementing an intermediate class of formulas between CTL^F [11] and FCTL [29]. Since all canonical form FCTL formulas can be translated to ESFCTL formulas, our implementation NuSMV^{sf} effectively enables model checking for canonical form FCTL formulas in NuSMV.

At present, *parity game solvers* appear to be the most powerful software available for μ-calculus model checking and satisfiability checking, with numerous algorithms implemented and optimized (*e.g.*, [20, 32, 35]). By an embedding

---

[2] Available online at https://git8.cs.fau.de/software/nusmvf.

of ESFCTL into the μ-calculus with alternation depth 2, model checking instances for ESFCTL formulas are equivalent to *Büchi games*, that is, parity games that involve just the priorities 1 (indicating least fixpoint formulas) and 2 (for all other formulas). Hence, as our third contribution, we illustrate by means of a series of examples and benchmarks the correspondence between compassionate NuSMV^{sf} specifications and equivalent parity games and study the respective performances of NuSMV^{sf} and various parity game solving tools (Sect. 5).

Direct comparisons of this kind between the two types of tools have not been undertaken often in the past, perhaps because translating previously available LTL fair specifications into the μ-calculus can be computationally costly. Our extension NuSMV^{sf} shows promising performance, outperforming parity game solvers by a large margin in selected cases, apparently due to the symbolic nature of its BDD-based model checking algorithm. We discuss the state of the art in parity game solving, and the future prospects of CTL-based model checking in Sect. 6.

In the present paper we focus on practical aspects, but we believe that there are interesting theoretical problems regarding SFCTL and ESFCTL. Examples include quasi-equational axiomatizations similar to those for CTL^f [22] or for the full μ-calculus [28,37], settling the question whether ESFCTL is contained in CTL*, or formal proofs of succinctness of our formalisms as compared to the one based on EM and its fragments [31].

2   Making CTL Fair and Compassionate

We begin by defining two extensions of CTL with operators along the lines of Emerson and Lei [17] that allow for expressing compassion properties. Next, we detail the relation of the obtained logics to other fair extensions of CTL.

Given some predefined collection of atoms At and a natural number n, *Extended Streett-Fair* CTL, which we denote by ESFCTL$_n$, is defined by the grammar

$$\varphi, \psi ::= \top \mid p \in \mathsf{At} \mid \neg\varphi \mid \varphi \wedge \psi \mid \mathsf{EX}\varphi \mid \mathsf{E}[\varphi\mathsf{U}\psi] \mid \langle \varphi_1 \triangleright \psi_1, \ldots, \varphi_n \triangleright \psi_n \rangle.$$

Apart from the usual defined operators, we also have

$$\mathsf{E}(\varphi_1 \blacktriangleright \psi_1, \ldots, \varphi_n \blacktriangleright \psi_n)\mathsf{G}\chi := \mathsf{E}[\chi\mathsf{U}\langle \varphi_1 \triangleright \psi_1, \ldots, \varphi_n \triangleright \psi_n, \neg\chi \triangleright \bot \rangle],$$

expressing the existence of a compassionate path that globally satisfies χ. Taken as a primitive, this last connective yields *Streett-Fair* CTL. In other words, SFCTL$_n$ is the fragment of ESFCTL$_{n+1}$ defined by the following grammar

$$\varphi, \psi ::= \top \mid p \mid \neg\varphi \mid \varphi \wedge \psi \mid \mathsf{EX}\varphi \mid \mathsf{E}[\varphi\mathsf{U}\psi] \mid \mathsf{E}(\varphi_1 \blacktriangleright \psi_1, \ldots, \varphi_n \blacktriangleright \psi_n)\mathsf{G}\chi.$$

ESFCTL and SFCTL denote the languages where the corresponding primitives are not restricted to any specific n.

Definition 2.1 (Reachability, Fairness and Compassion).

- A *transition system* is a triple $\mathcal{M} := (S, \longrightarrow, L)$, where
    - S is a finite collection of *states*,
    - $\longrightarrow \subseteq S \times S$ is a non-terminating *transition relation*, that is, we require that for all $s \in S$ for which there is some $s' \in S$ such that $s' \longrightarrow s$, there is some $t \in S$ such that $s \longrightarrow t$.
    - $L : S \to \wp(\mathsf{At})$ is a *labelling function*, assigning sets of atoms to states.
- A *path* in $\mathcal{M}$ is a function $\pi : \mathbb{N} \to S$ such that for all $n \in \mathbb{N}$, we have $\pi(n) \longrightarrow \pi(n+1)$. We write $\Pi_\mathcal{M}(s)$ for the set of all π such that $\pi(0) = s$ and $\Pi_\mathcal{M}$ for the set of all paths in $\mathcal{M}$; we drop the subscripts $\mathcal{M}$ whenever possible. We define a *finite path* analogously, restricting the domain to a finite interval of $\mathbb{N}$. Given any n, any $\pi \in \Pi$ divides into the *finite prefix* up to $\pi(n)$ and the *infinite suffix* in $\Pi(\pi(n))$.
- Given a non-terminating relation $\rightsquigarrow \subseteq \longrightarrow$, we say that its *domain* $dom(\rightsquigarrow)$ is the collection of all states $s \in S$ s.t. there exists $t \in S$ with $s \rightsquigarrow t$.
- We say that t is $\longrightarrow$-*reachable* (*strictly* $\longrightarrow$-*reachable*) *from* s if for some $\pi \in \Pi(s)$ there is $n \geq 0$ ($n \geq 1$, respectively) such that $\pi(n) = t$.
- Given $X, Y \subseteq S$, we say that $\pi \in \Pi$ is (X, Y)-*compassionate* if whenever π passes infinitely often through X, it also passes infinitely often through Y.

Definition 2.2 (Semantics of ESFCTL). We inductively define the relation of satisfaction $\vDash$ between *pointed* models (*i.e.*, models $\mathcal{M} := (S, \longrightarrow, L)$ with a distinguished state $s \in S$) and formulas; we also write $s \in [\varphi]^\mathcal{M}$ for $\mathcal{M}, s \vDash \varphi$.

- $\mathcal{M}, s \vDash \top$ always, $\mathcal{M}, s \vDash p$ if $p \in L(s)$, $\mathcal{M}, s \vDash \neg\varphi$ if $\mathcal{M}, s \nvDash \varphi$,
- $\mathcal{M}, s \vDash \varphi \wedge \psi$ if $\mathcal{M}, s \vDash \varphi$ and $\mathcal{M}, s \vDash \psi$,
- $\mathcal{M}, s \vDash \mathsf{EX}\varphi$ if there is $t \in S$ such that $s \longrightarrow t$ and $\mathcal{M}, t \vDash \varphi$,
- $\mathcal{M}, s \vDash \mathsf{E}[\varphi \mathsf{U} \psi]$ if there are $\pi \in \Pi(s)$ and $j \in \mathbb{N}$ such that $\mathcal{M}, \pi(j) \vDash \psi$ and for all $0 \leq i < j$, we have $\mathcal{M}, \pi(i) \vDash \varphi$.
- $\mathcal{M}, s \vDash \langle \varphi_1 \triangleright \psi_1, \ldots, \varphi_n \triangleright \psi_n \rangle$ if there is a non-terminating relation $\rightsquigarrow \subseteq \longrightarrow$ such that $s \in dom(\rightsquigarrow)$ and such that for all $1 \leq i \leq n$ and all t that are $\rightsquigarrow$-reachable from s, if some $u \in [\varphi_i]^\mathcal{M}$ is $\rightsquigarrow$-reachable from t, then some $v \in [\psi_i]^\mathcal{M}$ is strictly $\rightsquigarrow$-reachable from t.

The crucial last clause comes with the intuition that if $\langle \varphi_1 \triangleright \psi_1, \ldots, \varphi_n \triangleright \psi_n \rangle$ is satisfied at s, then a strongly connected subcomponent of $\mathcal{M}$ is reachable from s that, for all $1 \leq i \leq n$, contains some state satisfying ψ_i if it contains a state satisfying φ_i.

We leave out semantic brackets and superscript $\mathcal{M}$ wherever possible, notationally conflating a formula with its denotation. E.g., instead of writing that π is "$([\varphi_i]^\mathcal{M}, [\psi_i]^\mathcal{M})$-compassionate", we write π is "(φ_i, ψ_i)-compassionate". We also say that π is a φ-*path* if $\mathcal{M}, \pi(n) \vDash \varphi$ for every n. We have:

Lemma 2.3 (Semantics of ESFCTL).

- $\mathcal{M}, s \vDash \langle \varphi_1 \triangleright \psi_1, \ldots, \varphi_n \triangleright \psi_n, \neg\chi \triangleright \bot \rangle$ *implies that there is a* χ-*path in* $\Pi(s)$ *that is* (φ_i, ψ_i)-*compassionate for every* i.

- $\mathcal{M}, s \models \mathsf{E}(\varphi_1 \blacktriangleright \psi_1, \ldots, \varphi_n \blacktriangleright \psi_n) \mathsf{G} \chi$ *if and only if there is a χ-path in $\Pi(s)$ that is (φ_i, ψ_i)-compassionate for every i.*

Proof. For the first item, use the assumption and pick a witnessing non-terminating relation $\rightsquigarrow \subseteq \longrightarrow$ such that $s \in dom(\rightsquigarrow)$ and for all $i \leq n$ and all t that are $\rightsquigarrow$-reachable from s, if some $u \in [\varphi_i]^{\mathcal{M}}$ is $\rightsquigarrow$-reachable from t, then some $v \in [\psi_i]^{\mathcal{M}}$ is strictly $\rightsquigarrow$-reachable from t. Consider the strongly $\rightsquigarrow$-connected components that are $\rightsquigarrow$-reachable from s. Define the natural partial order between them as $Y \leq_{\mathsf{SCC}} Z$ if Y is reachable from Z (that is, there is a state in Y that is $\rightsquigarrow$-reachable from a state in Z). Pick an arbitrary such strongly connected component X that is minimal w.r.t. $\leq_{\mathsf{SCC}}$ and pick a finite path ending in some $u \in X$. The remaining infinite suffix of the compassionate path we have to construct is obtained as the infinite unfolding of a finite $\rightsquigarrow$-path ρ of the form $x_1 = u, \ldots, x_m = u$ and consists solely of states lying in X. We construct ρ stepping through $i \in \{1, \ldots, n\}$. We can ignore every i s.t. $X \cap [\varphi_i]^{\mathcal{M}} = \emptyset$, as the corresponding condition $\varphi_i \triangleright \psi_i$ is then satisfied automatically. For any other i, assuming that $x_1, \ldots, x_j$ have already been constructed, we pick a finite path $x_j, \ldots, x_k$ s.t. $x_k \in [\psi_i]^{\mathcal{M}}$ and append it to the part constructed so far, starting with x_{j+1}. By assumption, such a finite path always exists. We finish the construction by looping back to u.

For the second item, let $\theta := \mathsf{E}(\varphi_1 \blacktriangleright \psi_1, \ldots, \varphi_n \blacktriangleright \psi_n) \mathsf{G} \chi$. In one direction, pick a χ-path $\pi \in \Pi(s)$ which is (φ_i, ψ_i)-compassionate for every i. Let j be the minimal number for which, for each $1 \leq i \leq n$ such that ψ_i does not hold infinitely often on π, we have $\mathcal{M}, \pi(j') \not\models \varphi_i$ for all $j' \geq j$. We have $\mathcal{M}, s \models \theta$ if $\mathcal{M}, \pi(j) \models \langle \varphi_1 \triangleright \psi_1, \ldots, \varphi_n \triangleright \psi_n, \neg \chi \triangleright \bot \rangle$. Let $\rightsquigarrow$ be the restriction of $\longrightarrow$ to the suffix of π starting at j. Assume that $\pi(k) \models \varphi_i$ for some $k \geq j$. By our choice of j, this means that ψ_i holds infinitely often on π. Thus, as the witness of strict $\rightsquigarrow$-reachability, we can pick any $k' > k$ such that $\pi(k') \models \psi_i$. The part for $\neg \chi \triangleright \bot$ is trivial. For the opposite direction, assume

$$s \models \mathsf{E}[\chi \mathsf{U} \langle \varphi_1 \triangleright \psi_1, \ldots, \varphi_n \triangleright \psi_n, \neg \chi \triangleright \bot \rangle]$$

and pick $\pi \in \Pi(s)$ and $n \in \mathbb{N}$ s.t. $\forall i < n. \mathcal{M}, \pi(i) \models \chi$ and moreover

$$\mathcal{M}, \pi(n) \models \langle \varphi_1 \triangleright \psi_1, \ldots, \varphi_n \triangleright \psi_n, \neg \chi \triangleright \bot \rangle.$$

Now use the first item of the Lemma.   ⊣

We write $\varphi \leq \psi$ if, for all $\mathcal{M} := (S, \longrightarrow, L)$ and all $s \in S$, we have that $\mathcal{M}, s \models \varphi$ implies $\mathcal{M}, s \models \psi$. Moreover, we write $\varphi \equiv \psi$ if $\varphi \leq \psi$ and $\psi \leq \varphi$. We have

$$\langle \varphi_1 \triangleright \psi_1, \ldots, \varphi_n \triangleright \psi_n, \neg \chi \triangleright \bot \rangle \leq \mathsf{E}(\varphi_1 \blacktriangleright \psi_1, \ldots, \varphi_n \blacktriangleright \psi_n) \mathsf{G} \chi$$

since $\varphi \leq \mathsf{E}[\psi \mathsf{U} \varphi]$ for all φ, ψ.

Example 2.4. For the model shown to the left below, we have, e.g., that $x \models \mathsf{E}(a \blacktriangleright b, c \blacktriangleright d) \mathsf{G} e$ since the e-path $x, y, z, y, z, \ldots$ is both (a, b)-compassionate (since it satisfies b infinitely often) and (c, d)-compassionate (since it satisfies c

only finitely often). On the other hand, we have $x \not\models \langle a \rhd b, c \rhd d, \neg e \rhd \bot \rangle$ since we have $x \models c$ but no state satisfying d is reachable from x. However, we have $y \models \langle a \rhd b, c \rhd d, \neg e \rhd \bot \rangle$ and thus $x \models \mathsf{E}[e \,\mathsf{U}\, \langle a \rhd b, c \rhd d, \neg e \rhd \bot \rangle]$ (see Corollary 3.3).

For the model to the right, we have $v \models \mathsf{E}(a \blacktriangleright b, c \blacktriangleright d)\mathsf{G}\top$ as can be seen by looking at the compassionate path $v, u, u, \ldots$. Alternatively, the path $v, w, w, \ldots$ can be taken as a witness for satisfaction of the formula as well. We also have $v \models \langle a \rhd b, c \rhd d \rangle$ since $v \models a$ and $v \models c$, and since there are (different!) states satisfying b and d that are strictly reachable from v. Here, the atoms a and c that are satisfied at v trigger the *independent* requirements on eventually reaching states that satisfy b and d, respectively. This indicates that the operators $\langle \varphi_1 \rhd \psi_1, \ldots, \varphi_n \rhd \psi_n \rangle$ specify graphs (or sets of paths) rather than single paths. This non-determinism however is restricted to finite prefixes of paths so that skipping finite prefixes by means of the operator EF yields formulas $\mathsf{EF}\langle \varphi_1 \rhd \psi_1, \ldots, \varphi_n \rhd \psi_n \rangle \equiv \mathsf{E}(\varphi_1 \blacktriangleright \psi_1, \ldots, \varphi_n \blacktriangleright \psi_n)\mathsf{G}\top$ that specify single paths (again, see Corollary 3.3).

We define the remaining standard connectives of fair CTL as abbreviations:

$$\mathsf{EG}\varphi := \mathsf{E}(\top \blacktriangleright \top)\mathsf{G}\varphi \qquad \mathsf{EGF}\varphi := \mathsf{E}(\top \blacktriangleright \varphi)\mathsf{G}\top \qquad \mathsf{EF}\varphi := \mathsf{E}[\top \mathsf{U}\varphi]$$
$$\mathsf{AF}\varphi := \neg\mathsf{EG}\neg\varphi \qquad \mathsf{AG}\varphi := \neg\mathsf{EF}\neg\varphi \qquad \mathsf{AX}\varphi := \neg\mathsf{EX}\neg\varphi$$

and also $\mathsf{A}[\varphi \mathsf{U}\psi] := \neg\mathsf{E}[\neg\psi \mathsf{U}(\neg\varphi \wedge \neg\psi)] \wedge \mathsf{AF}\psi$. As an additional connective, we define a binary variant of EG by $\mathsf{E}\varphi\mathsf{G}\psi := \mathsf{E}(\top \blacktriangleright \varphi)\mathsf{G}\psi$. Corollary 2.5 below shows that it is precisely the fair connective of $\mathsf{CTL}^{\mathsf{f}}$ proposed recently (for theoretical reasons independent of model-checking concerns) by Ghilardi and van Gool [22]. There is an obvious n-ary generalization:

$$\mathsf{E}(\varphi_1, \ldots, \varphi_n)\mathsf{G}\psi := \mathsf{E}(\top \blacktriangleright \varphi_1, \ldots, \top \blacktriangleright \varphi_n)\mathsf{G}\psi.$$

A similar connective has been proposed by Rabinovich and Schnoebelen [31]. In our language, it is definable as

$$\mathsf{EM}(\varphi_1, \ldots, \varphi_n) := \mathsf{E}(\top \blacktriangleright \varphi_1, \ldots, \top \blacktriangleright \varphi_n)\mathsf{G}(\varphi_1 \vee \ldots \vee \varphi_n).$$

As a corollary of Lemma 2.3, this definition captures precisely the intended semantics of EM.

Corollary 2.5 (Semantics of Additional Operators).

- $\mathcal{M}, s \models \mathsf{E}(\varphi_1, \ldots, \varphi_n)\mathsf{G}\psi$ if and only if $\Pi(s)$ contains a ψ-path on which each φ_i holds infinitely often.
- $\mathcal{M}, s \models \mathsf{EM}(\varphi_1, \ldots, \varphi_n)$ if and only if $\Pi(s)$ contains a $(\varphi_1 \vee \cdots \vee \varphi_n)$-path on which each φ_i holds infinitely often.

When the arity of EM (or polyadic EG) is fixed, a reverse translation from SFCTL does not exist: Corollary 2.5 immediately implies

$$\mathsf{E}(\varphi_1, \ldots, \varphi_n)\mathsf{G}\psi \equiv \mathsf{EM}(\varphi_1 \wedge \psi, \ldots, \varphi_n \wedge \psi, \psi)$$

and it has been established by Rabinovich and Schnoebelen [31] that for every fixed n, the extension of CTL with n-ary EM is strictly less expressive than the one with $n+1$-ary EM.[3] In the limit, the logics determined by either the sequence of EG's with arbitrary arity, or by the sequence of EM's of arbitrary arity do have the same expressive power as SFCTL. However, a direct proof of this fact entails an exponential blowup. Let us illustrate this for the case where $n = 2$:

$$\mathsf{E}(\varphi_1 \blacktriangleright \psi_1, \varphi_2 \blacktriangleright \psi_2)\mathsf{G}\chi \equiv \mathsf{E}[\chi\mathsf{U}\mathsf{EG}(\neg\varphi_1 \wedge \neg\varphi_2 \wedge \chi)] \vee \mathsf{E}(\psi_1, \psi_2)\mathsf{G}\chi$$
$$\vee \mathsf{E}[\chi\mathsf{U}\mathsf{E}\psi_2\mathsf{G}(\neg\varphi_1 \wedge \chi)] \vee \mathsf{E}[\chi\mathsf{U}\mathsf{E}\psi_1\mathsf{G}(\neg\varphi_2 \wedge \chi)].$$

Each possible combination of $\neg\varphi_1$ or ψ_1 and $\neg\varphi_2$ or ψ_2 requires an individual EG operator. However, SFCTL succinctly embeds into a fragment of ECTL^+ (*cf.* [14–16,31]). Using informally ECTL^+ syntax, we can state this as

$$\mathsf{E}(\varphi_1 \blacktriangleright \psi_1, \ldots, \varphi_n \blacktriangleright \psi_n)\mathsf{G}\chi \equiv \mathsf{E}[(\mathsf{GF}\varphi_1 \to \mathsf{GF}\psi_1) \wedge \cdots \wedge (\mathsf{GF}\varphi_n \to \mathsf{GF}\psi_n) \wedge \mathsf{G}\chi].$$

3   Streett-Fair CTL and the μ-Calculus

The modal μ-calculus [28] extends standard modal logic with general extremal fixpoint operators and thus encompasses many temporal logics. For example, the CTL formula $\mathsf{EF}\,p$ can be expressed by the μ-calculus formula $\mu Y.\,(p \vee \mathsf{EX}\,Y)$, where Y is a fixpoint variable and the *least fixpoint operator* μY applied to its argument $p \vee \mathsf{EX}Y$ picks the least solution of the equation $Y = p \vee \mathsf{EX}Y$. Hence, the formula is satisfied at all states from which a state satisfying p is reachable. Dually, *greatest fixpoint* formulas $\nu Y.\,\varphi(Y)$ pick the greatest solution of the equation induced by $\varphi(Y)$, so that we can express, *e.g.*, the formula $\mathsf{AG}\,p$ by $\nu Y.\,(p \wedge \mathsf{AX}\,Y)$. We assume that the definitions from Sect. 2 are extended to accommodate fixpoint operators in the usual way and follow the ideas from [17] to embed our logics ESFCTL and SFCTL into the modal μ-calculus.

Definition 3.1. For $C = \{(\varphi_1, \psi_1), \ldots, (\varphi_n, \psi_n)\}$, we put

$$\tau_C(Y) := \bigwedge_{1 \leq i \leq n} \left(\mathsf{EX}(\mu Z.\,(\psi_i \wedge Y) \vee (Y \wedge \mathsf{EX}Z)) \vee (\neg\varphi_i \wedge \mathsf{EX}\,Y)\right).$$

Then we have $x \in [\![\tau_C(Y)]\!]$ if and only if, for all $1 \leq i \leq n$, a state satisfying ψ_i can be reached from x by a path of length at least 1 that does not leave Y, or φ_i is not satisfied at x and some successor of x is contained in Y. The

---

[3] An intuitive explanation: requiring that, *e.g.*, φ_1 and φ_2 are witnessed infinitely often on a given path does not amount to requiring that $\varphi_1 \wedge \varphi_2$ holds infinitely often, whereas EX in front of either conjunct could deviate from the path in question.

formula $\nu Y. \tau_C(Y)$ then expresses that the current state is contained within a non-terminating graph such that, for all i and all states satisying φ_i, a state satisfying ψ_i is reachable within the graph.

The following lemma and its corollaries can be derived from results given (without proofs) by Emerson and Lei [17, Lemma 4.8].

Lemma 3.2. $\langle \varphi_1 \triangleright \psi_1, \ldots, \varphi_n \triangleright \psi_n, \neg \chi \triangleright \bot \rangle \equiv \nu Y. (\chi \wedge \tau_C(Y))$.

Proof. For one direction, let $\mathcal{M}, x \vDash \nu Y. (\chi \wedge \tau_C(Y))$. Put $S' = \llbracket \nu Y. (\chi \wedge \tau_C(Y)) \rrbracket$; we will informally treat it as another variable. For each $y \in S'$, we have that $\mathcal{M}, y \vDash \chi$ and for all $1 \leq i \leq n$, we have $\mathcal{M}, y \vDash \mathsf{EX} \mathsf{E}[S' \mathsf{U} (\psi_i \wedge S')]$ or $\mathcal{M}, y \vDash \neg \varphi_i \wedge \mathsf{EX} S'$. Consequently, there is an $\longrightarrow$-successor z of y such that $\mathcal{M}, z \vDash \mathsf{E}[S' \mathsf{U} (\psi_i \wedge S')]$ or $\mathcal{M}, z \vDash S'$. Let $\rightsquigarrow \, \subseteq \, \longrightarrow$ consist of all edges (y, z) that are enforced in this way. It is clearly a non-terminating relation and $x \in dom(\rightsquigarrow)$. We also have that for each node $y \in S'$ and for all $1 \leq i \leq n$, if ψ_i is not strictly $\rightsquigarrow$-reachable from y (that is, if $\mathcal{M}, y \nvDash \mathsf{EX} \mathsf{E}[S' \mathsf{U} (\psi_i \wedge S')])$, then we have $\mathcal{M}, y \vDash \neg \varphi_i \wedge \mathsf{EX} S'$. Since ψ_i is not strictly $\rightsquigarrow$-reachable from y, ψ_i is also not strictly $\rightsquigarrow$-reachable from any $\rightsquigarrow$-successor y' of y. Hence we also have $\mathcal{M}, y' \vDash \neg \varphi_i \wedge \mathsf{EX} S'$. Repeat this argumentation to see that φ_i does not hold anywhere on any path $\pi \in \Pi_\rightsquigarrow(y)$, i.e., that φ_i is not $\rightsquigarrow$-reachable from y.

For the converse direction, let $\mathcal{M}, x \vDash \langle \varphi_1 \triangleright \psi_1, \ldots, \varphi_n \triangleright \psi_n, \neg \chi \triangleright \bot \rangle$ so that we can pick a non-terminating relation $\rightsquigarrow \, \subseteq \, \longrightarrow$ such that $x \in dom(\rightsquigarrow)$ and for each $y \in dom(\rightsquigarrow)$ and for all $1 \leq i \leq n$, we have that if ψ_i is not strictly $\rightsquigarrow$-reachable from y, then all $\rightsquigarrow$-paths that start at y globally satisfy $\neg \varphi_i$; also we have that all $\rightsquigarrow$-paths that start at y globally satisfy $\neg(\neg \chi)$. The latter follows from the requirement $\neg \chi \triangleright \bot$ since $\bot$ is not satisfied at any state. Then we have that χ holds everywhere in $S' := dom(\rightsquigarrow)$, that is, $S' \subseteq \llbracket \chi \rrbracket$. By coinduction, it suffices to show that S' is a postfixpoint of $\chi \wedge \tau_C$, that is, that $S' \subseteq \llbracket \chi \rrbracket \cap \tau_C(S')$. Since we have $S' \subseteq \llbracket \chi \rrbracket$, it remains to show $S' \subseteq \tau_C(S')$. Pick $y \in S'$. If ψ_i is strictly $\rightsquigarrow$-reachable from y, then it is also strictly $\longrightarrow$-reachable from y, and thus we have $\mathcal{M}, y \vDash \mathsf{EX} \mathsf{E}[S' \mathsf{U} (\psi_i \wedge S')]$. If ψ_i is not strictly $\rightsquigarrow$-reachable from y, then all $\rightsquigarrow$-paths that start at y globally satisfy $\neg \varphi_i$ by assumption and as y lies on some $\rightsquigarrow$-path that starts at y, we have $\mathcal{M}, y \vDash \neg \varphi_i \wedge \mathsf{EX} S'$. $\quad \dashv$

Corollary 3.3 (Fixpoint Characterizations for SFCTL and ESFCTL).

$$\langle \varphi_1 \triangleright \psi_1, \ldots, \varphi_n \triangleright \psi_n \rangle \equiv \nu Y. \tau_C(Y)$$
$$\mathsf{E}(\varphi_1 \blacktriangleright \psi_1, \ldots, \varphi_n \blacktriangleright \psi_n) \mathsf{G} \chi \equiv \mathsf{E}[\chi \mathsf{U} \nu Y. (\chi \wedge \tau_C(Y))]$$

Proof. For the first item, put $\chi = \top$ in Lemma 3.2. The second item follows immediately from that Lemma and the definition of the connective. $\quad \dashv$

This yields a translation of SFCTL and ESFCTL into a relatively simple fragment of the μ-calculus in which the nesting depth of alternating extremal fixpoints is bounded by 2 (see, e.g., [30] for a detailed definition of *alternation depth*):

$$(\top)^\mu := \top \qquad (p)^\mu := p \qquad (\neg \varphi)^\mu := \neg \varphi^\mu$$
$$(\varphi \wedge \psi)^\mu := \varphi^\mu \wedge \psi^\mu \quad (\mathsf{EX} \varphi)^\mu := \mathsf{EX} \varphi^\mu \quad (\mathsf{E}[\varphi \mathsf{U} \psi])^\mu := \mu Z. (\psi^\mu \vee (\varphi^\mu \wedge \mathsf{EX} Z)),$$

and, crucially,

$$(\langle\varphi_1 \triangleright \psi_1, \ldots, \varphi_n \triangleright \psi_n\rangle)^\mu :=$$
$$\nu Y. \bigwedge_{1 \le i \le n} \left(\mathsf{EX}(\mu Z.((\psi_i^\mu \wedge Y) \vee (Y \wedge \mathsf{EX}Z))) \vee (\neg\varphi_i^\mu \wedge \mathsf{EX}Y)\right).$$

To see that the embedding of our logics into the μ-calculus indeed is succinct, let $\mathsf{Cl}(\theta)$ denote the *closure* of a given μ-calculus formula θ, that is, the set of all its subformulas and let $|\psi|$ denote the *size* of formulas.

Lemma 3.4 (Size of the Translation). *Let $n > 1$. For every ESFCTL$_n$ formula ψ, we have $|\mathsf{Cl}(\psi^\mu)| \le (9n + 6)|\psi|$.*

Proof. The proof is by induction over ψ; we just consider the case where $\psi = \langle\varphi_1 \triangleright \psi_1, \ldots, \varphi_n \triangleright \psi_n\rangle$. We have $|\psi| = 1 + \sum_{1 \le i \le n}(|\varphi_i| + |\psi_i|)$ and, for

$$C := \{\psi^\mu, \quad \bigwedge_{1 \le i \le n} \left(\mathsf{EX}\mu Z.((Y \wedge \mathsf{EX}Z) \vee (\psi_i^\mu \wedge Y)) \vee (\neg\varphi_i^\mu \wedge \mathsf{EX}Y)\right),$$
$$\mathsf{EX}Y, \ Y, \ Y \wedge \mathsf{EX}Z, \ Z\}$$

and

$$D_i := \{\mathsf{EX}\mu Z.((Y \wedge \mathsf{EX}Z) \vee (\psi_i^\mu \wedge Y)) \vee (\neg\varphi_i^\mu \wedge \mathsf{EX}Y),$$
$$\mathsf{EX}\mu Z.(Y \wedge \mathsf{EX}Z) \vee (\psi_i^\mu \wedge Y), \ \neg\varphi_i^\mu \wedge \mathsf{EX}Y,$$
$$\mu Z.(Y \wedge \mathsf{EX}Z) \vee (\psi_i^\mu \wedge Y), \ \neg\varphi_i^\mu,$$
$$(Y \wedge \mathsf{EX}Z) \vee (\psi_i^\mu \wedge Y), \ \varphi_i^\mu, \ \psi_i^\mu \wedge Y, \ \psi_i^\mu\},$$

we have

$$\mathsf{Cl}(\psi^\mu) = C \cup \bigcup_{i \le n} D_i \cup \bigcup_{i \le n} \mathsf{Cl}(\varphi_i^\mu) \cup \bigcup_{i \le n} \mathsf{Cl}(\psi_i^\mu).$$

Hence we get $|\mathsf{Cl}(\psi^\mu)| = 6 + 9n + \sum_{1 \le i \le n}(|\mathsf{Cl}(\varphi_i^\mu)| + |\mathsf{Cl}(\psi_i^\mu)|)$, as $|C| = 6$ and $|D_i| = 9$ for $1 \le i \le n$. By the induction hypothesis,

$$|\mathsf{Cl}(\psi^\mu)| \le 6 + 9n + \sum_{1 \le i \le n}(6 + 9n)(|\varphi_i| + |\psi_i|)$$
$$= (9n + 6)(1 + \sum_{1 \le i \le n}(|\varphi_i| + |\psi_i|)) = (9n + 6)|\psi|. \qquad \dashv$$

Similar bounds can be established for the fragments of ESFCTL discussed above.

It is well-known (*e.g.*, [23,34]) that model checking μ-calculus formulas is linear-time equivalent to solving *parity games* in which the number of priorities correspond to the alternation depth of the input formulas. Furthermore, parity games with k priorities and m nodes can be solved in time $\mathcal{O}(m^{\frac{k}{2}})$ (see, e.g., [26]) so that solving parity games with a fixed number of priorities is a tractable problem. This suffices for our purposes since all parity games that we consider below have at most 2 priorities, that is, we always have $k \leq 2$. The size of the model checking game for a μ-calculus formula θ against some model $\mathcal{M}$ is $m = |\mathcal{M}| \cdot |\mathsf{Cl}(\theta)|$. Hence the time bound on the model checking problem is linear in $|\psi|$ if we fix the arity n of the main operator $\langle \varphi_1 \triangleright \psi_1, \ldots, \varphi_n \triangleright \psi_n \rangle$ (or its counterparts for other fragments discussed above). Without a fixed constant bound on the arity of the operator, n has to be replaced with $|\psi|$, turning the linear dependency on formula sizes into a quadratic one:

Corollary 3.5. *Let $\mathcal{M}$ be a model, $n \in \mathbb{N}$ and x be a state in $\mathcal{M}$.*

- *For a $\mathsf{ESFCTL_n}$ formula ψ, checking whether $\mathcal{M}, x \vDash \psi$ can be done in time $\mathcal{O}(|\mathcal{M}| \cdot |\psi|)$.*
- *For a ESFCTL formula ψ, checking whether $\mathcal{M}, x \vDash \psi$ can be done in time $\mathcal{O}(|\mathcal{M}| \cdot |\psi|^2)$.*

4   NuSMV Implementation

The current release version (v2.6.0) of the symbolic model checker NuSMV has only limited support for model checking branching time formulas in combination with fairness objectives; for CTL it allows the use of the JUSTICE keyword to specify global unconditional fairness constraints of the form $\bigwedge_i \mathsf{GF}\varphi_i$ where the φ_i are boolean formulas over atoms. A stronger COMPASSION keyword is also available which allows to specify strong fairness constraints of the form $\bigwedge_i (\mathsf{GF}\varphi_i \to \mathsf{GF}\psi_i)$, where again the φ_i and ψ_i are boolean formulas over atoms. However, the use of this keyword is restricted to LTL model checking. Hence, NuSMV currently does not support model checking for CTL with strong fairness objectives.

To rectify this problem, we extend the implementation of CTL model checking within NuSMV to support full ESFCTL (and its fragments), adding the capability of model checking CTL in combination with strong fairness objectives; the sources of our implementation are available at https://git8.cs.fau.de/software/nusmvf. Thanks to the fixpoint characterizations (Corollary 3.3) of our new compassion connectives, it was relatively straightforward to add support of $\mathsf{E}(\varphi_1 \blacktriangleright \psi_1, \ldots, \varphi_n \blacktriangleright \psi_n)\mathsf{G}\chi$ and $\langle \varphi_1 \triangleright \psi_1, \ldots, \varphi_n \triangleright \psi_n \rangle$ (both for arbitrary n) to the model checking procedure of NuSMV. Our implementation adds a new keyword ESFCTLSPEC, whose parameter is a ESFCTL formula. The keyword disables all JUSTICE and COMPASSION keywords while checking ESFCTL formulas in favour of directly expressing the fairness objectives via the formula. Alternatively, the user may specify an ordinary CTL formula augmented with an arbitrary number of COMPASSION constraints, which then is internally translated into the corresponding ESFCTL formula. Additionally, we have extended the trace generation mechanism of NuSMV to also support trace generation for ESFCTL formulas which allow a counter-example in the form of a single path.

4.1 BDD-based Model Checking Within NuSMV

The symbolic NuSMV model checking procedure for ordinary CTL represents the transition relation of the input model as a binary decision diagram (BDD) (*e.g.*, [25, Section 6.3.2]). The procedure verifies the satisfaction of the input formula at a given set of initial states rather than at a single given state. To support fairness constraints, the model BDD is first narrowed down to just those paths of the input model that satisfy the specified fairness constraints, resulting in a fair model BDD. Then the truth set of the input formula within the fair model is computed recursively as a second BDD. During this computation, the fair model BDD is queried directly when evaluating propositional atoms and via a preimage operation for the *next state* connectives EX (and the dual connectives AX). Boolean connectives are mapped to raw BDD operations. For the evaluation of CTL connectives, the relevant fixpoints of the respective subformulas are computed directly by approximation in the case of EG and EU or—in the case of AU, AF and EF—using standard CTL equivalences (see, *e.g.*, [25]).

Our extension of the model checking procedure—to which we refer as NuSMV^{sf} in the following—adds functions computing the fixpoints induced (via the fixpoint characterizations from Corollary 3.3) by the $\mathsf{E}(\varphi_1 \blacktriangleright \psi_1, \ldots, \varphi_n \blacktriangleright \psi_n)\mathsf{G}\chi$ and $\langle \varphi_1 \triangleright \psi_1, \ldots, \varphi_n \triangleright \psi_n \rangle$ connectives. The pseudo-code depicted in Algorithm 4.1 shows how the extension of a formula $\langle \varphi_1 \triangleright \psi_1, \ldots, \varphi_n \triangleright \psi_n \rangle$ is computed as the result of $\textsc{ExtendedStreettFair}((\varphi_1, \psi_1), \ldots, (\varphi_n, \psi_n))$. We use Boolean connectives to denote the respective BDD operations, the functions EU and EX compute EU and EX in the usual way and the model is assumed to be available globally to the functions.

Algorithm 4.1. Evaluation of $\langle \varphi_1 \triangleright \psi_1, \ldots, \varphi_n \triangleright \psi_n \rangle$ operators.

function $\textsc{ExtendedStreettFair}((\varphi_1, \psi_1), \ldots, (\varphi_n, \psi_n))$
    $y \leftarrow$ BDD for 'false'
    $y' \leftarrow$ BDD for 'true'
    while $y \neq y'$ **do**
        $y \leftarrow y'$
        $y' \leftarrow$ BDD for 'true'
        for $i = 1 \ldots n$ **do**
            $z \leftarrow \mathrm{EU}(y, \psi_i \wedge y)$
            $y' \leftarrow y' \wedge (\mathrm{EX}(z) \vee (\neg\varphi_i \wedge \mathrm{EX}(y)))$
        end for
    end while
    return y
end function

Since the new operators can be used to express fairness constraints, we no longer have to restrict the model to just the fair paths in a precomputation step. Instead, we directly evaluate the given ESFCTL formula within the given model. Furthermore, the evaluation of fairness objectives by means of fixpoint computations enables straightforward extraction of witnesses and counterexamples.

We have implemented witness generation for formulas that have path witnesses, essentially extending the witness generation capabilities of NuSMV to cope with our new compassion operators.

5   Examples and Benchmarks

To demonstrate the viability of our approach, we conduct several experiments in which we model check ESFCTL formulas (or their respective μ-calculus encodings) against systems that are given as unlabelled transition systems. From the perspective of parity games, our experiments amount to solving model checking games with just the two priorities 1 (for formulas belonging to least fixpoints) and 2 (for all other formulas), i.e., Büchi games. We compare the runtime behaviour and memory requirements of our new tool NuSMV^{sf} (as described in the previous section), with the explicit parity game solvers PGSolver [20] and Oink [35] and (for some experiments) with the BDD-based parity game solvers introduced in [32]. It should be noted that parity game solvers support model checking for the full μ-calculus while our implementation is restricted to ESFCTL. Furthermore, parity game solvers typically implement various game solving algorithms.

- For PGSolver we conduct experiments with the implementations of
  - Zielonka's recursive algorithm [38] (referred to as PGSolver(zlk) below),
  - the local model checking algorithm due to Stevens and Stirling [33] (PGSolver(mc)) and
  - the strategy improvement algorithm [36] (PGSolver(sil)), using default optimizations.
- For Oink, we evaluate the implementations
  - of Zielonka's algorithm (Oink(zlk)) and
  - the priority promotion algorithm [2] (Oink(npp)), again using default optimizations;
- for NuSMV^{sf}, we use the optimizations -dynamic (enabling dynamic reordering of variables) and -iwls95 100000 (enabling BDD-partitioning); sometimes it is useful to *dis*able BDD-caching with set enable_sexp2bdd_caching 0 (we refer to our implementation with BDD-caching disabled as NuSMV$^{sf}_{nc}$).
- Furthermore, we conduct experiments with an implementation of symbolic variants of Zielonka's algorithm (BDD(zlk)) and the fixpoint iteration algorithm [3] (BDD(fpi)) that work over BDDs, as detailed in Sanchez et al. [32]. Since dynamic reordering of the BDD variables does not guarantee improved performance [32], we disable it. As suggested by Sanchez et al., we execute our experiments using the native Python BDD implementation to handle BDD operations.

All experiments have been conducted on a system with Intel Core i7 3.60 GHz CPU with 24 GB RAM; we generally use a timeout of 360 seconds and report the mean time for three runs for all experiments. *For most experiments, we show just the results for the fastest algorithm from each of the tools that we tested.* Below, we show graphical presentations of our results with the exception of examples where some tools perform very similar, in which case we report the results as tables, for readability.

5.1   Elevator Control System

Standard benchmark sets for parity game solvers [3, 27] include a simple *elevator* example, which models an elevator serving a building with n floors. When the elevator is requested at some level i (modelled by an atom isPressed(i)), the request for this floor is added to a queue, whose entries the elevator visits in either FIFO or LIFO order. The property to be tested, a strong fairness objective, is that however the system evolves, if the elevator is called to a floor infinitely often, then it visits this floor infinitely often as well (the latter event being modelled by an atom isAt(i)). In terms of our language SFCTL, we check against

$$\theta^e(n) := \mathsf{AG} \bigwedge_{i \leq n} \neg\mathsf{E}(\top \blacktriangleright \mathsf{isPressed}(i))\mathsf{G}\neg\mathsf{isAt}(i),$$

stating that there is no $i \leq n$ such that isPressed(i) can be visited infinitely often while visiting isAt(i) only finitely often. The property is satisfied if the elevator processes its waiting queue in a FIFO manner while it is not satisfied in the LIFO version of the system. To obtain benchmark results, we wrote a script to generate elevator models in SMV format and used PGSolver's own tool `elevators` to generate parity games, accordingly. The results of the measurements on time and memory usage are depicted in Tables 1 and 2, where $\dagger_T$ indicates a runtime of over 360 seconds and $\dagger_M$ an out-of-memory error.

Table 1. Runtime and memory requirements for Elevator FIFO (n stages)

n	PGSolver(zlk)		PGSolver(sil)		Oink(zlk)		Oink(npp)		NuSMV^{sf}	
	Time	Memory	Time	Memory	Time	Memory	Time	Memory	Time	Memory
3	0.009	9836	0.026	10 824	0.002	5080	0.003	5052	0.009	17 272
4	0.046	12 656	1.041	21 144	0.003	5672	0.003	5464	0.028	0:028
5	1.252	33 888	113.450	83 608	0.009	7800	0.008	7524	0.112	19 832
6	73.370	168 624	$\dagger_T$	$\dagger_T$	0.070	27 824	0.062	25 148	0:758	25 480
7	$\dagger_T$	$\dagger_T$	$\dagger_T$	$\dagger_T$	0.771	189 980	0.728	169 360	2.904	50 792
8	$\dagger_T$	$\dagger_T$	$\dagger_M$	$\dagger_M$	6:812	1 671 940	6.410	1 484 552	69.815	67 672
9	$\dagger_M$	$\dagger_M$	$\dagger_M$	$\dagger_M$	$\dagger_M$	$\dagger_M$	79.915	14 812 208	$\dagger_T$	$\dagger_T$

Table 2. Runtime and memory requirements for Elevator LIFO (n stages)

n	PGSolver(zlk)		PGSolver(sil)		Oink(zlk)		Oink(npp)		NuSMV$^{sf}_{nc}$	
	Time	Memory	Time	Memory	Time	Memory	Time	Memory	Time	Memory
3	0.007	9440	0.009	9644	0.002	5184	0.003	4992	0.012	17 260
4	0.022	12 664	0.017	12 712	0.004	5676	0.003	5404	0.033	17 836
5	0.149	30 652	0.081	27 320	0.012	8324	0.009	7660	0.137	19 748
6	1.440	171 440	0.558	97 296	0.084	30 916	0.077	27 624	0.477	26 824
7	14.744	1 434 396	4.510	740 788	4.005	203 280	0.916	188 224	2.073	53 876
8	167.345	13 605 024	46.996	6 785 520	11.249	1 772 448	8.977	1 664 240	71.507	69 800

All the tools show relatively similar performance in this example (with NuSMV^{sf} generally being faster than PGSolver but somewhat slower than Oink). For the LIFO variant of the experiment, disabling BDD-caching roughly halves the runtime of NuSMV^{sf}, so we show just the results for NuSMV$^{sf}_{nc}$. While symbolic model checking does not seem to provide a measurable advantage regarding runtimes in the elevator example, we observe that NuSMV^{sf} uses a significantly smaller amount of memory than the parity game solvers, possibly due to succinct BDD-encoding of models and truth sets.

5.2   Non-emptiness for Random Büchi Automata

To further compare our implementation with existing parity game solvers, we devise several series of models and formulas from the domain of automata theory. Automata on infinite words—such as *Büchi*, *parity* or *Streett automata* [23, Ch. 1]—are graphs with atoms that identify *accepting/non-accepting states*, the *priorities* of states or containment in components of *acceptance pairs*. A run of an automaton thus is just an infinite path through the corresponding graph. We first focus on Büchi automata (BA), for which accepting runs visit some accepting state infinitely often. A state in an automaton is *non-empty* if some accepting run starts at the state and the *non-emptiness region* of automata consists of their non-empty states. While automata on infinite words typically have labelled edges so that runs correspond to infinite words over some alphabet, we restrict our development to models with unlabelled edges (corresponding to automata with a single letter alphabet); this is justified by the fact that edge labels do not affect the (non-)emptiness of states. Using f to indicate accepting states, the SFCTL formula $\theta^{BA} := E(\top \blacktriangleright f)G\top$ then specifies the non-emptiness region of BA by expressing the existence of a path on which some accepting state is visited infinitely often.

We compare the tools by checking random (non-)empty BA for non-emptiness. To this end, we construct random automata and in the non-empty case we randomly pick a single state that lies on some loop, marking it as accepting; the tools then have to find this state and verify that it is contained in some loop. Figures 1 and 2 show the runtimes of the various tools for (non)-empty automata of increasing size. Oink consistently shows the best performance and uses the least amount of memory on these random automata. Our implementation NuSMV^{sf} and the BDD-based parity game solvers [32] are the slowest tools in this example. We argue that this is due to the weakness of the BDD-based approach on random input models which are typically not well-structured and rarely allow for a concise BDD representation. Similar effects have also been observed by Sanchez *et al.* [32]. This point seems to be substantiated by the fact that for all random models in our experiments, the model BBDs in NuSMV^{sf} are at least 3 times larger than the corresponding explicit model representations.

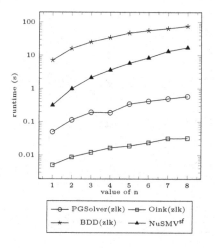

Fig. 1. Non-empty BA ($n \times 1000$ states)

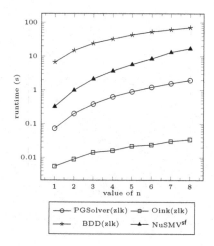

Fig. 2. Empty BA ($n \times 1000$ states)

5.3 Non-emptiness for Tree-Like Parity and Streett Automata

We now turn our attention to non-emptiness checking for parity and Streett automata with a certain tree-like structure that can be exploited by symbolic model checking algorithms. Since these automata can be transformed to equivalent (nondeterministic) Büchi automata, we can define their accepting runs by means of an SFCTL formula. The resulting model checking games then have a Büchi winning condition instead of a parity or Streett condition. Due to the strictness of the alternation hierarchy of the μ-calculus (*cf.*, *e.g.*, [23, Ch. 11]) we can use this straightforward reduction of parity and Streett conditions to Büchi conditions for *automata*, but not for *games* [13]. Hence we restrict our attention to non-emptiness checking for automata. Runs of parity automata (PA) are accepting if the highest *priority* that they visit infinitely often is even. To solve the non-emptiness problem for parity automata with k priorities by fair model checking, we require that each state has exactly one of the priorities 0 (encoded by p_0) to k (encoded by p_k). The non-emptiness region of parity automata then can defined by the SFCTL formula

$$\theta_k^{\mathsf{PA}} := \mathsf{EF} \bigvee_{i \leq k,\, i \text{ even}} \mathsf{E}(\top \blacktriangleright p_i)\mathsf{G}\left(\bigwedge_{j>i} \neg p_j\right)$$

which expresses that, eventually, a state is reached, for which there is some even priority i such that there is a path on which priority i is visited infinitely often and no priority greater than i is ever visited. While θ_k^{PA} mentions k priorities, the μ-calculus formula $(\theta_k^{\mathsf{PA}})^\mu$ has alternation depth just 2.

As indicated above, we run experiments on *tree-like* automata, that is, perfect binary trees of depth $n \geq 1$ with additional back edges from each leaf to the root state; all inner nodes of the tree have priority 0 while the 2^{n-1} leafs have the priorities 1 to 2^{n-1}. Figure 3 depicts the runtimes for model checking non-empty

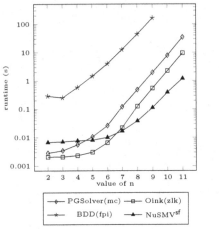

Fig. 3. Non-empty PA (depth n)   **Fig. 4.** Totally accepting PA (depth n)

tree-like parity automata of depth n and with 2^{n-1} priorities against the formula $\theta_{2^{n-1}}^{\mathsf{PA}}$; all trees satisfy the respective formula. We also run experiments for total acceptance of parity automata, expressed by the formula

$$\theta_k^{\mathsf{TPA}} := \mathsf{AG} \bigwedge\nolimits_{i \leq k,\, i \text{ odd}} \neg \mathsf{E}(\top \blacktriangleright p_i)\mathsf{G}(\bigwedge\nolimits_{j>i} \neg p_j)$$

which states that every run is accepting. Figure 4 depicts the results for checking tree-like parity automata of depth n and with 2^{n-1} priorities against $\theta_{2^{n-1}}^{\mathsf{TPA}}$; in this series, we choose automata to be totally accepting so that the formulas are satisfied.

All of the tools appear to exhibit exponential runtime behaviour on both series of tree-like parity automata, in accordance with the exponentially growing sizes of the models and formulas. Yet our implementation NuSMV^{sf} compares favourable to all parity game solvers in this example. We conjecture that the main reason for this lies in the BDD-encoding of models as discussed above (and in *e.g.*, [5] and [32]): in cases, where the input allows for a succinct encoding of the model as a BDD, symbolic model checkers have a structural advantage over tools that use explicit encoding of the input. To substantiate this conjecture, we measure the numbers of nodes in model BDDs and of nodes in explicit model representations. For trees of depth n, we denote the former number by $f(n)$ and the latter number by $g(n)$. We find that $f(n) \leq 15n$ but $g(n) \geq 2^n - 1$ in all our tree-like models. The model BDDs apparently grow linearly with n while the explicit models grow exponentially with n; we made the same observations with the tree-like Streett automata considered below. Interestingly, we did not observe the benefit on runtime that the symbolic approach provides in our experiments when testing the BDD-based parity game solvers of Sanchez *et al.* [32] (*cf.* the plot for BDD(fpi) in Fig. 3). The performance of symbolic model checkers appears to be highly dependent on the structure of the BDD-encoding of the model and the used variable ordering; there may be BDD-encodings of our tree-like automata which are more suitable for such tools.

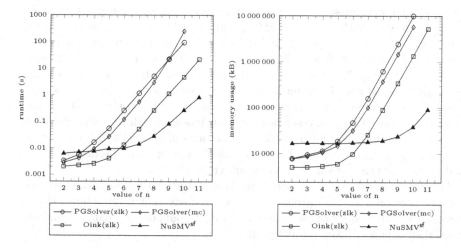

Fig. 5. Non-empty SA, runtime   **Fig. 6.** Non-empty SA, memory usage

Runs in Streett automata (SA) are accepting if, for each *acceptance pair* (P, Q), whenever some state from P is visited infinitely often along the run, then a state from Q is visited infinitely often as well. To check Streett automata for non-emptiness, we assume k acceptance pairs (P_i, Q_i), $i \leq k$, where containment in the respective component of a pair is modelled by atoms p_i, q_i. The non-emptiness region of Streett automata is then defined by the SFCTL formula

$$\theta_k^{\mathsf{SA}} := \mathsf{E}\,(p_1 \blacktriangleright q_1, \ldots, p_k \blacktriangleright q_k)\mathsf{G}\,\top$$

which states the existence of a path that is strongly fair for each acceptance pair. Figures 5 and 6 show the runtimes and the memory requirements, respectively, of the various tools when checking tree-like Streett automata of depth n and with 2^{n-1} acceptance pairs against the formula $\theta_{2^n-1}^{\mathsf{SA}}$. Here, we use non-empty automata in which acceptance pairs $(\{v_0\}, \{l_i\})$ require that if the root node v_0 is visited infinitely often, then the leaf l_i is visited infinitely often; hence the formula is satisfied in all cases. We observe that our tool again decisively outperforms all parity game solvers in this example, possibly due to the concise encoding of tree-like structures as BDDs; the results regarding memory usage are similarly pronounced.

5.4 Alternating Bit Protocol

As another example, we evaluate the performance of NuSMV[sf] with a version of the *Alternating Bit Protocol* [24] which is also included in the parity game benchmarking set [27]. The protocol describes communication of two agents via channels which might lose or duplicate data, a circumstance which it tries to overcome by sending a control bit along with each message which is flipped on successful transmission. The model is parameterized by a set of data elements D that can be sent over communication channels. Keiren's tool chain [27] uses a model written in the mCRL2 specification language to generate equivalent parity games. We start from the same file and generate an SMV model. The time for converting from mCRL2 to the respective format has not been measured. The resulting SMV model encodes the labelled transition system underlying the original model naively, resulting in only two variables *state* and *transition*, where the former represents a state of the system by a number and the latter can take values from the set of transition labels (which are obtained from the mCRL2 description as all possible combinations of actions and their parameters) in the original model. Thus, in NuSMV we can state propositions like `state = 42 & transition = next(transition)`.

Whereas *loc. cit.* performs model checking against several formulas, we concentrate here on a strong fairness statement, namely that if an action $r1(d)$—denoting that the sender reads a datum d from the outside—is enabled infinitely often, then it is also taken infinitely often:

$$\theta(D) := \mathsf{AG} \bigwedge_{d \in D} \neg \mathsf{E}(\top \blacktriangleright \mathsf{EX}(transition = r1(d)))\mathsf{G}\neg(transition = r1(d))$$

The property is satisfied in none of the models.

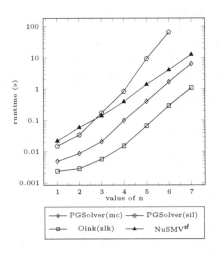

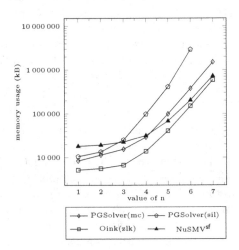

Fig. 7. Runtimes for ABP, $\theta(D)$ for $|D| = 2^n$ data elements

Fig. 8. Memory usage for ABP, $\theta(D)$ for $|D| = 2^n$ data elements

We present our findings in Figs. 7 and 8. It is worth noting that the largest NuSMV model (with $|D| = 2^7$) is around 512 kB in size, whereas the corresponding parity game is much larger at 53 MB.

6 Conclusions

Our work resulted in an extension of the popular tool NuSMV, fixing its known limitations in handling fair CTL specifications, *i.e.*, not only providing the previously missing COMPASSION keyword for CTL and overcoming the restriction to fairness constraints, but also supporting counterexample extraction. Furthermore, the evaluation of our extension so far has shown that for select examples, the advantages of the BDD-based approach seem to extend readily from CTL model checking to model checking with Streett fairness objectives. In general, we conjecture that if the input model can be succinctly encoded as a BDD, this compression leads to significantly reduced runtime and memory usage in comparison to state-of-the art (explicit) parity game solvers. However, a detailed evaluation of this claim (using, *e.g.*, large numbers of model checking instances from practical problems) remains for future work. Despite our promising initial evaluation, the recent progress on parity game solving, both in theory (*e.g.*, the quasipolynomial upper time bounds on explicit [6] and symbolic [8] parity game solving) and in practice [32,35] calls into question the long-term perspectives of the SMV line of tools, at least when it comes to CTL-based model checking.

The central advantage of NuSMV and related tools in comparison to parity game solvers has been the succinct internal representation of models and formulas in terms of BDDs [5]. However, parity game solvers have recently caught up in this area (see, *e.g.*, [7,8,32]), essentially reaching eye level with NuSMV. On a related note, the mCRL2 framework [4] supports model checking for the full μ-calculus by solving parity games and comes with a powerful description language, equaling or surpassing NuSMV regarding the readability and succinctness of the model specification language. Nevertheless, while symbolic parity game solving algorithms are available in theory and have been tested in repositories supporting recent submissions, it appears that they are not (yet) a part of the standard mCRL2 development.

For the time being, our implementation (NuSMV^{sf}) provides a unique combination of an expressive and succinct specification language with symbolic model checking for CTL formulas including Streett fairness objectives. On the practical side, NuSMV^{sf} could be further optimized by adding support for on-the-fly (that is, local) model checking (*e.g.*, [33]). Regarding theoretical aspects, we listed several challenges in the concluding sentence of Sect. 1.1.

The datasets generated and analyzed during the current study are available at https://doi.org/10.6084/m9.figshare.9977510 and have be verified using the virtual machine available at https://doi.org/10.6084/m9.figshare.9977510.

Acknowledgments. We would like to acknowledge discussions with Tim A.C. Willemse on symbolic parity game solving and with Marco Roveri on the NuSMV model checker. Furthermore, we would like to thank the referees for feedback.

References

1. Baier, C., Katoen, J.-P.: Principles of Model Checking (Representation and Mind Series). The MIT Press (2008)

2. Benerecetti, M., Dell'Erba, D., Mogavero, F.: A delayed promotion policy for parity games. Inf. Comput. **262**, 221–240 (2018). Special issue GandALF 2016

3. Bruse, F., Falk, M., Lange, M.: The fixpoint-iteration algorithm for parity games. In: Proceedings of the Fifth International Symposium on Games, Automata, Logics and Formal Verification (GandALF 2014), pp. 116–130 (2014)

4. Bunte, O., et al.: The mCRL2 toolset for analysing concurrent systems. In: Vojnar, T., Zhang, L. (eds.) TACAS 2019. LNCS, vol. 11428, pp. 21–39. Springer, Cham (2019). https://doi.org/10.1007/978-3-030-17465-1_2

5. Burch, J.R., Clarke, E.M., McMillan, K.L., Dill, D.L., Hwang, L.J.: Symbolic model checking: 10^{20} states and beyond. Inf. Comput. **98**(2), 142–170 (1992)

6. Calude, C.S., Jain, S., Khoussainov, B., Li, W., Stephan, F.: Deciding parity games in quasipolynomial time. In: Proceedings of the 49th Annual ACM SIGACT Symposium on Theory of Computing (STOC 2017), pp. 252–263 (2017)

7. Chatterjee, K., Dvořák, W., Henzinger, M., Loitzenbauer, V.: Improved set-based symbolic algorithms for parity games. In: Proceedings of the 26th EACSL Annual Conference on Computer Science Logic (CSL 2017), pp. 18:1–18:21 (2017)

8. Chatterjee, K., Dvořák, W., Henzinger, M., Svozil, A.: Quasipolynomial set-based symbolic algorithms for parity games. In: Proceedings of the 22nd International Conference on Logic for Programming, Artificial Intelligence and Reasoning (LPAR-22), pp. 233–253 (2018)

9. Chatterjee, K., Dvořák, W., Henzinger, M., Svozil, A.: Near-linear time algorithms for Streett objectives in graphs and MDPs. In: Proceedings of the 30th International Conference on Concurrency Theory (CONCUR 2019), pp. 7:1–7:16 (2019)

10. Cimatti, A., et al.: NuSMV 2: an opensource tool for symbolic model checking. In: Brinksma, E., Larsen, K.G. (eds.) CAV 2002. LNCS, vol. 2404, pp. 359–364. Springer, Heidelberg (2002). https://doi.org/10.1007/3-540-45657-0_29

11. Clarke, E.M., Emerson, E.A., Sistla, A.P.: Automatic verification of finite-state concurrent systems using temporal logic specifications. ACM Trans. Program. Lang. Syst. **8**(2), 244–263 (1986)

12. Clarke, E.M., Emerson, E.A.: Design and synthesis of synchronization skeletons using branching time temporal logic. In: Kozen, D. (ed.) Logic of Programs 1981. LNCS, vol. 131, pp. 52–71. Springer, Heidelberg (1982). https://doi.org/10.1007/BFb0025774

13. Dawar, A., Grädel, E.: The descriptive complexity of parity games. In: Kaminski, M., Martini, S. (eds.) CSL 2008. LNCS, vol. 5213, pp. 354–368. Springer, Heidelberg (2008). https://doi.org/10.1007/978-3-540-87531-4_26

14. Emerson, E.A., Clarke, E.M.: Characterizing correctness properties of parallel programs using fixpoints. In: de Bakker, J., van Leeuwen, J. (eds.) ICALP 1980. LNCS, vol. 85, pp. 169–181. Springer, Heidelberg (1980). https://doi.org/10.1007/3-540-10003-2_69

15. Emerson, E.A., Halpern, J.Y.: "Sometimes" and "Not Never" revisited: on branching versus linear time. In: Proceedings of the 10th ACM SIGACT-SIGPLAN Symposium on Principles of Programming Languages (POPL 1983), pp. 127–140 (1983)

16. Emerson, E.A., Halpern, J.Y.: "Sometimes" and "Not Never" revisited: on branching versus linear time temporal logic. J. ACM **33**(1), 151–178 (1986)

17. Emerson, E.A., Lei, C.-L.: Efficient model checking in fragments of the propositional mu-calculus (extended abstract). In: Proceedings of the Symposium on Logic in Computer Science (LICS 1986), pp. 267–278 (1986)

18. Emerson, E.A., Lei, C.-L.: Modalities for model checking: branching time logic strikes back. Sci. Comput. Prog. **8**(3), 275–306 (1987)

19. Francez, N.: Fairness. Springer, Heidelberg (1986)

20. Friedmann, O., Lange, M.: The PGSolver collection of parity game solvers (2010). https://github.com/tcsprojects/pgsolver/blob/master/doc/pgsolver.pdf
21. Gabbay, D., Pnueli, A., Shelah, S., Stavi, J.: On the temporal analysis of fairness. In: Proceedings of the 7th ACM SIGPLAN-SIGACT Symposium on Principles of Programming Languages (POPL 1980), pp. 163–173 (1980)
22. Ghilardi, S., van Gool, S.: Monadic second order logic as the model companion of temporal logic. In: Proceedings of the 31st Annual ACM/IEEE Symposium on Logic in Computer Science (LICS 2016), pp. 417–426 (2016)
23. Mazala, R.: Infinite games. In: Grädel, E., Thomas, W., Wilke, T. (eds.) Automata Logics, and Infinite Games. LNCS, vol. 2500, pp. 23–38. Springer, Heidelberg (2002). https://doi.org/10.1007/3-540-36387-4_2
24. Groote, J.F., Mousavi, M.R.: Modeling and Analysis of Communicating Systems. MIT Press (2014)
25. Huth, M., Ryan, M.D.: Logic in Computer Science – Modelling and Reasoning about Systems, 2 edn. Cambridge University Press (2004
26. Jurdziński, M.: Small progress measures for solving parity games. In: Reichel, H., Tison, S. (eds.) STACS 2000. LNCS, vol. 1770, pp. 290–301. Springer, Heidelberg (2000). https://doi.org/10.1007/3-540-46541-3_24
27. Keiren, J.J.A.: Benchmarks for parity games. In: Dastani, M., Sirjani, M. (eds.) FSEN 2015. LNCS, vol. 9392, pp. 127–142. Springer, Cham (2015). https://doi.org/10.1007/978-3-319-24644-4_9
28. Kozen, D.: Results on the propositional μ-calculus. Theoret. Comput. Sci. **27**, 333–354 (1983)
29. Laroussinie, F., Markey, N., Schnoebelen, P.: Model checking CTL^+ and FCTL is hard. In: Honsell, F., Miculan, M. (eds.) FoSSaCS 2001. LNCS, vol. 2030, pp. 318–331. Springer, Heidelberg (2001). https://doi.org/10.1007/3-540-45315-6_21
30. Niwiński, D.: On fixed-point clones. In: Kott, L. (ed.) ICALP 1986. LNCS, vol. 226, pp. 464–473. Springer, Heidelberg (1986). https://doi.org/10.1007/3-540-16761-7_96
31. Rabinovich, A., Schnoebelen, P.: BTL_2 and the expressive power of $ECTL^+$. Inf. Comput. **204**(7), 1023–1044 (2006)
32. Sanchez, L., Wesselink, W., Willemse, T.A.C.: A comparison of BDD-based parity game solvers. In: Proceedings of the 9th International Symposium on Games, Automata, Logics, and Formal Verification (GandALF 2018), pp. 103–117 (2018)
33. Stevens, P., Stirling, C.: Practical model-checking using games. In: Proceedings of the 4th International Conference on Tools and Algorithms for the Construction and Analysis of Systems (TACAS 1998), pp. 85–101 (1998)
34. Stirling, C.: Games and modal mu-calculus. In: Proceedings of the 2nd International Workshop on Tools and Algorithms for Construction and Analysis of Systems (TACAS 1996), pp. 298–312 (1996)
35. Dijk, T.: Oink: an implementation and evaluation of modern parity game solvers. In: Beyer, D., Huisman, M. (eds.) TACAS 2018. LNCS, vol. 10805, pp. 291–308. Springer, Cham (2018). https://doi.org/10.1007/978-3-319-89960-2_16
36. Vöge, J., Jurdziński, M.: A discrete strategy improvement algorithm for solving parity games. In: Emerson, E.A., Sistla, A.P. (eds.) CAV 2000. LNCS, vol. 1855, pp. 202–215. Springer, Heidelberg (2000). https://doi.org/10.1007/10722167_18
37. Walukiewicz, I.: Completeness of Kozen's axiomatisation of the propositional mu-calculus. In: Proceedings of the 10th Annual IEEE Symposium on Logic in Computer Science (LICS 1995), pp. 14–24 (1995)
38. Zielonka, W.: Infinite games on finitely coloured graphs with applications to automata on infinite trees. Theoret. Comput. Sci. **200**(1–2), 135–183 (1998)

A Cooperative Parallelization Approach for Property-Directed k-Induction

Martin Blicha[1,2(✉)], Antti E. J. Hyvärinen[1],
Matteo Marescotti[1], and Natasha Sharygina[1]

[1] Università della Svizzera italiana (USI), Lugano, Switzerland
{martin.blicha,antti.hyvarinen,matteo.marescotti,
natasha.sharygina}@usi.ch
[2] Faculty of Mathematics and Physics, Charles University, Prague, Czech Republic

Abstract. Recently presented, IC3-inspired symbolic model checking algorithms strengthen the procedure for showing inductiveness of lemmas expressing reachability of states. These approaches show an impressive performance gain in comparison to previous state-of-the-art, but also present new challenges to portfolio-based, lemma sharing parallelization as the solvers now store lemmas that serve different purposes. In this work we formalize this recent algorithm class for lemma sharing parallel portfolios using two central engines, one for checking inductiveness and the other for checking bounded reachability, and show when the respective engines can share their information. In our implementation based on the PD-KIND algorithm, the approach provides a consistent speedup already in a multi-core environment, and surpasses in performance the winners of a recent solver competition by a comfortable margin.

Keywords: Parallel model checking · Lemma sharing · Property-directed k-induction · IC3/PDR · Craig interpolation

1 Introduction

Safe inductive invariants of symbolically described, infinite-state transition systems are valuable artefacts when proving safety for example in software model checking. Algorithms suitable for obtaining such invariants include those based on k-induction [27,32] and IC3 [8]. These algorithms rely on descriptions in propositional or first-order logic that are solved with SAT and SMT solvers enhanced with over-approximation techniques based on Craig interpolation [7,12]. The elusive goal of such algorithms is to minimize the need for user intervention in model checking through well-defined tasks that can be turned into a symbolic traversal of a search space at the expense of increased computational cost.

Solvers for this problem have often a substantial heuristic component enabling different strategies in the algorithm execution. Recent results [10,24,30]

© Springer Nature Switzerland AG 2020
D. Beyer and D. Zufferey (Eds.): VMCAI 2020, LNCS 11990, pp. 270–292, 2020.
https://doi.org/10.1007/978-3-030-39322-9_13

show the use of varied strategies to be a powerful tool for parallelizing model-checking algorithms using algorithm portfolios. The abstract nature of the algorithmic components enables literally infinite possibilities for adjusting the model-checking algorithms, and the changes are known to affect dramatically not only the algorithm run time but also its convergence. However, the key to truly scalable solving is the sharing of information among the solvers of the portfolio (see, e.g., [24]), a usually much more complicated task than constructing the portfolio.

This paper describes a parallelization approach for a recently introduced class (see [15,20]) of model-checking algorithms that combines the strength of k-induction with IC3-style search in finding safe inductive invariants. The algorithms consist of two components, the *induction-checking* engine and the *finite reachability* engine. We describe what information sharing means in a portfolio of instances of this class, and show with a robust experimental analysis on our implementation that the class can profit greatly from this type of parallelization already in a multi-core environment, surpassing in performance the state-of-the-art. While in the following we refer to the class with the acronym IcE/FiRE, we point out the two existing implementation that we are aware of, PD-KIND [20] and KIC3 [15].

An instance of determining the safety of a transition system S consists of a triple of predicates (I, T, P), where I describes the initial states of the system, T describes its transition relation, and P is a set of states to be tested to contain all reachable states of S. The predicates are defined over a fixed set of state variables X, and, in the case of T, a copy X' of X. A solution to the instance, if one exists, is a predicate R containing I such that $R(X) \land T(X, X') \implies R(X')$ and R is contained in P.

In this paper we are studying a general class of algorithms that work on an over-approximation $\mathcal{F}$ of the states of S reachable in n steps or less for some $n \geq 1$. The idea is to maintain the invariant that predicate $\mathcal{F}$ does not intersect with $\neg P$, while trying to prove that $\mathcal{F}$ is (k-)inductive. When $\mathcal{F}$ is represented symbolically as a set of formulas, individual elements of $\mathcal{F}$ can be checked for inductiveness relative to $\mathcal{F}$ instead of checking $\mathcal{F}$ as a whole. Successfully checked elements are collected in a new set $\mathcal{G}$ which represents an over-approximation of the states of S reachable in m steps or less, for $m > n$. When $\mathcal{G} = \mathcal{F}$, such an $\mathcal{F}$ (or $\mathcal{G}$) has the properties of R and therefore is a solution for (I, T, P). This new class of algorithms, introduced in [20] and further refined in [15], is based on an observation that it is, from a pragmatic point of view, better to use an engine for k-induction instead of regular induction in showing $\mathcal{F}$ inductive. The class can be described as a combination of the algorithms based on k-induction and IC3. Intuitively it generalizes IC3, since k-induction is stronger than regular induction. In addition, instances from this class perform well in experimentations. For example, the model checker SALLY [20], which implements PD-KIND, won the transition system division of the 2019 edition of the CHC competition.[1]

In this paper we describe a parallelization approach for the IcE/FiRE class of algorithms. We show that the algorithms allow sharing both the formulas

---

[1] See https://chc-comp.github.io.

constructed for $\mathcal{F}$ and the formulas inside the finite reachability engine. Our parallel algorithm, implemented for multi-core environments on top of PD-KIND [20], performs better than the state-of-the-art parallel and sequential solvers P3 [24], Z3/Spacer [22], and PD-KIND itself [20]. The implementation shows surprisingly good, consistent, close to linear speed-up at least up to nine cores that is visible already for instances with run times as low as two seconds and tends to become more pronounced for higher run times. We show that both types of formula sharing are useful: the parallel solver solves more instances within our timeout and solves the easier instances faster. The implementation is particularly good at showing systems safe.

2   Related Work

Parallelization is a natural way of improving scalability of model-checking algorithms, for example when facing the complexity of real-world problems. We therefore review below only the work that we deem most relevant to our results.

In [24] we presented the P3 system for parallelizing the IC3-inspired algorithm IC3/PDR for computing clusters using portfolio of lemma-sharing solvers and search-space partitioning. The current work differs from that in several important aspects. First, we study a different class of algorithms, based on a combination of IC3 and k-induction. Second, in the implementation our emphasis in this work is on multicore environments instead of computing clusters. We also target a different application domain, studying transition systems instead of general constrained Horn clauses. Finally, in comparing the current system against P3 we measure a significant improvement on the set of instances that both tools can solve, providing practical evidence on the importance of the contribution.

Approaches for parallel IC3 were suggested, for example, in the original publication [8], and more recently in [10]. The current system differs from both, in addition to basing on k-induction, by allowing constraints expressible in first-order logic through an SMT encoding instead of purely propositional encoding, therefore being more readily applicable in software model checking.

The Tarmo system [34] allows SAT-based bounded model checkers to share learned clauses between queries of different execution bounds. The approach could be applied at least in the FiRE systems underlying our bounded reachability queries by allowing the SMT solvers to share clauses as in [18,25]. However, we leave the study of performance effects of such a technique for future work.

A system presented in [31] follows a different approach of determining the feasibility of symbolic execution paths in parallel. Our approach is more symbolic in the sense that it does not require the explicit enumeration of, in general, an exponential number of paths done in [31]. Algorithms for parallel LTL model checking are presented in [1]. The general approach relies on an automata-theoretic formulation of reducing model checking to determining the emptiness of Büchi automata. The parallelization idea focuses on using algorithms based on DFS and BFS for this purpose. We consider this approach orthogonal to ours, and leave it for future work to study the possible synergies. In [21] the authors use three processes to parallelize a standard k-induction algorithm enriched with invariants generated from predefined templates. This approach was generalized in [3] where program analysis with dynamic precision refinement generates continuously-refined invariants for the k-induction. Our approach is based on the more general IcE/FiRE class, and allows scalability to arbitrary number of cores. In [30] the authors present a more general approach of parallelizing model checking by running several model checkers in parallel. However, the paper does not address the problem of sharing information between the solvers, a topic central to the current discussion.

Finally, our approach is greatly inspired by the sequential approaches combining k-induction with IC3, in particular the PD-KIND algorithm [20] but also the KIC3 framework [15]. In this work we aim at capturing the class of these algorithms from the point of view of information sharing between different solvers, and apply these results on parallelizing these algorithms.

A very recent, not yet published work [2] presents another approach of combining k-induction and IC3/PDR. It extends the framework of [3] and employs IC3/PDR (not only) for generation of auxiliary invariants for k-induction.

Combining and unifying different approaches to software verification, such as IC3/PDR [8,14], k-induction [32] and BMC [5], is becoming increasingly popular [3,4,9,15,20]. Both combination and parallelization techniques benefit from relentless continuous improvements [6,11,16,23,33] of the original algorithms.

3 Preliminaries

Let X denote a finite set of typed variables and let X' denote the set of primed versions of variables from X, i.e., the next-state variables. Then a *state formula* $F(X)$ is any quantifier-free formula over variables from X and a *transition formula* $T(X, X')$ is any quantifier-free formula over variables from both X and X'. A *transition system* S (over X) is a pair $\langle I, T \rangle$, where I is a state formula denoting the initial states of the system and T is a transition formula. A *state* s^X is a type-consistent assignment of variables from X, i.e., $s^X(x) \in Dom(x)$ for all $x \in X$. When clear from context, we omit X and write simply s. A state formula F holds in a state s if it evaluates to true under s, that is, $s \vDash F$. The states s such that $s \vDash F$ are called the F-*states*. A sequence of states $\langle s_0, s_1, \ldots, s_k \rangle$ is called a *trace* if $s_{i-1}^X, s_i^{X'} \vDash T(X, X')$ for all $1 \leq i \leq k$. A state s is k-*reachable* in S (reachable in k steps) if there exists a trace $\langle s_0, s_1, \ldots, s_k \rangle$ such that $s_0 \vDash I$ and $s_k = s$. A state is *reachable* if it is k-reachable for some finite k.

A state formula F is a k-*invariant* of the system if it holds in all states reachable in k or less steps. If F is a k-invariant then $\neg F$ is not reachable in k steps or less and we say that $\neg F$ is k-*inconsistent* with S. When a concrete k is not important or not determined, or when we refer to multiple k-invariants but with different values of k, we use a more general term *bounded invariants*. A bounded invariant F is thus a state formula for which there exists k such that F is a k-invariant. Similarly to IC3, we also use the term *lemma* to refer to a bounded invariant.

Given a transition system $S = \langle I, T \rangle$, a state formula P and a set of state formulas $\mathcal{F}$, we say that P is $\mathcal{F}^k$-*inductive* if

$$\bigwedge_{i=0}^{k-1} ((\mathcal{F}(X_i) \land P(X_i)) \land T(X_i, X_{i+1})) \implies P(X_k) \qquad (1)$$

If $\mathcal{F} = \{P\}$ and P is a $(k-1)$-invariant, then P is a k-*inductive invariant* of S, meaning it is valid in all reachable states of S. When P is not $\mathcal{F}^k$-inductive, the negation of (1) is satisfiable and each satisfying assignment defines a trace $\langle s_0, \ldots, s_k \rangle$ of $k+1$ states called a *counter-example to (k-)induction* (CTI). We say that a CTI is reachable in S when s_0 is reachable. A central task of the algorithm presented in this paper is to check if elements of $\mathcal{F}$ are $\mathcal{F}^k$-inductive. Checking this for an element P of $\mathcal{F}$ and placing P to another set $\mathcal{G}$ if P is $\mathcal{F}^k$-inductive is referred to as *pushing* P to $\mathcal{G}$.

Given a transition system S and a state formula P, the goal of verification is to prove that P is valid on all reachable states of S, or equivalently that $\neg P$ is not reachable. We say that the system is *safe* with respect to P if P is indeed an invariant of the system, and we say that it is *unsafe* if there exists a finite trace starting from an initial state and ending in a $\neg P$-state. For the rest of the paper we make the assumption that the problem is non-trivial, meaning that the initial states satisfy the property P, or more formally, that $I \implies P$ is valid.

4   The IcE/FiRE Framework

This section formalizes a general approach for checking safety of symbolically represented transition systems in a way that allows us to present naturally our parallelization techniques. The approach splits the reasoning about the safety into two separate components (Fig. 1). The first, main, component is an *induction-checking engine* (IcE), also referred to shortly as induction engine. The goal of the induction engine is to decide the safety problem. It searches for a k-inductive strengthening of the property P being checked. If it finds such a strengthening it reports the system as safe. During the search it may discover that no such strengthening exists since the negation of the property is reachable from the initial states. In this case it reports the system as unsafe. To make progress in its search, to remove spurious counterexamples to induction, and to confirm real ones, IcE relies on the services of the second component – *finite reachability engine* (FiRE). The role of FiRE is to answer *bounded reachability queries* issued by IcE. Given a state formula s and a number n, a bounded reachability query asks if any s-state is reachable from initial states in exactly n steps. The finite reachability engine answers these queries and provides a reason for the answer. In case of reachability, the reason is a trace of $n + 1$ states leading from an initial state to an s-state. In case of unreachability, the reason is an n-invariant blocking s.

The cooperation of these two engines is depicted on Fig. 1. During the run, FiRE accumulates knowledge about the system in the form of bounded invariants. This knowledge helps it to answer the subsequent queries faster. The

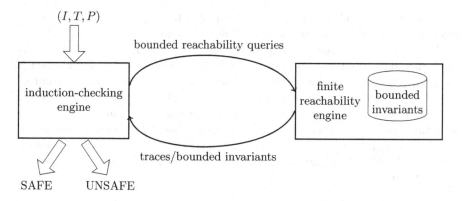

(I, T, P)

bounded reachability queries

induction-checking engine

finite reachability engine

bounded invariants

traces/bounded invariants

SAFE   UNSAFE

Fig. 1. The IcE/FiRE framework for solving safety of transition systems

progress of IcE during its run is modelled using a set of rules that capture and evolve the state of IcE. We discuss the rules in the next section and discuss how IcE relies on FiRE when applying these rules.

The idea of separate components for inductive and bounded reachability reasoning is present already in [20]. However, our formalization enables us to easily extend the framework to parallel setting with information sharing and reason about its correctness. In addition, thanks to its abstract nature, it covers not only PD-KIND [20], but also other algorithms, such as KIC3 [15]. We show this for PD-KIND in Sect. 5, but omit the similar proof for KIC3 due to lack of space.

4.1   Induction-Checking Engine

Given a safety problem for a transition system (I, T, P) the induction-checking engine (IcE) searches for k-inductive strengthening of P. It maintains two distinct sets of state formulas: a *base* frame $\mathcal{F}$ and a *successor* frame $\mathcal{G}$. In addition, it maintains information about its current level n. Intuitively, if IcE is currently working on level n, it already knows that the system is safe up to level n, i.e., $\neg P$ is not reachable in n steps or less. The base frame $\mathcal{F}$ serves both as a witness that $\neg P$ is not reachable, as well as a candidate for the inductive strengthening of P. IcE maintains an invariant that on level n every element of $\mathcal{F}$ is an n-invariant. Moreover, P is always an element of $\mathcal{F}$. The successor frame $\mathcal{G}$ collects those elements of $\mathcal{F}$ that are $\mathcal{F}^k$-inductive for some fixed $k \leq n+1$. Since $\bigwedge \mathcal{F}$ is an n-invariant, this means that all elements of $\mathcal{G}$ are at least $(n+1)$-invariants. When all elements of the base frame are checked and either successfully pushed to $\mathcal{G}$ or dropped, and no termination condition has been hit, $\mathcal{G}$ becomes the new base frame and the successor frame is emptied. If at any point $\mathcal{F} = \mathcal{G}$ then $\mathcal{F}$ is a k-inductive strengthening of P, proving that P holds in the system (as shown later in Lemma 1). In addition to the two frames IcE maintains a queue Q. The queue contains the elements of $\mathcal{F}$ that still need to be processed at the current level. We also refer to the elements of Q as *obligations*.

We now formalize the workings of the induction engine as a set of rules that work on and modify the current state of IcE. The current state of IcE is a 5-tuple $\langle \mathcal{F}, \mathcal{G}, n, k, Q \rangle$ with $\mathcal{F}$ being the base frame, $\mathcal{G}$ the successor frame, n the current level, Q the current queue of obligations, and k defining the current depth of induction. We refer to the state of IcE as *configuration*. For brevity we also sometimes refer to the elements of $\mathcal{F}$ as lemmas instead of bounded invariants. The initial configuration of IcE is $\langle \{P\}, \emptyset, 0, 1, \{P\} \rangle$ and IcE makes progress by applying the following rules. Note that the rules **Safe** and **Unsafe** are special, *terminating* rules.

Safe:
$$\frac{\langle \mathcal{F}, \mathcal{G}, n, k, \emptyset \rangle}{SAFE} \qquad \text{if } \left\{ \mathcal{F} = \mathcal{G} \right.$$

Unsafe:
$$\frac{\langle \mathcal{F}, \mathcal{G}, n, k, Q \rangle}{UNSAFE} \qquad \text{if } \left\{ \neg P \text{ is reachable in } [n+1, n+k] \text{ steps.} \right.$$

Next-Level:
$$\frac{\langle \mathcal{F}, \mathcal{G}, n, k, \emptyset \rangle}{\langle \mathcal{G}, \emptyset, n', k', \mathcal{G} \rangle} \qquad \text{if } \begin{cases} \mathcal{F} \neq \mathcal{G} \\ n' > n \\ \bigwedge \mathcal{G} \text{ is } n'\text{-invariant} \\ 1 \leq k' \leq n'+1 \end{cases}$$

Push-Lemma:
$$\frac{\langle \mathcal{F}, \mathcal{G}, n, k, Q \cup \{l\} \rangle}{\langle \mathcal{F}, \mathcal{G} \cup \{l\}, n, k, Q \rangle} \qquad \text{if } \left\{ l \text{ is } \mathcal{F}^k\text{-inductive} \right.$$

Add-Lemma:
$$\frac{\langle \mathcal{F}, \mathcal{G}, n, k, Q \rangle}{\langle \mathcal{F} \cup \{l\}, \mathcal{G}, n, k, Q \cup \{l\} \rangle} \qquad \text{if } \left\{ l \text{ is an } n\text{-invariant} \right.$$

Drop-Lemma:
$$\frac{\langle \mathcal{F}, \mathcal{G}, n, k, Q \cup \{l\} \rangle}{\langle \mathcal{F}, \mathcal{G}, n, k, Q \rangle} \qquad \text{if } \left\{ l \neq P \right.$$

The rules of IcE, namely **Add-Lemma** and **Drop-Lemma**, are abstract in the sense that we do not prescribe when or how are the new lemmas learnt, nor when they should be dropped. In sequential setting, new lemmas are typically learnt from FiRE when a counter-example to induction of some obligation is showed to be unreachable by FiRE. We discuss this in detail in Sect. 5 when we instantiate the abstract IcE for a concrete algorithm.

One specific thing that we would like to point out is that **Add-Lemma** is general enough to cover not only the *internal* learning, but also *external* learning.

By internal learning we mean the learning of lemmas from FiRE. The external learning means that the lemmas can come from any other source. This is important for parallelization as it enables incorporating bounded invariants discovered by other instances working on the same problem.

Correctness of the Induction-Checking Engine. The abstract nature of the rules of IcE allows us to easily prove it correctness. That is, if the engine terminates by applying the rule **Safe** (**Unsafe**) then the system really is safe (unsafe).

Given our assumption that $I \implies P$, the following invariants are valid for the initial configuration and are maintained by every rule (excluding the terminating rules **Safe**, **Unsafe**):

1. $P \in \mathcal{F}$
2. For each $l \in \mathcal{F} \cup \mathcal{G} \cup Q$ at level n, l is an n-invariant of $\mathcal{S}$.
3. For each $l \in \mathcal{G}$, l is $\mathcal{F}^k$-inductive.

It is easy to verify that all invariants are valid for the initial configuration. The first invariant is trivially preserved by all rules except **Next-Level** as $\mathcal{F}$ either stays the same or grows. When **Next-Level** is applied that it must hold that $P \in \mathcal{G}$ since it is put in Q at the beginning of each level and can never be dropped. Since Q is empty when **Next-Level** is being applied, P must have been successfully pushed to $\mathcal{G}$ using **Push-Lemma**.

The second invariant is preserved by the rules **Next-Level**, **Push-Lemma** and **Drop-Lemma** since the set of formulas in consideration stays the same or becomes smaller. The invariant is also preserved by **Add-Lemma** because of the condition of the rule.

The third invariant trivially holds after applying **Next-Level** as the successor frame is empty at that moment. For the other rules, let us use $\mathcal{G}'$ to denote the successor frame after a rule has been applied. The invariant is also preserved by rules **Add-Lemma** and **Drop-Lemma** since $\mathcal{G}' = \mathcal{G}$. Finally, the invariant is preserved by **Push-Lemma** because of the condition of the rule.

Lemma 1. *When the algorithm terminates by applying **Safe**, the system satisfies the property P and $\bigwedge \mathcal{F}$ is a safe k-inductive invariant. When the algorithm terminates by applying **Unsafe**, the system can reach a state where P does not hold.*

Proof. The first part follows from the invariants. When **Safe** is applied, then it must be the case that $\mathcal{F} = \mathcal{G}$. This means that $\mathcal{F}$ is $\mathcal{F}^k$-inductive and consists of n-invariants of the system with $k \leq n+1$. It follows that $\bigwedge \mathcal{F}$ is a k-inductive invariant of the system. Moreover, $P \in \mathcal{F}$, so P is an invariant. The second part follows trivially from the condition of the rule **Unsafe**.   □

4.2   Finite Reachability Engine

The finite reachability engine (FiRE) is responsible for answering *bounded reachability queries* issued by IcE. A bounded reachability query for a system $\mathcal{S}$ is simply a pair $\langle s, i \rangle$ where s is a state formula and i is a natural number. It represents a question if any s-state is reachable in $\mathcal{S}$ by exactly i steps. This is naturally generalized to queries of the form $\langle s, [i, j] \rangle$, meaning reachability in at least i and at most j steps. An answer to a bounded reachability query $\langle s, i \rangle$ is either an i-invariant l such that $l \implies \neg s$ in case of unreachability, or a trace of $i + 1$ states starting from an initial state and ending in an s-state in case of reachability.

We do not prescribe how FiRE should be implemented, but we note two known instances: bounded model checking [5] and IC3/PDR [8]. An interesting observation [20] is that when IC3/PDR only needs to answer bounded reachability queries then the requirements on the frames it maintains can be relaxed. The frames do not need to be inductive nor form a monotone sequence.

From the parallelization perspective the advantage of FiRE based on bounded invariants is two-fold. First, the correctness of FiRE is maintained when bounded invariants are exchanged between different instances. Second, there is freedom in generalizing the bounded invariants computed as certificates of unreachability and this freedom can be exploited for portfolio approach to discover a variety of interesting bounded invariants across multiple instances.

4.3   Cooperation of Multiple Instances

We base our parallelization on the portfolio approach running multiple instances of the same algorithm with different parameters on a single problem. However, we aim to go beyond that. We want the instances to *cooperate* and to *share* information they discover about the problem they are solving. Our approach to cooperation of multiple instances of IcE/FiRE framework is depicted in Fig. 2.

In our approach, several instances of IcE/FiRE framework (see Fig. 1) work on the same problem and share information among themselves. However, the communication is split to that between the finite reachability engines and to that between induction-checking engines.

Cooperation of FiREs. Each reachability engine is gradually building and refining its representation of the state space by discovering and accumulating bounded invariants of the system. Since all instances work on the same transition system, a bounded invariant discovered by one instance is valid for other instances as well. Thus, multiple reachability engines can share their information through a global database of bounded invariants. Additionally, in this setting each FiRE has a *filter* which controls which invariants are sent and received. The filter can be set to send and receive all or none invariants, or it can implement a heuristic. For example, it might be beneficial to send out only sufficiently small invariants to avoid burdening the other instances too much.

Cooperation of IcEs. Unlike FiREs, it is not immediately obvious what information IcEs could share between themselves. Natural candidates are elements of the base frame or the successor frame. However, one needs to be careful since different IcEs could be working on different levels and thus directly including lemmas from other instance might violate the invariants of these frames. Our

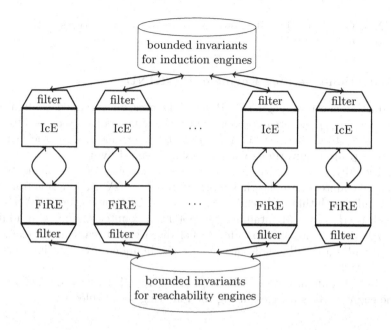

Fig. 2. Multiple instances of IcE/FiRE framework sharing information

solution is to accept external information in a way that can be modelled using the rule **Add-Lemma** and thus guarantee to preserve the correctness of the engine. Each engine sends out elements of the successor frame $\mathcal{G}$. When an engine is working on a level n and a lemma is pushed to $\mathcal{G}$, it is guaranteed to be at least $(n+1)$-invariant. Moreover, it is an *interesting* bounded invariant in the sense that this engine so far believes it should be part of the inductive strengthening. The engine sends such lemma to the global pool for other instances to see. When another engine receives this $(n+1)$-invariant, it checks if it can apply **Add-Lemma** to add it to its base frame. If the engine's current working level is higher than $n+1$, such bounded invariant cannot be added. Moreover, our preliminary experiments showed that it is better to have additional checks in the filter for incoming lemmas in order not to spend too much time processing useless external lemmas. We discuss our implementation and the experimental results with different settings of sharing information in Sect. 6.

5   PD-KIND as an Instance of IcE/FiRE

In this section we reformulate the original description of PD-KIND [20] in terms of our IcE/FiRE framework. This reformulation enables us to identify the freedom in the algorithm that can be utilized for the portfolio approach to parallelization. Additionally, the techniques mentioned in Sect. 4 for sharing information between cooperating instances will become directly applicable for

PD-KIND. On top of that, it allows us to prove the correctness of the parallel version of the algorithm.

5.1   Induction-Checking Engine of PD-KIND

The induction-checking engine of PD-KIND uses an extended configuration $\langle \mathcal{F}, \mathcal{G}, n, k, Q, n_{CTI} \rangle$, where n_{CTI} remembers the number of steps needed to reach a non-$\mathcal{F}$ state from an $\mathcal{F}$ state. This helps to determine $n' > n$ such that all elements of $\mathcal{G}$ are n'-invariants when applying **Next-Level**.

Additionally, IcE of PD-KIND maintains a mapping CEX of elements of $\mathcal{F}$ to potential counter-examples they block. Formally, CEX is a function from $\mathcal{F}$ to state formulas such that for each $l \in \mathcal{F}, l \implies \neg CEX(l)$ and every $CEX(l)$-state can reach a $\neg P$-state. Maintaining the potential counter-examples in addition to the bounded invariants allows for earlier discovery of real counter-examples. It also provides a possible fall-back in case the bounded invariant is too strong to be inductive.

The initial configuration of IcE is $\langle \{P\}, \emptyset, 0, 1, \{P\}, 1 \rangle$, with $CEX(P) = \neg P$, and the engine makes progress using the following set of rules.

Safe:
$$\frac{\langle \mathcal{F}, \mathcal{G}, n, k, \emptyset, n_{CTI} \rangle}{SAFE} \quad \text{if } \left\{ \mathcal{F} = \mathcal{G} \right.$$

Next-Level:
$$\frac{\langle \mathcal{F}, \mathcal{G}, n, k, \emptyset, n_{CTI} \rangle}{\langle \mathcal{G}, \emptyset, n', k', \mathcal{G}, n' + k' \rangle} \quad \text{if } \begin{cases} \mathcal{F} \neq \mathcal{G} \\ n' = n + n_{CTI} \\ 1 \leq k' \leq n' + 1 \end{cases}$$

Push-Lemma:
$$\frac{\langle \mathcal{F}, \mathcal{G}, n, k, Q \cup \{l\}, n_{CTI} \rangle}{\langle \mathcal{F}, \mathcal{G} \cup \{l\}, n, k, Q, n_{CTI} \rangle} \quad \text{if } \left\{ l \text{ is } \mathcal{F}^k\text{-inductive} \right.$$

Unsafe:
$$\frac{\langle \mathcal{F}, \mathcal{G}, n, k, Q \cup \{l\}, n_{CTI} \rangle}{UNSAFE} \quad \text{if } \left\{ CEX(l) \text{ is reachable in } [n+1, n+k] \text{ steps} \right.$$

Add-Lemma:
$$\frac{\langle \mathcal{F}, \mathcal{G}, n, k, Q, n_{CTI} \rangle}{\langle \mathcal{F} \cup \{l'\}, \mathcal{G}, n, k, Q \cup \{l'\}, n_{CTI} \rangle} \quad \text{if } \begin{cases} \exists l \in Q \text{ s.t.} \\ \neg CEX(l) \text{ is not } \mathcal{F}^k\text{-inductive} \\ \text{with } c' \text{ being its } CTI \\ \textbf{Unsafe} \text{ is not applicable} \\ l' \text{ is } n\text{-invariant that blocks } c' \\ CEX(l') = c' \end{cases}$$

Bad-Lemma:

$$\frac{\langle \mathcal{F}, \mathcal{G}, n, k, Q \cup \{l\}, n_{CTI} \rangle}{\langle \mathcal{F} \cup \{l'\}, \mathcal{G} \cup \{l'\}, n, k, Q, n'_{CTI} \rangle} \quad \text{if} \quad \begin{cases} N \in [n+1, n+k] \\ \neg l \text{ reachable in } N \text{ steps} \\ l' = \neg CEX(l) \\ \neg CEX(l) \text{ is } \mathcal{F}^k\text{-inductive} \\ n'_{CTI} = min(N, n_{CTI}) \end{cases}$$

Strengthen-Lemma:

$$\frac{\langle \mathcal{F}, \mathcal{G}, n, k, Q \cup \{l\}, n_{CTI} \rangle}{\langle \mathcal{F} \cup \{l'\}, \mathcal{G}, n, k, Q \cup \{l'\}, n_{CTI} \rangle} \quad \text{if} \quad \begin{cases} \neg CEX(l) \text{ is } \mathcal{F}^k\text{-inductive} \\ l \text{ is not } \mathcal{F}^k\text{-inductive} \\ \text{with } c' \text{ being } CTI \\ \textbf{Bad-Lemma is not applicable} \\ l' \text{ is } n\text{-lemma s.t.} \\ l' \implies l \land \neg c' \\ CEX(l') = CEX(l) \end{cases}$$

A run of the engine starts from the initial configuration and applies the rules until **Safe** or **Unsafe** is applicable (which is generally not guaranteed to happen). The engine can be viewed as operating on a certain level, defined by the parameter n. At each level, the engine attempts to prove that the n-invariants from $\mathcal{F}$ are $\mathcal{F}^k$-inductive, strengthening the frame in the process if necessary or giving up on n-invariants that do not hold for higher levels. When all elements of the (refined) frame $\mathcal{F}$ have been processed two cases can happen. Either the whole frame $\mathcal{F}$ has been pushed, in which case the engine can terminate using **Safe**, or some element could not be pushed and thus **Next-Level** is applied.

If all elements have not been pushed yet, that is, Q is not empty, then an n-invariant l from Q is picked and processed in the following way: When l is $\mathcal{F}^k$-inductive then l, and consequently $\neg CEX(l)$, is in fact at least $(n+1)$-invariant. In this case **Push-Lemma** is applied and l is removed from Q.

If **Push-Lemma** is not applicable and $\neg CEX(l)$ is not $\mathcal{F}^k$-inductive then there exists a CTI witnessing this. This CTI can be either real (reachable in $\mathcal{S}$) or spurious (not reachable in $\mathcal{S}$). A bounded reachability query is issued to FiRE to determine the status. If it is real, the system $\mathcal{S}$ is unsafe because $CEX(l)$ is reachable and $\neg P$ is reachable from $CEX(l)$. In this case the algorithm terminates by applying **Unsafe**. If CTI is spurious then a new lemma blocking it is returned from FiRE and added to $\mathcal{F}$ by applying **Add-Lemma**.

The last possibility is that l is not $\mathcal{F}^k$-inductive but $\neg CEX(l)$ is $\mathcal{F}^k$-inductive. Now the reachability query regarding the CTI for l is issued to FiRE. If it is not reachable then l is strengthened using the reason of unreachability returned by FiRE – **Strengthen-Lemma** is applied. If it is reachable then l is not an invariant of the system and must be discarded. **Bad-Lemma** is applied and l is replaced by $\neg CEX(l)$. Since we already know that $\neg CEX(l)$ is $\mathcal{F}^k$-inductive, it can be immediately pushed to the next frame.

This formalization of PD-KIND allows us to prove its correctness, building on the correctness of the abstract induction-checking engine (see Lemma 1). We extend the proof for parallel version in Sect. 5.3.

Lemma 2. *If* PD-KIND *terminates using the rule* **Safe (Unsafe)***, the transition system is safe (unsafe).*

Proof. For **Safe**, notice that PD-KIND's run can be viewed as a run of the abstract engine (Sect. 4.1). To avoid name clashes we use a prime to denote the PD-KIND's rules in this proof. All four rules **Safe'**, **Push-Lemma'**, **Next-Level'** and **Add-Lemma'** directly map to their abstract counterpart. **Bad-Lemma** is just **Drop-Lemma** applied on l followed by **Add-Lemma** and **Push-Lemma** on $\neg CEX(l)$. Finally, **Strengthen-Lemma** is **Drop-Lemma** applied on l, followed by **Add-Lemma** applied on l'. Consequently, each PD-KIND's run terminating with **Safe'** is mapped to an abstract engine's run terminating with **Safe**. By Lemma 1, the system is safe.

For **Unsafe**, we show that the following invariant is preserved throughout the run: For each l in $\mathcal{F} \cup \mathcal{G} \cup Q$, $CEX(l)$ can reach $\neg P$. The invariant holds for the initial configuration since $\mathcal{F} \cup \mathcal{G} \cup Q = \{P\}$ and $CEX(P) = \neg P$. **Add-Lemma** preserves the invariant since for the only new lemma l', $CEX(l')$ can reach $CEX(l)$, which can reach $\neg P$ by the induction hypothesis. The invariant is also preserved by **Bad-Lemma** and **Strengthen-Lemma** as $CEX(l') = CEX(l)$ for the only new lemma l' and an old lemma l. As the other rules do not change the set $\mathcal{F} \cup \mathcal{G} \cup Q$, we can conclude that the invariant is always preserved. Thus, when the algorithm terminates by rule **Unsafe**, $\neg P$ is reachable and the system is unsafe. □

5.2 Finite Reachability Engine of PD-KIND

The finite reachability engine used in PD-KIND [20] can be described as IC3-like algorithm. It answers the bounded reachability queries using a sequence of *reachability frames* and local reasoning only, i.e., it does not unroll the transition relation. A *reachability frame* at level n, $\mathcal{R}_n$, is a set of n-invariants. Consequently, the set of $\mathcal{R}_n$-states over-approximates the set of states reachable in n steps or less. Unlike IC3, there is no further condition on the reachability frames. They do not need to be monotone nor form an inductive sequence. Like IC3, when FiRE receives a query $\langle s, i \rangle$, it checks if it is reachable in one step from $\mathcal{R}_{i-1}$ using a simple satisfiability query $\mathcal{R}_{i-1} \wedge T \wedge s'$. If it is unreachable, then FiRE generalizes the reason for unreachability using *Craig interpolation* and returns the answer together with the reason. If it is reachable, then FiRE computes a predecessor t of s and recursively calls itself with query $\langle t, i-1 \rangle$. If this predecessor turns out to be unreachable, the $(i-1)$-invariant witnessing the unreachability is used to refine $\mathcal{R}_{i-1}$ and s is checked again. If the recursive sequences of calls ever reaches an initial state, then the information about reachability, together with the trace made of the predecessors is gradually returned.

Note that the only condition required for reachability frame $\mathcal{R}_n$ is that it consists of n-invariants. In sequential setting FiRE learns new bounded invariants on its own as it processes more and more reachability queries. However, in parallel setting it can also receive bounded invariants from external source. More specifically, it can receive bounded invariants discovered by other instances of the same engine working in parallel on the same problem. Additionally, different interpolation algorithms can be used in different instances, thus allowing the engines to spread the search for useful bounded invariants.

5.3 Parallel PD-KIND

Since PD-KIND is an instantiation of the IcE/FiRE framework, it can be readily plugged into the abstract parallel framework with information sharing described in Sect. 4.3.

The bounded reachability information is stored in form of reachability frames consisting of bounded invariants. Whenever FiRE learns new bounded invariant as a response to bounded reachability query made by IcE, it can send it to the other instances. It can also periodically query the common pool for new bounded invariants and when it receives an external i-invariant, it can directly add it to its reachability frame $\mathcal{R}_i$.

Similarly, IcE sends out bounded invariants when it manages to push them to the successor frame. When it receives an external bounded invariant, it must check the necessary condition for adding it to the base frame. If the condition is not met, it simply drops the lemma. Otherwise, it uses a heuristic to determine usefulness of the lemma. Since PD-KIND assumes that each element of the base frame is associated with a potential counter-example through the mapping CEX, each bounded invariant l that is sent out by IcE must also be accompanied by its companion $CEX(l)$.

It is important for the success of a parallel approach to *diversify* the search for the solution. It was not possible to discuss this for the abstract framework as it requires the concrete algorithm with its concrete settings that drive the behaviour of the algorithm. Here we identify the key points where the behaviour of PD-KIND can be adjusted and finally give an algorithm capturing PD-KIND as an instance of IcE/FiRE framework in the parallel setting.

Choosing the Depth of Induction. When the induction engine moves to the next level n by applying **Next-Level** there is freedom to choose a new value k of the induction depth from the interval $[1, n+1]$. The behaviour of the algorithm can be greatly influenced by the value of the induction depth it uses. For example, choosing large k requires large unwinding of the transition relation when SAT/SMT solver is used and the inductive checks become slower. On the other hand preferring larger k can lead to faster exploration of the search space. Moreover an obligation might be $\mathcal{F}^k$-inductive, and thus successfully pushed, but not $\mathcal{F}^{k'}$-inductive for $k' < k$. We denote the strategy to choose the new value of induction depth whenever **Next-Level** is applied as κ.

Obligation Processing Strategy. Several rules might be applicable given a configuration with nonempty queue of obligations Q. However, once the obligation to be processed is chosen, there is no more freedom. The conditions of the rules are mutually exclusive for a fixed obligation $l \in Q$. Which rule applies for a particular obligation l is determined by its properties and the properties of $CEX(l)$. Therefore, the behaviour of the algorithm can be controlled through the strategy determining the obligation to pick from the queue. We denote the strategy to pick the next obligation from Q by ω.

Learning Strategy. The finite reachability engine computes bounded invariants as certificates of unreachability. Theoretically, the certificate of unreachability for a query $\langle s, i \rangle$ could be $\neg s$. However, this leads to terrible performance in practice as it excludes only s and nothing else. Therefore, FiRE uses more sophisticated techniques to compute bounded invariants that are stronger and exclude more unreachable states. FiRE of PD-KIND uses Craig interpolation for computation of bounded invariants. However, Craig interpolant for a given problem is in general not unique and there exist techniques for computing different interpolants in propositional logic and in theories of first-order logic. The use of different interpolation algorithms leads to different bounded invariants and this can have a huge influence on the performance of the whole algorithm (see Sect. 6). We denote the strategy for computing the bounded invariants as σ.

Algorithm 1. PD-KIND in the parallel setting of IcE/FiRE

1: **procedure** $\text{RUN}(\mathcal{S}, \kappa, \omega, \sigma)$
2:     $C = \langle \mathcal{F}, \mathcal{G}, n, k, Q, n_{CTI} \rangle \leftarrow \langle \{P\}, \emptyset, 0, 1, \{P\}, 1 \rangle$ ▷ Initial configuration
3:     **while** True **do**
4:        **if** $Q = \emptyset$ **then**
5:           **if** $\mathcal{F} = \mathcal{G}$ **then return** SAFE   ▷ Terminate using rule **Safe**
6:           **else**
7:              Apply **Next-Level** on C with κ
8:              **continue**
9:           **end if**
10:        **end if**
11:        $\text{FiRE.SENDRECEIVE}()$ ▷ FiRE sends and receives bounded invariants
12:        $C \leftarrow \text{IcE.RECEIVE}(C)$ ▷ IcE receives bounded invariants
13:        $l \leftarrow \omega(Q)$ ▷ Pick obligation to process
14:        $c \leftarrow CEX(l)$
15:        **switch** $\langle l, c \rangle$ ▷ Pick rule based on properties of l, c
16:           **case** l is $\mathcal{F}^k$-inductive
17:              Apply **Push-Lemma** for l on C
18:              $\text{IcE.SEND}(\langle l, c, n+1 \rangle)$ ▷ IcE sends pushed bounded invariant
19:           **case** c is reachable in $[n+1, n+k]$ steps
20:              **return** UNSAFE   ▷ Terminate using rule **Unsafe**
21:           **case** $\neg c$ is not $\mathcal{F}^k$-inductive
22:              Apply **Add-Lemma** with σ on C
23:           **case** $\neg l$ is reachable in $[n+1, n+k]$ steps
24:              Apply **Bad-Lemma** for l
25:           **case** None of the above condition is met
26:              Apply **Strengthen-Lemma** with σ on C for l
27:        **end while**
28: **end procedure**

The run of a single instantiation of IcE/FiRE as PD-KIND in a parallel setting with information sharing is presented in pseudocode as Algorithm 1. The input is a triple $S = \langle I, T, P \rangle$ representing the transition system and the property together with the three strategies κ, ω, σ that determine the behaviour of the algorithm at the previously identified non-deterministic steps.

Lemma 3. *The parallel version of* PD-KIND *with information exchange is correct. If it reports SAFE (UNSAFE), the system is safe (unsafe).*

Proof. The correctness of exchanging the bounded invariants between reachability engines has been discussed already in Sect. 4.3. The only new step IcE does is incorporating an external lemma l from another PD-KIND instance, together with a potential counter-example that it blocks. This is done only if the condition of the abstract rule **Add-Lemma** is satisfied and thus the invariants ensuring the correctness of SAFE answer are preserved. Moreover, the invariant from the proof of Lemma 2 is preserved and thus also UNSAFE answer is correct.   □

6   Implementation and Experiments

Our implementation of the parallel PD-KIND algorithm is based on the open-source model checker SALLY [20] and uses the SMTS framework [26] for parallelization and information exchange. We have extended SALLY with API for sending and receiving information. In our experiments SALLY was using YICES [13] for checking satisfiability and OPENSMT [17] for the interpolation queries.[2]

The benchmarks were taken from the transition systems category of CHC COMP 2019[3], where the problem is encoded using the theory of linear real arithmetic. Out of 244 benchmarks, 7 problematic ones were excluded due to reasons such as the presence of a non-linear operation. All experiments were run on a single multi-core machine with 16 Intel® Xeon® X5687 @ 3.6 GHz CPUs and 180 GB of RAM. The resources were restricted to 1000 s of timeout and 6 GB of memory *per one instance* of SALLY. This means that configurations with more instances are effectively granted more memory and CPU time. This choice is in line with our goal of improving the solver's wall clock time.

All instances use the default strategy of SALLY when they are choosing the depth of induction (κ from Algorithm 1). The obligation processing strategy ω is a priority queue based on a score assigned to obligations, randomized to diversify the behaviour of different instances. The learning strategy σ is diversified primarily by using different interpolation algorithms in OPENSMT and secondary by using different random seed for the SMT search. Three different LRA interpolation algorithms were used: Farkas interpolation algorithm [28], dual Farkas, and an interpolation algorithm based on decomposing Farkas interpolants [7]. We denote these as PF, DF and PD, respectively.

---

[2] All benchmarks, tools and results are bundled together in an artifact available at https://doi.org/10.5281/zenodo.3484097.

[3] https://github.com/chc-comp/chc-comp19-benchmarks/tree/master/lra-ts.

In the experiments we seek answers to the following questions:

1. How does the system compare to the state-of-the-art?
2. How important is the sharing of information between various instances?
3. How does the approach scale when the number of instances is increased?
4. How do different interpolation algorithms contribute to the overall performance?

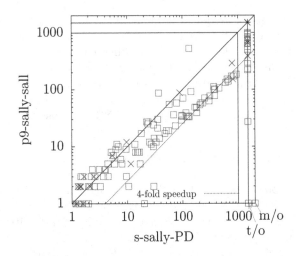

Fig. 3. Best parallel configuration against the winner of LRA-TS category of CHC COMP 2019

Comparison to the State-of-the-Art. The main result of the experiments is summarized in Fig. 3 that compares the performance of the winner of the transition systems category of CHC COMP 2019 (sequential SALLY using PD interpolation algorithm in OPENSMT) with our parallel implementation with nine instances sharing information between IcEs and between FiREs. The parallel implementation achieves 4-fold speedup on a significant number of instances and solves 224 instances compared to 197 instances solved by the sequential version.

We also compared our parallel implementation to P3 [24], the parallel implementation of SPACER [22] that also allows sharing information between solver instances. We also add the comparison with the sequential SPACER, the default Horn clause engine in Z3 [29].[4] The results are summarized in Fig. 4. Our framework significantly outperforms SPACER on safe instances. Interestingly, SPACER seems to fare better on unsafe instances.

Information Sharing. Figure 5 summarizes the performance of 4 configurations: no information sharing (sno), sharing between FiREs only (sreach), sharing

---

[4] Results for Z3-4.8.5 with default settings.

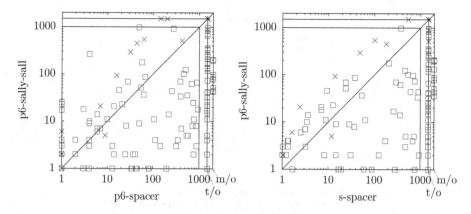

Fig. 4. Comparison of parallel SALLY and parallel SPACER using 6 communicating instances

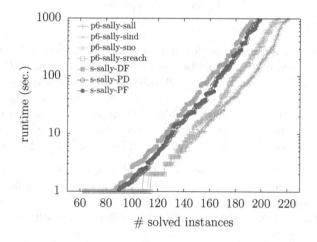

Fig. 5. The effect of sharing information

between IcEs only (sind), and all sharing enabled (sall). In these configurations six instances were running in parallel (two instances for each interpolation algorithm PF, DF and PD). For comparison, the figure includes results of sequential versions with different interpolation algorithms. Note that the runtimes of the parallel implementation were rounded to the whole seconds and this creates an effect of "stairs" for the low runtimes in cactus plots with logarithmic scale. There is also a significant number of instances solved almost instantly and for this reason the axes start at 1 s runtime and 50 instances solved.

A clear gap is visible between the best sequential version and the parallel versions indicating that the parallel approach yields a significant improvement even without information sharing. Sharing information between FiREs is helpful, but the effect is not that significant compared to sharing information between IcEs,

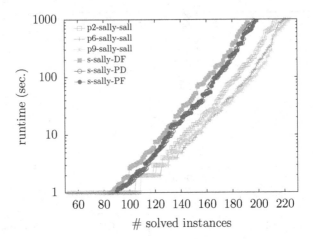

Fig. 6. Scalability experiments

which is crucial for improving performance on many benchmarks. Configurations with sharing reachability information disabled (**p6-sally-sno**, **p6-sally-sind**) do not profit much from enabling it (**p6-sally-sreach**, **p6-sally-sall**). However, some hard benchmarks could only be solved by allowing reachability information to be shared. On the other hand, enabling the sharing of induction information does boost the performance significantly. We conclude that the best performance was achieved by enabling sharing information between both IcEs and FiREs.

Scalability. We compared the performance of one, two, six and nine instances with all information sharing enabled. The results, summarized in Fig. 6, show that adding more instances improves the performance, both decreasing the runtime and solving more benchmarks with the configurations solving 197, 213, 221 and 224 instances, respectively.

The Effect of Interpolation. The large jump when moving from sequential solving to two instances running in parallel can be in part contributed to different interpolation algorithms. We investigate this further in Fig. 7. We compared configurations using six instances when the interpolation algorithm varies (**p6-sally-sall**), when the interpolation algorithm is fixed to PF for all instance (**p6-sally-sall-PF**), and when it is fixed to PD (**p6-sally-sall-PD**). We also added a configuration of just two instances (one with PF, one with PD). The results show that varying the interpolation algorithm is very important as the performance of **p2-sally-sall** is comparable to that of **p6-sally-sall-PD** and **p6-sally-sall-PF** while **p6-sally-sall** performs significantly better.

The experiments show that our parallel algorithm performs substantially better than its sequential version. Its success can be contributed to more than one factor: The use of different interpolation algorithms helps to solve more benchmarks compared to a single interpolation algorithm used by all instances. Sharing information between solver instances can significantly reduce the runtime and

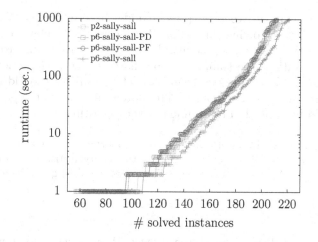

Fig. 7. The effect of using different interpolation algorithms

thus solve more instances within the time limit. The major part of this can be contributed to the sharing of induction information, but sharing reachability information does help as well. The scalability experiments show continuing improvement up to nine instances. Additionally, our algorithm compares favorably with the state-of-the-art parallel implementation of SPACER, outperforming it significantly on the safe instances. Since SPACER is performing better on unsafe instances, the integration of the two algorithms within the SMTS framework to get the best of both tools is an interesting possibility for the future work.

7 Conclusions

The IC3 algorithm [8] has arguably given a significant boost to symbolic model checking as witnessed by the number of new algorithms it has inspired. An early observation first made in [8] and later independently verified for example in [10,24] states that these algorithms are particularly amenable for parallelization. A recent pragmatic addition to the base algorithmic idea aims at obtaining higher quality reachability lemmas by k-induction and naturally splits the IC3 algorithm into two engines, one for induction and the other for computing bounded reachability.

This idea changes the way a lemma sharing parallel portfolio can be implemented for the class of algorithms, a question that was fundamental in IC3 from the beginning. In this work we provide the IcE/FiRE architecture that addresses this question by separating the two engines and their lemma storages and allowing parallel running solvers to share lemmas among their respective engines. We show experimentally that this approach provides a good speed-up in multi-core environments, and that the solver surpasses in speed and number of instances solved the current state-of-the-art on proving safety of transitions systems.

In future we plan to extend the presented idea in several ways. We will generalize the approach to solving constrained Horn clauses. We plan to study closer possible heuristics for sharing lemmas between the solvers, and to determine under what conditions the lemmas can be shared between an induction engine and a reachability engine. Aside from parallel portfolio, we would also like to study how search space partitioning and approaches such as the *parallelization tree* [19] could be applied in the context of the algorithm.

Acknowledgements. This work was partially supported by the Czech Science Foundation project nr. 18-17403S, by the Charles University institutional funding SVV 260451 and by the Swiss National Science Foundation (SNSF) grant 200020_166288.

References

1. Barnat, J., et al.: Parallel model checking algorithms for linear-time temporal logic. Handbook of Parallel Constraint Reasoning, pp. 457–507. Springer, Cham (2018). https://doi.org/10.1007/978-3-319-63516-3_12
2. Beyer, D., Dangl, M.: Software verification with PDR: implementation and empirical evaluation of the state of the art (2019)
3. Beyer, D., Dangl, M., Wendler, P.: Boosting k-induction with continuously-refined invariants. In: Kroening, D., Păsăreanu, C.S. (eds.) CAV 2015. LNCS, vol. 9206, pp. 622–640. Springer, Cham (2015). https://doi.org/10.1007/978-3-319-21690-4_42
4. Beyer, D., Dangl, M., Wendler, P.: A unifying view on SMT-based software verification. J. Autom. Reason. **60**(3), 299–335 (2018)
5. Biere, A., Cimatti, A., Clarke, E., Zhu, Y.: Symbolic model checking without BDDs. In: Cleaveland, W.R. (ed.) TACAS 1999. LNCS, vol. 1579, pp. 193–207. Springer, Heidelberg (1999). https://doi.org/10.1007/3-540-49059-0_14
6. Birgmeier, J., Bradley, A.R., Weissenbacher, G.: Counterexample to induction-guided abstraction-refinement (CTIGAR). In: Biere, A., Bloem, R. (eds.) CAV 2014. LNCS, vol. 8559, pp. 831–848. Springer, Cham (2014). https://doi.org/10.1007/978-3-319-08867-9_55
7. Blicha, M., Hyvärinen, A.E.J., Kofroň, J., Sharygina, N.: Decomposing Farkas interpolants. In: Vojnar, T., Zhang, L. (eds.) TACAS 2019. LNCS, vol. 11427, pp. 3–20. Springer, Cham (2019). https://doi.org/10.1007/978-3-030-17462-0_1
8. Bradley, A.R.: SAT-based model checking without unrolling. In: Jhala, R., Schmidt, D. (eds.) VMCAI 2011. LNCS, vol. 6538, pp. 70–87. Springer, Heidelberg (2011). https://doi.org/10.1007/978-3-642-18275-4_7
9. Brain, M., Joshi, S., Kroening, D., Schrammel, P.: Safety verification and refutation by k-invariants and k-induction. In: Blazy, S., Jensen, T. (eds.) SAS 2015. LNCS, vol. 9291, pp. 145–161. Springer, Heidelberg (2015). https://doi.org/10.1007/978-3-662-48288-9_9
10. Chaki, S., Karimi, D.: Model checking with multi-threaded IC3 portfolios. In: Jobstmann, B., Leino, K.R.M. (eds.) VMCAI 2016. LNCS, vol. 9583, pp. 517–535. Springer, Heidelberg (2016). https://doi.org/10.1007/978-3-662-49122-5_25
11. Cimatti, A., Griggio, A.: Software model checking via IC3. In: Madhusudan, P., Seshia, S.A. (eds.) CAV 2012. LNCS, vol. 7358, pp. 277–293. Springer, Heidelberg (2012). https://doi.org/10.1007/978-3-642-31424-7_23
12. Craig, W.: Three uses of the Herbrand-Gentzen theorem in relating model theory and proof theory. J. Symb. Logic **22**(3), 269–285 (1957)

13. Dutertre, B.: Yices 2.2. In: Biere, A., Bloem, R. (eds.) CAV 2014. LNCS, vol. 8559, pp. 737–744. Springer, Cham (2014). https://doi.org/10.1007/978-3-319-08867-9_49
14. Een, N., Mishchenko, A., Brayton, R.: Efficient implementation of property directed reachability. In: Proceedings of the International Conference on Formal Methods in Computer-Aided Design, FMCAD 2011, pp. 125–134. FMCAD Inc., Austin (2011)
15. Gurfinkel, A., Ivrii, A.: K-induction without unrolling. In: Stewart, D., Weissenbacher, G. (eds.) Proceedings of FMCAD 2017, pp. 148–155. IEEE (2017)
16. Hoder, K., Bjørner, N.: Generalized property directed reachability. In: Cimatti, A., Sebastiani, R. (eds.) SAT 2012. LNCS, vol. 7317, pp. 157–171. Springer, Heidelberg (2012). https://doi.org/10.1007/978-3-642-31612-8_13
17. Hyvärinen, A.E.J., Marescotti, M., Alt, L., Sharygina, N.: OpenSMT2: an SMT solver for multi-core and cloud computing. In: Creignou, N., Le Berre, D. (eds.) SAT 2016. LNCS, vol. 9710, pp. 547–553. Springer, Cham (2016). https://doi.org/10.1007/978-3-319-40970-2_35
18. Hyvärinen, A.E.J., Marescotti, M., Sharygina, N.: Search-space partitioning for parallelizing SMT solvers. In: Heule, M., Weaver, S. (eds.) SAT 2015. LNCS, vol. 9340, pp. 369–386. Springer, Cham (2015). https://doi.org/10.1007/978-3-319-24318-4_27
19. Hyvärinen, A.E.J., Wintersteiger, C.M.: Parallel satisfiability modulo theories. Handbook of Parallel Constraint Reasoning, pp. 141–178. Springer, Cham (2018). https://doi.org/10.1007/978-3-319-63516-3_5
20. Jovanovic, D., Dutertre, B.: Property-directed k-induction. In: Piskac, R., Talupur, M. (eds.) Proceedings of FMCAD 2016, pp. 85–92. IEEE (2016)
21. Kahsai, T., Tinelli, C.: PKind: a parallel k-induction based model checker. Electron. Proc. Theor. Comput. Sci. **72**, 55–62 (2011)
22. Komuravelli, A., Gurfinkel, A., Chaki, S.: SMT-based model checking for recursive programs. In: Biere, A., Bloem, R. (eds.) CAV 2014. LNCS, vol. 8559, pp. 17–34. Springer, Cham (2014). https://doi.org/10.1007/978-3-319-08867-9_2
23. Lange, T., Prinz, F., Neuhäußer, M.R., Noll, T., Katoen, J.-P.: Improving generalization in software IC3. In: Gallardo, M.M., Merino, P. (eds.) SPIN 2018. LNCS, vol. 10869, pp. 85–102. Springer, Cham (2018). https://doi.org/10.1007/978-3-319-94111-0_5
24. Marescotti, M., Gurfinkel, A., Hyvärinen, A.E.J., Sharygina, N.: Designing parallel PDR. In: Stewart, D., Weissenbacher, G. (eds.) 2017 Formal Methods in Computer Aided Design (FMCAD), pp. 156–163. IEEE Press (2017)
25. Marescotti, M., Hyvärinen, A.E.J., Sharygina, N.: Clause sharing and partitioning for cloud-based SMT solving. In: Artho, C., Legay, A., Peled, D. (eds.) ATVA 2016. LNCS, vol. 9938, pp. 428–443. Springer, Cham (2016). https://doi.org/10.1007/978-3-319-46520-3_27
26. Marescotti, M., Hyvärinen, A.E.J., Sharygina, N.: SMTS: distributed, visualized constraint solving. In: LPAR-22, 22nd International Conference on Logic for Programming, Artificial Intelligence and Reasoning, Awassa, Ethiopia, pp. 16–21 (November 2018)
27. McMillan, K.L.: Interpolation and SAT-based model checking. In: Hunt, W.A., Somenzi, F. (eds.) CAV 2003. LNCS, vol. 2725, pp. 1–13. Springer, Heidelberg (2003). https://doi.org/10.1007/978-3-540-45069-6_1
28. McMillan, K.L.: An interpolating theorem prover. Theor. Comput. Sci. **345**(1), 101–121 (2005)

29. de Moura, L., Bjørner, N.: Z3: an efficient SMT solver. In: Ramakrishnan, C.R., Rehof, J. (eds.) TACAS 2008. LNCS, vol. 4963, pp. 337–340. Springer, Heidelberg (2008). https://doi.org/10.1007/978-3-540-78800-3_24

30. Palikareva, H., Cadar, C.: Multi-solver support in symbolic execution. In: Sharygina, N., Veith, H. (eds.) CAV 2013. LNCS, vol. 8044, pp. 53–68. Springer, Heidelberg (2013). https://doi.org/10.1007/978-3-642-39799-8_3

31. Rakadjiev, E., Shimosawa, T., Mine, H., Oshima, S.: Parallel SMT solving and concurrent symbolic execution. In: 2015 IEEE Trustcom/BigDataSE/ISPA, vol. 3, pp. 17–26 (August 2015)

32. Sheeran, M., Singh, S., Stålmarck, G.: Checking safety properties using induction and a SAT-solver. In: Hunt, W.A., Johnson, S.D. (eds.) FMCAD 2000. LNCS, vol. 1954, pp. 127–144. Springer, Heidelberg (2000). https://doi.org/10.1007/3-540-40922-X_8

33. Vediramana Krishnan, H.G., Vizel, Y., Ganesh, V., Gurfinkel, A.: Interpolating strong induction. In: Dillig, I., Tasiran, S. (eds.) CAV 2019. LNCS, vol. 11562, pp. 367–385. Springer, Cham (2019). https://doi.org/10.1007/978-3-030-25543-5_21

34. Wieringa, S., Niemenmaa, M., Heljanko, K.: Tarmo: a framework for parallelized bounded model checking. In: Brim, L., van de Pol, J. (eds.) Proceedings of PDMC 2009, EPTCS, vol. 14, pp. 62–76 (2009)

Generalized Property-Directed Reachability for Hybrid Systems

Kohei Suenaga[1,2]([⊠]) and Takuya Ishizawa[1]

[1] Kyoto University, Kyoto, Japan
ksuenaga@gmail.com
[2] JST PRESTO, Tokyo, Japan

Abstract. *Generalized property-directed reachability* (GPDR) belongs to the family of the model-checking techniques called IC3/PDR. It has been successfully applied to software verification; for example, it is the core of Spacer, a state-of-the-art Horn-clause solver bundled with Z3. However, it has yet to be applied to hybrid systems, which involve a continuous evolution of values over time. As the first step towards GPDR-based model checking for hybrid systems, this paper formalizes HGPDR, an adaptation of GPDR to hybrid systems, and proves its soundness. We also implemented a semi-automated proof-of-concept verifier, which allows a user to provide hints to guide verification steps.

Keywords: Hybrid systems · Property-directed reachability · IC3 · Model checking · Verification

1 Introduction

A *hybrid system* is a dynamical system that exhibits both continuous-time dynamics (called a *flow*) and discrete-time dynamics (called a *jump*). This combination of flows and jumps is an essential feature of *cyber-physical systems (CPS)*, a physical system governed by software. In the modern world where safety-critical CPS are prevalent, their correctness is an important issue.

Model checking [14,19] is an approach to guaranteeing hybrid system safety. It tries to prove that a given hybrid system does not violate a specification by abstracting its behavior and by exhaustively checking that the abstracted model conforms to the specification.

In the area of software model checking, an algorithm called *property-directed reachability (PDR)*, also known as *IC3*, is attracting interest [5,7,12]. IC3/PDR was initially proposed in the area of hardware verification; it was then transferred to software model checking by Cimatti et al. [10]. Its effectiveness for software model checking is now widely appreciated. For example, the SMT solver Z3 [29] comes with a Horn-clause solver Spacer [21] that uses PDR internally; Horn-clause solving is one of the cutting-edge techniques to verify functional programs [6,8,17] and programs with loops [6].

© Springer Nature Switzerland AG 2020
D. Beyer and D. Zufferey (Eds.): VMCAI 2020, LNCS 11990, pp. 293–313, 2020.
https://doi.org/10.1007/978-3-030-39322-9_14

We propose a model checking method for hybrid automata [3] based on the idea of PDR; the application of PDR to hybrid automata is less investigated compared to its application to software systems. Concretely, we propose an adaptation of a variant of PDR called *generalized property-directed reachability (GPDR)* proposed by Hoder and Bjørner [20]. Unlike the original PDR, which is specialized to jump-only automata-based systems, GPDR is parametrized over a map over predicates on states (i.e., a *forward predicate transformer*); the detail of the underlying dynamic semantics of a verified system is encapsulated into the forward predicate transformer. This generality of GDPR enables the application of PDR to systems outside the scope of the original PDR by itself; for example, Hoder et al. [20] show how to apply GPDR to programs with recursive function calls.

An obvious challenge in an adaptation of GPDR to hybrid automata is how to deal with flow dynamics that do not exist in software systems. To this end, we extend the logic on which the forward predicate transformer is defined so that it can express flow dynamics specified by an ordinary differential equation (ODE). Our extension, inspired by the differential dynamic logic ($d\mathcal{L}$) proposed by Platzer [32], is to introduce *continuous reachability predicates (CRP)* of the form $\langle \mathcal{D} \mid \varphi_I \rangle \varphi$ where $\mathcal{D}$ is an ODE and φ_I and φ are predicates. This CRP is defined to hold under valuation σ if there is a continuous transition from σ to certain valuation σ' that satisfies the following conditions: (1) the continuous transition is a solution of $\mathcal{D}$, (2) the valuation σ' makes φ true, and (3) φ_I is true at every point on the continuous transition. With this extended logic, we define a forward predicate transformer that faithfully encodes the behavior of a hybrid automaton. We find that we can naturally extend GPDR to hybrid automata by our predicate transformer.

We formalize our adaptation of GPDR to hybrid automata, which we call HGPDR. In the formalization, we define a forward predicate transformer that precisely expresses the behavior of hybrid automata [3] using $d\mathcal{L}$. We prove the soundness of HGPDR. We also describe our proof-of-concept implementation of HGPDR and show how it verifies a simple hybrid automaton with human intervention.

In order to make this paper self-contained, we detail GPDR for discrete-time systems before describing our adaptation to hybrid automata. After fixing the notations that we use in Sect. 2, we define a discrete-time transition system and hybrid automata in Sect. 3. Section 4 then reviews the GPDR procedure. Section 5 presents HGPDR, our adaptation of GPDR to hybrid automata, and states the soundness of the procedure. We describe a proof-of-concept implementation in Sect. 6. After discussing related work in Sect. 7, we conclude in Sect. 8.

For readability, several definitions and proofs are presented in the appendices.

2   Preliminary

We write $\mathbb{R}$ for the set of reals. We fix a finite set $V := \{x_1, \ldots, x_N\}$ of *variables*. We often use primed variables x' and x''. The prime notation also applies to a set of variables; for example, we write V' for $\{x'_1, \ldots, x'_N\}$. We use metavariable

x for a finite sequence of variables. We write **Fml** for the set of quantifier-free first-order formulas over $V \cup V' \cup V''$; its elements are ranged over by φ. We call elements of the set $\Sigma := (V \cup V' \cup V'') \to \mathbb{R}$ a *valuations*; they are represented by metavariable σ. We use the prime notation for valuations. For example, if $\sigma \in V \to \mathbb{R}$, then we write σ' for $\{x'_1 \mapsto \sigma(x_1), \ldots, x'_N \mapsto \sigma(x_N)\}$. We write $\sigma[x \mapsto r]$ for the valuation obtained by updating the entry for x in σ with r. We write $\sigma \models \varphi$ if σ is a model of φ; $\sigma \not\models \varphi$ if $\sigma \models \varphi$ does not hold; $\models \varphi$ if $\sigma \models \varphi$ for any σ; and $\not\models \varphi$ if there exists σ such that $\sigma \not\models \varphi$. We sometimes identify a valuation σ with a logical formula $\bigwedge_{x \in V} x = \sigma(x)$.

3   State-Transition Systems and Verification Problem

We review the original GPDR for discrete-time systems [20] in Sect. 4 before presenting our adaptation for hybrid systems in Sect. 5. This section defines the models used in these explanations (Sects. 3.1 and 3.2) and formally states the verification problem that we tackle (Sect. 3.3).

3.1   Discrete-Time State-Transition Systems (DTSTS)

We model a discrete-time program by a state-transition system.

Definition 3.1. *A* discrete-time state-transition system (DTSTS) *is a tuple* $\langle Q, q_0, \varphi_0, \delta \rangle$. *We use metavariable* $\mathcal{S}_D$ *for DTSTS.* $Q = \{q_0, q_1, q_2, \ldots\}$ *is a set of* locations. q_0 *is the initial location.* φ_0 *is the formula that has to be satisfied by the initial valuation.* $\delta \subseteq Q \times \mathbf{Fml} \times \mathbf{Fml} \times Q$ *is the transition relation. We write* $\langle q, \sigma_1 \rangle \to_\delta \langle q', \sigma_2 \rangle$ *if* $\langle q, \varphi, \varphi_c, q' \rangle \in \delta$ *where* $\sigma_1 \models \varphi$ *and* $\sigma_1 \cup \sigma'_2 \models \varphi_c$; *we call relation* $\to_\delta$ *the* jump transition. *A* run *of a DTSTS* $\langle Q, q_0, \varphi_0, \delta \rangle$ *is a finite sequence* $\langle q^0, \sigma_0 \rangle, \langle q^1, \sigma_1 \rangle, \ldots, \langle q^N, \sigma_N \rangle$ *where (1)* $q^0 = q_0$, *(2)* $\sigma_0 \models \varphi_0$, *and (3)* $\langle q^i, \sigma_i \rangle \to_\delta \langle q^{i+1}, \sigma_{i+1} \rangle$ *for any* $i \in [0, N-1]$.

$\langle q, \varphi, \varphi_c, q' \rangle \in \delta$ intuitively means that, if the system is at the location q with valuation σ_1 and $\sigma_1 \models \varphi$, then the system can make a transition to the location q' and change its valuation to σ'_2 such that $\sigma_1 \cup \sigma'_2 \models \varphi_c$. We call φ the *guard* of the transition. φ_c is a predicate over $V \cup V'$ that defines the *command* of the transition; it defines how the value of the variables may change in this transition. The elements of V represent the values before the transition whereas those of V' represent the values after the transition.

$$x > 0 \wedge sum' = sum + x \wedge x' = x - 1$$

$$x \geq 0 \wedge sum = 0 \longrightarrow \boxed{q_0} \xrightarrow{x \leq 0} \boxed{q_1}$$

Fig. 1. An example of DTSTS

Example 3.2. Figure 1 is an example of a DTSTS that models a program to compute the value of $1 + \cdots + x$; $Q := \{q_0, q_1\}$ and $\varphi_0 := x \geq 0 \wedge$ $sum = 0$. In the transition from q_0 to q_0, the guard is $x > 0$; the command is $sum' = sum + x \wedge x' = x - 1$. In the transition from q_0 to q_1, the guard is $x \leq 0$; the command is $x' = x \wedge sum' = sum$ because this transition does not change the value of x and sum. Therefore, the transition relation $\delta = \{\langle q_0, x > 0, sum' = sum + x \wedge x' = x - 1, q_0 \rangle, \langle q_0, x \leq 0, x' = x \wedge sum' = sum, q_1 \rangle\}$. The finite sequence $\langle q_0, \{x \mapsto 3, sum \mapsto 0\}\rangle, \langle q_0, \{x \mapsto 2, sum \mapsto 3\}\rangle, \langle q_0, \{x \mapsto 1, sum \mapsto 5\}\rangle, \langle q_0, \{x \mapsto 0, sum \mapsto 6\}\rangle,$ $\langle q_1, \{x \mapsto 0, sum \mapsto 6\}\rangle$ is a run of the DTSTS Fig. 1.

3.2   Hybrid Automaton (HA)

We model a hybrid system by a hybrid automaton (HA) [3]. We define an HA as an extension of DTSTS as follows.

Definition 3.3. *A hybrid automaton (HA) is a tuple $\langle Q, q_0, \varphi_0, F, inv, \delta \rangle$. The components Q, q_0, φ_0, and δ are the same as Definition 3.1. We use metavariable S_H for HA. F is a map from Q to ODE on V that specifies the flow dynamics at each location; inv is a map from Q to **Fml** that specifies the* stay condition[1] *at each state.*

A state of a hybrid automaton is a tuple $\langle q, \sigma \rangle$. A run of $\langle Q, q_0, \varphi_0, F, inv, \delta \rangle$ is a sequence of states $\langle q_0, \sigma_0 \rangle \langle q_1, \sigma_1 \rangle \ldots \langle q_n, \sigma_n \rangle$ where $\sigma_0 \models \varphi_0$. The system is allowed to make a transition from $\langle q_i, \sigma_i \rangle$ to $\langle q_{i+1}, \sigma_{i+1} \rangle$ if (1) σ_i reaches a valuation σ' along with the flow dynamics specified by $F(q_i)$, (2) $inv(q_i)$ holds at every point on the flow, and (3) $\langle q_i, \sigma' \rangle$ can jump to $\langle q_{i+1}, \sigma_{i+1} \rangle$ under the transition relation δ. In order to define the set of runs formally, we need to define the continuous-time dynamics that happens within each location.

Definition 3.4. *Let $\mathcal{D}$ be an ordinary differential equation (ODE) on V and let $x_1(t), \ldots, x_n(t)$ be a solution of $\mathcal{D}$ where t is the time. Let us write $\sigma^{(t)}$ for the valuation $\{x_1 \mapsto x_1(t), \ldots, x_n \mapsto x_n(t)\}$. We write $\sigma \rightarrow_{\mathcal{D}, \varphi} \sigma'$ if (1) $\sigma = \sigma^{(0)}$ and (2) there exists $t' \geq t$ such that $\sigma' = \sigma^{(t')}$ and $\sigma^{(t'')} \models \varphi$ for any $t'' \in (0, t']$. We call relation $\rightarrow_{\mathcal{D}, \varphi}$ the flow transition.*

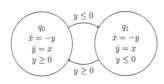

Fig. 2. An example of a hybrid automaton.

Intuitively, the relation $\sigma \rightarrow_{\mathcal{D}, \varphi} \sigma'$ means that there is a trajectory from the state represented by σ to that represented by σ' such that (1) the trajectory is a solution of $\mathcal{D}$ and (2) φ holds at any point on the trajectory. For example, let $\mathcal{D}$ be $\dot{x} = v, \dot{v} = 1$, where x and v are time-dependent variables; $\dot{x}$ and $\dot{v}$ are their time derivative. The solution of $\mathcal{D}$ is $v = t + v_0$ and

---

[1] We use the word "stay condition" instead of the standard terminology "invariant" following Kapur et al. [23].

$x = \frac{t^2}{2} + v_0 t + x_0$ where t is the elapsed time, x_0 is the initial value of x, and v_0 is the initial value of v. Therefore, $\{x \mapsto 0, v \mapsto 0\} \to_{\mathcal{D}, true} \{x \mapsto \frac{1}{2}, v \mapsto 1\}$ holds because $(x, v) = (\frac{1}{2}, 1)$ is the state at $t = 1$ on the above solution with $x_0 = 0$ and $v_0 = 0$. $\{x \mapsto 0, v \mapsto 0\} \to_{\mathcal{D}, x \geq 0} \{x \mapsto \frac{1}{2}, v \mapsto 1\}$ also holds because the condition $x \geq 0$ continues to hold along with the trajectory from $(x, v) = (0, 0)$ to $(\frac{1}{2}, 1)$. However, $\{x \mapsto 0, v \mapsto 0\} \to_{\mathcal{D}, x \geq \frac{1}{4}} \{x \mapsto \frac{1}{2}, v \mapsto 1\}$ does *not* hold because the condition $x \geq \frac{1}{4}$ does not hold for the initial $\frac{1}{\sqrt{2}}$ seconds in this trajectory.

Using this relation, we can define a run of an HA as follows.

Definition 3.5. *A finite sequence* $\langle q^0, \sigma_0 \rangle, \langle q^1, \sigma_1 \rangle, \ldots, \langle q^N, \sigma_N \rangle$ *is called a run of an HA* $\langle Q, q_0, \varphi_0, F, inv, \delta \rangle$ *if (1)* $q^0 = q_0$, *(2)* $\sigma_0 \models \varphi_0$, *(3) for any* i, *if* $0 \leq i \leq N - 2$, *there exists* $\langle q^i, \varphi_i, \varphi_c^i, q^{i+1} \rangle \in \delta$ *and* σ^I *such that* $\sigma_i \to_{F(q^i), inv(q^i)} \sigma^I$ *and* $\sigma^I \models \varphi_i$ *and* $\langle q^i, \sigma^I \rangle \to_\delta \langle q^{i+1}, \sigma_{i+1} \rangle$, *and (4)* $\sigma_{N-1} \to_{F(q^{N-1}), inv(q^{N-1})} \sigma_N$.

Remark 3.6. This definition is more complicated than that of runs of DTSTS because we need to treat the last transition from $\langle q^{N-1}, \sigma_{N-1} \rangle$ to $\langle q^N, \sigma_N \rangle$ differently than the other transitions. Each transition from $\langle q^i, \sigma_i \rangle$ to $\langle q^{i+1}, \sigma_{i+1} \rangle$, if $0 \leq i \leq N - 2$, is a flow transition followed by a jump transition; however, the last transition consists only of a flow transition.

Example 3.7. Figure 2 shows a hybrid automaton with $Q := \{q_0, q_1\}$ schematically. Each circle represents a location q; we write $F(q)$ for the ODE associated with each circle. Each edge between circles represents a transition; we present the guard of the transition on each edge. We omit the φ_c part; it is assumed to be the do-nothing command represented by $\wedge_{x \in V} x' = x$.

Both locations are equipped with the same flow that is the anticlockwise circle around the point $(x, y) = (0, 0)$ on the xy plane. The system can stay at q_0 as long as $y \geq 0$ and at q_1 as long as $y \leq 0$. $y = 0$ holds whenever a transition is invoked. Indeed, for example, $inv(q_0) = y \geq 0$ and the guard from q_0 to q_1 is $y \leq 0$; therefore, when the transition is invoked, $inv(q_0) \wedge y \leq 0$ holds, which is equivalent to $y = 0$.

Starting from the valuation $\sigma_0 := \{x \mapsto 1, y \mapsto 0\}$ at location q_0, the system reaches $\sigma_1 := \{x \mapsto -1, y \mapsto 0\}$ by the flow $F(q_0)$ along which $inv(q_0) \equiv y \geq 0$ continues to hold; then the transition from q_0 to q_1 is invoked. After that, the system reaches $\sigma_2 := \{x \mapsto 0, y \mapsto -1\}$ by $F(q_1)$. Therefore, $\langle q_0, \sigma_0 \rangle \langle q_1, \sigma_1 \rangle \langle q_1, \sigma_2 \rangle$ is a run of this HA.

3.3 Safety Verification Problem

Definition 3.8. *We say that* σ *is reachable in DTSTS* $\mathcal{S}_D$ *(resp., HA* $\mathcal{S}_H$) *if there is a run of* $\mathcal{S}_D$ *(resp.,* $\mathcal{S}_H$) *that reaches* $\langle q, \sigma \rangle$ *for some* q. *A safety verification problem (SVP) for a DTSTS* $\langle \mathcal{S}_D, \varphi \rangle$ *(resp., HA* $\langle \mathcal{S}_H, \varphi \rangle$) *is the problem to decide whether* $\sigma' \models \varphi$ *holds for all the reachable valuation* σ' *of the given* $\mathcal{S}_D$ *(resp.,* $\mathcal{S}_H$).

If an SVP is affirmatively solved, then the system is said to be *safe*; otherwise, the system is said to be *unsafe*. One of the major strategies for proving the safety of a system is discovering its *inductive invariant*.

Definition 3.9. – *Let* $\langle \mathcal{S}_D, \varphi_P \rangle$ *be an SVP for DTSTS where* $\mathcal{S}_D = \langle Q, q_0, \varphi_0, \delta \rangle$. *Then, a function* $R : Q \to \mathbf{Fml}$ *is called an inductive invariant if (1)* $\models \varphi_0 \implies R(q_0)$; *(2) if* $\sigma \models R(q)$ *and* $\langle q, \sigma \rangle \to_\delta \langle q', \sigma' \rangle$, *then* $\sigma' \models R(q')$; *and (3)* $\models R(q) \implies \varphi_P$ *for any q.*
- *Let* $\langle \mathcal{S}_H, \varphi_P \rangle$ *be an SVP for HA where* $\mathcal{S}_H = \langle Q, q_0, \varphi_0, F, inv, \delta \rangle$. *Then, a function* $R : Q \to \mathbf{Fml}$ *is called an inductive invariant if (1)* $\models \varphi_0 \implies R(q_0)$; *(2) if* $\sigma \models R(q)$ *and* $\langle q, \sigma \rangle \to_{F(q), inv(q)} \langle q'', \sigma'' \rangle$ *and* $\langle q'', \sigma'' \rangle \to_\delta \langle q', \sigma' \rangle$, *then* $\sigma' \models R(q')$; *and (3)* $\models R(q) \implies \varphi_P$ *for any q.*

Unsafety can be proved by discovering a *counterexample*.

Definition 3.10. *Define* $\mathcal{S}_D$, φ_P, *and* $\mathcal{S}_H$ *as in Definition 3.9. A run* $\langle \sigma_0, q_0 \rangle \ldots \langle \sigma_N, q_N \rangle$ *of* $\mathcal{S}_D$ *(resp.* $\mathcal{S}_H$*) is called a counterexample to the SVP* $\langle \mathcal{S}_D, \varphi_P \rangle$ *(resp.* $\langle \mathcal{S}_H, \varphi_P \rangle$*) if* $\sigma_N \models \neg\varphi_P$.

GPDR is a procedure that tries to find an inductive invariant or a counterexample to a given SVP. SVP is in general undecidable. Therefore, the original GPDR approach [20] and our extension with hybrid systems presented in Sect. 5 do not terminate for every input.

4   GPDR for DTSTS

Before presenting our extension of GPDR with hybrid systems, we present the original GPDR procedure by Hoder and Bjørner [20] in this section. (The GPDR presented here, however, is slightly modified from the original one; see Remark 4.4.)

Given a safety verification problem $\langle \mathcal{S}_D, \varphi_P \rangle$ where $\mathcal{S}_D = \langle Q, q_0, \varphi_0, \delta \rangle$, GPDR tries to find (1) an inductive invariant to prove the safety of $\mathcal{S}_D$, or (2) a counterexample to refute the safety. To this end, GPDR (nondeterministically) manipulates a data structure called *configurations*. A configuration is either **Valid**, **Model** M, or an expression of the form $M \parallel R_0, \ldots, R_N; N$. We explain each component of the expression $M \parallel R_0, \ldots, R_N; N$ in the following. (**Valid** and **Model** M are explained later.)

- $R_0, \ldots, R_N$ is a finite sequence of maps from Q to $\mathbf{Fml}$ (i.e., elements of $\mathbf{Fml}$). Each R_i is called a *frame*. The frames are updated during an execution of GPDR so that $R_i(q_j)$ is an overapproximation of the states that are reachable within i steps from the initial state in $\mathcal{S}_D$ and whose location is q_j.
- N is the index of the last frame.
- M is a finite sequence of the form $\langle \sigma_i, q_i, i \rangle, \langle \sigma_i, q_i, i+1 \rangle, \ldots, \langle \sigma_N, q_N, N \rangle$. This sequence is a candidate partial counterexample that starts from the one that is i-step reachable from the initial state and that ends up with a state $\langle \sigma_N, q_N \rangle$ such that $\sigma_N \models \neg\varphi_P$. Therefore, in order to prove the safety of $\mathcal{S}_D$, a GPDR procedure needs to prove that $\langle q_i, \sigma_i \rangle$ is unreachable within i steps from an initial state.

In order to formalize the above intuition, GPDR uses a *forward predicate transformer* determined by $\mathcal{S}_D$. In the following, we fix an SVP $\langle \mathcal{S}_D, \varphi_P \rangle$.

Definition 4.1. $\mathcal{F}(R)(q')$, *where* $\mathcal{F}$ *is called the* forward predicate transformer *determined by* $\mathcal{S}_D$, *is the following formula:*

$$(q' = q_0 \wedge \varphi_0) \vee \bigvee_{(q,\varphi,\varphi_c,q') \in \delta} \exists \boldsymbol{x}''. \left(\begin{array}{c} [\boldsymbol{x}''/\boldsymbol{x}]R(q) \\ \wedge\, [\boldsymbol{x}''/\boldsymbol{x}]\varphi \wedge [\boldsymbol{x}/\boldsymbol{x}', \boldsymbol{x}''/\boldsymbol{x}]\varphi_c \end{array} \right),$$

where $\boldsymbol{x}''$ *is the sequence* $x_1'', \ldots, x_N''$.

Notice that $\mathcal{F}(\lambda q.false)$ is equivalent to φ_0. Intuitively, $\sigma' \models \mathcal{F}(R)(q')$ holds if $\langle q', \sigma' \rangle$ is an initial state (i.e., $q' = q_0$ and $\sigma' \models \varphi_0$) or $\langle q', \sigma' \rangle$ is reachable in 1-step transition from a state that satisfies R. The latter case is encoded by the second disjunct of the above definition: The valuation σ' satisfies the second disjunct if there are q, φ, and φ_c such that $(q, \varphi, \varphi_c, q') \in \delta$ (i.e., q' is 1-step after q in δ) and there is a valuation σ such that $\sigma \models R(q) \wedge \varphi$ (i.e., σ satisfies the precondition $R(q)$ and the guard φ) and σ' is a result of executing command c under σ.

The following lemma guarantees that $\mathcal{F}$ soundly approximates the transition of an DTSTS.

Lemma 4.2. *If* $\sigma_1 \models R(q_1)$ *and* $\langle q_1, \sigma_1 \rangle \rightarrow_\delta \langle q_2, \sigma_2 \rangle$, *then* $\sigma_2 \models \mathcal{F}(R)(q_2)$.

Proof. Assume $\sigma_1 \models R(q_1)$ and $\langle q_1, \sigma_1 \rangle \rightarrow_\delta \langle q_2, \sigma_2 \rangle$. Then, by definition, $(q_1, \varphi, \varphi', q_2) \in \delta$ and $\sigma_1 \models \varphi$ and $\sigma_1 \cup \sigma_2' \models \varphi_c$ for some φ and φ_c. $\sigma_1'' \cup \sigma_2 \models [\boldsymbol{x}''/\boldsymbol{x}]R(q_1)$ follows from $\sigma_1 \models R(q_1)$. $\sigma_1'' \cup \sigma_2 \models [\boldsymbol{x}''/\boldsymbol{x}]\varphi$ follows from $\sigma_1 \models \varphi$. $\sigma_1'' \cup \sigma_2 \models [\boldsymbol{x}/\boldsymbol{x}', \boldsymbol{x}''/\boldsymbol{x}]\varphi_c$ follows from $\sigma_1 \cup \sigma_2' \models \varphi_c$. Therefore, $\sigma_1'' \cup \sigma_2 \models [\boldsymbol{x}''/\boldsymbol{x}]R(q_1) \wedge [\boldsymbol{x}''/\boldsymbol{x}]\varphi \wedge [\boldsymbol{x}/\boldsymbol{x}', \boldsymbol{x}''/\boldsymbol{x}]\varphi_c$. Hence, we have $\sigma_2 \models \exists \boldsymbol{x}''.[\boldsymbol{x}''/\boldsymbol{x}]R(q) \wedge [\boldsymbol{x}''/\boldsymbol{x}]\varphi \wedge [\boldsymbol{x}/\boldsymbol{x}', \boldsymbol{x}''/\boldsymbol{x}]\varphi_c$ as required.

By using the forward predicate transformer $\mathcal{F}$, we can formalize the intuition about configuration $M \parallel R_0, \ldots, R_N; N$ explained so far as follows.

Definition 4.3. *Let* $\mathcal{S}_D$ *be* $\langle Q, q_0, \varphi_0, \delta \rangle$, $\mathcal{F}$ *be the forward predicate transformer determined by* $\mathcal{S}_D$, *and* φ_P *be the safety condition to be verified. A configuration* C *is said to be* consistent *if it is (1) of the form* **Valid**, *(2) of the form* **Model** $\langle \sigma, q_0, 0 \rangle\, M$, *or (3) of the form* $M \parallel R_0, \ldots, R_N; N$ *that satisfies all of the following conditions:*

- *(Con-A)* $R_0(q_0) = \varphi_0$ *and* $R_0(q_i) = false$ *if* $q_i \neq q_0$;
- *(Con-B)* $\models R_i(q) \implies R_{i+1}(q)$ *for any* q;
- *(Con-C)* $\models R_i(q) \implies \varphi_P$ *for any* q *and* $i < N$;
- *(Con-D)* $\models \mathcal{F}(R_i)(q) \implies R_{i+1}(q)$ *for any* $i < N$ *and* q;
- *(Con-E) if* $\langle \sigma, q, N \rangle \in M$, *then* $\sigma \models R_N(q) \wedge \neg \varphi_P{}^2$; *and*
- *(Con-F) if* $\langle \sigma_1, q_1, i \rangle, \langle \sigma_2, q_2, i+1 \rangle \in M$ *and* $i < N$, *then* $\langle q_1, \varphi, \varphi_c, q_2 \rangle \in \delta$ *and* $\sigma_1, \sigma_2' \models R_i(q_1) \wedge \varphi \wedge \varphi_c$.

If C *is consistent, we write* **Con**(C).

INITIALIZE $\quad\rightsquigarrow \emptyset \parallel \langle R_0 := \mathcal{F}(\lambda q.false); N := 0\rangle$
$\qquad\qquad\qquad\qquad$ if $\forall q \in Q. \models R_0(q) \implies \varphi_P$

VALID $\qquad\quad M \parallel A \rightsquigarrow$ **Valid**
$\qquad\qquad\qquad\qquad$ if $\exists i < N. \forall q \in Q. \models R_i(q) \implies R_{i-1}(q)$

UNFOLD $\qquad M \parallel A \rightsquigarrow \emptyset \parallel A[R_{N+1} := \lambda q.true; N := N + 1]$
$\qquad\qquad\qquad\qquad$ if $\forall q \in Q. \models R_N(q) \implies \varphi_P$

INDUCTION $\quad M \parallel A \rightsquigarrow \emptyset \parallel A[R_j := \lambda q. R_j(q) \wedge R(q)]_{j=1}^{i+1}$
$\qquad\qquad\qquad\qquad$ if $\forall q \in Q. \models \mathcal{F}(\lambda q. R_i(q) \wedge R(q))(q) \implies R(q)$

CANDIDATE $\quad \emptyset \parallel A \rightsquigarrow \langle \sigma, q, N \rangle \parallel A$
$\qquad\qquad\qquad\qquad$ if $\sigma \models R_N(q) \wedge \neg\varphi_P$

DECIDE $\quad \langle \sigma_2, q_2, i + 1 \rangle M \parallel A \rightsquigarrow \langle \sigma_1, q_1, i \rangle \langle \sigma_2, q_2, i + 1 \rangle M \parallel A$
$\qquad\qquad\qquad\qquad$ if $\langle q_1, \varphi, \varphi_c, q_2 \rangle \in \delta$ and $\sigma_1, \sigma_2' \models R_i(q_1) \wedge \varphi \wedge \varphi_c$

MODEL $\qquad \langle \sigma, q_0, 0 \rangle M \parallel A \rightsquigarrow$ **Model** $\langle \sigma, q_0, 0 \rangle M$

CONFLICT $\quad \langle \sigma', q', i + 1 \rangle M \parallel A \rightsquigarrow \emptyset \parallel A[R_j \leftarrow \lambda q. R_j(q) \wedge R(q)]_{j=1}^{i+1}$
$\qquad\qquad\qquad\qquad$ if $\models R(q') \implies \neg\sigma'$ and $\forall q \in Q. \models \mathcal{F}(R_i)(q) \implies R(q)$

Fig. 3. The rules for the original PDR. Recall that $\neg\sigma'$ in the rule CONFLICT denotes the formula $\neg \left(\bigwedge_{x \in V} x = \sigma'(x) \right)$.

The GPDR procedure rewrites a configuration following the (nondeterministic) rewriting rules in Fig. 3. We add a brief explanation below; for more detailed exposition, see [20]. Although the order of the applications of the rules in Fig. 3 is arbitrary, we fix one scenario of the rule applications in the following for explanation.

1. The procedure initializes M to $\emptyset$, R_0 to $\mathcal{F}(\lambda q.false)$, and N to 0 (INITIALIZE).
2. If there are a valuation σ and a location q such that $\sigma \models R_N(q) \wedge \neg\varphi_P$ (CANDIDATE), then the procedure adds $\langle \sigma, q, N \rangle$ to M. The condition $\sigma \models R_N(q) \wedge \neg\varphi_P$ guarantees that the state $\langle q, \sigma \rangle$ violates the safety condition φ_P; therefore, the candidate $\langle \sigma, q, N \rangle$ needs to be refuted. If not, then the frame sequence is extended by setting N to $N + 1$ and R_{N+1} to $\lambda q.true$ (UNFOLD); this is allowed since $\forall q \in Q. \models R_N(q) \implies \varphi_P$ in this case.
3. The discovered $\langle q, \sigma \rangle$ is backpropagated by successive applications of DECIDE: In each application of DECIDE, for $\langle q_2, \sigma_2, i + 1 \rangle$ in M, the procedure tries to find σ and q such that $\langle q_1, \varphi, \varphi_c, q_2 \rangle \in \delta$ and $\sigma_1, \sigma_2' \models R_i(q_1) \wedge \varphi \wedge \varphi_c$ where σ_2' is the valuation obtained by replacing the domain of σ_2 with their primed counterpart. These conditions in combination guarantee $\langle q_1, \sigma_1 \rangle \rightarrow_\delta \langle q_2, \sigma_2 \rangle$ and $\sigma_1 \models R_i(q_1)$.
   (a) If this backpropagation reaches R_0 (the rule MODEL), then it reports the trace of the backpropagation returning **Model** M.
   (b) If it does not reach R_0, in which case there exists i such that $\sigma' \wedge \mathcal{F}(R_i)(q')$ is not satisfiable, then we pick a frame R such that $\models R(q') \implies \neg\sigma'$ and $\models \mathcal{F}(R_i)(q) \implies R(q)$ for any q (the rule CONFLICT). Intuitively, R is a frame that separates (1) the union of the initial states denoted by φ_0 and the states that are one-step reachable from a state denoted by $R_i(q')$ and

---

[2] We hereafter write $\langle \sigma, q, i \rangle \in M$ to express that the element $\langle \sigma, q, i \rangle$ exists in the sequence M although M is a sequence, not a set.

(2) the state denoted by $\langle q', \sigma' \rangle$. In a GPDR term, R is a *generalization* of $\neg \sigma'$. This formula is used to strengthen R_j for $j \in \{1, \ldots, i+1\}$.

4. The frame R obtained in the application of the rule CONFLICT is propagated forward by applying the rule INDUCTION. The condition $\forall q \in Q. \models \mathcal{F}(\lambda q.R_i(q) \wedge R(q))(q) \implies R(q)$ forces that R holds in the one-step transition from a states that satisfies R_i. If this condition holds, then R holds for $i+1$ steps (Theorem 4.5); therefore, we conjoin R to $R_1(q), \ldots, R_{i+1}(q)$. In order to maintain the consistency conditions (Con-E) and (Con-F), this rule clears M to the empty set to keep its consistency to the updated frames.[3]

5. If $\forall q \in Q. \models R_i(q) \implies R_{i-1}(q)$ for some $i < N$, then the verification succeeds and R_i is an inductive invariant (VALID). If such i does not exist, then we go back to Step 2.

Remark 4.4. One of the differences of the above GPDR from the original one [20] is that ours deals with the locations of a given DTSTS explicitly. In the original GPDR, information about locations are assumed to be encoded using a variable that represents the program counter. Although such extension was proposed for IC3 by Lange et al. [26], we are not aware of a variant of GPDR that treats locations explicitly.

Soundness. We fix one DTSTS $\langle Q, q_0, \varphi_0, \delta \rangle$ in this section. The correctness of the GPDR procedure relies on the following lemmas.

Lemma 4.5. Con *is invariant to any rule application of Fig. 3.*

Theorem 4.6. *If the GPDR procedure is started from the rule* INITIALIZE *and leads to* **Valid***, then the system is safe. If the GPDR procedure is started from the rule* INITIALIZE *and leads to* **Model** $\langle \sigma_0, q_0, 0 \rangle \ldots \langle \sigma_N, q_N, N \rangle$*, then the system is unsafe.*

5 HGPDR

We now present our procedure HGPDR that is an adaptation of the original GPDR to hybrid systems. An adaptation of GPDR to hybrid systems requires the following two challenges to be addressed.

1. The original definition of $\mathcal{F}$ (Definition 4.1) captures only a discrete-time transition. In our extension of GPDR, we need a forward predicate transformer that can mention a flow transition.

2. A run of an HA (Definition 3.5) differs from that of DTSTS in that its last transition consists only of flow dynamics; see Remark 3.6.

In order to address the first challenge, we extend the logic on which $\mathcal{F}$ is defined to be able to mention flow dynamics and define $\mathcal{F}$ on the extended logic (Sect. 5.1). To address the second challenge, we extend the configuration used by GPDR so that it carries an overapproximation of the states that are reachable from the last frame by a flow transition; the GPDR procedure is also extended to maintain this information correctly (Sect. 5.2).

---

[3] We could filter M so that it is consistent for the updated frame. We instead discard M here for simplicity.

5.1 Extension of Forward Predicate Transformer

In order to extend $\mathcal{F}$ to accommodate flow dynamics, we extend the logic on which $\mathcal{F}$ is defined with *continuous reachability predicates (CRP)* inspired by the differential dynamic logic $(d\mathcal{L})$ proposed by Platzer [33].

Definition 5.1. *Let $\mathcal{D}$ be an ODE over $Y := \{y_1, \ldots, y_k\} \subseteq V$. Let us write σ for $\{y_1 \mapsto e_1, \ldots, y_k \mapsto e_k\}$ and σ' for $\{y_1 \mapsto e'_1, \ldots, y_k \mapsto e'_k\}$. We define a predicate $\langle \mathcal{D} \mid \varphi \rangle \varphi'$ by: $\sigma \models \langle \mathcal{D} \mid \varphi \rangle \varphi'$ iff. $\exists \sigma'.\sigma \to_{\mathcal{D},\varphi} \sigma' \wedge \sigma' \models \varphi'$. We call a predicate of the form $\langle \mathcal{D} \mid \varphi_I \rangle \varphi$ a* continuous reachability predicate (CRP).

Using the above predicate, we extend $\mathcal{F}$ as follows.

Definition 5.2. *For an HA $\langle Q, q_0, \varphi_0, F, inv, \delta \rangle$, the forward predicate transformer $\mathcal{F}_{\mathcal{H}}(R)(q')$ is the following formula:*

$$(q' = q_0 \wedge \varphi_0) \vee$$
$$\bigvee_{(q,\varphi,\varphi_c,q') \in \delta} \exists \boldsymbol{x}''. \left(\begin{array}{l} [\boldsymbol{x}''/\boldsymbol{x}]R(q) \\ \wedge \langle [\boldsymbol{x}''/\boldsymbol{x}]F(q) \mid [\boldsymbol{x}''/\boldsymbol{x}]inv(q) \rangle ([\boldsymbol{x}''/\boldsymbol{x}]\varphi \wedge [\boldsymbol{x}/\boldsymbol{x}', \boldsymbol{x}''/\boldsymbol{x}]\varphi_c) \end{array} \right).$$

In the above definition, $[\boldsymbol{x}''/\boldsymbol{x}]F(q)$ is the ODE obtained by renaming the variables $\boldsymbol{x}$ that occur in ODE $F(q)$ with $\boldsymbol{x}''$.

We also define predicate $\mathcal{F}_C(R)(q')$ as follows:

$$\exists \boldsymbol{x}''.([\boldsymbol{x}''/\boldsymbol{x}]R(q') \wedge \langle [\boldsymbol{x}''/\boldsymbol{x}]F(q') \mid [\boldsymbol{x}''/\boldsymbol{x}]inv(q') \rangle \boldsymbol{x} = \boldsymbol{x}'').$$

Intuitively, $\sigma' \models \mathcal{F}_{\mathcal{H}}(\varphi)(q')$ holds if either (1) $\langle q', \sigma' \rangle$ is an initial state or (2) it is reachable from R by a flow transition followed a jump transition. Similarly, $\sigma' \models \mathcal{F}_C(R)(q')$ holds if σ' is reachable in a flow transition (not followed by a jump transition) from a state denoted by $R(q')$. This definition of $\mathcal{F}_{\mathcal{H}}$ is an extension of Definition 4.1 in that it encodes the "flow-transition" part of the above intuition by the CRP. In the case of $\mathcal{F}_C$, the postcondition part of the CRP is $\boldsymbol{x} = \boldsymbol{x}''$ because we do not need a jump transition in this case.

Lemma 5.3. *If $\sigma_1 \models R(q_1)$ and $\sigma_1 \to_{F(q_1), inv(q_1)} \sigma^I$ and $\langle q_1, \sigma^I \rangle \to_\delta \langle q_2, \sigma_2 \rangle$, then $\sigma_2 \models \mathcal{F}_{\mathcal{H}}(R)(q_2)$.*

Proof. Assume (1) $\sigma_1 \models R(q_1)$, (2) $\sigma_1 \to_{F(q_1), inv(q_1)} \sigma^I$, and (3) $\langle q_1, \sigma^I \rangle \to_\delta \langle q_2, \sigma_2 \rangle$. Then, by definition, (4) $(q_1, \varphi, \varphi_c, q_2) \in \delta$ and (5) $\sigma^I \models \varphi$ and (6) $\sigma^I \cup \sigma'_2 \models \varphi_c$ for some φ and φ_c. We show $\exists \boldsymbol{x}''.([\boldsymbol{x}''/\boldsymbol{x}]R(q) \wedge \langle [\boldsymbol{x}''/\boldsymbol{x}]F(q) \mid [\boldsymbol{x}''/\boldsymbol{x}]inv(q) \rangle ([\boldsymbol{x}''/\boldsymbol{x}]\varphi \wedge [\boldsymbol{x}/\boldsymbol{x}', \boldsymbol{x}''/\boldsymbol{x}]\varphi_c))$. (5) implies (7) $\sigma^I \cup \sigma'_2 \models \varphi$. (6) and (7) imply (8) $\sigma^{I''} \cup \sigma'_2 \models [\boldsymbol{x}''/\boldsymbol{x}]\varphi \wedge [\boldsymbol{x}''/\boldsymbol{x}]\varphi_c$. (2) implies (9) $\sigma_1'' \to_{[\boldsymbol{x}''/\boldsymbol{x}]F(q_1), [\boldsymbol{x}''/\boldsymbol{x}]inv(q_1)} \sigma^{I''}$. Therefore, from (8) and (9), we have (10) $\sigma_1'' \cup \sigma_2 \models \langle [\boldsymbol{x}''/\boldsymbol{x}]F(q_1) \mid [\boldsymbol{x}''/\boldsymbol{x}]inv(q_1) \rangle ([\boldsymbol{x}''/\boldsymbol{x}]\varphi \wedge [\boldsymbol{x}''/\boldsymbol{x}, \boldsymbol{x}/\boldsymbol{x}']\varphi_c)$. (Note that the variables in $\boldsymbol{x}'$ appear only in φ_c.) $\sigma_1'' \cup \sigma_2 \models [\boldsymbol{x}''/\boldsymbol{x}]R(q_1)$ follows from (1); therefore, we have $\sigma_1'' \cup \sigma_2 \models [\boldsymbol{x}''/\boldsymbol{x}]R(q_1) \wedge \langle [\boldsymbol{x}''/\boldsymbol{x}]F(q_1) \mid [\boldsymbol{x}''/\boldsymbol{x}]inv(q_1) \rangle ([\boldsymbol{x}''/\boldsymbol{x}]\varphi \wedge [\boldsymbol{x}''/\boldsymbol{x}, \boldsymbol{x}/\boldsymbol{x}']\varphi_c)$. This implies $\exists \boldsymbol{x}''.([\boldsymbol{x}''/\boldsymbol{x}]R(q) \wedge \langle [\boldsymbol{x}''/\boldsymbol{x}]F(q) \mid [\boldsymbol{x}''/\boldsymbol{x}]inv(q) \rangle ([\boldsymbol{x}''/\boldsymbol{x}]\varphi \wedge [\boldsymbol{x}/\boldsymbol{x}', \boldsymbol{x}''/\boldsymbol{x}]\varphi_c))$ as required.

$$\text{INITIALIZE} \qquad\qquad \leadsto \emptyset \parallel \langle R_0 := \mathcal{F}_\mathcal{H}(\lambda q.false); R_{rem} := \lambda q.true; N := 0\rangle$$
$$\qquad\qquad\qquad\qquad\qquad \text{if } \forall q \in Q. \models R_0(q) \implies \varphi_P$$
$$\text{VALID} \qquad\qquad M \parallel A \leadsto \textbf{Valid}$$
$$\qquad\qquad\qquad\qquad\qquad \text{if } \exists i < N. \forall q \in Q. \models R_i(q) \implies R_{i-1}(q)$$
$$\text{UNFOLD} \qquad\qquad M \parallel A \leadsto \emptyset \parallel A[R_{N+1} := \lambda q.true; R_{rem} := \lambda q.true; N := N+1]$$
$$\qquad\qquad\qquad\qquad\qquad \text{if } \forall q \in Q. \models R_{rem}(q) \implies \varphi_P$$
$$\text{INDUCTION} \qquad M \parallel A \leadsto \emptyset \parallel A[R_j := \lambda q.R_j(q) \wedge R(q)]_{j=1}^{i+1}$$
$$\qquad\qquad\qquad\qquad\qquad \text{if } \forall q \in Q. \models \mathcal{F}_\mathcal{H}(\lambda q.R_i(q) \wedge R(q))(q) \implies R(q)$$
$$\text{DECIDE} \qquad \langle \sigma_2, q_2, i+1\rangle M \parallel A \leadsto \langle \sigma_1, q_1, i\rangle \langle \sigma_2, q_2, i+1\rangle M \parallel A$$
$$\qquad\qquad\qquad\qquad\qquad \text{if } \langle q_1, \varphi, \varphi_c, q_2\rangle \in \delta \text{ and } \sigma_1, \sigma_2' \models R_i(q_1) \wedge \langle F(q_1) \mid inv(q_1)\rangle(\varphi \wedge \varphi_c)$$
$$\text{MODEL} \qquad \langle \sigma, q_0, 0\rangle M \parallel A \leadsto \textbf{Model } \langle \sigma, q_0, 0\rangle M$$
$$\text{CONFLICT} \qquad \langle \sigma', q', i+1\rangle M \parallel A \leadsto \emptyset \parallel A[R_j := \lambda q.R_j(q) \wedge R(q)]_{j=1}^{i+1}$$
$$\qquad\qquad\qquad\qquad\qquad \text{if } \models R(q') \implies \neg\sigma' \text{ and } \forall q \in Q. \models \mathcal{F}_\mathcal{H}(R_i)(q) \implies R(q)$$
$$\text{PROPAGATECONT} \qquad M \parallel A \leadsto M \parallel A[R_{rem} := \lambda q.R_{rem}(q) \wedge R(q)]$$
$$\qquad\qquad\qquad\qquad\qquad \text{if } \forall q \in Q. \models R_N(q) \vee \mathcal{F}_\mathcal{C}(R_N)(q) \implies R(q)$$
$$\text{CANDIDATECONT} \qquad \emptyset \parallel A \leadsto \langle \sigma, q, rem\rangle \parallel A$$
$$\qquad\qquad\qquad\qquad\qquad \text{if } \sigma \models R_{rem}(q) \wedge \neg\varphi_P$$
$$\text{DECIDECONT} \qquad \langle \sigma_2, q, rem\rangle \parallel A \leadsto \langle \sigma_1, q, N\rangle \langle \sigma_2, q, rem\rangle \parallel A$$
$$\qquad\qquad\qquad\qquad\qquad \text{if } \sigma_1, \sigma_2' \models R_N(q) \wedge \langle F(q) \mid inv(q)\rangle(\boldsymbol{x} = \boldsymbol{x}')$$
$$\text{CONFLICTCONT} \qquad \langle \sigma', q', rem\rangle \parallel A \leadsto \emptyset \parallel A[R_{rem} := \lambda q.R_{rem}(q) \wedge R(q)]$$
$$\qquad\qquad\qquad\qquad\qquad \text{if } R(q') \implies \neg\sigma', \text{ and } \models R_N(q') \vee \mathcal{F}_\mathcal{C}(R_N)(q') \implies R(q')$$

Fig. 4. The rules for HGPDR.

Lemma 5.4. *If* $\sigma_1 \models R(q_1)$ *and* $\sigma_1 \rightarrow_{F(q_1), inv(q_1)} \sigma_2$, *then* $\sigma_2 \models \mathcal{F}_\mathcal{C}(R)(q_1)$.

Proof. Almost the same argument as the proof of Lemma 5.3.

5.2   Extension of GPDR

We present our adaptation of GPDR for hybrid systems, which we call HGPDR. Recall that the original GPDR in Sect. 4 maintains a configuration of the form $M \parallel R_0, \ldots, R_N; N$. HGPDR uses a configuration of the form $M \parallel R_0, \ldots, R_N; R_{rem}; N$. In addition to the information in the original configurations, we add R_{rem} which we call *remainder frame*. R_{rem} overapproximates the states that are reachable from R_N within one flow transition.

Figure 4 presents the rules for HGPDR. The rules from INITIALIZE to CONFLICT are the same as Fig. 3 except that (1) INITIALIZE and UNFOLD are adapted so that they set the remainder frame to $\lambda q.true$ and (2) CANDIDATE is dropped. We explain the newly added rules.

– PROPAGATECONT discovers a fact that holds in R_{rem}. The side condition $\models R_N(q) \vee \mathcal{F}_\mathcal{C}(R_N)(q) \implies R(q)$ for any q guarantees that $R(q)$ is true at the remainder frame; hence R is conjoined to R_{rem}.
– CANDIDATECONT replaces CANDIDATE in the original procedure. It tries to find a candidate from the frame R_{rem}. The candidate $\langle q, \sigma\rangle$ found here is added to M in the form $\langle \sigma, q, rem\rangle$ to denote that $\langle q, \sigma\rangle$ is found at R_{rem}.
– DECIDECONT propagates a counterexample $\langle \sigma', q', rem\rangle$ found at R_{rem} to the previous frame R_N. This rule computes the candidate to be added to M by deciding $\sigma \cup \sigma' \models R_N(q) \wedge \langle F(q) \mid inv(q)\rangle(\boldsymbol{x} = \boldsymbol{x}')$, which guarantees that σ evolves to σ' under the flow dynamics determined by $F(q)$ and $inv(q)$.
– CONFLICT uses $\mathcal{F}_\mathcal{H}$ instead of $\mathcal{F}$ in the original GPDR. As in the rule CONFLICT in GPDR, the frame R in this rule is a generalization of $\neg\sigma'$ which is not backward reachable to R_i.

– CONFLICTCONT is the counterpart of CONFLICT for the frame R_{rem}. This rule is the same as CONFLICT except that it uses $\mathcal{F}_C$ instead of $\mathcal{F}_\mathcal{H}$; hence, R separates σ' from both the states denoted by φ_0 and the states that are reachable from R_i in a flow transition (*not* followed by a jump transition).

5.3 Soundness

In order to prove the soundness of HGPDR, we adapt the definition of **Con** in Definition 4.3 for HGPDR.

Definition 5.5. *Let S_H be $\langle Q, q_0, \varphi_0, F, inv, \delta \rangle$, $\mathcal{F}_\mathcal{H}$ and $\mathcal{F}_C$ be the forward predicate transformers determined by S_H, and φ_P be the safety condition to be verified. A configuration C is said to be* consistent *if it is* **Valid**, **Model** $\langle \sigma, q_0, 0 \rangle\, M$, *or* $\mathbf{Con}_H(M \parallel R_0, \ldots, R_N; R_{rem}; N)$ *that satisfies all of the following:*

- *(Con-A) $R_0(q_0) = \varphi_0$ and $R_0(q_i) = false$ if $q_i \neq q_0$;*
- *(Con-B-1) $\models R_i(q) \implies R_{i+1}(q)$ for any q and $i < N$;*
- *(Con-B-2) $\models R_N(q) \implies R_{rem}(q)$ for any q;*
- *(Con-C) $\models R_i(q) \implies \varphi_P$ if $i < N$;*
- *(Con-D-1) $\models \mathcal{F}_\mathcal{H}(R_i)(q) \implies R_{i+1}(q)$ for any $i < N$ and q;*
- *(Con-D-2) $\models \mathcal{F}_C(R_N)(q) \implies R_{rem}(q)$ for any q;*
- *(Con-E) if $\langle \sigma, q, rem \rangle \in M$, then $\sigma \models R_{rem}(q) \wedge \neg \varphi_P$;*
- *(Con-F-1) if $\langle \sigma_1, q_1, i \rangle, \langle \sigma_2, q_2, i+1 \rangle \in M$ and $i < N$, then $\langle q_1, \varphi, \varphi_c, q_2 \rangle \in \delta$ and $\sigma_1, \sigma_2' \models R_i(q_1) \wedge \varphi \wedge \varphi_c$; and*
- *(Con-F-2) if $\langle \sigma_1, q_1, N \rangle, \langle \sigma_2, q_2, rem \rangle \in M$, then $\langle q_1, \varphi, \varphi_c, q_2 \rangle \in \delta$ and $\sigma_1, \sigma_2' \models R_i(q_1) \wedge \varphi \wedge \varphi_c$.*

The soundness proof follows the same strategy as that of the original GPDR.

Lemma 5.6. $\mathbf{Con}_H$ *is invariant to any rule application of Fig. 4.*

Theorem 5.7. *If HGPDR is started from the rule INITIALIZE and leads to VALID, then the system is safe. If HGPDR is started from the rule INITIALIZE and leads to* **Model** $\langle \sigma_0, q_0, 0 \rangle \ldots \langle \sigma_N, q_N, N \rangle \langle \sigma_{rem}, q_{rem}, rem \rangle$, *then the system is unsafe.*

5.4 Operational Presentation of HGPDR

The definition of HGPDR in Fig. 4 is declarative and nondeterministic. For the sake of convenience of implementation, we derive an operational procedure from HGPDR; we call the operational version DETHYBRIDPDR, whose definition is in Algorithm 1.

Input: Hybrid automaton $\mathcal{S}_H := \langle Q, q_0, \varphi_0, F, inv, \delta \rangle$
Output: Model(M) if $\mathcal{S}_H$ is unsafe; M is a witnessing trace. **Valid**(R) if $\mathcal{S}_H$ is
     safe; R is an inductive invariant.

```
   // INITIALIZE
 1 N := 0; R_0 := λq.(if q = q_0 then φ_0 else false)
 2 R_1 := true; R_rem := true; M := ∅
 3 while true do
 4 │   for q ∈ Q do
 5 │   │   switch querySat(R_rem(q) ∧ ¬φ_P) do
 6 │   │   │   case Sat(σ') do
   │   │   │   │   // CANDIDATECONT
 7 │   │   │   │   M := ⟨q, σ, rem⟩
 8 │   │   │   │   switch RemoveTrace(M, R_0, ..., R_N, R_rem, N) do
 9 │   │   │   │   │   case Valid(R) do
10 │   │   │   │   │   │   return Valid(R)
11 │   │   │   │   │   case Cont(R_0, ..., R_N, R_rem) do
12 │   │   │   │   │   │   M := ∅
13 │   │   │   │   │   │   Update R_0, ..., R_N, R_rem to the returned frames
14 │   │   │   │   │   case Model(M) do
15 │   │   │   │   │   │   return Model(M)
16 │   │   │   │   end
17 │   │   │   case Unsat do
   │   │   │   │   // UNFOLD
18 │   │   │   │   M := ∅; R_{N+1} := λq.true; R_rem := λq.true; N := N + 1
19 │   │   end
20 │   end
21 end
```

Algorithm 1. Definition of DETHYBRIDPDR.

Discharging Verification Conditions. An implementation of HGPDR needs to discharge verification conditions during verification. In addition to verification conditions expressed as a satisfiability problem of a first-order predicate, which can be discharged by a standard SMT solver, DETHYBRIDPDR needs to discharge conditions including a CRP predicate. Specifically, DETHYBRIDPDR needs to deal with the following three types of problems.

– Checking whether $\delta := \psi \wedge \langle \mathcal{D} \mid \varphi_I \rangle (\wedge_{x \in V} x = \sigma'(x))$ is satisfiable or not for given first-order predicates ψ and φ_I, an ODE $\mathcal{D}$, and a valuation σ'. DETHYBRIDPDR needs to discharge this type of predicates when it decides which of DECIDECONT and CONFLICTCONT should be applied if the top of M is $\langle \sigma', q', rem \rangle$. We use Algorithm 3 for discharging δ. This algorithm searches for a valuation σ_i that witnesses the satisfiability of δ by using a time-inverted simulation of $\mathcal{D}$ as follows. Concretely, this algorithm numerically simulates $\mathcal{D}^{-1}$, the time-inverted ODE of $\mathcal{D}$, starting from the point $\{x \mapsto \sigma'(x)\}$. If it reaches a point σ_i that satisfies ψ and if all $\sigma_{i+1} \ldots \sigma'$ in the obtained solution satisfy φ_I, then σ_i witnesses the satisfiability of δ. If such σ_i does

Input: Hybrid automaton $\mathcal{S}_H := \langle Q, q_0, \varphi_0, F, inv, \delta \rangle$; Trace of counterexamples M; Frames
$R_0, \ldots, R_N, R_{rem}$; Natural number N.
Output:

```
 1  while M ≠ ∅ do
 2      if M = ⟨q′, σ′, rem⟩ M′ then
 3          switch querySat_C(R_N(q′) ∧ ⟨F(q′) | inv(q′)⟩(x = σ′(x)) do
                // DecideCont
 4              case Sat(σ) do
 5              |   M := ⟨q′, σ, N⟩ M
                // ConflictCont
 6              case Unsat(R) do
 7                  M := ∅; R_{rem} := λq.R_{rem}(q) ∧ R(q)
                    // PropagateCont
 8                  for ψ ∈ Formulas(R_N(q′)) do
 9                      switch querySat_C(R_N(q′) ∧ ⟨F(q′) | inv(q′)⟩¬ψ) do
10                          case Unsat do
11                          |   R_{rem}(q′) := R_{rem}(q′) ∧ ψ
12                          end
13                  end
14          end
15      else if M = ⟨q′, σ′, 0⟩ M′ then
                // Model
16          return Model(M)
17      else if M = ⟨q′, σ′, i⟩ M′ and 0 < i ≠ rem then
18          for ⟨q, φ, φ_c, q′⟩ ∈ δ do
19              switch querySat_C(R_{i−1}(q) ∧ ⟨F(q) | inv(q)⟩(φ ∧ φ_c ∧ x = σ′(x))) do
                    // Decide
20                  case Sat(σ) do
21                  |   M := ⟨q, σ⟩ M
                    // Conflict
22                  case Unsat(R) do
23                      for j ∈ [1, i + 1] do
24                      |   R_j := λq.R_j(q) ∧ R(q); M := ∅;
25                      end
                        // Induction
26                      for i ∈ [1, N − 1], ψ ∈ Formulas(R_i(q′)) do
27                          switch querySat_C(R_i(q′) ∧ ψ ∧ ⟨F(q′) | inv(q′)⟩¬ψ) do
28                              case Unsat do
29                              |   R_j(q′) := R_j(q′) ∧ ψ for j ∈ [1, i + 1]
30                          end
31                      end
32                  end
33          end
34      end
35  end
36  if There exists i such that ∀q. ⊨ R_{i+1}(q) ⟹ R_i(q) then
        // Valid
37      return Valid(R_i)
38  else
        // Inductive invariant is not reached yet.
39      return Cont(R_0, . . . , R_N, R_{rem})
40  end
```

Algorithm 2. Definition of *RemoveTrace*.

not exist but there is σ_i such that $\sigma_i \not\models \varphi_I$, then ψ is not backward reachable from σ' and hence δ is unsatisfiable. In this case, Algorithm 3 needs to return a predicate that can be used as ψ' in the rule CONFLICTCONT in Fig. 4. Currently, we assume that the user provides this predicate. We expect that we can help this step of discovering ψ' by using techniques for analyzing

Input: Formula $\delta := \psi \wedge \langle \mathcal{D} \mid \varphi_I \rangle (\wedge_{x \in V} x = \sigma'(x))$ to be discharged; Number $T > 0$.
Output: $Sat(\sigma_i)$ if $\sigma_i \models \delta$; $Unsat(\psi')$ if δ is unsatisfiable and ψ' is a generalization of σ';
          aborts if satisfiability nor unsatisfiability is proved.
// $\mathcal{D}^{-1}$ is the time-inverted ODE of $\mathcal{D}$. Therefore, p is the backward solution of $\mathcal{D}$
       from σ'.

1   $\mathcal{D}^{-1} :=$ the ODE obtained by replacing all the occurrences of the variable t corresponding
       to the time to $-t$ and negating each time derivative;
2   Solve $\mathcal{D}^{-1}$ numerically from the initial point $\sigma_0 := \sigma'$;
3   Let $p := \sigma_0 \sigma_1 \ldots \sigma_{T-1}$ be the solution obtained at the Step 2;
      // i_1 is set to ∞ if there is no such i.
4   $i_1 :=$ the minimum i such that $\sigma_j \models \varphi_I$ for any $j < i$ and $\sigma_i \models \psi$;
      // i_2 is set to ∞ if there is no such i.
5   $i_2 :=$ the minimum i such that $\sigma_j \models \varphi_I$ for any $j < i$;
6   **if** $i_1 < \infty$ **then**
       // σ_{i_1} witnesses the satisfiability of δ.
7   **return** $Sat(\sigma_{i_1})$
8   **else if** $i_2 < \infty$ **then**
       // σ_{i_2} is the end point of the $\mathcal{D}^{-1}$ with the stay condition φ_I, but $\sigma_{i_2} \not\models \psi$.
       Therefore, ψ is not backward reachable from σ' along with $\mathcal{D}$. Currently, the
       user needs to provide a predicate that can be used for further refinement.
9   Obtain ψ' such that $\models \exists x_0.[x_0/x]\psi \wedge \langle [x_0/x]\mathcal{D} \mid [x_0/x]\varphi_I \rangle x_0 = x \implies \psi'$ and
       $\sigma' \not\models \psi'$ from the user;
10   **return** $Unsat(\psi')$
11 **end**
      // Cannot conclude neither satisfiability nor unsatisfibililty.
12 **abort**

Algorithm 3. Algorithm for discharging $\delta := \psi \wedge \langle \mathcal{D} \mid \varphi_I \rangle (\wedge_{x \in V} x = \sigma'(x))$.

continuous dynamics (e.g., automated synthesizer of barrier certificates [34] and Flow* [9] in combination with Craig interpolant synthesis procedures [2, 31]). If neither holds, then we give up the verification by aborting; this may happen if, for example, the value of T is too small.

- Checking whether $\delta' := \psi \wedge \langle F(q) \mid inv(q) \rangle (\varphi \wedge \varphi_c \wedge x = \sigma'(x))$ is satisfiable or not. DETHYBRIDPDR needs to solve this problem in the choice between DECIDE and CONFLICT. This query is different from the previous case in that the formula that appears after $\langle F(q) \mid inv(q) \rangle$ in δ' is $\varphi \wedge \varphi_c \wedge x = \sigma'(x)$, not $x = \sigma'(x)$; therefore, we cannot use numerical simulation to discharge δ'. Although it is possible to adapt Algorithm 3 to maintain the sequence of *predicates* $\alpha_0 \alpha_1 \ldots \alpha_{T-1}$ instead of *valuations* so that each α_i becomes the preimage of α_{i-1} by $\mathcal{D}$, the preimage computation at each step is prohibitively expensive. Instead, the current implementation restricts the input system so that there exists at most one σ such that $\sigma \models \varphi \wedge \varphi_c \wedge x = \sigma'(x)$ for any σ'; if this is met, then one can safely use Algorithm 3 for discharging δ'. Concretely, we allow only φ_c that corresponds to the command whose syntax is given by $c:: = \mathbf{skip} \mid x := r_1 x + r_2 \mid x := r_1 x - r_2$ where $\mathbf{skip}$ is a command that does nothing; r_1 and r_2 are real constants.
- Checking whether $\varphi_1 \wedge \langle \mathcal{D} \mid \varphi_I \rangle \neg \varphi_2$ is unsatisfiable. DETHYBRIDPDR needs to discharge this type of queries when it applies INDUCTION or PROPAGATECONT. This case is different from the previous case in that (1) DETHYBRIDPDR may answer *Otherwise* without aborting the entire verification if unsatisfiability nor satisfiability is proved, and (2) DETHYBRIDPDR

Input: Formula $\varphi_1 \wedge \langle \dot{x} = f(x) \mid \varphi_I \rangle \neg \varphi_2$ to be discharged; Number $r > 0$.

Output: *Unsat* or *Otherwise*; if *Unsat* is returned then the input formula is unsatisfiable.

1 **if** $\varphi_1 \wedge \varphi_2$ *is satisfiable* **then**
2 | **return** *Otherwise*
3 **end**
4 Let dt be a fresh symbol;
    // Checking φ_1 is invariant throughout the dynamics determined by
    $\dot{x} = f(x)$ and $\models \varphi_1 \implies \neg\varphi_2$.
5 **if** $r > dt > 0 \wedge \varphi_1 \wedge \varphi_I \wedge \neg[x + f(x)dt/x]\varphi_1$ *and* $\varphi_1 \wedge \varphi_2$ *are unsatisfiable* **then**
6 | **return** *Unsat*
7 **end**
    // Checking $\neg\varphi_2$ is invariant throughout in the dynamics determined
    by $\dot{x} = f(x)$ and $\models \varphi_1 \implies \neg\varphi_2$.
8 **if** $r > dt > 0 \wedge \neg\varphi_2 \wedge \varphi_I \wedge [x + f(x)dt/x]\varphi_2$ *and* $\varphi_1 \wedge \varphi_2$ *are unsatisfiable* **then**
9 | **return** *Unsat*
10 **end**
11 **return** *Otherwise*

Algorithm 4. Algorithm for discharging $\varphi_1 \wedge \langle \dot{x} = f(x) \mid \varphi_I \rangle \neg \varphi_2$.

does not need to return a generalization if the given predicate is unsatisfiable. We use Algorithm 4 to discharge this type of queries. This algorithm first checks the satisfiability of $\varphi_1 \wedge \varphi_2$ in Step 1; if it is satisfiable, then so is the entire formula. Then, Step 5 tries to prove that the entire formula is unsatisfiable by proving (1) φ_1 is invariant with respect to the dynamics specified by $\mathcal{D}$ and φ_I and (2) $\varphi_1 \wedge \varphi_2$ is unsatisfiable. In order to prove the former, the algorithm tries the following sufficient condition: For any positive dt that is smaller than a positive real number r, $\models \varphi_i \wedge \varphi_I \implies [x + f(x)dt/x]\varphi_1$, where $\mathcal{D} \equiv \dot{x} = f(x)$.[4] Step 8 tries the same strategy but tries to prove that $\neg\varphi_2$ is invariant. If both attempts fail, then the algorithm returns *Otherwise*.[5] This algorithm could be further enhanced by incorporating automated invariant-synthesis procedures [15,28,35]; exploration of this possibilities is left as future work.

6 Proof-of-Concept Implementation

We implemented DETHYBRIDPDR as a semi-automated verifier. We note that the current implementation is intended to be a proof of concept; extensive experiments are left as future work. The snapshot of the source code as of writing can be found at https://github.com/ksuenaga/HybridPDR/tree/master/src.

---

[4] This strategy is inspired by the previous work by one of the authors on nonstandard programming [18,30,36,37].

[5] If the flow specified by $\mathcal{D}$ is a linear or a polynomial, then we can apply the procedure proposed by Liu et al. [28], which is proved to be sound and complete for such a flow.

The verifier takes a hybrid automaton $\mathcal{S}_H$ specified with SPACEEX modeling language [27], the initial location q_0, the initial condition φ_0, and the safety condition φ_P as input; then, it applies DETHYBRIDPDR to discover an inductive invariant or a counterexample. The frontend of the verifier is implemented with OCaml; in the backend, the verifier uses Z3 [29] and ODEPACK [1] to discharge verification conditions.

As we mentioned in Sect. 5.4, when a candidate counterexample $\langle q', \sigma', i + 1 \rangle$ turns out to be backward unreachable to R_i, then our verifier asks for a generalization of σ' to the user; concretely, for example in an application of the rule CONFLICT, the user is required to give ψ such that $\models \psi \implies \neg \sigma'$ and $\models (q, \varphi, \varphi_c, q') \in \delta \wedge [\boldsymbol{x_0}/\boldsymbol{x}]R_i(q) \wedge \langle [\boldsymbol{x_0}/\boldsymbol{x}]F(q) \mid [\boldsymbol{x_0}/\boldsymbol{x}]inv(q)\rangle[\boldsymbol{x_0}/\boldsymbol{x}, \boldsymbol{x_0}/\boldsymbol{x}](\varphi \wedge \varphi_c) \implies \psi$ and $\models R_0(q') \implies \psi$. Instead of throwing this query at the user in this form, the verifier asks the following question in order to make this process easier for the user for each $(q, \varphi, \varphi_c, q') \in \delta$:

Pre:$R_i(q)$; Flow:$F(q)$; Stay:$inv(q)$; Guard:φ; Cmd:φ_c; CE:σ'; Init:$R_0(q')$.

In applying CONFLICTCONT, the verifier omits the fields Guard and Cmd.

We applied the verifier to the hybrid automaton in Fig. 2 with several initial conditions and the safety condition $\varphi_P := x \leq 1$. We remark that the outputs from the verifier presented here are post-processed for readability. We explain how verification is conducted in each setting; we write $\mathcal{D}$ for the ODE $\dot{x} = -y, \dot{y} = x$.

- Initial condition $x = 0 \wedge y = 0$ at location q_0: The verifier finds the inductive invariant $\{q_0 \mapsto x = 0 \wedge y = 0, q_1 \mapsto x = 0 \wedge y = 0\}$ after asking for proofs of unsatisfiability to the user 5 times.
- Initial condition $x \leq \frac{1}{2}$ at location q_0: The verifier finds a counterexample $\{x \mapsto 0.490533, y \mapsto 1.93995\}$, from which the system reaches $\{x \mapsto 2.00100, y \mapsto 0\}$. The verifier asks 5 questions, one of which is the following:

  > Pre: $(x \leq 1 \wedge y \geq 0) \vee x \leq 0.5$; Flow: $\mathcal{D}$; Stay: $y \geq 0$;
  > Guard: $y \leq 0$; Cmd: skip; CE: $\{x \mapsto 0.998516; y \mapsto -1.889365\}$;
  > Init: $x \leq 0.5$.

  Notice that the stay condition is $y \geq 0$ and the guard is $y \leq 0$; therefore the predicate $y = 0$ holds when a jump transition happens. Since the flow specified by $\mathcal{D}$ is an anticlockwise circle whose center is $\{x \mapsto 0, y \mapsto 0\}$ with the stay condition $y \geq 0$, the states after the flow dynamics followed by a jump transition is $x \leq 0.5 \wedge y = 0$, which indeed does not intersect with $x = 0.998516 \wedge y = -1.889365$. The verification proceeds by giving $y \geq 0$ as a generalization in this case.
- Initial condition $0 \leq x \leq \frac{1}{2} \wedge 0 \leq y \leq \frac{1}{2}$ at location q_0: The verifier finds an inductive invariant

$$R := \left\{ \begin{array}{l} q_0 \mapsto (y = 0 \wedge 0 \leq x \leq 0.707107) \vee (0 \leq x \leq 0.5 \wedge 0 \leq y \leq 0.5), \\ q_1 \mapsto y = 0 \wedge -0.707107 \leq x \leq 0 \end{array} \right\}$$

after asking for 8 generalizations to the user. This is indeed an inductive invariant. Noting $0.707107 \approx \frac{1}{\sqrt{2}}$, we can confirm that (1) the states that are reachable by flow dynamics followed by a jump transition is the set denoted by $R(q_0)$; the same holds for the transition from $R(q_1)$; (2) it contains the initial condition $0 \leq x \leq 0.5 \wedge 0 \leq y \leq 0.5$ at location q_0; and (3) it does not intersect with the unsafe region $x > 1$. The following is one of the questions that are asked by the verifier:

Pre: $(y = 0 \wedge -0.707107 \leq x \leq 0) \vee (0 \leq x \leq 0.5 \wedge 0 \leq y \leq 0.5)$;
Flow: $\mathcal{D}$; Stay: $y \leq 0$; CE: $\{x \mapsto 0.998516; y \mapsto -1.889365\}$;
Init: *false*.

Instead of a precise overapproximation $(x^2 + y^2 = 0.5 \wedge y \leq 0) \vee (0 \leq x \leq 0.5 \wedge 0 \leq y \leq 0.5)$ of the reachable states, we give $(-0.707107 \leq y \leq 0 \wedge -0.707107 \leq x \leq 0.707107) \vee (0 \leq x \leq 0.5 \wedge 0 \leq y \leq 0.5)$, which progresses the verification.

7   Related Work

Compared to its success in software verification [5,10,12,20,21], IC3/PDR for hybrid systems is less investigated. HyComp [11,13] is a model checker that can use several techniques (e.g., IC3, bounded model checking, and k-induction) in its backend. Before verifying a hybrid system, HyComp discretizes its flows so that the verification can be conducted using existing SMT solvers that do not directly deal with continuous-time dynamics. Compared to HyComp, HGPDR does not necessarily require prior discretization for verification. We are not aware of an IC3/PDR-based model checking algorithm for hybrid systems that does not require prior discretization.

Kindermann et al. [24,25] propose an application of PDR for a timed system—a system that is equipped with *clock variables*; the flow dynamics of a clock variable c is limited to $\dot{c} = 1$. A clock variable may be also reset to a constant in a jump transition. Kindermann et al. finitely abstract the state space of clock variables by using region abstraction [38]. The abstracted system is then verified using the standard PDR procedure. Later Isenberg et al. [22] propose a method that abstracts clock variables by using zone abstraction [4]. They do not deal with a hybrid system whose flow behavior at each location cannot be described by $\dot{c} = 1$; the system in Fig. 2 is out of the scope of their work.

Our continuous-reachability predicates (CRP) are inspired by Platzer's $d\mathcal{L}$ [33]. We may be able to use the theorem prover KeYmaera X for $d\mathcal{L}$ predicates [16] for our purpose of discharging CRP.

8   Conclusion

We proposed an adaptation of GPDR to hybrid systems. For this adaptation, we extended the logic on which the forward predicate transformer is defined with the continuous reachability predicates $\langle \mathcal{D} \mid \varphi_I \rangle \varphi$ inspired by the differential dynamic logic $d\mathcal{L}$. The extended forward predicate transformer can precisely express the behavior of hybrid systems. We formalized our procedure HGPDR and proved its soundness. We also implemented it as a semi-automated procedure, which proves the safety of a simple hybrid system in Fig. 2.

On top of the current proof-of-concept implementation, we plan to implement a GPDR-based model checker for hybrid systems. We expect that we need to improve the heuristic used in the application of the rule INDUCTION, where we currently check sufficient conditions of the verification condition. We are also looking at automating part of the work currently done by human in verification; this is essential when we apply our method to a system with complex continuous-time dynamics.

Acknowledgements. We appreciate the comments from the anonymous reviewers, John Toman, and Naoki Kobayashi. This work is partially supported by JST PRESTO Grant Number JPMJPR15E5, JSPS KAKENHI Grant Number 19H04084, and JST ERATO MMSD project.

References

1. Hindmarsh, A.C.: ODEPACK, a systematized collection of ODE solvers. In: Stepleman, R.S., et al. (eds.) Scientific Computing, North-Holland, Amsterdam, vol. 1 of IMACS Transactions on Scientific Computation, pp. 55–64 (1983). http://www.llnl.gov/CASC/nsde/pubs/u88007.pdf
2. Albarghouthi, A., McMillan, K.L.: Beautiful interpolants. In: Sharygina, N., Veith, H. (eds.) CAV 2013. LNCS, vol. 8044, pp. 313–329. Springer, Heidelberg (2013). https://doi.org/10.1007/978-3-642-39799-8_22
3. Alur, R., Courcoubetis, C., Henzinger, T.A., Ho, P.-H.: Hybrid automata: an algorithmic approach to the specification and verification of hybrid systems. In: Grossman, R.L., Nerode, A., Ravn, A.P., Rischel, H. (eds.) HS 1991-1992. LNCS, vol. 736, pp. 209–229. Springer, Heidelberg (1993). https://doi.org/10.1007/3-540-57318-6_30
4. Behrmann, G., Bouyer, P., Larsen, K.G., Pelánek, R.: Lower and upper bounds in zone-based abstractions of timed automata. STTT **8**(3), 204–215 (2006)
5. Birgmeier, J., Bradley, A.R., Weissenbacher, G.: Counterexample to induction-guided abstraction-refinement (CTIGAR). In: Biere, A., Bloem, R. (eds.) CAV 2014. LNCS, vol. 8559, pp. 831–848. Springer, Cham (2014). https://doi.org/10.1007/978-3-319-08867-9_55
6. Bjørner, N., Gurfinkel, A., McMillan, K., Rybalchenko, A.: Horn clause solvers for program verification. In: Beklemishev, L.D., Blass, A., Dershowitz, N., Finkbeiner, B., Schulte, W. (eds.) Fields of Logic and Computation II. LNCS, vol. 9300, pp. 24–51. Springer, Cham (2015). https://doi.org/10.1007/978-3-319-23534-9_2
7. Bradley, A.R.: SAT-based model checking without unrolling. In: Jhala, R., Schmidt, D. (eds.) VMCAI 2011. LNCS, vol. 6538, pp. 70–87. Springer, Heidelberg (2011). https://doi.org/10.1007/978-3-642-18275-4_7
8. Champion, A., Chiba, T., Kobayashi, N., Sato, R.: ICE-based refinement type discovery for higher-order functional programs. In: Beyer, D., Huisman, M. (eds.) TACAS 2018. LNCS, vol. 10805, pp. 365–384. Springer, Cham (2018). https://doi.org/10.1007/978-3-319-89960-2_20

9. Chen, X., Ábrahám, E., Sankaranarayanan, S.: Flow*: an analyzer for non-linear hybrid systems. In: Sharygina, N., Veith, H. (eds.) CAV 2013. LNCS, vol. 8044, pp. 258–263. Springer, Heidelberg (2013). https://doi.org/10.1007/978-3-642-39799-8_18

10. Cimatti, A., Griggio, A.: Software model checking via IC3. In: Madhusudan, P., Seshia, S.A. (eds.) CAV 2012. LNCS, vol. 7358, pp. 277–293. Springer, Heidelberg (2012). https://doi.org/10.1007/978-3-642-31424-7_23

11. Cimatti, A., Griggio, A., Mover, S., Tonetta, S.: Parameter synthesis with IC3. In: Formal Methods in Computer-Aided Design, FMCAD 2013, Portland, OR, USA, October 20–23, 2013, pp. 165–168 (2013). http://ieeexplore.ieee.org/document/6679406/

12. Cimatti, A., Griggio, A., Mover, S., Tonetta, S.: IC3 modulo theories via implicit predicate abstraction. In: Ábrahám, E., Havelund, K. (eds.) TACAS 2014. LNCS, vol. 8413, pp. 46–61. Springer, Heidelberg (2014). https://doi.org/10.1007/978-3-642-54862-8_4

13. Cimatti, A., Griggio, A., Mover, S., Tonetta, S.: HyComp: an SMT-based model checker for hybrid systems. In: Baier, C., Tinelli, C. (eds.) TACAS 2015. LNCS, vol. 9035, pp. 52–67. Springer, Heidelberg (2015). https://doi.org/10.1007/978-3-662-46681-0_4

14. Clarke Jr., E.M., Grumberg, O., Peled, D.A.: Model Checking. MIT Press, Cambridge (1999)

15. Colón, M.A., Sankaranarayanan, S., Sipma, H.B.: Linear invariant generation using non-linear constraint solving. In: Hunt, W.A., Somenzi, F. (eds.) CAV 2003. LNCS, vol. 2725, pp. 420–432. Springer, Heidelberg (2003). https://doi.org/10.1007/978-3-540-45069-6_39

16. Fulton, N., Mitsch, S., Quesel, J.-D., Völp, M., Platzer, A.: KeYmaera X: an axiomatic tactical theorem prover for hybrid systems. In: Felty, A.P., Middeldorp, A. (eds.) CADE 2015. LNCS (LNAI), vol. 9195, pp. 527–538. Springer, Cham (2015). https://doi.org/10.1007/978-3-319-21401-6_36

17. Hashimoto, K., Unno, H.: Refinement type inference via horn constraint optimization. In: Blazy, S., Jensen, T. (eds.) SAS 2015. LNCS, vol. 9291, pp. 199–216. Springer, Heidelberg (2015). https://doi.org/10.1007/978-3-662-48288-9_12

18. Hasuo, I., Suenaga, K.: Exercises in *nonstandard static analysis* of hybrid systems. In: Madhusudan, P., Seshia, S.A. (eds.) CAV 2012. LNCS, vol. 7358, pp. 462–478. Springer, Heidelberg (2012). https://doi.org/10.1007/978-3-642-31424-7_34

19. Henzinger, T.A., Ho, P., Wong-Toi, H.: HYTECH: a model checker for hybrid systems. STTT 1(1–2), 110–122 (1997). https://doi.org/10.1007/s100090050008

20. Hoder, K., Bjørner, N.: Generalized property directed reachability. In: Cimatti, A., Sebastiani, R. (eds.) SAT 2012. LNCS, vol. 7317, pp. 157–171. Springer, Heidelberg (2012). https://doi.org/10.1007/978-3-642-31612-8_13

21. Hoder, K., Bjørner, N., de Moura, L.: μZ – an efficient engine for fixed points with constraints. In: Gopalakrishnan, G., Qadeer, S. (eds.) CAV 2011. LNCS, vol. 6806, pp. 457–462. Springer, Heidelberg (2011). https://doi.org/10.1007/978-3-642-22110-1_36

22. Isenberg, T., Wehrheim, H.: Timed automata verification via IC3 with zones. In: Merz, S., Pang, J. (eds.) ICFEM 2014. LNCS, vol. 8829, pp. 203–218. Springer, Cham (2014). https://doi.org/10.1007/978-3-319-11737-9_14

23. Kapur, A., Henzinger, T.A., Manna, Z., Pnueli, A.: Proving safety properties of hybrid systems. In: Langmaack, H., de Roever, W.-P., Vytopil, J. (eds.) FTRTFT 1994. LNCS, vol. 863, pp. 431–454. Springer, Heidelberg (1994). https://doi.org/10.1007/3-540-58468-4_177

24. Kindermann, R.: SMT-based verification of timed systems and software. Ph. D. thesis, Aalto University, Helsinki, Finland (2014). https://aaltodoc.aalto.fi/handle/123456789/19852
25. Kindermann, R., Junttila, T., Niemelä, I.: SMT-based induction methods for timed systems. In: Jurdziński, M., Ničković, D. (eds.) FORMATS 2012. LNCS, vol. 7595, pp. 171–187. Springer, Heidelberg (2012). https://doi.org/10.1007/978-3-642-33365-1_13
26. Lange, T., Neuhäußer, M.R., Noll, T.: IC3 software model checking on control flow automata. In: Formal Methods in Computer-Aided Design, FMCAD 2015, Austin, Texas, USA, September 27–30, 2015, pp. 97–104 (2015)
27. Lebeltel, O., Cotton, S., Frehse, G.: The SpaceEx modeling language (December 2010)
28. Liu, J., Zhan, N., Zhao, H.: Computing semi-algebraic invariants for polynomial dynamical systems. In: Proceedings of the 11th International Conference on Embedded Software, EMSOFT 2011, Part of the Seventh Embedded Systems Week, ESWeek 2011, Taipei, Taiwan, October 9–14, 2011, pp. 97–106 (2011). https://doi.org/10.1145/2038642.2038659
29. de Moura, L., Bjørner, N.: Z3: an efficient SMT solver. In: Ramakrishnan, C.R., Rehof, J. (eds.) TACAS 2008. LNCS, vol. 4963, pp. 337–340. Springer, Heidelberg (2008). https://doi.org/10.1007/978-3-540-78800-3_24
30. Nakamura, H., Kojima, K., Suenaga, K., Igarashi, A.: A nonstandard functional programming language. In: Chang, B.-Y.E. (ed.) APLAS 2017. LNCS, vol. 10695, pp. 514–533. Springer, Cham (2017). https://doi.org/10.1007/978-3-319-71237-6_25
31. Okudono, T., Nishida, Y., Kojima, K., Suenaga, K., Kido, K., Hasuo, I.: Sharper and simpler nonlinear interpolants for program verification. In: Chang, B.-Y.E. (ed.) APLAS 2017. LNCS, vol. 10695, pp. 491–513. Springer, Cham (2017). https://doi.org/10.1007/978-3-319-71237-6_24
32. Platzer, A.: Differential dynamic logic for hybrid systems. J. Autom. Reason. **41**(2), 143–189 (2008). https://doi.org/10.1007/s10817-008-9103-8
33. Platzer, A.: Differential dynamic logics. KI **24**(1), 75–77 (2010). https://doi.org/10.1007/s13218-010-0014-6
34. Prajna, S., Jadbabaie, A.: Safety verification of hybrid systems using barrier certificates. In: Alur, R., Pappas, G.J. (eds.) HSCC 2004. LNCS, vol. 2993, pp. 477–492. Springer, Heidelberg (2004). https://doi.org/10.1007/978-3-540-24743-2_32
35. Sankaranarayanan, S., Sipma, H., Manna, Z.: Non-linear loop invariant generation using gröbner bases. In: Proceedings of the 31st ACM SIGPLAN-SIGACT Symposium on Principles of Programming Languages, POPL 2004, Venice, Italy, January 14–16, 2004, pp. 318–329 (2004). https://doi.org/10.1145/964001.964028
36. Suenaga, K., Hasuo, I.: Programming with infinitesimals: a WHILE-language for hybrid system modeling. In: Aceto, L., Henzinger, M., Sgall, J. (eds.) ICALP 2011. LNCS, vol. 6756, pp. 392–403. Springer, Heidelberg (2011). https://doi.org/10.1007/978-3-642-22012-8_31
37. Suenaga, K., Sekine, H., Hasuo, I.: Hyperstream processing systems: nonstandard modeling of continuous-time signals. In: The 40th Annual ACM SIGPLAN-SIGACT Symposium on Principles of Programming Languages, POPL 2013, Rome, Italy - January 23–25, 2013, pp. 417–430 (2013). https://doi.org/10.1145/2429069.2429120
38. Wang, F.: Efficient verification of timed automata with bdd-like data structures. STTT **6**(1), 77–97 (2004). https://doi.org/10.1007/s10009-003-0135-4

Language Inclusion for Finite Prime Event Structures

Andreas Fellner[1,2], Thorsten Tarrach[1], and Georg Weissenbacher[2(✉)]

[1] AIT Austrian Institute of Technology,
1210 Vienna, Austria
{andreas.fellner,thorsten.tarrach}@ait.ac.at
[2] TU Wien, 1040 Vienna, Austria
georg.weissenbacher@tuwien.ac.at

Abstract. We study the problem of language inclusion between finite, labeled prime event structures. Prime event structures are a formalism to compactly represent concurrent behavior of discrete systems. A labeled prime event structure induces a language of sequences of labels produced by the represented system. We study the problem of deciding inclusion and membership for languages encoded by finite prime event structures and provide complexity results for both problems. We provide a family of examples where prime event structures are exponentially more succinct than formalisms that do not take concurrency into account. We provide a decision algorithm for language inclusion that exploits this succinctness. Furthermore, we provide an implementation of the algorithm and an evaluation on a series of benchmarks. Finally, we demonstrate how our results can be applied to mutation-based test case generation.

Keywords: Event structures · Language inclusion · Concurrency · Mutation-based test case generation

1 Introduction

Language inclusion is a fundamental problem in computer science which arises in numerous application domains. In its most familiar form the problem is

This work has received funding from the Electronic Component Systems for European Leadership Joint Undertaking under grant agreement No 737459 (project Productive 4.0), which receives support from the European Union Horizon 2020 research and innovation program and Germany, Austria, France, Czech Republic, Netherlands, Belgium, Spain, Greece, Sweden, Italy, Ireland, Poland, Hungary, Portugal, Denmark, Finland, Luxembourg, Norway, Turkey, from the by ECSEL Joint Undertaking under the project H2020 737469 AutoDrive—Advancing failaware, fail-safe, and fail-operational electronic components, systems, and architectures for fully automated driving to make future mobility safer, affordable, and end-user acceptable, from the LogiCS doctoral program W1255-N23 of the Austrian Science Fund (FWF) and by the Vienna Science and Technology Fund (WWTF) through the projects Heisenbugs project VRG11-005.

D. Beyer and D. Zufferey (Eds.): VMCAI 2020, LNCS 11990, pp. 314–336, 2020.
https://doi.org/10.1007/978-3-030-39322-9_15

instantiated with regular languages and finite automata [23]; an incarnation frequently occurring in formal verification and model checking is language inclusion (and intersection, respectively) for ω-regular languages and Büchi automata [9, Chapter 7]. In the latter application, the goal is to check whether a transition system conforms to a specification given in linear temporal logic. One challenge arising in automata-based model checking is that the verification of concurrent systems relies on the explicit construction of a product automaton whose size can be exponential in the number of processes. Partial Order Reduction (POR, see [20,41] and [9, Chapter 12], for instance) addresses this problem by exploiting independence between transitions to avoid the construction of the full product automaton: the reduction identifies equivalence classes of words in the language (i.e., executions) obtained by reordering commutative edges/transitions [31] and restricts the exploration to representative members of these classes. POR in its simplest form can be used to check reachability and deadlock problems; for checking temporal logic properties only transitions whose labels are "invisible" to the property are assumed to be independent [9, Chapter 12]. This renders the approach impractical for language inclusion if the alphabets of both languages are the same, e.g., when checking whether a modification is language-preserving – a question arising in the applications that motivated our work (see below).

In this paper, we focus on language inclusion for finite, labeled prime event structures, a representation of bounded executions of concurrent systems in which dependence (and independence) of transitions is made explicit. This representation can be exponentially more succinct than finite automata, as shown in Sect. 4: there are event structures with n events, such that the smallest NFA expressing the same language has at least 2^n states.

We provide an analysis of the computational complexity of checking language membership as well as inclusion between two event structures, showing that the former is NP-complete and the latter is Π_2^p-complete (Sect. 3). While a similar results to the former was proven earlier for trace languages [3], to the best of our knowledge, the latter result is novel even in the related domains of bounded trace languages and bounded labeled Petri nets.

Besides showing the complexity of the decision problems, we provide a practical decision algorithm for solving event structure language inclusion in Sect. 4. By finding suitable embeddings of one event structure in another, the algorithm determines whether the language of the former is included in the language of the latter. The algorithm iteratively refines the event structure whenever two labels occur unordered in the former structure but ordered in the latter. Moreover, the algorithm can provide counterexamples to inclusion encoded as event structures representing words that occur in the former language but not in the latter.

Section 5 provides a qualitative analysis of our representation and an experimental evaluation that highlights advantages and disadvantages of event structures in comparison to an automaton-based representation (for which language inclusion is PSPACE-complete).

Our inclusion algorithm decides whether two systems, represented as event structures, have the same behavior in terms of bounded words over a common vocabulary. This scenario arises in a range of applications: refinement or model checking, where an implementation is compared against a specification; upgrade or regression checking, where a fixed version of a software is compared against the original version; or mutation-based test case generation, where a small modification (or bug) is introduced in code to obtain a "mutant" of the original program, and the counterexample to inclusion then represents a test case which discriminates between mutant and original. We use the latter scenario, which motivated our research on language inclusion, as an exemplary application of our approach in our experiments (Sect. 5).

2 Preliminaries

In this section we introduce labeled prime event structures. Throughout this work, we assume that every set of labels $\mathcal{X}$ contains a distinct label ε, which denotes the empty symbol. Concatenation of ε to a word does not change the word.

Definition 1 (FLES). *Given a set of labels $\mathcal{X}$, a finite, $\mathcal{X}$-labeled prime event structure (FLES) is a tuple $\mathcal{E} := \langle E, <, \#, h \rangle$ where E is a finite set of events, $< \subseteq E \times E$ is a strict partial order on E, called* causality relation, *$h : E \to \mathcal{X}$ labels every event with an element of $\mathcal{X}$, and $\# \subseteq E \times E$ is the symmetric, irreflexive* conflict relation *that is* closed under $<$, *i.e. for all $e, e', e'' \in E$, if $e \# e'$ and $e' < e''$, then $e \# e''$.*

For an event e, we use $\lceil e \rceil$ to denote the history of e as the set of events that must happen before e according to $<$, formally $\lceil e \rceil := \{e' \in E \mid e' < e\}$. We require that there is a special event $\bot \in E$, such that $\lceil \bot \rceil = \varnothing$, for all events $e \in E : \bot < e$, and $h(\bot) = \varepsilon$. We define the direct successors *dsucc* of event e as the set of events that depend on e without there being another event in-between, formally $dsucc(e) = \{e' \in E \mid e < e' \land \nexists e'' : e < e'' < e'\}$. We say that two events $e, e' \in E$ are *concurrent* if $e \neq e'$, not $(e < e')$, not $(e > e')$, and not $(e \# e')$.

A central concept in assigning event structures a semantic is the notion of configurations:

Definition 2 (Configuration). *For a FLES $\mathcal{E} := \langle E, <, \#, h \rangle$, a configuration of $\mathcal{E}$ is a set of events $C = \{e_1, \ldots, e_n\} \subseteq E$ that is both*

- *Left closed: $\forall e \in C : \forall e' \in E$ such that $e' < e \implies e' \in C$, and*
- *Conflict free: $\forall e, e' \in C : \neg(e \# e')$*

A configuration C is *maximal*, if there is no configuration C' such that $C \subseteq C'$ and $C \neq C'$. We denote by $\mathcal{MC}(\mathcal{E})$ the set of all maximal configurations of an event structure $\mathcal{E}$. A *trace* τ of C is a sequence of events $\langle e_1, \ldots, e_n \rangle$, where every event $e \in C$ occurs exactly once in the sequence and for all $e_i, e_j \in \tau : e_i < e_j \implies i < j$. We denote the set of all traces of a configuration C with $T(C)$.

(a) LES with one maximal configuration   (b) Event structure with conflicts

Fig. 1. Event structures

Let $f : C \to X$ be a mapping on C to some set X. For a trace τ of C, we denote by $f(\tau)$ the sequence resulting from point-wise application of f on the elements of τ. Finally, we extend T to event structures by defining it as the union of traces over all maximal configurations. That is, $T(\mathcal{E}) := \bigcup_{C \in \mathcal{MC}(\mathcal{E})} T(C)$.

A finite, labeled prime event structure $\mathcal{E}$ represents a finite set of bounded words over an alphabet $\mathcal{X}$, where the bound for the length of words is given by the size of the largest maximal configuration. We call this set the language $\mathcal{L}(\mathcal{E})$.

Definition 3 (Language of C and $\mathcal{E}$). *The language of configuration C of $\mathcal{E}$ is $\mathcal{L}(C) := \{h(\tau) \mid \tau \in T(C)\}$. The language of $\mathcal{E}$ is $\mathcal{L}(\mathcal{E}) := \{h(\tau) \mid \tau \in T(\mathcal{E})\}$.*

To illustrate this definition we give a small example.

Example 1 (Event structure and configurations). We show two event structures in Fig. 1a and b. Boxes depict events. Inside every box is its event's identifier, above or below the box is its event's label. If there is no label we implicitly assume the label to be ε. Solid arrows depict direct successors of an event. Dashed lines depict immediate conflicts. Two events e, e' are in immediate conflict if $e \# e'$ and there are no $e_1, e_2 \in E$ such that $e_1 < e \wedge e_1 \# e'$ or $e_2 < e' \wedge e \# e_2$. For better readability, we omit all other causalities and conflicts.

Figure 1a and b both represent the language $\{AB, BA\}$. The event structure in Fig. 1a has a single maximal configuration consisting of events $\{\bot, e_1, e_2\}$. The event structure in Fig. 1b has two maximal configurations: $\{\bot, e_1, e_2\}$ and $\{\bot, e_3, e_4\}$ (due to the conflict between e_1 and e_3 these two events cannot appear in the same configuration).

3   Language Inclusion Problem and Complexity Results

The language inclusion problem for two event structures $\mathcal{E}_1, \mathcal{E}_2$ is to decide whether $\mathcal{L}(\mathcal{E}_1) \subseteq \mathcal{L}(\mathcal{E}_2)$. In this section we prove a complexity bound for the language inclusion problem. As an intermediate step we look at the membership problem.

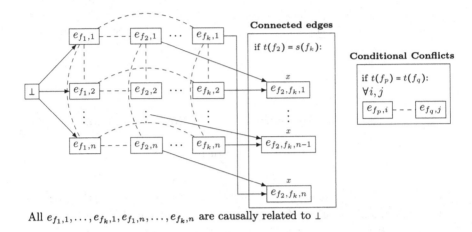

All $e_{f_1,1}, \ldots, e_{f_k,1}, e_{f_1,n}, \ldots, e_{f_k,n}$ are causally related to $\perp$

Fig. 2. $\mathcal{E}^G$ for Theorem 2

3.1 Language Membership Is NP-complete

The *finite prime event structure language membership problem* for word w and FLES $\mathcal{E}$ is the problem of deciding whether $w \in \mathcal{L}(\mathcal{E})$. Surprisingly, deciding membership is NP-complete. In contrast, trace membership $\tau \in T(\mathcal{E})$ can be decided in polynomial time. Trace membership can be decided simply by verifying that the set of events of τ forms a maximal configuration of $\mathcal{E}$, which requires to verify left-closure, conflict-freedom, and maximality. All of those can be checked in polynomial time (linear time, assuming linear conflict lookup).

Intuitively, the hardness of language membership comes from the fact that the labeling function does not need to be injective and the role of conflicts, which together rule out a greedy algorithm that consumes the word in question symbol by symbol in a unique way.

Theorem 1. *Finite prime event structure language membership is in NP.*

Proof. Let $\mathcal{E} = \langle E, <, \#, h \rangle$ be an $\mathcal{X}$-labeled FLES and $w = \langle \sigma_1, \ldots, \sigma_n \rangle \in \mathcal{X}^*$ be a word. A trace τ is a polynomially sized certificate for $w \in \mathcal{L}(\mathcal{E})$. Checking that $\tau \in T(\mathcal{E})$ can be done in polynomial time, and checking whether $h(\tau) = w$ can be done in linear time. $\qquad\square$

To prove NP-hardness we reduce the Hamiltonian cycle (HC) problem to the membership problem. HC is known to be NP-hard [26]. It is the problem of deciding whether for a directed graph there exists a path that visits all vertices once and that ends in the vertex it started. We use $s(f)$ and $t(f)$ to denote the source and target of a directed edge f.

Theorem 2. *Finite prime event structure language membership is NP-hard.*

Proof. For a directed graph $G = (\{v_1, \ldots, v_n\}, \{f_1, \ldots, f_k\})$ we construct an event structure $\mathcal{E}^G$, such that $x^n \in \mathcal{L}(\mathcal{E}^G)$ iff G has a Hamiltonian cycle. $\mathcal{E}^G$ is shown in Fig. 2 and we present the main arguments why this reduction is correct here. A detailed, formal proof is given in the appendix of [14].

Configurations of the event structure encode a sequence of n edges. If event $e_{f,i}$ is included in the configuration it means that edge f is at position i in the sequence of edges. To ensure that every vertex is visited, edges with the same target are in conflict. Since n edges need to be selected, there are n vertices, and every vertex is a target of some selected edge, every vertex is visited once by the selected edges. To ensure that the sequence of edges actually forms a cycle they need to be connected. Events $e_{f,i}$ and $e_{f',i+1\bmod n}$ for which the target of f is the source of f' cause an x-labeled event $e_{f,f',i}$. Therefore, only configurations that represent a cycle form the word x^n.

In summary, checking the membership of x^n amounts to checking whether there exists a Hamiltonian cycle in G. The reduction clearly is polynomial. $\square$

3.2   Language Inclusion Is Π_2^p-complete

The *finite prime event structure language inclusion problem* for FLES $\mathcal{E}_1$ and $\mathcal{E}_2$ is the problem of deciding whether $\mathcal{L}(\mathcal{E}_1) \subseteq \mathcal{L}(\mathcal{E}_2)$.

Π_2^p is a complexity class from the polynomial hierarchy. It intuitively represents a $\forall\exists$ quantifier alternation. To show inclusion, we use the definition of Π_2^p given by Wrathall [46], providing semantics for the complexity class in terms of formal languages. These languages should not be confused with the particular type of languages we discuss in this work. In contrast, such languages encode problem instances and candidate witnesses.

Formally, a language L is in Π_2^p iff there exists a polynomially decidable language L', such that $x \in L \Leftrightarrow \forall y_1 \exists y_2 [\langle x, y_1, y_2 \rangle \in L']$. A language L' is polynomially decidable if $w \in L'$ can be decided in polynomial time. The x represents an encoding of the problem instance as a string. The y_1 and y_2 represent string encodings of witnesses to a sub-problem.

We fix two $\mathcal{X}$-labeled FLES $\mathcal{E}_1 = \langle E_1, <_1, \#_1, h_1 \rangle$ and $\mathcal{E}_2 = \langle E_2, <_2, \#_2, h_2 \rangle$.

Theorem 3. *Finite prime event structure language inclusion is in Π_2^p.*

Proof. Language inclusion $\mathcal{L}(\mathcal{E}_1) \subseteq \mathcal{L}(\mathcal{E}_2)$ amounts to checking whether $\forall w \in \mathcal{L}(\mathcal{E}_1) \Rightarrow w \in \mathcal{L}(\mathcal{E}_2)$. In terms of traces this can be expressed as $\forall \tau_1 \in T(\mathcal{E}_1). \exists \tau_2 \in T(\mathcal{E}_2). h_1(\tau_1) = h_2(\tau_2)$, meaning that for every trace in $\mathcal{E}_1$ there has to be a trace in $\mathcal{E}_2$ corresponding to the same word in the common alphabet $\mathcal{X}$.

We define $L := \{\langle \mathcal{E}_1, \mathcal{E}_2 \rangle \mid \mathcal{L}(\mathcal{E}_1) \subseteq \mathcal{L}(\mathcal{E}_2)\}$ and $L' := \{\langle \langle \mathcal{E}_1, \mathcal{E}_2 \rangle, \tau_1, \tau_2 \rangle \mid \tau_1 \in T(\mathcal{E}_1) \Rightarrow (h_1(\tau_1) = h_2(\tau_2) \wedge \tau_2 \in T(\mathcal{E}_2))\}$. By the argument above, we obtain the desired form $x \in L$ iff $\forall y_1 \exists y_2 [\langle x, y_1, y_2 \rangle \in L']$ to show Π_2^p inclusion. Furthermore, L' can be decided deterministically in polynomial time, because trace membership, as well as label equality, can be decided in polynomial time. $\square$

To show Π_2^p hardness, we present a reduction from the Dynamic Hamiltonian Cycle (DHC) problem to the finite prime event structure language inclusion problem. Given an undirected graph $G = (V, F)$ and a set $B \subseteq F$, graph G

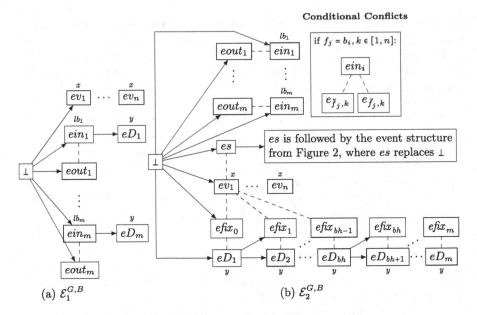

Fig. 3. Event structures for the language inclusion hardness proof. We use ... to indicate omitted events.

and B form a DHC if for every set $D \subseteq B$ with $|D| \le |B|/2$, the graph $G_D = (V, F \setminus D)$ has a Hamiltonian cycle. We define $n := |V|$, $k := |F|$, $m := |B|$, and $bh := \lfloor |B|/2 \rfloor$. Essentially DHC, in comparison to HC, has an additional universal quantifier over subsets of B. DHC is known to be Π_2^p-complete [27].

Theorem 4. *Finite prime event structure language inclusion is Π_2^p-hard.*

Proof. For an undirected graph $G = (V, F)$ and set $B = \{b_1, \ldots, b_m\} \subseteq F$ we construct event structures $\mathcal{E}_1^{G,B}$ and $\mathcal{E}_2^{G,B}$, such that $\mathcal{L}(\mathcal{E}_1^{G,B}) \subseteq \mathcal{L}(\mathcal{E}_2^{G,B})$ iff G, B satisfy DHC. $\mathcal{E}_1^{G,B}$ and $\mathcal{E}_2^{G,B}$ are shown in Fig. 3 and we present the main arguments why this reduction is correct here. A detailed, formal proof, as well as an example, are given in the appendix of [14].

The idea of the proof is to encode subsets D of B via events ein_i and $eout_i$ with $i \in [1, m]$ in both $\mathcal{E}_1^{G,B}$ and $\mathcal{E}_2^{G,B}$. Events ein_i are labeled with lb_i and represent $b_i \in D$, whereas $eout_i$ are labeled with ε and represent $b_i \notin D$. Furthermore, the cardinality of D is encoded in $\mathcal{E}_1^{G,B}$ via y-labeled events eD_i. In contrast y-labeled events eD_i in $\mathcal{E}_2^{G,B}$ are not used to count $|D|$, but to differentiate whether or not a Hamiltonian cycle is required to show DHC (i.e. whether $|D| \le \frac{|B|}{2}$). For every $i \in [1, m]$, event $efix_i$ is used to guarantee the existence of maximal configurations in $\mathcal{E}_2^{G,B}$ with i y-labeled events. In case a Hamiltonian cycle is required to show DHC for some set D, we encode G_D using the same event structure as in the proof of Theorem 2, excluding edges from D via conflicts of events ein_i.

Our Hamiltonian cycle encoding used in the proof of Theorem 2 operates on directed edges, but DHC is defined for undirected graphs. Therefore, we replace every edge f in G with two edges in opposing directions, denoted by $\vec{f}$ and $\overleftarrow{f}$. Clearly, every Hamiltonian cycle in the directed version corresponds to a Hamiltonian cycle in the undirected graph. In order to faithfully represent restricted graphs G_D, we make sure always to exclude all directed edges corresponding to edges in D when looking for a Hamiltonian cycle in G_D.

Every subset D of B is encoded by some word in $\mathcal{L}(\mathcal{E}_1^{G,B})$ via labels lb_i of events ein_i. Since ein_i is in conflict with $eout_i$ maximal configurations can only include one or the other. That is, words exactly enumerate all subsets D of B. Furthermore, similarly as for the proof of Theorem 2, every $w \in \mathcal{L}(\mathcal{E}_1^{G,B})$ contains n times the label x.

Membership of words of $\mathcal{L}(\mathcal{E}_1^{G,B})$ in $\mathcal{L}(\mathcal{E}_2^{G,B})$ only depends on whether the encoded subset $F \setminus D$ induces a Hamiltonian cycle: Words that encode a D such that $|D| > \frac{|B|}{2}$ are always in $\mathcal{L}(\mathcal{E}_2^{G,B})$, because they are trivially accepted by events ev_i. In contrast, for D such that $|D| \le \frac{|B|}{2}$ the event $efix_{|D|}$ is in conflict with ev_1, thereby preventing a trivial acceptance of words in $\mathcal{L}(\mathcal{E}_1^{G,B})$. Therefore, x labels of words in $\mathcal{L}(\mathcal{E}_2^{G,B})$ that encode D such that $|D| \le \frac{|B|}{2}$ must be of events caused by es. The events caused by es exactly encode Hamiltonian cycles in G_D, similarly to the proof of Theorem 2.

Since the two cases are exhaustive and cover every subset D of B, we get $\mathcal{L}(\mathcal{E}_1^{G,B}) \subseteq \mathcal{L}(\mathcal{E}_2^{G,B})$ iff G and B satisfy DHC. The reduction is polynomial as can be easily observed by the event structures in Fig. 3.   □

4   Deciding Language Inclusion

In this section, we introduce a decision algorithm for the FLES language inclusion problem. Furthermore, we provide a language preserving translation of event structures into non-deterministic finite automata (NFAs), which allows us to compare our algorithm to NFA language inclusion. We start by introducing necessary concepts for our decision algorithm.

Configuration as an Event Structure. Given an event structure $\mathcal{E} = \langle E, <, \#, h \rangle$ and a configuration C, we denote its corresponding event structure as $\mathcal{E}^C := \langle C, <_{\lceil C \times C}, \emptyset, h_{\lceil C} \rangle$, where $X_{\lceil Y}$ denotes the restriction of X to Y. For ease of presentation, when describing our algorithms, we abuse notation and do not differentiate between a configuration and its corresponding event structure. Furthermore, in the following presentation of the algorithms, we assume that the causality relations and labeling functions of configurations C_i for $i \in \{1, 2\}$ are implicitly given by the event structure interpretation over $\mathcal{E}_i$.

ε-free configurations. For every configuration C, there is a configuration with the same language whose only ε-labeled event is $\bot$. This ε-free configuration can be obtained simply by removing all ε-labeled events besides $\bot$ from its corresponding event structure, in particular from C and $<_{\lceil C \times C}$. The resulting ε-free

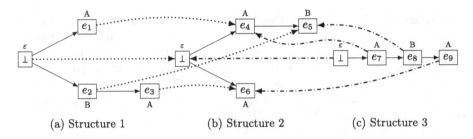

(a) Structure 1   (b) Structure 2   (c) Structure 3

Fig. 4. Necessary and sufficient embeddings.
$\varphi : \bot \mapsto \bot; e_1 \mapsto e_4; e_2 \mapsto e_5; e_3 \mapsto e_6$ is a necessary embedding (dotted arrows).
$\varphi : \bot \mapsto \bot; e_7 \mapsto e_4; e_8 \mapsto e_5; e_9 \mapsto e_6$ is a sufficient embedding (dash-dotted arrows).

configuration has the same language as the initial configuration, because the causality relation is transitive. Furthermore, ε-labeled events do not modify the words and thus removing them does not influence the language of the configuration. Therefore, in order to improve readability, from hereon we assume without loss of generality that configurations are ε-free. We keep the $\bot$ event to improve readability, even though for our purpose this event is not required neither. Note that ε-labeled events are useful during the construction phase of the event structure representing, for example, hidden transitions or non-deterministic choices.

Embeddings. An embedding is a structure-preserving one-to-one mapping between events of two configurations from different event structures. We consider two different types of embeddings that vary in their strictness in terms of structure preservation. Since embeddings are defined between configurations, conflicts do not play a role in these considerations. In order to use these embeddings for deciding language inclusion between two FLES, we assume that in a step prior to searching for embeddings, the maximal configurations of both $\mathcal{E}_1$ and $\mathcal{E}_2$ are computed. This can, for example, be achieved with the algorithm presented in [38].

In the following we consider two configurations C_1 and C_2 of two $\mathcal{X}$-labeled FLES $\mathcal{E}_1 = \langle E_1, <_1, \#_1, h_1 \rangle$ respectively $\mathcal{E}_2 = \langle E_2, <_2, \#_2, h_2 \rangle$.

Definition 4 (Necessary Embedding). *A mapping $\varphi : C_1 \to C_2$ is a necessary embedding if (A) φ is bijective, (B) $\forall e \in C_1 : h_1(e) = h_2(\varphi(e))$, and (C) $\forall e \in C_1 : \neg (e(<_1 \cup <_2^\varphi)^+ e)$, where .$^+$ denotes transitive closure and $<_2^\varphi$ denotes the relation $<_2$ mapped to the events of C_1. Formally $<_2^\varphi := \{(\varphi^{-1}(e_1), \varphi^{-1}(e_2)) \mid \exists e_1, e_2 \in C_2. \ e_1 <_2 e_2\}$. For a necessary embedding φ from C_1 to C_2, we write $C_1 \sim_N^\varphi C_2$. We write $C_1 \sim_N C_2$ if there exists a necessary embedding φ such that $C_1 \sim_N^\varphi C_2$.*

A necessary embedding implies that the two configurations have a common word, by requiring they have the same number of events with the same labels and that their partial orders are not contradicting each other. Note that the relation $\sim_N$ is symmetric, since for a necessary embedding $\varphi : C_1 \to C_2$, φ^{-1} is a necessary embedding from C_2 onto C_1.

Example 2. Consider the configurations in Fig. 4a and b. There are only two label-preserving bijections between the configurations: $\varphi_1 : \bot \mapsto \bot; e_1 \mapsto e_6; e_2 \mapsto e_5; e_3 \mapsto e_4$ and $\varphi_2 : \bot \mapsto \bot; e_1 \mapsto e_4; e_2 \mapsto e_5; e_3 \mapsto e_6$.

The mapping φ_1 is not a necessary embedding, since $e_2(<_1 \cup <_2^\varphi)e_2$, which violates C). To see this, consider the chain of events $e_2 <_1 e_3 <_2^\varphi e_2$, where $e_3 = \varphi^{-1}(e_4), e_2 = \varphi^{-1}(e_5)$, and $e_4 <_2 e_5$. In contrast, φ_2 is a necessary embedding and a witness to the common word ABA of both configurations.

Lemma 1. *Let C_1 and C_2 be maximal configuration of FLES $\mathcal{E}_1$ respectively $\mathcal{E}_2$. $C_1 \sim_N C_2$ if and only if $\mathcal{L}(C_1) \cap \mathcal{L}(C_2) \neq \varnothing$.*

The following corollary gives rise to a termination criterion of the decision algorithm. If we find a configuration C in $\mathcal{E}_1$, such that there exists no configuration in $\mathcal{E}_2$ that shares a word with C, we can abort the search and report non-inclusion.

Corollary 1. *Let $C, C_1, \ldots, C_n$ be configurations such that $C \neq \varnothing$. If $(\forall i = 1, \ldots, n : C_i \not\sim_N C)$ then $\mathcal{L}(C) \not\subseteq \bigcup_{i=1}^n \mathcal{L}(C_i)$.*

The second type of embedding has a stronger requirement on structure preservation. Intuitively, it requires that the source of such an embedding is at least as strict in terms of causality as the target.

Definition 5 (Sufficient Embedding). *A mapping $\varphi : C_1 \to C_2$ is a sufficient embedding if (A) φ is bijective, (B) $\forall e \in C_1 : h_1(e) = h_2(\varphi(e))$, and (C) $\forall e_1, e_2 \in C_1 : \varphi(e_1) <_2 \varphi(e_2) \implies e_1 <_1 e_2$. If there exists a sufficient embedding φ from C_1 to C_2, we write $C_1 \sqsubseteq_S^\varphi C_2$. We write $C_1 \sqsubseteq_S C_2$ if there exists sufficient embedding φ, such that $C_1 \sqsubseteq_S^\varphi C_2$.*

A sufficient embedding is a witness to language inclusion between configurations. The reason to work with two kinds of embeddings is that we can construct necessary embeddings using a backtracking algorithm. It is easy to check whether a necessary embedding is also sufficient, whereas it is not straight forward to construct a sufficient embedding from scratch.

Example 3. Consider the configurations in Fig. 4b and c. The mapping $\varphi_1 : \bot \mapsto \bot; e_7 \mapsto e_4; e_8 \mapsto e_5; e_9 \mapsto e_6$ is a sufficient embedding. The only non-trivial causality to check is $e_4 <_2 e_5$, for which we have $\varphi_1^{-1}(e_4) = e_7 <_3 e_8 = \varphi_1^{-1}(e_5)$. In contrast, $\varphi_2 : \bot \mapsto \bot; e_7 \mapsto e_6; e_8 \mapsto e_5; e_9 \mapsto e_4$ is not a sufficient embedding, since in this case $e_4 <_2 e_5$ and $\varphi_1^{-1}(e_4) = e_9 \not<_3 e_8 = \varphi_1^{-1}(e_5)$. This shows that the language of the event structure in Fig. 4c is included in language of the event structure in Fig. 4b.

The following Lemma provides a connection between sufficient embeddings and language inclusion. In case there exists a sufficient embedding, the respective languages are included.

Lemma 2. *Let C_1 and C_2 be maximal configurations of FLES $\mathcal{E}_1$ and $\mathcal{E}_2$ respectively. If $C_1 \sqsubseteq_S C_2$ then $\mathcal{L}(C_1) \subseteq \mathcal{L}(C_2)$.*

The converse statement is not always true. To see this, consider a configuration $C_1 = \{\perp, e_1, e'_1\}$ such that e_1 and e'_1 are concurrent and $h(e_1) = h(e'_1) = A$. Furthermore, consider a configuration $C_2 = \{\perp, e_2, e'_2\}$ such that e_2 and e'_2 are sequential and $h(e_2) = h(e'_2) = A$. Clearly, the configurations have the same language $\{AA\}$. However, there is no sufficient embedding from C_1 to C_2.

Our decision algorithm performs an additional refinement step in such a case and concludes language inclusion only after checking the refined configurations. In the appendix of [14], we provide a proof that in the case of unique labels, the converse statement also holds.

Splits. Our language inclusion decision algorithm continuously performs configuration refinement steps that we call splits. To be precise, we refine the causality relation of its corresponding event structure.

Definition 6 (Split). *Let C be a configuration of event structure $\langle E, <, \#, h \rangle$ and let $e_1, e_2 \in C$ be two concurrent events. The split of C on e_1 before e_2 is $C_{e_1 < e_2} := \langle C, (< \cup \{(e_1, e_2)\})^+_{\lceil C \times C}, \varnothing, h_{\lceil C} \rangle$ where $.^+$ denotes transitive closure.*

A split on two concurrent events e_1 and e_2 simply adds an additional ordering constraint between the two events. In our algorithm, we always split both ways, creating two new configurations that order concurrent events e_1 and e_2 one way and the other. Note that in order to avoid duplication of events, in practice splits can be implemented via additional, optional causalities on the event structure. The following lemma states that splitting a configuration in both ways produces two new configurations with languages whose union is the original language.

Lemma 3. *Let C be a configuration and $e_1, e_2 \in C$ be concurrent events, then $\mathcal{L}(C) = \mathcal{L}(C_{e_1 < e_2}) \cup \mathcal{L}(C_{e_2 < e_1})$. If h is injective (labels are unique), then $\mathcal{L}(C_{e_1 < e_2}) \cap \mathcal{L}(C_{e_2 < e_1}) = \varnothing$.*

The following lemma guarantees progress of our algorithm. It states that if we find a necessary, but not sufficient embedding, there are events that can be used to split C_1. The goal is that after a finite number of splits a sufficient embedding can be established.

Lemma 4. *Let C_1, C_2 be maximal configuration of FLES $\mathcal{E}_1$ respectively $\mathcal{E}_2$. Furthermore, let $C_1 \sim^\varphi_N C_2$ and $C_1 \not\#^\varphi_S C_2$. Then there are concurrent events $e, e' \in C_1$, such that $\varphi(e) <_2 \varphi(e')$.*

4.1   Language Inclusion Decision Algorithm

We present our decision algorithm in Algorithm 1. Inputs to the algorithm are finite, labeled prime event structures $\mathcal{E}_1$ and $\mathcal{E}_2$.

The first step of the algorithm is to calculate the maximal configurations of the event structure, which can be done with the algorithm described in [38]. For every maximal configuration C_1 of $\mathcal{E}_1$, the function Check() attempts to

---

Algorithm 1. Language inclusion decision algorithm

Input: Finite, labeled Prime Event Structures $\mathcal{E}_1$ and $\mathcal{E}_2$
Result: $\mathcal{L}(\mathcal{E}_1) \subseteq \mathcal{L}(\mathcal{E}_2)$

1 $\{C_1^1, \ldots, C_1^n\}, \{C_2^1, \ldots, C_2^m\} \leftarrow$ all maximal configurations of $\mathcal{E}_1$ respectively $\mathcal{E}_2$
2 **return** $\bigwedge_{C_1 \in \{C_1^1, \ldots, C_1^n\}}$ Check$(C_1, \{C_2^1, \ldots, C_2^m\})$
3 **Function** Check$(C_1, \{C_2^{i_1}, \ldots, C_2^{i_l}\})$:

    Result: $\mathcal{L}(C_1) \subseteq \bigcup_{j=1}^l \mathcal{L}(C_2^{i_j})$

4   *Candidates* $\leftarrow \{C_2^{i_1}, \ldots, C_2^{i_l}\}$
5   **foreach** $C_2 \in \{C_2^{i_1}, \ldots, C_2^{i_l}\}$ **do**
6   **if** $\exists \varphi : C_1 \to C_2.\ C_1 \sim_N^\varphi C_2$ **then**
7   **return** SuffOrSplit$(C_1, C_2, \varphi, Candidates)$
8   **else**
9   *Candidates* $\leftarrow$ *Candidates* $\setminus \{C_2\}$
10   **return** false   ▷ **counter-example** C_1
11 **Function** SuffOrSplit$(C_1, C_2, \varphi, Candidates)$:
12   **if** $C_1 \sqsubseteq_S^\varphi C_2$ **then**
13   **return** true
14   Let $e, e' \in C_1$ be concurrent and $\varphi(e) <_2 \varphi(e')$ ▷ **always exist (Lemma 4)**
15   **return** SuffOrSplit$(C_{e<e'}, C_2, \varphi, Candidates) \wedge$ Check$(C_{e'<e}, Candidates)$

---

show that $\mathcal{L}(C_1)$ is a subset of $\mathcal{L}(\mathcal{E}_2)$. This is achieved by searching for sufficient embeddings from (refined versions of) C_1 to maximal configurations of $\mathcal{E}_2$.

In order to construct candidate sufficient embeddings, in Line 6 the algorithm attempts to construct necessary embeddings, using Algorithm 2. In the following line, function SuffOrSplit() checks whether a necessary embedding φ is also sufficient. This can be done by checking $\forall e \in C_2 : \forall e' \in dsucc(e) : \varphi^{-1}(e)$ is not concurrent with $\varphi^{-1}(e')$. In case φ is not a sufficient embedding, such a pair of events is guaranteed to exist by Lemma 4. For efficiency, this check can already be done during construction of the necessary embedding.

In case φ is not sufficient, Lemma 4 guarantees the existence of a pair of concurrent events that can be split. The resulting split configurations are recursively checked for language inclusion in Line 15. Lemma 4 guarantees us that φ is a necessary embedding for one of the splits (say $C_{e<e'}$). Therefore, for $C_{e<e'}$ we do not need to construct a new necessary embedding again, but can immediately check whether φ is a sufficient embedding for $C_{e<e'}$.

In case no necessary embedding can be found for some configuration C_1 and its candidates, according to Lemma 1, we can conclude $\mathcal{L}(C_1) \cap \mathcal{L}(\mathcal{E}) = \varnothing$, i.e. all words in C_1 are counter-examples to language inclusion. Once Line 10 is reached we know that C_1 does not share any word with any $\{C_2^1, \ldots, C_2^m\}$, therefore C_1 is a counter-example to language inclusion.

The algorithm terminates, because the notions of necessary and sufficient embedding collapse in case the configuration contains only a single trace, which

---

Algorithm 2. $\sim_N$ decision algorithm

Input: Configurations C_1, C_2

Result: $\varphi : C_1 \rightarrow C_2$ if $C_1 \sim_N^\varphi C_2$, None otherwise

1 **if** $\exists x \in \mathcal{X}.\ |\{e \in C_1 \mid h_1(e) = x\}| \neq |\{e \in C_2 \mid h_2(e) = x\}|$ **then**

2 | **return** false

3 **return** NEmbedding($\{\bot_1\}, \{\bot_1 \mapsto \bot_2\}$)

4 NEmbedding(*frontier*, φ):

    Input: *frontier* stack of events C_1

    Input: $\varphi : C_1 \rightarrow C_2$ (partial mapping)

    Result: $\varphi : E_1 \rightarrow E_2$ if $C_1 \sim_N^\varphi C_2$, None otherwise

5   **if** *frontier* $= \varnothing$ **then**

6 | **return** φ

7     $e \leftarrow$ *frontier*.pop()

8   **foreach** $e' \in dsucc_{\mathcal{E}C_1}(e)$ **do**   ▷ direct successors of e in C_1

9 | *frontier*.push(e')

10   **foreach** $e'' \in C_2$ such that $h_1(e) = h_2(e'') \wedge e'' \notin range(\varphi)$ **do**

11 | $\varphi' \leftarrow \varphi \cup \{e \mapsto e''\}$

12 | **if** $\nexists e_1, e_2 \in E_1.\ e_1 <_1 e_2 \wedge \varphi'(e_2) <_2 \varphi'(e_1)$ **then**   ▷ check for cycle

13 | | $\varphi'' \leftarrow$ NEmbedding(*frontier*, φ')

14 | | **if** $\varphi'' \neq$ None **then**

15 | | | **return** φ''

16   **return** None

---

is the case when the causality relation is a total order on the events of the configuration (see [14], Lemma 6).

As the algorithm recursively searches for sufficient embeddings, for efficiency, we can reduce the set of candidate configurations, because in case there is no necessary embedding between two configurations, there is clearly also no necessary embedding between any of their split configurations.

We present the algorithm to construct necessary embeddings in Algorithm 2. Intuitively, the algorithm is a combined depth first search over the causality relation, as well as the space of possible bijective, label-preserving mappings.

The algorithm starts by dismissing configurations that can never have a necessary embedding because the number of events with the same label differs (Line 1). The actual embedding is established with the recursive function NEmbedding(). The recursion maintains a frontier of events that are yet to be explored and a partial mapping of already explored events. It ends if the frontier becomes empty (Line 5). The exploration is done on C_1 by adding the successors of the current event e to the frontier (Line 8). Then for every event e'' in C_2 with the same label as e a mapping φ' is created and a cycle check performed. If this mapping does not introduce a cycle we recurs on it (Line 13). The first valid (not None) mapping that is returned by a recursion is returned. If no such mapping is found, then None is returned. The cycle check in Line 12 basically checks if the two causality relations $<_1$ and $<_2$ are compatible for the mapped events, in the sense that the events can be brought in an order that respects both causality relations. The procedure can be implemented using any of the well known cycle detection algorithms over the graph with nodes being events of C_1 and edges being causalities $<_1 \cup <_2^\varphi$.

The worst-case runtime of the decision algorithm is exponential in $O(2^{2n})$, where $n = |E_1| + |E_2|$, which is not surprising for an algorithm solving a Π_2^p hard problem. There are two dominant factors of the exponential complexity.

First, the number of maximal configurations can be exponential in n and Algorithm 1 potentially has to compare all pairs of maximal configurations. The CCNFS benchmark in Sect. 5 is an example for an event structure with an exponential number of maximal configurations in n.

Second, the number of mappings between configurations that need to be considered as candidates for necessary embeddings can be exponential in n. That is, algorithm Algorithm 2 has worst case runtime exponential in n. Note that for a fixed mapping, the algorithm performs a linear search over the configuration and the combined causality relation.

Note that the number of possible embeddings decreases with the number of calls to Check and the size of maximal configurations decreases relative to n with the number of maximal configurations. Therefore, the amortized runtime should be much better than the worst case complexity.

4.2   Automaton Based Language Inclusion

We provide a language preserving encoding of event structures into non-deterministic finite automata (NFA). The encoding allows us to compare our algorithm to well researched language inclusion algorithms in our evaluation (Sect. 5).

The encoding has a state for every configuration of the event structure. There is a transition between two states, if the difference between the corresponding configurations is just one event. The transition is labeled with the label of that event. In essence, the encoding is an automaton representation of what is known as the configuration structure of a prime event structure [19].

Definition 7 (Automaton Encoding). *Let* $\mathcal{E} = \langle E, <, \#, h \rangle$ *be a finite prime event structure with labels* $\mathcal{X}$. *We define the non-deterministic finite automaton* $\mathcal{A}^{\mathcal{E}} = \langle Q^{\mathcal{E}}, \Omega^{\mathcal{E}}, \delta^{\mathcal{E}}, q_0^{\mathcal{E}}, F^{\mathcal{E}} \rangle$ *as* $Q^{\mathcal{E}} = \{q_C^{\mathcal{E}} \mid C$ *is a configuration of* $\mathcal{E}\}$, $\Omega^{\mathcal{E}} = \mathcal{X}$, $(q_{C_1}^{\mathcal{E}}, \sigma, q_{C_2}^{\mathcal{E}}) \in \delta^{\mathcal{E}}$ *iff there is* $e \in E$, *such that* $C_1 \cup \{e\} = C_2$ *and* $h(e) = \sigma$, $q_0^{\mathcal{E}} := q_{\{\perp\}}^{\mathcal{E}}$, *and* $F^{\mathcal{E}} = \{q_C^{\mathcal{E}} \mid C$ *is maximal*$\}$.

Lemma 5. *Let* $\mathcal{E}$ *be a labeled, finite prime event structure, then* $\mathcal{L}(\mathcal{E}) = \mathcal{L}(\mathcal{A}^{\mathcal{E}})$.

The provided encoding is not optimal in general due to conflicts and the fact that events of prime event structures are caused in a unique way, which is a well known caveat of prime event structures [43]. However, for the family of event structures that consists of the $\perp$ event and n concurrent events (c.f. the proof of Theorem 5 in the appendix of [14]), our encoding contains exactly $2^n + 1$ states, which is one state more than the provably optimal NFA accepting the language of the event structure. Furthermore, in our experiments, we apply optimized NFA reduction techniques [30] before checking language inclusion on automata.

Theorem 5. *There is a family of event structures $\mathcal{E}_n$ with events E_n, such that $|E_n| = n+1$, $|\mathcal{L}(\mathcal{E}_n)| = n!$, and $|Q^{\mathcal{E}}| = 2^n + 1$. Every NFA $\mathcal{A}$ with $\mathcal{L}(\mathcal{A}) = \mathcal{L}(\mathcal{E}_n)$ has at least 2^n states.*

5   Application and Evaluation

Our motivation to investigate event structures and language inclusion was model-based mutation testing. The goal of *model-based testing* (MBT) is to derive test-cases from a model of a system. The model may, for example, be a UML state machine and the test may be a sequence of inputs and outputs of the system. The simplest way of obtaining such test cases would be to randomly explore the state machine and record the produced input/output (IO) sequences. These tests can then be run against an implementation at a later point.

Model-based mutation testing (MBMT) compares the original model to a mutated version of it, where a mutation is a small change in the model, such as removing or adding a transition. A test case is only generated if an observable difference between the original and the mutated model can be witnessed. This form of test case generation can be easily expressed using language inclusion between the two versions of the system: The test is exactly the word that is a member of the mutant, but not of the original.

The application of finite prime event structures to this problem is motivated by three factors. Firstly, models often use concurrent state machine that synchronize rarely. Secondly, mutation analysis on reactive models can be performed by exploring models in bounded segments [13], where a bounded segment refers to all events occurring between two consecutive inputs. These bounded segments can be represented as finite event structures. Thirdly, it is desirable express independence in test cases in order to produce minimal test suites that do not need to list all variations of a test that differ only in terms of independent events. Such test cases can be obtained as counter-examples to language inclusion, as discussed in Sect. 4.

To this end, we implemented the presented prime event structure language inclusion algorithm in the model-based mutation testing tool MoMuT [13]. MoMuT accepts models written as object-oriented action systems (OOAS). The models can be understood as labeled transition systems, where labels are either observable, controllable or hidden (ε). OOAS models can model highly concurrent systems. In order to construct test cases for such concurrent models efficiently, we need to apply partial order reduction during model exploration. In [38] a partial order reduction based algorithm for constructing labeled prime event structures from transition systems is given. We implemented this algorithm, using a static dependency relation based on variable reads and writes, and use it during model exploration, obtaining finite labeled event structures representing bounded segments of the model. Each segment corresponds to all output or hidden transitions following some input until either a new input is required by the model to progress further or the model is in a terminating state. We operate on models that exclude infinite sequences of outputs or hidden transitions. Thus, the discussed segments are indeed bounded in our case.

The event structures constructed during partial order reduction are labeled with (potentially hidden) transitions of the explored model. However, for mutation analysis, we want to find observable differences between event structures for given controllable inputs, in contrast to any difference in transition labels. Therefore, in addition to using transition labels during partial order reduction, we use projected, visible (input & output) labels and perform language inclusion on the languages over the latter kind.

During model exploration, which is described in detail in [13], we construct event structures $\mathcal{E}_B$ of the original model and $\mathcal{E}_A$ of mutants, representing bounded segments (as described above) following the same sequence of inputs. We perform language inclusion checks $\mathcal{L}(\mathcal{E}_A) \subseteq \mathcal{L}(\mathcal{E}_B)$ using Algorithm 1 to decide whether the corresponding mutant is killed by the sequence of inputs and a test case can be produced.

In our experimental evaluation, we report measurements of these language inclusion checks during test case generation on a sequence of benchmark models. For comparison and in addition to event structure based language inclusion, we perform language inclusion via automaton encoding, as described in Sect. 4.2. To this end, we encode the produced event structures as NFAs and check language inclusion using the tool RABIT [30].

5.1   Benchmarks and Results

We use the following benchmarks for our experimental evaluation. All benchmark models, scripts to instantiate the models for any parameter value, and the version of MoMuT used in the experiments can be found in the publicly available artifact of this paper [15], which can be run with the virtual machine provided in [8].

- The **Paxos** (n, m, k) benchmark models the Paxos distributed consensus protocol [28] with n proposers, m acceptors, and k learners. The protocol specifies how the different actors can exchange certain messages to achieve consensus on some proposed value. The actions of the actors are largely independent of each other, which introduces lots of concurrency to the model. Furthermore, test cases extracted from our method should be interesting to concertize and run against implementations of the Paxos algorithm.
- The **Semaphore** (n) benchmark models n threads that are synchronized by a semaphore. Exactly $n - 1$ threads are allowed to enter and compute in a critical section at the same time. The amount of parallelism of this model is proportional to n. Furthermore, the model exhibits lots of conflicts, as all operations on the semaphore are in conflict with each other.
- The **ParSum** (n) benchmark models a parallel summation algorithm. The sequence $0, \dots, n^2 - 1$ is split into n equally sized chunks, which are summed up concurrently. Then the partial results are summed up centrally when all parallel threads are finished.

Table 1. Benchmark results for language inclusion checks $\mathcal{L}(\mathcal{E}_A) \subseteq \mathcal{L}(\mathcal{E}_B)$ respectively $\mathcal{L}(\mathcal{A}^{\mathcal{E}_A}) \subseteq \mathcal{L}(\mathcal{A}^{\mathcal{E}_B})$.

Name	$|\mathcal{E}_B|$	PC	Inclusion		Non-Incl.		$|\mathcal{A}^{\mathcal{E}_B}|$	Inclusion		Non-Incl.	
			Time	Num	Time	Num		Time	Num	Time	Num
Paxos (2, 3, 1)	80	4.1	–	0	$4.1 \cdot 10^3$	65	23469	TO	TO	TO	TO
Paxos (3, 6, 1)	716	4.1	–	0	$4.0 \cdot 10^3$	94	TO	TO	TO	TO	TO
Semaphore (3)	9	1.2	–	0	23.8	78	5	–	0	324.0	78
Semaphore (11)	25	2.3	3.5	2	48.9	84	9	–	0	564.2	80
ParSum (3)	18	2.2	1.1	80	170.5	92	218	$2.5 \cdot 10^3$	80	$9.3 \cdot 10^3$	84
ParSum (5)	38	3.8	342.0	84	67.6	94	TO	TO	TO	TO	TO
ParSum (10)	123	8.2	–	0	12.6	23	TO	TO	TO	TO	TO
CCNFS (3)	15	1.7	3.9	88	1.2	88	9	262.7	88	610.9	88
CCNFS (6)	77	2.7	501.8	108	84.0	92	65	379.7	108	$1.2 \cdot 10^3$	92
CCNFS (10)	1045	4.0	$303 \cdot 10^3$	98	$17 \cdot 10^3$	102	59050	TO	TO	TO	TO
AllPar (10)	12	4.0	1.4	56	8.6	144	1025	$10 \cdot 10^3$	56	$82 \cdot 10^3$	144
AllPar (50)	52	17.3	3.2	44	93.3	156	TO	TO	TO	TO	TO
AllPar (500)	502	167.3	361.9	40	$7.7 \cdot 10^3$	160	TO	TO	TO	TO	TO
Sharing (5, 20)	111	1.0	7.2	26	4.2	174	23	338.1	26	$1.1 \cdot 10^3$	174
Sharing (50, 50)	2601	1.0	$1.9 \cdot 10^3$	38	527.2	162	53	255.4	38	$1.5 \cdot 10^3$	162

- The **CCNFS** (n) benchmark models a system with n events and unique labels, such that the $2i'th$ event is in conflict exactly with the $2i+1'th$ event. Every set of independent events induces an event resetting the state. This benchmark is interesting, because its number of maximal configurations $2^{\lfloor \frac{n}{2} \rfloor}$ (each configuration contains either $2i$ or $2i+1$ for each $i = 1 \ldots \lfloor \frac{n}{2} \rfloor$) is exponential in the number of events n. Due to the high number of maximal configurations, this benchmark is challenging for our algorithm.
- The **AllPar** (n) benchmark models a system with n independent events and unique labels. The benchmark is the ideal case for our algorithm, because its event structure consists of only one maximal configuration with all events in parallel. In contrast, the benchmark is a very bad case for NFA language inclusion, as the smallest NFA to encode all permutations of n symbols is exponential in n (Theorem 5).
- The **Sharing** (n, m) benchmark models a system that has n different prefixes that all share the same suffix of length m. The benchmark particularly exhibits the well known shortcoming of event structures not being able to encode shared causes. The NFA is able to express the common suffix more succinct in comparison to the event structure.

We present the results of our experimental evaluation in Table 1. For every benchmark, we report measurements of language inclusion checks for the largest bounded segment encountered during model exploration. As described above, every such bounded segment corresponds to all output and hidden transitions following some input transition. We report measurements of event structure based language inclusion $\mathcal{L}(\mathcal{E}_A) \subseteq \mathcal{L}(\mathcal{E}_B)$ and automaton based language inclusion $\mathcal{L}(\mathcal{A}^{\mathcal{E}_A}) \subseteq \mathcal{L}(\mathcal{A}^{\mathcal{E}_B})$. We separate the results into the cases where language inclusion holds (**Inclusion**) respectively does not hold (**Non-Incl.**). Column $|\mathcal{E}_\mathbf{B}|$ shows the size of $\mathcal{E}_B$ in terms of the number of its events. Column $|\mathcal{A}^{\mathcal{E}_\mathbf{B}}|$ shows the size of $\mathcal{A}^{\mathcal{E}_B}$ in terms of the number of its states. Columns Num show the number of inclusion checks performed on the respective bounded segment (which is the number of mutants relevant in the segment). Columns Time show the average time for the inclusion checks in milliseconds. Finally, column **PC** shows a measurement of the degree of concurrency. For a single configuration C, the measurement is defined as $|C|/max_{e \in C} depth(e)$ and we report the average measurement of all maximal configurations in the respective event structure.

The reported time for language inclusion of event structures is the time for calculation of the maximal configurations plus the time for the actual language inclusion check. The reported time for language inclusion of automata is the time for the language inclusion check on a pre-reduced automaton. The construction and minimization of the NFAs is not included.

The results show that our language inclusion algorithm performs well on models with a lot of concurrency, i.e. those with high ParCoeff. Furthermore, the automaton translation clearly fails in cases with lots of concurrency that are easy for our method (c.f. the **AllPar** benchmark). For these examples our algorithm is very useful. This result is not surprising, since our method exploits concurrency, whereas the NFA encoding does not include any notion of concurrency. Nevertheless, the result demonstrates that the benefits of exploiting concurrency with our method outweigh optimizations and fine-tuning of a well established language inclusion algorithm that has no notion of concurrency.

However, as the **Sharing** benchmark shows, the inability of prime event structures to encode shared causes of events is a limitation of the approach. In contrast, the reduced automaton representation can be significantly more compact than the event structure representation, rendering the automaton-based language inclusion superior.

6   Related Work

Prime event structures are a widely used formalism to express concurrency of discrete systems [43] that can be obtained from transition systems via the method presented in [38], or its extended version in [34]. There are multiple other variants of event structures, such as stable event structures [43] and flow event structures [5]. Studying language inclusion for these event structure variants is interesting future work.

Event structure containment based on causality and conflict refinement is considered in [43,44]. However, as we demonstrate in our work, causality preservation is not necessary for language inclusion. In [18,42] equivalence of event structures under action refinement is investigated. This line of research is orthogonal to our approach, as it considers refinement of event structures, while we compare event structures that can be obtained in multiple different ways. Moreover, there is almost never language inclusion between an event structure and the event structure with refined actions by design.

Model checking over particular types of event structures has been studied in [36] for event structures labeled with atomic propositions and in [29] for event structures labeled with trace languages. However, the proposed model-checking methods are not based on language inclusion, which is one of the interesting future directions for our research. Instead, formulas are directly interpreted over the event structure.

Several formalisms to express concurrency of discrete systems have been proposed and their relationships have been worked out in [45]. In particular, trace languages and Petri nets are formalisms closely related to event structures, for which languages and language related problems have been studied.

The theory of trace languages [31,32] studies closure of string languages under independence relations. [6] presents an efficient method to show trace language inclusion over languages defined by non-deterministic finite automata. In [7] decidability results of rational trace languages are studied. In particular, it is shown that language inclusion of rational (closed under union, concatenation, and Kleene-star) trace languages is decidable if and only if the common independence relation is transitive. Language membership for context free and regular trace languages was shown to be NP-complete in [3]. In [4], comparison of concurrent programs via trace languages is studied. The suggested trace languages abstract the program executions by considering statement ordering, as well as read and write accesses on a subset of relevant variables and synchronization primitives. Trace language refinement is then reduced to assertion checking. Interestingly, for Boolean programs this refinement check has complexity Δ_2^P for bounded abstraction precision and Σ_2^P for unbounded abstraction precision. In contrast to arbitrary event labels considered in our work, the authors of [4] consider refinement on languages of a more concrete program and dependency model.

Our problem is orthogonal to trace language inclusion in three aspects. Firstly, we do not assume the independence relations of the compared systems to be equal. Secondly, we do not require the independence relation to be defined over labels. That is, we can study systems where two labels occur concurrently in one place, while the labels occur sequentially in another. This can occur because different events can have the same label. Finally, in contrast to automata, which are often used to define trace languages, event structures are acyclic. Therefore, event structures are less expressive than automata. However, the price of the additional expressivity is that trace language inclusion over automata is undecidable in general [2], whereas our problem is decidable.

Petri nets are a formalism for concurrent systems that is closely related to event structures [35]. A manifold of complexity questions have been studied for Petri nets, see [10,11,25] for surveys. In particular, language related problems of labeled Petri nets have been studied, see [17,37] for an overview over the types of considered languages and complexity results. Since Petri nets typically describe languages on infinite words and many Petri net related problems are undecidable, complexity results on language related Petri nets problems focus on establishing the boundary between decidability and undecidability. Language inclusion and equivalence were shown to be undecidable for a wide range of types of Petri nets [11,21,24]. Language inclusion is decidable for languages of firing of regular Petri nets [40] and certain types of deterministic Petri nets [17]. In contrast, language membership is decidable for a large class of Petri nets and language types [22,37]. Similarly to trace languages, the additional expressivity of Petri nets over finite prime event structures manifests in increased complexity of solving language inclusion. However, as we demonstrated with our application, finite prime event structures are sufficient for interesting practical problems.

Finite asynchronous automata [12] express concurrent systems succinctly in the same spirit as prime event structures. Furthermore, asynchronous automata accept trace languages [47]. However, to the best of our knowledge, there is neither an algorithm, nor a tool to check language inclusion for (loop free) finite asynchronous automata.

Language inclusion of regular languages is a classic problem of computer science [16,23,33,39]. Algorithms for the problem are well studied and highly optimized [1,6,30]. However, as we demonstrate in the evaluation section, our procedure can outperform these algorithms in the realm of highly concurrent systems. Adapting methods for classic automaton based language inclusions to event structures is interesting future work.

7   Conclusion and Future Work

In this paper we showed that the language inclusion problem between two event structures is computationally hard, but our application and evaluation show that there are numerous benchmarks where the use of event structures and their comparison is beneficial. However, the experiments also manifested a well known shortcoming of prime event structures, namely their inability to succinctly encode shared causes of events.

Interesting future work includes adapting our language inclusion method to different variants of event structures that do not suffer this problem. Furthermore, we want to study whether our language inclusion procedure can be used to perform model checking over event structures. Finally, we want to further study the test cases generated for the Paxos distributed consensus algorithm. Concertizing the resulting test cases and running them against an implementation of the protocol might yield interesting results.

References

1. Abdulla, P.A., Chen, Y.-F., Holík, L., Mayr, R., Vojnar, T.: When simulation meets antichains. In: Esparza, J., Majumdar, R. (eds.) TACAS 2010. LNCS, vol. 6015, pp. 158–174. Springer, Heidelberg (2010). https://doi.org/10.1007/978-3-642-12002-2_14
2. Bertoni, A., Mauri, G., Sabadini, N.: Equivalence and membership problems for regular trace languages. In: Nielsen, M., Schmidt, E.M. (eds.) ICALP 1982. LNCS, vol. 140, pp. 61–71. Springer, Heidelberg (1982). https://doi.org/10.1007/BFb0012757
3. Bertoni, A., Mauri, G., Sabadini, N.: Membership problems for regular and context-free trace languages. Inf. Comput. **82**(2), 135–150 (1989)
4. Bouajjani, A., Enea, C., Lahiri, S.K.: Abstract semantic diffing of evolving concurrent programs. In: Ranzato, F. (ed.) Proceedings of the Static Analysis - 24th International Symposium, SAS 2017, New York, NY, USA, 30 August–1 September 2017, LNCS, vol. 10422, pp. 46–65. Springer (2017). https://doi.org/10.1007/978-3-319-66706-5_3
5. Boudol, G.: Flow event structures and flow nets. In: Guessarian, I. (ed.) LITP 1990. LNCS, vol. 469, pp. 62–95. Springer, Heidelberg (1990). https://doi.org/10.1007/3-540-53479-2_4
6. Černý, P., et al.: From non-preemptive to preemptive scheduling using synchronization synthesis. Formal Methods Syst. Des. **50**(2), 97–139 (2017)
7. Diekert, V., Métivier, Y.: Partial commutation and traces. In: Rozenberg, G., Salomaa, A. (eds.) Handbook of Formal Languages, pp. 457–533. Springer, Heidelberg (1997). https://doi.org/10.1007/978-3-642-59126-6_8
8. Dietsch, D., Jakobs, M.C.: VMCAI 2020 virtual machine, November 2019. https://doi.org/10.5281/zenodo.3533104
9. Clarke, J.E.M., Grumberg, O., Kroening, D., Peled, D., Veith, H.: Model Checking. 2nd edn. MIT Press (2018)
10. Esparza, J.: Decidability and complexity of Petri net problems — an introduction. In: Reisig, W., Rozenberg, G. (eds.) ACPN 1996. LNCS, vol. 1491, pp. 374–428. Springer, Heidelberg (1998). https://doi.org/10.1007/3-540-65306-6_20
11. Esparza, J., Nielsen, M.: Decidability issues for Petri nets - a survey. Bull. EATCS **52**, 244–262 (1994)
12. Fatès, N.: A guided tour of asynchronous cellular automata. In: Kari, J., Kutrib, M., Malcher, A. (eds.) AUTOMATA 2013. LNCS, vol. 8155, pp. 15–30. Springer, Heidelberg (2013). https://doi.org/10.1007/978-3-642-40867-0_2
13. Fellner, A., Krenn, W., Schlick, R., Tarrach, T., Weissenbacher, G.: Model-based, mutation-driven test-case generation via heuristic-guided branching search. ACM Trans. Embed. Comput. Syst. **18**(1), 4:1–4:28 (2019)
14. Fellner, A., Tarrach, T., Weissenbacher, G.: Language inclusion for finite prime event structures (2019). https://arxiv.org/abs/1911.06355
15. Fellner, A., Tarrach, T., Weissenbacher, G.: Language Inclusion for Finite Prime Event Structures. Artifact (2019). https://doi.org/10.5281/zenodo.3514619
16. Friedman, E.P.: The inclusion problem for simple languages. Theor. Comput. Sci. **1**(4), 297–316 (1976)
17. Gaubert, S., Giua, A.: Petri net languages and infinite subsets of Nm. J. Comput. Syst. Sci. **59**(3), 373–391 (1999). https://doi.org/10.1006/jcss.1999.1634

18. van Glabbeek, R., Goltz, U.: Refinement of actions in causality based models. In: de Bakker, J.W., de Roever, W.-P., Rozenberg, G. (eds.) REX 1989. LNCS, vol. 430, pp. 267–300. Springer, Heidelberg (1990). https://doi.org/10.1007/3-540-52559-9_68

19. van Glabbeek, R.J., Plotkin, G.D.: Configuration structures, event structures and Petri nets. Theor. Comput. Sci. **410**(41), 4111–4159 (2009)

20. Godefroid, P.: Partial-order methods for the verification of concurrent systems (1996)

21. Grabowski, J.: The unsolvability of some Petri net language problems. Inf. Process. Lett. **9**(2), 60–63 (1979). https://doi.org/10.1016/0020-0190(79)90128-5

22. Hack, M.: Decidability questions for Petri Nets. Ph.D. thesis, Massachusetts Institute of Technology, Cambridge, MA, USA (1976). http://hdl.handle.net/1721.1/27441

23. Hopcroft, J.E., Motwani, R., Ullman, J.D.: Introduction to Automata Theory, Languages, and Computation. 3rd edn. Pearson (2013)

24. Jancar, P.: Nonprimitive recursive complexity and undecidability for Petri net equivalences. Theor. Comput. Sci. **256**(1–2), 23–30 (2001). https://doi.org/10.1016/S0304-3975(00)00100-6

25. Jones, N.D., Landweber, L.H., Lien, Y.E.: Complexity of some problems in Petri nets. Theor. Comput. Sci. **4**(3), 277–299 (1977). https://doi.org/10.1016/0304-3975(77)90014-7

26. Karp, R.M.: Reducibility among combinatorial problems. In: Miller, R.E., Thatcher, J.W., Bohlinger, J.D. (eds.) Complexity of Computer Computations. The IBM Research Symposia Series, pp. 85–103. Springer, Boston (1972). https://doi.org/10.1007/978-1-4684-2001-2_9

27. Ko, K.I., Lin, C.L.: On the complexity of min-max optimization problems and their approximation. In: Du, D.Z., Pardalos, P.M. (eds.) Minimax and Applications. Nonconvex Optimization and Its Applications, vol. 4, pp. 219–239. Springer, Boston (1995). https://doi.org/10.1007/978-1-4613-3557-3_15

28. Lamport, L., et al.: Paxos made simple. ACM SIGACT News **32**(4), 18–25 (2001)

29. Madhusudan, P.: Model-checking trace event structures. In: Proceedings of the 18th IEEE Symposium on Logic in Computer Science (LICS 2003), Ottawa, Canada, 22–25 June 2003, pp. 371–380. IEEE Computer Society (2003). https://doi.org/10.1109/LICS.2003.1210077

30. Mayr, R., Clemente, L.: Advanced automata minimization. In: ACM SIGPLAN Notices, vol. 48, pp. 63–74. ACM (2013)

31. Mazurkiewicz, A.: Trace theory. In: Brauer, W., Reisig, W., Rozenberg, G. (eds.) ACPN 1986. LNCS, vol. 255, pp. 278–324. Springer, Heidelberg (1987). https://doi.org/10.1007/3-540-17906-2_30

32. Mazurkiewicz, A.: Introduction to trace theory. In: The Book of Traces, pp. 3–41 (1995)

33. Meyer, A.R., Stockmeyer, L.J.: The equivalence problem for regular expressions with squaring requires exponential space. In: SWAT (FOCS), pp. 125–129 (1972)

34. Nguyen, H.T.T., Rodríguez, C., Sousa, M., Coti, C., Petrucci, L.: Quasi-optimal partial order reduction. In: Chockler, H., Weissenbacher, G. (eds.) CAV 2018. LNCS, vol. 10982, pp. 354–371. Springer, Cham (2018). https://doi.org/10.1007/978-3-319-96142-2_22

35. Nielsen, M., Plotkin, G., Winskel, G.: Petri nets, event structures and domains, part I. Theor. Comput. Sci. **13**(1), 85–108 (1981)

36. Penczek, W.: Model-checking for a subclass of event structures. In: Brinksma, E. (ed.) TACAS 1997. LNCS, vol. 1217, pp. 145–164. Springer, Heidelberg (1997). https://doi.org/10.1007/BFb0035386

37. Peterson, J.: Petri Net Theory and the Modeling of Systems. Independently Published (2019). https://books.google.at/books?id=IthLyAEACAAJ

38. Rodríguez, C., Sousa, M., Sharma, S., Kroening, D.: Unfolding-based partial order reduction. In: 26th International Conference on Concurrency Theory (CONCUR 2015), pp. 456–469 (2015)

39. Stearns, R.E., Hunt III, H.B.: On the equivalence and containment problems for unambiguous regular expressions, regular grammars and finite automata. SIAM J. Comput. **14**(3), 598–611 (1985)

40. Valk, R., Vidal-Naquet, G.: Petri nets and regular languages. J. Comput. Syst. Sci. **23**(3), 299–325 (1981). https://doi.org/10.1016/0022-0000(81)90067-2

41. Valmari, A.: Stubborn sets for reduced state space generation. In: Rozenberg, G. (ed.) ICATPN 1989. LNCS, vol. 483, pp. 491–515. Springer, Heidelberg (1991). https://doi.org/10.1007/3-540-53863-1_36

42. Van Glabbeek, R., Goltz, U.: Refinement of actions and equivalence notions for concurrent systems. Acta Informatica **37**(4–5), 229–327 (2001)

43. Winskel, G.: An introduction to event structures. In: de Bakker, J.W., de Roever, W.-P., Rozenberg, G. (eds.) REX 1988. LNCS, vol. 354, pp. 364–397. Springer, Heidelberg (1989). https://doi.org/10.1007/BFb0013026

44. Winskel, G.: Event structures, stable families and concurrent games (2016)

45. Winskel, G., Nielsen, M.: Handbook of logic in computer science. In: Models for Concurrency, vol. 4, pp. 1–148. Oxford University Press Inc., New York (1995). http://dl.acm.org/citation.cfm?id=218623.218630

46. Wrathall, C.: Complete sets and the polynomial-time hierarchy. Theor. Comput. Sci. **3**(1), 23–33 (1976)

47. Zielonka, W.: Notes on finite asynchronous automata. RAIRO-Theor. Inf. Appl. **21**(2), 99–135 (1987)

Promptness and Bounded Fairness in Concurrent and Parameterized Systems

Swen Jacobs[1]([✉]) [iD], Mouhammad Sakr[1,2] [iD], and Martin Zimmermann[3] [iD]

[1] CISPA Helmholtz Center for Information Security, Saarbrücken, Germany
jacobs@cispa.saarland
[2] Saarland University, Saarbrücken, Germany
[3] University of Liverpool, Liverpool, UK

Abstract. We investigate the satisfaction of specifications in Prompt Linear Temporal Logic (Prompt-LTL) by concurrent systems. Prompt-LTL is an extension of LTL that allows to specify parametric bounds on the satisfaction of eventualities, thus adding a quantitative aspect to the specification language. We establish a connection between bounded fairness, bounded stutter equivalence, and the satisfaction of Prompt-LTL\\$\mathbf{X}$ formulas. Based on this connection, we prove the first cutoff results for different classes of systems with a parametric number of components and quantitative specifications, thereby identifying previously unknown decidable fragments of the parameterized model checking problem.

1 Introduction

Concurrent systems are notoriously hard to get correct, and are therefore a promising application area for formal methods like model checking or synthesis. However, these methods usually give correctness guarantees only for systems with a given, fixed number of components, and the state explosion problem prevents us from using them for systems with a large number of components. To ensure that desired properties hold for systems with a very large or even an *arbitrary* number of components, methods for *parameterized* model checking and synthesis have been devised.

While parameterized model checking is undecidable even for simple safety properties and systems with uniform finite-state components [33], there exist a number of methods that decide the problem for specific classes of systems [2,10,12–15,17,20,29], some of which have been collected in surveys of the literature recently [8,16]. Additionally, there are semi-decision procedures that are successful in many interesting cases [9,11,25,28,30]. However, most of these approaches only support safety properties, or their support for progress or liveness properties is limited, e.g., because global fairness properties are not

---

Partially funded by grant EP/S032207/1 from the Engineering and Physical Sciences Research Council (EPSRC).

D. Beyer and D. Zufferey (Eds.): VMCAI 2020, LNCS 11990, pp. 337–359, 2020.
https://doi.org/10.1007/978-3-030-39322-9_16

considered and cannot be expressed in the supported logic (cp. Außerlechner et al. [5]).

In this paper, we investigate cases in which we can guarantee that a system with an arbitrary number of components satisfies strong liveness properties, including a quantitative version of liveness called *promptness*. The idea of promptness is that a desired event should not only happen at *some* time in the future, but there should exist a *bound* on the time that can pass before it happens. We consider specifications in Prompt-LTL, an extension of LTL with an operator that expresses prompt eventualities [27], i.e., the logic puts a symbolic bound on the satisfaction of the eventuality, and the model checking problem asks if there is a value for this symbolic bound such that the property is guaranteed to be satisfied with respect to this value. In many settings, adding promptness comes for free in terms of asymptotic complexity [27], e.g., model checking and synthesis [24].[1] Hence, here we study *parameterized* model checking for Prompt-LTL and show that in many cases adding promptness is also free for this problem.

More precisely, as is common in the analysis of concurrent systems, we abstract concurrency by an interleaving semantics and consider the satisfaction of a specification *up to stuttering*. Therefore, we limit our specifications to Prompt-LTL**X**, an extension of the stutter-insensitive logic LTL**X** that does not have the next-time operator. Determining satisfaction of Prompt-LTL**X** specifications by concurrent systems brings new challenges and has not been investigated in detail before.

Motivating Example. For instance, consider the reader-writer protocol on the right which models access to shared data between processes. If a process wants to "read", it enters the state **tr** ("try-read") that has a direct transition to the reading state **r**. However, this transition is guarded by $\forall\neg$**w**, which stands for the set of all states except

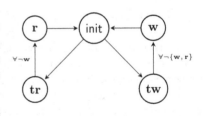

w, the "writing" state. That is, the transition is only enabled if no other process is currently in state **w**. Likewise, if a process wants to enter **w** it has to go through **tw**, but the transition to **w** is enabled only if no other process is reading or writing.

For such systems, previous results [5,14] provide cutoff results for parameterized verification of properties from LTL**X**, e.g.,

$$\forall i.\mathbf{G}\left((tr_i \rightarrow \mathbf{F}r_i) \wedge (tw_i \rightarrow \mathbf{F}w_i)\right),$$

---

[1] Prompt-LTL can be seen as a fragment of parametric LTL, a logic introduced by Alur et al. [1]. However, since most decision problems for parametric LTL, including model checking, can be reduced to those for Prompt-LTL, we can restrict our attention to the simpler logic.

In this paper we investigate whether the same cutoffs still hold if we consider specifications in Prompt-LTL\$\X$, e.g., if we substitute the LTL eventually operator $\mathbf{F}$ above with the prompt-eventually operator $\mathbf{F_p}$, while imposing a bounded fairness assumption on the scheduler.

Contributions. As a first step, we note that Prompt-LTL\$\X$ is not a stutter-insensitive logic, since unbounded stuttering could invalidate a promptness property. This leads us to define the notion of *bounded stutter equivalence*, and proving that Prompt-LTL\$\X$ is *bounded stutter insensitive*.

This observation is then used in an investigation of existing approaches that solve parameterized model checking by the *cutoff* method, which reduces problems from systems with an arbitrary number of components to systems with a fixed number of components. More precisely, these approaches prove that for every trace in a large system, a stutter-equivalent trace in the cutoff system exists, and vice versa. We show that in many cases, modifications of these constructions allow us to obtain traces that are *bounded* stutter equivalent, and therefore the cutoff results extend to specifications in Prompt-LTL\$\X$. The types of systems for which we prove these results include *guarded protocols*, as introduced by Emerson and Kahlon [14], and *token-passing systems*, as introduced by Emerson and Namjoshi [13] for uni-directional rings, and by Clarke et al. [10] for arbitrary topologies. Parameterized model checking for both of these system classes has recently been further investigated [2,3,5,22,31,32], but thus far not in a context that includes promptness properties. Due to space constraints, we omit detailed proofs in some cases. They can be found in the full version of the paper [23].

2 Prompt-LTL\X and Bounded Stutter Equivalence

We assume that the reader is aware of standard notions such as finite-state transition systems and linear temporal logic (LTL) [6].

We consider concurrent systems that are represented as an interleaving composition of finite-state transition systems, possibly with synchronizing transitions where multiple processes take a step at the same time. In such systems, a process may stay in the same state for many global transitions while other processes are moving. From the perspective of that process, these are *stuttering steps*.

Stuttering is a well-known phenomenon, and temporal languages that include the next-time operator $\mathbf{X}$ are *stutter sensitive*: they can require some atomic proposition to hold at the next moment in time, and the insertion of a stuttering step may change whether the formula is satisfied or not. On the other hand, LTL \ $\mathbf{X}$, which does not have the $\mathbf{X}$ operator, is stutter-insensitive: two words that only differ in stuttering steps cannot be distinguished by the logic [6].

In the following, we introduce Prompt-LTL\$\X$, an extension of LTL\$\X$, and investigate its properties with respect to stuttering.

2.1   Prompt-LTL\X

Let AP be the set of atomic propositions. The syntax of Prompt-LTL\X formulas over AP is given by the following grammar:

$$\varphi ::= a \mid \neg a \mid \varphi \vee \varphi \mid \varphi \wedge \varphi \mid \mathbf{F_p}\varphi \mid \varphi \mathbf{U}\varphi \mid \varphi \mathbf{R}\varphi, \text{where } a \in AP$$

The semantics of Prompt-LTL\X formulas is defined over infinite words $w = w_0 w_1 \ldots \in (2^{AP})^\omega$, positions $i \in \mathbb{N}$, and bounds $k \in \mathbb{N}$. The semantics of the prompt-eventually operator $\mathbf{F_p}$ is defined as follows:

$$(w, i, k) \models \mathbf{F_p}\varphi \text{ iff there exists } j \text{ such that } i \leq j \leq i + k \text{ and } (w, j, k) \models \varphi.$$

All other operators ignore the bound k and have the same semantics as in LTL, moreover we define $\mathbf{F}$ and $\mathbf{G}$ in terms of $\mathbf{U}$ and $\mathbf{R}$ as usual.

2.2   Prompt-LTL and Stuttering

Our first observation is that Prompt-LTL\X is stutter sensitive: to satisfy the formula $\varphi = \mathbf{GF_p}q$ with respect to a bound k, q has to appear at least once in every k steps. Given a word w that satisfies φ for some bound k, we can construct a word that does not satisfy φ for any bound k by introducing an increasing (and unbounded) number of stuttering steps between every two appearances of q. In the following, we show that Prompt-LTL\X is stutter insensitive if and only if there is a bound on the number of consecutive stuttering steps.

Bounded Stutter Equivalence. A finite word $w \in (2^{AP})^+$ is a *block* if $\exists \alpha \subseteq AP$ such that $w = \alpha^{|w|}$. Two blocks $w, w' \in (2^{AP})^+$ are *d-compatible* if $\exists \alpha \subseteq AP$ such that $w = \alpha^{|w|}, w' = \alpha^{|w'|}$, $|w| \leq d \cdot |w'|$ and $|w'| \leq d \cdot |w|$. Two infinite sequences of blocks $w_0 w_1 w_2 \ldots$, $w_0' w_1' w_2' \ldots$ are *d-compatible* if w_i, w_i' are d-compatible for all i.

Two words $w, w' \in (2^{AP})^\omega$ are *d-stutter equivalent*, denoted $w \equiv_d w'$, if they can be written as d-compatible sequences of blocks. They are *bounded stutter equivalent* if they are d-stutter equivalent for some d. We denote by $\hat{w}$ a sequence of blocks that corresponds to a word w.

Given an infinite sequence of blocks $\hat{w} = w_0, w_1, w_2 \ldots$, let $N_i^{\hat{w}} = \{\sum_{l=0}^{i-1} |w_l|, \ldots, \sum_{l=0}^{i-1} |w_l| + |w_i| - 1\}$ be the set of positions of the ith block. Given a position n, there is a unique i such that $n \in N_i^{\hat{w}}$.

To prove that Prompt-LTL\X is *bounded stutter insensitive*, i.e., it cannot distinguish two words that are bounded stutter equivalent, we define a function that maps between positions in two d-compatible sequences of blocks: given two infinite d-stutter equivalent words w, w' such that $\hat{w}, \hat{w}'$ are d-compatible, define the function $f : \mathbb{N} \to 2^{\mathbb{N}}$ where: $f(j) = N_i^{\hat{w}'} \Leftrightarrow j \in N_i^{\hat{w}}$. Note that $\forall j' \in f(j)$ we have $w(j) = w'(j')$, where $w(i)$ denotes the ith symbol in w. For an infinite word w, let $w[i, \infty)$ denote its suffix starting at position i, and $w[i : j]$ its infix starting at i and ending at j. Then we can state the following.

Remark 1. Given two words w and w', if $w \equiv_d w'$, then $\forall j \in \mathbb{N} \ \forall j' \in f(j)$: $w[j, \infty) \equiv_d w'[j', \infty)$.

Now, we can state our first theorem.

Theorem 1 (Prompt-LTL\X is Bounded Stutter Insensitive). *Let w, w' be d-stutter equivalent words, φ a Prompt-LTL\X formula, and f as defined above. Then $\forall i, k \in \mathbb{N}$:*

$$(w, i, k) \models \varphi \Rightarrow \forall j \in f(i) : (w', j, d \cdot k) \models \varphi$$

Proof. The proof works inductively over the structure of φ. Let $\hat{w} = w_0, w_1, \ldots$ and $\hat{w}' = w'_0, w'_1, \ldots$ be two d-compatible sequences of w and w'. We denote by n_i, m_i the number of elements inside $N_i^w, N_i^{w'}$ respectively. We consider two cases, the other cases are trivial or similar to Case 2:

Case 1: $\varphi = \mathbf{F_p}\varphi$. $(w, i, k) \models \mathbf{F_p}\varphi \Leftrightarrow \exists e, x : i \leq e \leq i + k, e \in N_x^{\hat{w}}$, and $(w, e, k) \models \varphi$ where $(\sum_{l=0}^{x-1} n_l) \leq e < (\sum_{l=0}^{x} n_l)$. Then by induction hypothesis we have: $\forall j \in f(e)(w', j, d \cdot k) \models \varphi$. Let s be the smallest position in $f(e)$, then $s = \sum_{l=0}^{x-1} m_l$. There exists $y \in \mathbb{N}$ s.t. $i \in N_y^{\hat{w}}$ then $s = \sum_{l=0}^{y-1} m_l + \sum_{l=y}^{x-1} m_l \leq \sum_{l=0}^{y-1} m_l + \sum_{l=y}^{x-1} n_l.d \leq \sum_{l=0}^{y-1} m_l + d.(\sum_{l=y}^{x-1} n_l) \leq \sum_{l=0}^{y-1} m_l + k \cdot d$ (note that $i \in N_y^{\hat{w}}$ and $(w, i, k) \models \mathbf{F_p}\varphi$). As $\sum_{l=0}^{y-1} m_l$ is the smallest position in $f(i)$, then $\forall j \in f(i) : (w', j, d \cdot k) \models \mathbf{F_p}\varphi$.

Case 2: $\varphi = \varphi_1 \mathbf{U} \varphi_2$. $(w, i, k) \models \varphi_1 \mathbf{U} \varphi_2 \Leftrightarrow \exists j \geq i : (w, j, k) \models \varphi_2$ and $\forall e < j : (w, e, k) \models \varphi_1$. Then, by induction hypothesis we have: $\forall e < j \ \forall l \in f(e) : (w', l, d \cdot k) \models \varphi_1$ and $\forall l \in f(j) : (w', l, d \cdot k) \models \varphi_2$, therefore $\forall j \in f(i) : (w', j, d \cdot k) \models \varphi_1 \mathbf{U} \varphi_2$. $\qquad \square$

Our later proofs will be based on the existence of counterexamples to a given property, and will use the following consequence of Theorem 1.

Corollary 1. *Let w, w' be d-stutter equivalent words, φ a Prompt-LTL\X formula, and f as defined above. Then $\forall k \in \mathbb{N}$:*

$$(w, i, k) \not\models \varphi \Rightarrow \forall j \in f(i) : (w', j, k/d) \not\models \varphi$$

3 Guarded Protocols and Parameterized Model Checking

In the following, we introduce a system model for concurrent systems, called guarded protocols. However, we will see that some of our results are of interest for other classes of concurrent and parameterized systems, e.g., the token-passing systems that we investigate in Sect. 6.

3.1   System Model: Guarded Protocols

We consider systems of the form $A\|B^n$, consisting of one copy of a process template A and n copies of a process template B, in an interleaving parallel composition. We distinguish objects that belong to different templates by indexing them with the template. E.g., for process template $U \in \{A, B\}$, Q_U is the set of states of U. For this section, fix a finite set of states $Q = Q_A \,\dot{\cup}\, Q_B$ and a positive integer n, and let $\mathcal{G} = \{\exists, \forall\} \times 2^Q$ be the set of guards.

Processes. A *process template* is a transition system $U = (Q_U, \mathrm{init}_U, \delta_U)$ where

– $Q_U \subseteq Q$ is a finite set of states including the initial state init_U,
– $\delta_U \subseteq Q_U \times \mathcal{G} \times Q_U$ is a guarded transition relation.

Guarded Protocols. The semantics of $A\|B^n$ is given by the transition system $(S, \mathrm{init}_s, \Delta)$, where[2]

– $S = Q_A \times (Q_B)^n$ is the set of (global) states,
– $\mathrm{init}_S = (\mathrm{init}_A, \mathrm{init}_B, \dots, \mathrm{init}_B)$ is the global initial state, and
– $\Delta \subseteq S \times S$ is the global transition relation. Δ will be defined by local guarded transitions of the process templates A and B in the following.

We distinguish different copies of process template B in $A\|B^n$ by subscript, and each B_i is called a *B-process*. We denote the set $\{A, B_1, \dots, B_n\}$ as $\mathcal{P}$, and a process in $\mathcal{P}$ as p. For a global state $s \in S$ and $p \in \mathcal{P}$, let the *local state of p in s* be the projection of s onto that process, denoted $s(p)$.

Then a local transition (q, g, q') of process $p \in \mathcal{P}$ is *enabled* in global state s if $s(p) = q$ and either

– $g = (\exists, G)$ and $\exists p' \in \mathcal{P} \setminus \{p\} : s(p') \in G$, or
– $g = (\forall, G)$ and $\forall p' \in \mathcal{P} \setminus \{p\} : s(p') \in G$.

Finally, $(s, s') \in \Delta$ if there exists $p \in \mathcal{P}$ such that $(s(p), g, s'(p)) \in \delta_p$ is enabled in s, and $s(p') = s'(p')$ for all $p' \in \mathcal{P} \setminus \{p\}$. We say that the transition (s, s') *is based* on the local transition $(s(p), g, s'(p))$ of p.

Disjunctive and Conjunctive Systems. We distinguish disjunctive and conjunctive systems, as defined by Emerson and Kahlon [14]. In a *disjunctive process template*, every guard is of the form $(\exists, G)$ for some $G \subseteq Q$. In a *conjunctive process template*, every guard is of the form $(\forall, G)$, and $\{\mathrm{init}_A, \mathrm{init}_B\} \subseteq G$, i.e., initial states act as neutral states for all transitions. A *disjunctive (conjunctive) system* consists of only disjunctive (conjunctive) process templates. For conjunctive

---

[2] By similar arguments as in Emerson and Kahlon [14], our results can be extended to systems with an arbitrary (but fixed) number of process templates. The same holds for *open* process templates that can receive inputs from an environment, as considered by Außerlechner et al. [5].

systems we additionally assume that processes are *initializing*, i.e., any process that moves infinitely often visits its initial state infinitely often.[3]

Runs. A *path* of a system $A\|B^n$ is a sequence $x = s_0 s_1 \dots$ of global states such that for all $i < |x|$ there is a transition $(s_i, s_{i+1}) \in \Delta$ based on a local transition of some process $p \in \mathcal{P}$. We say that p *moves* at *moment* i. A path can be finite or infinite, and a *maximal path* is a path that cannot be extended, i.e., it is either infinite or ends in a global state where no local transition is enabled, also called a *deadlock*. A *run* is a maximal path starting in init_S. We write $x \in A\|B^n$ to denote that x is a run of $A\|B^n$.

Given a path $x = s_0 s_1 \dots$ and a process p, the *local path* of p in x is the projection $x(p) = s_0(p) s_1(p) \dots$ of x onto local states of p. It is a *local run* of p if x is a run. Additionally we denote by $x(p_1, \dots, p_k)$ the projection $s_0(p_1, \dots, p_k) s_1(p_1, \dots, p_k) \dots$ of x onto the processes $p_1, \dots, p_k \in \mathcal{P}$.

Fairness. We say a process p is *enabled* in global state s if at least one of its transitions is enabled in s, otherwise it is *disabled*. Then, an infinite run x of a system $A\|B^n$ is

- *strongly fair* if for every process p, if p is enabled infinitely often, then p moves infinitely often.
- *unconditionally fair*, denoted u-fair(x), if every process moves infinitely often.
- *globally b-bounded fair*, denoted b-gfair(x), for some $b \in \mathbb{N}$, if

$$\forall p \in \mathcal{P} \; \forall m \in \mathbb{N} \; \exists j \in \mathbb{N} : m \le j \le m + b \text{ and } p \text{ moves at moment } j.$$

- *locally b-bounded fair* for $E \subseteq \mathcal{P}$, denoted b-lfair(x, E), if it is unconditionally fair and

$$\forall p \in E \; \forall m \in \mathbb{N} \; \exists j \in \mathbb{N} : m \le j \le m + b \text{ and } p \text{ moves at moment } j.$$

Bounded-fair System. We consider systems that keep track of bounded fairness explicitly by running in parallel to $A\|B^n$ one counter for each process. In a step of the system where process p moves, the counter of p is reset, and all other counters are incremented. If one of the counters exceeds the bound b, the counter goes into a failure state from which no transition is enabled. We call such a system a *bounded-fair system*, and denote it $A\|_b B^n$.

A *path* of a bounded-fair system $A\|_b B^n$ is given as $x = (s_0, b_0)(s_1, b_1) \dots$, and extends a path of $A\|B^n$ by valuations $b_i \in \{0, \dots, b\}^{n+1}$ of the counters. Note that a run (i.e., a maximal path) of $A\|_b B^n$ is finite iff either it is deadlocked (in which case also its projection to a run of $A\|B^n$ is deadlocked) or a failure state is reached. Thus, the projection of all infinite runs of $A\|_b B^n$ to $A\|B^n$ are exactly the globally b-bounded fair runs of $A\|B^n$.

---

[3] This restriction has already been considered by Außerlechner et al. [5], and was necessary to support global fairness assumptions.

3.2 Parameterized Model Checking and Cutoffs

Prompt-LTL\X Specifications. Given a system $A\|B^n$, we consider specifications over $AP = Q_A \cup (Q_B \times \{1, \ldots, n\})$, i.e., states of processes are used as atomic propositions. For $i_1, \ldots, i_c \in \{1, \ldots, n\}$, we write $\varphi(A, B_{i_1}, \ldots, B_{i_c})$ for a formula that contains only atomic propositions from $Q_A \cup (Q_B \times \{i_1, \ldots, i_c\})$.

In the absence of fairness considerations, we say that $A\|B^n$ satisfies φ if

$$\exists k \in \mathbb{N} \; \forall x \in A\|B^n : (x, 0, k) \models \varphi.$$

We say that $A\|B^n$ satisfies $\varphi(A, B_1, \ldots, B_c)$ *under global bounded fairness*, written $A\|B^n \models_{gb} \varphi(A, B_1, \ldots, B_c)$, if

$$\forall b \in \mathbb{N} \; \exists k \in \mathbb{N} \; \forall x \in A\|B^n : b\text{-gfair}(x) \Rightarrow (x, 0, k) \models \varphi(A, B_1, \ldots, B_c).$$

Finally, for local bounded fairness we usually require bounded fairness for all processes that appear in the formula $\varphi(A, B_1, \ldots, B_c)$. Thus, we say that $A\|B^n$ satisfies $\varphi(A, B_1, \ldots, B_c)$ *under local bounded fairness*, written $A\|B^n \models_{lb} \varphi(A, B_1, \ldots, B_c)$, if

$$\forall b \in \mathbb{N} \; \exists k \in \mathbb{N} \; \forall x \in A\|B^n : b\text{-lfair}(x, \{1, \ldots, c\}) \Rightarrow (x, 0, k) \models \varphi(A, B_1, \ldots, B_c).$$

Parameterized Specifications. A *parameterized specification* is a Prompt-LTL\X formula with quantification over the indices of atomic propositions. A *h-indexed formula* is of the form $\forall i_1, \ldots, \forall i_h.\varphi(A, B_{i_1}, \ldots, B_{i_h})$. Let $f \in \{gb, lb\}$, then for given $n \geq h$,

$$A\|B^n \models_f \forall i_1, \ldots, \forall i_h.\varphi(A, B_{i_1}, \ldots, B_{i_h})$$

$$\Leftrightarrow$$

$$\forall j_1 \neq \ldots \neq j_h \in \{1, \ldots, n\} : A\|B^n \models_f \varphi(A, B_{j_1}, \ldots, B_{j_h}).$$

By symmetry of guarded protocols, this is equivalent (cp. [14]) to $A\|B^n \models_f \varphi(A, B_1, \ldots, B_h)$. The latter formula is denoted by $\varphi(A, B^{(h)})$, and we often use it instead of the original $\forall i_1, \ldots, \forall i_h.\varphi(A, B_{i_1}, \ldots, B_{i_h})$.

(Parameterized) Model Checking Problems. For $n \in \mathbb{N}$, a specification $\varphi(A, B^{(h)})$ with $n \geq h$, and $f \in \{gb, lb\}$:

– the *model checking problem* is to decide whether $A\|B^n \models_f \varphi(A, B^{(h)})$,
– the *parameterized model checking problem* (PMCP) is to decide whether $\forall m \geq n : A\|B^m \models_f \varphi(A, B^{(h)})$.

Cutoffs and Decidability. We define cutoffs with respect to a class of systems (either disjunctive or conjunctive), a class of process templates P, e.g., templates of bounded size, and a class of properties, e.g. satisfaction of h-indexed Prompt-LTL\X formulas under a given fairness notion.

A *cutoff* for a given class of systems with processes from P, a fairness notion $f \in \{lb, gb\}$ and a set of Prompt-LTL\$\mathbf{X}$ formulas Φ is a number $c \in \mathbb{N}$ such that

$$\forall A, B \in P \ \forall \varphi \in \Phi \ \forall n \geq c : A\|B^n \models_f \varphi \Leftrightarrow A\|B^c \models_f \varphi.$$

Note that the existence of a cutoff implies that the PMCP is *decidable* iff the model checking problem for the cutoff system $A\|B^c$ is decidable. Decidability of model checking for finite transition systems with specifications in Prompt-LTL\$\mathbf{X}$ and bounded fairness follows from the fact that bounded fairness can be expressed in Prompt-LTL\$\mathbf{X}$, and from results on decidability of assume-guarantee model checking for Prompt-LTL (cf. Kupferman et al. [27] and Faymonville and Zimmermann [19][Lemmas 8, 9]).

4 Cutoffs for Disjunctive Systems

In this section, we prove cutoff results for disjunctive systems under bounded fairness and stutter-insensitive specifications with or without promptness. To this end, in Sect. 4.1 we prove two lemmas that show how to simulate, up to bounded stuttering, local runs from a system of given size n in a smaller or larger disjunctive system. We then use these two lemmas in Subsects. 4.2 and 4.3 to obtain cutoffs for specifications in LTL\$\mathbf{X}$ and Prompt-LTL\$\mathbf{X}$, respectively.

Moreover for the proofs of these two lemmas we utilize the same construction techniques that were used in [4,5,14], but in addition we analyze their effects on bounded fairness and bounded stutter equivalence. Note that we will only consider formulas of the form $\varphi(A, B^{(1)})$, however, as in previous work [4,14], our results extend to specifications over an arbitrary number h of B-processes.

Table 1 summarizes the results of this section: for specifications in LTL\$\mathbf{X}$ and Prompt-LTL\$\mathbf{X}$ we obtain a cutoff that depends on the size of process template B, as well as on the number h of quantified index variables. The table states generalizations of Theorems 2 and 3 from the 2-indexed case to the h-indexed case for arbitrary $h \in \mathbb{N}$. For one of the cases we were not able to obtain a cutoff result (as explained in the full version [23]).

Simple Reader-Writer Example. Consider the disjunctive system $W\|R^n$, where W is a writer process (Fig. 2), and R is a reader process (Fig. 1). Let the specification φ be $\forall i \ \mathbf{G}(\mathbf{w} \rightarrow \mathbf{F_p}[(\mathbf{w} \wedge \mathbf{nr}_i)])$, i.e., if process W is in state $\mathbf{w}$, then eventually all the R processes will be in state $\mathbf{nr}$, while W is in $\mathbf{w}$. According to Table 1, the cutoff for checking whether $W\|R^n \models_{lb} \varphi$ is 5.

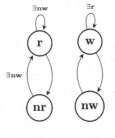

Fig. 1.
Reader

Fig. 2.
Writer

Table 1. Cutoffs for disjunctive systems

	Local bounded fairness	Global bounded fairness
h-indexed LTL$\backslash$**X**	$2|Q_B| + h$	$2|Q_B| + h$
h-indexed Prompt-LTL$\backslash$**X**	$2|Q_B| + h$	-

4.1 Simulation up to Bounded Stutter Equivalence

Definitions. Fix a run $x = x_0 x_1 ...$ of the disjunctive system $A \| B^n$. Our constructions are based on the following definitions, where $q \in Q_B$:

- appears$^{B_i}(q)$ is the set of all moments in x where process B_i is in state q: appears$^{B_i}(q) = \{m \in \mathbb{N} \mid x_m(B_i) = q\}$.
- appears(q) is the set of all moments in x where at least one B-process is in state q: appears$(q) = \{m \in \mathbb{N} \mid \exists i \in \{1, \ldots, n\} : x_m(B_i) = q\}$.
- f_q is the first moment in x where q appears: $f_q = min(\text{appears}(q))$, and first$_q \in \{1, \ldots, n\}$ is the index of a B-process where q appears first, i.e., with $x_{f_q}(B_{\text{first}_q}) = q$.
- if appears(q) is finite, then $l_q = max(\text{appears}(q))$ is the last moment where q appears, and last$_q \in \{1, \ldots, n\}$ is a process index with $x_{l_q}(B_{\text{last}_q}) = q$
- let Visited$^{inf} = \{q \in Q_B \mid \exists B_i \in \{B_2, \ldots, B_n\} : \text{appears}^{B_i}(q) \text{ is infinite}\}$ and Visited$^{fin} = \{q \in Q_B \mid \forall B_i \in \{B_2, \ldots, B_n\} : \text{appears}^{B_i}(q) \text{ is finite}\}$.
- $Set(x_i)$ is the set of all state that are visited by some process at moment i: $Set(x_i) = \{q | q \in (Q_A \cup Q_B) \text{ and } \exists p \in \mathcal{P} : x_i(p) = q\}$.

Our first lemma states that any behavior of processes A and B_1 in a system $A \| B^n$ can be simulated up to bounded stuttering in a system $A \| B^{n+1}$. This type of lemma is called a *monotonicity lemma*.

Lemma 1 (Monotonicity Lemma for Bounded Stutter Equivalence).
Let A, B be disjunctive process templates, $n \geq 2$, $b \in \mathbb{N}$ and $x \in A \| B^n$ with b-lfair$(x, \{A, B_1\})$. Then there exists $y \in A \| B^{n+1}$ with $2b$-lfair$(y, \{A, B_1\})$ and $x(A, B_1) \equiv_2 y(A, B_1)$.

Proof. Let x be a run of $A \| B^n$ where b-lfair$(x, \{A, B_1\})$. Let $y(A) = x(A)$ and $y(B_j) = x(B_j)$ for all $B_j \in \{B_1, \ldots, B_n\}$ and let the new process B_{n+1} copy one of the B-processes of $A \| B^n$, i.e., $y(B_{n+1}) = x(B_i)$ for some $i \in \{1, \ldots, n\}$. Copying a local run violates the interleaving semantics as two processes will be moving at the same time. To solve this problem, we split every transition (y_l, y_{l+1}) where the interleaving semantics is violated by B_i and B_{n+1} executing local transitions (q_i, g, q_i') and (q_{n+1}, g, q_{n+1}'), respectively. To do this, replace (y_l, y_{l+1}) with two consecutive transitions $(y_l, u)(u, y_{l+1})$, where (y_l, u) is based on the local transition (q_i, g, q_i') and (u, y_{l+1}) is based on the local transition (q_{n+1}, g, q_{n+1}'). Note that both of these local transitions are enabled in the constructed run y since the transition (q_i, g, q_i') is enabled in the original run x. Moreover, run y inherits unconditional fairness from x. Finally, it is easy to see that for every local transition of process B_i in x, establishing interleaving semantics has added one additional stuttering step to every local run in y including processes A and B_1. Therefore we have that $2b$-lfair$(y, \{A, B_1\})$ and $x(A, B_1) \equiv_2 y(A, B_1)$. $\qquad\square$

Reader-Writer Example. Consider the run x of the system $W \| R^2$ in Fig. 3 where W and R are as defined in Figs. 1 and 2. We construct a run y of the system $W \| R^3$ (see Fig. 4) such that $x(W, R_1) \equiv_2 y(W, R_1)$. The local run of process R_3 is obtained by (i) copying the run of R_2, and (ii) establishing the interleaving semantics as in the proof of Lemma 1.

t	W	R_1	R_2
0	nw	nr	nr
1	nw	**r**	nr
2	nw	r	**r**
3	**w**	r	r
4	**nw**	r	r
5	nw	**r**	r
6	nw	r	**r**

t	W	R_1	R_2	R_3
0	nw	nr	nr	nr
1	nw	**r**	nr	nr
2	nw	r	**r**	nr
3	nw	r	r	**r**
4	**w**	r	r	r
5	**nw**	r	r	r
6	nw	**r**	r	r
7	nw	r	**r**	r
8	nw	r	r	**r**

Fig. 3. Run: $W \| R^2$ **Fig. 4.** Run: $W \| R^3$

As mentioned in the above construction, if a local run of x is d-bounded fair for some $d \in \mathbb{N}$, then it will be $2d$-bounded fair in the constructed run y. This observation leads to the following corollary.

Corollary 2. *Let A, B be disjunctive process templates, $n \geq 2$, $b \in \mathbb{N}$ and $x \in A \| B^n$ with b-gfair(x). Then there exists $y \in A \| B^{n+1}$ with $2b$-gfair(y) and $x(A, B_1) \equiv_2 y(A, B_1)$.*

Our second lemma is a *bounding lemma* which states that any behavior of processes A and B_1 in a disjunctive system $A \| B^n$ can be simulated up to bounded stuttering in a system $A \| B^c$, if c is chosen to be sufficiently large and $n \geq c$.

Lemma 2 (Bounding Lemma for Bounded Stutter Equivalence). *Let A, B be disjunctive process templates, $c = 2|Q_B| + 1$, $n \geq c$, $b \in \mathbb{N}$ and $x \in A \| B^n$ with b-lfair$(x, \{A, B_1\})$. Then there exists $y \in A \| B^c$ with $(b \cdot c)$-lfair$(y, \{A, B_1\})$ and $x(A, B_1) \equiv_c y(A, B_1)$.*

Proof. Let x be a run of $A \| B^n$ where b-lfair$(x, \{A, B_1\})$. We show how to construct a run y of $A \| B^c$ where $(b \cdot c)$-lfair$(y, \{A, B_1\})$ and $x(A, B_1) \equiv_c y(A, B_1)$.

The basic idea is that, in order to ensure that all transitions in y are enabled at the time they are taken, we "flood" every state q that is visited in x with one or more processes that enter q and stay there. Additionally, we need to take care of fairness, which requires a more complicated construction that allows every such process to move infinitely often. Therefore, some processes have to leave the state they have flooded (if that state only appears finitely often in the original run), and every process needs to eventually enter a loop that allows it to move infinitely often. In the following, we construct such runs formally.

Construction:

1. **(Flooding with evacuation):** To every $q \in \mathsf{Visited}^{fin}(x)$, devote one process B_{i_q} that copies B_{first_q} until the time f_q, then stutters in q until time l_q where it starts copying B_{last_q} forever. Formally:

$$y(B_{i_q}) = x(B_{\mathsf{first}_q})[0 : f_q].(q)^{l_q - f_q}.x(B_{last_q})[l_q + 1 : \infty]$$

2. **(Flooding with fair extension):** For every $q \in \mathsf{Visited}^{inf}(x)$, let B_q^{inf} be a process that visits q infinitely often in x. We devote to q two processes $B_{i_{q_1}}$ and $B_{i_{q_2}}$ that both copy B_{first_q} until the time f_q, and then stutter in q until B_q^{inf} reaches q for the first time. After that, let $B_{i_{q_1}}$ and $B_{i_{q_2}}$ copy B_q^{inf} in turns as follows: $B_{i_{q_1}}$ copies B_q^{inf} until it reaches q while $B_{i_{q_2}}$ stutters in q, then $B_{i_{q_2}}$ copies B_q^{inf} until it reaches q while $B_{i_{q_1}}$ stutters in q and so on.
3. Establish interleaving semantics as in the proof of Lemma 1.

After steps 1 and 2, the following property holds: at any time t we have that $Set(x_t) \subseteq Set(y_t)$, which guarantees that every transition along the run is enabled. Note that establishing the interleaving semantics preserves this property.

Finally, establishing interleaving semantics could introduce additional stuttering steps to the local runs of processes A and B_1 whenever steps 1 or 2 of the construction use the same local run from x more than once (e.g. if $\exists q_i, q_j \in Q_B$ with $\mathsf{first}_{q_i} = \mathsf{first}_{q_j}$). A local run of x can be used in the above construction at most $2|Q_B|$ times, therefore we have $x(A, B_1) \equiv_c y(A, B_1)$. Moreover, since the upper bound of consecutive stuttering steps in A or B_1 is $(2|Q_B| + 1) \cdot b$, we get $(b \cdot c)\text{-lfair}(y, \{A, B_1\})$.   □

Reader-Writer Example. Consider again the reader-writer system in Figs. 1 and 2. For any run x of $W\|R^n$, using the construction above we obtain a run y of $W\|R^5$ (or even a smaller system) with $x(W, R_1) \equiv_5 y(W, R_1)$.

4.2   Cutoffs for Specifications in LTL\X Under Bounded Fairness

The PMCP for disjunctive systems with specifications from LTL$\backslash$**X** has been considered in several previous works [5,14,22]. In the following we extend these results by proving cutoff results under bounded fairness.

Theorem 2 (Cutoff for LTL\X with Global Bounded Fairness). *Let A, B be disjunctive process templates, $c = 2|Q_B| + 1$, $n \geq c$, and $\varphi(A, B^{(1)})$ a specification with $\varphi \in LTL\backslash \mathbf{X}$. Then:*

$$\left(\forall b \in \mathbb{N} : A\|_b B^n \models \varphi(A, B^{(1)}) \right) \Leftrightarrow \left(\forall b' \in \mathbb{N} : A\|_{b'} B^c \models \varphi(A, B^{(1)}) \right)$$

We prove the theorem by proving two lemmas, one for each direction of the equivalence.

Lemma 3 (Monotonicity Lemma for LTL\X). *Let A, B be disjunctive process templates, $n \geq 1$, and $\varphi(A, B^{(1)})$ a specification with $\varphi \in LTL\backslash\mathbf{X}$. Then:*

$$\left(\exists b \in \mathbb{N} : A\|_b B^n \not\models \varphi(A, B^{(1)})\right) \Rightarrow \left(\exists b' \in \mathbb{N} : A\|_{b'} B^{n+1} \not\models \varphi(A, B^{(1)})\right)$$

Proof. Assume $\exists b \in \mathbb{N} : A\|_b B^n \not\models \varphi(A, B^{(1)})$. Then there exists a run x of $A\|B^n$ where x is b-gfair(x) and $x \not\models \varphi(A, B^{(1)})$. According to Corollary 2 there exists y of $A\|B^{n+1}$ where $2b$-gfair(y) and $x(A, B_1) \equiv_2 y(A, B_1)$, which guarantees that $y \not\models \varphi(A, B^{(1)})$. $\qquad\square$

For the corresponding bounding lemma, our construction is based on that of Lemma 2. However, the local runs resulting from that construction might stutter in some local states for an unbounded time (e.g. local runs devoted for states in Visited$_F^{fin}$). To bound stuttering in such constructions, given an arbitrary run of a system $A\|B^n$, we first show that whenever there exists a bounded-fair run that violates a specification in LTL\X, then there also exists an ultimately periodic run with the same property.

A (non-deterministic) *Büchi automaton* is a tuple $\mathcal{A} = (\Sigma, Q_\mathcal{A}, \delta, a_0, \alpha)$, where Σ is a finite alphabet, $Q_\mathcal{A}$ is a finite set of states, $\delta : Q_\mathcal{A} \times \Sigma \to 2^{Q_\mathcal{A}}$ is a transition function, $a_0 \in Q_\mathcal{A}$ is an initial state, and $\alpha \subseteq Q_\mathcal{A}$ is a Büchi acceptance condition. Given an LTL specification φ, we denote by A_φ the Büchi automaton that accepts exactly all words that satisfy φ [34].

Lemma 4 (Ultimately Periodic Counter-Example). *Let $\varphi \in LTL$ and $b \in \mathbb{N}$. If $A\|_b B^n \not\models \varphi$ then there exists a run $x = uv^\omega$ of $A\|B^n$ with b-gfair(x), and $x \not\models \varphi$, where u, v are finite paths, and $|u|, |v| \leq 2 \cdot |Q_A| \cdot |Q_B|^n \cdot b^{n+1} \cdot |Q_{A_{\neg\varphi}}|$.*

Now, we have all the ingredients to prove the bounding lemma for the case of LTL\X specifications and (global) bounded fairness.

Lemma 5 (Bounding Lemma for LTL\X). *Let A, B be disjunctive process templates, $c = 2|Q_B| + 1$, $n \geq c$, and $\varphi(A, B^{(1)})$ a specification with $\varphi \in LTL\backslash\mathbf{X}$. Then:*

$$\left(\exists b \in \mathbb{N} : A\|_b B^n \not\models \varphi(A, B^{(1)})\right) \Rightarrow \left(\exists b' \in \mathbb{N} : A\|_{b'} B^c \not\models \varphi(A, B^{(1)})\right)$$

Proof. Assume $\exists b \in \mathbb{N} : A\|_b B^n \not\models \varphi(A, B^{(1)})$. Then by Lemma 4 there is a run $x = uv^\omega$ of $A\|B^n$, where b-gfair(x) and $|u|, |v| \leq 2 \cdot |Q_A| \cdot |Q_B|^n \cdot b^{n+1} \cdot |Q_{A_{\neg\varphi}}|$. According to Lemma 2, we can construct out of x a run y of $A\|B^c$ where b''-lfair(y, $\{A, B_1\}$), and $x(A, B_1) \equiv_d y(A, B_1)$ with $d = 2|Q_B| + 1$ and $b'' = b \cdot d$. The latter guarantees that $y \not\models \varphi(A, B^{(1)})$. We still need to show that b'-gfair(y) for some $b' \in \mathbb{N}$. As $x = uv^\omega$, we observe that the construction of Lemma 2 ensures the following:

- The number of consecutive stuttering steps per process introduced in step 1 is bounded by $|u|$.

- The number of consecutive stuttering steps introduced in step 2 for a given process is bounded by $|u| + 2|v|$ because B_q^{inf} needs up to $|u| + |v|$ steps to reach q, and one of the processes has to wait for up to $|v|$ additional global steps before it can move.

In addition to the stuttering steps introduced in step 1 and 2, if more than one of the constructed processes simulate the same local run of x then establishing the interleaving semantics would be required, which in turn introduces additional stuttering steps. Therefore the upper bound of consecutive stuttering steps introduced in step 3 of the construction is $(2|Q_B| + 1) \cdot b$. Therefore b'-gfair(y) where $b' = (2|Q_B| + 1) \cdot b + 6 \cdot |Q_A| \cdot |Q_B|^n \cdot b^{n+1} \cdot |Q_{A_{\neg\varphi}}|$.   □

Remark 2. With a more complex construction that uses a stutter-insensitive automaton $\mathcal{A}$ [18] to represent the specification and considers runs of the composition of system and automaton, we can obtain a much smaller b' that is also independent of n. This is based on the observation that if in y some process is consecutively stuttering for more than $|A\|B^c \times \mathcal{A}|$ steps, then there must be a repetition of states from the product in this time, and we can simply cut the infix between the repeating states from the constructed run y.

4.3   Cutoffs for Specifications in Prompt-LTL\X

LTL specifications cannot enforce boundedness of the time that elapses before a liveness property is satisfied. Prompt-LTL solves this problem by introducing the prompt-eventually operator explained in Sect. 2.1. Since we consider concurrent asynchronous systems, the satisfaction of a Prompt-LTL formula can also depend on the scheduling of processes. If scheduling can introduce unbounded delays for a process, then promptness can in general not be guaranteed. Hence, nontrivial Prompt-LTL specifications can *only* be satisfied under the assumption of bounded fairness, and therefore this is the only case we consider here.

Theorem 3 (Cutoff for Prompt-LTL\X with Local Bounded Fairness). *Let A, B be disjunctive process templates, $c = 2|Q_B| + 1$ $n \geq c$, and $\varphi(A, B^{(1)})$ a specification with $\varphi \in$ Prompt-LTL\X. Then:*

$$A\|B^c \models_{lb} \varphi(A, B^{(1)}) \;\Leftrightarrow\; A\|B^n \models_{lb} \varphi(A, B^{(1)}).$$

Again, we prove the theorem by proving a monotonicity and a bounding lemma. Note that $A\|B^n \not\models_{lb} \varphi(A, B^{(1)})$ iff

$$\exists b \in \mathbb{N} \; \forall k \in \mathbb{N} \; \exists x \in A\|B^n \text{:} b\text{-lfair}(x, \{A, B^{(1)}\}) \wedge (x, 0, k) \not\models \varphi(A, B^{(1)}).$$

Lemma 6 (Monotonicity Lemma for Prompt-LTL\X). *Let A, B be disjunctive process templates, $n \geq 2$, and $\varphi(A, B^{(1)})$ a specification with $\varphi \in$ Prompt-LTL\X. Then:*

$$A\|B^n \not\models_{lb} \varphi(A, B^{(1)}) \;\Rightarrow\; A\|B^{n+1} \not\models_{lb} \varphi(A, B^{(1)}).$$

Proof. Assume $A\|B^n \not\models_{lb} \varphi(A, B^{(1)})$. Then there exists $b \in \mathbb{N}$ such that $\forall k \in \mathbb{N}$ there is a run x of $A\|B^n$ where b-lfair$(x, \{A, B^{(1)}\})$, and $(x, 0, 2 \cdot k) \not\models \varphi(A, B^{(1)})$. Then according to Lemma 1 there exists y of $A\|B^{n+1}$ where $2b$-lfair$(y, \{A, B^{(1)}\})$ and $x(A, B_1) \equiv_2 y(A, B_1)$, which guarantees, according to Corollary 1, that $(y, 0, k) \not\models \varphi(A, B^{(1)})$. As a consequence there exists $b \in \mathbb{N}$ such that $\forall k \in \mathbb{N}$ there is a run y of $A\|B^c$ where $2b$-lfair$(y, \{A, B^{(1)}\})$ and $(y, 0, k) \not\models \varphi(A, B^{(1)})$, thus $A\|B^c \not\models_{lb} \varphi(A, B^{(1)})$. $\qquad\square$

Using the same argument of the above proof but by using Corollary 2 instead of Lemma 1 to construct the globally bounded fair counter example, we obtain the following:

Corollary 3 *Let A, B be disjunctive process templates, $n \geq 2$, and $\varphi(A, B^{(1)})$ a specification with $\varphi \in$ Prompt-LTL$\setminus \mathbf{X}$. Then:*

$$A\|B^n \not\models_{gb} \varphi(A, B^{(1)}) \;\Rightarrow\; A\|B^{n+1} \not\models_{gb} \varphi(A, B^{(1)}).$$

Lemma 7 (Bounding Lemma for Prompt-LTL$\setminus \mathbf{X}$). *Let A, B be disjunctive process templates, $c = 2|Q_B| + 1$, $n \geq c$, and $\varphi(A, B^{(1)})$ a specification with $\varphi \in$ Prompt-LTL$\setminus \mathbf{X}$. Then:*

$$A\|B^n \not\models_{lb} \varphi(A, B^{(1)}) \;\Rightarrow\; A\|B^c \not\models_{lb} \varphi(A, B^{(1)}).$$

Proof. Assume $A\|B^n \not\models_{lb} \varphi(A, B^{(1)})$. Then there exists $b \in \mathbb{N}$ such that $\forall k \in \mathbb{N}$ there is a run x of $A\|B^n$ where b-lfair$(x, \{A, B^{(1)}\})$ and $(x, 0, d \cdot k) \not\models \varphi(A, B^{(1)})$ with $d = (2|Q_B|+1)$. According to Lemma 2 we can construct for every such x a run y of $A\|B^c$ where $(d \cdot b)$-lfair$(y, \{A, B^{(1)}\})$, and $x(A, B_1) \equiv_d y(A, B_1)$, which guarantees that $(y, 0, k) \not\models \varphi(A, B^{(1)})$ (see Corollary 1). Thus, there exists $b \in \mathbb{N}$ such that $\forall k \in \mathbb{N}$ there is a run y of $A\|B^c$ where $(d \cdot b)$-lfair$(y, \{A, B^{(1)}\})$ and $(y, 0, k) \not\models \varphi(A, B^{(1)})$, thus $A\|B^c \not\models_{lb} \varphi(A, B^{(1)})$. $\qquad\square$

5 Cutoffs for Conjunctive Systems

In this section we investigate cutoff results for conjunctive systems under bounded fairness and specifications in Prompt-LTL$\setminus \mathbf{X}$. Table 2 summarizes the results of this section, as generalizations of Theorems 4 and 5 to h-indexed specifications. Note that for results marked with a $*$ we require processes to be *bounded initializing*, i.e., that every cycle in the process template contains the initial state.[4]

5.1 Cutoffs Under Local Bounded Fairness

Theorem 4 (Cutoff for Prompt-LTL$\setminus \mathbf{X}$ with Local Bounded Fairness). *Let A, B be conjunctive process templates, $n \geq 2$, and $\varphi(A, B^{(1)})$ a specification with $\varphi \in$ Prompt-LTL$\setminus \mathbf{X}$. Then:*

$$A\|B^2 \models_{lb} \varphi(A, B^{(1)}) \;\Leftrightarrow\; A\|B^n \models_{lb} \varphi(A, B^{(1)}).$$

---

[4] This is only slightly more restrictive than the assumption that they are initializing, as stated in the definition of conjunctive systems in Sect. 3.1.

Table 2. Cutoffs for conjunctive systems

	Local bounded fairness	Global bounded fairness
h-indexed LTL$\backslash$**X**	$h+1$	$h+1^*$
h-indexed Prompt-LTL$\backslash$**X**	$h+1$	$h+1^*$

We prove the theorem by proving two lemmas, one for each direction of the equivalence. Note that $A\|B^n \not\models_{lb} \varphi(A, B^{(1)})$ iff $\exists b \in \mathbb{N} \; \forall k \in \mathbb{N} \; \exists x \in A\|B^n :$ $b\text{-gfair}(x) \wedge (x, 0, k) \not\models \varphi(A, B^{(1)})$.

Lemma 8 (Monotonicity Lemma, Prompt-LTL$\backslash$X with Local Bounded Fairness). *Let A, B be conjunctive process templates, $n \geq 2$, and $\varphi(A, B^{(1)})$ a specification with $\varphi \in$ Prompt-LTL$\backslash$**X**. Then:*

$$A\|B^n \not\models_{lb} \varphi(A, B^{(1)}) \;\Rightarrow\; A\|B^{n+1} \not\models_{lb} \varphi(A, B^{(1)}).$$

Proof. Assume $A\|B^n \not\models_{lb} \varphi(A, B^{(1)})$. Then there exists $b \in \mathbb{N}$ such that $\forall k \in \mathbb{N}$ there is a run x of $A\|B^n$ where $b\text{-gfair}(x)$ and $(x, 0, k) \not\models \varphi(A, B^{(1)})$. For every such x, we construct a run y of $A\|B^{n+1}$ with $b\text{-lfair}(y)$ and $(y, 0, k) \not\models \varphi(A, B^{(1)})$. Let $y(A) = x(A)$ and $y(B_j) = x(B_j)$ for all $B_j \in \{B_1, \ldots, B_n\}$ and let the new process B_{n+1} "share" a local run $x(B_i)$ with an existing process B_i of $A\|B^{n+1}$ in the following way: one process stutters in $init_B$ while the other makes transitions from $x(B_i)$, and whenever $x(B_i)$ enters $init_B$ the roles are reversed. Since this changes the behavior of B_i, B_i cannot be a process that is mentioned in the formula, i.e. we need $n \geq 2$ for a formula $\varphi(A, B^{(1)})$. Then we have $b\text{-lfair}(y, \{A, B_1\})$ as the run of B_{n+1} inherits the unconditional fairness behavior from the local run of the process B_i in x. Note that it is not guaranteed that the local runs $y(B_i)$ and $y(B_{n+1})$ are bounded fair as the time between two occurrences of $init_B$ in $x(B_i)$ is not bounded. Moreover we have $x(A, B_1) \equiv_1 y(A, B_1)$, which according to Corollary 1 implies $(y(A, B_1), k) \not\models \varphi(A, B^{(1)})$. $\square$

Lemma 9 (Bounding Lemma, Prompt-LTL$\backslash$X, Local Bounded Fairness). *Let A, B be conjunctive process templates, $n \geq 1$, and $\varphi(A, B^{(1)})$ a specification with $\varphi \in$ Prompt-LTL$\backslash$**X**. Then:*

$$A\|B^n \not\models_{lb} \varphi(A, B^{(1)}) \;\Rightarrow\; A\|B^1 \not\models_{lb} \varphi(A, B^{(1)}).$$

Proof. Assume $A\|B^n \not\models_{lb} \varphi(A, B^{(1)})$. Then there exists $b \in \mathbb{N}$ such that $\forall k \in \mathbb{N}$ there is a run x of $A\|B^n$ where $b\text{-gfair}(x)$, and $(x, 0, b \cdot k) \not\models \varphi(A, B^{(1)})$. For every such x, we construct a run y in the cutoff system $A\|B^1$ by copying the local runs of processes A and B_1 in x and deleting stuttering steps. It is easy to see that $b\text{-gfair}(y)$ then we have $x(A, B_1) \equiv_b y(A, B_1)$, and by Corollary 1 $(y(A, B_1), k) \not\models \varphi(A, B^{(1)})$. $\square$

Note that this is the same proof construction as in Außerlechner et al. [5], and we simply observe that this construction preserves bounded fairness.

5.2 Cutoffs Under Global Bounded Fairness

As mentioned before, to obtain a result that preserves global bounded fairness, we need to restrict process template B to be bounded initializing.

Theorem 5 (Cutoff for Prompt-LTL\X with Global Bounded Fairness). *Let A, B be conjunctive process templates, where B is bounded initializing, $n \geq 2$, and $\varphi(A, B^{(1)})$ a specification with $\varphi \in$ Prompt-LTL\X. Then:*

$$A\|B^2 \models_{gb} \varphi(A, B^{(1)}) \iff A\|B^n \models_{gb} \varphi(A, B^{(1)}).$$

Again, the theorem can be separated into two lemmas.

Lemma 10 (Monotonicity Lemma, Prompt-LTL\X, Global Bounded Fairness). *Let A, B be conjunctive process templates, where B is bounded initializing, $n \geq 2$, and $\varphi(A, B^{(1)})$ a specification with $\varphi \in$ Prompt-LTL\X. Then:*

$$A\|B^n \not\models_{gb} \varphi(A, B^{(1)}) \implies A\|B^{n+1} \not\models_{gb} \varphi(A, B^{(1)}).$$

Proof. Assume $A\|B^n \not\models_{gb} \varphi(A, B^{(1)})$. Then there exists $b \in \mathbb{N}$ such that $\forall k \in \mathbb{N}$ there is a run x of $A\|B^n$ where b-gfair(x), and $(x, 0, (b+|Q_B|) \cdot k) \not\models \varphi(A, B^{(1)})$. For every such x, we construct a run y of $A\|B^{n+1}$ in the same way we did in the proof of Lemma 8. Then we have b'-gfair(y) with $b' = b + |Q_B|$ as $init_B$ is on every cycle of the process template B. Moreover we have $x(A, B_1) \equiv_1 y(A, B_1)$ which according to Corollary 1 implies that $(y(A, B_1), k) \not\models \varphi(A, B^{(1)})$. □

Lemma 11 (Bounding Lemma, Prompt-LTL\X, Global Bounded Fairness). *Let A, B be conjunctive process templates, where B is bounded initializing, $n \geq 1$, and $\varphi(A, B^{(1)})$ a specification with $\varphi \in$ Prompt-LTL\X. Then:*

$$A\|B^n \not\models_{gb} \varphi(A, B^{(1)}) \implies A\|B^1 \not\models_{gb} \varphi(A, B^{(1)}).$$

Proof. Under the given assumptions, we can observe that the construction from Lemma 9 also preserves global bounded fairness.

6 Token Passing Systems

In this section, we first introduce a system model for token passing systems and then show how to obtain cutoff results for this class of systems.

6.1 System Model

Processes. A *token passing process* is a transition system $T = (Q_T, I_T, \Sigma_T, \delta)$ where

- $Q_T = \overline{Q_T} \times \{0, 1\}$ is a finite set of states. $\overline{Q_T}$ is a finite non-empty set. The boolean component $\{0, 1\}$ indicates the possession of the token.
- I_T is the set of initial states with $I_T \cap (\overline{Q_T} \times \{0\}) \neq \emptyset$ and $I_T \cap (\overline{Q_T} \times \{1\}) \neq \emptyset$.

- $\Sigma_T = \{\epsilon, rcv, snd\}$ is the set of actions, where ϵ is an asynchronous action, and $\{rcv, snd\}$ are the actions to receive and send the token.
- $\delta_T = Q_T \times \Sigma_T \times Q_T$ is a transition relation, such that $((q, b), a, (q', b')) \in \delta_T$ iff all of the following hold:
  - $a = \epsilon \Rightarrow b = b'$.
  - $a = snd \Rightarrow b = 1$ and $b' = 0$
  - $a = rcv \Rightarrow b = 0$ and $b' = 1$

Token Passing System. Let $G = (V, E)$ be a finite directed graph without self loops where $V = \{1, \ldots, n\}$ is the set of vertices, and $E \subseteq V \times V$ is the set of edges. A *token passing system* T_G^n is a concurrent system containing n instances of process T where the only synchronization between the processes is the sending/receiving of a token according to the graph G. Formally, $T_G^n = (S, init_S, \Delta)$ with:

- $S = (Q_T)^n$.
- $init_S = \{s \in (I_T)^n$ such that exactly one process holds the token$\}$,
- $\Delta \subseteq S \times S$ such that $((q_1, \ldots, q_n), (q_1', \ldots, q_n')) \in \Delta$ iff:
  - **Asynchronous Transition.** $\exists i \in V$ such that $(q_i, \epsilon, q_i') \in \delta_{T_i}$, and $\forall j \neq i$ we have $q_j = q_j'$.
  - **Synchronous Transition.** $\exists (i, j) \in E$ such that $(q_i, snd, q_i') \in \delta_{T_i}$, $(q_j, rcv, q_j') \in \delta_{T_j}$, and $\forall z \in V \setminus \{i, j\}$ we have $q_z = q_z'$.

Runs. A *configuration* of a system T_G^n is a tuple (s, ac) where $s \in S$, and either $ac = a_i$ with $a \in \Sigma_T$, and $i \in V$ is a process index, or $ac = (snd_i, rcv_j)$ where $i, j \in V$ are two process indices with $i \neq j$. A run is an infinite sequence of configurations $x = (s_0, ac_0)(s_1, ac_1) \ldots$ where $s_0 \in init_S$ and s_{i+1} results from executing action ac_i in s_i. Additionally we denote by $x(i, \ldots, j)$ the projection $(s_0(i, \ldots, j), ac_0(i, \ldots, j))(s_1(i, \ldots, j), ac_1(i, \ldots, j)) \ldots$ where $s_e(i, \ldots, j)$ is the projection of s_e on the local states of $(T_i, \ldots, T_j)$ and

$$ac(i, \ldots, j) = \begin{cases} \bot & \text{if } ac = a_m \text{ and } m \notin \{i, \ldots, j\} \\ \bot & \text{if } ac = (snd_m, rcv_n) \text{ and } m, n \notin \{i, \ldots, j\} \\ ac & otherwise \end{cases}$$

Bounded Fairness. A run x of a token passing system T_G^n is b-gfair(x) if for every moment m and every process T_i, T_i receives the token at least once between moments m and $m + b$.

Cutoffs for Complex Networks. In the presence of different network topologies, represented by the graph G, we define a cutoff to be a bound on the size of G that is sufficient to decide the PMCP. Note that, in order to obtain a decision procedure for the PMCP, we not only need to know the size of the graphs, but also which graphs of this size we need to investigate. This is straightforward if the graph always falls into a simple class, such as rings, cliques, or stars, but is more challenging if the graph can become more complex with increasing size.

6.2 Cutoff Results for Token Passing Systems

Table 3 summarizes the results of this section, generalizing Theorem 6 to the case of h-indexed specifications. Similar to previous sections, the specifications are over states of processes. The results for local bounded fairness follow from the results for global bounded fairness.

To prove the results of this section, we need some additional definitions.

Table 3. Cutoff results for token passing systems

	Local bounded fairness	Global bounded fairness
h-indexed LTL$\backslash$**X**	$2h$	$2h$
h-indexed Prompt-LTL$\backslash$**X**	$2h$	$2h$

Connectivity Vector [10]. Given two indices $i, j \in V$ in a finite directed graph G, we define the connectivity vector $v(G, i, j) = (u_1, u_2, u_3, u_4, u_5, u_6)$ as follows:

- $u_1 = 1$ if there is a non-empty path from i to i that does not contain j. $u_1 = 0$ otherwise.
- $u_2 = 1$ if there is a path from i to j via vertices different from i and j. $u_2 = 0$ otherwise.
- $u_3 = 1$ if there is a direct edge from i to j. $u_3 = 0$ otherwise.
- u_4, u_5, u_6 are defined like u_1, u_2, u_3, respectively where i is replaced by j and vice versa.

Immediately Sends. Given a token passing process T, we fix two local states q^{snd} and q^{rcv}, such that there is (i) a local path $q^{init}, \dots, q^{rcv}$ where $q^{init} \in I_T \cap (\overline{Q_T} \times \{0\})$, (ii) a local path $q^{rcv}, \dots, q^{snd}$ that starts with a receive action, and (iii) a local path $q^{snd}, \dots, q^{rcv}$ that starts with a send action.

When constructing a local run for a process T_i that is currently in local state q^{rcv}, we say that T_i *immediately sends the token* if and only if:

1. T_i executes consecutively all the actions on a simple path $q^{rcv}, \dots, q^{snd}$, then sends the token, and then executes consecutively all the actions on a simple path $q^{snd}, \dots, q^{rcv}$.
2. All other processes remain idle until T_i reaches q^{rcv}.

Note that, when T_i *immediately* sends the token, it executes at most $|Q_T|$ actions, since the two paths cannot share any states except q^{rcv} and q^{snd}.

Theorem 6 (Cutoff for Prompt-LTL$\backslash$X). *Let T^n_G be a token-passing system, $g, h \in V$, and $\varphi(T_g, T_h)$ a specification with $\varphi \in$ Prompt-LTL$\backslash$**X**. Then there exists a system $T^4_{G'}$ with $G' = (V', E')$ and $i, j \in V'$ such that $v(G, g, h) = v(G', i, j)$, and*

$$T^n_G \models_{gb} \varphi(T_g, T_h) \Leftrightarrow T^4_{G'} \models_{gb} \varphi(T_i, T_j).$$

We prove the theorem by proving two lemmas, one for each direction of the equivalence. Note that $T_G^n \not\models_{gb} \varphi(T_g, T_h)$ iff $\exists b \in \mathbb{N}\ \forall k \in \mathbb{N}\ \exists x \in T_G^n :$ b-gfair$(x) \wedge (x, 0, k) \not\models \varphi(T_g, T_h)$.

Lemma 12 (Monotonicity Lemma). *Let T_G^n be a token-passing system with $n \geq 3$ and $g, h \in V$, and $\varphi(T_g, T_h)$ a specification with $\varphi \in$ Prompt-LTL$\setminus \mathbf{X}$. Then there exists a system $T_{G'}^{n+1}$ with $G' = (V', E')$ and $i, j \in V'$ such that $v(G, g, h) = v(G', i, j)$ and*

$$T_G^n \not\models_{gb} \varphi(T_g, T_h) \ \Rightarrow\ T_{G'}^{n+1} \not\models_{gb} \varphi(T_i, T_j).$$

Proof. Let a be a vertex of G with $a \notin \{g, h\}$. Then we construct G' from G as follows: Let $V' = V \cup \{n + 1\}$, and $E' = (E \cup \{(n + 1, m)|(a, m) \in E$ for some $m \in V\} \cup \{(a, n + 1)\}) \setminus \{(a, m)|(a, m) \in E$ for some $m \in V\}$, i.e. we copy all the outgoing edges of a to the vertex $n + 1$, and replace all the outgoing edges of a by one outgoing edge to $n + 1$.

Assume $T_G^n \not\models_{gb} \varphi(T_g, T_h)$. Then there exists $b \in \mathbb{N}$ such that $\forall k' \in \mathbb{N}$ there is a run x of T_G^n where b-gfair(x), and $(x, 0, |Q_T| \cdot k') \not\models \varphi(T_g, T_h)$. Let $b' = b + (b - n + 2) \cdot |Q_T|$, and $d = |Q_T| + 1$. We will construct for every such run x a run y of $T_{G'}^{n+1}$ where b'-gfair(y), and $x(T_g, T_h) \equiv_d y(T_i, T_j)$ which guarantees that $(y, 0, k') \not\models \varphi(T_i, T_j)$ (see Corollary 1).

Construction. The construction is such that we keep the local paths of the n existing processes up to bounded stuttering, and we add a process T_{n+1} that always immediately sends the token after receiving it, with q^{rcv}, q^{snd} and the corresponding paths as defined above. In the following, as a short-hand notation, if $s = (q_1, \ldots, q_n)$ is a global state of T_G^n and $q \in Q_T$, we write (s, q) for $(q_1, \ldots, q_n, q)$.

Let $x = (s_0, ac_0)(s_1, ac_1) \ldots$ and $y' = ((s_0, q^{rcv}), ac_0)((s_1, q^{rcv}), ac_1) \ldots$. Note that y' is a sequence of configurations of $T_{G'}^{n+1}$, but not a run. To obtain a run, first let $y'' = ((s_0, q^{init}), \epsilon) \ldots ((s_0, q^{rcv}), ac_0)((s_1, q^{rcv}), ac_1) \ldots$. Finally, replace every occurrence of a pair of consecutive configurations $((s, q^{rcv}), (snd_a, rcv_z)), ((s', q^{rcv}), ac')$, where $s, s' \in Q_T^n, z \in V, ac' \in \Sigma$, with the sequence $((s, q^{rcv}), (snd_a, rcv_{n+1})) \ldots ((s, q^{snd}), (snd_{n+1}, rcv_z)) \ldots ((s', q^{rcv}), ac')$.

In other words, instead of sending the token to T_z, T_a sends the token to T_{n+1}, and T_{n+1} sends the token immediately to T_z. Furthermore, in x between moments t and $t + b$, T_a can send the token at most $b - n + 1$ times, and whenever T_{n+1} receives the token, it takes at most $|Q_T|$ steps before reaching q^{rcv} again. Finally, note that the number of steps T_{n+1} takes to reach q^{rcv} for the first time is also bounded by $|Q_T|$. Therefore we have b'-gfair(y) and $x(T_g, T_h) \equiv_d y(T_i, T_j)$ (as $b' \leq b \cdot d$) which by Corollary 1 implies that $(y, 0, k') \not\models \varphi(T_i, T_j)$. $\qquad\square$

Lemma 13 (Bounding Lemma). *Let T_G^n be a system with $n \geq 4$ and $g, h \in V$, and $\varphi(T_g, T_h)$ a specification with $\varphi \in Prompt\text{-}LTL \backslash \mathbf{X}$. Then there exists a system $T_{G'}^4$ with $G' = (V', E')$ and $i, j \in V'$ such that $v(G, g, h) = v(G', i, j)$ and*

$$T_G^n \not\models_{gb} \varphi(T_g, T_h) \;\Rightarrow\; T_{G'}^4 \not\models_{gb} \varphi(T_i, T_j).$$

Proof (Proof idea). First, note that the existence of G' and $i, j \in V'$ with $v(G, g, h) = v(G', i, j)$ follows directly from Proposition 1 in Clarke et al. [10]. As usual, assuming that $T_G^n \not\models_{gb} \varphi(T_g, T_h)$, we need to construct counterexample runs of $T_{G'}^4$ for some $b' \in \mathbb{N}$ and all $k' \in \mathbb{N}$.

The construction is based on the same ideas as in the proof of Lemma 12, with the following modifications: (i) instead of keeping all local runs of a run $x \in T_G^n$, we only keep the local runs of T_g and T_h (now assigned to T_i and T_j), (ii) instead of constructing one local run for the new process, we now construct local runs for two new processes T_k and T_l (basically, each of them is responsible for passing the token to T_i or T_j, respectively), and (iii) the details of the construction of these runs depend on the connectivity vector $v(G, g, h)$, which essentially determines which of the new processes holds the token when neither T_i nor T_j have it.

As usual, the construction ensures that y is globally bounded fair and that $y(T_i, T_j) \equiv_d x(T_g, T_h)$ for some d, which by Corollary 1 implies that $(y, 0, k') \not\models \varphi(T_i, T_j)$. $\square$

7 Conclusions

We have investigated the behavior of concurrent systems with respect to promptness properties specified in Prompt-LTL$\backslash \mathbf{X}$. Our first important observation is that Prompt-LTL$\backslash \mathbf{X}$ is not stutter insensitive, so the standard notion of stutter equivalence is insufficient to compare traces of concurrent systems if we are interested in promptness. Based on this, we have defined *bounded stutter equivalence*, and have shown that Prompt-LTL$\backslash \mathbf{X}$ is *bounded stutter insensitive*.

We have shown how this allows us to obtain cutoff results for guarded protocols and token-passing systems, and have obtained cutoffs for Prompt-LTL$\backslash \mathbf{X}$ (with locally or globally bounded fairness) that are the same as those that were previously shown for LTL$\backslash \mathbf{X}$ (with unbounded fairness). This implies that, for the cases where we do obtain cutoffs, the PMCP for Prompt-LTL$\backslash \mathbf{X}$ has the same asymptotic complexity as the PMCP for LTL$\backslash \mathbf{X}$.

One case that we investigated remains open: disjunctive systems with global bounded fairness. In future work, we will try to solve this open problem, and investigate whether other cutoff results in the literature can also be lifted from LTL$\backslash \mathbf{X}$ to Prompt-LTL$\backslash \mathbf{X}$.

Finally, we note that together with methods for distributed synthesis from Prompt-LTL$\backslash \mathbf{X}$ specifications, our cutoff results enable the synthesis of parameterized systems based on the *parameterized synthesis* approach [21] that has been used to solve challenging synthesis benchmarks by reducing them to systems with a small number of components [7, 26].

References

1. Alur, R., Etessami, K., La Torre, S., Peled, D.A.: Parametric temporal logic for "model measuring". ACM Trans. Comput. Log. **2**(3), 388–407 (2001). https://doi. org/10.1145/377978.377990

2. Aminof, B., Jacobs, S., Khalimov, A., Rubin, S.: Parameterized model checking of token-passing systems. In: McMillan, K.L., Rival, X. (eds.) VMCAI 2014. LNCS, vol. 8318, pp. 262–281. Springer, Heidelberg (2014). https://doi.org/10.1007/978-3-642-54013-4_15

3. Aminof, B., Kotek, T., Rubin, S., Spegni, F., Veith, H.: Parameterized model checking of rendezvous systems. Distrib. Comput. **31**(3), 187–222 (2018). https:// doi.org/10.1007/s00446-017-0302-6

4. Außerlechner, S., Jacobs, S., Khalimov, A.: Tight cutoffs for guarded protocols with fairness. CoRR abs/1505.03273 (2015). http://arxiv.org/abs/1505.03273

5. Außerlechner, S., Jacobs, S., Khalimov, A.: Tight cutoffs for guarded protocols with fairness. In: Jobstmann, B., Leino, K.R.M. (eds.) VMCAI 2016. LNCS, vol. 9583, pp. 476–494. Springer, Heidelberg (2016). https://doi.org/10.1007/978-3-662-49122-5_23

6. Baier, C., Katoen, J.P.: Principles of Model Checking. vol. 26202649. MIT press Cambridge (2008)

7. Bloem, R., Jacobs, S., Khalimov, A.: Parameterized synthesis case study: AMBA AHB. In: SYNT. EPTCS, vol. 157, pp. 68–83 (2014). https://doi.org/10.4204/EPTCS.157.9

8. Bloem, R., et al.: Decidability of Parameterized Verification. Synthesis Lectures on Distributed Computing Theory, Morgan & Claypool Publishers (2015). https:// doi.org/10.2200/S00658ED1V01Y201508DCT013

9. Bouajjani, A., Jonsson, B., Nilsson, M., Touili, T.: Regular model checking. In: Emerson, E.A., Sistla, A.P. (eds.) CAV 2000. LNCS, vol. 1855, pp. 403–418. Springer, Heidelberg (2000). https://doi.org/10.1007/10722167_31

10. Clarke, E., Talupur, M., Touili, T., Veith, H.: Verification by network decomposition. In: Gardner, P., Yoshida, N. (eds.) CONCUR 2004. LNCS, vol. 3170, pp. 276–291. Springer, Heidelberg (2004). https://doi.org/10.1007/978-3-540-28644-8_18

11. Clarke, E., Talupur, M., Veith, H.: Proving ptolemy right: the environment abstraction framework for model checking concurrent systems. In: Ramakrishnan, C.R., Rehof, J. (eds.) TACAS 2008. LNCS, vol. 4963, pp. 33–47. Springer, Heidelberg (2008). https://doi.org/10.1007/978-3-540-78800-3_4

12. Emerson, E.A., Kahlon, V.: Model checking guarded protocols. In: LICS, pp. 361–370. IEEE Computer Society (2003). https://doi.org/10.1109/LICS.2003.1210076

13. Emerson, E.A., Namjoshi, K.S.: On reasoning about rings. Found. Comput. Sci. **14**(4), 527–549 (2003). https://doi.org/10.1142/S0129054103001881

14. Emerson, E.A., Kahlon, V.: Reducing model checking of the many to the few. In: McAllester, D. (ed.) CADE 2000. LNCS (LNAI), vol. 1831, pp. 236–254. Springer, Heidelberg (2000). https://doi.org/10.1007/10721959_19

15. Esparza, J., Finkel, A., Mayr, R.: On the verification of broadcast protocols. In: LICS, pp. 352–359. IEEE Computer Society (1999). https://doi.org/10.1109/LICS. 1999.782630

16. Esparza, J.: Keeping a crowd safe: on the complexity of parameterized verification (invited talk). In: STACS. LIPIcs, vol. 25, pp. 1–10. Schloss Dagstuhl - Leibniz-Zentrum fuer Informatik (2014). https://doi.org/10.4230/LIPIcs.STACS.2014.1

17. Esparza, J., Ganty, P., Majumdar, R.: Parameterized verification of asynchronous shared-memory systems. J. ACM **63**(1), 10:1–10:48 (2016). https://doi.org/10.1145/2842603
18. Etessami, K.: Stutter-invariant languages, ω-automata, and temporal logic. In: Halbwachs, N., Peled, D. (eds.) CAV 1999. LNCS, vol. 1633, pp. 236–248. Springer, Heidelberg (1999). https://doi.org/10.1007/3-540-48683-6_22
19. Faymonville, P., Zimmermann, M.: Parametric linear dynamic logic. Inf. Comput. **253**, 237–256 (2017). https://doi.org/10.1016/j.ic.2016.07.009
20. German, S.M., Sistla, A.P.: Reasoning about systems with many processes. J. ACM **39**(3), 675–735 (1992). https://doi.org/10.1145/146637.146681
21. Jacobs, S., Bloem, R.: Parameterized synthesis. Log. Methods Comput. Sci. **10**, 1–29 (2014). https://doi.org/10.2168/LMCS-10(1:12)2014
22. Jacobs, S., Sakr, M.: Analyzing guarded protocols: better cutoffs, more systems, more expressivity. Verification, Model Checking, and Abstract Interpretation. LNCS, vol. 10747, pp. 247–268. Springer, Cham (2018). https://doi.org/10.1007/978-3-319-73721-8_12
23. Jacobs, S., Sakr, M., Zimmermann, M.: Promptness and bounded fairness in concurrent and parameterized systems. CoRR abs/1911.03122 (2019). http://arxiv.org/abs/1911.03122
24. Jacobs, S., Tentrup, L., Zimmermann, M.: Distributed synthesis for parameterized temporal logics. Inf. Comput. **262**, 311–328 (2018). https://doi.org/10.1016/j.ic.2018.09.009
25. Kaiser, A., Kroening, D., Wahl, T.: Dynamic cutoff detection in parameterized concurrent programs. In: Touili, T., Cook, B., Jackson, P. (eds.) CAV 2010. LNCS, vol. 6174, pp. 645–659. Springer, Heidelberg (2010). https://doi.org/10.1007/978-3-642-14295-6_55
26. Khalimov, A., Jacobs, S., Bloem, R.: Towards efficient parameterized synthesis. In: Giacobazzi, R., Berdine, J., Mastroeni, I. (eds.) VMCAI 2013. LNCS, vol. 7737, pp. 108–127. Springer, Heidelberg (2013). https://doi.org/10.1007/978-3-642-35873-9_9
27. Kupferman, O., Piterman, N., Vardi, M.Y.: From liveness to promptness. Formal Methods Syst. Des. **34**(2), 83–103 (2009)
28. Kurshan, R.P., McMillan, K.L.: A structural induction theorem for processes. Inf. Comput. **117**(1), 1–11 (1995). https://doi.org/10.1006/inco.1995.1024
29. Namjoshi, K.S.: Symmetry and completeness in the analysis of parameterized systems. In: Cook, B., Podelski, A. (eds.) VMCAI 2007. LNCS, vol. 4349, pp. 299–313. Springer, Heidelberg (2007). https://doi.org/10.1007/978-3-540-69738-1_22
30. Pnueli, A., Ruah, S., Zuck, L.: Automatic deductive verification with invisible invariants. In: Margaria, T., Yi, W. (eds.) TACAS 2001. LNCS, vol. 2031, pp. 82–97. Springer, Heidelberg (2001). https://doi.org/10.1007/3-540-45319-9_7
31. Spalazzi, L., Spegni, F.: Parameterized model-checking of timed systems with conjunctive guards. In: Giannakopoulou, D., Kroening, D. (eds.) VSTTE 2014. LNCS, vol. 8471, pp. 235–251. Springer, Cham (2014). https://doi.org/10.1007/978-3-319-12154-3_15
32. Spalazzi, L., Spegni, F.: On the existence of cutoffs for model checking disjunctive timed networks. In: CEUR Workshop Proceedings ICTCS/CILC, vol. 1949, pp. 174–185. CEUR-WS.org (2017)
33. Suzuki, I.: Proving properties of a ring of finite state machines. Inf. Process. Lett. **28**(4), 213–214 (1988). https://doi.org/10.1016/0020-0190(88)90211-6
34. Vardi, M.Y., Wolper, P.: An automata-theoretic approach to automatic program verification. In: LICS, pp. 322–331. IEEE Computer Society (1986)

Solving LIA* Using Approximations

Maxwell Levatich[1,2,3], Nikolaj Bjørner[1,2,3(✉)], Ruzica Piskac[1,2,3], and Sharon Shoham[1,2,3]

[1] Yale, New Haven, USA
{maxwell.levatich,ruzica.piskac}@yale.edu
[2] Microsoft Research, Redmond, USA
nbjorner@microsoft.com
[3] Tel Aviv University, Tel Aviv, Israel
sharon.shoham@gmail.com

Abstract. Linear arithmetic with stars, LIA*, is an extension of Presburger arithmetic that allows forming indefinite summations over values that satisfy a formula. It has found uses in decision procedures for multi-sets and for vector addition systems. LIA* formulas can be translated back into Presburger arithmetic, but with non-trivial space overhead. In this paper we develop a decision procedure for LIA* that checks satisfiability of LIA* formulas. By refining on-demand under and over-approximations of LIA* formulas, it can avoid the space overhead that is integral to previous approaches. We have implemented our procedure in a prototype and report on encouraging results that suggest that LIA* formulas can be checked for satisfiability without computing a prohibitively large equivalent Presburger formula.

1 Introduction

Decision procedures for Presburger arithmetic, also known as linear integer arithmetic, LIA, are fundamental to many uses of SMT solvers. LIA is a first-order theory of integers that includes addition and subtraction, but does not include multiplication between variables. Reasoning about linear integer arithmetic is widely used in verification. Furthermore, there are several decidable theories for which the satisfiability problem reduces to reasoning in LIA [13,16]. Yet, LIA is a mild subset of the highly undecidable Peano arithmetic.

In this paper, we pursue an extension of LIA called LIA*. LIA* extends LIA by admitting predicates of the form $x \in \{y \mid F\}^*$, where F is a LIA (or in the nested case, a LIA*) formula. The set of x that satisfy the formula are sums of values that satisfy F, thus $x = \sum_{i=0}^{n} v_i$, for some $n \geq 0$ and such that $F(v_i)$ for each v_i. We describe an efficient algorithm, also empirically tested in practice, for reasoning about LIA*. To our knowledge it is the first available approach for solving LIA* without requiring eagerly computing a semilinear set representation explicitly or using a large template as suggested in [17]. Our algorithm maintains under- and over-approximations of a star formula in the form of LIA formulas. The approximations are refined iteratively until they converge

© Springer Nature Switzerland AG 2020
D. Beyer and D. Zufferey (Eds.): VMCAI 2020, LNCS 11990, pp. 360–378, 2020.
https://doi.org/10.1007/978-3-030-39322-9_17

LIA* formulas: $\varphi ::= F_1 \wedge \boldsymbol{x_1} \in \{\boldsymbol{x_2} \mid F_2\}^\star$
    such that $dim(\boldsymbol{x_1}) = dim(\boldsymbol{x_2})$ and $\textit{free-vars}(F_2) \subseteq \boldsymbol{x_2}$
LIA formulas:
    $F ::= A \mid F_1 \wedge F_2 \mid F_1 \vee F_2 \mid \neg F_1 \mid \exists x.\ F \mid \forall x.\ F$
    $A ::= T_1 \leq T_2 \mid T_1 = T_2$
    $T ::= x \mid C \mid T_1 + T_2 \mid C \cdot T_1 \mid \text{ite}(F, T_1, T_2)$
terminals: x - integer variable; C - integer constant

Fig. 1. Presburger Arithmetic and an extension with the Star Operator.

to the actual solution: the under-approximation may determine satisfiability, while the over-approximation may determine unsatisfiability. Technically, the under-approximation is weakened by extending an underapproximate semilinear representation of the formula, while the over-approximation is strengthened via interpolation exploiting a characterization of the star operator as a solution to a set of Constraint Horn Clauses (CHCs). In the limit, the algorithm creates a semilinear set representation of a LIA formula, but only if it is unable to determine satisfiability using an approximation. The algorithm we present considers the class of formulas studied in [17]. They involve only a single star formula in a conjunction. Handling these formulas suffices for an evaluation based on multi-set formulas, as well as formulas from the more specialized theory of Boolean Algebra over Presburger Arithmetic, BAPA [12].

We have also investigated how to handle *full* LIA* allowing an arbitrary nesting of star operators with negations, other Boolean connectives and quantifiers. Full LIA* extends the $\exists$LIA* fragment from [9], which does not admit alternating negations and universal quantifiers with stars. The generalization, which we do not describe in this paper, can be accomplished using a scheme that also works with under- and over-approximations of each subformula. We plan to describe this generalization in future work. While the lower bound complexity of $\exists$LIA* is known [9], we do not know the lower bound complexity of full LIA*.

2   Linear Integer Arithmetic with the Star Operator

In this section we introduce LIA* formally. The definition of the LIA* logic relies on the crucial new operator, the star operator, defined over a set of integer vectors S, as follows:

$$S^\star \triangleq \left\{ \sum_{i=1}^{n} \boldsymbol{s}_i \mid \forall i. 1 \leq i \leq n.\ \boldsymbol{s}_i \in S \right\} \tag{1}$$

In other words, the set $S^\star$ is a set of all linear combinations of vectors from S. Implicitly, $\boldsymbol{0} \in S^\star$, for every set S. Figure 1 contains the definition of the LIA* logic. A LIA* formula is a conjunction of a LIA formula F_1 and a star formula

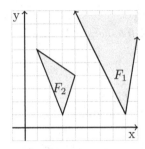
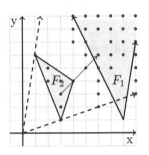

(a) Integer solutions of formulas F_1 and F_2 lie within the shaded areas. Note that the solution set for F_1 is unbounded.

(b) The vector $(6,6)$ is a solution for $F_1(x,y) \land F_2^*(x,y)$

Fig. 2. An illustration of a LIA* formula $F_1(x,y) \land F_2^*(x,y)$, such that $F_1(x,y) \Leftrightarrow y + 2x \geq 17 \land 6x - y \leq 47$ and $F_2(x,y) \Leftrightarrow 5x + 2y \geq 17 \land 3x - y \leq 8 \land 2x + 3y \leq 20$.

$x_1 \in \{x_2 \mid F_2\}^*$ that states that the vector x_1 is a linear combination of solution vectors x_2 of the LIA formula F_2. General LIA* formulas allow arbitrary Boolean combinations as well as nesting of the star operator.

Through the rest of the paper we often use $\varphi^*(x_1)$, or simply φ^*, as a shorthand for $x_1 \in \{x_2 \mid \varphi\}^*$.

Example 1. Consider a simple LIA* example given in Fig. 2. The solid lines indicate borders within which lie integer solutions of each formula. As it is clear from Fig. 2a, formula $F_1(x,y) \land F_2(x,y)$ is unsatisfiable. However, the LIA* formula $F_1(x,y) \land F_2^*(x,y)$ is satisfiable. The dashed lines in Fig. 2b outline the borders within which lie integer vectors satisfying $F_2^*(x,y)$ – they are indicated by the points. Consider, for example, the vector $(6,6)$: it satisfies $F_1(6,6)$, while at the same time $(6,6) = 2 * (3,3)$ and $F_2(3,3)$ holds.

Checking satisfiability of a LIA* formula is decidable [16]. Furthermore, when restricting the underlying LIA formulas to be quantifier free, it is an NP complete problem [17]. The key insight is that (i) the set of solutions of every LIA formula is a semilinear set, as proved in [8], and (ii) the representation of the solutions as a semilinear set allows to eliminate the star operator (cf. Theorem 2).

Definition 1. *A linear set $LS(a, B)$ is defined by an integer vector a and a finite set of integer vectors $B = \{b_1, \ldots, b_n\}$, all of the same dimension, as follows:*

$$LS(a, B) \triangleq \left\{ a + \sum_{i=1}^{n} \lambda_i b_i \mid \bigwedge_{i=1}^{n} \lambda_i \geq 0 \right\} \tag{2}$$

The vector a is called the shift *vector, and the vectors $b_1, \ldots, b_n \in B$ are called the* offset *vectors.*

A semilinear set $SLS(ls_1, \ldots, ls_n)$ is a finite union of linear sets $ls_1, \ldots, ls_n$, i.e., $SLS(ls_1, \ldots, ls_n) = \bigcup_{i=1}^{n} ls_i$.

A linear set $LS(a, B)$ can be seen as Minkowski sum $\{a\} + B^*$. In the sequel, we often view B as a matrix and use λB as a shorthand for $\sum_{i=1}^{n} \lambda_i b_i$.

Theorem 1 (Theorem 1.3 in [8]). *Let f be a LIA formula. Then the set of vectors that satisfy f forms a semilinear set. Furthermore, any semilinear set $U = SLS(LS(a_1, B_1), \ldots, LS(a_k, B_k))$ can be characterized by a LIA formula, defined as follows:*

$$\text{LIA}(U)(x) \quad \triangleq \quad \bigvee_{i=1}^{k} \exists \lambda \geq 0 \ . \ x = a_i + \lambda B_i \tag{3}$$

Theorem 2 (Lemmas 2 and 3 in [17]). *Let f be a LIA formula and let $U = SLS(LS(a_1, B_1), \ldots, LS(a_k, B_k))$ be the semilinear set of vectors that satisfy f. Then $f^*(x) \equiv \text{STARLIA}(U)(x)$, where $\text{STARLIA}(U)$ is a LIA formula that characterizes U^* and is defined as follows:*

$$\text{STARLIA}(U)(x) \quad \triangleq \quad \exists \mu_1 \geq 0, \ldots, \mu_k \geq 0, \lambda_1 \geq 0, \ldots \lambda_k \geq 0 \ .$$
$$x = \sum_{i=1}^{k} \mu_i a_i + \lambda_i B_i \wedge \bigwedge_{i=1}^{k} (\mu_i = 0 \rightarrow \lambda_i = 0) \tag{4}$$

Given a LIA* formula $F_1 \wedge x \in \{y \mid F_2\}^*$, where F_1 and F_2 are LIA formulas, Theorem 1 ensures that there is a semilinear set describing the set of solutions of F_2. Theorem 2 shows how to use that semilinear set to eliminate the star operator. The resulting LIA formula is equivalent to $x \in \{y \mid F_2\}^*$, thereby reducing satisfiability checking to LIA.

3   Reasoning About Multisets as a LIA* Problem

Multisets can be seen as a generalization of sets: they are mathematical objects where an element can appear multiple times in a collection. For example, if a set contains an element, adding that same element to the set does not change the set. However, in the same scenario, adding an element to a *multiset* results in a different multiset. Formally, a multiset can be defined as a function from some unbounded set of elements $\mathbb{E}$ to the set of natural numbers $\mathbb{N}$. Formulas involving multisets with cardinality constraints naturally arise in verification when a container data structure is abstracted in a way that it only tracks the elements appearing in the data structure. While there are several decision procedures for multisets [15–17,20], they were essentially impractical, until now.

Multisets And Presburger Arithmetic (MAPA) formulas allow an arbitrary Boolean combination of atomic formulas that compare multisets for equality $(m_1 = m_2)$ or inclusion $(m_1 \subseteq m_2)$, and quantifier-free LIA formulas, where arithmetic terms are extended with a cardinality operator for multisets; The syntax is given in Fig. 3. The cardinality operator returns the number of elements in the multiset; the same elements are counted as many times as they appear. To count the number of distinct elements in a multiset m, we can use

top-level formulas:
$$F ::= A \mid F \wedge F \mid F \vee F \mid \neg F$$
$$A ::= M{=}M \mid M \subseteq M \mid F_{\text{LIA}}$$
quantifier-free linear arithmetic formulas:
$$F_{\text{LIA}} ::= A_{\text{LIA}} \mid F_{\text{LIA}} \wedge F_{\text{LIA}} \mid F_{\text{LIA}} \vee F_{\text{LIA}} \mid \neg F_{\text{LIA}}$$
$$A_{\text{LIA}} ::= t \le t \mid t{=}t$$
linear arithmetic terms:
$$t ::= x \mid |M| \mid C \mid t + t \mid C \cdot t \mid \text{ite}(F_{\text{LIA}}, t, t)$$
multiset expressions:
$$M ::= m \mid \emptyset \mid M \cap M \mid M \cup M \mid M \uplus M \mid M \setminus M \mid M \setminus\!\setminus M \mid \text{set}(M)$$
terminals:
m - multiset variables; x - integer variable; C - integer constant

Fig. 3. MAPA: quantifier-free multiset constraints with cardinality operator

the expression $|\text{set}(m)|$. The $\text{set}(\cdot)$ function converts a multiset into a set. As an illustration, two different multisets $\{a, a, a, b, b\}$ and $\{a, a, b, b, b\}$ as sets are the same: $\text{set}(\{a, a, a, b, b\}) = \text{set}(\{a, a, b, b, b\}) = \{a, b\}$. Using the $\text{set}(\cdot)$ function, we can easily express standard BAPA benchmarks as MAPA benchmarks. All standard set expressions are also defined on multisets. In addition the disjoint union, $\uplus$, operator produces a multiset where the multiplicity of elements are added. Figure 3 provides a grammar for quantifier-free MAPA.

The semantics of MAPA is provided in Fig. 4, which describes how every MAPA formula can be reduced to an equisatisfiable LIA* formula in linear time. The reduction follows a sequence of rewriting steps corresponding to the definitions of multiset operators. A justification for this translation is provided in [16].

Example 2. Consider the following constraint: if an element is removed from a multiset, its size will decrease by one. In MAPA, this property can be expressed as $s \subseteq L \wedge |s| = 1 \Rightarrow |L \setminus s| = |L| - 1$. To prove its validity, we apply the algorithm given in Fig. 4 to check the satisfiability of the formula $s \subseteq L \wedge |s| = 1 \wedge |L \setminus s| \ne |L| - 1$. The first step flattens the formula and we introduce new variables for all non-trivial expressions:

$$x_1 \ne x_2 - 1 \wedge x_3 = 1 \wedge |m| = x_1 \wedge |L| = x_2 \wedge |s| = x_3 \wedge m = L \setminus s \wedge s \subseteq L$$

The resulting formula has three parts: a part that is a pure LIA, a part which defines cardinality constraints, and a part that is only about multisets without cardinality constraints. Every MAPA formula can be reduced to this form.

The next step is to translate the resulting formula into a LIA* formula. For every multiset variable M we introduce an integer variable $\widetilde{M}$. After some basic simplifications the above formula becomes:

$$x_1 \ne x_2 - 1 \wedge x_3 = 1 \wedge (x_1, x_2, x_3) \in \{(\widetilde{m}, \widetilde{L}, \widetilde{s}) \mid \widetilde{m} = \widetilde{L} - \widetilde{s} \wedge \widetilde{s} \le \widetilde{m}\}^*$$

For brevity, we suppress the sign constraints $\widetilde{m} \ge 0, \widetilde{L} \ge 0$ and $\widetilde{s} \ge 0$.

INPUT: a multiset formula in the syntax of Figure 3
OUTPUT: an equisatisfiable LIA* formula

1. Occurrences of multiset equalities $M_1 = M_2$ that are not top-level are rewritten to $|M_1| = |M_2| \land |M_1 \setminus M_2| = 0 \land |M_2 \setminus M_1| = 0$, and similar with $M_1 \subseteq M_2$.
2. Flatten all expressions e where e is one of the expressions $\emptyset$, $M_1 \cup M_2$, $M_1 \cup M_2$, $M_1 \uplus M_2$, $M_1 \setminus M_2$, $M_1 \setminus\setminus M_2$, $\text{set}(M_1)$, $|M_1|$, and where the occurrence of e is not already in a top-level conjunct $x = e$ or $e = x$ for some variable x:

$$C[e] \rightsquigarrow (x_f = e \land C[x_f]), \text{ where } x_f \text{ is a fresh variable.}$$

3. Furthermore, for multi-set variable M_i introduce a top-level conjunction $x_i = |M_i|$ if it doesn't already exist for fresh x_i.
4. Create a LIA* formula. The step eliminates all multisets M_i using a corresponding fresh integer variable $\widetilde{M_i}$. Let $x_1 = |M_1|, \ldots, x_n = |M_n|$ be the cardinality equalities, then the integer variables are $\widetilde{M_1}, \ldots, \widetilde{M_n}$. All the rewrite steps are applying the following schema:

$$F \land F_{mul} \rightsquigarrow F \land (x_1, \ldots, x_n) \in \{(\widetilde{M_1}, \ldots, \widetilde{M_n}) \mid F_{\text{LIA}} \land \bigwedge_i \widetilde{M_i} \geq 0\}^*$$

The schema is applied to the following pairs of multiset and LIA formula:

$$
\begin{aligned}
&F_{mul} : M_0 = \emptyset & &\rightsquigarrow F_{\text{LIA}} : \widetilde{M_0} = 0 \\
&F_{mul} : M_0 = M_1 \cap M_2 & &\rightsquigarrow F_{\text{LIA}} : \widetilde{M_0} = \text{ite}(\widetilde{M_1} \leq \widetilde{M_2}, \widetilde{M_1}, \widetilde{M_2}) \\
&F_{mul} : M_0 = M_1 \cup M_2 & &\rightsquigarrow F_{\text{LIA}} : \widetilde{M_0} = \text{ite}(\widetilde{M_1} \leq \widetilde{M_2}, \widetilde{M_2}, \widetilde{M_1}) \\
&F_{mul} : M_0 = M_1 \uplus M_2 & &\rightsquigarrow F_{\text{LIA}} : \widetilde{M_0} = \widetilde{M_1} + \widetilde{M_2} \\
&F_{mul} : M_0 = M_1 \setminus M_2 & &\rightsquigarrow F_{\text{LIA}} : \widetilde{M_0} = \text{ite}(\widetilde{M_1} \leq \widetilde{M_2}, 0, \widetilde{M_1} - \widetilde{M_2}) \\
&F_{mul} : M_0 = M_1 \setminus\setminus M_2 & &\rightsquigarrow F_{\text{LIA}} : \widetilde{M_0} = \text{ite}(\widetilde{M_2} = 0, \widetilde{M_1}, 0) \\
&F_{mul} : M_0 = \text{set}(M_1) & &\rightsquigarrow F_{\text{LIA}} : \widetilde{M_0} = \text{ite}(1 \leq \widetilde{M_1}, 1, 0) \\
&F_{mul} : M_1 \subseteq M_2 & &\rightsquigarrow F_{\text{LIA}} : \widetilde{M_1} \leq \widetilde{M_2} \\
&F_{mul} : M_1 = M_2 & &\rightsquigarrow F_{\text{LIA}} : \widetilde{M_1} = \widetilde{M_2} \\
&F_{mul} : x_i = |M_i| & &\rightsquigarrow \text{true}
\end{aligned}
$$

Fig. 4. Algorithm for converting MAPA formulas to LIA* formulas.

The final step is the elimination of the star operator. A semilinear set describing all the solutions of the formula $\widetilde{m} = \widetilde{L} - \widetilde{s} \land \widetilde{s} \leq \widetilde{m}$ is a linear set $LS((0,0,0), \{(1,1,0), (0,1,1)\})$. Having the zero vector as the shift vector, simplified the process of eliminating the star operator:

$$(x_1, x_2, x_3) \in \{(\widetilde{m}, \widetilde{L}, \widetilde{s}) \mid \widetilde{m} = \widetilde{L} - \widetilde{s} \land \widetilde{s} \leq \widetilde{m}\}^* \Leftrightarrow$$

$$\exists \lambda_1, \lambda_2.(x_1, x_2, x_3) = \lambda_1(1,1,0) + \lambda_2(0,1,1)$$

The final formula $x_1 \neq x_2 - 1 \wedge x_3 = 1 \wedge (x_1, x_2, x_3) = \lambda_1(1,1,0) + \lambda_2(0,1,1)$ is unsatisfiable, proving that the originally given formula was valid.

4 Checking Satisfiability of LIA* Formulas by Approximating from Above and Below

In this section, we explain our algorithm for checking satisfiability of LIA* formulas.

We fix a LIA* formula $g \wedge x \in \{y \mid f\}^*$. Observe that the set of solutions of f^* is the least fixpoint of the following set of equations (Constrained Horn Clauses):

$$
\begin{aligned}
x = 0 &\longrightarrow f^*(x) \\
f^*(y) \wedge f(z) \wedge x = y + z &\longrightarrow f^*(x)
\end{aligned}
\tag{5}
$$

However, to determine unsatisfiability of $g \wedge f^*$, it suffices to find an over-approximation o of f^* such that $g \wedge o$ is UNSAT, while satisfiability may be determined based on satisfiability of an under-approximation u. As such, rather than computing a LIA formula that captures f^*, the algorithm approximates this set and uses the approximations for checking satisfiability of $g \wedge f^*$. To do so, the algorithm maintains:

- A LIA formula u that underapproximates f^*, i.e., $u \to f^*$.
- A LIA formula o that overapproximates f^*, i.e., $f^* \to o$.

Algorithm 1 displays the steps for checking satisfiability of $g \wedge f^*$ as a set of inference rules. The algorithm manipulates three types of states: *initial states* of the form $\langle g, \varphi \rangle$, *internal states* of the form $\langle g, u, \varphi, o \rangle$ and *terminal states* $[u, o]$, where $g, u, o, f \in$ LIA and $\varphi = f^*$. The formulas u and o are under- and overapproximations, respectively, of φ, and as such every state satisfies the invariant that $u \to \varphi \to o$.

On input $g \wedge f^*$, the algorithm starts at the initial state $\langle g, f^* \rangle$. From the initial state it follows the $\star$-INIT rule and transitions to the internal state $\langle g, x = 0, f^*, \text{true} \rangle$ that maintains in addition to g and f^* also approximations of f^*. $\star$-INIT initializes the underapproximation of f^* to include only $\mathbf{0}$, and initializes the overapproximation to true.

Transitions between (internal) states refine the approximations according to the inference rules: weaken the underapproximation of f^* (rule $\star$-WEAKEN) or strengthen its overapproximation (rule $\star$-STRENGTHEN). These transitions take the form

$$
\langle g, u, \varphi, o \rangle \implies \langle g, u', \varphi, o' \rangle \qquad \text{such that} \qquad u \to u' \to \varphi \to o' \to o .
$$

We explain $\star$-STRENGTHEN in Sect. 4.1, and $\star$-WEAKEN in Sect. 4.2.

The $\star$-CONVERGE rule identifies the case where the underapproximation u has become an over-approximation of f^*. This happens when u satisfies Eq. (5)

Algorithm 1. Procedure for checking satisfiability of a LIA* formula $g \wedge x \in \{y \mid f\}^\star$.

Initial states: $\langle g, \varphi \rangle \in \text{LIA} \times \text{LIA}^\star$
Internal states: $\langle g, u, \varphi, o \rangle \in \text{LIA} \times \text{LIA} \times \text{LIA}^\star \times \text{LIA}$ s.t. $o \rightarrow \varphi \rightarrow u$
Terminal states: $[u, o] \in \text{LIA} \times \text{LIA}$

$$\langle g, f^\star \rangle \implies \langle g, x = 0, f^\star, \text{true} \rangle \qquad \star\text{-INIT}$$

$$\frac{g \wedge o \text{ is UNSAT}}{\langle g, u, f^\star, o \rangle \implies [u, o]} \text{ EXIT-UNSAT} \qquad \frac{g \wedge u \text{ is SAT}}{\langle g, u, f^\star, o \rangle \implies [u, o]} \text{ EXIT-SAT}$$

$$\frac{f(x) \wedge \neg u(x) \text{ is UNSAT}}{\langle g, u, f^\star, o \rangle \implies \langle g, u, f^\star, u \rangle} \star\text{-CONVERGE}$$

$$\frac{\begin{array}{c} x = v \models f(x) \wedge \neg u(x) \\ u' = \text{WEAKENUNDER}(u, v) \end{array}}{\langle g, u, f^\star, o \rangle \implies \langle g, u', f^\star, o \rangle} \star\text{-WEAKEN}$$

$$\frac{\begin{array}{c} u(x) \wedge f^{\leq 2n}(y) \wedge g(x + y) \text{ is UNSAT} \\ o' = \text{STRENGTHENOVER}(o, u, f^{\leq n}, g) \end{array}}{\langle g, u, f^\star, o \rangle \implies \langle g, u, f^\star, o' \rangle} \star\text{-STRENGTHEN}$$

(recall that $f^\star$ is the least solution of these equations). $\star$-CONVERGE recognizes this case by unsatisfiability of the test $f(x) \wedge \neg u(x)$ since this test is equi-satisfiable to the "inductiveness" test $u(y) \wedge f(x) \wedge \neg u(x + y)$ (because $u(0)$ and u is closed under addition, as we will see in Sect. 4.2). When this condition holds, it indicates that the under-approximation has converged to a LIA formula that is equivalent to $f^\star$, and satisfiability of $g \wedge f^\star$ reduces to satisfiability of $g \wedge u$, as they are equi-satisfiable.

In fact, u need not be equivalent to $f^\star$ to enable determining satisfiability of $g \wedge f^\star$. Equi-satisfiability of u and $f^\star$ with respect to g is a sufficient condition for that, which is in turn ensured by equi-satisfiability of u and o with respect to g (since $u \rightarrow f^\star \rightarrow o$). Accordingly, we say that:

Definition 2. *An internal state* $\langle g, u, \varphi, o \rangle$ *is* determined *when* $g \wedge u$ *and* $g \wedge o$ *are equi-satisfiable.*

Such a state is called determined since equi-satisfiability of the under- and over-approximations with respect to g implies that they are both equi-satisfiable to $f^\star$ with respect to g. Equivalently, the under-approximation is satisfiable or the over-approximation is unsatisfiable when conjoined with g:

Lemma 1. *An internal state* $\langle g, u, \varphi, o \rangle$ *is determined if and only if* $g \wedge u$ *is SAT or* $g \wedge o$ *is UNSAT.*

Algorithm 2. STRENGTHENOVER($o, u, f^{\leq n}, g$)

/* Procedure for computing an over-approximation o of $f^\star$ */

1 $f_1 := u(y) \wedge f^{\leq n}(z) \wedge x = y + z$; $f_2 := \neg(x = y' + z' \wedge f^{\leq n}(y') \wedge g(z'))$
2 **if** $f_1 \rightarrow f_2$ **then**
3     $Itp(x) :=$ interpolant between f_1 and f_2
4     $C :=$ conjunction of all interpolants produced so far
5     $o :=$ the maximal subset of C such that $o(x) \wedge f(y) \rightarrow o(x + y)$
6 **return** o

The EXIT-SAT and EXIT-UNSAT rules establish these cases as exit criteria that lead to terminal states.

Note that the exit rules may be applicable before the approximations converge to a formula that is equivalent to $f^\star$. However, in the worst case the algorithm terminates after $\star$-CONVERGE is applied.

We discuss correctness and termination of the algorithm in Sect. 4.3, after we fill in the missing details for weakening and strengthening the approximations.

4.1 Computing Over-Approximations of $f^\star$

Our approach for obtaining an over-approximation of $f^\star$, depicted in Algorithm 2, is through reverse interpolation against g. Recall that $f^\star$ is the least solution of Eq. (5). Hence, any solution to these equations is an overapproximation of $f^\star$. Recall further that the overapproximation o is used for early detection of unsatisfiability of $g \wedge f^\star$ (rule EXIT-UNSAT). Hence, the "optimal" overapproximation (in case $g \wedge f^\star$ is unsatisfiable) is a solution for the following set of equations:

$$x = 0 \longrightarrow o(x)$$
$$o(y) \wedge f(z) \wedge x = y + z \longrightarrow o(x)$$
$$o(x) \longrightarrow \neg g(x)$$

As a step towards finding such a solution, we use interpolation. For a given underapproximation u that covers in general an unbounded number of $f^\star$ solutions (including $x = 0$) and where $u(y) \wedge f(z) \wedge x = y + z \wedge g(x)$ is UNSAT, we can query an interpolation procedure for a predicate $Itp(x)$ such that

$$u(y) \wedge f(z) \wedge x = y + z \rightarrow Itp(x) \qquad \text{and} \qquad Itp(x) \rightarrow \neg g(x),$$

The interpolant $Itp(x)$ is disjoint from g. However, it is not in general an over-approximation of $f^\star(x)$; rather, it is an over-approximation of a single unfolding of f from u. We therefore do not use Itp as is, but use it as the basis for obtaining an overapproximation of $f^\star$.

Similar to how IC3 propagates clauses through frames that represent increasing unfoldings of the transition relation, and in the essence of the Houdini approach for learning conjunctions of inductive predicates from a candidate set of predicates, our approach is to use conjunctions generated from all the interpolation queries to strengthen a global "inductive invariant", i.e., a formula $o(x)$ such that $x = 0 \longrightarrow o(x)$ and $o(y) \wedge f(z) \wedge x = y + z \longrightarrow o(x)$. Such a formula may not be disjoint from g but it is guaranteed to overapproximate $f^\star$ (which is the least solution of these equations). Our task of producing a global invariant concludes when it implies $\neg g(x)$; or $u(x)$ witnesses satisfiability.

A drawback of posing the interpolation query with only one unfolding of f is that it could easily find a biased interpolant based on $g(x)$ or $u(x)$. We therefore pose more general interpolation queries that are forced to produce separating predicates that generalize beyond 0 or 1 unfoldings with f as follows. We consider n unfoldings of f:

Definition 3 $(f^{\leq n}(y))$.

$$f^{\leq 0}(y) \triangleq y = 0$$
$$f^{\leq n+1}(y) \triangleq y = 0 \vee (\exists y_1, y_2 \cdot y = y_1 + y_2 \wedge f(y_1) \wedge f^{\leq n}(y_2))$$

Given some choice of n such that $u(y) \wedge f^{\leq 2n}(x) \wedge g(x + y)$ is unsatisfiable, Algorithm 2 computes an interpolant:

$$u(y) \wedge f^{\leq n}(z) \wedge x = y + z \rightarrow Itp(x) \qquad \text{and}$$
$$Itp(x) \rightarrow \neg(x = y' + z' \wedge f^{\leq n}(y') \wedge g(z'))$$

and uses it as the basis for computing an over approximation as explained above. (If the above formula is satisfiable, the over approximation is not modified.)

4.2 Computing Under-Approximations of $f^\star$

The procedure WEAKENUNDER extends the current under-approximation u of $f^\star$ to include a solution v of f (and hence also of $f^\star$) that is not yet covered by u. Recall that such a solution also establishes that u is not yet inductive since the test $f(x) \wedge \neg u(x)$ is equi-satisfiable to the test $u(y) \wedge f(x) \wedge \neg u(x + y)$. The procedure returns a weaker under-approximation u' such that $u \rightarrow u' \rightarrow f^\star$ and $x = v \models u'$. The procedure relies on (i) computing a semilinear set U that underapproximates the solutions of f and includes v, and (ii) using Theorem 2 to express its star using a LIA formula. Since the star operator is monotone, we are guaranteed that applying the star operator on the underapproximation of f results in an underapproximation of $f^\star$.

We start by describing a procedure, called LIA2SLS, for computing a semilinear representation of the LIA formula f with access to a LIA oracle only. WEAKENUNDER does not invoke that procedure per se, but it uses some of its ingredients, where it acts as the LIA oracle, as we explain in the sequel.

Definition 4 (LIA oracle). *By a LIA oracle we will understand a decision procedure for LIA, which, given a LIA formula f, returns a model for f if it is satisfiable, and returns UNSAT otherwise.*

Generating Semilinear Representation of a LIA *Formula via Underapproximations.* The LIA2SLS procedure, displayed in Algorithm 3, generates increasing under-approximations of f in the form of semilinear sets that converge to a representation of f.

One should observe that at any given point, LIA2SLS maintains a semilinear set $SLS(LS(a_1, B_1), \ldots, LS(a_k, B_k))$ that under-approximates (the set of solutions of) f. The semilinear set is represented as a set U of linear sets $LS(a_i, B_i)$, where each of them is represented by its shift vector and offset vectors. In the sequel, we sometimes identify U with the semilinear set. Using this terminology, an invariant of the procedure is that $\text{LIA}(U) \to f$ (where $\text{LIA}(U)$ denotes the formula associated with the semilinear set, as defined in Eq. (3)).

Initially, the under-approximation U is the empty set (rule **Init**). The procedure then augments the under-approximation until $f \to \text{LIA}(U)$, in which case $f \equiv \text{LIA}(U)$ and U is its representation as a semilinear set (rule **Exit**). As long as this is not the case, **Augment** extends U by adding a solution of f that is not yet covered, followed by a saturation procedure. Saturation applies the rules **Merge**, **Shift Down** and **Offset Down** that use coordinate-wise comparison between vectors, defined below, in order to minimize shift and offset vectors and, as we will see, ensure termination.

Definition 5 ($a \preceq b$). *For two integer vectors a and b define*

$$a \preceq b \;\triangleq\; \bigwedge_{0 < i \le \dim(a)} (0 \le a_i \le b_i \lor 0 \ge a_i \ge b_i) \tag{6}$$

Algorithm 3. LIA2SLS

Init $U := \emptyset$.

Augment Let v be a solution to $f(x) \land \neg\text{LIA}(U)(x)$. Add the linear set $LS(v, \emptyset)$ to U, and apply $\text{SATURATE}(U)$ until convergence.

Exit If $f \land \neg\text{LIA}(U)$ is UNSAT, then return $\text{LIA}(U)$.

$\text{SATURATE}(U)$:

Merge Let $LS(a_1, B_1)$ and $LS(a_2, B_2)$ be two linear sets in U such that $a_2 \preceq a_1$. If $\forall \lambda_1, \lambda_2, \lambda_3 \,.\, f(a_2 + \lambda_1 B_1 + \lambda_2 B_2 + \lambda_3(a_1 - a_2))$ is valid (equivalently, $\neg f(a_2 + \lambda_1 B_1 + \lambda_2 B_2 + \lambda_3(a_1 - a_2))$ is unsatisfiable) then replace the two linear sets by $LS(a_2, B_1 \cup B_2 \cup \{a_1 - a_2\})$ in U.

Shift Down Let $LS(a_1, B_1)$ be a linear set in U. If there is a $b \in B_1$, such that $b \preceq a_1$ and $\forall \lambda \,.\, f(a_1 - b + \lambda B_1)$ is valid, then replace $LS(a_1, B_1)$ by $LS(a_1 - b, B_1)$.

Offset Down Let $LS(a_1, B_1)$ be a linear set in U. If there are $b_1, b_2 \in B_1$, such that $b_2 \preceq b_1$ and $\forall \lambda \,.\, f(a_1 + \lambda B_1')$ is valid for $B_1' := (B_1 \setminus \{b_1\}) \cup \{b_1 - b_2\}$, then replace $LS(a_1, B_1)$ by $LS(a_1, B_1')$ in U.

It follows by inspecting the steps that the procedure always augments U to an improved under-approximation of f. In other words, it maintains the invariant $\text{LIA}(U) \to f$.

Lemma 2. *Let U be the set computed after any number of steps of Algorithm 3, and let $\text{LIA}(U)$ be the formula associated with it (per Eq. (3)). Then $\text{LIA}(U) \to f$.*

Proof (sketch). The **Augment** rule adds to U a single solution of f. Any of the other rules checks whether the newly added linear set, when converted into a LIA formula via Eq. (3), implies f.

In each step, the under-approximation is improved as it has more solutions or a smaller representation. Termination is obtained since $\preceq$ is a *well quasi order* (wqo) [11] (a reflexive and transitive relation where any infinite sequence of elements $v_1, v_2, \ldots$ contains an increasing pair $v_i \preceq v_j$ with $i < j$).

Lemma 3 (Termination). *Algorithm 3 terminates in a finite number of steps.*

Proof. Observe that $\preceq$ is a pointwise application of well quasi orders. Hence, by Dickson's lemma [7], it is also a well quasi order. This ensures that for any finite set U, any of the rules **Merge, Shift Down** and **Offset Down** may only be applied finitely many times (since a wqo does not have infinite descending sequences). Hence, to establish termination it remains to show that **Augment** cannot be applied infinitely many times. Assume to the contrary that **Augment** generates an infinite sequence $v_1, v_2, \ldots$. Each vector in the sequence belongs to one of the finitely many linear sets defining f. Hence, there is an infinite subsequence of $v_1, v_2, \ldots$ where all vectors are members of the same linear set $L(a, B)$, and further are all merged together by **Merge**. Further, since $\preceq$ is a wqo, this subsequence has an infinite increasing subsequence $v_{i_1} \preceq v_{i_2} \preceq \ldots$.

For each vector v_{i_j}, we denote by $set(i_j) = LS(a_{i_j}, B_{i_j})$ the linear set in U to which v_{i_j} belongs after the (single) application of **Augment** that generated it followed by an iterative application of **Merge, Offset Down, Shift Down**, until they converge. An invariant that follows by induction is that $a_{i_j} = a + \lambda B$ for some λ and, similarly, each vector in B_{i_j} is a linear combination of vectors in B, i.e., is equal to λB for some λ (it is easy to verify that **Offset Down** and **Shift Down** preserve this property; for **Merge** we rely on our choice of vectors). The vector a_{i_j} may be decreased only finitely many times, hence at some point it stabilizes to some vector $\widetilde{a}$. Similarly, each vector b in B_{i_j} may be decreased by **Offset Down** at most finitely many times. Hence, for each B_{i_j} there exists a time step after which all the vectors that originated from it are no longer decremented. Denote the set that contains the vectors originating from B_{i_j} after stabilization by $\widetilde{B}_{i_j}$.

Hence, the infinite sequence $v_{i_1} \preceq v_{i_2} \preceq \ldots$ gives rise to an infinite sequence of sets of vectors $\widetilde{B}_{i_1} \subseteq \widetilde{B}_{i_2}, \ldots$ as defined above (inclusion follows since the vectors in $\widetilde{B}_{i_j}$ no longer evolve). Note that by construction, $LS(\widetilde{a}, \bigcup_j \widetilde{B}_{i_j})$ spans all vectors in $v_{i_1}, v_{i_2}, \ldots$. Further, $\bigcup \widetilde{B}_{i_j}$ must be finite since all the vectors in it are incomparable (as all vectors have stabilized) and $\preceq$ is a wqo. However,

---

Algorithm 4. WEAKENUNDER(u,v)

$U := \text{GETSLS}(u)$
Add $LS(v, \emptyset)$ to U and apply SATURATE(U) until convergence.
Return STARLIA(U).

---

this implies that $LS(\widetilde{a}, \bigcup_j \widetilde{B}_{i_j})$ is added to U after a finite number of steps, after which no vector from $v_1, v_2, \ldots$ may be generated by **Augment**, in contradiction to our assumption that infinitely many of them are generated.   □

Note that by strengthening the queries into the LIA oracle to find minimal solutions modulo $\preceq$ we can effectively bound the number of queries that produce new vectors to be the same as the size of a minimal semilinear set representation. Our proof doesn't assume minimality of vectors and therefore relies on using properties of well quasi orderings.

Computing Under-Approximations of $f^\star$. WEAKENUNDER (Algorithm 4) relies on Algorithm 3 to generate a semilinear set U that under-approximates f. From U it produces an under-approximation STARLIA(U) of $f^\star$ through Eq. (4).

In order to compute U, WEAKENUNDER first extracts from u, the current under-approximation of f, the semilinear set U such that $u = \text{STARLIA}(U)$. Since all underapproximations are computed by WEAKENUNDER, all of them follow Eq. (4), which makes it easy to extract U from u. WEAKENUNDER then simulates an iteration of Algorithm 3 (a step of **Augment** followed by saturation) that extends U based on a new solution to f, except that it uses the provided uncovered solution v of f rather than obtaining one from the LIA-oracle.

Recall that the solution v provided to WEAKENUNDER is taken from $x = v \models f(x) \wedge \neg u(x)$. Hence, v is a solution to f that is not yet covered by u. This means that v is not yet covered neither by U nor by $U^\star$.

Iteratively applying WEAKENUNDER results in a variant of Algorithm 3, where in each iteration, U is extended not with an arbitrary solution of $f \wedge \neg \text{LIA}(U)$ (that may or may not be covered by $U^\star$), but rather with a solution of $f \wedge \neg \text{STARLIA}(U)$ as the algorithm is geared towards computing a representation of $f^\star$. Similarly to Algorithm 3, iterative application of WEAKENUNDER is guaranteed to converge to a precise representation U of f within a finite number of iterations, in which case STARLIA(U), returned as the under-approximation of $f^\star$, is also precise (i.e., equivalent to $f^\star$). It may terminate earlier, as STARLIA(U) may be equivalent to $f^\star$ even though LIA(U) is not yet equivalent to f.

4.3   Correctness

The following lemma is a simple corollary of the invariants maintained by the algorithm.

Lemma 4 (Partial Correctness). *If* $\langle g, f^\star \rangle \Longrightarrow^\star [u, o]$ *then* $g \wedge u$, $g \wedge o$ *and* $g \wedge f^\star$ *are all equi-satisfiable.*

To argue termination of Algorithm 1, we must require a fair scheduling of the transitions: namely, each of the rules must be scheduled infinitely often.

Lemma 5 (Termination). *Any fair execution of Algorithm 1 starting from state* $\langle g, f^\star \rangle$ *terminates in a finite number of steps.*

As explained in the previous section, iterative application of weakening, which gradually refines u, mimics Algorithm 3. Hence, u must converge to a LIA formula that is equivalent to $f^\star$ within a finite number of steps, in which case when Algorithm 1 applies $\star$-CONVERGE it reaches a determined state, and terminates in one of the exit rules. Note that the termination argument relies only on the under-approximations and their convergence to $f^\star$. However, in practice, the over-approximations are also important for termination as they facilitate early termination without convergence to a LIA formula that is equivalent to $f^\star$.

5 Evaluation

To empirically test our decision procedure, we implemented Algorithm 1. In addition, we also implemented the translation algorithm given in Fig. 4. This way we can evaluate our tool on real-world MAPA problems. The implementation is written in Python, using the Python binding for Z3 as our LIA oracle. The implementation and benchmarks are publicly available at https://github.com/mlevatich/sls-reachability.

As it was pointed out in [18], there is a lack of native MAPA benchmarks. For our evaluation, we tested the code on 240 BAPA benchmarks derived from a set of benchmarks used for reasoning about distributed algorithms [1]. Since the BAPA problems involve reasoning about sets and not multisets, we used the set$(\cdot)$ operator which explicitly states that a multiset variable M is a set, meaning that an element can appear at most once.

Before we expand further upon the results for each table presented here, we divide the benchmarks into classes based on their size, where the size of a benchmark is determined by the number of conjunctions in its LIA* representation. Due to our translation, this value also scales evenly with the number of free variables in the formula, and is a rough measure of a problem's complexity. For each class, we give the number of benchmarks in that class, and how many of them were sat or unsat, or timed out. We provide average statistics for the solved examples in that class about the size of the final computed semilinear set (measured as total number of vectors in its linear sets, including the offset vector for each set), the number of calls made to z3, and the total runtime of the algorithm. For all evaluations, we arbitrarily chose a timeout of 50 s.

The results of our initial evaluation are given by Table 1. We found that our tool handled the BAPA benchmarks very effectively – most benchmarks finished quickly and severely under-approximated the full semilinear set representation of the problem. This experiment used a single unfolding when computing interpolants in Algorithm 2.

We noticed that the set(·) operator and at-most-one appearance constraints increase each benchmark's difficulty, reflected by the larger semilinear sets, many Z3 calls, and longer average running times. To test how our decision procedure performs on its native theory, MAPA. We converted all 240 of the BAPA benchmarks into genuine MAPA problems by simply omitting the set(·) constraints from the translation. This change means that the set variables in the original benchmarks are no longer considered sets but multisets. Our only intent in doing this was to create suitable benchmarks for evaluating our tool – we are not concerned with whether or not MAPA is suitable for modeling the same problems as the original benchmarks. By turning the BAPA benchmarks into MAPA benchmarks, we could exercise true multiset reasoning. The results of MAPA benchmarks are given by Table 2, in which we see a considerable speedup – even though multisets are more complex objects than sets, the omission of the multiplicity constraints results in a shorter and more efficient representation, showing the effectiveness of our tool on genuine MAPA problems.

Using the MAPA representation of the benchmarks, we further studied the reverse interpolation procedure for computing over-approximations. We applied the unfolding method given by Definition 3 with $n = 5$ to produce more general interpolants. Table 3 presents the performance of the benchmarks with unfolding added (also using MAPA semantics). By unfolding, we force Z3 to generate interpolants which are more likely to be inductive, resulting in a significant speedup and the ability to solve far more of the hard problems in the 13–16 size range.

To demonstrate the need for interpolation, we also ran our procedure with no interpolation at all. Without interpolation, unsatisfiability can only be shown when the entire semilinear set representation is computed, which is prohibitively expensive. The summary of the results is given in Table 4 (for MAPA semantics). In this case, the algorithm struggles to prove that complex examples are unsatisfiable, and must resort to generating larger semilinear sets.

Table 1. BAPA evaluation summary for $n = 1$ unfoldings.

Problem size	# of Problems	Sat/Unsat/TO	SLS size	Z3 Invocations	Time (s)
6	106	76/30/0	6	76	1.6
7–9	64	34/30/0	7	75	1.8
10–12	13	1/9/3	18	575	21.7
13–16	46	3/0/43	20	780	33.9
19–22	11	0/0/11	N/A	N/A	N/A

Finally, in Table 5 we provide the running times of our procedure, giving the average time spent by each evaluation on different parts of the procedure. In general, the algorithm performs very well for smaller problem sizes and the intrinsic complexity of the problem is visible on the problems of a bigger size.

Table 2. MAPA evaluation summary for $n = 1$ unfoldings.

Problem size	# of Problems	Sat/Unsat/TO	SLS size	Z3 Invocations	Time (s)
6	106	76/30/0	4	22	0.6
7–9	64	34/30/0	5	30	0.9
10–12	13	2/8/3	11	225	7.5
13–16	46	2/2/42	10	200	8.4
19–22	11	0/0/11	N/A	N/A	N/A

Table 3. MAPA evaluation summary for $n = 5$ unfoldings.

Problem size	# of Problems	Sat/Unsat/TO	SLS size	Z3 Invocations	Time (s)
6	106	76/30/0	4	17	0.6
7–9	64	34/30/0	3	15	0.7
10–12	13	0/11/2	2	11	0.8
13–16	46	3/15/28	4	76	7.9
19–22	11	0/0/11	N/A	N/A	N/A

Table 4. MAPA evaluation summary without interpolation.

Problem size	# of Problems	Sat/Unsat/TO	SLS size	Z3 Invocations	Time (s)
6	106	76/30/0	5	18	0.6
7–9	64	34/30/0	5	20	0.7
10–12	13	0/0/13	N/A	N/A	N/A
13–16	46	8/0/38	10	93	4.7
19–22	11	0/0/11	N/A	N/A	N/A

Table 5. Runtime performance profile of the procedure.

	Augmentation (s)	Interpolation (s)	Reduction (s)	Sat checking (s)
BAPA	0.23	0.87	0.92	1.09
MAPA	0.07	0.48	0.17	0.33
UNFOLD-5	0.04	0.86	0.07	0.17
NO-INTERP	0.08	0	0.2	0.32

One observation is that the MAPA evaluation is much faster than BAPA – while our algorithm generalizes to BAPA, the set($\cdot$) operator results in the increase of the ite($\cdot, \cdot, \cdot$) expressions, which can potentially lead to an exponential blow up in size of the input formula. On the positive side, our efficient representation means that modeling multisets is comparatively easy despite their complexity, opening the opportunity for easy use of multisets in verification.

The MAPA evaluation, when compared to NO-INTERP (Table 4), also showcases the benefits of using the semilinear set over-approximation. NO-INTERP was unable to prove a single complex problem unsatisfiable, because the full semilinear set representation that witnesses unsatisfiability is too large to compute even with our reduction and augmentation cycle. NO-INTERP solved slightly more satisfiable examples than MAPA, since the algorithm could spend more time growing the semilinear set before timing out (because it was not interpolating).

The most effective evaluation was UNFOLD-5 (Table 3). Compared to MAPA, UNFOLD-5 solved 14 more of the problems of size 13–16, out of 46 total, and was faster on average for all classes of problems. The general interpolants that unfolding demands are far more likely to be inductive and, for many real-world MAPA problems, can prove unsatisfiability almost instantly. The trade-off is that the interpolation problems become heavier, as shown in Table 5, and because interpolants serve as over-approximations, they do not help for satisfiable problems.

It is possible that by tuning the unfolding by experimenting more thoroughly with different values for n, we could increase the speed and effectiveness of the algorithm even further. We can also apply the benefits of unfolding to satisfiable MAPA problems by introducing unfoldings when checking for satisfiability – even before the semilinear set underapproximation is able to reach a solution, a finite unfolding allows it to flexibly step outside itself and look for nearby solutions.

Overall, our initial results are quite promising, and there is still room for potential optimizations to be made to the basic algorithm.

6   Related Work

Several decidable extensions of LIA have been studied, such as LIA with divisibility constraints [10] and Büchi arithmetic [4,5] that has a predicate that can distinguish whether a number is a power of two. The existential fragment of $LIA^\star$ with unbounded nesting of stars, $\exists LIA^\star$, was established to be NEXP-complete in [9]. Although quantifier-free LIA formulas with bounded nesting of star operators lie in the NP-complete fragment, as established in [17], there is no implementation and the proposed algorithm relies on computing the semilinear representation of the solution, which is mainly unfeasible in practice. In general semilinear sets require a number of generators that is exponential in the size of the input LIA formula [19]. There are algorithms that are based on enumerative search for possible generators of a semilinear set [6], following the size ordering and yielding a potentially doubly exponential number of vectors that need to be considered. The other approach, suggested in [19], uses the bounds on the vectors in a standard basis (as obtained from a Hilbert basis). The fact that the number of basis vectors easily explodes precludes implementations that can efficiently find semilinear sets for a given formula.

To avoid explicit computation of semilinear sets, Piskac and Kuncak [17] devised a novel decision procedure that for a given $LIA^\star$ formula $F_1 \wedge x \in \{y \mid F_2\}^\star$, constructs an equisatisfiable LIA formula $F_1 \wedge F_2'$ by using only solution vectors for formula F_2. The number of the solution vectors is high: it is bounded by $\mathcal{O}(n^2 \log n)$, where n is the size of the formula. Although this approach does not compute semilinear sets, the algorithm was still not applicable in practice.

The decision procedure constructs formula F_2' in a monolithic way, producing immediately a very large formula that could not be solved by existing tools, not even for the most simple cases. It should be clear that for modest values of n, the bound $n^2 \log n$ grows very quickly.

Zarba [20] studied a combination of multisets and linear integer arithmetic. The logic did not support the cardinality operator, but there was a count operator that would return how many times an element appears in a multiset. Lugiez [15] considered a logic of multisets with a limited cardinality operator that would return only the number of distinct elements. Piskac and Kuncak [16] introduced a more general logic that allows the standard definition of the cardinality operator. We use MAPA, a simplified, but equally expressive version of their logic. This name is chosen to also indicate that MAPA can be seen as a generalization of BAPA (Boolean Algebra and Presburger Arithmetic) [12,13], a logic that is used to express properties about sets with cardinality constraints. The BAPA logic is used in verification of data structures [3] and distributed protocols [1].

7   Conclusion

In this paper we developed and evaluated a decision procedure for LIA*. The evaluation, using our prototype, suggested that samples extracted from BAPA applications benefited from the incremental nature of our solver. In addition, it suggested that interpolants based on bounded unfoldings were useful for finding over-approximations that were helpful determining unsatisfiability. The prototype could be improved in many ways, including notably a tighter integration within a native LIA* solver. The benefits of a native integration includes incrementality, access to preprocessing simplifications, and alternative heuristics such as sampling f for creating a large initial basis, and sound, but incomplete, inference rules. Nevertheless, we feel encouraged by the overall approach given the promising results from the prototype.

While our initial motivation for this work was to find an efficient decision procedure for reasoning about multisets with cardinality constraints, reasoning about LIA* formulas suggested new application areas. For instance, there are numerous classes of integer vector addition systems with states (VASS), where the set of reachable states is described with a semilinear set (for a classification of VASS see for example [2,14]). We conjecture that our solver for LIA* formulas could be used for checking VASS reachability for those classes.

References

1. Berkovits, I., Lazić, M., Losa, G., Padon, O., Shoham, S.: Verification of threshold-based distributed algorithms by decomposition to decidable logics. In: Dillig, I., Tasiran, S. (eds.) CAV 2019. LNCS, vol. 11562, pp. 245–266. Springer, Cham (2019). https://doi.org/10.1007/978-3-030-25543-5_15

2. Blondin, M., Haase, C., Mazowiecki, F.: Affine extensions of integer vector addition systems with states. In: CONCUR, volume 118 of LIPIcs, pp. 14:1–14:17. Schloss Dagstuhl - Leibniz-Zentrum fuer Informatik (2018)
3. Bouillaguet, C., Kuncak, V., Wies, T., Zee, K., Rinard, M.: Using first-order theorem provers in the jahob data structure verification system. In: Cook, B., Podelski, A. (eds.) VMCAI 2007. LNCS, vol. 4349, pp. 74–88. Springer, Heidelberg (2007). https://doi.org/10.1007/978-3-540-69738-1_5
4. Bruyère, V., Hansel, G., Michaux, C., Villemaire, R.: Logic and p-recognizable sets of integers. Bull. Belg. Math. Soc. 1, 191–238 (1994)
5. Büchi, J.R.: Weak second-order arithmetic and finite automata. Math. Logic Q. 6(1–6), 66–92 (1960)
6. Contejean, E., Devie, H.: An efficient incremental algorithm for solving systems of linear Diophantine equations. Inf. Comput. 113(1), 143–172 (1994)
7. Dickson, L.E.: Finiteness of the odd perfect and primitive abundant numbers with n distinct prime factors. Am. J. Math. 35, 413–422 (1913)
8. Ginsburg, S., Spanier, E.H.: Semigroups, Presburger formulas, and languages. Pac. J. Math. 16(2), 285–296 (1966)
9. Haase, C., Zetzsche, G.: Presburger arithmetic with stars, rational subsets of graph groups, and nested zero tests. In: LICS, pp. 1–14. IEEE (2019)
10. Jovanovic, D., de Moura, L.: Cutting to the chase - solving linear integer arithmetic. J. Autom. Reason. 51(1), 79–108 (2013)
11. Kruskal, J.B.: The theory of well-quasi-ordering: a frequently discovered concept. J. Comb. Theory Ser. A 13(3), 297–305 (1972)
12. Kuncak, V., Nguyen, H.H., Rinard, M.: An algorithm for deciding BAPA: Boolean algebra with Presburger arithmetic. In: Nieuwenhuis, R. (ed.) CADE 2005. LNCS (LNAI), vol. 3632, pp. 260–277. Springer, Heidelberg (2005). https://doi.org/10.1007/11532231_20
13. Kuncak, V., Nguyen, H.H., Rinard, M.C.: Deciding Boolean algebra with Presburger arithmetic. J. Autom. Reason. 36(3), 213–239 (2006)
14. Leroux, J.: The general vector addition system reachability problem by Presburger inductive invariants. Logic. Methods Comput. Sci. 6(3) (2010)
15. Lugiez, D.: Multitree automata that count. Theor. Comput. Sci. 333(1–2), 225–263 (2005)
16. Piskac, R., Kuncak, V.: Decision procedures for multisets with cardinality constraints. In: Logozzo, F., Peled, D.A., Zuck, L.D. (eds.) VMCAI 2008. LNCS, vol. 4905, pp. 218–232. Springer, Heidelberg (2008). https://doi.org/10.1007/978-3-540-78163-9_20
17. Piskac, R., Kuncak, V.: Linear arithmetic with stars. In: Gupta, A., Malik, S. (eds.) CAV 2008. LNCS, vol. 5123, pp. 268–280. Springer, Heidelberg (2008). https://doi.org/10.1007/978-3-540-70545-1_25
18. Piskac, R., Kuncak, V.: MUNCH - automated reasoner for sets and multisets. In: Giesl, J., Hähnle, R. (eds.) IJCAR 2010. LNCS (LNAI), vol. 6173, pp. 149–155. Springer, Heidelberg (2010). https://doi.org/10.1007/978-3-642-14203-1_13
19. Pottier, L.: Minimal solutions of linear diophantine systems: bounds and algorithms. In: Book, R.V. (ed.) RTA 1991. LNCS, vol. 488, pp. 162–173. Springer, Heidelberg (1991). https://doi.org/10.1007/3-540-53904-2_94
20. Zarba, C.G.: Combining multisets with integers. In: Voronkov, A. (ed.) CADE 2002. LNCS (LNAI), vol. 2392, pp. 363–376. Springer, Heidelberg (2002). https://doi.org/10.1007/3-540-45620-1_30

Formalizing and Checking Multilevel Consistency

Ahmed Bouajjani[1], Constantin Enea[1], Madhavan Mukund[2,3],
Gautham Shenoy R.[2], and S. P. Suresh[2,3(✉)]

[1] Université Paris Diderot, Paris, France
{abou,cenea}@irif.fr
[2] Chennai Mathematical Institute, Chennai, India
{madhavan,gautshen,spsuresh}@cmi.ac.in
[3] CNRS UMI 2000 ReLaX, Chennai, India

Abstract. Developers of distributed data-stores must trade consistency for performance and availability. Such systems may in fact implement weak consistency models, e.g., causal consistency or eventual consistency, corresponding to different costs and guarantees to the clients. We consider the case of distributed systems that offer not just one level of consistency but multiple levels of consistency to the clients. This corresponds to many practical situations. For instance, popular data-stores such as Amazon DynamoDB and Apache's Cassandra allow applications to tag each query within the same session with a separate consistency level. In this paper, we provide a formal framework for the specification of multilevel consistency, and we address the problem of checking the conformance of a computation to such a specification. We provide a principled algorithmic approach to this problem and apply it to several instances of models with multilevel consistency.

1 Introduction

To achieve availability and scalability, modern data-stores (key-value stores) rely on optimistic replication, allowing multiple clients to issue operations on shared data on a number of replicas, which communicate changes to each other using message passing. One benefit of such architectures is that the replicas remain locally available to clients even when network connections fail. Unfortunately, the famous CAP theorem [15] shows that such high Availability and tolerance to network Partitions are incompatible with strong Consistency, i.e., the illusion of a single centralized replica handling all operations. For this reason, modern replicated data-stores often provide weaker forms of consistency such as eventual consistency [23] or causal consistency [19], which have been formalized only recently [6,7,10,22].

Programming applications on top of weakly-consistent data-stores is difficult. Some form of synchronization is often unavoidable to preserve correctness.

Partially supported by CEFIPRA DST-Inria-CNRS Project 2014-1, AVeCSo.

D. Beyer and D. Zufferey (Eds.): VMCAI 2020, LNCS 11990, pp. 379–400, 2020.
https://doi.org/10.1007/978-3-030-39322-9_18

Therefore, popular data-stores such as Amazon DynamoDB and Apache's Cassandra provide different levels of consistencies, ranging from weaker forms to strong consistency. Applications can tag queries to the data-store with a suitable level of consistency depending on their needs.

Implementations of large-scale data-stores are difficult to build and test. For instance, they must account for partial failures, where some components or the network can fail and produce incomplete results. Ensuring fault-tolerance relies on intricate protocols which are difficult to design and reason about. The black-box testing framework Jepsen[1] found a remarkably large number of subtle problems in many production distributed data-stores.

Testing a data-store raises two issues: (1) deriving a suitable set of testing scenarios, e.g., faults to inject into the system and the set of operations to be executed, and (2) efficient algorithms for checking whether a given execution satisfies the considered consistency models. The Jepsen framework shows that the first issue can be solved using randomization, e.g., introducing faults at random and choosing the operations randomly. The effectiveness of this solution has been proved formally in recent work [21]. The second issue is dependent on a suitable formalization of the consistency models.

In this work, we consider the problem of specifying data-stores which provide multiple levels of consistency and derive algorithms to check whether a given execution adheres to such a multilevel consistency specification.

We build on the specification framework in [10] which formalizes consistency models using two auxiliary relations: (i) a *visibility* relation, which specifies the set of operations observed by each operation, and (ii) an *arbitration order*, which specifies the order in which concurrent operations should be viewed by all replicas. An execution is said to satisfy a consistency criterion if there exists a visibility relation and an arbitration order that obey an associated set of constraints. For the case of a data-store providing multiple levels of consistency, we consider multiple visibility relations and arbitration orders, one for each level of consistency. Then, we consider a set of formulas which specifies each consistency level in isolation, and also, how visibility relations and arbitration orders of different consistency levels are related.

Based on this formalization, we investigate the problem of checking whether a given execution satisfies a certain multilevel consistency specification. In general, this problem is known to be NP-COMPLETE [6]. However, we show that for executions where each value is written at most once to a key, this problem is polynomial time for many practically-interesting multilevel consistency specifications. Since practical data-store implementations are data-independent [24], i.e., their behaviour doesn't depend on the concrete values read or written in the transactions, it suffices to consider executions where each value is written at most once. This complexity result uses the idea of *bad patterns* introduced in [6] for the case of causal consistency. Intuitively, a bad pattern is a set of operations occurring in a particular order corresponding to a consistency violation. In this paper, we provide a *systematic methodology* for deriving bad patterns characterizing a wide range of consistency models and combinations thereof.

---

[1] Available at http://jepsen.io.

Our contributions form an effective algorithmic framework for the verification of modern data-stores providing multiple levels of consistency. To the best of our knowledge, we are the first to investigate the asymptotic complexity for such a wide class of consistency models and their combinations, despite their prevalence in practice.

The paper is organized as follows. We begin with some real-life examples of multilevel consistency. In Sect. 3, we present a formal model for specifying and reasoning about multilevel consistency. Section 4 describes algorithms for verifying multilevel consistency. We conclude with a discussion of related work. Detailed proofs can be found in the technical report [8].

2 Multilevel Consistency in the Wild

In this section we present some real-world instances of multilevel consistency. We restrict our attention to distributed read-write key-value data-stores (henceforth referred to as read-write stores), consisting of unique memory locations addressed by *keys* or *variables*. We use *keys* and *variables* interchangeably in this work. The contents of these memory locations come from a domain, called *values*.

The read-write data-store provides two APIs to access and modify the contents of a particular memory location. The API to read the content of a particular memory location is typically named *Read* or *Get*, and the API to store a value into a particular memory location is typically named *Write* or *Put*. In this paper, we refer to these two methods as Read and Write respectively. The Read method does not update the state of the data-store and only reveals part of the state to the application session which invokes the method. The Write method on the other hand modifies the state of the data-store.

Typically, an application reads a location of the data-store, performs some local computation and writes a value back to the data-store. A sequence of related read and write operations performed by an application is called a *session*.

Applications expect some sort of consistency guarantee from the data-store in terms of how *fresh* or *stale* the data value is that they read from the data-store. They also seek some guarantees pertaining to monotonicity of the results that are presented to them. These guarantees provided by the data-store to the applications are called *consistency criterion*. Some of the popular consistency criteria include:

- **Read-Your-Writes:** The effects of prior operations in the session will be visible to later operations in the same session.
- **Monotonic Reads:** Once the effect of an operation becomes visible within a session, it remains visible to all subsequent operations in that session.
- **Monotonic Writes:** If the effect of a remote operation is visible in a session, then the effects of all prior operations in the session of the remote operation are also visible.
- **Causal consistency:** Effects of prior operations in a session are always visible to later operations. Further, if the effect of an operation is visible to

another operation, then every operation that has seen the effects of the latter would have seen the effects of the former.
- **Sequential Consistency:** Effects of the operations can be explained from a single sequential execution obtained by interleaving the reads and writes performed at individual sessions.

Most of the existing literature on testing the behaviour of read-write stores focuses on testing the correctness with respect to specific consistency criteria [6,7,14]. However, there are cases where data-stores such as DynamoDB and Cassandra offer to applications the choice of specifying the consistency level per read-operation [11]. There are distributed data-store libraries that allow consistency rationing [18] and also allow incremental consistency guarantees for the read operations [17]. In each of these cases we need to reason about the correctness of the behaviour of the data-store with respect to more than one consistency criterion.

We now look at some examples of multilevel consistency in the real world. In this work, we assume that the Read and the Write APIs are as follows.

Definition 1 (Read and Write APIs). *Let x be a key/variable, val denote a value read-from/written-to the data-store and level denote the consistency level.*

- Write(x, val) : *Updates the content of the memory location addressed by the key/variable x with the value val.*
- Read($x, val, level$) : *The content of the memory location whose key is x is val with respect to the consistency level level.*

Read-Write Stores with Strong and Weak Reads

Consider the case of the data-store Cassandra, which allows the application a more fine grained choice of consistency levels, such as ANY, ONE, QUORUM, ALL. It achieves this by ensuring that when the Read is executed with ANY, the return value is provided by consulting any available replica of the data store. Similarly, if the Read operation is submitted with ONE, the return value is provided by consulting a replica that is known to contain at least one value for that key. On the other hand, if the Read is executed with QUORUM, the data-store returns the value after consulting a majority of the replicas. Finally, if Read is executed with ALL, then all the replicas are consulted before returning the response. Clearly, ANY is the weakest consistency criterion while ALL is the strongest consistency criterion. In general, a data-store offers responses pertaining to different consistency criteria by consulting the required subset of replicas to answer the query.

Typically a read operation under the stronger consistency criterion will take more time, since it might have to wait for all pending operations to become visible, or run a consensus protocol before returning the result. In certain cases, applications may be satisfied with Read operations that return values that are correct with respect to some weaker consistency criterion. Consider a web-application that displays the available seats in a movie theater. The application can choose to read the available seats based on a weaker consistency criterion, since:

- The number of users attempting to book seats is usually more than the seats available. Waiting for a consensus or a quorum can slow down the reads for everyone. So a quicker response is desirable.
- There is a lag between the time the user gets to see available seats and the time when the user decides to book particular seats. Since concurrent bookings are ongoing, the data displayed can become stale by the time the user books the seat.
- Users can change their minds before finally settling on a set of seats, and paying for them.

Thus, the web-application can opt for a read satisfying a weaker consistency criterion while allowing the user to pick a seat, and then perform a read satisfying a stronger consistency criterion only when the user pays for it.

Consider the example in Fig. 1 where all write requests are processed at the same replica. For each session, there is a (potentially different) designated replica from which the responses to the weak reads are returned.

Session 1	Session 2	Session 3
A : Write$(x, 5)$	G : Write$(x, 4)$	I : Write$(x, 6)$
$\downarrow$ so	$\downarrow$ so	
B : Read$(x, 5, \mathsf{st})$	H : Write$(y, 3)$	
$\downarrow$ so		
C : Read$(x, 4, \mathsf{wk})$		
$\downarrow$ so		
D : Read$(y, 3, \mathsf{st})$		
$\downarrow$ so		
E : Read$(x, 6, \mathsf{st})$		
$\downarrow$ so		
F : Read$(x, 4, \mathsf{wk})$		

Fig. 1. An example of a read-write store behaviour with strong and weak reads. The so relation relates read and write operations from the same session in the order in which they happened in that session.

In this scenario, the strong reads (corresponding to the consistency level ALL) satisfy sequential consistency while the weak reads obey monotonic reads consistency. Hence, the fragment consisting of all the writes and the weak reads should be correct with respect to monotonic reads. Similarly, the fragment consisting of all the writes and the strong reads should be correct with respect to sequential consistency.

The weak fragment corresponding to the example in Fig. 1 can be seen in Fig. 2(a). This fragment is correct with respect to monotonic reads; once the write G is visible at session 1 to the read C, it remains visible throughout the session. The write I is not visible to any of the other sessions yet.

The strong fragment is represented in Fig. 2(b). This is correct with respect to sequential consistency, where the order of the operations obtained by consensus is $A \rightarrow B \rightarrow G \rightarrow H \rightarrow I \rightarrow D \rightarrow E$.

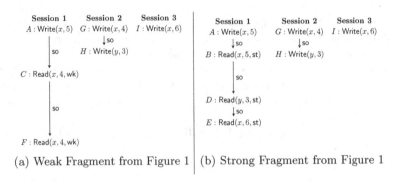

(a) Weak Fragment from Figure 1   (b) Strong Fragment from Figure 1

Fig. 2. Strong and Weak fragments of the hybrid behaviour

However, since the strong reads correspond to the level ALL where all the replicas have seen the prior writes and have agreed on the order of the concurrent writes, it behooves a weak read following a strong read to take into consideration the effects seen by the earlier strong read. Thus the data-store imposes an additional constraint. Once a write is visible to a strong read in a session, it is visible to all the subsequent weak reads in that session. This ensures that the weaker reads do incorporate the prior results seen by the session. Similarly, a write visible to a weak read is made from a replica which participates in the subsequent strong reads corresponding to the level ALL. Thus the effects visible to the prior weak reads in a session are also visible to the subsequent strong reads.

With these additional constraints, we can no longer explain the read operation F, since the effects of writes G and I are both visible at read F. The strong consistency criterion has already guaranteed that write I has happened after write G, thereby effectively overwriting the value 4 with the value 6. Hence this behaviour is incorrect in the multilevel setting.

Now consider the behaviour of Cassandra where writes are performed at one of the replicas (corresponds to the level ONE), weak reads are performed at one of the replicas (corresponds to the level ONE) and strong reads are performed at a quorum of replicas (corresponds to the level QUORUM). In this situation, it is not necessary that the effects of writes visible to prior weaker reads are visible at subsequent stronger reads, since the replica from which the weaker read is performed may be missing from the quorum of replicas from which the stronger read is made. Similarly, the effects of writes visible to prior stronger reads of a session need not be visible to the subsequent weaker reads in the session, as the writes from the quorum may not have reached the replica from which the weaker read is performed. Thus, the stronger and weaker reads can be independent of each other.

Finally consider the case of Amazon DynamoDB Accelerator (DAX) [1], which contains a write-through cache sitting between the application and the DynamoDB backend. Every write made by the application is first submitted to the DynamoDB backend and also updated at the cache. By default, the reads are eventually consistent, i.e., the reads are performed from the cache. If the item does not exist in the cache, then it is fetched from the backend data-store and the cache is updated with the item before the value is returned to the application. However, the application can also request strongly consistent reads by invoking ConsistentRead. In this case, the value is read from the backend and returned to the application, without caching the results. Any subsequent eventually consistent reads made by the application may not reflect the value returned by the prior strongly consistent read. In the case of DAX, it can be observed that the effects of the writes visible to the weak eventually consistent reads are also visible to the subsequent strongly consistent reads as those writes are also present in the DynamoDB backend. However, it is not necessary that the effects of writes visible to the strongly consistent reads are visible to the subsequent weak eventually consistent reads.

From these examples of multilevel consistency, we can see that the presence of another consistency criterion can impose additional constraints on the choice of the visibility and arbitration relations chosen to explain the correctness of the history. In the next section, we provide a formal framework for modelling behaviours of read-write data-stores with multiple consistency levels.

3   Formalizing Multilevel Consistency

We extend the formal framework provided in [9] for modelling the behaviours of read-write stores. Each operation submitted to the data-store by the application is either a Read or a Write operation whose signature is given in Definition 1.

We denote the set of all variables in the read-write store by *Vars* and assume that each value written to the read-write store is a natural number $val \in \mathbb{N}$. We assume that all variables are initially undefined, with value $\perp$.

For simplicity, we assume only two consistency levels, weak and strong, denoted by wk and st, respectively, where the consistency criterion corresponding to wk-level is strictly weaker than then the consistency criterion corresponding to the st-level. Comparison between consistency criteria is formally defined in Definition 7.

The behaviour of the read-write data-store as observed by an application is the sequence of reads and writes that it performs on the stores. The sequence of related read and write operations is termed a *session*. Thus the behaviour of the read-write store seen by each session is a total order of read/write operations performed in that session.

The behaviour of the read-write store is the collection of behaviours seen by all the sessions. In Fig. 1 we saw the behaviour of the data-store as observed by the three sessions accessing the data-store. We call such a behaviour a *hybrid history*, formally defined as follows:

Definition 2 (Hybrid History). *A hybrid history of a read-write store is a pair $H = (\mathcal{O}, \text{so})$ where $\mathcal{O}$ is the set of read-write operations and so is a collection of total orders called session orders.*

For a history H, we define the following subsets of $\mathcal{O}$.

- $\mathcal{O}_{\text{Read}}$ *is the set of read operations occurring in H.*
- $\mathcal{O}_{\text{Write}}$ *is the set of write operations occurring in H.*
- $\mathcal{O}_{\text{wk}} = \mathcal{O}_{\text{Write}} \cup \{\text{Read}(x, val, level) \in \mathcal{O}_{\text{Read}} \mid level = \text{wk}\}$ *(the set of weak operations occurring in H).*
- $\mathcal{O}_{\text{st}} = \mathcal{O}_{\text{Write}} \cup \{\text{Read}(x, val, level) \in \mathcal{O}_{\text{Read}} \mid level = \text{st}\}$ *(the set of strong operations occurring in H).*

The weak fragment of the history H is denoted H_{wk} and defined to be $(\mathcal{O}_{\text{wk}}, \text{so} \cap (\mathcal{O}_{\text{wk}} \times \mathcal{O}_{\text{wk}}))$. Similarly the strong fragment of the history H is denoted H_{st} and is defined to be $(\mathcal{O}_{\text{st}}, \text{so} \cap (\mathcal{O}_{\text{st}} \times \mathcal{O}_{\text{st}}))$. Note that we take the write operations to be part of both the strong and weak fragments.

- *For $X \subseteq \mathcal{O} \times \mathcal{O}$ and $\ell \in \{\text{Read}, \text{Write}, \text{wk}, \text{st}\}$, $X \restriction_\ell = X \cap (\mathcal{O}_\ell \times \mathcal{O}_\ell)$.*
- *For $X, Y \subseteq \mathcal{O} \times \mathcal{O}$, $X; Y = \{(x, y) \mid \exists z : (x, z) \in X \text{ and } (z, y) \in Y\}$ is the composition of X and Y.*
- *For $X \subseteq \mathcal{O} \times \mathcal{O}$, $\text{total}(X)$ is used to mean that X is a total order.*

When a replica of the read-write store receives an operation from an application, it decides how the effects of the older operations known to the replica (either received from applications, or from other replicas of the data-store) should be made visible to the new operation. A visibility relation over a history specifies the set of operations visible to an operation.

Definition 3 (Visibility Relation). *A visibility relation vis over a history $H = (\mathcal{O}, \text{so})$ is an acyclic relation over $\mathcal{O}$. For $o, o' \in \mathcal{O}$, we write $o \xrightarrow{\text{vis}} o'$ to indicate that the effects of the operation o are visible to the operation o'.*

If a pair of operations o, o' are not related by vis, we term them concurrent operations, denoted by $o \parallel_{\text{vis}} o'$.

We define the view *of an operation o with respect to a visibility relation vis, denoted $\text{View}_{\text{vis}}(o)$ to be the set of all the Write operations visible to it.*

For the history in Fig. 1, we can define a visibility relation to be

$$\{A \xrightarrow{\text{vis}} B, G \xrightarrow{\text{vis}} C, G \xrightarrow{\text{vis}} D, H \xrightarrow{\text{vis}} D, G \xrightarrow{\text{vis}} E, H \xrightarrow{\text{vis}} E, I \xrightarrow{\text{vis}} E, G \xrightarrow{\text{vis}} F\}$$

When the replicas communicate with each other, they need to reconcile the effects of concurrent write operations in order to converge to the same state eventually. In case of convergent data-stores this is done using a rule such as *Last Writer Wins* which totally orders all write operations. This is abstracted by an arbitration relation, which is a total order over all write operations in the history. We will denote the arbitration relation by arb. We assume that the arbitration relation is consistent with the visibility relation, in the sense that for a pair of writes o and o', if o is visible to o' then o is before o' in arb.

Definition 4 (Arbitration Relation). *An arbitration relation arb over a hybrid history $H = (\mathcal{O}, \text{so})$ is a total order over $\mathcal{O}_{\text{Write}}$. For $o_i, o_j \in \mathcal{O}$, we say $o_i \xrightarrow{\text{arb}} o_j$ to indicate that operation o_i has been ordered before the operation operation o_j.*

For the history in Fig. 1 the arbitration relation can be the total order

$$A \xrightarrow{\text{arb}} G \xrightarrow{\text{arb}} H \xrightarrow{\text{arb}} I$$

We define the correctness of a hybrid history in terms of the *functional specification* of read-write stores.

Let H be a hybrid history. Let vis and arb be visibility and arbitration relations over H.

We say that a write operation o' is a *related-write* of a read operation o iff o' is in the view of o and both o and o' operate on the same variable. The set of all related writes of o, denoted $RelWrites_{\text{vis}}(o)$, is defined to be the set $\{o' \in \text{View}_{\text{vis}}(o) \mid o \text{ and } o' \text{ operate on the same variable}\}$.

$MaxRelWrites_{\text{vis}}(o)$, the set of maximal elements among these related writes with respect to vis, is defined to be

$$\{o' \in RelWrites_{\text{vis}}(o) \mid \forall o'' \in RelWrites_{\text{vis}}(o) : o'' \xrightarrow{\text{vis}} o' \vee o'' \parallel_{\text{vis}} o'\}$$

The effective write of a read-operation o, denoted by $EffWrite_{\text{vis}}^{\text{arb}}(o)$ is defined to be the maximum write operation from the set of maximal related writes of o as per the arbitration relation.

$$EffWrite_{\text{vis}}^{\text{arb}}(o) = \begin{cases} max(\text{arb} \restriction_{MaxRelWrites_{\text{vis}}(o)}) & \text{if } MaxRelWrites_{\text{vis}}(o) \neq \emptyset \\ \bot & \text{otherwise} \end{cases}$$

Definition 5 (Functional Correctness for Read-Write Stores). *Let $H = (\mathcal{O}, \text{so})$ be a hybrid history of a read-write data store with visibility relation* vis *and arbitration relation* arb. *We say that $(H, \text{vis}, \text{arb})$ is* functionally correct *iff for every read operation $o = \text{Read}(x, val, level)$, the following conditions hold.*

- *$EffWrite_{\text{vis}}^{\text{arb}}(o) = \bot$ iff $val = \bot$ (i.e., there was no write operation on x when o happened).*
- *If $o' = EffWrite_{\text{vis}}^{\text{arb}}(o)$ then o' wrote the value val.*

Next, we formally define *consistency criteria* in terms of a set of formulas. Our definition is adapted from the definitions of constraints in [13].

Definition 6 (Consistency Criteria). *A relation term τ is a composition of the form $r_1; \cdots ; r_k$ ($k \geq 1$), where each $r_i \in \{so, vis\}$. A consistency criterion is a subset of*

$$\{\tau \subseteq vis \mid \tau \text{ is a relation term}\} \cup \{\text{total}(vis)\}.$$

Thus a consistency criterion is a possibly empty collection of visibility constraints and an optional totality constraint. For simplicity of notation, we usually write a constraint as a conjunction.

Note that so and vis are variables which are usually interpreted as restrictions of the so and vis relations in a history. As we will see below, we always require an additional constraint that $vis \restriction_{\text{Write}} \subseteq arb$ (and hence it is not explicitly included in the consistency criteria).

For a consistency criterion α, *RelTerms*(α) is the set of all relation terms occurring in α, and *VisBasic*(α) is the collection of all visibility constraints in α excluding the totality constraint total(vis).

Definition 7 (Consistency Criterion in a history). *Let* $H = (\mathcal{O}, \text{so})$ *be a hybrid history, let* vis *and* arb *be a visibility and arbitration relation over* H, *and let* α *be a consistency criterion. We say that* $H, \text{vis} \models \alpha$ *iff:*

1. *for every* $\tau \subseteq vis$ *in* α, $\tau[so := \text{so}, vis := \text{vis}] \subseteq \text{vis}$, *and*
2. *if* total(vis) $\in \alpha$, *then* total(vis) *holds.*

Further we say that $H, \text{vis}, \text{arb} \models \alpha$ *iff* $H, \text{vis} \models \alpha$ *and* vis$\restriction_{\text{Write}} \subseteq$ arb.

Some well known consistency criteria are given in Table 1.

Table 1. Well known consistency criteria

Name	Description
Basic Eventual Consistency (BEC)	$\top$
Read Your Writes (RYW)	$so \subseteq vis$
Monotonic Reads (MR)	$vis; so \subseteq vis$
Monotonic Writes (MW)	$so; vis \subseteq vis$
Strong Eventual Consistency (SEC)	$so \subseteq vis \ \wedge \ vis; so \subseteq vis$
FIFO Consistency (FIFO)	$so \subseteq vis \ \wedge \ vis; so \subseteq vis \ \wedge \ so; vis \subseteq vis$
Causal Consistency (CC)	$so \subseteq vis \ \wedge \ vis; vis \subseteq vis$
Sequential Consistency (SEQ)	$so \subseteq vis \ \wedge \ vis; vis \subseteq vis \ \wedge \ \text{total}(vis)$

We say that a consistency criterion α is at least as *strong* as another consistency criterion α' if for every history H, visibility relation vis, and arbitration relation arb over H, if $H, \text{vis}, \text{arb} \models \alpha$ then $H, \text{vis}, \text{arb} \models \alpha'$.

Suppose $H = (\mathcal{O}, \text{so})$ is a hybrid history. Let α_w and α_s respectively be the wk and st consistency criteria. We then want to choose wk and st visibility relations vis$_{\text{wk}}$, vis$_{\text{st}}$, respectively, and an arbitration relations arb such that $H_{\text{wk}}, \text{vis}_{\text{wk}}, \text{arb} \models \alpha_w$ and $H_{\text{st}}, \text{vis}_{\text{st}}, \text{arb} \models \alpha_s$.

As we had noted in the previous section, in a multilevel setting, it is not sufficient to separately satisfy the constraints corresponding to the wk and st consistency criteria. We now proceed to modelling multilevel consistency constraints.

Modelling Multilevel Consistency

Taking inspiration from DAX [1] and the cache-hierarchy in modern processors, we can model multilevel consistency as a series of data-stores arranged in increasing order of the consistency they guarantee, such that the data-store offering the weakest level of consistency is closest to the application, and the data-store offering the strongest level of consistency is farthest away from the application. We shall further assume that these data-stores use the same arbitration strategy to order concurrent write operations and every weaker data-store has the capability to update its state to match that of a stronger data-store.

For the purpose of this paper, since we are restricting ourselves to only two levels, namely wk and st, this will reduce to having just two data-stores, where the data-store corresponding to the weaker consistency criterion sits as a cache between the application and the data-store corresponding to the stronger consistency criterion.

All the wk-reads are performed from the wk data-store.

There are two possible ways in which the writes can be performed.

1. Write-Through: The write is first performed at the st-data-store and eventually will be propagated to the wk-data-store.
2. Write-Back: The write is first performed at the wk-data-store and eventually will be propagated to the st-data-store.

There are two possible ways in which st-reads can be performed.

(a) Read-Through: The result of the st-read performed at the st-data-store is directly sent to the application bypassing the wk-data-store.
(b) Read-Back: The result of the st-read is updated at the wk-data-store before it is propagated to the application.

Thus, the system picks one of two ways to perform the write, and one of the two ways to perform the st-read.

Note that a system which picks the Write-Through strategy for performing the write will ensure that any write visible at the wk data-store will also be visible to the st data-store, as all the writes are first performed at the st data-store before they are propagated to the wk one. Hence, the effects of write operations visible to a wk-read operation are also visible to the subsequent st-operations in the session.

Similarly a system which picks the Read-Back strategy for performing the st-reads will ensure that any write that is visible to a *strong*-read will also be visible at a subsequent wk-read in the session as before returning the result of the st-read to the application, the result is merged into the wk data-store.

However, the Write-Back and Read-Through strategies do not provide any guarantees between the effects of writes visible to wk (resp. st) reads in relation to the subsequent st (resp. wk) reads in that session.

We now define the guarantees provided by each of these four strategies in the form of a constraint.

Definition 8 (Multilevel Constraints). *We define the following formulas:*

- $\psi_{thru}^{write} := (vis^{wk}; so) \restriction_{st} \subseteq vis^{st}$
- $\psi_{back}^{write} := \top$
- $\psi_{thru}^{read} := \top$

– $\psi_{back}^{read} := (vis^{st}; so) \lceil_{\mathsf{wk}} \subseteq vis^{wk}$

A multilevel constraint φ is a conjunction of the form $\psi^{read} \wedge \psi^{write}$, where $\psi^{read} \in \{\psi_{thru}^{read}, \psi_{back}^{read}\}$ and $\psi^{write} \in \{\psi_{thru}^{write}, \psi_{back}^{write}\}$.

Suppose $H = (\mathcal{O}, \mathsf{so})$ is a history, and $\mathsf{vis_{wk}}$ and $\mathsf{vis_{st}}$ are two visibility relations respectively over $\mathcal{O}_{\mathsf{wk}}$ and $\mathcal{O}_{\mathsf{st}}$. Let φ be a multilevel constraint. We say that $H, \mathsf{vis_{wk}}, \mathsf{vis_{st}} \models \varphi$ iff $\varphi[so := \mathsf{so}, vis^{wk} := \mathsf{vis_{wk}}, vis^{st} := \mathsf{vis_{st}}]$ is true.

The formula ψ_{thru}^{write} imposes the constraint that the strong operations see the effects seen by the prior weak operations in the session. Similarly, the formula ψ_{back}^{read} imposes the constraint that the weak operations see the effects seen by the prior strong operations in the session. These two guarantee that the effect seen by reads of one consistency level remain monotonically visible to the subsequent reads of another consistency level.

Consider Cassandra's multilevel consistency with writes performed at level ONE, weak-reads at level ONE and strong-reads at level ALL which ensure that weaker reads see the effects visible to prior stronger reads and vice-versa. This can be modelled using $\psi_{thru}^{write} \wedge \psi_{back}^{read}$.

On the other hand, Cassandra's multilevel consistency with writes performed at level ONE, weak-reads at level ONE and strong-reads at level QUORUM neither ensures that weaker reads see the effects visible to prior stronger reads nor the converse. This can be modelled using $\psi_{back}^{write} \wedge \psi_{thru}^{read}$.

The DynamoDB's DAX case can be modelled using $\psi_{thru}^{write} \wedge \psi_{thru}^{read}$ which only allows for the effects of prior weak reads to be visible to subsequent stronger reads, but not the converse.

We now formally define when a hybrid history is correct.

Definition 9 (Multilevel Correctness of a Hybrid History). A hybrid history $H = (\mathcal{O}, \mathsf{so})$ of a read-write store is said to be multilevel correct with respect to a wk-consistency criterion α_w, st-consistency criterion α_s and multilevel consistency constraint φ, iff there exists visibility relations $\mathsf{vis_{wk}}$ and $\mathsf{vis_{st}}$ over H_{wk} and H_{st} respectively and arbitration relation arb such that

- $(H_{\mathsf{wk}}, \mathsf{vis_{wk}}, \mathsf{arb})$ and $(H_{\mathsf{st}}, \mathsf{vis_{st}}, \mathsf{arb})$ are functionally correct,
- $H_{\mathsf{wk}}, \mathsf{vis_{wk}}, \mathsf{arb} \models \alpha_w$,
- $H_{\mathsf{st}}, \mathsf{vis_{st}}, \mathsf{arb} \models \alpha_s$, and
- $H, \mathsf{vis_{wk}}, \mathsf{vis_{st}} \models \varphi$.

4 Testing Multilevel Correctness of a Hybrid History

Given a read-write hybrid history $H = (\mathcal{O}, \mathsf{so})$, we want to test it for multi-level correctness with respect to weak and strong consistency criteria α_w and α_s and multilevel constraints given by φ.

We note that for the history to be correct, for every read operation that returns a value that is not $\perp$, there should exist a write operation writing the same value to the variable that was read. The *reads-from* relation associates a write operation to the read that reads its effect. Our strategy for testing the multilevel correctness of H is to enumerate all such *reads-from* relations rf, for each rf we find visibility relations vis_{wk} and vis_{st}, respectively, containing rf_{wk} and rf_{st}, such that they satisfy the visibility constraints imposed by the individual consistency criteria, as well as the multilevel constraints, i.e., $H_{wk}, vis_{wk} \models \alpha_w$, $H_{st}, vis_{st} \models \alpha_s$ and $H, vis_{wk}, vis_{st} \models \varphi$. We then check for the presence of a finite number of *bad-patterns* in these visibility relations. The presence of a bad-pattern implies that for every arbitration relation arb, there is some level $\ell \in \{wk, st\}$ such that either the arbitration constraint $vis_\ell \lceil_{Write} \subseteq arb$ is not satisfied, or the history (H_ℓ, vis_ℓ, arb) is not functionally correct.

If the history is multi-level correct, then we will find a witness consisting of a *reads-from* relation rf and visibility relations vis_{wk} and vis_{st} extending rf_{wk} and rf_{st} such that all the constraints are satisfied and there are no bad-patterns. If the history is not multi-level correct, then for every pair of weak and strong visibility relation extending every *reads-from* relation, either some constraint is not satisfied or there exists a bad-pattern.

We present the bad-pattern characterization for multilevel correctness of a hybrid history in the next subsection. In the following subsection, we provide a procedure for computing the minimal visibility relations vis_{wk} and vis_{st} for a given *reads-from* relation rf that satisfies α_w, α_s and φ.

4.1   Bad Pattern Characterization for Multilevel Correctness

We now characterize the correctness of hybrid histories based on the non-existence of certain bad patterns. This is a generalization of the bad-pattern characterization for causal consistency in [6].

Given a hybrid history, we can associate each Read with a unique write operation from the history whose effect the Read operation reads from. We call this the *reads-from* relation.

Definition 10 (Reads-From). *A* reads-from *relation* rf *over a history* $H = (\mathcal{O}, so)$ *is a binary relation such that*

1. $(o_i, o_j) \in rf \implies o_i$ *is a* Write, o_j *is a* Read, *both on the same variable, such that the value returned by* o_j *is the value written by* o_i.
2. $(o_i, o_j) \in rf \land (o_k, o_j) \in rf \implies o_i = o_k$.
3. *For all* $o_j = \mathsf{Read}(x, val, level) \in \mathcal{O}_{Read}$

$$[\exists \, o \in \mathcal{O}_{Write} \text{ which writes } val \text{ to } x \implies \exists \, o_i \in \mathcal{O}_{Write} : (o_i, o_j) \in rf.]$$

Condition 1 associates a read operation with a write operation only if they operate on the same variable and that the return value of the read operation matches the argument of the write operation.

Condition 2 ensures that a read operation is associated with at most one write operation.

Finally, Condition 3 insists that if a Read is not related to any Write via rf, it is only because there is no matching Write in the hybrid history (i.e. a write of the same value to the same variable).

Let rf be a *reads-from* relation on a hybrid history $H = (\mathcal{O}, \mathsf{so})$. For a Read operation $o \in \mathcal{O}$, if there exists a Write operation o' such that $(o', o) \in \mathsf{rf}$, then we say that $\mathsf{rf}^{-1}(o) = o'$. If no such o' exists, we set $\mathsf{rf}^{-1}(o) = \bot$.

Further, we denote by $\mathsf{rf}_{\mathsf{wk}}$ and $\mathsf{rf}_{\mathsf{st}}$ the *reads-from* relation restricted to H_{wk} and H_{st} respectively.

Suppose rf_ℓ is a *reads-from* relation over H_ℓ. We say that a visibility relation vis_ℓ over H_ℓ *extends* rf_ℓ iff $\mathsf{rf}_\ell \subseteq \mathsf{vis}_\ell$. Suppose arb is an arbitration relation over H_ℓ. Then, we say that $(\mathsf{vis}_\ell, \mathsf{arb})$ *realize* rf_ℓ iff for all read operations $o \in \mathcal{O}_\ell$, $\mathsf{rf}_\ell^{-1}(o) = \mathit{EffWrite}_{\mathsf{vis}_\ell}^{\mathsf{arb}}(o)$.

Given a *reads-from* relation rf_ℓ and a visibility relation vis_ℓ that extends it, we can define a conflict relation that orders all the remaining maximal related writes in $\mathit{MaxRelWrites}_{\mathsf{vis}_\ell}(o)$ of a read-operation o before the write-operation $\mathsf{rf}_\ell^{-1}(o)$. The conflict relation captures the essence of the arbitration relation for a given *reads-from* relation and a visibility relation extending it.

Definition 11 (Conflict Relation). *Let $H_\ell = (\mathcal{O}_\ell, \mathsf{so}_\ell)$ be a history. Let rf_ℓ be a reads-from relation over H_ℓ. Let $\mathsf{vis}_\ell \supseteq \mathsf{rf}_\ell$ be a visibility relation over H_ℓ. We define the conflict relation for rf_ℓ and vis_ℓ, denoted $\mathsf{CF}(\mathsf{rf}_\ell, \mathsf{vis}_\ell)$, as the set*

$$\{(o'', o') \mid \exists o \in \mathcal{O}_\ell \!\upharpoonright_{\mathsf{Read}}: o'', o' \in \mathit{MaxRelWrites}_{\mathsf{vis}}(o) \wedge o' = \mathsf{rf}_\ell^{-1}(o)\}.$$

We now define the bad patterns that characterize the correctness of the hybrid history.

Definition 12 (Bad Patterns for a hybrid history). *Let $H = (\mathcal{O}, \mathsf{so})$ be a hybrid history with weak and strong consistency criteria α_w and α_s respectively and multilevel constraints φ. Let rf be a reads-from relation over H. For $\ell \in \{\mathsf{wk}, \mathsf{st}\}$, let vis_ℓ be a relation over $\mathcal{O}_\ell$ with $\mathsf{vis}_\ell \supseteq \mathsf{rf}_\ell$ such that $H_{\mathsf{wk}}, \mathsf{vis}_{\mathsf{wk}} \models \alpha_w$, $H_{\mathsf{st}}, \mathsf{vis}_{\mathsf{st}} \models \alpha_s$ and $H, \mathsf{vis}_{\mathsf{wk}}, \mathsf{vis}_{\mathsf{st}} \models \varphi$. We define the following bad patterns for $(H, \mathsf{rf}, \mathsf{vis}_{\mathsf{wk}}, \mathsf{vis}_{\mathsf{st}})$. For some $\ell \in \{\mathsf{wk}, \mathsf{st}\}$:*

- BADVISIBILITY: $\mathsf{Cyclic}(\mathsf{vis}_\ell)$
- THINAIR: $\exists o \in \mathcal{O}_{\mathsf{Read}} \!\upharpoonright_\ell$: *$o$ returns a value that is not $\bot$, but* $\mathsf{rf}_\ell^{-1}(o) = \bot$
- BADINITREAD: $\exists o \in \mathcal{O}_{\mathsf{Read}} \!\upharpoonright_\ell$: *$o$ returns $\bot$ but* $\mathit{RelWrites}_{\mathsf{vis}_\ell}(o) \neq \emptyset$
- BADREAD: $\exists o \in \mathcal{O}_{\mathsf{Read}} \!\upharpoonright_\ell$: $\mathsf{rf}_\ell^{-1}(o) \notin \mathit{MaxRelWrites}_{\mathsf{vis}_\ell}(o)$
- BADARB: $\mathsf{Cyclic}(\bigcup\limits_{\ell \in \{\mathsf{wk}, \mathsf{st}\}} (\mathsf{CF}(\mathsf{rf}_\ell, \mathsf{vis}_\ell) \cup (\mathsf{vis}_\ell)_{\mathsf{Write}}))$

BADVISIBILITY says that one of the visibility relations has a cycle.

THINAIR says that there exists a read in the history which reads a non-initial value which is not written by any write operation in the hybrid history.

BADINITREAD says that there is a read operation on a variable which reads the initial value despite having a non-initial write to that variable in its view.

BADREAD says that the write operation from which the read-operation reads is not a maximal write, and there are other writes in the view of the read operation that would have overwritten the value written by that write.

BADARB says that the union of the conflict relations along visibility relation restricted to only the Write operations has a cycle indicating that there exists no total-order arb over $\mathcal{O}_{\text{Write}}$, such that $(\text{vis}_\ell, \text{arb})$ realizes rf_ℓ.

Multi-level correctness of a hybrid history can be characterized in terms of non-existence of these bad patterns. The proof can be found in the full version of this paper [8].

Theorem 1 (Bad patterns characterization). *A hybrid history $H = (\mathcal{O}, \text{so})$ is said to be multilevel correct with respect to weak and strong consistency criteria α_w, α_s and multilevel constraint φ iff there exists a reads-from relation rf, and relations $\text{vis}_{\text{wk}} \supseteq \text{rf}_{\text{wk}}$ and $\text{vis}_{\text{st}} \supseteq \text{rf}_{\text{st}}$ respectively over $\mathcal{O}_{\text{wk}}$ and $\mathcal{O}_{\text{st}}$ such that $H_{\text{wk}}, \text{vis}_{\text{wk}} \models \alpha_w$, $H_{\text{st}}, \text{vis}_{\text{st}} \models \alpha_s$ and $H, \text{vis}_{\text{wk}}, \text{vis}_{\text{st}} \models \varphi$ and no bad pattern exists in $(H, \text{rf}, \text{vis}_{\text{wk}}, \text{vis}_{\text{st}})$.*

4.2 Constructing Minimal Visibility Relations

Suppose $H = (\mathcal{O}, \text{so})$ is a hybrid history. Let α_w and α_s be the formulas defining the weak and strong consistency criteria, and let φ be the formula defining the multilevel constraints. Let $\alpha'_w = VisBasic(\alpha_w)$ and $\alpha'_s = VisBasic(\alpha_s)$.

We provide a procedure that iterates over all the possible *reads-from* relations and constructs a minimal visibility relation extending the *reads-from* relation such that it satisfies α_w, α_s and φ. The pseudo-code for the procedure is presented in Algorithm 1 and 2.

Algorithm 1 Constructing minimal visibility relations

```
1   MinVisOne(𝒪ℓ, soℓ, visℓ, αℓ):
2       Let vis₀ := visℓ;
3
4       while (True):
5           Let visₚ := vis₀;
6           for τ ∈ RelTerms(αℓ):
7               visₙ := visₚ ∪ τ[soℓ, visₚ];
8               visₚ := visₙ;
9           if (visₙ == vis₀)
10              return visₙ
11          vis₀ := visₙ
12
13
14  ComputeVisSet(𝒪ℓ, soℓ, visℓ, αℓ)
15      if total(vis) is a subformula in αℓ:
16          visSetℓ := {totvis|totvis
                        is a
                        total order over
                        𝒪ℓ such that
                        visℓ ⊆ totvis}
17      else :
18          visSetℓ := {visℓ}
19
20      return visSetℓ
```

```
21  MinVisMulti(𝒪, so, vis_wk, vis_st, ψ)
22      if ψ ∈ {ψ_back^write, ψ_thru^read}:
23          return (vis_wk, vis_st)
24      else if ψ ∈ {ψ_thru^write}:
25          Let ℓ = st, ℓ' = wk;
26      else if ψ ∈ {ψ_back^read}:
27          Let ℓ = wk, ℓ' = st;
28
29      Let vis_ℓ^o := vis_ℓ;
30      Let vis_ℓ'^o := vis_ℓ';
31
32      if ψ ∈ {ψ_thru^write, ψ_back^read}:
33          Let vis_ℓ^n := vis_ℓ^o ∪ (vis_ℓ'^o ; so) ↾ℓ;
34          Let vis_ℓ'^n := vis_ℓ'^o;
35
36      if ψ ∈ {ψ_back^read}:
37          return (vis_ℓ^n, vis_ℓ'^n)
38      else if ψ ∈ {ψ_thru^write}:
39          return (vis_ℓ'^n, vis_ℓ^n)
```

In Lines 1–12 we have a method MinVisOne that takes as input a visibility relation vis_ℓ for the history $(\mathcal{O}_\ell, \text{so}_\ell)$ and constructs an extension vis_n that satisfies the formula $VisBasic(\alpha_\ell)$. We achieve this by iterating over the $RelTerms$ appearing in $RelTerms(\alpha_\ell)$ (Line 6) and extending the previous visibility relation vis_p with the evaluation of the term (Line 7). We do this until we obtain a relation vis_n which we can no longer extend (Line 9). This final visibility relation vis_n extends vis_ℓ and satisfies the formula $VisBasic(\alpha_\ell)$.

In Lines 21–40, we have the procedure MinVisMulti which takes as inputs the hybrid history $(\mathcal{O}, so)$, visibility relations vis_{wk} and vis_{st} and an individual conjunct ψ appearing in the multilevel constraint φ. Since every visibility relation trivially satisfies ψ_{back}^{write} or ψ_{thru}^{read}, for these multilevel constraint, we simply return without modifying vis_{wk} or vis_{st} (Lines 22–23). In the remaining cases, when the multi-level constraint is either ψ_{back}^{write} or ψ_{thru}^{read}, for $\ell, \ell' \in \{wk, st\}$, the multilevel constraints relates the write operations visible to the operations of level ℓ in terms of the writes seen by operations of level ℓ' that have occured previously in the session. Depending on the conjunct ψ, we set ℓ and ℓ' appropriately(Lines 24–27). We then extend the visibility relation for level ℓ by relating each ℓ-operation to the Writes that have been seen by any of the ℓ'-operations prior to the ℓ-operation in its session (Line 33). The visibility relation for level ℓ' remains unchanged in this case (Line 34).

We return these extended visibility relations as a pair, where the wk visibility extension is followed by st visibility extension (Lines 36–39).

Algorithm 2 Testing multilevel correctness of a hybrid history

---

```
43  ComputeStableExt(O, so, vis_wk, vis_st, α_w, α_s, φ):
44      Let vis⁰_wk := vis_wk,
            vis⁰_st := vis_st
45
46      while (True):
47          Let vis^p_wk := vis⁰_wk,
                vis^p_st := vis⁰_st
48
49          Let vis^n_wk :=
                MinVisOne(O_wk, so_wk, vis^p_wk, α_w);
50
51          Let vis^n_st :=
                MinVisOne(O_st, so_st, vis^p_st, α_s);
52
53          for each subformula ψ_i
                in the conjunction φ:
54              vis^p_wk := vis^n_wk, vis^p_st := vis^n_st
55
56              (vis^n_wk, vis^n_st) =
                MinVisMulti(O, so, vis^p_wk, vis^p_st, ψ_i)
57
58          if vis^n_wk = vis⁰_wk and vis^n_st = vis⁰_st:
59              return (vis^n_wk, vis^n_st)
60
61          vis⁰_wk := vis^n_wk, vis⁰_st := vis^n_st

62  TestMultiCorrect(O, so, α_w, α_s, φ):
63      Let rfSet := {rf | rf is a reads-from
                        relation over (O, so)}
64      for rf ∈ rfSet:
65          Let vis^min_wk :=
                MinVisOne(O_wk, so_wk, rf_wk, α_w);
66          Let visSet_wk :=
            ComputeVisSet(O_wk, so_wk, vis^min_wk, α_w);
67
68          Let vis^min_st :=
                MinVisOne(O_wk, so_st, rf_st, α_s);
69          Let visSet_st :=
            ComputeVisSet(O_st, so_st, vis^min_st, α_s);
70
71          for vis_wk ∈ visSet_wk, vis_st ∈ visSet_st:
72              Let (vis^stb_wk, vis^stb_st) :=
                    ComputeStableExt(O, so, vis_wk,
                                    vis_st, α_w, α_s, φ);
73
74              if NoBadPatterns(O, so, rf,
                                vis^stb_wk, vis^stb_st) :
75                  return (rf, vis^stb_wk, vis^stb_st)
76
77      return BadHistory
```

In Lines 43–61 we have the procedure ComputeStableExt which takes history $(\mathcal{O}, so)$ a pair of visibility relations vis_{wk} and vis_{st} and extends it to vis^n_{wk} and vis^n_{st} such that they individually satisfy $VisBasic(\alpha_w)$ (Line 49) and $VisBasic(\alpha_s)$

(Line 51) respectively and jointly satisfy φ (Lines 53–56). We repeat this till we can extend these relations no longer, which implies that they have satisfied all the constraints (Lines 58–59).

The procedure TestMultiCorrect in Lines 42–57 takes as input a hybrid history $H = (\mathcal{O}, \mathsf{so})$ whose multilevel correctness we want to check with respect to formulas α_w, α_s and φ.

We first enumerate the set of possible *reads-from* relations on the history (line 43). We then iterate through each of the *reads-from* relations rf to see whether it can be extended to construct a minimal visibility relation satisfying all the constraints and having no bad-patterns (Lines 44–55). For each rf, we construct minimal visibility relations $\mathsf{vis}_{\mathsf{wk}}^{\mathsf{min}}$ and $\mathsf{vis}_{\mathsf{st}}^{\mathsf{min}}$ extending $\mathsf{rf}_{\mathsf{wk}}$ and $\mathsf{rf}_{\mathsf{st}}$ respectively and satisfying the subformulas $VisBasic(\alpha_w)$ and $VisBasic(\alpha_s)$ respectively (Lines 45, 48).

If α_w (resp. α_s) contains the subformula total(vis), we enumerate the set of all the total orders extending $\mathsf{vis}_{\mathsf{wk}}^{\mathsf{min}}$ (resp. $\mathsf{vis}_{\mathsf{st}}^{\mathsf{min}}$) in the set visSet$_{\mathsf{wk}}$ (resp. visSet$_{\mathsf{st}}$) in Line 46 (resp. Line 49). If α_w (resp. α_s) does not contain the subformula total(vis), then, visSet$_{\mathsf{wk}}$ (resp. visSet$_{\mathsf{st}}$) will contain the only minimum visibility relation extending $\mathsf{rf}_{\mathsf{wk}}$ (resp. $\mathsf{rf}_{\mathsf{st}}$), i.e., $\mathsf{vis}_{\mathsf{wk}}^{\mathsf{min}}$ (resp. $\mathsf{vis}_{\mathsf{st}}^{\mathsf{min}}$.).

For each pair of visibility relations from visSet$_{\mathsf{wk}}$ and visSet$_{\mathsf{st}}$ we compute their stable extensions $\mathsf{vis}_{\mathsf{wk}}^{\mathsf{stb}}$ and $\mathsf{vis}_{\mathsf{st}}^{\mathsf{stb}}$ which individually satisfy α_w and α_s, respectively, and jointly satisfy φ (line 52). We then check if this computed extension has a bad pattern (Line 54). If no bad patterns are found, we return the (rf, $\mathsf{vis}_{\mathsf{wk}}$, $\mathsf{vis}_{\mathsf{st}}$) as the witness.

If none of the rf can be extended to obtain the required visibility relation, we declare that the history is a bad history. We formally prove the correctness of TestMultiCorrect in the full version of this work [8].

Theorem 2 (Correctness of TestMultiCorrect procedure). *For a hybrid read-write history $H = (\mathcal{O}, \mathsf{so})$ with weak and strong consistency criteria given by α_w and α_s, respectively, and multilevel constraints given by φ, the procedure* TestMultiCorrect *returns a witness* (rf, $\mathsf{vis}_{\mathsf{wk}}$, $\mathsf{vis}_{\mathsf{st}}$) *over H iff H is multi-level correct with respect to α_w, α_s and φ.*

4.3   Complexity

Suppose $H = (\mathcal{O}, \mathsf{so})$ is history with $|\mathcal{O}| = N$.

We note that in the procedure ComputeStableExt, at the end of every iteration of the outer **while**-loop, the values of $\mathsf{vis}_{\mathsf{wk}}^{\mathsf{n}}$ and $\mathsf{vis}_{\mathsf{st}}^{\mathsf{n}}$ monotonically increase from the end of the previous iteration. Since they are binary relations over finite history $H = (\mathcal{O}, \mathsf{so})$ their size is upper bounded by $O(N^2)$. The time taken to evaluate each term in $RelTerms(\alpha_\ell)$ is again polynomial in N. Hence, the time-complexity of ComputeStableExt is polynomial in N, say $f(N)$.

We can observe from the procedure TestMultiCorrect that the main part that adds to the complexity is iterating through all the *reads-from* relation, as well as the total orders if α_w or α_s contain the subformula total(vis). Suppose the number of read operations are k. Then the number of write operations is $N - k$, and there are $O((N-k)^k)$ *reads-from* relations. Since $k = O(N)$, this can be bound by $O(2^{N \log N})$. Furthermore, for a given rf, if any of the levels $\ell \in \{\mathsf{wk}, \mathsf{st}\}$ require that the visibility relation be a total order, then we iterate over all the total-orders containing the minimal visibility relation extending rf. Iterating through this requires time bounded by $O(2^{N \log N})$. Thus the worst case time complexity of the procedure is $O(f(N).2^{N \log N})$.

In general, the problem of testing the correctness of a hybrid history is in NP. We need to guess the *reads-from* relation, and then, extend it to obtain the minimal visibility relations satisfying the visibility constraints of the wk and the st consistency criteria. If the visibility relation is required to be a total order, we can guess the order. Extending this to derive fixed-point minimal visibility relations that satisfy all the visibility constraints via ComputeStableExt requires polynomial time. Subsequently checking for each of the bad-patterns requires polynomial time.

Note that we can reduce the testing of the correctness of a regular history (that contains only a single level of Read and Write operations) with respect to consistency criterion α to this procedure by defining the level of all the read operations to st. We set α_s to α, α_w to $\top$, and φ to $\psi_{back}^{write} \wedge \psi_{thru}^{read}$. For any *reads-from* relation rf, $\mathsf{rf}_{\mathsf{wk}} = \emptyset$. Thus $\mathsf{vis}_{\mathsf{wk}} = \emptyset$, trivially satisfying α_w as well as φ. Thus, the lower bound for testing the correctness of the hybrid history H is the complexity of testing the correctness of the H_{wk} and H_{st} with respect to their respective consistency criteria. It has been shown in [14] that testing the correctness of a read-write history with respect to sequential consistency is NP-COMPLETE. In [6], the authors use the same reduction to show that testing the correctness with respect to causal consistency is NP-COMPLETE. However, it can be shown that the reduction works for any consistency criterion stronger than FIFO consistency, and checking correctness with respect to such a consistency criterion is NP-COMPLETE. Thus, in general, though testing the multi-level correctness of a hybrid history is a hard problem, the hardness is not due to the multilevel constraints but due to the constraints of the individual consistency criteria and the read-write specification.

In [6], the authors identify the class of read-write data-stores called *data-independent* data-stores whose behaviour is not dependent on the exact values written to the keys. Thus, for such stores, if there is a bad history, there is an equivalent bad *differentiated history* where a particular value is written to a particular memory location at most once. Thus, we can restrict our testing to only the correctness of differentiated histories. The authors show that the problem of testing the correctness of differentiated-histories with respect to causal consistency is solvable in polynomial time.

Note that for differentiated histories, there is exactly one *reads-from* relation which associates every Read operation with at most one Write operation which has written that value to the memory location read by the Read operation. Thus, if neither of α_w or α_s contain the subformula total(vis), the procedure TestMultiCorrect terminates in polynomial time. Thus, our procedure generalizes the result from [6] to all the consistency criteria defined in terms of the set of formulas involving only visibility, but not totality constraints. Our procedure checks the multi-level correctness of hybrid histories where the individual consistency levels do not require the visibility relation to be a total order, in polynomial time.

On the other hand, if one of α_w or α_s contains total(vis), then the worst case complexity remains $O(2^{N \log N})$. Once again, this does not come as a surprise, since the problem of testing the correctness of a differentiated history w.r.t. sequential consistency is not known to have a polynomial time solution.

5   Related Work

There is prior work that illustrates the need for multiple levels of consistency provided by the distributed data-stores to provide a trade off between consistency and availability/latency [2,17,18,20]. The work by Kraska et al. [18] provides a transactional paradigm that allows applications to define the consistency level on data instead of transactions, and also allows the application to switch consistency guarantees at runtime. In the work by Guerraoui et al. [17], the authors provide a generic library that allows applications to request multiple responses to the same query, where the response that comes later in time is *more-correct* than the prior responses. Thus, later responses are supposed to have more knowledge of the state of the system compared to earlier responses. In our work, we have defined multilevel constraints, which can model the requirement of incremental consistency guarantees by requiring that subsequent strong responses see the effects observed by prior weak responses.

Burckhardt [9] provides a generic methodology for formalizing the specification of distributed data-stores in terms of histories, visibility and arbitration orders and provides an axiomatic characterization for consistency criteria. In our work, we have derived the specification for read-write stores based on this formalism. We have adapted this characterization to define consistency criteria as a conjunction of individual formulas. Our work extends [9] in terms of the definition of hybrid histories and provides a definition of multi-level correctness for read-write stores.

There is prior work on verifying the correctness of a behaviour with respect to individual consistency criteria. Examples include [7], which deals with verifying the correctness with respect to eventual consistency, [5], which investigates the feasibility of checking a concurrent implementation with respect to a consistency criterion that has a sequential specification, including sequential consistency, linearizability and conflict-serializability and [6], which focusses on correctness with respect to causal consistency. Our work provides a generic procedure for checking the correctness of read-write histories for all these individual consistency criteria. Further, [6] show that verification of correctness of a history with respect to causal consistency is NP-COMPLETE. However, for differentiated histories, the problem is solvable in polynomial time. In our work, we generalize the technique of computing the minimal visibility relation and checking for the absence of bad patterns for all the consistency criteria defined using our syntax. In [12], the authors model quiescent consistency using Mazurkiewicz Trace

Theory. They show that the testing problem (which they call the membership problem) for a history is NP-COMPLETE. We cannot model quiescent consistency in our framework since we cannot model a quiescent point. In [14], the authors present a detailed complexity analysis of the problem of testing the correctness of a history with respect to various consistency criteria. Our findings are consistent with the results from [14] with respect to hardness of testing consistency criteria that require the visibility relation to be a total order. In a recent work [13], the authors provide a technique for testing the correctness of a history of a data-store with respect to a weak consistency criterion. That work also characterizes correctness in terms of minimal visibility relation extending the session order (called program-order there) and the happened-before relation (called returns-before relation in [9]). Our work applies this concept to read-write stores, where we observe that correctness with respect to visibility constraints can be satisfied by constructing a minimal visibility relation while the correctness with respect to read-write specifications and arbitration constraints can be reduced to checking for absence of certain bad patterns. In particular, our characterization of the arbitration relation in terms of the conflict relation saves the step of searching through all possible arbitration relations which is used in [13].

[16] deals with verification of *red-blue* consistency where, in a history, a subset of operations are labelled *red* while the remaining are labelled *blue*. The *blue* operations are expected to satisfy a weaker consistency criterion, while the *red* operations are supposed to satisfy a stronger consistency criterion. The effects of the strong operations and weak operations are visible to each other. We can model this by setting $\varphi = \psi_{thru}^{write} \wedge \psi_{back}^{read}$.

Our work should also be contrasted with [3], which addresses the problem of checking the consistency of CRDTs against their specifications, and covers a wide range of CRDTs including replicated sets, flags, counters, registers, etc. The relevant data structure in our case is registers, where the results are comparable (checking w.r.t. the weaker consistency criterion is tractable). However, we also consider registers with multiple consistency criteria in this paper, which is not considered there.

Another related work is [4], which uses the reads-from relation (called the *write-read* relation there) to show that testing the correctness of an execution (containing transactions) with respect to various consistency criteria like Read Committed (RC), Read Atomic (RA), Causal Consistency (CC), Prefix Consistency, and Snapshot Isolation. The key difference in the current work is that we consider histories having multiple consistency levels simultaneously while [4] considers executions consisting of transactions, under a single consistency criterion.

References

1. Amazon DynamoDB Developer Guide (API Version 2012–08–10): DAX and DynamoDB consistency Models (2018). https://docs.aws.amazon.com/amazondynamodb/latest/developerguide/DAX.consistency.html. Accessed 26 Sep 2019

2. Bailis, P., Ghodsi, A., Hellerstein, J.M., Stoica, I.: Bolt-on causal consistency. In: Proceedings of the 2013 ACM SIGMOD International Conference on Management of Data, SIGMOD 2013, pp. 761–772. ACM, New York (2013). https://doi.org/10.1145/2463676.2465279

3. Biswas, R., Emmi, M., Enea, C.: On the complexity of checking consistency for replicated data types. In: Dillig, I., Tasiran, S. (eds.) CAV 2019. LNCS, vol. 11562, pp. 324–343. Springer, Cham (2019). https://doi.org/10.1007/978-3-030-25543-5_19

4. Biswas, R., Enea, C.: On the complexity of checking transactional consistency. Proc. ACM Program. Lang. **3**(OOPSLA), 165:1–165:28 (2019). https://doi.org/10.1145/3360591

5. Bouajjani, A., Emmi, M.: Analysis of recursively parallel programs. ACM Trans. Program. Lang. Syst. **35**(3), 10:1–10:49 (2013). https://doi.org/10.1145/2518188

6. Bouajjani, A., Enea, C., Guerraoui, R., Hamza, J.: On verifying causal consistency. In: Proceedings of the 44th ACM SIGPLAN Symposium on Principles of Programming Languages, POPL 2017, pp. 626–638. ACM, New York (2017). https://doi.org/10.1145/3009837.3009888

7. Bouajjani, A., Enea, C., Hamza, J.: Verifying eventual consistency of optimistic replication systems. In: The 41st Annual ACM SIGPLAN-SIGACT Symposium on Principles of Programming Languages, POPL 2014, San Diego, CA, USA, January 20–21, 2014, pp. 285–296 (2014). https://doi.org/10.1145/2535838.2535877

8. Bouajjani, A., Enea, C., Mukund, M., Shenoy, R.G., Suresh, S.P.: Formalizing and checking multilevel consistency. Tech. rep., Chennai Mathematical Institute (2019). http://www.cmi.ac.in/~spsuresh/pdfs/vmcai2020-tr.pdf

9. Burckhardt, S.: Principles of eventual consistency. Found. Trends Program. Lang. **1**(1–2), 1–150 (2014). https://doi.org/10.1561/2500000011

10. Burkhardt, S., Gotsman, A., Yang, H., Zawirski, M.: Replicated data types: specification, verification, optimality. In: The 41st Annual ACM SIGPLAN-SIGACT Symposium on Principles of Programming Languages, POPL 2014, San Diego, CA, USA, January 20–21, 2014, pp. 271–284 (2014)

11. Damien: DynamoDB vs Cassandra (2017). https://www.beyondthelines.net/databases/dynamodb-vs-cassandra/. Accessed 16 Nov 2018

12. Dongol, B., Hierons, R.M.: Decidability and complexity for quiescent consistency. In: Proceedings of the 31st Annual ACM/IEEE Symposium on Logic in Computer Science, LICS 2016, pp. 116–125. ACM, New York (2016). https://doi.org/10.1145/2933575.2933576

13. Emmi, M., Enea, C.: Monitoring weak consistency. In: Chockler, H., Weissenbacher, G. (eds.) CAV 2018. LNCS, vol. 10981, pp. 487–506. Springer, Cham (2018). https://doi.org/10.1007/978-3-319-96145-3_26

14. Furbach, F., Meyer, R., Schneider, K., Senftleben, M.: Memory model-aware testing - a unified complexity analysis. In: 14th International Conference on Application of Concurrency to System Design, ACSD 2014, Tunis La Marsa, Tunisia, June 23–27, 2014, pp. 92–101 (2014). https://doi.org/10.1109/ACSD.2014.27

15. Gilbert, S., Lynch, N.A.: Brewer's conjecture and the feasibility of consistent, available, partition-tolerant web services. SIGACT News **33**(2), 51–59 (2002)

16. Gotsman, A., Yang, H., Ferreira, C., Najafzadeh, M., Shapiro, M.: 'cause i'm strong enough: reasoning about consistency choices in distributed systems. In: Proceedings of the 43rd Annual ACM SIGPLAN-SIGACT Symposium on Principles of Programming Languages, POPL 2016, St. Petersburg, FL, USA, January 20–22, 2016, pp. 371–384 (2016). https://doi.org/10.1145/2837614.2837625

17. Guerraoui, R., Pavlovic, M., Seredinschi, D.A.: Incremental consistency guarantees for replicated objects. In: Proceedings of the 12th USENIX Conference on Operating Systems Design and Implementation, OSDI 2016, pp. 169–184. USENIX Association, Berkeley (2016). http://dl.acm.org/citation.cfm?id=3026877.3026891

18. Kraska, T., Hentschel, M., Alonso, G., Kossmann, D.: Consistency rationing in the cloud: pay only when it matters. PVLDB **2**(1), 253–264 (2009). http://www.vldb.org/pvldb/2/vldb09-759.pdf

19. Lamport, L.: How to make a multiprocessor computer that correctly executes multiprocess programs. IEEE Trans. Comput. **28**(9), 690–691 (1979)

20. Li, C., Porto, D., Clement, A., Gehrke, J., Preguiça, N., Rodrigues, R.: Making geo-replicated systems fast as possible, consistent when necessary. In: Proceedings of the 10th USENIX Conference on Operating Systems Design and Implementation, OSDI 2012, pp. 265–278. USENIX Association, Berkeley (2012). http://dl.acm.org/citation.cfm?id=2387880.2387906

21. Ozkan, B.K., Majumdar, R., Niksic, F., Befrouei, M.T., Weissenbacher, G.: Randomized testing of distributed systems with probabilistic guarantees. PACMPL **2**(OOPSLA), 160:1–160:28 (2018). https://doi.org/10.1145/3276530

22. Perrin, M., Mostefaoui, A., Jard, C.: Causal consistency: beyond memory. In: Proceedings of the 21st ACM SIGPLAN Symposium on Principles and Practice of Parallel Programming, PPoPP 2016, pp. 26:1–26:12. ACM, New York (2016)

23. Terry, D.B., Theimer, M., Petersen, K., Demers, A.J., Spreitzer, M., Hauser, C.: Managing update conflicts in bayou, a weakly connected replicated storage system. In: Proceedings of the Fifteenth ACM Symposium on Operating System Principles, SOSP 1995, Copper Mountain Resort, Colorado, USA, December 3–6, 1995, pp. 172–183 (1995). https://doi.org/10.1145/224056.224070

24. Wolper, P.: Expressing interesting properties of programs in propositional temporal logic. In: Conference Record of the Thirteenth Annual ACM Symposium on Principles of Programming Languages, St. Petersburg Beach, Florida, USA, January 1986, pp. 184–193 (1986). https://doi.org/10.1145/512644.512661

Practical Abstractions for Automated Verification of Shared-Memory Concurrency

Wytse Oortwijn[1]([⊠]), Dilian Gurov[2]([⊠]), and Marieke Huisman[3]([⊠])

[1] Department of Computer Science, ETH Zürich, Zürich, Switzerland
woortwijn@inf.ethz.ch
[2] KTH Royal Institute of Technology, Stockholm, Sweden
dilian@kth.se
[3] University of Twente, Enschede, The Netherlands
m.huisman@utwente.nl

Abstract. Modern concurrent and distributed software is highly complex. Techniques to reason about the correct behaviour of such software are essential to ensure its reliability. To be able to reason about realistic programs, these techniques must be modular and compositional as well as practical by being supported by automated tools. However, many existing approaches for concurrency verification are theoretical and focus on expressivity and generality. This paper contributes a technique for verifying behavioural properties of concurrent and distributed programs that makes a trade-off between expressivity and usability. The key idea of the approach is that program behaviour is abstractly modelled using process algebra, and analysed separately. The main difficulty is presented by the typical abstraction gap between program implementations and their models. Our approach bridges this gap by providing a deductive technique for formally linking programs with their process-algebraic models. Our verification technique is modular and compositional, is proven sound with Coq, and has been implemented in the automated concurrency verifier VerCors. Moreover, our technique is demonstrated on multiple case studies, including the verification of a leader election protocol.

1 Introduction

Modern software is typically composed of multiple concurrent components that communicate via shared or distributed interfaces. The concurrent nature of the interactions between (sub)components makes such software highly complex as well as notoriously difficult to develop correctly. To ensure the reliability of modern software, verification techniques are much-needed to aid software developers to comprehend all possible concurrent system behaviours. To be able to reason about *realistic* programs, these techniques must be modular and compositional, but must also be practical by being supported by automated verifiers.

Even though verification of concurrent and distributed software is a very active research field [11,13,30,41,44,50], most work is theoretical and focuses

© Springer Nature Switzerland AG 2020
D. Beyer and D. Zufferey (Eds.): VMCAI 2020, LNCS 11990, pp. 401–425, 2020.
https://doi.org/10.1007/978-3-030-39322-9_19

primarily on expressivity and generality. This paper contributes a scalable and practical technique for verifying global behavioural properties of concurrent and distributed programs that makes a trade-off between expressivity and usability: rather than aiming for a unified approach to concurrency reasoning, we propose a powerful sound technique that is implemented in an automated verification tool, to reason automatically about realistic programs.

Reasoning about complex concurrent program behaviours is only practical if conducted at a suitable level of abstraction that hides irrelevant implementation details. This is because any real concurrent programming language with shared memory, threads and locks, has only very little algebraic behaviour. In contrast, *process algebra* offers an abstract, mathematically elegant way of expressing program behaviour. For this reason, many believe that process algebra provides a language for modelling and reasoning about the behaviour of concurrent programs at a suitable level of abstraction [1]. Our approach therefore uses process algebra as a language for *specifying* program behaviour. Such a specification can be seen as a model, the properties of which can additionally be checked (say, by model checking against temporal logic formulas). The main difficulty of this approach is dealing with the typical abstraction gap between program implementations and their models. The unique contribution of our approach is that it bridges this gap by providing a deductive technique for formally linking programs with their process-algebraic models. These formal links preserve *safety* properties; we leave the preservation of liveness properties for future work.

The key idea of the approach rests in the use of concurrent separation logic to reason not only about data races and memory safety, which is standard, but also about process-algebraic models (i.e., specified program behaviours), viewing the latter as *resources* that can be split and consumed. This results in a modular and compositional approach to establish that a program behaves as specified by its abstract model. Our approach is formally justified by correctness results that have mechanically been proven using Coq, including a machine-checked soundness proof of the proof system, stating that any verified program is a refinement of its abstract model. The verification technique has been been implemented in the VerCors verifier for automated deductive verification of concurrent software [6]. Finally, the approach has been applied on various case studies [34], including a leader election protocol that is included in this paper.

We also recently successfully applied the techniques presented in this paper on an industrial case study, concerning the formal verification of a safety-critical traffic tunnel control system that is currently in use in Dutch traffic [36]. For this case study we made a process algebraic model of the control software that we analysed with mCRL2, and used the techniques presented in this paper to prove that this model is a sound abstraction of the program's behaviour.

An extended version of this paper is available as a technical report [46], which contains more details on the formalisation of the approach and the case study.

Contributions. This paper contributes a verification technique to reason about the behaviour of shared-memory concurrent programs that is modular, compositional, sound (proven with Coq), and implemented in an automated verifier.

First Sect. 2 illustrates the technique on a small Owicki–Gries example. Then Sect. 3 gives theoretical justification of the verification technique, as a concurrent separation logic with special constructs to handle process-algebraic models. Section 4 gives more details on the Coq embedding of the program logic and its soundness proof, and on its implementation in VerCors. Section 5 demonstrates the approach on a larger case study: the verification of a leader election protocol. Finally, Sect. 6 discusses related work and Sect. 7 concludes.

2 Approach

We first illustrate the approach on a simple example. In short, we abstractly specify concurrent program behaviour as process algebra terms. Process algebra terms are composed of atomic, indivisible *actions*. In our approach the actions are *logical descriptions of shared-memory modifications*: they describe what changes are allowed to a specified region of shared memory in the program. Actions are then *linked* to the concrete instructions in the program code that compute the memory updates. These links between the program and its abstract model are established deductively, using a concurrent separation logic that is presented later. Well-known techniques for process-algebraic reasoning can then be applied to guarantee safety properties over all possible state changes, as described by their compositions of actions. The novelty of the approach is that these safety properties can then be relied upon in the program logic due to the established formal connection between the program and its process-algebraic model.

Example Program. Consider the following program, which is a simple variant of the classical concurrent Owicki–Gries example [38].

$$\textbf{atomic} \left\{ X := [E];\ [E] := X + 4 \right\} \quad \Big\|\quad \textbf{atomic} \left\{ Y := [E];\ [E] := Y * 4 \right\}$$

This program consists of two concurrent threads: one that atomically increments the value at heap location E by four, while the other atomically multiplies the value at E by four. The notation $[E]$ denotes *heap dereferencing*, where E is an expression whose evaluation determines the heap location to dereference.

The challenge is to modularly deduce the classical Owicki-Gries postcondition: after termination of both threads, the value at heap location E is either $4 * (old_E + 4)$ or $(4 * old_E) + 4$ (depending on the interleaving of threads), where old_E is the old value at E—the value of E at the pre-state of the computation.

Well-known classical approaches to deal with such concurrent programs [42] include auxiliary state [38] and interference abstraction via rely-guarantee reasoning [20]. Modern program logics employ more intricate constructs, like atomic Hoare triples [41] in the context of TaDa, or higher-order ghost state [23] in the context of Iris. However, the mentioned classical approaches typically do not scale well, whereas such modern, theoretical approaches are hard to integrate into (semi-)automated verifiers like VeriFast or VerCors.

In contrast, our approach is a balanced trade-off between expressivity and usability: it is scalable as well as implemented in an automated deductive verifier. The approach consists of the following three steps: (1) defining a process-algebraic model $OG = incr(4) \parallel mult(4)$ that is composed out of two actions, incr and mult, that abstract the atomic sub-programs; (2) verifying the Owicki–Gries postcondition algorithmically on the OG process; and (3) deductively verifying that OG is a correct behavioural specification of the program's execution flow (i.e., verifying that all atomic state changes in the program have a corresponding action in OG).The following paragraphs give more detail on these three steps.

Step 1: Specifying Program Behaviour. The first step is to construct a behavioural specification OG of the example program. This process is defined as the parallel composition of the actions $incr(4)$ and $mult(4)$, which specify the behaviour of the atomic increment and multiplication in the program, respectively. In our approach, program behaviour is specified logically, by associating a *contract* to every action. For our example program, incr and mult have the following contract:

requires true;
ensures $x = \old(x) + n$;
action incr(**int** n);

requires true;
ensures $x = \old(x) * n$;
action mult(**int** n);

The variable x is a free, *process-algebraic variable* that is later linked to a concrete heap location in the program (namely E). Moreover, the increment and multiplication of 4 has now been generalised to an arbitrary integer n.

These two actions may be composed into a full behavioural specification of the example program, by also assigning a top-level contract to OG:

requires true;
ensures $x = (\old(x) + n) * n \lor x = (\old(x) * n) + n$;
process OG(**int** n) := incr(n) $\parallel$ mult(n);

Step 2: Process-Algebraic Reasoning. The next step is to verify that OG satisfies its contract, which can be reduced to standard process-algebraic analysis. We say that OG satisfies its contract if all finite, action contract-complying traces of OG satisfy the ensures clause. The standard approach to analyse OG is to first linearise it to the bisimilar process term $incr(n) \cdot mult(n) + mult(n) \cdot incr(n)$, and then to prove its correctness by analysing all branches. VerCors currently does the analysis by encoding the linearised process as input to the Viper verifier [29]. VerCors can indeed automatically establish that OG satisfies its postcondition.

Step 3: Deductively Linking Processes to Programs. The key idea of our approach is that, by analysing how contract-complying action sequences change the values of process-algebraic variables, we may indirectly reason about how the content

```
1  old_E := [E];
2  M := process OG(4) over {x ↦ E};
```

```
3  atomic {                      ‖   9  atomic {
4    X := [E];                   ‖  10    Y := [E];
5    action incr(4) do {         ‖  11    action mult(4) do {
6      [E] := X + 4;             ‖  12      [E] := Y * 4;
7    }                           ‖  13    }
8  }                             ‖  14  }
```

```
15  finish M;
16  assert E ↪¹ (old_E + 4) * 4 ∨ E ↪¹ (old_E * 4) + 4;
```

Fig. 1. The annotated Owicki–Gries example (the annotations are coloured blue). (Color figure online)

at heap location E evolves over time. So the final step is to project this process-algebraic reasoning onto program behaviour, by annotating the program.

Figure 1 shows the required program annotations. First, x is connected to E by initialising a new model M on line 2 that executes according to OG(4). The actions incr and mult are then linked to the corresponding subprograms on lines 5–7 and 11–13 by identifying *action blocks* in the code, using special program annotations. We use these **action** annotations to verify in a thread-modular way that the left thread performs the incr(4) action (on lines 5–7) and that the right thread performs mult(4) (lines 11–13). As a result, when the program reaches the **finish** annotation on line 15 all the actions of OG will have been performed. This indirectly means that the content at heap location E has evolved as described by OG, thus allowing the asserted postcondition on line 16 to be derived.

3 Formalisation

This section gives theoretical justification of the verification approach and explains the underlying logical machinery. First, Sects. 3.1 and 3.2 briefly discuss the syntax and semantics of process algebraic models and programs, respectively. Then Sect. 3.3 presents the program logic as a concurrent separation logic with assertions that allow to specify program behaviour as a process algebraic model. Section 3.4 discusses the proof rules. Finally, Sect. 3.6 discusses soundness of the approach. All these components have been fully formalised in Coq.

Due to space constraints, the technical presentation assumes a certain familiarity with process algebra and separation logic. For more details we refer to the accompanying technical report or to the Coq formalisation [46].

3.1 Process Algebraic Models

Process algebraic models are defined by the language *Proc* as follows, with $a, b, \cdots \in Act$ the domain of *actions*, $x, y, z, \cdots \in ProcVar$ the domain of *process algebraic variables*, and $m, n, \cdots \in Lit$ the domain of *literals*.

Successful termination

$$\varepsilon\downarrow \qquad \frac{P\downarrow \quad Q\downarrow}{P\cdot Q\downarrow} \qquad \frac{P\downarrow}{P+Q\downarrow} \qquad \frac{Q\downarrow}{P+Q\downarrow} \qquad \frac{P\downarrow \quad Q\downarrow}{P\parallel Q\downarrow} \qquad P^*\downarrow$$

Small-step reduction rules (excerpt)

PSTEP-SEQ-L

$$\frac{(P,\sigma) \xrightarrow{a} (P',\sigma')}{(P\cdot Q,\sigma) \xrightarrow{a} (P'\cdot Q,\sigma')}$$

PSTEP-SEQ-R

$$\frac{P\downarrow \quad (Q,\sigma) \xrightarrow{a} (Q',\sigma')}{(P\cdot Q,\sigma) \xrightarrow{a} (Q',\sigma')}$$

PSTEP-ACT

$$\frac{[\![\mathsf{pre}(a)]\!](\sigma) \quad [\![\mathsf{post}(a)]\!](\sigma')}{(a,\sigma) \xrightarrow{a} (\varepsilon,\sigma')}$$

Fig. 2. The small-step operational semantics of process algebraic models.

Definition 1 (Process expressions, Process conditions, Processes).

$$e \in \mathit{ProcExpr} ::= m \mid x \mid e+e \mid e-e \mid \cdots$$
$$b \in \mathit{ProcCond} ::= \mathsf{true} \mid \mathsf{false} \mid \neg b \mid b \wedge b \mid e = e \mid e < e \mid \cdots$$
$$P,Q \in \mathit{Proc} ::= \varepsilon \mid \delta \mid a \mid P\cdot Q \mid P+Q \mid P\parallel Q \mid P^*$$

As usual, ε is the empty process that has no behaviour, whereas δ is the deadlocked process that neither progresses nor terminates. The process $P\cdot Q$ is the sequential composition of P and Q, while $P+Q$ denotes their non-deterministic choice. The process $P\parallel Q$ is the parallel composition P and Q. Finally, P^* is the Kleene iteration of P and denotes a sequence of zero or more P's.

The verification approach uses process algebraic models in the presence of data, implemented via *action contracts*. These action contracts make the process algebra language non-standard. Action contracts consist of pre- and postconditions that logically describe the state changes imposed by the action. Each action is assumed to have an associated contract that can be obtained via the functions pre, post : $\mathit{Act} \to \mathit{ProcCond}$. All pre- and postconditions are of type $\mathit{ProcCond}$, which is the domain of Boolean expressions over process algebraic variables.

Semantics. The operational semantics of processes is expressed as a binary reduction relation $\cdot \longrightarrow \cdot \subseteq \mathit{ProcConf} \times \mathit{Act} \times \mathit{ProcConf}$ over *process configurations* $\mathit{ProcConf} \triangleq \mathit{Proc} \times \mathit{ProcStore}$, labelled with actions from Act. The notion of data is implemented via *process stores* $\sigma \in \mathit{ProcStore} \triangleq \mathit{ProcVar} \to \mathit{Val}$ that map process algebraic variables to a semantic domain Val of *values*.

Most of the reduction rules are standard. Figure 2 gives an overview of the non-standard rules. All other transition rules are deferred to [46].

To define the transition rule PSTEP-SEQ-R for sequential composition, it is common in process algebra with ε to use an explicit notion of *successful termination* [4]. Successful termination $P\downarrow$ of any process P intuitively means that P has the choice to have no further behaviour and thus to behave as ε. Furthermore, the PSTEP-ACT transition rule for action handling permits state to change in any way that complies with the corresponding action contract.

STEP-PROC-INIT
$(X := \textbf{process } P \textbf{ over } \Pi, h, s) \rightsquigarrow (\textbf{skip}, h, s)$

STEP-PROC-FINISH
$(\textbf{finish } X, h, s) \rightsquigarrow (\textbf{skip}, h, s)$

STEP-ACT

$$\frac{(C, h, s) \rightsquigarrow (C', h', s')}{(\textbf{action } X.a \textbf{ do } C, h, s) \rightsquigarrow (\textbf{action } X.a \textbf{ do } C', h', s')}$$

STEP-ACT-FINISH
$(\textbf{action } X.a \textbf{ do skip}, h, s) \rightsquigarrow (\textbf{skip}, h, s)$

Fig. 3. An excerpt of the small-step operational semantics of programs.

The program logic allows one to handle process algebraic models *up to bisimulation*. We write $P \cong Q$ to denote that P and Q are *bisimilar* (i.e., behaviourally equivalent). Bisimilarity is a congruence with respect to all process algebraic connectives. Moreover, we indeed have that $P \downarrow$ implies $P \cong P + \varepsilon$ for any P.

3.2   Programs

Our approach is formalised on the following simple concurrent pointer language, where $X, Y, Z, \cdots \in \textit{Var}$ are *(program) variables*.

Definition 2 (Expressions, Conditions, Programs).

$$E \in \textit{Expr} ::= n \mid X \mid E + E \mid E - E \mid \cdots$$
$$B \in \textit{Cond} ::= \textsf{true} \mid \textsf{false} \mid \neg B \mid B \wedge B \mid E = E \mid E < E \mid \cdots$$
$$\Pi \in \textit{AbstrBinder} ::= \{x_0 \mapsto E_0, \ldots, x_n \mapsto E_n\}$$
$$C \in \textit{Cmd} ::= \textbf{skip} \mid X := E \mid X := [E] \mid [E] := E \mid C; C \mid C \parallel C$$
$$\mid X := \textbf{alloc } E \mid \textbf{dispose } E \mid \textbf{atomic } C$$
$$\mid \textbf{if } B \textbf{ then } C \textbf{ else } C \mid \textbf{while } B \textbf{ do } C$$
$$\mid X := \textbf{process } P \textbf{ over } \Pi \mid \textbf{action } X.a \textbf{ do } C \mid \textbf{finish } X$$

This language is a variation of the language proposed by [9,32], extended with *specification-only* commands (displayed in blue) for handling process algebraic models in the logic. These commands are ignored during program execution.

Specification-wise, $X := \textbf{process } P \textbf{ over } \Pi$ initialises a new process algebraic model that is represented by the process term P, with Π a finite mapping from process algebraic variables to heap locations. Π is used to connect abstract state (i.e., the state of process algebraic models) to concrete program state (i.e., heap entries) and is therefore referred to as an *abstraction binder*.

The **finish** X command *concludes* the model that is identified by X, given that the associated process successfully terminates. By *concludes* we mean that the model's postcondition can be relied upon and used in the proof system.

Finally, **action** $X.a$ **do** C executes the command C in the context of the abstract model X as the action a. In particular, this specification command states that, by executing C (according to the operational semantics of programs), the action a is executed in the specified process algebraic model.

Semantics. The operational semantics of programs is expressed as a small-step reduction relation $\cdot \rightsquigarrow \cdot \subseteq Conf \times Conf$, between *(program) configurations* $Conf \triangleq Cmd \times Heap \times Store$. Program configurations $(C, h, s) \in Conf$ consist of a program C, as well as a heap $h \in Heap \triangleq Val \rightharpoonup_{\mathsf{fin}} Val$ that models shared memory and a store $s \in Store \triangleq Var \rightarrow Val$ that models thread-local memory.

Figure 3 shows an excerpt of the new reduction rules for ghost commands. All other reduction rules are standard in spirit and are deferred to [46].

Most importantly, all ghost commands are specification constructs: they do not affect the program state and are essentially handled as if they were comments. However, observe that STEP-PROC-FINISH and STEP-ACT-FINISH are auxiliary transition steps that reduce a finished process or action to **skip**. These are not strictly needed, but make it more convenient to prove soundness of the logic.

3.3   Program Logic

Our program logic builds on *intuitionistic*[1] concurrent separation logic (CSL), where the assertion language is defined by the following grammar.

Definition 3 (Assertions).

$$t \in PointsToType ::= \mathsf{std} \mid \mathsf{proc} \mid \mathsf{act}$$
$$\mathcal{P}, \mathcal{Q}, \mathcal{R}, \cdots \in Assn ::= B \mid \forall X.\mathcal{P} \mid \exists X.\mathcal{P} \mid \mathcal{P} \vee \mathcal{Q} \mid \mathcal{P} * \mathcal{Q} \mid \mathcal{P} \mathbin{-\!*} \mathcal{Q}$$
$$\mid \mathbin{*}_{i \in I} \mathcal{P}_i \mid E \xrightarrow{\pi}_t E \mid \mathsf{Proc}_\pi(X, b, P, \Pi)$$

The assertion $\mathcal{P} * \mathcal{Q}$ is the separating conjunction of separation logic and states that $\mathcal{P}$ and $\mathcal{Q}$ hold on *disjoint* parts of the heap. This for example means that $\mathcal{P}$ and $\mathcal{Q}$ cannot both express write access to the same heap entry. The assertion $\mathbin{*}_{i \in I} \mathcal{P}_i$ is the *iteration of* $*$ and is equivalent to $\mathcal{P}_0 * \cdots * \mathcal{P}_n$ given that $I = \{0, \ldots, n\}$. Furthermore, the $\mathbin{-\!*}$ connective from separation logic is known as the *magic wand* and expresses hypothetical modifications of the current state.

Apart from these standard CSL connectives, the assertion language contains three different heap ownership predicates $\xrightarrow{\pi}_t$, with $\pi \in (0, 1]_\mathbb{Q}$ a *fractional permission* in the style of Boyland [8] and t the *heap ownership type*, where:

- $E \xrightarrow{\pi}_{\mathsf{std}} E'$ is the *standard heap ownership predicate* from separation logic, that provides read-only access for $0 < \pi < 1$ and write access in case $\pi = 1$.
- $E \xrightarrow{\pi}_{\mathsf{proc}} E'$ is the *process heap ownership predicate*, which indicates that the heap location E is bound to an active process algebraic model, but in a *read-only* manner: it only provides read-only access, even when $\pi = 1$.

---

[1] This intuitively means that the program logic is able to "forget" about resources, which fits naturally with garbage collecting languages like Java and C#.

- $E \xrightarrow{\pi}_{\text{act}} E'$ is the *action heap ownership predicate*, which indicates that the heap location E is bound by an active process algebraic model and is used in the context of an action block, in a *read/write* manner.

The distinction between different types of heap ownership is needed for the program logic to be sound, for example to disallow the deallocation of memory that is bound by a process algebraic model. Moreover, observe that $E \xrightarrow{\pi}_{\text{proc}} E'$ predicates never provide write access to E. However, we shall later see that the proof system allows one to upgrade $\xrightarrow{\pi}_{\text{proc}}$ predicates to $\xrightarrow{\pi}_{\text{act}}$ inside **action** blocks, and $\xrightarrow{\pi}_{\text{act}}$ again provides write access if $\pi = 1$. This system of upgrading enforces that all modifications to E happen in the context of **action** $X.a$ **do** C commands, and can therefore be recorded in the model X as the action a.

Finally, the $\mathsf{Proc}_\pi(X, b, P, \Pi)$ assertion expresses ownership of the program model that is identified by X and is represented by the process P. The condition b is the postcondition of the abstract model. Furthermore, Π connects the abstract model to the concrete program, by mapping the models' process algebraic variables to heap locations in the program. And last, the fractional permission π is needed to implement the ownership system of program models. Fractional permissions are only used here to be able to reconstruct the full Proc_1 predicate.

Semantics of Assertions. The interpretation of assertions is defined as a modelling relation $ph, pm, s, g \models \mathcal{P}$, where the models (ph, pm, s, g) consist of the following four components:

- A *permission heap*, $ph \in PermHeap \triangleq Var \rightarrow \mathsf{free} \mid \langle v \rangle_t^\pi$, that maps values (heap locations) to either free (unoccupied) or to occupied entries $\langle v \rangle_t^\pi$. Occupied heap cells store a value v, as well as a type t to associate heap cells to the three different kinds of heap ownership predicates used in the logic.
- A *process map*, $pm \in ProcMap \triangleq Var \rightarrow \mathsf{free} \mid \langle b, P, \Lambda \rangle^\pi$, defined as a total mapping from values (process identifiers) to *process map entries*. Occupied entries have the form $\langle b, P, \Lambda \rangle^\pi$ and model ownership of process algebraic models in the program logic. The components $\Lambda \in ProcVar \rightharpoonup_{\text{fin}} Val$ in turn define the models of the abstraction binders (that were defined in Definition 2).
- Two stores, $s, g \in Store$, that gives an interpretation to all variables used in program and ghost code, respectively. Ghost variables do not interfere with regular program execution and are therefore separated from program variables and maintained in an extra store g, referred to as the *ghost store*.

The semantics of assertions is defined as a modelling relation $\cdot \models \cdot$ between models of the logic $PermHeap \times ProcMap \times Store^2$ and assertions $Assn$ as follows:

Definition 4 (Semantics of assertions (excerpt)). *The interpretation of assertions $ph, pm, s, g \models \mathcal{P}$ is defined by structural recursion on $\mathcal{P}$ in the standard way, except for the following two cases:*

$\hookrightarrow$-SPLITMERGE
$$E_1 \xrightarrow{\pi_1+\pi_2}_t E_2 \dashv\vdash E_1 \xrightarrow{\pi_1}_t E_2 * E_1 \xrightarrow{\pi_2}_t E_2$$

PROC-SPLITMERGE
$$\mathsf{Proc}_{\pi_1+\pi_2}(X, b, P_1 \parallel P_2, \Pi) \dashv\vdash \mathsf{Proc}_{\pi_1}(X, b, P_1, \Pi) * \mathsf{Proc}_{\pi_2}(X, b, P_2, \Pi)$$

PROC-$\cong$
$$\frac{P \cong Q}{\mathsf{Proc}_\pi(X, b, P, \Pi) \dashv\vdash \mathsf{Proc}_\pi(X, b, Q, \Pi)}$$

Fig. 4. Selected entailment rules of the program logic.

$$ph, pm, s, g \models E_1 \xrightarrow{\pi}_t E_2 \qquad \textit{iff} \qquad ph(\llbracket E_1 \rrbracket(s)) = \langle \llbracket E_2 \rrbracket(s) \rangle_t^{\pi'} \wedge \pi \leq \pi'$$

$$ph, pm, s, g \models \mathsf{Proc}_\pi(X, b, P, \Pi) \qquad \textit{iff} \qquad \exists P' . pm(g(X)) = \langle b, P \parallel P', \llbracket \Pi \rrbracket(s) \rangle^{\pi'}$$
$$\wedge \pi \leq \pi' \wedge (\pi = 1 \implies P' = \varepsilon)$$

The full definition of the semantics of assertions can be found in [46].

Clarifying the non-standard cases, $E \xrightarrow{\pi}_t E'$ is satisfied if ph holds an entry at location E that matches with the ownership type t, with an associated fractional permission that is at least π. Process ownership assertions $\mathsf{Proc}_\pi(X, b, P, \Pi)$ are satisfied if pm holds a matching entry with a fractional permission at least π, as well as a process that has at least the behaviour of P. The denotation $\llbracket \Pi \rrbracket(s)$ gives the model of the abstraction binder Π, and is defined as follows:

Definition 5 (Semantics of abstraction binders).

$$\llbracket \{x_0 \mapsto E_0, \ldots, x_n \mapsto E_n\} \rrbracket(s) \triangleq \{x_0 \mapsto \llbracket E_0 \rrbracket(s), \ldots, x_n \mapsto \llbracket E_n \rrbracket(s)\}$$

3.4 Entailment Rules

Figure 4 shows the non-standard entailment rules of the program logic. All other, standard rules can be found in [46]. The notation $\mathcal{P} \dashv\vdash \mathcal{Q}$ is a shorthand notation for $\mathcal{P} \vdash \mathcal{Q}$ and $\mathcal{Q} \vdash \mathcal{P}$, and indicates that the rule can be used in both directions. All rules have shown to be sound in the standard sense, using Coq.

Clarifying the entailment rules, $\hookrightarrow$-SPLITMERGE expresses that heap ownership predicates $\xrightarrow{\pi}_t$ of any type t may be *split* (in the left-to-right direction) and be *merged* (right-to-left) along π. This allows one to distribute heap ownership among the different threads in the program. Likewise, PROC-SPLITMERGE allows one to split and merge process ownership along parallel compositions inside abstract models, to distribute them over different threads. More specifically, by splitting a predicate $\mathsf{Proc}_{\pi_1+\pi_2}(X, b, P_1 \parallel P_2, \Pi)$ into two, both parts can be distributed over different concurrent threads, so that thread i can establish that it executes as prescribed by its part $\mathsf{Proc}_{\pi_i}(X, b, P_i, \Pi)$ of the abstraction. Afterwards, when the threads join again, the remaining partial abstractions can be

HT-PROCINIT

$$\frac{\begin{array}{c} \mathsf{fv}(b_1) \subseteq \mathsf{dom}(\Pi) = \{x_0, \ldots, x_n\} \\ I = \{0, \ldots, n\} \qquad X \notin \mathsf{fv}(\mathcal{R}, E_0, \ldots, E_n) \qquad B = b_1[x_i/E_i]_{\forall i \in I} \end{array}}{\Gamma, \{b_1\} P \{b_2\}; \mathcal{R} \vdash \begin{array}{c} \left\{ *_{i \in I} \Pi(x_i) \stackrel{1}{\hookrightarrow}_{\mathsf{std}} E_i * B \right\} \\ X := \mathbf{process}\, P\, \mathbf{over}\, \Pi \\ \left\{ \begin{array}{c} *_{i \in I} \Pi(x_i) \stackrel{1}{\hookrightarrow}_{\mathsf{proc}} E_i * B * \\ \mathsf{Proc}_1(X, b_2, P, \Pi) \end{array} \right\} \end{array}}$$

HT-PROCUPDATE

$$\frac{\begin{array}{c} \mathsf{fv}(a) = \{x_0, \ldots, x_n\} \subseteq \mathsf{dom}(\Pi) \qquad I = \{0, \ldots, n\} \\ B_1 = \mathsf{pre}(a)[x_i/E_i]_{\forall i \in I} \qquad B_2 = \mathsf{post}(a)[x_i/E_i]_{\forall i \in I} \\ \Gamma; \mathcal{R} \vdash \{*_{i \in I} \Pi(x_i) \stackrel{\pi_i}{\hookleftarrow}_{\mathsf{act}} E_i * B_1 * \mathcal{P}\}\, C\, \{*_{i \in I} \Pi(x_i) \stackrel{\pi_i}{\hookleftarrow}_{\mathsf{act}} E_i' * B_2 * \mathcal{Q}\} \end{array}}{\Gamma; \mathcal{R} \vdash \begin{array}{c} \left\{ \begin{array}{c} *_{i \in I} \Pi(x_i) \stackrel{\pi_i}{\hookleftarrow}_{\mathsf{proc}} E_i * B_1 * \\ \mathsf{Proc}_\pi(X, b, a \cdot P + Q, \Pi) * \mathcal{P} \end{array} \right\} \\ \mathbf{action}\, X.a\, \mathbf{do}\, C \\ \left\{ \begin{array}{c} *_{i \in I} \Pi(x_i) \stackrel{\pi_i}{\hookleftarrow}_{\mathsf{proc}} E_i' * B_2 * \\ \mathsf{Proc}_\pi(X, b, P, \Pi) * \mathcal{Q} \end{array} \right\} \end{array}}$$

HT-PROCFINISH

$$\frac{\mathsf{fv}(b) \subseteq \mathsf{dom}(\Pi) = \{x_0, \ldots, x_n\} \qquad I = \{0, \ldots, n\} \qquad B = b[x_i/E_i]_{\forall i \in I} \qquad P \downarrow}{\Gamma; \mathcal{R} \vdash \left\{ \begin{array}{c} *_{i \in I} \Pi(x_i) \stackrel{1}{\hookrightarrow}_{\mathsf{proc}} E_i * \\ \mathsf{Proc}_1(X, b, P, \Pi) \end{array} \right\} \mathbf{finish}\, X \left\{ *_{i \in I} \Pi(x_i) \stackrel{1}{\hookrightarrow}_{\mathsf{std}} E_i * B \right\}}$$

Fig. 5. The non-standard Hoare proof rules related to abstract models.

merged back into a single predicate. This system thus provides a compositional way of verifying that programs meet their abstract models.

Finally, PROC-$\cong$ allows one to replace program abstractions by bisimilar ones. This rule is used to rewrite processes in a canonic form used by some other rules.

3.5 Program Judgments

Judgments of programs are defined as sequents of the form $\Gamma; \mathcal{R} \vdash \{\mathcal{P}\} C \{\mathcal{Q}\}$, where $\mathcal{R}$ is a *resource invariant* [9], and Γ is a *process environment*:

Definition 6 (Process environment).

$$\Gamma ::= \emptyset \mid \Gamma, \{b\} P \{b\}$$

Process environments are defined in the style of *interface specifications* [33], and are essentially a series of Hoare-triples $\{b_1\} P \{b_2\}$ for processes P, that constitute the top-level contracts of the programs' abstract models.

The intuitive meaning of a program judgment $\Gamma; \mathcal{R} \vdash \{\mathcal{P}\} C \{\mathcal{Q}\}$ is that, starting from any state satisfying $\mathcal{P} * \mathcal{R}$, the invariant $\mathcal{R}$ is maintained throughout execution of C, and any final state upon termination of C will satisfy $\mathcal{Q} * \mathcal{R}$. Moreover, the proof derivation of C may use any abstract model that is in Γ.

Figure 5 presents the proof rules that handle process algebraic abstractions. All other proof rules are deferred to [46] due to space constraints.

The HT-PROCINIT rule handles initialisation of an abstract model P over a set of heap locations as specified by Π. Standard points-to predicates with write-permission are required for any heap location that is to be bound by P, and these are converted to $\stackrel{1}{\hookrightarrow}_{\mathsf{proc}}$. Moreover, HT-PROCINIT requires that the precondition of P holds, which is constructed from b_1 by replacing all process variables by the symbolic values at the corresponding heap locations. A Proc_1 predicate with full permission is ensured, containing the postcondition b_2 of the abstract model.

The HT-PROCUPDATE rule handles updates to program abstractions, by performing an action a in the context of an **action** $X.a$ **do** C program, provided that C respects the contract of a. As a precondition, a predicate of the form $\mathsf{Proc}_\pi(X, b, a \cdot P + Q, \Pi)$ is required for some π. The process component of this predicate must be of the form $a \cdot P + Q$ to allow performing the a action. After performing a, this process component will be reduced to P, thereby discarding Q as the choice is made not to follow execution as prescribed by Q. In order to get process components into the required format $a \cdot P + Q$, the PROC-$\cong$ rule can be used to rewrite process components up to bisimilarity. Furthermore, $\stackrel{\pi}{\hookrightarrow}_{\mathsf{proc}}$ predicates are required for any heap location that is bound by Π. These points-to predicates are needed to resolve the pre- and postcondition of a.

Finally, HT-PROCFINISH handles finalisation of program models that successfully terminate. A predicate $\mathsf{Proc}_1(X, b, P, \Pi)$ with *full* permission is required, which means that no other thread can have any fragment of the model. This predicate is exchanged for the postcondition of the abstraction. This postcondition can be established, since (i) the contracts of processes in Γ are assumed as their validity is checked externally, and b is a postcondition of one of these contracts; (ii) the abstraction has been initialised in a state satisfying the precondition of that contract; and (iii) the leftover process P is able to successfully terminate. Lastly, all $\stackrel{1}{\hookrightarrow}_{\mathsf{proc}}$ predicates are converted back to $\stackrel{1}{\hookrightarrow}_{\mathsf{std}}$ to indicate that the associated heap locations are no longer bound by the abstraction.

3.6   Soundness

The soundness proof of the program logic has been fully mechanised using the Coq proof assistant, as a deep embedding that is inspired by [53]. The overall Coq implementation comprises roughly 15.000 lines of code. Proving soundness was non-trivial and required substantial auxiliary definitions. The Coq development and its documentation can be found at [46].

The soundness theorem relates program judgments to the operational semantics of programs, and amounts to the following: if a proof $\Gamma; \mathcal{R} \vdash \{\mathcal{P}\} C \{\mathcal{Q}\}$ can be derived for any program C, and if the contracts in Γ of all abstract models of C are satisfied, then C *executes safely for any number of computation steps*. To concretise this, we first define the semantics of program judgments.

Definition 7 (Semantics of program judgments).

$$\Gamma; \mathcal{R} \models \{\mathcal{P}\} \, C \, \{\mathcal{Q}\} \; \triangleq \; \models \Gamma \implies \forall n, ph, pm, s, g \, .$$
$$ph, pm, s, g \models \mathcal{P} \implies \mathsf{safe}^n_\Gamma(C, ph, pm, s, g, \mathcal{R}, \mathcal{Q})$$

The entailment $\models \Gamma$ intuitively means that, for any Hoare triple $\{b_1\} \, P \, \{b_2\}$ in Γ and for any σ such that $[\![b_1]\!](\sigma)$, we have that any run $(P, \sigma) \longrightarrow^* (P', \sigma')$ that terminates (i.e., $P' \!\downarrow$) ends up with a store σ' for which $[\![b_2]\!](\sigma')$ holds.

The predicate safe^n_Γ defines execution safety for n computation steps, meaning that the program is: data-race free, memory safe, complies with its pre- and postconditions, and refines its process algebraic models, for n computation steps. This definition extends the well-known inductive definition of configuration safety of Vafeiadis [53] by adding machinery to handle process algebraic models. The most important extension is a *simulation argument* between program execution (with respect to $\rightsquigarrow$) and the execution of all active models (with respect to $\xrightarrow{a}$). However, as the reduction steps of these two semantics do not directly correspond one-to-one, this simulation is established via an intermediate, instrumented semantics. This intermediate semantics is defined in terms of $\rightsquigarrow_{\mathsf{ghost}}$ transitions that define the *lock-step execution* of program transitions $\rightsquigarrow$ and the transitions $\xrightarrow{a}$ of their abstractions. Our definition of "*executing safely for n execution steps*" includes that all $\rightsquigarrow$ steps can be simulated by $\rightsquigarrow_{\mathsf{ghost}}$ steps and vice versa, for n execution steps. Thus, the end-result is a refinement between programs and their abstract models.

Theorem 1 (Soundness). $\Gamma; \mathcal{R} \vdash \{\mathcal{P}\} \, C \, \{\mathcal{Q}\} \implies \Gamma; \mathcal{R} \models \{\mathcal{P}\} \, C \, \{\mathcal{Q}\}$

The underlying idea of the above definition, i.e., having a continuation-passing style definition for program judgments, has first been applied in [2] and has further been generalised in [16] and [17]. Moreover, the idea of defining (program) execution safety in terms of an inductive predicate originates from [3]. These two concepts have been reconciled in [53] into a formalisation for the classical CSL of Brookes [9], that has been encoded and mechanically been proven in both Isabelle and Coq. Our definition builds on the latter, by having a refinement between programs and abstractions encoded in safe.

4 Implementation

The verification approach has been implemented in the VerCors verifier, which specialises in automated verification of parallel and concurrent programs written in high-level languages, like (subsets of) Java and C [6]. VerCors applies a correctness-preserving translation of the input program into a sequential imperative language, and delegates the generation of verification conditions to the Viper verifier [29] and their verification ultimately to Z3.

Tool support for our technique has been implemented in VerCors for languages with fork/join concurrency and statically-scoped parallel constructs [34]. This is done defining an axiomatic domain for processes in Viper, consisting of constructors for all process-algebraic connectives, supported by standard process-algebraic axioms. The Proc_π assertions are encoded as predicates over these process types. The three different ownership types $\xrightarrow{\pi}_t$ are encoded by defining extra fields that maintain the ownership status t for each global reference.

To analyse process-algebraic models, VerCors first linearises all processes and then encodes the linear processes and their contracts into Viper. The linearisation algorithm is based on a rewrite system that uses a subset of the standard process-algebraic axioms as rewrite rules [51] to eliminate parallel connectives.

The VerCors implementation of the abstraction approach is much richer than the simple language of Sect. 3 that is used to formalise the approach on. Notably, the abstraction language in VerCors supports general recursion instead of Kleene iteration, and allows parameterising process and action declarations by data. VerCors also has support for several axiomatic data types that enrich the expressivity of reasoning with abstractions, like (multi)sets and sequences.

5   Case Study

Finally, we demonstrate our verification approach on a well-known version of the leader election protocol [35] that is based on shared memory. Most importantly, this case study shows how our approach bridges the typical abstraction gap between process algebraic models and program implementations. In particular, it shows how a high-level process algebraic model of a leader election protocol, together with a contract for this model (checked with mCRL2 for various inputs), is formally connected to an actual program implementation of the protocol.

The protocol is performed by N concurrent workers that are organised in a ring, so that worker i only sends to worker $i + 1$ and only receives from worker $i - 1$, modulo N. The goal is to determine a leader among these workers. To find a leader, the election procedure assumes that each worker i receives a unique integer value to start with, and then operates in N rounds. In every round (i) each worker sends the highest value it encountered so far to its right neighbour, (ii) receives a value from its left neighbour, and (iii) remembers the highest of the two. The result after N rounds is that all workers know the highest unique value in the network, allowing its original owner to announce itself as leader.

The case study has been verified with VerCors using the presented approach. All workers communicate via two standard non-blocking operations for message passing: $\mathsf{mp\_send}(r, msg)$ for sending a message msg to the worker with rank r^2, and $msg := \mathsf{mp\_recv}(r)$ for receiving a message from worker r. The election protocol is implemented on top of this message passing system.

The main challenge of this case study is to define a message passing system on the process algebra level that matches this implementation. To design such a system we follow the ideas of [35]; by defining two actions, $\mathsf{send}(r, msg)$ and $\mathsf{recv}(r, msg)$, that abstractly describe the behaviour of the concrete implementations in $\mathsf{mp\_send}$ and $\mathsf{mp\_recv}$, respectively. Moreover, *process algebraic summation* $\Sigma_{x \in D} P$ is used to quantify over the possible messages that $\mathsf{mp\_recv}$ might

---

[2] The identifiers of workers are typically called *ranks* in message passing terminology.

```
1  seq⟨seq⟨Msg⟩⟩ chan; // communication channels between workers
2  int lead; // rank of the worker that is announced as leader
3
4  /* Action for sending messages. */
5  requires 0 ≤ rank < |chan|;
6  ensures chan[rank] = \old(chan[rank]) + {msg};
7  ensures ∀r′ : int . (0 ≤ r′ < |chan| ∧ r′ ≠ rank) ⇒ chan[r′] = \old(chan[r′]);
8  action send(int rank, Msg msg);
9
10 /* Action for receiving messages. */
11 requires 0 ≤ rank < |chan|;
12 ensures {msg} + chan[rank] = \old(chan[rank]);
13 ensures ∀r′ : int . (0 ≤ r′ < |chan| ∧ r′ ≠ rank) ⇒ chan[r′] = \old(chan[r′]);
14 action recv(int rank, Msg msg);
15
16 /* Action for announcing a leader. */
17 requires 0 ≤ rank < |chan|;
18 ensures lead = rank;
19 action announce(int rank);
20
21 /* Local behavioural specification for each worker. */
22 requires 0 ≤ n ≤ |chan| ∧ 0 ≤ rank < |chan|;
23 process Elect(int rank, Msg v₀, Msg v, int n) ≜
24     if 0 < n then send((rank + 1) % |chan|, v) ·
25        Σ_{v′∈Msg} recv(rank, v′) · Elect(rank, v₀, max(v, v′), n − 1)
26     else (if v = v₀ then announce(rank) else ε);
27
28 /* Global behavioural specification of the election protocol. */
29 requires |vs| = |chan|;
30 requires ∀i, j : int . (0 ≤ i < |vs| ∧ 0 ≤ j < |vs| ∧ vs[i] = vs[j]) ⇒ i = j;
31 ensures |vs| = |chan| ∧ 0 ≤ lead < |vs|;
32 ensures ∀i : int . (0 ≤ i < |vs|) ⇒ vs[i] ≤ vs[lead];
33 process ParElect(seq⟨Msg⟩ vs) ≜
34     Elect(0, vs[0], vs[0], |vs|) ‖ · · · ‖ Elect(|vs|−1, vs[|vs|−1], vs[|vs|−1], |vs|);
```

Fig. 6. Behavioural specification of the leader election protocol.

receive. The summation operator $\Sigma_{x\in D} P$ quantifies over a set $D = \{d_0, \ldots, d_n\}$ of data and is defined as the (finite) sequence $P[x/d_0] + \cdots + P[x/d_n]$ of non-deterministic choices. The following two rules illustrate how the abstract send and recv actions are connected to mp_send and mp_recv (observe that both these actions are parameterised by data[3]).

---

[3] Recall that the VerCors implementation of our abstraction technique is much richer than the simple language of Sect. 3 that is used to formalise the approach on.

$$\{\mathsf{send}(r, msg) \cdot P\}\, \mathtt{mp\_send}(r, msg)\, \{P\}$$
$$\{\Sigma_{x \in Msg}\mathsf{recv}(r, x) \cdot P\}\, msg := \mathtt{mp\_recv}(r)\, \{P[x/msg]\}$$

Finally, we construct a process-algebraic model of the election protocol using send and recv, and verify that the implementation adheres to this model. This model has been analysed with mCRL2 for various inputs (since mCRL2 is essentially finite-state) to establish the global property of announcing the correct leader. The deductive proof of the program can then rely on this property.

5.1   Behavioural Specification

Our main goal is proving that the implementation determines the correct leader upon termination. To prove this, we first define a *behavioural specification* of the election protocol that hides all irrelevant implementation details, and prove the correctness property on this specification. Process algebra provides a proper abstraction level that suits our needs well, as the behaviour of leader election can concisely be specified in terms of sequences of sends and receives.

Figure 6 presents the process algebraic specification. In particular, ParElect specifies the *global* behaviour whereas Elect specifies the *thread-local* behaviour. The ParElect process encodes the parallel composition of all eligible participants. ParElect takes a sequence *vs* of initial values as argument, whose length equals the total number of workers by its precondition. ParElect's postcondition states that *lead* must be a valid rank after termination and that *vs*[*lead*] be the highest initial worker value. It follows that worker *lead* is the correctly chosen leader.

The Elect process takes four arguments, which are: the rank of the worker, the initial unique value v_0 of that worker, the current highest value v encountered by that worker, and finally the number n of remaining rounds. The rounds are implemented via general recursion. In each round all workers send their current highest value v to their right neighbour (on line 24), receive a value v' in return from their left neighbour (line 25), and continue with the highest of the two. The extra announce action is declared and used to announce the leader after n rounds. The postcondition of announce is that *lead* stores the leader's rank.

The contracts of send and recv describe the behaviour of standard non-blocking message passing. Communication on the specification level is implemented via *message queues*. Message queues are defined as sequences of messages that are taken from a finite domain *Msg*. Since workers are organised in a ring in this case, every worker can do with only a single queue and the global communication channel architecture can be defined as a sequence of message queues: *chan* in the figure. The action contract of send(*r, msg*) expresses enqueuing the message *msg* onto the message queue *chan*[*r*] of the worker with rank r. The postcondition of send is that *msg* has been enqueued onto *chan*[*r*] and that the queues *chan*[*r'*] for any $r' \neq r$ have not been altered. Likewise, the contract of recv(*r, msg*) expresses dequeuing *msg* from *chan*[*r*]. The expression \old(e) indicates that e is to be evaluated with respect to the pre-state of computation.

```
1  global seq⟨seq⟨Msg⟩⟩ C; // implementation of communication channels
2  global int N; // total number of workers
3  global int L; // rank of the leader to be announced
4
5  lock_invariant L ↪¹⟶proc − * ∃c : seq⟨seq⟨Msg⟩⟩ . C ↪¹⟶proc c * N ↪^½⟶proc |c|;
6
7  given p, P, Q, Π, π, π';
8  context {chan ↦ C} ∈ Π * ∃n . N ↪^π⟶proc n * 0 ≤ rank < n;
9  requires Proc_π'(X, p, send(rank, msg) · P + Q, Π);
10 ensures Proc_π'(X, p, P, Π);
11 void mp_send(ref X, int rank, Msg msg) { /* omitted */ }
12
13 given p, P, Q, Π, π, π';
14 context {chan ↦ C} ∈ Π * ∃n . N ↪^π⟶proc n * 0 ≤ rank < n;
15 requires Proc_π'(X, p, Σ_{m∈Msg} recv(rank, m) · P + Q, Π);
16 ensures Proc_π'(X, p, P[m/\result], Π);
17 Msg mp_recv(ref X, int rank) { /* omitted */ }
18
19 given n, p, Π, π, π';
20 context {lead ↦ L, chan ↦ C} ∈ Π * N ↪^π⟶proc n * 0 ≤ rank < n;
21 requires Proc_π'(X, p, Elect(rank, v₀, v, n), Π);
22 ensures Proc_π'(X, p, ε, Π);
23 void elect(ref X, int rank, Msg v₀, Msg v) {
24   loop_invariant 0 ≤ i ≤ n;
25   loop_invariant Proc_π'(X, p, Elect(rank, v₀, v, n − i), Π);
26   for (int i := 0 to N) {
27     mp_send(X, (rank + 1) % N, v) with {
28       P := Σ_{x∈Msg} recv(rank, x) · Elect(rank, v₀, max(v, x), n − i − 1),
29       Q := ε, p := p, Π := Π, π := π, π' := π'
30     };
31     Msg v' := mp_recv(X, rank) with {
32       P := Elect(rank, v₀, max(v, v'), n − i − 1),
33       Q := ε, p := p, Π := Π, π := π, π' := π'
34     };
35     v := max(v, v');
36   }
37   if (v = v₀) {
38     atomic { action X.announce(rank) do L := rank; }
39   }
40 }
```

Fig. 7. The annotated implementation of the leader election protocol. Annotations of the form **context** $\mathcal{P}$ are shorthand for **requires** $\mathcal{P}$; **ensures** $\mathcal{P}$.

```
41  given p, Π;
42  context N ⊂⅟₂→proc |vs| * 0 < |vs|;
43  requires Proc₁(X, p, ParElect(vs), Π);
44  ensures Proc₁(X, p, ε, Π);
45  void parelect(ref X, seq⟨Msg⟩ vs) {
46    context 0 ≤ rank < |vs|;
47    requires Proc₁/|vs|(X, p, Elect(rank, vs[rank], vs[rank], |vs|), Π′);
48    ensures Proc₁/|vs|(X, p, ε, Π);
49    par (int rank := 0 to N) {
50      elect(X, vs[rank], vs[rank]) with {
51        n := N, p := p, Π := Π, π := 1/(4|vs|), π′ := 1/|vs|
52      };
53    }
54  }
55
56  context N ⊂¹→std − * C ⊂¹→std − * L ⊂¹→std −;
57  requires ∀i, j : int . (0 ≤ i < |vs| ∧ 0 ≤ j < |vs| ∧ vs[i] = vs[j]) ⇒ i = j;
58  ensures 0 ≤ \result < |vs|;
59  ensures ∀i : int . (0 ≤ i < |vs|) ⇒ vs[i] ≤ vs[\result];
60  int main(seq⟨Msg⟩ vs) {
61    N := |vs|, C := initialiseChannels(N);
62    X := process ParElect(vs) over {chan ↦ C, lead ↦ L};
63    commitLock(); // initialise the lock invariant
64    parelect(X, vs) with { p := ParElect(vs), Π := {chan ↦ C, lead ↦ L} };
65    uncommitLock(); // reclaim the lock invariant
66    finish X; // obtain the global correctness property from the abstraction
67    return L; // return rank of leader
68  }
```

Fig. 8. Bootstrap procedures of the leader election protocol.

5.2   Protocol Implementation

Figure 7 presents the annotated implementation of the election protocol[4]. The
elect method contains the code that is executed by every worker. The contract
of elect(X, $rank$, v_0, v) states that the method body adheres to the behavioural
description Elect($rank$, v_0, v, N) of the election protocol. Each worker performing elect enters a **for**-loop that iterates N times, whose loop invariant states
that, at iteration i, the remaining program behaves as prescribed by the process
Elect($rank$, v_0, v, $i - 1$). The invocations to mp_send and mp_recv on lines 27 and
31 are annotated with **with** clauses that resolve the assignments required by the

---

[4] It should be noted that the presentation is slightly different from the version that is
verified by VerCors, to better connect to the theory discussed in the earlier sections to
the case study. Notably, VerCors uses Implicit Dynamic Frames [27] as the underlying
logical framework, which is equivalent to separation logic [39] but handles ownership
slightly differently. The details of this are deferred to [6,21].

given clauses in the contracts of mp_send and mp_recv. The **given** $\overline{\eta}$ annotation expresses that the parameter list $\overline{\eta}$ are extra ghost arguments for the sake of specification. After N rounds all workers with $v = v_0$ announce themselves as leader. However, since the initial values are chosen to be unique there can only be one such worker. Finally, we can verify that at the post-state of elect the abstract model has been fully executed and thus reduced to ε.

The mp_send(X, *rank*, *msg*) method implements the operation of enqueuing *msg* onto the message queue of worker *rank*. Its implementation has been omitted for brevity. The contract of mp_send expresses that the enqueuing operation is encapsulated as a send(*rank*, *msg*) action that is prescribed by an abstract model identified by X. The mp_recv(X, *rank*) function implements the operation of dequeuing and returns the first message of the message queue of worker *rank*. The receive is prescribed as the recv action on the abstraction level, where the potential received message is ranged over by the summation on lines 15.

Figure 8 presents bootstrapping code for the implementation of message passing. The main function initialises the communication channels whereas parelect spawns all worker threads. main(*vs*) additionally initialises and finalises the abstraction ParElect(*vs*) on the specification level (on line 62 and 66, respectively), whose analysis allows one to establish the postconditions of main. The function parelect(X, *vs*) implements the abstract model ParElect(*vs*) by spawning N workers that all execute the elect program. The contract associated to the parallel block (lines 46–48) is called an *iteration contract* and assigns pre- and postconditions to every parallel instance. For more details on iteration contracts we refer to [5]. Most importantly, the iteration contract of each parallel worker states (on line 47) that the worker behaves as specified by Elect. Thus, we deductively verify in a *thread-modular way* that the program implements its behavioural specification. Lastly, all the required ownership for the global fields and the $Proc_1$ predicate is split and distributed among the individual workers via the iteration contract and the **with** clause on lines 50–52.

6 Related Work

Significant progress has been made on the theory of concurrent software verification over the last years [11–13,30,41,48–50]. This line of research proposes advanced program logics that all provide some notion of expressing and restricting thread interference of various complexity, via *protocols* [24]: formal descriptions of how shared-memory is allowed to evolve over time. In our approach protocols have the form of process algebraic abstractions.

The original work on CSL [32] allows specifying simple thread interference in shared-memory programs via resource invariants and critical regions. Later, RGSep [54] merges CSL with rely-guarantee reasoning to enable describing more fine-grained inter-thread interference by identifying atomic concurrent actions. Many modern program logics build on these principles and propose even more advanced ways of verifying shared-memory concurrency. For example, TaDa [41] and CaReSL [50] express thread interference protocols through state-transition systems. iCAP [48] and Iris [25] propose a more unified approach by accepting user-defined monoids to express protocols on shared state, together with invariants restricting these protocols. Iris provides reasoning support for proving language properties in Coq, where our focus is on proving programs correct.

In the distributed setting, Disel [44] allows specifying protocols for distributed systems. Disel builds on dependent type theory and is implemented as a shallow embedding in Coq. Even though their approach is more expressive than ours, it can only semi-automatically be applied in the context of Coq. Villard et al. [55] present a program logic for message passing concurrency, where threads may communicate over channels using native send/receive primitives. This program logic allows specifying protocols via *contracts*, which are state-machines in the style of Session Types [18], to describe channel behaviour. Our technique is more general, as the approach of Villard et al. is tailored specifically to basic shared-memory message passing. Actor Services [47] is a program logic with assertions to express the consequences of asynchronous message transfers between actors. However, the meta-theory of Actor Services has not been proven sound.

Most of the related work given so far is essentially theoretical and mainly focuses on expressiveness and generality. Our approach is a trade-off between expressivity and usability. It allows specifying process algebraic protocols over a general class of concurrent systems, while also allowing the approach to be implemented in automated verifiers for concurrency like VerCors. Related concurrency verifiers are SmallfootRG [10], VeriFast [19], CIVL [45], THREADER [14] and Viper [22,29]; the latter tool is used as the main back-end of VerCors. SmallfootRG is a memory-safety verifier based on RGSep. VeriFast is a rich toolset for verifying (multi-threaded) Java and C programs using separation logic. Notably, Penninckx et al. [40] extend VeriFast with a Petri-net extension to reason about the I/O behaviour of programs. This Petri-net approach is similar to ours, however our technique supports reasoning about abstract models and allows reasoning about more than just I/O behaviour. The CIVL framework can reason about race-freedom and functional correctness of MPI programs written in C [28,57]. The reasoning is done via bounded model checking combined with symbolic execution. THREADER is an automated verifier for multi-threaded C, based on model checking and counterexample-guided abstraction refinement.

Apart from the proposed technique, VerCors also allows using process algebraic abstractions as *histories* [7,56]. Also related in this respect are the time-stamped histories of [43], which records atomic state changes in concurrent programs as a history, which are, likewise to our approach, handled as resources in the logic. However, history recording is only suitable for terminating programs.

Finally, there is a lot of more general work on proving linearisability [15,26,52], which essentially allows reasoning about fine-grained concurrency by using sequential verification techniques. Our technique, as well as the history-based technique of [7], uses process algebraic linearisation to do so.

7   Conclusion

To reason effectively about realistic concurrent and distributed software, we have presented a verification technique that performs the reasoning at a suitable level of abstraction that hides irrelevant implementation details, is scalable to realistic programs by being modular and compositional, and is practical by being supported by automated tools. The approach is expressive enough to allow reasoning about realistic software as is demonstrated by the case study as well as by [36], and can be implemented as part of an automated deductive program verifier (viz. VerCors). The proof system underlying our technique has mechanically been proven sound using Coq. Our technique is therefore supported by a strong combination of theoretical justification and practical usability.

We consider the presented technique as just the beginning of a comprehensive verification framework that aims to capture many different concurrent and distributed programming paradigms. To illustrate, we recently adapted the presented approach to the distributed case, by allowing process algebraic models to describe message passing behaviour of distributed programs [37].

We are currently further investigating the use of mCRL2 and Ivy to reason algorithmically about program abstractions, e.g., [31]. Moreover, we are planning to investigate the preservation of liveness properties in addition to safety.

Acknowledgements. This work is partially supported by the NWO VICI 639.023.710 Mercedes project and by the NWO TOP 612.001.403 VerDi project.

References

1. Aldini, A., Bernardo, M., Corradini, F.: A Process Algebraic Approach to Software Architecture Design. Springer, London (2010). https://doi.org/10.1007/978-1-84800-223-4
2. Appel, A.W., Blazy, S.: Separation logic for small-step CMINOR. In: Schneider, K., Brandt, J. (eds.) TPHOLs 2007. LNCS, vol. 4732, pp. 5–21. Springer, Heidelberg (2007). https://doi.org/10.1007/978-3-540-74591-4_3
3. Appel, A., Melliès, P., Richards, C., Vouillon, J.: A very modal model of a modern, major, general type system. In: POPL, vol. 42, pp. 109–122. ACM (2007). https://doi.org/10.1145/1190216.1190235
4. Baeten, J.: Process Algebra with Explicit Termination. Eindhoven University of Technology, Department of Mathematics and Computing Science (2000)
5. Blom, S., Darabi, S., Huisman, M.: Verification of loop parallelisations. In: Egyed, A., Schaefer, I. (eds.) FASE 2015. LNCS, vol. 9033, pp. 202–217. Springer, Heidelberg (2015). https://doi.org/10.1007/978-3-662-46675-9_14
6. Blom, S., Darabi, S., Huisman, M., Oortwijn, W.: The VerCors tool set: verification of parallel and concurrent software. In: Polikarpova, N., Schneider, S. (eds.) IFM 2017. LNCS, vol. 10510, pp. 102–110. Springer, Cham (2017). https://doi.org/10.1007/978-3-319-66845-1_7
7. Blom, S., Huisman, M., Zaharieva-Stojanovski, M.: History-based verification of functional behaviour of concurrent programs. In: Calinescu, R., Rumpe, B. (eds.) SEFM 2015. LNCS, vol. 9276, pp. 84–98. Springer, Cham (2015). https://doi.org/10.1007/978-3-319-22969-0_6

8. Boyland, J.: Checking interference with fractional permissions. In: Cousot, R. (ed.) SAS 2003. LNCS, vol. 2694, pp. 55–72. Springer, Heidelberg (2003). https://doi.org/10.1007/3-540-44898-5_4

9. Brookes, S.: A semantics for concurrent separation logic. Theor. Comput. Sci. **375**(1–3), 227–270 (2007). https://doi.org/10.1016/j.tcs.2006.12.034

10. Calcagno, C., Parkinson, M., Vafeiadis, V.: Modular safety checking for fine-grained concurrency. In: Nielson, H.R., Filé, G. (eds.) SAS 2007. LNCS, vol. 4634, pp. 233–248. Springer, Heidelberg (2007). https://doi.org/10.1007/978-3-540-74061-2_15

11. Dinsdale-Young, T., Dodds, M., Gardner, P., Parkinson, M.J., Vafeiadis, V.: Concurrent abstract predicates. In: D'Hondt, T. (ed.) ECOOP 2010. LNCS, vol. 6183, pp. 504–528. Springer, Heidelberg (2010). https://doi.org/10.1007/978-3-642-14107-2_24

12. Feng, X.: Local rely-guarantee reasoning. In: POPL, vol. 44, pp. 315–327. ACM (2009). https://doi.org/10.1145/1480881.1480922

13. Feng, X., Ferreira, R., Shao, Z.: On the relationship between concurrent separation logic and assume-guarantee reasoning. In: De Nicola, R. (ed.) ESOP 2007. LNCS, vol. 4421, pp. 173–188. Springer, Heidelberg (2007). https://doi.org/10.1007/978-3-540-71316-6_13

14. Gupta, A., Popeea, C., Rybalchenko, A.: Threader: a constraint-based verifier for multi-threaded programs. In: Gopalakrishnan, G., Qadeer, S. (eds.) CAV 2011. LNCS, vol. 6806, pp. 412–417. Springer, Heidelberg (2011). https://doi.org/10.1007/978-3-642-22110-1_32

15. Herlihy, M., Wing, J.: Linearizability: a correctness condition for concurrent objects. TOPLAS **12**(3), 463–492 (1990). https://doi.org/10.1145/78969.78972

16. Hobor, A.: Oracle semantics. Ph.D. thesis, Princeton University (2008)

17. Hobor, A., Appel, A.W., Nardelli, F.Z.: Oracle semantics for concurrent separation logic. In: Drossopoulou, S. (ed.) ESOP 2008. LNCS, vol. 4960, pp. 353–367. Springer, Heidelberg (2008). https://doi.org/10.1007/978-3-540-78739-6_27

18. Honda, K., Vasconcelos, V.T., Kubo, M.: Language primitives and type discipline for structured communication-based programming. In: Hankin, C. (ed.) ESOP 1998. LNCS, vol. 1381, pp. 122–138. Springer, Heidelberg (1998). https://doi.org/10.1007/BFb0053567

19. Jacobs, B., Smans, J., Philippaerts, P., Vogels, F., Penninckx, W., Piessens, F.: VeriFast: a powerful, sound, predictable, fast verifier for C and Java. In: Bobaru, M., Havelund, K., Holzmann, G.J., Joshi, R. (eds.) NFM 2011. LNCS, vol. 6617, pp. 41–55. Springer, Heidelberg (2011). https://doi.org/10.1007/978-3-642-20398-5_4

20. Jones, C.: Tentative steps toward a development method for interfering programs. TOPLAS **5**(4), 596–619 (1983). https://doi.org/10.1145/69575.69577

21. Joosten, S., Oortwijn, W., Safari, M., Huisman, M.: An exercise in verifying sequential programs with VerCors. In: Summers, A. (ed.) FTfJP, pp. 40–45. ACM (2018). https://doi.org/10.1145/3236454.3236479

22. Juhasz, U., Kassios, I., Müller, P., Novacek, M., Schwerhoff, M., Summers, A.: Viper: a verification infrastructure for permission-based reasoning. Technical report, ETH Zürich (2014)

23. Jung, R., Krebbers, R., Birkedal, L., Dreyer, D.: Higher-order ghost state. In: ICFP, vol. 51, pp. 256–269. ACM (2016). https://doi.org/10.1145/2951913.2951943

24. Jung, R., et al.: Iris: monoids and invariants as an orthogonal basis for concurrent reasoning. In: POPL, vol. 50, pp. 637–650. ACM (2015). https://doi.org/10.1145/2676726.2676980

25. Krebbers, R., Jung, R., Bizjak, A., Jourdan, J.-H., Dreyer, D., Birkedal, L.: The essence of higher-order concurrent separation logic. In: Yang, H. (ed.) ESOP 2017. LNCS, vol. 10201, pp. 696–723. Springer, Heidelberg (2017). https://doi.org/10.1007/978-3-662-54434-1_26

26. Krishna, S., Shasha, D., Wies, T.: Go with the flow: compositional abstractions for concurrent data structures. POPL **2**, 1–31 (2017). https://doi.org/10.1145/3158125

27. Leino, K.R.M., Müller, P., Smans, J.: Verification of concurrent programs with Chalice. In: Aldini, A., Barthe, G., Gorrieri, R. (eds.) FOSAD 2007-2009. LNCS, vol. 5705, pp. 195–222. Springer, Heidelberg (2009). https://doi.org/10.1007/978-3-642-03829-7_7

28. Luo, Z., Zheng, M., Siegel, S.: Verification of MPI programs using CIVL. In: EuroMPI. ACM (2017). https://doi.org/10.1145/3127024.3127032

29. Müller, P., Schwerhoff, M., Summers, A.J.: Viper: a verification infrastructure for permission-based reasoning. In: Jobstmann, B., Leino, K.R.M. (eds.) VMCAI 2016. LNCS, vol. 9583, pp. 41–62. Springer, Heidelberg (2016). https://doi.org/10.1007/978-3-662-49122-5_2

30. Nanevski, A., Ley-Wild, R., Sergey, I., Delbianco, G.A.: Communicating state transition systems for fine-grained concurrent resources. In: Shao, Z. (ed.) ESOP 2014. LNCS, vol. 8410, pp. 290–310. Springer, Heidelberg (2014). https://doi.org/10.1007/978-3-642-54833-8_16

31. Neele, T., Willemse, T.A.C., Groote, J.F.: Solving parameterised Boolean equation systems with infinite data through quotienting. In: Bae, K., Ölveczky, P.C. (eds.) FACS 2018. LNCS, vol. 11222, pp. 216–236. Springer, Cham (2018). https://doi.org/10.1007/978-3-030-02146-7_11

32. O'Hearn, P.: Resources, concurrency and local reasoning. Theor. Comput. Sci. **375**(1–3), 271–307 (2007). https://doi.org/10.1016/j.tcs.2006.12.035

33. O'Hearn, P., Yang, H., Reynolds, J.: Separation and information hiding. In: POPL, vol. 39, pp. 268–280. ACM (2004). https://doi.org/10.1145/964001.964024

34. Oortwijn, W., Blom, S., Gurov, D., Huisman, M., Zaharieva-Stojanovski, M.: An abstraction technique for describing concurrent program behaviour. In: Paskevich, A., Wies, T. (eds.) VSTTE 2017. LNCS, vol. 10712, pp. 191–209. Springer, Cham (2017). https://doi.org/10.1007/978-3-319-72308-2_12

35. Oortwijn, W., Blom, S., Huisman, M.: Future-based static analysis of message passing programs. In: Programming Language Approaches to Concurrency- & Communication-cEntric Software (PLACES), pp. 65–72. Open Publishing Association (2016). https://doi.org/10.4204/EPTCS.211.7

36. Oortwijn, W., Huisman, M.: Formal verification of an industrial safety-critical traffic tunnel control system. In: Ahrendt, W., Tapia Tarifa, S.L. (eds.) IFM 2019. LNCS, vol. 11918, pp. 418–436. Springer, Cham (2019). https://doi.org/10.1007/978-3-030-34968-4_23

37. Oortwijn, W., Huisman, M.: Practical abstractions for automated verification of message passing concurrency. In: Ahrendt, W., Tapia Tarifa, S.L. (eds.) IFM 2019. LNCS, vol. 11918, pp. 399–417. Springer, Cham (2019). https://doi.org/10.1007/978-3-030-34968-4_22

38. Owicki, S., Gries, D.: An axiomatic proof technique for parallel programs. Acta Informatica **6**, 319–340 (1975)

39. Parkinson, M.J., Summers, A.J.: The relationship between separation logic and implicit dynamic frames. In: Barthe, G. (ed.) ESOP 2011. LNCS, vol. 6602, pp. 439–458. Springer, Heidelberg (2011). https://doi.org/10.1007/978-3-642-19718-5_23

40. Penninckx, W., Jacobs, B., Piessens, F.: Sound, modular and compositional verification of the input/output behavior of programs. In: Vitek, J. (ed.) ESOP 2015. LNCS, vol. 9032, pp. 158–182. Springer, Heidelberg (2015). https://doi.org/10. 1007/978-3-662-46669-8_7

41. da Rocha Pinto, P., Dinsdale-Young, T., Gardner, P.: TaDA: a logic for time and data abstraction. In: Jones, R. (ed.) ECOOP 2014. LNCS, vol. 8586, pp. 207–231. Springer, Heidelberg (2014). https://doi.org/10.1007/978-3-662-44202-9_9

42. da Rocha Pinto, P., Dinsdale-Young, T., Gardner, P.: Steps in modular specifications for concurrent modules. In: MFPS, pp. 3–18 (2015). https://doi.org/10.1016/ j.entcs.2015.12.002

43. Sergey, I., Nanevski, A., Banerjee, A.: Specifying and verifying concurrent algorithms with histories and subjectivity. In: Vitek, J. (ed.) ESOP 2015. LNCS, vol. 9032, pp. 333–358. Springer, Heidelberg (2015). https://doi.org/10.1007/978-3-662-46669-8_14

44. Sergey, I., Wilcox, J., Tatlock, Z.: Programming and proving with distributed protocols. POPL **2**, 1–30 (2017). https://doi.org/10.1145/3158116

45. Siegel, S., et al.: CIVL: the concurrency intermediate verification language. In: International Conference for High Performance Computing, Networking, Storage and Analysis (SC), p. 61. ACM (2015). https://doi.org/10.1145/2807591.2807635

46. Supplementary Material. The supplementary material for this paper, consisting of a technical report, the Coq formalisation and the case study, can be found online at https://github.com/wytseoortwijn/VMCAI20-SharedMemAbstr

47. Summers, A.J., Müller, P.: Actor services – modular verification of message passing programs. In: Thiemann, P. (ed.) ESOP 2016. LNCS, vol. 9632, pp. 699–726. Springer, Heidelberg (2016). https://doi.org/10.1007/978-3-662-49498-1_27

48. Svendsen, K., Birkedal, L.: Impredicative concurrent abstract predicates. In: Shao, Z. (ed.) ESOP 2014. LNCS, vol. 8410, pp. 149–168. Springer, Heidelberg (2014). https://doi.org/10.1007/978-3-642-54833-8_9

49. Svendsen, K., Birkedal, L., Parkinson, M.: Modular reasoning about separation of concurrent data structures. In: Felleisen, M., Gardner, P. (eds.) ESOP 2013. LNCS, vol. 7792, pp. 169–188. Springer, Heidelberg (2013). https://doi.org/10.1007/978-3-642-37036-6_11

50. Turon, A., Dreyer, D., Birkedal, L.: Unifying refinement and Hoare-style reasoning in a logic for higher-order concurrency. In: ICFP, pp. 377–390. ACM (2013). https://doi.org/10.1145/2500365.2500600

51. Usenko, Y.: Linearization in μCRL. Technische Universiteit Eindhoven (2002)

52. Vafeiadis, V.: Automatically proving linearizability. In: Touili, T., Cook, B., Jackson, P. (eds.) CAV 2010. LNCS, vol. 6174, pp. 450–464. Springer, Heidelberg (2010). https://doi.org/10.1007/978-3-642-14295-6_40

53. Vafeiadis, V.: Concurrent separation logic and operational semantics. In: MFPS, volume 276 of ENTCS, pp. 335–351 (2011). https://doi.org/10.1016/j.entcs.2011. 09.029

54. Vafeiadis, V., Parkinson, M.: A marriage of rely/guarantee and separation logic. In: Caires, L., Vasconcelos, V.T. (eds.) CONCUR 2007. LNCS, vol. 4703, pp. 256–271. Springer, Heidelberg (2007). https://doi.org/10.1007/978-3-540-74407-8_18

55. Villard, J., Lozes, É., Calcagno, C.: Proving copyless message passing. In: Hu, Z. (ed.) APLAS 2009. LNCS, vol. 5904, pp. 194–209. Springer, Heidelberg (2009). https://doi.org/10.1007/978-3-642-10672-9_15
56. Zaharieva-Stojanovski, M.: Closer to reliable software: verifying functional behaviour of concurrent programs. Ph.D. thesis, University of Twente (2015). https://doi.org/10.3990/1.9789036539241
57. Zheng, M., Rogers, M., Luo, Z., Dwyer, M., Siegel, S.: CIVL: formal verification of parallel programs. In: ASE, pp. 830–835. IEEE (2015). https://doi.org/10.1109/ASE.2015.99

How to Win First-Order Safety Games

Helmut Seidl[1], Christian Müller[1,2(✉)], and Bernd Finkbeiner[2]

[1] Technische Universität München, Munich, Germany
{seidl,christian.mueller}@in.tum.de
[2] Saarland University, Saarbrücken, Germany
finkbeiner@cs.uni-saarland.de

Available   Functional

Abstract. First-order (FO) transition systems have recently attracted attention for the verification of parametric systems such as network protocols, software-defined networks or multi-agent workflows like conference management systems. Functional correctness or noninterference of these systems have conveniently been formulated as safety or hypersafety properties, respectively. In this article, we take the step from verification to synthesis—tackling the question whether it is possible to automatically synthesize predicates to enforce safety or hypersafety properties like noninterference. For that, we generalize FO transition systems to FO safety games. For FO games with monadic predicates only, we provide a complete classification into decidable and undecidable cases. For games with non-monadic predicates, we concentrate on universal first-order invariants, since these are sufficient to express a large class of properties—for example noninterference. We identify a non-trivial subclass where invariants can be proven inductive and FO winning strategies be effectively constructed. We also show how the extraction of weakest FO winning strategies can be reduced to SO quantifier elimination itself. We demonstrate the usefulness of our approach by automatically synthesizing nontrivial FO specifications of messages in a leader election protocol as well as for paper assignment in a conference management system to exclude unappreciated disclosure of reports.

Keywords: First order safety games · Universal invariants · First Order Logic · Second order quantifier elimination

1 Introduction

Given a network of processes, can we synthesize the content of messages to be sent to elect a single leader? Given a conference management system, can we

The project has received funding from the European Research Council (ERC) under the European Union's Horizon 2020 research and innovation programme under grant agreement No. 787367 (PaVeS) as well as grant agreement No. 683300 (OSARES). This work was also partially supported by the German Research Foundation (DFG) as part of the Collaborative Research Center "Foundations of Perspicuous Software Systems" (TRR 248, 389792660).

D. Beyer and D. Zufferey (Eds.): VMCAI 2020, LNCS 11990, pp. 426–448, 2020.
https://doi.org/10.1007/978-3-030-39322-9_20

automatically synthesize a strategy for paper assignment so that no PC member is able to obtain illegitimate information about reports? Parametric systems like conference management systems can readily be formalized as first order (FO) transition systems where the attained states of agents are given as a FO structure, i.e., a finite set of relations. This approach was pioneered by abstract state machines (ASMs) [15], and has found many practical applications, for example in the verification of network protocols [27], software defined networks [3], and multi-agent workflows [12,13,23]. FO transition systems rely on *input* predicates to receive information from the environment such as network events, interconnection topologies, or decisions of agents. In addition to the externally provided inputs, there are also *internal* decisions that are made to ensure well-behaviour of the system. This separation of input predicates into these two groups turns the underlying transition system into a two-player *game*. In order to systematically explore possibilities of synthesizing message contents in protocols or strategies in workflows, we generalize FO transition systems to FO games.

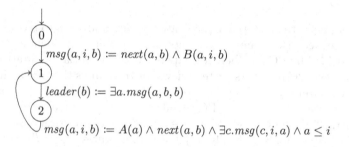

Fig. 1. FO safety game for the running leader election example

Example 1. Figure 1 shows a slightly simplified version of the network leader election protocol from [27] turned into a FO game. The topology of the network, here a ring, is given by the predicates *next* and $\leq$, which are appropriately axiomatized. The participating agents communicate via messages through the predicate *msg* but are only allowed to send messages to the next agent in the ring topology. In the first step, agents can send any message (determined via the input predicate B) to their neighbor. Afterwards they check if they have received a message containing their own id. If so, they declare themselves leader and add themselves to the *leader* relation. Then, a subset of processes determined by the input predicate A decides to send any id to their next neighbor that they have received which is not exceeded by their own.

At no point more than one process should have declared itself leader—regardless of the size of the ring. This property is enforced, e.g., if the initial message to be sent is given by the id of the sending process itself, i.e., $B(a,i,b)$ is given by the literal $(i = a)$.   □

Example 2. Consider the workflow of a conference management system as specified in Fig. 2. The specification maintains the binary predicates *Conflict* and

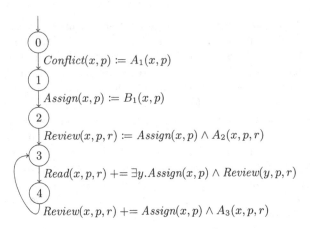

Fig. 2. FO safety game for the running conference management example

Assign together with the ternary predicates *Review* and *Read* to record conflicts of interest between PC members and papers, the paper assignment as well as the reports provided by PC members for papers. After the initial declaration of conflicts of interest, PC members write reviews for the papers they are assigned and update them after reading the other reviews to the same paper. The predicates A_1, A_2, A_3 represent choices by PC members, while the predicate B_1 is under control of the PC chair. The operator $+=$ adds tuples to a relation instead of replacing all contents. Specifically, $R\bar{y} += \varphi$ abbreviates $R\bar{y} := R\bar{y} \vee \varphi$. □

One property to be checked in Example 2 is that no PC member can learn anything about papers she has declared conflict with. *Noninterference* properties like this one can be formalized as *hyper-safety* properties, but can be reduced to *safety* properties of suitable *self-compositions* of the system in question [23]. This reduction is explained in the appendix at [31]. A plain safety property in this example would be, e.g., the more humble objective that no PC member x is going to read a report on a paper p which she herself has authored, i.e.,

$$\forall x, p, r. \neg(\mathit{Conflict}(x, p) \wedge \mathit{Read}(x, p, r))$$

Obvious choices for B_1 to enforce this property are

$$B_1(x, p) := \neg\mathit{Conflict}(x, p) \qquad \text{or}$$
$$B_1(x, p) := \mathit{false}$$

The second choice is rather trivial. The first choice, on the other hand, which happens to be the *weakest* possible, represents a meaningful strategy.

In this paper, we therefore investigate cases where *safety* is decidable and winning strategies for safety player are effectively computable and as weak as possible. For FO transition systems as specified by the Relational Modeling Language (RML) [27], typed update commands are restricted to preserve Bernays-Schönfinkel-Ramsey (also called *effectively propositional*) formulas. As a consequence, inductiveness of a universal invariant can be checked automatically. We show that this observation can be extended to FO safety *games*—given that appropriate winning strategies for safety player are either provided or can be effectively constructed (see Sect. 5). We also provide sufficient conditions under which a *weakest* such strategy can be constructed (see Sect. 6).

The question arises whether a similar transfer of the decidability of the logic to the decidability of the verification problem is possible for other decidable fragments of FO logic. A both natural and useful candidate is *monadic* logic. Interestingly, this transfer is only possible for specific *fragments* of monadic FO safety games, while in general safety is undecidable. For FO safety games using arbitrary predicates, we restrict ourselves to FO universal invariants only, since the safety properties, e.g., arising from noninterference can be expressed in this fragment. For universal invariants, we show how general methods for second order quantifier elimination can be instantiated to compute winning strategies. Existential SO quantifier elimination, though, is not always possible. Still, we provide a non-trivial class of universal invariants where optimal strategies can be synthesized. In the general case and, likewise, when existential FO quantifiers are introduced during game solving, we resort to *abstraction* as in [23]. This allows us to automatically construct strategies that guarantee safety or, in the case of information-flow, to enforce noninterference.

The paper is organized as follows. In Sects. 2 and 3, the notion of first-order safety games is introduced. We prove that safety player indeed has a positional winning strategy, whenever the game is safe. We also prove that safety of *finite* games is already inter-reducible to SO predicate logic. In Sect. 4, we consider the important class of FO safety games where all predicates are either monadic or boolean flags. Despite the fact that this logic is decidable and admits SO quantifier elimination, safety for this class is undecidable. Nonetheless, we identify three subclasses of monadic games where decidability is retained. Section 5 proves that even when a universally quantified FO candidate for an inductive invariant of the safety game is already provided, checking whether or not the candidate invariant is inductive, can be reduced to SO existential quantifier elimination. Section 6 provides background techniques for SO universal as well as existential quantifier elimination. It proves that for universal FO formulas, the construction of a *weakest* SO Hilbert choice operator can be reduced to SO quantifier elimination itself. Moreover, it provides sufficient conditions when a universal invariant for a FO safety game can effectively proven inductive and a corresponding weakest strategy for safety player be extracted. Based on the candidates for the second-order Hilbert choice operator from Sect. 6, and abstraction techniques from [23], a practical implementation is presented in Sect. 7 which allows to infer inductive invariants and FO definable winning strategies for safety player. Finally, Sect. 8 provides a more detailed comparison with related work while Sect. 9 concludes.

2   First-Order Transition Systems

Assume that we are given finite sets $\mathcal{R}_{state}, \mathcal{R}_{input}, \mathcal{C}$ of relation symbols and constants, respectively. A first-order (FO) transition system $\mathcal{S}$ (over $\mathcal{R}_{state}, \mathcal{R}_{input}$

and $\mathcal{C}$) consists of a control-flow graph (V, E, v_0) underlying $\mathcal{S}$ where V is a finite set of program points, $v_0 \in V$ is the start point and E is a finite set of edges between vertices in V. Each edge thereby is of the form (v, θ, v') where θ signifies how the first-order structure for program point v' is determined in terms of a first-order structure at program point v. Thus, θ is defined as a mapping which provides for each predicate $R \in \mathcal{R}_{state}$ of arity r, a first-order formula $R\theta$ with free variables from $\mathcal{C}$ as well as a dedicated sequence of fresh FO variables $\bar{y} = y_1 \ldots y_r$. Each formula $R\theta$ may use FO quantification, equality or disequality literals as well as predicates from $\mathcal{R}_{state}$. Additionally, we allow occurrences of dedicated *input* predicates from $\mathcal{R}_{input}$. For convenience, we denote a substitution θ of predicates $R_1, \ldots, R_n$ with $\varphi_1, \ldots, \varphi_n$ by

$$\theta = \{R_1\bar{y}_1 := \varphi_1, \ldots, R_n\bar{y}_n := \varphi_n\}$$

where $\bar{y}_j = y_1 \ldots y_{r_j}$ are the formal parameters of R_i and may occur free in φ_i.

Example 3. In the example from Fig. 2, the state predicates in $\mathcal{R}_{state}$ are *Conflict*, *Assign*, *Review* and *Read*, while the input predicates $\mathcal{R}_{input}$ consist of A_1, A_2, A_3 and B_1. As there are no global constants, $\mathcal{C}$ is empty. For the edge from node 2 to node 3, θ maps *Review* to the formula $Assign(y_1, y_2) \wedge A_2(y_1, y_2, y_3)$ and each other predicate R from $\mathcal{R}_{state}$ to itself (applied to the appropriate list of formal parameters). Thus, θ maps, e.g., *Conflict* to $Conflict(y_1, y_2)$. □

Let U be some universe and $\rho : \mathcal{C} \to U$ be a valuation of the globally free variables. Let $\mathcal{R}_{state}^n$ denote the set of predicates with arity n. A *state* $s : \bigcup_{n \geq 0} \mathcal{R}_{state}^n \times U^n \to \mathbb{B}$ is an evaluation of the predicates $\mathcal{R}_{state}$ by means of relations over U. Let States_U denote the set of all states with universe U. For an edge (v, θ, v'), a valuation ω of the input predicates, and states s, s', there is a transition from (v, s) to (v', s') iff for each predicate $R \in \mathcal{R}_{state}$ of arity r together with a vector $\bar{y} = y_1 \ldots y_r$ and an element $u \in U^r$

$$s', \rho \oplus \{y \mapsto u\} \models Ry \text{ iff } s \oplus \omega, \rho \oplus \{y \mapsto u\} \models (R\theta)$$

holds. Here, the operator "$\oplus$" is meant to update the assignment in the left argument with the variable/value pairs listed in the second argument. The set of all pairs $((v, s), (v', s'))$ constructed in this way, constitute the *transition relation* $\Delta_{U,\rho}$ of $\mathcal{S}$ (relative to universe U and valuation ρ). A finite *trace* from (v, s) to (v', s') is a finite sequence $(v_0, s_0), \ldots, (v_n, s_n)$ with $(v, s) = (v_0, s_0)$ and $(v_n, s_n) = (v', s')$ such that for each $i = 0, \ldots, n-1$, $((v_i, s_i), (v_{i+1}, s_{i+1})) \in \Delta_{U,\rho}$ holds. We denote the set of all finite traces of a transition system $\mathcal{S}$ as $\text{Traces}(\mathcal{S})$.

Example 4. Let us instantiate the running example from Fig. 2 for the universe $\{x_1, x_2, p_1, p_2, r_1\}$. A possible state attainable at node 2 could have *Conflict* $= \{(x_1, p_1)\}$, *Assign* $= \{(x_1, p_2), (x_2, p_1), (x_2, p_2)\}$ and all other relations empty. For the valuation $A_2 = \{(x_2, p_2, r_1)\}$ of the input predicate, there would be a transition to node 3 and a state where *Review* $= \{(x_2, p_2, r_1)\}$, with *Conflict* and *Assign* unchanged and *Read* still empty. □

3   First-Order Safety Games

For a first-order transition system, a FO *assertion* is a mapping I that assigns to each program point $v \in V$ a FO formula $I[v]$ with relation symbols from $\mathcal{R}_{state}$ and free variables from $\mathcal{C}$. Assume that additionally we are given a FO formula Init (also with relation symbols from $\mathcal{R}_{state}$ and free variables from $\mathcal{C}$) describing the potential initial states. The assertion I *holds* if for all universes U, all valuations ρ, all states s with $s, \rho \models$ Init and all finite traces τ from (v_0, s) to (v, s'), we have that $s', \rho \models I[v]$. In that case, we say that I is an *invariant* of the transition system (w.r.t. the initial condition Init).

Example 5. For our running example from Fig. 2, the initial condition specifies that all relations R in $\mathcal{R}_{state}$ are empty, i.e., Init $= \bigwedge_{R \in \mathcal{R}_{state}} \forall \bar{y}. \neg R \bar{y}$ where we assume that the length of the sequence of variables $\bar{y}$ matches the rank of the corresponding predicate R. Since the example assertion should hold everywhere, we have for every u, $I[u] = \forall x, p, r. \neg (\mathit{Conflict}(x, p) \wedge \mathit{Read}(x, p, r))$.   □

We now generalize FO transition systems to *FO safety games*, i.e., 2-player games where reachability player $\mathcal{A}$ aims at violating the given assertion I while safety player $\mathcal{B}$ tries to establish I as an invariant. To do so, player $\mathcal{A}$ is able to choose the universe, which outgoing edges are chosen at a given node and all interpretations of relations under his control. Accordingly, we partition the set of input predicates $\mathcal{R}_{input}$ into subsets $\mathcal{R}_{\mathcal{A}}$ and $\mathcal{R}_{\mathcal{B}}$. While player $\mathcal{B}$ controls the valuation of the predicates in $\mathcal{R}_{\mathcal{B}}$, player $\mathcal{A}$ has control over the valuations of predicates in $\mathcal{R}_{\mathcal{A}}$ as well as over the universe and the valuation of the FO variables in $\mathcal{C}$. For notational convenience, we assume that each substitution θ in the control-flow graph contains at most one input predicate, and that all these are distinct[1]. Also we consider a partition of the set E of edges into the subsets $E_{\mathcal{A}}$ and $E_{\mathcal{B}}$ where the substitutions only at edges from $E_{\mathcal{B}}$ may use predicates from $\mathcal{R}_{\mathcal{B}}$. Edges in $E_{\mathcal{A}}$ or $E_{\mathcal{B}}$ will also be called $\mathcal{A}$-edges or $\mathcal{B}$-edges, respectively. For a particular universe U and valuation ρ, a trace τ starting in some (v_0, s) with $s, \rho \models$ Init and ending in some pair (v, s') is considered a *play*. For a given play, player $\mathcal{A}$ *wins* iff $s', \rho \not\models I[v]$ and player $\mathcal{B}$ wins otherwise.

A *strategy* σ for player $\mathcal{B}$ is a mapping which for each $\mathcal{B}$-edge $e = (u, \theta, v)$ with input predicate B_e (of some arity r), each universe U, valuation ρ, each state s and each play τ reaching (u, s), returns a relation $B' \subseteq U^r$. Thus, σ provides for each universe, the history of the play and the next edge controlled by $\mathcal{B}$, a possible choice. σ is *positional* or *memoryless*, if it depends on the universe U, the valuation ρ, the state s and the $\mathcal{B}$-edge (u, θ, v) only.

A play τ *conforms* to a strategy σ for safety player $\mathcal{B}$, if all input relations at $\mathcal{B}$-edges occurring in τ are chosen according to σ. The strategy σ is *winning* for $\mathcal{B}$ if $\mathcal{B}$ wins all plays that conform to σ. An FO safety game can be won by $\mathcal{B}$ iff there exists a winning strategy for $\mathcal{B}$. In this case, the game is *safe*.

---

[1] In general, edges may use multiple input predicates of the same type. This can, however, always be simulated by a sequence of edges that stores the contents of the input relations in auxiliary predicates from $\mathcal{R}_{state}$ one by one, before realizing the substitution of the initial edge by means of the auxiliary predicates.

Example 6. In the running conference management Example 2, player $\mathcal{A}$, who wants to reach a state where the invariant from Example 5 is violated (a state where someone reads a review to his own paper before the official release) has control over the predicates A_1, A_2, A_3 and thus provides the values for the predicates *Conflict* and *Review* and also determines how often the loop body is iterated. Player $\mathcal{B}$ only has control over predicate B_1 which is used to determine the value of predicate *Assign*. This particular game is *safe*, and player $\mathcal{B}$ has several winning strategies, e.g., $B_1(x,p) := \neg Conflict(x,p)$.   □

Lemma 1. *If there exists a winning strategy for player $\mathcal{B}$, then there also exists a winning strategy that is positional.*

Proof. Once a universe U is fixed, together with a valuation ρ of the globally free variables, the FO safety game G turns into a reachability game $G_{U,\rho}$ where the positions are given by all pairs $(v,s) \in V \times \mathsf{States}_U$ (controlled by reachability player $\mathcal{A}$) together with all pairs $(s,e) \in \mathsf{States}_U \times E$ controlled by safety player $\mathcal{B}$ if $e \in E_\mathcal{B}$ and by $\mathcal{A}$ otherwise. For an edge $e = (v, \theta, v')$ in G, $G_{U,\rho}$ contains all edges $(v,s) \to (s,e)$, together with all edges $(s,e) \to (v',s')$ where s' is a successor state of s w.r.t. e and ρ.

Let $\mathsf{Init}_{U,\rho}$ denote the set of all positions (v_0, s) where $s, \rho \models \mathsf{Init}$, and $I_{U,\rho}$ the set of all positions (v,s) where $s, \rho \models I[v]$ together with all positions (s,e) where $s, \rho \models I[v]$ for edges e starting in v. Then $G_{U,\rho}$ is safe iff safety player $\mathcal{B}$ has a strategy $\sigma_{U,\rho}$ to force each play started in some position $\mathsf{Init}_{U,\rho}$ to stay within the set $I_{U,\rho}$. Assuming the axiom of choice for set theory, the set of positions can be well-ordered. Therefore, the strategy $\sigma_{U,\rho}$ for safety player $\mathcal{B}$ can be chosen positionally, see, e.g., Lemma 2.12 of [21]. Putting all positional strategies $\sigma_{U,\rho}$ for safety player $\mathcal{B}$ together, we obtain a single positional strategy for $\mathcal{B}$.   □

In case the game is safe, we are interested in strategies that can be included into the FO transition system itself, i.e., are themselves first-order definable. Lemma 1 as is, gives no clue whether or not there is a winning strategy which is positional and can be expressed in FO logic, let alone be effectively computed.

Theorem 1. *There exist safe FO safety games where no winning strategy is expressible in FO logic.*

Proof. Consider a game with $\mathcal{R}_{state} = \{E, R_1, R_2\}$, $\mathcal{R}_\mathcal{A} = \{A_1, A_2\}$ and $\mathcal{R}_\mathcal{B} = \{B_1\}$, performing three steps in sequence:

$$E(x,y) := A_1(x,y); \quad R_1(x,y) := B_1(x,y); \quad R_2(x,y) := A_2(x,y)$$

In this example, reachability player $\mathcal{A}$ chooses an arbitrary relation E, then safety player $\mathcal{B}$ chooses R_1 and player $\mathcal{A}$ chooses R_2. The assertion I ensures that at the endpoint R_1 is at least the transitive closure of E and R_1 is smaller or equal to R_2 (provided $\mathcal{A}$ chose R_2 to include the closure of E) i.e.,

$$\mathsf{closure}(R_2, E) \to (\mathsf{closure}(R_1, E) \wedge \forall x, y. (R_1(x,y) \to R_2(x,y)))$$

where $\mathsf{closure}(R, E)$ is given by $\forall x, y.R(x, y) \leftarrow (E(x, y) \lor \exists z.R(x, z) \land E(z, y))$. The only winning strategy for safety player $\mathcal{B}$ (choosing R_1) is to select the smallest relation R_1 satisfying $closure(R_1, E)$, which is the transitive closure of E. In this case, no matter what reachability player $\mathcal{A}$ chooses for R_2, safety player $\mathcal{B}$ wins, but the winning strategy for $\mathcal{B}$ is not expressible in FO logic. $\square$

Despite this negative result, effective means are sought for of computing FO definable strategies, whenever they exist. In order to do so, we rely on a *weakest precondition* operator $[\![e]\!]^\top$ corresponding to edge $e = (u, \theta, v)$ of the control-flow graph of a FO safety game $\mathcal{T}$ by

$$[\![e]\!]^\top \Psi = \begin{cases} \forall A_e.(\Psi\theta) \text{ if } e \ \mathcal{A}\text{-edge} \\ \exists B_e.(\Psi\theta) \text{ if } e \ \mathcal{B}\text{-edge} \end{cases}$$

The weakest pre-condition operator captures the minimal requirement at the start point of an edge to meet the post-condition Ψ at the end point. That operator allows to define the following iteration: Let $\mathcal{T}$ denote a game and I an assertion. For $h \geq 0$, let the assignment $\Psi^{(h)}$ of program points v to formulas be

$$\begin{aligned}
\Psi^{(0)}[v] &= I[v] \\
\Psi^{(h)}[v] &= \Psi^{(h-1)}[v] \land \bigwedge_{e \in out(v)} [\![e]\!]^\top \Psi^{(h-1)} \quad \text{for } h > 0
\end{aligned} \tag{1}$$

where $out(v)$ are the outgoing edges of node v. Then the following holds:

Theorem 2. *A FO safety game $\mathcal{T}$ is safe iff $\mathsf{Init} \to \Psi^{(h)}[v_0]$ holds for all $h \geq 0$.*

The proof can be found in the appendix at [31]. The characterization of safety due to Theorem 2 is precise—but may require to construct infinitely many $\Psi^{(h)}$. Whenever, though, the safety game $\mathcal{T}$ is *finite*, i.e., the underlying control-flow graph of G is acyclic, then G is safe iff $\mathsf{Init} \to \Psi^{(h)}[v_0]$ where h equals the length of the longest path in the control-flow graph of G starting in v_0. As a result, we get that *finite* first order safety games are as powerful as second order logic.

Theorem 3. *Deciding a finite FO safety game with predicates from $\mathcal{R}_{state}$ is inter-reducible to satisfiability of SO formulas with predicates from $\mathcal{R}_{state}$.*

Proof. We already showed that solving a finite FO safety game can be achieved by solving the SO formula $\psi^{(h)}$ for some sufficiently large h. For the reverse implication, consider an arbitrary closed formula φ in SO Logic. W.l.o.g., assume that φ has no function symbols and is in prenex normal form where no SO Quantifier falls into the scope of a FO quantifier [19]. Thus, φ is of the form $Q_1C_1 \ldots Q_nC_n. \psi$ where all Q_n are SO quantifiers and ψ is a relational formula in FO logic.

We then construct a FO safety game $\mathcal{T}$ as follows. The set $\mathcal{R}_{state}$ of predicates consists of all predicates that occur freely in φ together with copies R_i' of all quantified relations C_i. The control-flow graph consists of $n+1$ nodes $v_0, \ldots, v_n$, together with edges (v_{i-1}, θ_i, v_i) for $i = 1, \ldots, n$. Thus, the maximal length of any path is exactly n. An edge $e = (v_{i-1}, \theta_i, v_i)$ is used to simulate the quantifier $Q_i C_i$. The substitution θ_i is the identity on all predicates from $\mathcal{R}_{state}$ except R'_i which is mapped to C_i. If Q_i is a universal quantifier, C_i is included into $\mathcal{R}_\mathcal{A}$, and e is an $\mathcal{A}$-edge. Similarly, if Q_i is existential, C_i is included into $\mathcal{R}_\mathcal{B}$ and e is a $\mathcal{B}$-edge. Assume that ψ' is obtained from ψ by replacing every relation R_i with R'_i. As FO assertion I, we then use $I[v_i] = true$ for $i = 0, \ldots, n-1$ and $I[v_n] = \psi'$. Then $\Psi^{(n)}[v_n] = \varphi$. Accordingly for $\mathsf{Init} = true$, player $\mathcal{B}$ can win the game iff φ is universally true. $\qquad\square$

Theorem 3 implies that a FO definable winning strategy for safety player $\mathcal{B}$ (if it exists) can be constructed whenever the SO quantifiers introduced by the choices of the respective players can be eliminated. Theorem 3, though, gives no clue *how* to decide whether or not safety player $\mathcal{B}$ has a winning strategy and if so, whether it can be effectively represented.

4 Monadic FO Safety Games

Assuming that the universe is finite and bounded in size by some $h \geq 0$, then FO games reduce to finite games (of tremendous size, though). This means that, at least in principle, both checking of invariants as well as the construction of a winning strategy (in case that the game is safe) is effectively possible. A more complicated scenario arises when the universe consists of several disjoints *sorts* of which some are bounded in size and some are unbounded.

We will now consider the special case where each predicate has at most one argument which takes elements of an unbounded sort. In the conference management example, we could, e.g., assume that PC members, papers and reports constitute disjoint sorts of bounded cardinalities, while the number of (versions of) reviews is unbounded. By encoding the tuples of elements of finite sorts into predicate names, we obtain FO games where all predicates are either nullary or *monadic*. Monadic FO logic is remarkable since satisfiability of formulas in that logic is decidable, and monadic SO quantifiers can be effectively eliminated [4,35]. Due to Theorem 3, we therefore conclude for *finite* monadic safety games that safety is decidable. Moreover, in case the game is safe, a positional winning strategy for safety player $\mathcal{B}$ can be effectively computed.

Monadic safety games which are not finite, turn out to be very close in expressive power to *multi-counter machines*, for which reachability is undecidable [17,29]. The first statement of the following theorem has been communicated to us by Igor Walukiewicz:

Theorem 4. *For monadic safety games, safety is undecidable when one of the following conditions is met:*

1. *there are both $\mathcal{A}$-edges as well as $\mathcal{B}$-edges;*
2. *there are $\mathcal{A}$-edges and substitutions with equalities or disequalities;*
3. *there are $\mathcal{B}$-edges and substitutions with equalities or disequalities.*

The proof of statement (1) is by using monadic predicates to simulate the counters of a multi-counter machine. Statements (2) and (3) follow from the observation that one player in this simulation can be replaced by substitutions using equality or disequality literals (see [31] for details of the simulation).

There are, though, interesting cases that do not fall into the listed classes and can be effectively decided. Let us first consider monadic safety games where no predicate is under the control of either player, i.e., $\mathcal{R}_\mathcal{A} = \mathcal{R}_\mathcal{B} = \emptyset$, but both equalities and disequalities are allowed. Then, safety of the game collapses to the question if player $\mathcal{A}$ can pick universe and control-flow such that the assertion is violated at some point. For this case, we show that the conjunction of preconditions from Sect. 3 necessarily stabilizes.

Theorem 5. *Assume that $\mathcal{T}$ is a monadic safety game, possibly containing equalities and/or disequalities with $\mathcal{R}_\mathcal{A} = \mathcal{R}_\mathcal{B} = \emptyset$. Then for some $h \geq 0$, $\Psi^{(h)} = \Psi^{(h+1)}$. Therefore, safety of $\mathcal{T}$ is decidable.*

Theorem 5 relies on the observation that when applying substitutions alone, i.e., without additional SO quantification, the number of equalities and disequalities involving FO variables, remains bounded. Our proof relies on variants of the *counting quantifier normal form* for monadic FO formulas [4] (see the appendix of [31]).

Interestingly, decidability is also retained for assertions I that only contain disequalities, if no equalities between bound variables are introduced during the weakest precondition computation. This can only be guaranteed if safety player $\mathcal{B}$ does not have control over any predicates.[2]

Theorem 6. *Assume that $\mathcal{T}$ is a monadic safety game without $\mathcal{B}$-edges (i.e. $\mathcal{R}_\mathcal{B} = \emptyset$) and*

1. *there are no disequalities between bound variables in I,*
2. *in all literals $x = y$ or $x \neq y$ in Init and substitutions θ, $x \in \mathcal{C}$ or $y \in \mathcal{C}$.*

Then it is decidable whether $\mathcal{T}$ is safe.

The proof is based on the following observation: Assume that $\mathcal{C}$ is a set of variables of cardinality d, and formulas φ_1, φ_2 have free variables only from $\mathcal{C}$. If φ_1, φ_2 contain no disequalities between bound variables, then φ_1, φ_2 are equivalent for all models and all valuations ρ iff they are equivalent for models and valuations with *multiplicity* exceeding d. Here, the *multiplicity* $\mu(s)$ of a model s is the minimal cardinality of a non-empty equivalence class of U w.r.t. *indistinguishability*. We call two elements u, u' of the universe U indistinguishable in a model s iff $(s, \{x \mapsto u\} \models Rx) \leftrightarrow (s, \{x \mapsto u'\} \models Rx)$ for all relations R. Then, when computing $\Psi^{(h)}$, we use an *abstraction* by formulas without equalities, which is shown to be a *weakest strengthening* (see the appendix at [31]).

Analogously, decidability is retained for assertions that only contain positive equalities if there are no disequalities introduced during the weakest precondition

---

[2] Predicates under the control of player $\mathcal{B}$ can be used to introduce equalities through SO existential quantifier elimination (see [31]).

computation. This is only the case when $\mathcal{R}_{\mathcal{A}} = \emptyset$, i.e., reachability player $\mathcal{A}$ only selects universe and control-flow path. As a consequence, we obtain:

Theorem 7. *Assume that $\mathcal{T}$ is a monadic safety game without $\mathcal{A}$-edges where*

1. *there are no equalities between bound variables in I,*
2. *in all literals $x = y, x \neq y$ in* Init *and substitutions θ, either $x \in \mathcal{C}$ or $y \in \mathcal{C}$.*

Then it is decidable whether $\mathcal{T}$ is safe.

The proof is analogous to the Proof of Theorem 6 where the abstraction of equalities now is replaced with an abstraction of disequalities (see [31]). In summary, we have shown that even though monadic logic is decidable, 2-player monadic FO safety games are undecidable in general. However, for games where one of the players does not choose interpretations for any relation, decidability can be salvaged if the safety condition has acceptable equality/disequality literals only and neither Init, nor the transition relation introduce further equality/disequality literals between bound variables.

5   Proving Invariants Inductive

Even though the general problem of verification is already hard for monadic FO games, there are useful incomplete algorithms to still prove general FO safety games safe. One approach for verifying infinite state systems is to come up with a candidate invariant which then is proven *inductive* (see, e.g., [27]). This idea can be extended to *safety games* where, additionally strategies must either be provided or extracted.

In the context of FO safety games, an invariant Ψ is called *inductive* iff for all edges $e = (u, \theta, v)$, $\Psi[u] \to \llbracket e \rrbracket^{\top}(\Psi[v])$ holds. We have:

Lemma 2. *Assume that Ψ is inductive, and $\Psi[v] \to I[v]$ for all nodes v. Then*

1. *For all $h \geq 0$, $\Psi[v] \to \Psi^{(h)}[v]$;*
2. *The game G is safe, whenever* Init $\to \Psi[v_0]$ *holds.*

We remark that, under the assumptions of Lemma 2, a *positional* winning strategy σ for safety player $\mathcal{B}$ exists. Checking an FO safety game $\mathcal{T}$ for safety thus boils down to the following tasks:

1. Come up with a candidate invariant Ψ so that
   - $\Psi[v] \to I[v]$ for all nodes v, and
   - Init $\to \Psi[v_0]$ hold;
2. Come up with a strategy σ which assigns some FO formula to each predicate in $\mathcal{R}_{\mathcal{B}}$;
3. Prove that Ψ is inductive for the FO transition system $\mathcal{T}\sigma$ which is obtained from $\mathcal{T}$ by substituting each occurrence of B with $\sigma(B)$ for all $B \in \mathcal{R}_{\mathcal{B}}$.

For monadic FO safety games, we thereby obtain:

Theorem 8. *Assume that $\mathcal{T}$ is a monadic FO safety game with initial condition* Init *and assertion I. Assume further that Ψ is a monadic FO invariant, i.e., maps each program point to a monadic formula. Then the following holds:*

1. *It is decidable whether* Init $\rightarrow \Psi[v_0]$ *as well as $\Psi[v] \rightarrow I[v]$ holds for each program point v;*
2. *It is decidable whether Ψ is inductive, and if so, an FO definable strategy σ can be constructed which upholds Ψ.*

The proof is by showing that all formulas fall into a decidable fragment—in this case Monadic Second Order logic. A *monadic* FO safety game can thus be proven safe by providing an appropriate monadic FO invariant Ψ: the winning strategy itself can be effectively computed.

Another important instance is when the candidate invariant Ψ as well as I consists of universal FO formulas only, while Init is in the *Bernays-Schönfinkel-Ramsey* (BSR) fragment[3].

Theorem 9. *Let $\mathcal{T}$ denote a safety game where each substitution θ occurring at edges of the control-flow graph uses non-nested FO quantifiers only. Let Ψ denote a universal FO invariant for $\mathcal{T}$, i.e., $\Psi[v]$ is a universal FO formula for each node v.*

1. *It is decidable whether* Init $\rightarrow \Psi[v_0]$ *as well as $\Psi[v] \rightarrow I[v]$ holds for each program point v;*
2. *Assume that no $B \in \mathcal{R}_\mathcal{B}$ occurs in the scope of an existential FO quantifier, and σ is a strategy which provides a universal FO formula for each $B \in \mathcal{R}_\mathcal{B}$. Then it is decidable whether or not Ψ is inductive for $\mathcal{T}\sigma$.*

The proof is by showing that all mentioned formulas can be solved by checking satisfiability of a formula in the decidable fragment $\exists^*\forall^*$FOL. Theorem 9 states that (under mild restrictions on the substitutions occurring at $\mathcal{B}$-edges), the candidate invariant Ψ can be checked for inductiveness—at least when a positional strategy of $\mathcal{B}$ is provided which is expressed by means of universal FO formulas. In particular, this implies decidability for the case when the set $E_\mathcal{B}$ is empty. The proof works by showing that all verification conditions fall into the BSR fragment of FO Logic. For the verification of inductive invariants for FO transition systems (no $\mathcal{B}$ edges), the IVY system essentially relies on the observations summarized in Theorem 9 [27].

Besides finding promising strategies σ, the question remains how for a given assertion I a suitable *inductive* invariant can be inferred. One option is to iteratively compute the sequence $\Psi^{(h)}, h \geq 0$ as in (1). In general that iteration may never reach a fixpoint. Here, however, FO definability implies termination:

---

[3] The Bernays-Schönfinkel-Ramsey fragment contains all formulas of First Order Logic that have a quantifier prefix of $\exists^*\forall^*$ and do not contain function symbols. Satisfiability of formulas in BSR is known to be decidable [28].

Theorem 10. *Assume that for all program points u and $h \geq 0$, $\Psi^{(h)}[u]$ is FO definable as well as the infinite conjunction $\bigwedge_{h \geq 0} \Psi^{(h)}[u]$. Then there exists some $m \geq 0$ such that $\Psi^{(m)} = \Psi^{(m+k)}$ holds for each $k \geq 0$. Thus, $\bigwedge_{h \geq 0} \Psi^{(h)}[u] = \Psi^{(m)}[u]$ for all u.*

Proof. Let φ_u denote the first order formula which is equivalent $\bigwedge_{h \geq 0} \Psi^{(h)}[u]$. In particular, this means that $\varphi_u \rightarrow \Psi^{(h)}[u]$ for each $h \geq 0$. On the other hand, we know that $\bigwedge_{h \geq 0} \Psi^{(h)}[u]$ implies φ_u. Since φ_u as well as each $\Psi^{(h)}[u]$ are assumed to be FO definable, it follows from Gödel's compactness theorem that there is a *finite* subset $J \subseteq \mathcal{N}$ such that $\bigwedge_{h \in J} \Psi^{(h)}[u]$ implies φ_u. Let m be the maximal element in J. Then, $\bigwedge_{h \in J} \Psi^{(h)}[u] = \Psi^{(m)}[u]$ since the $\Psi^{(h)}[u]$ form a decreasing sequence of formulas. Together, this proves that φ_u is equivalent to $\Psi^{(m)}[u]$. $\square$

Theorem 10 proves that if there exists an inductive invariant proving a given FO game safe, then fixpoint iteration will definitely terminate and find it.

For the case of *monadic* FO safety games, this means that the corresponding infinite conjunction is not always FO definable—otherwise decidability would follow. In general, not every invariant I can be strengthened to an inductive Ψ, and universal strategies need not be sufficient to win a universal safety game. Nonetheless, there is a variety of non-trivial cases where existential SO quantifiers can be effectively eliminated, e.g., by Second Order quantifier elimination algorithms SCAN or DLS* (see the overview in [14]). In our case, in addition to plain elimination we need an explicit construction of the corresponding strategy, expressed as a FO formula. We remark that following Theorem 9, it is not necessary to perform *exact* quantifier elimination: instead, a sufficiently weak *strengthening* may suffice. Techniques for such *approximate* SO existential quantifier elimination are provided in the next section.

6   Hilbert's Choice Operator for Second Order Quantifiers

In this section, we concentrate on formulas with universal FO quantifiers only. First, we recall the following observation:

Lemma 3. (see Fact 1, [23]). *Consider a disjunction c of the form*

$$F \vee \bigvee_{i=1}^{k} A\bar{z}_i \vee \bigvee_{j=1}^{l} \neg A\bar{z}'_i$$

for some formula F without occurrences of predicate A. Then $\forall A.c$ is equivalent to $F \vee \bigvee_{i,j}(\bar{z}_i = \bar{z}'_j)$ for sequences of variables $\bar{z}_i = z_{i1} \ldots z_{ir}$, $\bar{z}'_j = z'_{j1} \ldots z'_{jr}$, where $\bar{z}_i = \bar{z}_j$ is an abbreviation for $\bigwedge_{k=1}^{r} z_{ik} = z'_{jk}$. $\square$

As a consequence, universal SO quantification can always be eliminated from universal formulas.

Example 7. Consider the assertion $I = \forall x, p, r. \neg (\mathit{Conflict}(x, p) \wedge \mathit{Review}(x, p, r))$ and substitution θ from the edge between program points 2 and 3 in Fig. 2, given by $\mathit{Review}(x, p, r) := \mathit{Assign}(x, p) \wedge A_3(x, p, r)$ and $\mathit{Conflict}(x, p) := \mathit{Conflict}(x, p)$. Since $I\theta$ contains only negative occurrences of A_3, we obtain:

$$\forall A_3.(I\theta) = \forall x, p, r. \forall A_3. \neg \mathit{Conflict}(x, p) \vee \neg \mathit{Assign}(x, p) \vee \neg A_3(x, p, r)$$
$$= \forall x, p, r. \neg \mathit{Conflict}(x, p) \vee \neg \mathit{Assign}(x, p)$$

□

As we have seen in Sect. 5, checking whether a universal FO invariant is inductive can be reduced to SO existential quantifier elimination. While universal SO quantifiers can always be eliminated in formulas with universal FO quantifiers only, this is not necessarily the case for existential SO quantifiers. As already observed by Ackermann [1], the formula

$$\exists B. \, Ba \wedge \neg Bb \wedge \forall x, y. \neg Bx \vee \neg Rxy \vee By$$

expresses that b is not reachable from a via the edge relation R and thus cannot be expressed in FO logic. This negative result, though, does not exclude that in a variety of meaningful cases, equivalent FO formulas can be constructed. For formulas with universal FO quantifiers only, we provide a simplified algorithm for existential SO quantifier elimination. Moreover, we show that the construction of a *weakest* SO *Hilbert choice operator* can be reduced to existential SO quantifier elimination itself. In terms of FO safety games, the latter operator enables us to extract *weakest* winning strategies for safety player $\mathcal{B}$. For an in-depth treatment on SO existential quantifier elimination, we refer to [14].

Let φ denote some universally quantified formula, possibly containing a predicate B of arity r. Let $\bar{y} = y_1 \ldots y_r$, and $\bar{y}' = y_1' \ldots y_r'$. We remark that for *any* formula ψ with free variables in y, $\varphi[\psi/B] \rightarrow \exists B. \varphi$ holds. Here, this SO substitution means that every literal $B\bar{z}$ and every literal $\neg B\bar{z}'$ is replaced with $\psi[\bar{z}/\bar{y}]$ and $\neg \psi[\bar{z}'/\bar{y}]$, respectively. Let $H_{B,\varphi}$ denote the set of *all* FO formulas ψ such that $\exists B. \varphi$ is equivalent to $\varphi[\psi/B]$. A general construction for B and φ (at least from some suitably restricted class of formulas) of some FO formula $\psi \in H_{B,\varphi}$ is an instance of Hilbert's (second-order) *choice* operator. If it exists, we write $\psi = \mathcal{H}_B(\varphi)$. In order to better understand the construction of such operators, we prefer to consider universal FO formulas in *normal form*.

Lemma 4. *Every universal FO formula φ possibly containing occurrences of B is equivalent to a formula*

$$E \wedge (\forall \bar{y}.F \vee B\bar{y}) \wedge (\forall \bar{y}'.G \vee \neg B\bar{y}') \wedge (\forall \bar{y}\bar{y}'.H \vee B\bar{y} \vee \neg B\bar{y}') \qquad (2)$$

where E, F, G, H are universal formulas without B.

For the corresponding construction see [31]. The construction introduces disequalities between variables as well as fresh auxiliary variables $\bar{y}$ and $\bar{y}'$, where the sequence $\bar{y}'$ is only required when both positive and negative B literals occur within the same clause. In case these are missing, the formula is said to be in *simple* normal form. For that case, Ackermann's lemma applies:

Lemma 5. (Ackermann's lemma [1]). *Assume that φ is in simple normal form $E \wedge (\forall \bar{y}.F \vee B\bar{y}) \wedge (\forall \bar{y}.G \vee \neg B\bar{y})$. Then we have:*

1. *$\exists B.\varphi = E \wedge (\forall \bar{y}.F \vee G)$;*
2. *For every FO formula ψ, $\exists B.\varphi = \varphi[\psi/B]$ iff $(E \wedge \neg F) \to \psi$ and $\psi \to (\neg E \vee G)$.*   □

For formulas in simple normal form a Hilbert choice operator thus is given by:

$$\mathcal{H}_B\varphi = \neg E \vee G \tag{3}$$

—which is the *weakest* ψ for which $\exists B.\varphi$ is equivalent to $\varphi[\psi/B]$.

Example 8. For the invariant from Example 5, the weakest precondition w.r.t. the second statement amounts to: $\exists B_1.\forall x, p.\neg Conflict(x, p) \vee \neg B_1(x, p)$ which is *true* for any formula Ψ for B_1 (with free x, p) implying $\neg Conflict(x, p)$.   □

The *strongest* solution according to Example 8 thus is that the PC chair decides to assign papers to *no* PC member. While guaranteeing safety, this choice is not very useful. The *weakest* choice on the other hand, provides us here with a decent strategy. In the following we therefore will aim at constructing as *weak* strategies as possible.

Ackermann's Lemma gives rise to a nontrivial class of safety games where existential SO quantifier elimination succeeds. We call $B \in \mathcal{R}_B$ *ackermannian* in the substitution θ iff for every predicate $R \in \mathcal{R}_{state}$, if $\theta(R)$ contains B literals, $\theta(R)$ is quantifierfree and its CNF does not contain clauses with both positive and negative B literals.

Theorem 11. *Assume we are given a FO Safety Game $\mathcal{T}$ where all substitutions contain nonnested quantifiers only, and a universal inductive invariant Ψ. Assume further that the following holds:*

1. *All predicates B under the control of safety player $\mathcal{B}$ are ackermannian in all substitutions θ;*
2. *For every $\mathcal{B}$-edge $e = (u, \theta, v)$, every clause of $\Psi[v]$ contains at most one literal with a predicate R where $\theta(R)$ has a predicate from $\mathcal{R}_B$.*

Then the weakest FO strategy for safety player $\mathcal{B}$ can be effectively computed for which Ψ is inductive.

Proof. Consider an edge (u, θ, v) where the predicate B under control of safety player occurs in θ. Assume that $\Psi[v] = \forall \bar{z}.\Psi'$ where Ψ' is quantifierfree and in conjunctive normal form. Since θ is ackermannian and due to the restrictions given for Ψ', Ψ' can be written as $\Psi' = \Psi_0 \wedge \Psi_1 \wedge \Psi_2$ where Ψ_0, Ψ_1, Ψ_2 are the conjunctions of clauses c of Ψ' where $\theta(c)$ contains none, only positive or only negative occurrences of B-literals, respectively. In particular, $\theta(\Psi_0)$ is a FO formula without nested quantifiers. The formula $\theta(\Psi_1)$ is equivalent to a conjunction of formulas of the form $F \vee B\bar{y}_1 \vee \ldots B\bar{y}_r$ where F has non-nested quantifiers only, which thus are equivalent to

$$\forall \bar{y}.F \vee (\bar{y}_1 \neq \bar{y}) \wedge \ldots \wedge (\bar{y}_r \neq \bar{y}) \vee B\bar{y}$$

Likewise, $\theta(\Psi_2)$ is equivalent to a conjunction of formulas of the form $G \vee \neg B\bar{y}_1 \vee \ldots \neg B\bar{y}_r$ where G has non-nested quantifiers only, which thus are equivalent to

$$\forall \bar{y}.G \vee (\bar{y}_1 \neq \bar{y}) \wedge \ldots \wedge (\bar{y}_r \neq \bar{y}) \vee \neg B\bar{y}$$

Therefore, we can apply Ackermann's lemma to obtain a formula $\bar{\Psi}$ in $\forall^* \exists^*$FOL equivalent to $\exists B. \theta(\Psi[v])$. Likewise, we obtain a weakest FO formula φ for B so that $\theta(\Psi[v])[\varphi/B] = \bar{\Psi}$. Since $\Psi[u]$ only contains universal quantifiers, $\Psi[u] \to \bar{\Psi}$ is effectively decidable. □

Example 9. Consider the leader election protocol from Example 1, together with the invariant from [27]. Therein, the predicate B is ackermannian, and *msg* appears once in two different clauses of the invariant. Thus by Theorem 11, the weakest safe strategy for player $\mathcal{B}$ can be effectively computed. Our solver, described in Sect. 7 finds it to be

$$B(a,i,b) := \neg E \vee \neg next(a,b) \vee \begin{pmatrix} \forall n. \ (i \geq n \vee b \neq i) \wedge \\ \forall n. \ (\neg between(b,i,n) \vee i > n) \end{pmatrix}$$

where E axiomatizes the ring architecture, i.e., the predicate *between* as the transitive closure of *next* together with the predicate $\leq$. The given strategy is weaker than the intuitive (and also safe) strategy of $(i = a)$, and allows for more behaviours—for example a can send messages that are greater than its own id in case they are not greater than the ids of nodes along the way from b back to a. □

In general, though, existential SO quantifier elimination must be applied to universally quantified formulas which cannot be brought into simple normal form. In particular, we provide a sequence of *candidates* for the Hilbert choice operator which provides the *weakest* Hilbert choice operator—whenever it is FO definable. Consider a formula φ in normal form (2). Therein, the sub-formula $\neg H$ can be understood as a binary predicate between the variables $\bar{y}'$ and $\bar{y}$ which may be composed, iterated, post-applied to predicates on $\bar{y}'$ and pre-applied to predicates on $\bar{y}$. We define H^k, $k \geq 0$, with free variables from $\bar{y}, \bar{y}'$ by

$$H^0 = \bar{y} \neq \bar{y}'$$
$$H^k = \forall \bar{y}_1.H^{k-1}[\bar{y}_1/\bar{y}'] \vee H[\bar{y}_1/\bar{y}] \qquad \text{for } k > 0$$

We remark that by this definition,

$$H^{k+l} = \forall y_1.H^k[\bar{y}_1/\bar{y}'] \vee H^l[\bar{y}_1/\bar{y}]$$

for all $k, l \geq 0$. Furthermore, we define the formulas:

$$G \circ H^k = \forall \bar{y}.G[\bar{y}/\bar{y}'] \vee H^k$$
$$G \circ H^k \circ F = \forall \bar{y}'.(G \circ H^k) \vee F[\bar{y}'/\bar{y}]$$

Then, we have:

Lemma 6. *If* $\exists B.\varphi$ *is FO definable, then it is equivalent to* $E \wedge \bigwedge_{i=0}^{k} G \circ H^i \circ F$ *for some* $k \geq 0$.

Starting from G and iteratively composing with H, provides us with a sequence of candidate SO Hilbert choice operators. Let

$$\gamma_k = \neg E \vee \bigwedge_{i=0}^{k}(G \circ H^i)[\bar{y}/\bar{y}'] \tag{4}$$

for $k \geq 0$. The candidate γ_k takes all *i*fold compositions of H with $i \leq k$ into account. Then the following holds:

Lemma 7. *For every* $k \geq 0$,

1. $\varphi[\gamma_k/B]$ *implies* $\exists B.\varphi$;
2. *If* $\exists B.\varphi$ *is equivalent to* $\varphi[\psi/B]$ *for some FO formula* ψ, *then* $\psi \to \gamma_k$.
3. $\gamma_{k+1} \to \gamma_k$, *and if* $\gamma_k \to \gamma_{k+1}$, *then* $\varphi[\gamma_k/B] = \exists B.\varphi$.

As a result, the γ_k form a decreasing sequence of candidate strategies for safety player $\mathcal{B}$. We remark that due to statement (2), the sequence γ_k results in the *weakest* Hilbert choice operator—whenever it becomes stable.

We close this section by noting that there is a SO Hilbert choice operator which can be expressed in SO logic itself. The following theorem is related to Corollary 6.20 of [14], but avoids the explicit use of fixpoint operators in the logic.

Theorem 12. *The weakest Hilbert choice operator* $\mathcal{H}_B\varphi$ *for the universal formula* (2) *is definable by the SO formula:*

$$\neg E \vee \exists B. B\bar{y} \wedge (\forall \bar{y}'.G \vee \neg B\bar{y}') \wedge (\forall \bar{y}\bar{y}'.H \vee B\bar{y} \vee \neg B\bar{y}')$$

The weakest Hilbert choice operator itself can thus be obtained by SO existential quantifier elimination. The proof is by rewriting the formula and can be found in [31].

7   Implementation

We have extended our solver NIWO for FO transition systems [23] to a solver for FO safety games which is able to verify inductive universal FO invariants and extract corresponding winning strategies for safety player $\mathcal{B}$. It has been packaged and published under [32]. Our solver supports *inference* of inductive invariants if the given candidate invariant is not yet inductive. For that it relies on the abstraction techniques from [23] to strengthen arbitrary FO formulas by means of FO formulas using universal FO quantifiers only. For the simplification of FO formulas as well as for satisfiability of BSR formulas, it relies on the EPR algorithms of the automated theorem prover Z3 [9].

We evaluate our solver on three kinds of benchmark problems. First, we consider FO games with safety properties such as the running example "Conference, Safety" from Fig. 2 and Example 5. For all of its variants, the fixpoint iteration

Name	Mode	Size	Invariant	#Str.	Max. inv.	Time
Conference, Safety	synthesis	6	inferred	4	50	736 ms
Leader Election	verification	4	inductive	0	42	351 ms
Leader Election	synthesis	4	inductive	0	42	346 ms
Conference, NI, stubborn	verification	6	inferred	4	850	6782 ms
Conference, NI, stubborn	synthesis	6	inferred	4	850	6817 ms
Conference acyclic, NI, causal	synthesis	8	inferred	4	137	1985 ms
Conference, NI, causal	verification	11	counterex.	7	-	2114 ms
Conference, NI, causal	synthesis	11	inferred	2	102	2460 ms
Conference, NI, causal, approx.	synthesis	11	inferred	8	5090	3359 ms

Fig. 3. Experimental results

(1) terminates in less than one second with a weakest winning strategy (w.r.t. the found inductive invariant) whenever possible. The second group "Leader Election" considers variants of the leader election protocol from Example 1, initially taken from [27]. Since the inductive invariant implies some transitively closed property, it cannot be inferred automatically by our means. Yet, our solver succeeds in proving the invariant from [27] inductive, and moreover, infers a FO definition for the message to be forwarded to arrive at a single leader. The third group "Conference, NI" deals with noninterference for variants of the conference management example where the acyclic version has been obtained by unrolling the loop twice. The difference between the *stubborn* and *causal* settings is the considered angle of attack (see [13] for an in-depth explanation). In the setting of stubborn agents, the attackers try to break the Noninterference property with no specific intent of working together. Here, the solver infers inductive invariants together with winning FO strategies (where possible) in 5–7 s. The setting of causal agents is inherently more complex as it allows for groups of unbounded size that are working together to extract secrets from the system. This allows for elaborate attacks where multiple agents conspire to defeat noninterference [12]. The weakest strategy that is safe for stubborn agents ($\neg Conflict(x, p)$ as a strategy for B_1) can no longer be proven correct—instead the solver finds a counterexample for universes of size ≥ 5. To infer an inductive invariant and a safe strategy for causal agents, multiple iterates of the fixpoint iteration from Sect. 3 must be computed. Each iteration requires formulas to be brought into conjunctive normal form—possibly increasing formula size drastically. To cope with that increase, formula simplification turns out not to be sufficient. We try two different approaches to overcome this challenge: First, we provide the solver with parts of the inductive invariant, so fewer strengthening steps are needed. Given the initial direction, inference terminates much faster and provides us with a useful strategy. For the second approach, we do not supply an initial invariant, but accelerate fixpoint iteration by further strengthening of formulas. This enforces termination while still verifying safety. The extracted strategy, though, is much stronger and essentially rules out all intended behaviours of the system.

All benchmarks were run on a workstation running Debian Linux on an Intel i7-3820 clocked at 3.60 GHz with 15.7 GiB of RAM. The results are summarized in Fig. 3. The table gives the group and type of experiment as well as the size of the transition system in the number of nodes of the graph. For the examples that regard Noninterference, the agent model is given. For verification benchmarks, the solver either proves the given invariant inductive or infers an inductive invariant if the property is not yet inductive. For synthesis benchmarks, it additionally extracts a universal formula for each $B \in \mathcal{R}_B$ to be used as a strategy. The remaining columns give the results of the solver: Could the given invariant be proven inductive, could an inductive strengthening be found, or did the solver find a counterexample violating the invariant? We list the number of times any label of the invariant needed to be strengthened during the inference algorithm, the size of the largest label formula of the inferred invariant measured in the number of nodes of the syntax tree and the time the solver needed in milliseconds (averaged over 10 runs).

Altogether, the experiments confirm that verification of provided invariants as well as synthesis of inductive invariants and winning strategies is possible for nontrivial transition systems with safety as well as noninterference objectives.

8   Related Work

In AI, First Order Logic has a long tradition for representing potentially changing states of the environment [7]. First-order transition systems have then been used to model reachability problems that arise in robot planning (see, e.g., chapters 8–10 in [30]). The system GOLOG [20], for instance, is a programming language based on FO logic. A GOLOG program specifies the behavior of the agents in the system. The program is then evaluated with a theorem prover, and thus assertions about the program can be checked for validity. Automated synthesis of predicates to enforce safety of the resulting system has not yet been considered.

There is a rich body of work on *abstract state machines* (ASMs) [15], i.e., state machines whose states are first-order structures. ASMs have been used to give comprehensive specifications of programming languages such as Prolog, C, and Java, and design languages, like UML and SDL (cf. [5]). A number of tools for the verification and validation of ASMs are available [6]. Known decidability results for ASMs require, however, on strong restrictions such as sequential nullary ASMs [33].

In [3,24], it is shown that the semantics of switch controllers of software-defined networks as expressed by *Core SDN* can be nicely compiled into FO transition systems. The goal then is to use this translation to verify given invariants by proving them inductive. Inductivity of invariants is checked by means of the theorem prover Z3 [9]. The authors report that, if their invariants are not already inductive, a single strengthening, corresponding to the computation of $\Psi^{(1)}$ is often sufficient. In [25], the difficulty of inferring universal inductive invariants is investigated for classes of transition systems whose transition relation is expressed by FO logic formulas over theories of data structures. The authors show that inferring universal inductive invariants is decidable when the transition relation is expressed by formulas with unary predicates and a single binary predicate restricted by the theory of linked lists and becomes undecidable as soon as the binary symbol is not restricted by background theory. By excluding the binary predicate, this result is related to our result for transition systems with monadic predicates, equality and disequality, but neither $\mathcal{A}$- nor $\mathcal{B}$-predicates. In [18], an inference method is provided for universal invariants as an extension of Bradley's PDR/IC3 algorithm for inference of propositional invariants [8]. The method is applied to variants of FO transition systems (no games) within a fragment of FO logic which enjoys the finite model property and is decidable. Whenever it terminates, it either returns a universal invariant which is inductive, or a counter-example. This line of research has led to the tool IVY which generally applies FO predicate logic for the verification of parametric systems [22,27]. Relying on a language similar to [3,24], it meanwhile has been used, e.g., for the verification of network protocols such as leader election in ring topologies and the PAXOS protocol [26].

In [12,13,23], hypersafety properties such as noninterference are studied for *multi-agent workflows*. These workflows are naturally generalized by our notion of FO transition systems. The transformation for reducing noninterference to universal invariants originates from [23] which also provides an approximative approach for inferring inductive invariants. When the attempt fails, a counter-example can be extracted—but might be spurious.

All works discussed so far are concerned with verification rather than synthesis. For synthesizing controllers for systems with an infinite state space, several approaches have been introduced that automatically construct, from a symbolic description of a given concrete game, a finite-state abstract game [2,10,11,16,34]. The main method to obtain the abstract state space is predicate abstraction, which partitions the states according to the truth values of a set of predicates. States that satisfy the same predicates are indistinguishable in the abstract game. The abstraction is iteratively refined by introducing new predicates. Applications include the control of real-time systems [11] and the synthesis of drivers for I/O devices [34]. In comparison, our approach provides a general modelling framework of First Order Safety Games to unify different applications of synthesis for infinite-state systems.

9 Conclusion

We have introduced *First Order Safety Games* as a model for reasoning about games on parametric systems where attained states are modeled as FO structures. We showed that this approach allows to model interesting real-world synthesis problems from the domains network protocols and information flow in multiagent systems. We examined the important case where all occurring predicates are monadic or nullary and provided a complete classification into decidable and undecidable cases. For the non-monadic case, we concentrated on *universal* FO safety properties. We provided techniques for certifying safety and also designed methods for synthesizing FO definitions of predicates as strategies to enforce the given safety objective. We have implemented our approach and succeeded to infer contents of particular messages in the leader election protocol from [27] in order to prove the given invariant inductive. Our implementation also allowed us to synthesize predicates for parametric workflow systems as in [23], to enforce noninterference in presence of declassification. In this application, however, we additionally must take into account that the synthesized formulas only depend on predicates whose values are independent of the secret. Restricting the subset of predicates possibly used by strategies, turns FO safety games into *partial information* safety games. It remains for future work, to explore this connection in greater detail in order, e.g., to determine whether strategies can be automatically synthesized which only refer to specific *admissible* predicates and, perhaps, also take the *history* of plays into account.

References

1. Ackermann, W.: Untersuchungen über das Eliminationsproblem der mathematischen Logik. Math. Ann. **110**, 390–413 (1935)
2. de Alfaro, L., Roy, P.: Solving games via three-valued abstraction refinement. In: Caires, L., Vasconcelos, V.T. (eds.) CONCUR 2007. LNCS, vol. 4703, pp. 74–89. Springer, Heidelberg (2007). https://doi.org/10.1007/978-3-540-74407-8_6
3. Ball, T., et al.: Vericon: towards verifying controller programs in software-defined networks. In: ACM Sigplan Notices, vol. 49, pp. 282–293. ACM (2014)
4. Behmann, H.: Beiträge zur Algebra der Logik, insbesondere zum Entscheidungsproblem. Math. Ann. **86**(3–4), 163–229 (1922)
5. Börger, E., Stärk, R.: History and survey of ASM research. In: Börger, E., Stärk, R. (eds.) Abstract State Machines, pp. 343–367. Springer, Berlin (2003). https://doi.org/10.1007/978-3-642-18216-7_9
6. Börger, E., Stärk, R.: Tool support for ASMs. In: Börger, E., Stärk, R. (eds.) Abstract State Machines, pp. 313–342. Springer, Berlin (2003). https://doi.org/10.1007/978-3-642-18216-7_8
7. Brachman, R.J., Levesque, H.J., Reiter, R.: Knowledge Representation. MIT Press, Cambridge (1992)
8. Bradley, A.R.: SAT-based model checking without unrolling. In: Jhala, R., Schmidt, D. (eds.) VMCAI 2011. LNCS, vol. 6538, pp. 70–87. Springer, Heidelberg (2011). https://doi.org/10.1007/978-3-642-18275-4_7
9. de Moura, L., Bjørner, N.: Z3: an efficient SMT solver. In: Ramakrishnan, C.R., Rehof, J. (eds.) TACAS 2008. LNCS, vol. 4963, pp. 337–340. Springer, Heidelberg (2008). https://doi.org/10.1007/978-3-540-78800-3_24
10. Dimitrova, R., Finkbeiner, B.: Abstraction refinement for games with incomplete information. In: IARCS Annual Conference on Foundations of Software Technology and Theoretical Computer Science FSTTCS, vol. 2008, pp. 175–186 (2008)
11. Dimitrova, R., Finkbeiner, B.: Counterexample-guided synthesis of observation predicates. In: Jurdziński, M., Ničković, D. (eds.) FORMATS 2012. LNCS, vol. 7595, pp. 107–122. Springer, Heidelberg (2012). https://doi.org/10.1007/978-3-642-33365-1_9
12. Finkbeiner, B., Müller, C., Seidl, H., Zalinescu, E.: Verifying security policies in multi-agent workflows with loops. In: Proceedings of the 2017 ACM SIGSAC Conference on Computer and Communications Security, CCS 2017, Dallas, TX, USA,

30 October–03 November 2017, pp. 633–645. IEEE (2017). https://doi.org/10.1145/3133956.3134080

13. Finkbeiner, B., Seidl, H., Müller, C.: Specifying and verifying secrecy in workflows with arbitrarily many agents. In: Artho, C., Legay, A., Peled, D. (eds.) ATVA 2016. LNCS, vol. 9938, pp. 157–173. Springer, Cham (2016). https://doi.org/10.1007/978-3-319-46520-3_11

14. Gabbay, D.M., Schmidt, R., Szalas, A.: Second Order Quantifier Elimination: Foundations. Computational Aspects and Applications. College Publications, Michigan (2008)

15. Gurevich, Y.: Evolving algebras 1993: Lipari guide. arXiv preprint arXiv:1808.06255 (2018)

16. Henzinger, T.A., Jhala, R., Majumdar, R.: Counterexample-guided control. In: Baeten, J.C.M., Lenstra, J.K., Parrow, J., Woeginger, G.J. (eds.) ICALP 2003. LNCS, vol. 2719, pp. 886–902. Springer, Heidelberg (2003). https://doi.org/10.1007/3-540-45061-0_69

17. Holzer, M., Kutrib, M., Malcher, A.: Complexity of multi-head finite automata: origins and directions. Theoret. Comput. Sci. **412**(1–2), 83–96 (2011)

18. Karbyshev, A., Bjørner, N., Itzhaky, S., Rinetzky, N., Shoham, S.: Property-directed inference of universal invariants or proving their absence. J. ACM (JACM) **64**(1), 7 (2017)

19. Miller, D.A., Nadathur, G.: Higher-order logic programming. In: Shapiro, E. (ed.) ICLP 1986. LNCS, vol. 225, pp. 448–462. Springer, Heidelberg (1986). https://doi.org/10.1007/3-540-16492-8_94

20. Levesque, H.J., Reiter, R., Lespérance, Y., Lin, F., Scherl, R.B.: GOLOG: a logic programming language for dynamic domains. J. Logic Programm. **31**(1), 59–83 (1997). https://doi.org/10.1016/S0743-1066(96)00121-5

21. Mazala, R.: Infinite games. In: Grädel, E., Thomas, W., Wilke, T. (eds.) Automata Logics, and Infinite Games. LNCS, vol. 2500, pp. 23–38. Springer, Heidelberg (2002). https://doi.org/10.1007/3-540-36387-4_2

22. McMillan, K.L., Padon, O.: Deductive verification in decidable fragments with ivy. In: Podelski, A. (ed.) SAS 2018. LNCS, vol. 11002, pp. 43–55. Springer, Cham (2018). https://doi.org/10.1007/978-3-319-99725-4_4

23. Müller, C., Seidl, H., Zalinescu, E.: Inductive invariants for noninterference in multi-agent workflows. In: 31st IEEE Computer Security Foundations Symposium, CSF 2018, Oxford, UK, 9–12 July 2018, pp. 247–261. IEEE (2018). https://doi.org/10.1109/CSF.2018.00025

24. Padon, O., Immerman, N., Karbyshev, A., Lahav, O., Sagiv, M., Shoham, S.: Decentralizing SDN policies. In: ACM SIGPLAN Notices, vol. 50, pp. 663–676. ACM (2015)

25. Padon, O., Immerman, N., Shoham, S., Karbyshev, A., Sagiv, M.: Decidability of inferring inductive invariants. In: Proceedings of the 43rd Annual ACM SIGPLAN-SIGACT Symposium on Principles of Programming Languages, POPL 2016, pp. 217–231. ACM (2016). https://doi.org/10.1145/2837614.2837640

26. Padon, O., Losa, G., Sagiv, M., Shoham, S.: Paxos made EPR: decidable reasoning about distributed protocols. Proc. ACM Programm. Lang. **1**(OOPSLA), 108 (2017)

27. Padon, O., McMillan, K.L., Panda, A., Sagiv, M., Shoham, S.: Ivy: safety verification by interactive generalization. ACM SIGPLAN Notices **51**(6), 614–630 (2016)

28. Ramsey, F.P.: On a problem of formal logic. In: Gessel, I., Rota, G.C. (eds.) Classic Papers in Combinatorics. MBC, pp. 1–24. Birkhäuser, Boston (2009). https://doi.org/10.1007/978-0-8176-4842-8_1

29. Rosenberg, A.L.: On multi-head finite automata. IBM J. Res. Dev. **10**(5), 388–394 (1966)
30. Russell, S.J., Norvig, P.: Artificial Intelligence: A Modern Approach. Pearson Education Limited, Kuala Lumpur (2016)
31. Seidl, H., Müller, C., Finkbeiner, B.: How to win first-order safety games. arXiv preprint arXiv:1908.05964 (2019)
32. Seidl, H., Müller, C., Finkbeiner, B.: How to win first order safety games - software artifact, October 2019. https://doi.org/10.5281/zenodo.3514277
33. Spielmann, M.: Abstract state machines: verification problems and complexity. Ph.D. thesis, RWTH Aachen University, Germany (2000). http://sylvester.bth. rwth-aachen.de/dissertationen/2001/008/01_008.pdf
34. Walker, A., Ryzhyk, L.: Predicate abstraction for reactive synthesis. In: 2014 Formal Methods in Computer-Aided Design (FMCAD), pp. 219–226, October 2014. https://doi.org/10.1109/FMCAD.2014.6987617
35. Wernhard, C.: Second-order quantifier elimination on relational monadic formulas – a basic method and some less expected applications. In: De Nivelle, H. (ed.) TABLEAUX 2015. LNCS (LNAI), vol. 9323, pp. 253–269. Springer, Cham (2015). https://doi.org/10.1007/978-3-319-24312-2_18

Improving Parity Game Solvers
with Justifications

Ruben Lapauw$^{(\boxtimes)}$, Maurice Bruynooghe, and Marc Denecker

Department of Computer Science, KU Leuven, 3001 Leuven, Belgium
{ruben.lapauw,maurice.bruynooghe,marc.denecker}@cs.kuleuven.be

Abstract. Parity games are infinite two-player games played on node-weighted directed graphs. Formal verification problems such as verifying and synthesizing automata, bounded model checking of LTL, CTL*, propositional μ-calculus, ... reduce to problems over parity games. The core problem of parity game solving is deciding the winner of some (or all) nodes in a parity game. In this paper, we improve several parity game solvers by using a justification graph. Experimental evaluation shows our algorithms improve upon the state-of-the-art.

1 Introduction

Parity games are infinite two player games played on node-weighted directed graphs without leaves. Priorities, the weights of the nodes, are integers in an interval $[1, d]$ with d a parameter of the parity game. All nodes belong to one player, either Even or Odd. The players play by moving one token from node to node following the edges of the graph. The owner of the node on which the token lands, plays next. The winner of this infinite path, a play, is Even if the maximal priority that occurs infinitely often is even, otherwise Odd wins. A parity game solver determines for each node the winner and a winning strategy. Many problems over boolean equation systems [5,13], μ-calculus [10,20], nested fixpoints [11] and temporal logics such as LTL, CTL and CTL* [10] reduce to parity games.

The algorithm with the best known time complexity [4,7] is quasi-polynomial in the number of weights. However, in practice, it is outperformed by several exponential algorithms, most notably: fixpoint induction [3], Zielonka's algorithm [21], multiple variants of strategy-improvement [16], priority promotion [1,2] and tangle learning [18]. Currently, Zielonka's algorithm and priority promotion are considered the two fastest algorithms though there is experimental evidence that tangle learning is faster on large random graphs [18].

R. Lapauw—Supported by a IWT research grant.

D. Beyer and D. Zufferey (Eds.): VMCAI 2020, LNCS 11990, pp. 449–470, 2020.
https://doi.org/10.1007/978-3-030-39322-9_21

Our contribution is to extend these algorithms with a justification graph data structure. For fixpoint induction this allows us to efficiently reconstruct winning strategies; more importantly, it enables optimizations in the computation of a solution. Furthermore, we applied these optimisations for Zielonka's algorithm, and tangle learning. As our experiments show, adding justifications to these algorithms improve their performance. Overall, tangle learning extended with justifications performs best over the whole of our benchmark set.

In Sect. 2, the preliminaries, we formally define the parity game problem, introduce the μ-formula [20] that determines the winners of a parity game and a parity game solving fixpoint algorithm by Bruse et al. [3]. In Sect. 3, we introduce justifications, integrate them in the fixpoint algorithm and argue correctness is preserved. In Sect. 4 this technique is applied to Zielonka's algorithm and tangle learning. Next, in Sect. 5, we evaluate our three justification based implementations. We round up in Sect. 6.

2 Preliminaries

2.1 Parity Games

A parity game is a two player game with players 0 (Even) and 1 (Odd). We use α to denote a player with $\alpha \in \{0,1\}$ and use $\bar{\alpha}$ to denote the opponent of player α. Formally, a parity game is a tuple $PG = (V, E, V_0, V_1, Pr)$ consisting of a finite game graph (V, E) with outgoing edges for every node, a partition $\{V_0, V_1\}$ of nodes V and a priority function $Pr : V \to P$, with P an interval of integer priorities $\{1 \ldots d\}$. In nodes of V_0, player Even plays, and in those of V_1, it is player Odd. Without loss of generality we assume d is even.

Given a set of nodes S, a player α, a priority i and a relation $\sim$ in the set $\{=, \neq, \leq, \geq, <, >, \equiv_2, \not\equiv_2\}$: $S|_\alpha$ denotes the set $S \cap V_\alpha$ and $S^{\sim i}$ denotes the set of nodes $\{v \in S | Pr(v) \sim i\}$. E.g., $V^{<i}$ is $\{v \in V | Pr(v) < i\}$ and $V^{\equiv_2 0}$ is the set of nodes with a priority which is equivalent – modulo 2 – with priority 0, i.e., the nodes with an even priority.

A play is an infinite sequence of nodes $\langle v_0 v_1 \ldots v_n \ldots \rangle$ where $\forall i \in \mathbb{N} : v_i \in V \wedge (v_i, v_{i+1}) \in E$. We use π to denote a play. Since every node has outgoing edges, there exist plays in every node. The winner of a play is the player with the parity of the highest priority that occurs infinitely often: $Winner(\pi) = \lim_{i \to +\infty} max \{Pr(v_j) | j \geq i\} \mod 2$.

A strategy for α is a partial function $\sigma_\alpha : V_\alpha \to V$ for which for every x in the domain of σ_α: $(x, \sigma_\alpha(x)) \in E$. A play π is consistent with σ_α if $v_{n+1} = \sigma_\alpha(v_n)$ for every v_n in the domain of σ_α. A strategy σ_α is winning in v if α is the winner of every play in v consistent with σ_α. A node v is won by α if there exists a strategy σ_α that is winning in v. The set of nodes won by α is denoted as $\mathcal{W}_\alpha$.

Strategies, as defined here, are *positional*: they do not depend on the history of the play. Furthermore, both players α have at least one strategy σ_α that is winning for every node in $\mathcal{W}_\alpha$. Such strategies are *winning*. Most algorithms in this paper compute winning strategies.

2.2   Nested Fixpoint Iteration for Parity Games

A basic algorithm for computing the winning positions of a parity game uses a nested fixpoint computation. For a given set T, an operator $\Phi : 2^T \rightarrow 2^T$ that is monotone with respect to $\subseteq$ has a least and a greatest fixpoint, denoted $\mu S.\Phi(S)$ resp. $\nu S.\Phi(S)$. The least fixpoint is the limit of the ascending sequence $\emptyset, \Phi(\emptyset), \Phi^2(\emptyset), \ldots$, while the greatest fixpoint is the limit of the descending sequence $T, \Phi(T), \Phi^2(T), \ldots$ For a given operator $\Phi : \left(2^T\right)^2 \rightarrow 2^T$ that is monotone in both arguments, it is not difficult to show that the functions $\Psi_\mu : S_2 \mapsto \mu S_1.\Phi(S_2, S_1)$ and $\Psi_\nu : S_2 \mapsto \nu S_1.\Psi(S_2, S_1)$ are monotone functions. Hence, their least and greatest fixpoints are well-defined and can be computed in the standard way, leading to a nested fixpoint computation.

Let Φ be d-ary operator of 2^T that is monotone in all its arguments. Then $\nu S_d.\mu S_{d-1}. \ldots \nu S_2.\mu S_1.\Phi(S_d, \ldots, S_1)$ is a unique and well-defined set that can be computed by a nested least and greatest fixpoint computation. This algorithm was originally used by Emerson and Lei [6] for evaluating μ-calculus formulae in transition systems. For a finite set T, Φ is evaluated $|T|^d$ times by the algorithm in the worst case. An improved algorithm by Long et al. [15] reduced the number of evaluations to $|T|^{\lceil d/2 \rceil}$.

Solving a parity game amounts to computing the positions won by Even and Odd and a winning strategy for both. Walukiewicz [20] characterized the winning positions of Even with a fixpoint calculation $\nu S_d.\mu S_{d-1}. \ldots \mu S_1.\Phi(S_d, \ldots, S_1)$ with

$$\Phi(S_d, \ldots, S_1) = \{v \in V_0 | \exists w : (v, w) \in E \wedge w \in S_i \text{ with } i = Pr(w)\} \cup$$
$$\{v \in V_1 | \forall w : (v, w) \in E \Rightarrow w \in S_i \text{ with } i = Pr(w)\}$$

Since the inner operator Φ is monotone in all of its arguments $S_d, \ldots, S_1$, the corresponding fixpoint computation has a unique and well-defined outcome which is also computed by Algorithm 1. Note that S_i is initialized with respectively V for even i (a greatest fixpoint), and $\emptyset$ for odd i (a least fixpoint).

Bruse et al. [3] observe that it suffices to store elements of priority i in S_i; indeed computing Φ only checks if $w \in S_i$ for $i = Pr(w)$, hence: $\Phi(S_d, \ldots, S_1) = \Phi(S_d^{=d}, \ldots, S_1^{=1})$. Omitting the irrelevant elements, all S_i can be combined in a single set $S = \cup_i S_i^{=i}$; finally, the operation $\Phi(S_d, \ldots, S_1)$ is to be replaced by:

$$\phi(S) = \{v \in V_0 | \exists w : (v, w) \in E \wedge w \in S\} \cup$$
$$\{v \in V_1 | \forall w : (v, w) \in E \Rightarrow w \in S\}$$

A second optimization, developed by Long et al. [15], partially eliminates re-initializations. Instead of resetting all nodes of lower priority than i to their initial state $(S_R^{<i} \leftarrow V^{<i} \cap V^{\equiv_2 0})$, only nodes with a priority of opposite parity are reset (Algorithm 2, Lines 9 to 12): If i is even then the nodes with even priority are kept and nodes with an odd priority are removed; analogously, if i is odd, odd nodes are kept and even nodes are added.

The first optimization reduces the memory use by a factor d, the second is, according to Seidl [17], sufficient to reduce the time complexity to

input: A parity game
output: S_d: nodes won by *Even*
1 **Func** $basic((V, E, V_0, V_1, Pr))$:
2   **for** $i \in \{1 \ldots d\}$ **do**
3   **if** i *is even* **then** $S_i \leftarrow V$;
4   **else** $S_i \leftarrow \emptyset$;
5   **do**
6     $S_\phi \leftarrow \Phi(S_d, \ldots, S_2, S_1)$
7     $i \leftarrow 1$
8   **while** $S_i = S_\phi \wedge i \leq d$ **do**
9       $i \leftarrow i + 1$
10   **if** $i \leq d$ **then**
11       $S_i \leftarrow S_\phi$
12   **for** $j \in \{i - 1 \ldots 1\}$ **do**
13   **if** j *is even* **then** $S_j \leftarrow V$;
14   **else** $S_j \leftarrow \emptyset$;
15   **until** $i = d + 1$;
16   **return** S_d

Algorithm 1. A basic fixpoint iteration algorithm

input: A parity game
output: S: the nodes won by *Even*
1 **Func** $time((V, E, V_0, V_1, Pr))$:
2   $S \leftarrow \{v \in V \mid Pr(v) \text{ is even}\}$
3   **while** $S \neq \phi(S)$ **do**
4     $S \leftarrow next(S)$
5   **return** S
6 **Func** $next(S)$:
7   $S_\phi \leftarrow \phi(S)$
8   $i \leftarrow min \{Pr(v) \mid v \in S \triangle S_\phi\}$
9   **if** i is even **then**
10     $S_R \leftarrow S \setminus V^{\equiv_2 1}$
11   **else**
12     $S_R \leftarrow S \cup V^{\equiv_2 0}$
13   **return** $S^{>i} \cup S_\phi^{=i} \cup S_R^{<i}$

Algorithm 2. The time- and memory-efficient algorithm of Bruse et al. [3]. $\triangle$ is the symmetric set difference.

$O(|E| \cdot n^{\lceil d/2 \rceil})$ with $n = |V|/d + 1$. These two optimizations result in Algorithm 2 which calculates the nodes won by Even as S.

The following example shows a simulation of Algorithm 2 for the small parity game in Fig. 1.

Example 1. Initially, the nodes won by Even are estimated as $S = \{v_6, v_4\}$. In the first iteration is $S_\phi = \{v_3, v_7\}$ and $S \triangle S_\phi = \{v_3, v_4, v_6, v_7\}$. Node v_3 is the only node of priority $i = 3$. Even wins v_3 by playing to v_4 and S is updated to $\{v_6, v_4, v_3\}$. Five iterations later is S, the current estimate for Even, equal to $\{v_7, v_6, v_4, v_3, v_1\}$. In the next iteration is $S_\phi = \{v_7, v_4, v_3, v_1\}$: node v_6 is won by Odd by playing to v_9. The reset operation removes nodes v_3 and v_1 (and adds v_4). The set S is now $\{v_7, v_4\}$. In the final iterations,

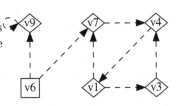

Fig. 1. A small parity game. The priority of node v_i is i. Even plays in diamond nodes and Odd in the square node v_6.

Even wins v_1 by playing to v_7, and wins v_3 by playing to v_4. Now, the estimate is $S = \{v_7, v_4, v_3, v_1\}$; as this is a fixpoint, this is the set of nodes won by Even.

It would be useful if we could construct a winning strategy from the previous calculation. However, this is tricky. E.g., in the final steps we derived that Even wins v_1 using its move to v_7, suggesting that in node v_1 Even should play to v_7. This is wrong: Even must play to v_3 to win.

Bruse et al. [3] then extended Algorithm 2 to compute winning strategies (with domain $\mathcal{W}_\alpha | \alpha$). The algorithm works by recording for every iteration, for every player, for every node of that player that is supposed to be won by that player in that iteration, a winning move for that node. After the run, for each player one global winning strategy, called the *eventually-positional winning strategy*, is extracted from this data structure. A disadvantage of this method is that its memory use is proportional to the running time. This leads to exponential memory consumption in terms of the parity games' size.

3   Speeding up Fixpoint Iteration with Justifications

The first contribution of this paper is to propose an algorithm that maintains an improved datastructure called a justification graph, to store a single (partial) winning strategy during execution. Justification graphs as we use it here, were first introduced in Hou et al. [11] in the context of a semantic study of nested least and greatest fixpoint definitions.

Below, we view the set S in Algorithm 2 as the current estimate of the nodes won by Even, and $V \setminus S$ as the nodes won by Odd. If $v \in S$, we say that v is won by Even according to S (or Even is the winner of v according to S), and if $v \notin S$, we say that v is won by Odd according to S.

Definition 1 (Justification). *A pair (S, J) is a justification if S is a set of nodes, an estimation of nodes won by Even, and J is a sub-graph of the game graph (V, E), an extended candidate winning strategy, satisfying two constraints:*

(i) *Each node v won according to S by its owner (i.e., $v \in S|_0 \cup (V \setminus S)|_1$) has either no outgoing edges or one outgoing edge.*

(ii) *Each node v won according to S by the opponent of its owner (i.e., $v \in S|_1 \cup (V \setminus S)|_0$) has either no outgoing edges or all outgoing edges of that node.*

If in J, the node v has outgoing edges, we call v *justified* in J, otherwise we call v *unjustified* in J. We denote the set of nodes that are unjustified in J as $U(J)$. A justification is *complete* if every node is justified.

Definition 2 (Winning justification). *A justification (S, J) is winning if all connected nodes are won by the same player according to S and if every infinite path in J starting in a node v is a play won by the winner of v according to S.*

Note that paths in winning justifications are fragments of winning strategies (for Even when it is a path of nodes in S and for Odd when it is a path of nodes outside S).

Lemma 1. *Let (S, J) be a complete and winning justification, $\sigma_0 = \{v \mapsto w : (v, w) \in J, v \in S|_0\}$ and $\sigma_1 = \{v \mapsto w : (v, w) \in J, v \in (V \setminus S)|_1\}$. Then every play starting in a node $v \in S$ and consistent with σ_0 is an infinite path in J and every play starting in a node $v \notin S$ and consistent with σ_1 is an infinite path in J. Furthermore, S equals $\mathcal{W}_0$, the set of nodes won by Even, and $V \setminus S$ equals $\mathcal{W}_1$, the set of nodes won by Odd and, σ_0 and σ_1 are global winning strategies for respectively Even and Odd.*

input: A parity game
$G = (V, E, V_0, V_1, Pr)$
output: S: nodes won by Even,
J: a justification

```
1  Func compute_J(G):
2  │ S←{v ∈ V|Pr(v) is even}
3  │ J ← ∅
4  │ while U(J) ≠ ∅ do
5  │ │ (S, J)←next(S, J)
6  │ return S, J
7  Func strategyα(S, U):
8  │ J←∅
9  │ for v ∈ U do
10 │ │ if v ∈ Vα then
11 │ │ │ Wv←{w|(v, w) ∈ E ∧ w ∈ S}
12 │ │ else
13 │ │ │ Wv←{w|(v, w) ∈ E ∧ w ∉ S}
14 │ │ if Wv ≠ ∅ then
15 │ │ │ w←choose(Wv)
16 │ │ │ J←J ∪ {(v, w)}
17 │ │ else
18 │ │ │ J←J ∪ {(v, w')|(v, w') ∈ E}
19 │ return J
```

```
1  Func next(S, J):
2  │ i←min {Pr(v)|v ∈ U(J)}
3  │ U←U(J)=i
4  │ Upd←(φ(S) △ S) ∩ U
5  │ if Upd ≠ ∅ then
6  │ │ R←Reaches(J, Upd)
7  │ │ if i is even then
8  │ │ │ SR←(S \ R≡²1) ∩ V<i
9  │ │ else
10 │ │ │ SR←(S ∪ R≡²0) ∩ V<i
11 │ │ Jt←J \ (R × V)
12 │ │ J'←Jt ∪ strategy0(S, Upd)
13 │ │ S'←S>i ∪ (S △ Upd) ∪ SR
14 │ else
15 │ │ J'←J ∪ strategy0(S, U)
16 │ │ S'←S
17 │ return (S', J')
```

Algorithm 3. *compute_J* determines winning strategies for both players

---

Proof. Let v_0 be won by α according to S and let $\pi = v_0 v_1 v_2 \ldots$ be an arbitrary play in v_0 consistent with σ_α. Since (S, J) is a complete justification, v_0 is justified in J. Let $v_0 v_1 v_2 \ldots v_i$ be an initial segment of π that is a path in J. All connected nodes in J share the same winner according to S, hence, also v_i is won by α according to S. Since (S, J) is complete, if $v_i \in V_\alpha$, v_i has one child in J, namely $\sigma_\alpha(v_i)$. Since π is consistent with σ_α, this node is v_{i+1}. If on the other hand $v_i \in V_{\bar{\alpha}}$, then J contains all outgoing edges from v_i in E, including v_{i+1}. Either way, $v_1 \ldots v_{i+1}$ is a path in J. Using induction on i, we conclude that the entire play π is an infinite path in J. Since (S, J) is winning, π is won by α. It follows that σ_α is a winning strategy for α in v_0. Hence, the elements of S belong to $\mathcal{W}_0$ and those of $V \setminus S$ to $\mathcal{W}_1$. We obtain $S = \mathcal{W}_0$ and $V \setminus S = \mathcal{W}_1$.

We now present an improved algorithm that makes use of justifications: Algorithm 3 extends Algorithm 2 with management of such justification graph J. It uses the auxiliaries $U(J)$, the set of unjustified nodes of J, and $Reaches(J, X)$, the set of nodes that have a path in J to an element of X. It also uses the auxiliary procedure $strategy_\alpha(S, X)$ which chooses justifications for nodes $v \in X \subseteq U^1$. The parameter α of the procedure is the player that wins the set S; here this is always Even (Lines 12 and 15 of *next*); in some later algorithms, it can be Odd. For the player that owns an unjustified node $v \in X$, σ_α selects a winning move

---

[1] To make $strategy_\alpha$ deterministic, **choose** can return, e.g., the smallest element.

if one exists (Line 11/13 with Lines 15, 16 of $strategy_\alpha$); otherwise, it selects all moves for v in E (Line 18).

Initially, J contains no edges. Subsequent calls to $next$ are made until all nodes are justified. At each iteration, the lowest priority i with non-empty set U of unjustified nodes is determined by Line 2. The subset Upd of nodes with a revised winner is determined $((\phi(S) \bigtriangleup S) \cap U)$. If Upd is not empty, the set R of nodes with a path to Upd is computed (Line 6). Such paths represent partial plays to leafs won according to S, but these paths are outdated now. Therefore, the winners of these nodes are reset to their initial values (Lines 7–10) and their justifications are removed (Line 11). It will be proven that nodes in R belong to $V^{<i}$ and that all nodes in R are won by $\alpha = i \bmod 2$ according to S. Thus, all nodes of R belong to S if i is even and to $V \setminus S$ if i is odd. Nodes in R need to be reset to their initial winner: if i is even, it suffices to remove the nodes of R of odd priority $(R^{\equiv_2 1})$ from S; if i is odd, it suffices to add nodes of R of even priority $(R^{\equiv_2 0})$ to S. The set S_R is computed as the result of this update to $S^{<i}$. After resetting the nodes in R, new justifications for the nodes in Upd are computed in Line 12. Finally, the updated set of nodes won by Even, S', is computed by applying the update Upd and by using the reset-update S_R (Line 13).

The other case, when Upd is empty, is simpler: no nodes at level i are revised, S is unchanged and J is extended with justifications for all nodes in U (Line 15).

When the algorithm is finished, the nodes in S are won by Even, non-elements of S are won by Odd and J is a complete justification. For both players, the strategy for a node is given by the unique edge in the justification of that node.

Example 2. We apply Algorithm 3 on the parity game of Fig. 1. The first iteration selects a justification for node v_1: v_1 is won by Odd by playing to v_3. The justification J is then $\{(v_1, v_3)\}$. The algorithm then follows Example 1. By choosing[2] node v_7 as winning move for v_6, the algorithm reaches an equivalent state after six iterations: S is $\{v_7, v_6, v_4, v_3, v_1\}$ and the solid edges in Fig. 2 express the current justification graph.

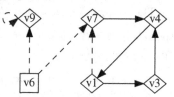

Fig. 2. The justification of Example 2 after 6 iterations.

The next iteration shows the crucial difference between the previous and the new algorithms. Node v_6 is the unjustified node with the lowest priority; it is won by Odd by playing to v_9. The previous algorithm resets nodes v_1 and v_3. However, since nodes v_1 and v_3 do not depend on v_6 they are not reset in Algorithm 3. The new justification consists of $S = \{v_7, v_4, v_3, v_1\}$ and $J = \{(v_1, v_3), (v_3, v_4), (v_4, v_1), (v_7, v_4), (v_6, v_9)\}$. The final iteration adds, for node v_9, the following justification to J: (v_9, v_9). The fixpoint has been reached and the final justification graph can be projected to a winning strategy. Note that, according to J, in node v_1 Even must play to v_3.

---

[2] Choosing v_9 as winning move for v_6 never resets node v_6, avoiding the difficulties of Example 1.

3.1   Correctness

The goal of the algorithm is to find a complete winning justification. We prove
the loop invariant that (S, J) is a wining justification at the end of every iteration
and that J grows monotonically to a complete justification w.r.t a finite order.
To bring this about we prove invariance for three additional properties: the
justification (S, J) in Algorithm 3 is coherent, dominating and default.

Definition 3 (Coherent). *A justification (S, J) is* coherent *if two connected
nodes in J are won by the same player:* $\forall (v, w) \in J : v \in S \Leftrightarrow w \in S$.

Definition 4 (Default). *The* default *winner of a node is Even if its priority
is even and Odd if its priority is odd. A justification (S, J) is* default *if every
unjustified node is won by the default winner of that node according to S : $\forall v \in
U(J) : v \in S \Leftrightarrow Pr(v) \equiv_2 0$.*

Definition 5 (Dominating). *A sub-graph J of a parity game is* dominating
*if every leaf of J (every $v \in U(J)$) has a priority strictly larger than the priority
of nodes on paths to that leaf. Formally: $\forall w \in U(J), \forall v \in Reaches(J, \{w\})$:
$Pr(v) < Pr(w)$.*

Adding a justification for an unjustified node v can introduce a cycle. If so,
dominance of J ensures that the priority of v is the highest priority in the cycle
and hence this priority determines the winner of this cycle. Moreover, if (S, J)
is default, then the winner of that new cycle is the winner according to S.

The following invariant of Algorithm 3 proves correctness:

Invariant 1. *The pair (S, J) for each iteration of the while-loop is a coherent,
dominating, default and winning justification.*

In the proof, we use the notation $J(v) = \{w \mid (v, w) \in J\}$, and likewise
$E(v) = \{w \mid (v, w) \in E\}$. Recall that (S, J) is a justification iff for every node
$v \in V$, $J(v) = \emptyset$ or v's owner wins in v according to S and $J(v)$ is a singleton
subset of $E(v)$ or v's owner looses in v according to S and $J(v) = E(v)$.

Proof. We prove this invariant by induction.

The initial pair $(S, J) = (\{v \in V \mid Pr(v) \text{ is even }\}, \emptyset)$ is, by construction, a
winning, coherent, dominating and default justification.

We prove in the induction step that if the justification (S, J) is winning,
coherent, dominating and default then so is $(S', J') = next(S, J)$:

Justification: This invariant is at risk at a node v when a justification is set to
v, or when v is added or removed from S since this modifies the assigned winner
of v. For unjustified nodes v in $U(J)^{=i}$, the calls to $strategy_0$ in Lines 12 and 15
create a correct justification for v for its winner according to $\phi(S)$. As for updates
of S, this occurs for nodes v in Upd and in the reset nodes in R. For $v \in Upd$, the
call to $strategy_0$ creates a correct justification for v while for reset nodes $v \in R$,
the justification of v is removed in Line 11 which also preserves the invariant.
As such (S', J') is a justification.

Coherent: It is easy to check that the edges returned by $strategy_0$ are coherent with $\phi(S)$. Thus the edges added to J will be coherent since $S' \cap U$ is exactly $\phi(S) \cap U$. We still need to prove that edges (v, w) in J preserved in J' remain coherent. This follows from the fact if the edge (v, w) is preserved in J, then also the winners of v and w according to S must be preserved. Indeed, whenever v or w is assigned a different winner, v ends up in R and its edge to w is removed.

Default: Initially, all nodes are unjustified and won, according to S, by their default winner. When the winner of an unjustified node changes according to S, then the node becomes justified. When a node becomes unjustified, the winner is reset to the default winner.

Dominating: If Upd is non-empty, then first for nodes v in $Reaches(J, Upd)$, the justification is removed and each becomes an unreachable leaf of J' (edges from and to v are removed). This preserves the invariant. Then for every node v in Upd, justifying edges (v, w) are created where w is won by the opposite player according to S. Since (S, J) is coherent and default, all reachable unjustified nodes from w are won by the opposite player, hence have a priority different than i and hence, strictly larger than i (i is the least priority with unjustified nodes). Thus, the newly reachable unjustified nodes from v, and from nodes that can reach v (which by dominance of J have priority $< i$), have priority $> i$. Hence, dominance is preserved. If Upd is empty, all nodes v with priority i are assigned a justification, and all newly reachable unjustified nodes from v and from nodes that could reach v have strictly higher priority than i. Again, dominance is preserved.

Winning: The first condition, all connected nodes have the same winner according to S', follows from coherence. The second condition remains to be proven: Let π be an infinite path of J' consisting of nodes won by α according to S'. It must be proven that α is the winner of π.

Assume π has an index j such that the tail $\langle v_j, v_{j+1}, \dots \rangle$ is a path in J. Since (S, J) is a winning justification, α is the winner of the tail, and hence of π itself.

Assume π does not have a tail preserved from J. Then π passes infinitely often over new edges $(v, w) \in J' \setminus J$, where $v \in U(J)$ and v has priority i. In the play π there exist two types of nodes: nodes unjustified in J, of priority i, and nodes justified in J. The justified nodes have a path in J along π to the next unjustified node which has priority i. Since J is dominating, it follows that these justified nodes have a priority less than i. So the highest priority of the play that occurs infinitely often is i and π is won by player $i \bmod 2$. From the proof of dominating, it follows that truly new infinite paths are only possible when Upd is empty. Since Upd is empty, player $i \bmod 2$ is, according to S', the winner of all nodes on π. Thus player α wins the play π. Therefore, (S', J') is a winning justification.

To ensure termination, we define the size of a justification and argue that the size decreases in every cycle until the justification is complete.

Definition 6 (Justification size). *The size of a justification, denoted* $size(J)$, *is a d-tuple* $(a_d, a_{d-1}, \ldots, a_1)$ *where each* a_i *counts the number of unjustified nodes of priority i. Justification sizes are ordered lexicographically:*
$$(a_d, a_{d-1}, \ldots, a_1) < (b_d, b_{d-1}, \ldots, b_1) \text{ iff } \exists i : a_i < b_i \wedge \forall j > i : a_j = b_j.$$

Theorem 1 (Total correctness). *Algorithm 3 terminates with a complete winning justification* (S, J).

Proof. If Upd is empty, the algorithm strictly reduces the number of unjustified nodes of priority i to zero. Otherwise, if Upd is not empty, the algorithm strictly reduces the number of unjustified nodes at priority i (and may increase the number of unjustified nodes at strictly lower levels). Either way, the size of J strictly decreases at each iteration. Hence, the algorithm terminates.

Furthermore, the algorithm terminates when no unjustified nodes exist. At this point, (S, J) is complete.

No improvements in time complexity are expected:

Theorem 2 (Time complexity). *Algorithm has time complexity* $O(|E| \cdot n^{\lceil d/2 \rceil})$ *with* $n = |V|/d + 1$.

Proof omitted.

4   Integrating Justifications in Other Algorithms

Currently, three algorithms are considered as state-of-the-art: Zielonka's algorithm [21], priority promotion [1,2] and tangle learning [19]. While studying related work the applicability of justifications to these algorithms was noticed: while all algorithms calculate a winning strategy, only region recovery, a priority promotion variant, and tangle learning use this strategy to improve the algorithm. In this section we sketch how to extend Zielonka's algorithm and tangle learning with justifications. While justifications do not improve the time complexity, one can expect a performance improvement. This is confirmed by the experimental evaluation. In the future work section we argue that applying justifications to priority promotion is an improvement of the region recovery variant.

Zielonka's Algorithm. Zielonka's algorithm determines the winners by recursively decomposing a game G in a smaller sub-game G' and first solving the sub-game. Once the winners of G' are determined, it returns to the nodes not in G' and, if needed, another sub-game is created and solved.

The algorithm is based on the notion of the *attracted node set* of a set S, denoted $Attr_\alpha(S)$. Informally, this is the set of all nodes from which α can force a play to S. Formally, this set can be computed using a least fixpoint computation:

$$Attr_\alpha(V, S) = \mu A.S \cup \{v \in V_\alpha | \exists w : (v, w) \in E \wedge w \in A\}$$
$$\cup \{v \in V_{\bar{\alpha}} | \forall w : (v, w) \in E \Rightarrow w \in A\}$$

In addition, Zielonka's algorithm computes a corresponding α-strategy σ_{Attr} : $A|_\alpha \setminus S \to A$ for all attracted nodes which shows how any play starting in a node $v \in A$ eventually ends in S.

For correctness, Zielonka's algorithm depends on two properties of $Attr_\alpha$: (i) if all nodes of S can be won by α then all attracted nodes are won by α and (ii) if all nodes in S have priority $p \equiv_2 \alpha$ and all attracted nodes have a lower (or equal) priority then all moves from S to $Attr_\alpha(S)$ are won by α.

For a game G and a set of nodes A we define $G \setminus A$ as the removal of A from all parts of G: the nodes, and edges, owners, and priorities.

In the original algorithm, Algorithm 4, empty games are immediately solved. For non-empty games, the maximal priority p is calculated. Then the algorithm calculates the set A together with a strategy σ_A for all nodes attracted to the *heads*, i.e., nodes with the maximal priority, $V^{=p}$. A play π starting in a head and consistent with σ_A has two options: either π stays in A and forms an infinite play with highest priority p, won by α, or π escapes to an unattracted node in $V \setminus A$. To finally determine the winner the sub-game $G \setminus A$ is recursively solved to determine W_0' and W_1' (Line 7). If all nodes in this sub-game are also won by α, then, in this case, all nodes of this game are won by α. All that remains is finding a strategy for the heads since the moves for these nodes are explicitly not included in σ_A (Line 10). In the other case, some nodes are won by the opponent: heads may be attracted or forced to $W_{\bar\alpha}'$ and consequently attract more nodes of A (Line 14). These nodes are attracted to a set B and removed to create a second sub-game $G \setminus B$. The solution of this sub-game together with nodes B won by $\bar\alpha$ and the corresponding strategy σ_B form the final solution of G.

Fig. 3. A small parity game. Nodes v_i have priority i. Even plays in v_4. Odd plays in v_1 and v_2.

One weakness of the algorithm is that it resets all attracted nodes if a single node is attracted to the opponent. For sufficient complex game this results in an increased number of solved sub-games:

Example 3. We simulate Algorithm 4 for the parity game in Fig. 3. Initially we solve the game with all three nodes. v_4 does not attract. This node is removed and the sub-game with nodes v_1, v_2 is solved. v_2 does not attract v_1; it is removed to solve the sub-game with one node, v_1. v_1 is the last node, the empty sub-game is solved trivially.

For the sub-game with only v_1, no nodes are won by $W_{\bar\alpha}$, v_1 is won by Odd by playing to itself. For the sub-game with v_1 and v_2, v_1 is won by $W_{\bar\alpha}$, v_1 does not attract v_2 thus the sub-game with only v_2 is solved. The steps of solving this game are skipped, v_2 is won by Even. For the sub-game with v_1 and v_2, v_1 is won

input: A parity game
$G = (V, E, V_0, V_1, Pr)$
output: W_0, W_1: winning nodes,
σ_0, σ_1: strategies

1 **Func** *zielonka*(G):
2   **if** $V = \emptyset$ **then**
3 | **return** $(\emptyset, \emptyset, \emptyset, \emptyset)$
4   $p \leftarrow max\{Pr(v)|v \in V\}$
5   $\alpha \leftarrow p \bmod 2$
6   $A, \sigma_A \leftarrow Attr_\alpha(V^{<p}, V^{=p})$
7   $W_0, W_1, \sigma_0, \sigma_1 \leftarrow zielonka(G \setminus A)$
8   **if** $W_{\bar\alpha} = \emptyset$ **then**
9     $W_\alpha \leftarrow W_\alpha \cup A$
10     $\sigma_F \leftarrow strategy_\alpha(W_\alpha, V^{=p} \cap V|_\alpha)$
11     $\sigma_\alpha \leftarrow \sigma_\alpha \cup \sigma_A \cup \sigma_F$
12   **return** $W_0, W_1, \sigma_0, \sigma_1$
13   **else**
14     $B, \sigma_B \leftarrow Attr_{\bar\alpha}(V, W_{\bar\alpha})$
15     $W_0', W_1', \sigma_0', \sigma_1' \leftarrow zielonka(G \setminus B)$
16     $W_{\bar\alpha}' \leftarrow W_{\bar\alpha}' \cup B$
17     $\sigma_{\bar\alpha}' \leftarrow \sigma_{\bar\alpha}' \cup \sigma_B$
18   **return** $W_0', W_1', \sigma_0', \sigma_1'$

Algorithm 4. Zielonka's algorithm

input: A parity game
$G = (V, E, V_0, V_1, Pr)$
output: W_0, W_1: winning nodes,
J: justification

1 **Func** *zielonka_j*(G):
2   **if** $V = \emptyset$ **then**
3 | **return** $(\emptyset, \emptyset, \emptyset)$
4   $p \leftarrow max\{Pr(v)|v \in V\}$
5   $\alpha \leftarrow p \bmod 2$
6   $W_\alpha \leftarrow V^{=p}, W_{\bar\alpha} \leftarrow \emptyset$
7   $R \leftarrow V^{<p}, J \leftarrow \emptyset$
8   **while** *true* **do**
9     $A, J_A \leftarrow Attr_\alpha(R, W_\alpha)$
10     $W_\alpha \leftarrow W_\alpha \cup A$
11     $G' \leftarrow (G \setminus W_\alpha) \setminus W_{\bar\alpha}$
12     $W_0', W_1', J_Z \leftarrow zielonka\_j(G')$
13     $(W_0, W_1) \leftarrow (W_0 \cup W_0', W_1 \cup W_1')$
14     $J \leftarrow J \cup J_Z \cup J_A$
15   **if** $W_{\bar\alpha}' = \emptyset$ **then**
16       $J_F \leftarrow strategy_\alpha(W_\alpha, W_\alpha \cap V^{=p})$
17   **return** $(W_0, W_1, J \cup J_F)$
18     $B, J_B \leftarrow Attr_{\bar\alpha}(V, W_{\bar\alpha})$
19     $R \leftarrow Reaches(J, B)$
20     $J \leftarrow (J \setminus (R \times V)) \cup J_B$
21     $W_\alpha \leftarrow W_\alpha \setminus R, W_{\bar\alpha} \leftarrow W_{\bar\alpha} \cup B$

Algorithm 5. Zielonka's algorithm
with justifications

by Odd, v_2 is won by Even. In the sub-game of v_1, v_2 and v_4, $W_{\bar\alpha}$ contains v_1. v_2 and v_4 are not attracted to v_1 thus the sub-game with v_2 and v_4 is solved. v_4 does not attract v_2, the sub-game with only v_2 is solved again. For the sub-game with v_2 and v_4, v_4 wins by playing to itself, v_2 is won by *Even* with either move. The game is solved: v_1 is won by Odd, v_2 and v_4 are won by Even.

This example shows that the sub-game with only v_2 is solved multiple times with the same results. Moreover, there was no reason to solve the sub-game with v_1 and v_2. Using justifications, we can do better by further partitioning $A \setminus B$ with the help of σ_A: the nodes that depended on nodes in B and safe nodes. Only the former nodes need to be recalculated in the new sub-game.

Algorithm 5 integrates a justification graph. The essential difference between the two algorithms is Line 19. To make this line useful the algorithm needs to be reformulated. First, the strategy variables σ_0, σ_1 are extended and merged into a single justification graph J which allows to easily calculate reachability. Second, the recursive tail-call in Algorithm 4 at Line 15 is transformed into a loop which is interrupted when $W_{\bar\alpha}' = \emptyset$. The iterative representation allows for a stateful algorithm to recover and modify previously calculated information.

After applying these two changes, the difference between the original algorithm and the justification variant is a single line: if R is overestimated as $W_\alpha^{\neq p}$ on Line 19 the behaviour of the algorithm reverts to the original Zielonka algorithm. In the justification variant of the algorithm the algorithm must, after attracting for the opponent (Line 18), create a new sub-game. It first calculates the set of nodes R that depended on nodes that changed winner (Line 19). Subsequently Line 20 fixes the justification J: it removes the justifications for all nodes in R and adds the justifications for nodes attracted for $\bar\alpha$. Then it removes these nodes from the set W_α, as the properties of $Attr$ have been lost for nodes in R, while adding the attracted nodes to $W_{\bar\alpha}$. Now the loop is ready to restart with first attracting reset nodes that have a different way of playing to W_α and then solving the sub-game of nodes that are still not attracted.

As for correctness, similarly to Algorithm 3, the pair (S, J) with $S = W_0 \cup (V^{\equiv_2 0} \setminus W_1)$ remains a coherent, dominating, default and winning justification while the size of the justification increases every iteration of the while-loop at Line 8. We omit further details.

Tangle Learning. Tangle learning [18,19] is a recent state-of-the-art algorithm based on deriving and attracting tangles. Tangles are sub-games won by a single player α with a strongly connected strategy:

Definition 7 (Tangles). *An α-tangle is a set of nodes $\tau \subset V$ for which there exists a tangle-strategy $\sigma : \tau|_\alpha \to \tau$ such that the graph (τ, E_τ) with $E_\tau = E \cap (\sigma \cup (\tau|_{\bar\alpha} \times \tau))$ has at least one edge, is strongly connected, and all cycles within (τ, E_τ) are won by α.*

A play starting in a node of an α-tangle can either stay within the tangle or $\bar\alpha$ can escape to a node in $Ext(\tau) = \{w|(v, w) \in E, v \in \tau|_{\bar\alpha}, w \notin \tau\}$. Thus if all escapes are won by α then all nodes in the α-tangle are won by α.

Integrating the tangles involves an extension to the attraction function used by Zielonka's algorithm. Recall that nodes are attracted for a player α if that player can force a play to a given set, rules (i) and (ii). For tangle learning the property is extended to either playing to the given set or α wins the infinite play. This property is satisfied for α-tangles: all nodes of an α-tangle are attracted if all escapes of the tangle are attracted, rule (iii).

Formally, given the set of tangles T (with the α-tangles of T denoted as $T|_\alpha$), the set of nodes V, the set of edges E, the subset of nodes attracted to S is:

$$
\begin{aligned}
TAttr_\alpha(T, V, E, S) = \mu A.\ &S \\
\cup\ &\{v \in V_\alpha | \exists w : (v, w) \in E \land w \in A\} && (i) \\
\cup\ &\{v \in V_{\bar\alpha} | \forall w : (v, w) \in E \Rightarrow w \in A\} && (ii) \\
\cup\ &\{v \in t \cap V | t \in T|_\alpha \land (Ext(t) \cap V) \neq \emptyset \land (Ext(t) \cap V) \subseteq A\} && (iii)
\end{aligned}
$$

The second part of the algorithm consists of learning tangles. They are found after attracting: Assume $A, \sigma_A = TAttr_\alpha(T, V, S)$. If a node $v \in S_\alpha$ can play within A or if a node $v \in S_{\bar\alpha}$ must play within A then the possibility of a cycle exists. Furthermore, if all nodes in S have the same priority $p \equiv_2 \alpha$ and all attracted nodes A have a lower priority then all cycles are won by α. The tangle learning algorithm will only attract nodes and tangles of a lower priority by invariant. Thus every non-trivial cycle will be an α-tangle. The problem then consists of determining the non-trivial strongly connected components in (A, E_A) with $E_A = E \cap (\sigma_A \cup (A_{\bar\alpha} \times A))$.

Tangle learning consists of first finding tangles and then, to progress, attracting them. If a tangle is used a second time, some work is saved. The more complex the tangle, the more work is saved. First a tangle learning algorithm without justifications is shown, then a new variant with justifications is discussed.

The original tangle learning algorithm (Algorithm 6). First, we explain some key variables: (i) tangles found so far: T, (ii) new tangles to be used in the next iteration, Y, and (iii) the region mappings: L. The solution of the parity game is accumulated in the output variables $W_0, W_1, \sigma_0, \sigma_1$.

The region mapping, $L : V \to P$, is a function that determines the priority to which every node is currently attracted. The notation $(L \setminus A) \cup (A \mapsto p)$ is used to map the value of the nodes in the set A with p. For a region mapping $L : V \to P$, a relation in the set $\{=, \neq, <, >, \equiv_2, \not\equiv_2\}$ and a priority $p \in P$ the notation $L^{-1}_{\sim p}$ denotes $\{v \in V | L(v) \sim p\}$.

The core loop of the algorithm runs from Lines 6 to 21: until all nodes have a region, the algorithm selects the highest priority among the nodes without a region, extends the set of nodes with this priority with all nodes attracted to them and computes all tangles in this set. The final winner can be assigned to such a tangle in case it has no externals (the for-loop at line 15) and the involved nodes will be removed from the game before the next iteration starts; other tangles are added to the set Y and all involved nodes are assigned region p. When all nodes have been assigned a region, at least one tangle has been found. The new tangles in Y are then "promoted" to the set T and the algorithm starts a new iteration with resetting L.

Similar to *Attr*, *TAttr* records how nodes are attracted as a strategy σ_A or as part of a justification J_A. The strategy for attracted nodes is unchanged while the strategy for attracted nodes of a tangle is determined by σ_t.

Given the strategy σ_A, the procedure *extract_tangles* returns the set of all promotable tangles within A. It obtains them by calculating all strongly connected components with, e.g., Tarjan's strongly connected component algorithm. A tangle is promotable if the regions of all its externals are larger than the priority of the tangle. Unpromotable tangles are not returned by *extract_tangles*.

Like Zielonka's algorithm, tangle learning removes all information depending on faulty assumptions; indeed, it empties the region information L (Line 5). By adding justifications, we can do better.

Tangle learning with justifications (Algorithm 7). Like the previous algorithms, the changes are centred around the reset-phase. This variant makes full use of the region information L. This information is never fully reset; instead, *impr* determines outdated information and the justification J is used to selectively withdraw invalid information.

input: A parity game
$$G = (V, E, V_0, V_1, Pr)$$
output: W_0, W_1: winning nodes,
σ_0, σ_1: strategies

1 **Func** $tangle\_learning(G)$:
2 $\quad T \leftarrow \emptyset$
3 $\quad W_0 \leftarrow \emptyset, W_1 \leftarrow \emptyset, \sigma_0 \leftarrow \emptyset, \sigma_1 \leftarrow \emptyset$
4 $\quad$**while** $V \neq \emptyset$ **do**
5 $\quad\quad L \leftarrow (V \mapsto \emptyset), Y \leftarrow \emptyset$
6 $\quad\quad$**while** $L^{-1}_{=\emptyset} \neq \emptyset$ **do**
7 $\quad\quad\quad V' \leftarrow V \cap L^{-1}_{=\emptyset}$
8 $\quad\quad\quad E' \leftarrow E \cap (V' \times V')$
9 $\quad\quad\quad p \leftarrow \max\{Pr(v) | v \in V'\}$
10 $\quad\quad\quad \alpha \leftarrow p \bmod 2$
11 $\quad\quad\quad A, \sigma_A \leftarrow TAttr_\alpha(T, V', E', V'^{=p})$
12 $\quad\quad\quad L \leftarrow L \cup (A \mapsto p)$
13 $\quad\quad\quad New \leftarrow extract\_tangles(A, \sigma_A)$
14 $\quad\quad\quad Dom \leftarrow \{t \in New | E_T(t) = \emptyset\}$
15 $\quad\quad\quad$**for** $(t, \sigma_t) \in Dom$ **do**
16 $\quad\quad\quad\quad D, \sigma \leftarrow TAttr_\alpha(T, V, t)$
17 $\quad\quad\quad\quad W_\alpha \leftarrow W_\alpha \cup D$
18 $\quad\quad\quad\quad \sigma_\alpha \leftarrow \sigma_\alpha \cup \sigma$
19 $\quad\quad\quad\quad L \leftarrow L \setminus D$
20 $\quad\quad\quad\quad V \leftarrow V \setminus D$
21 $\quad\quad\quad Y \leftarrow Y \cup (New \setminus Dom)$
22 $\quad\quad T \leftarrow T \cup Y$
23 $\quad$**return** $W_0, W_1, \sigma_0, \sigma_1$

Algorithm 6. Tangle learning

input: A parity game
$$G = (V, E, V_0, V_1, Pr)$$
output: W_0, W_1: winning nodes,
J: justification

1 **Func** $tl\_just(G)$:
2 $\quad L \leftarrow (V \mapsto \emptyset), T \leftarrow \emptyset$
3 $\quad W_0 \leftarrow \emptyset, W_1 \leftarrow \emptyset, J \leftarrow \emptyset$
4 $\quad$**while** $V \neq \emptyset$ **do**
5 $\quad\quad Y \leftarrow \emptyset$
6 $\quad\quad$**while** $impr(V, T, L) \neq \emptyset$ **do**
7 $\quad\quad\quad V' \leftarrow V \cap L^{-1}_{\leq p}$
8 $\quad\quad\quad E' \leftarrow E \cap (V' \times V')$
9 $\quad\quad\quad p \leftarrow \max(impr(V, T, L))$
10 $\quad\quad\quad \alpha \leftarrow p \bmod 2$
11 $\quad\quad\quad H \leftarrow L^{-1}_{=p} \cup (L^{-1}_{=\emptyset} \cap V^{=p})$
12 $\quad\quad\quad A, J_A \leftarrow TAttr_\alpha(T, V', E', H)$
13 $\quad\quad\quad R \leftarrow Reaches(J, A \cap L^{-1}_{<p, \neq 2p})$
14 $\quad\quad\quad J \leftarrow (J \setminus ((R \cup A) \times V)) \cup J_A$
15 $\quad\quad\quad L \leftarrow (L \setminus R) \cup (R \mapsto \emptyset)$
16 $\quad\quad\quad L \leftarrow (L \setminus A) \cup (A \mapsto p)$
17 $\quad\quad\quad New \leftarrow extract\_tangles(A, J_A)$
18 $\quad\quad\quad Dom \leftarrow \{t \in New | E_T(t) = \emptyset\}$
19 $\quad\quad\quad$**for** $(t, \sigma_t) \in Dom$ **do**
20 $\quad\quad\quad\quad D, J_D \leftarrow TAttr_\alpha(T, V, t)$
21 $\quad\quad\quad\quad W_\alpha \leftarrow W_\alpha \cup D$
22 $\quad\quad\quad\quad J_\alpha \leftarrow J_\alpha \cup J_D$
23 $\quad\quad\quad\quad L \leftarrow L \setminus D, V \leftarrow V \setminus D$
24 $\quad\quad\quad Y \leftarrow Y \cup (New \setminus Dom)$
25 $\quad\quad T \leftarrow T \cup Y$
26 $\quad$**return** W_0, W_1, J

Algorithm 7. Tangle learning
improved with justifications

The function *impr* determines for which nodes and tangles the region L can be improved. If no such nodes exist, either the algorithm is finished or some tangles must have been found which are not yet available for attraction; the inner while loop is exited, the new tangles are added to T and their region is reset to $\emptyset$ (Line 25). Otherwise we are interested in the nodes and tangles available for improvement that have the maximal priority p.

Line 9 identifies the maximal priority for which improvements are possible, Line 11 determines which nodes can be improved and Line 12 determines the attracting nodes. After resetting the nodes that become invalid (Lines 13 to 15), the improved region is assigned for all attracted nodes (Line 16). At this point, the set of nodes with region p is the same as in the non-justification algorithm (given the same set of tangles T). However, this does not guarantee that the set of extracted tangles will be the equal as it is possible that the chosen strategy σ_A and justification J differ.

As for correctness, similarly to Algorithm 3, the pair (S, J) with $S = W_0 \cup L^{\equiv_2 0} \cup (V^{\equiv_2 0} \setminus L^{\equiv_2 1} \setminus W_1)$ remains a coherent, dominating, default and winning justification while the size of the justification increases every iteration of the while-loop at Line 8. We omit further details.

Overall, the algorithm improves two facets of the attraction: first, unchanged regions are skipped and secondly even when extending the region, nodes already belonging to the region are not re-attracted.

5   Experimental Results

In the literature, we selected three parity game solving projects:

- PGSolver [8,9] (github.com/tcsprojects/pgsolver) is a collection of tools for solving parity games written in OCaml. We refer to its algorithms with `pgsolver-*`.
- Oink [18,19] (github.com/trolando/oink) is a recent parity game solver suite written in C++. We refer to its algorithms with `oink-*`.
- pbespgsolver (www.mcrl2.org) is part of the mCRL2 toolset [5], centred around formal verification of automata. We refer to its algorithms with `pbes-*`.

Each project implements several algorithms, among them are fixpoint iteration (referred as `*-fp`, Zielonka's algorithm (referred as `*-zlk`), priority promotion (referred as `*-pp`) and tangle learning (referred as `*-tl`). For example, with `oink-tl` we refer to the tangle learning algorithm in the Oink solver. In total, 13 algorithms are benchmarked, 8 from the above three solvers and 5 algorithms we implemented. One of them, `oink-zlk-just`, is a modification of the implementation of Zielonka's algorithm in Oink. The fixpoint iteration algorithm is only implemented in PGSolver which, as Table 1 shows, has the worst performance of all three solvers. So it looks as a bad idea to modify that implementation. Therefore, we implemented our own version of the fixpoint algorithm (`prty-fp`) and an extension with justifications (`prty-fp-just`). As for priority promotion and tangle learning, we did not have the time to extend both with justifications. We selected the best performing one, tangle learning. However, extending the Oink implementation was too involved: tangle learning is significantly more complex than Zielonka's algorithm. We started from scratch, implementing a baseline `prty-tl` and an extension with justifications (`prty-tl-just`). All `prty-*` solvers are implemented in Rust and are available at bitbucket.org/krr/prty.

In literature, we found information on two benchmarks. The parity game benchmark [14] and one with large random graphs used for benchmarking tangle learning [18]. These benchmarks[3] have been executed for the selected algorithms

---

[3] The benchmarks can be reproduced in the VMCAI 2020 virtual machine (https://doi.org/10.5281/zenodo.3533104) with the artifact at https://doi.org/10.5281/zenodo.3510292.

Table 1. Number of solved instances in less than 1, 10, and 100 s and par2 score (lower is better), sorted by the par2 score

Configuration 6 GB	Both benchmarks (1297 instances)			
	<1 s	<10 s	<100 s	par2 (s)
prty-tl-just	976	1215	1289	4912
prty-tl	959	1207	1288	5729
oink-tl	947	1209	1277	7193
oink-zlk-just	947	1206	1260	10464
oink-pp	952	1188	1245	13295
oink-zlk	932	1186	1239	14471
pbes-pp	919	1141	1205	21406
pbes-zlk	860	1072	1140	34437
prty-fp-just	863	1094	1134	34866
pgsolver-pp	698	1034	1138	36453
pgsolver-zlk	625	910	1035	56824
prty-fp	590	780	845	92529
pgsolver-fp	532	743	807	100616

with a time-limit of 100 s and a memory limit of 6 GB on a PC with an Intel 'i7-4770' CPU. A summary of the results for these benchmarks is reported in Table 1: the number of games solved within 1 s, 10 s, and within the time-limit. The par2 score is also reported, it is the sum of the run-times of all solved games and a penalty of twice the time-limit (200 s) for each unsolved game.

This benchmark ranks the base algorithms as follows: tangle learning performs best, priority promotion performs better than Zielonka's algorithm and fixpoint iteration is the worst algorithm. The frameworks can also be ranked by comparing different implementations of the same algorithm: Oink performs best, then pbespgsolver second-best and PGSolver ranks last. More interesting is the effect of adding justifications to various algorithms. The table shows that each justification variant performs better than the corresponding base algorithm.

The fixpoint algorithm `prty-fp-just` outperforms `prty-fp` with 289 additional solved instances. As it ranks below the best algorithms, we do not analyse it in more detail but focus on the other two implementations with justifications.

Figure 4 is a cactusplot of the 100 most time consuming instances; it zooms in on the top six algorithms. The figure shows that adding justifications results in a clear performance improvement for Zielonka's algorithm (`oink-zlk` vs `oink-zlk-just`) and tangle learning (`prty-tl` vs `prty-tl-just`). Both the table and the figure show that our baseline tangle learning algorithm, `prty-tl`, performs better than `oink-tl`. Further analysis learned us that the cause is a solvable memory inefficiency in Oink. To measure the effect more in detail we considered the 1277 instance solved by both versions: `oink-tl` needs 2626 s to solve them while our baseline, `prty-tl`, only needs 2541 s.

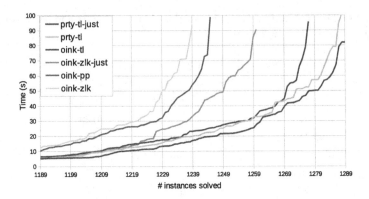

Fig. 4. Cactusplot showing runtime of the slowest 100 parity games for the top six algorithms

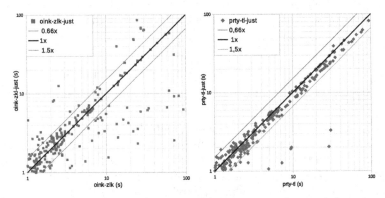

(a) Comparison for Zielonka's al-   (b) Comparison for tangle learning
gorithm

Fig. 5. Comparisons of run times

Figure 5 zooms in on the differences in run-time for all instances solved by both versions of an algorithm. Below the black line are instances for which the justification version is faster; above the line those for which the justification version is slower. Figure 5a compares `oink-zlk` with `oink-zlk-just`. While there are examples with a large speed-up, there are also examples with a significant slowdown. We assume that most of the variability is caused by the explicit representation of the justification graph that uses hashing for direct access to the inverse of the justification function. Indeed, performance analysis showed that a major chunk of time is spent maintaining this data structure. Overall, there are more examples with a significant speed-up than with a significant slowdown and the overall time for solving the 1233 common examples is reduced from 2629 s to 2293 s. Considering that `oink-zlk-just` solves 21 extra instances, we conclude that adding justifications improves Zielonka's algorithm.

Table 2. The reduction of runtime is coupled to a reduction in number of attracted nodes

Instance	Runtime (s)		# attracted nodes	
	prty-tl	-just	prty-tl	-just
jurdzinskigame(500,50)	2.8	0.7	663k	51k
jurdzinskigame(500,100)	7.2	1.3	2.6M	101k
jurdzinskigame(100,500)	9.4	1.9	13M	101k
jurdzinskigame(500,200)	28.6	2.0	10M	201k
jurdzinskigame(200,500)	30.2	3.3	25M	201k
jurdzinskigame(500,500)	(190)	7.7	63M	502k
ABP_Onebit_(3,1,1,weak-bisim)	70.6	66.7	177M	40M
rn-1000000-1000000-1-2-4	75.8	58.4	163M	157M
rn-1000000-1000000-1-2-9	79.0	62.6	168M	164M
SWP(4,3,infinitely_often_rw)	79.1	78.9	104M	27M
rn-700000-700000-1-2-5	94.6	81.9	217M	235M
rn-700000-700000-1-2-4	99.4	81.4	224M	220M

As the explicit justification graph used in Zielonka's algorithm caused a lot of variability in the run-time of individual instances, we opted for an implicit representation of the justification graph in tangle learning; it derives the justification graph from the existing information about nodes. Figure 5b, which compares prty-tl with prty-tl-just, indeed shows much less variability and we see, for instances requiring more than 10 s, a modest but almost consistent improvement. The overall time to solve the 1277 instances is reduced from 2541 s to 2159 s which is a 15% improvement.

The figure also shows a few examples with a significant speed-up while none with a significant slowdown. It turns out all these instances are so called Jurdzinski games [12]. A detailed profiling learned us that up to 80% of the time is spent on attracting nodes and that justifications reduce the number of attracted and reset nodes in Jurdzinski games with several orders of magnitude. Table 2 shows details about the Jurdzinski game instances as well as some other hard instances. It also includes the 500 by 500 Jurdzinski game, the most difficult Jurdzinski game in the data set, which is not part of Fig. 5b as it requires more than 100 s to solve. In this game, the number of attracted nodes is reduced from 126M to 501k nodes and the run-time from 190 s to less than 8 s. The other instances in Table 2 are representative for the instances in the top right of Fig. 5b. Justifications reduce the number of attracted nodes by only a fraction of the total. Still, there are a small improvements in run-time. We conclude that justifications are a significant improvement for tangle learning.

Conclusion. Our experiments demonstrate that adding a justification graph to a parity game solver algorithm is beneficial to the performance. Also, we have shown that `prty-tl-just`, a tangle learning solver with justifications, is improving upon the state of the art.

6   Conclusion

In this paper we explored the use of justification graphs in parity game solvers. We started with the nested fixpoint induction algorithm for parity games [3]. Besides storing the winning strategy of a node, the justification can also be used to save work. Indeed, upon each update of winning nodes, the basic algorithm resets all lower priority nodes to the static overestimation of their winner. The justification allows one to dynamically select the nodes for which the current winner is invalidated and only resets those nodes to the default assumption of their winner. Experimental evaluation showed that this results in a substantial speed-up of the algorithm.

Encouraged by these results we also explored the use of justifications in other algorithms. Our analysis learned us that also Zielonka's algorithm [21], priority promotion [1,2] and tangle learning [18] can potentially benefit from justifications as it allows one to reset fewer nodes to their default settings at the beginning of a new iteration. So far we could only implement two of these three algorithms, namely Zielonka's algorithm and tangle learning. Our evaluation meets our expectations, for both algorithms we obtained a good performance improvement for the whole of our benchmarkset. Moreover, our best algorithm improves upon the state of the art.

Future Work. For Zielonka's algorithm, we expect that replacing the explicit justification graph with an implicit one will improve the performance and will result in a more consistent speed-up over all instances of the benchmark.

We predict that adding justifications to priority promotion speed up the algorithm. Moreover, the region-recovery variant of priority promotion shows parallels to justification-based resetting: it uses the witness strategy to safeguard regions (a set of nodes) if none of the nodes depend on a reset region. This is, however, coarser than justifications: if a single nodes depends on a reset region then all nodes in that region are reset which cascades for all dependent regions. We predict that games improved by region recovery are also improved when using a justifications-based algorithm.

There is a need to develop a benchmark set with harder instances: The best algorithm solves 1289 out of 1297 instances and solves all instances in 400 s with 15 GB of memory. Furthermore, only 82 instances need more than 10 s to solve.

Finally, one can imagine that justifications are excellent for incremental parity game solving. When a small part of a parity game is revised, justifications allows one to identify the affected part of the solution, to reset the nodes in that part to the default winners and to start the search for a solution form there. So far we are not aware of applications that could use such an incremental parity game solver.

References

1. Benerecetti, M., Dell'Erba, D., Mogavero, F.: Improving priority promotion for parity games. In: Bloem, R., Arbel, E. (eds.) HVC 2016. LNCS, vol. 10028, pp. 117–133. Springer, Cham (2016). https://doi.org/10.1007/978-3-319-49052-6_8

2. Benerecetti, M., Dell'Erba, D., Mogavero, F.: Solving parity games via priority promotion. In: Chaudhuri, S., Farzan, A. (eds.) CAV 2016. LNCS, vol. 9780, pp. 270–290. Springer, Cham (2016). https://doi.org/10.1007/978-3-319-41540-6_15. ISBN 978-3-319-41539-0

3. Bruse, F., Falk, M., Lange, M.: The fixpoint-iteration algorithm for parity games. In: Peron, A., Piazza, C. (eds.) Proceedings Fifth International Symposium on Games, Automata, Logics and Formal Verification, GandALF 2014. EPTCS, Verona, Italy, 10–12 September 2014, vol. 161, pp. 116–130 (2014)

4. Calude, C.S., et al.: Deciding parity games in quasipolynomial time. In: Hatami, H., McKenzie, P., King, V. (eds.) Proceedings of the 49th Annual ACM SIGACT Symposium on Theory of Computing, STOC 2017, Montreal, QC, Canada, 19–23 June 2017, pp. 252–263. ACM (2017). ISBN 978-1-4503-4528-6

5. Cranen, S., et al.: An overview of the mCRL2 toolset and its recent advances. In: Piterman, N., Smolka, S.A. (eds.) TACAS 2013. LNCS, vol. 7795, pp. 199–213. Springer, Heidelberg (2013). https://doi.org/10.1007/978-3-642-36742-7_15. ISBN 978-3-642-36742-7

6. Emerson, E.A., Lei, C.-L.: Efficient model checking in fragments of the propositional mu-calculus (extended abstract). In: Proceedings of the Symposium on Logic in Computer Science (LICS 1986), Cambridge, Massachusetts, USA, 16–18 June 1986. IEEE Computer Society, pp. 267–278 (1986). ISBN 0-8186-0720-3

7. Fearnley, J., et al.: An ordered approach to solving parity games in quasi polynomial time and quasi linear space. In: Erdogmus, H., Havelund, K. (eds.) Proceedings of the 24th ACM SIGSOFT International SPIN Symposium on Model Checking of Software, Santa Barbara, CA, USA, 10–14 July 2017, pp. 112–121. ACM (2017). ISBN 978-1-4503-5077-8

8. Friedmann, O., Lange, M.: Solving parity games in practice. In: Liu, Z., Ravn, A.P. (eds.) ATVA 2009. LNCS, vol. 5799, pp. 182–196. Springer, Heidelberg (2009). https://doi.org/10.1007/978-3-642-04761-9_15. ISBN 978-3-642-04760-2

9. Friedmann, O., Lange, M.: The PGSolver collection of parity game solvers. University of Munich (2009)

10. Grädel, E., Thomas, W., Wilke, T. (eds.): Automata Logics, and Infinite Games: A Guide to Current Research. LNCS, vol. 2500. Springer, Heidelberg (2002). https://doi.org/10.1007/3-540-36387-4. ISSN 3-540-00388-5

11. Hou, P., De Cat, B., Denecker, M.: FO(FD): extending classical logic with rule-based fixpoint definitions. TPLP 10(4–6), 581–596 (2010)

12. Jurdziński, M.: Small progress measures for solving parity games. In: Reichel, H., Tison, S. (eds.) STACS 2000. LNCS, vol. 1770, pp. 290–301. Springer, Heidelberg (2000). https://doi.org/10.1007/3-540-46541-3_24. ISBN 3-540-67141-1

13. Kant, G., van de Pol, J.: Efficient instantiation of parameterised Boolean equation systems to parity games. In: Wijs, A., Bosnacki, D., Edelkamp, S. (eds.) Proceedings First Work-Shop on GRAPH Inspection and Traversal Engineering, GRAPHITE 2012. EPTCS, Tallinn, Estonia, 1st April 2012, vol. 99, pp. 50–65 (2012)

14. Keiren, J.J.A.: Benchmarks for parity games. In: Dastani, M., Sirjani, M. (eds.) FSEN 2015. LNCS, vol. 9392, pp. 127–142. Springer, Cham (2015). https://doi.org/10.1007/978-3-319-24644-4_9. ISBN 978-3-319-24643-7

15. Long, D.E., Browne, A., Clarke, E.M., Jha, S., Marrero, W.R.: An improved algorithm for the evaluation of fixpoint expressions. In: Dill, D.L. (ed.) CAV 1994. LNCS, vol. 818, pp. 338–350. Springer, Heidelberg (1994). https://doi.org/10.1007/3-540-58179-0_66. ISBN 3-540-58179-6
16. Schewe, S.: An optimal strategy improvement algorithm for solving parity and payoff games. In: Kaminski, M., Martini, S. (eds.) CSL 2008. LNCS, vol. 5213, pp. 369–384. Springer, Heidelberg (2008). https://doi.org/10.1007/978-3-540-87531-4_27. ISBN 978-3-540-87530-7
17. Seidl, H.: Fast and simple nested fixpoints. Inf. Process. Lett. **59**(6), 303–308 (1996)
18. Dijk, T.: Attracting tangles to solve parity games. In: Chockler, H., Weissenbacher, G. (eds.) CAV 2018. LNCS, vol. 10982, pp. 198–215. Springer, Cham (2018). https://doi.org/10.1007/978-3-319-96142-2_14. ISBN 978-3-319-96141-5
19. Dijk, T.: Oink: an implementation and evaluation of modern parity game solvers. In: Beyer, D., Huisman, M. (eds.) TACAS 2018. LNCS, vol. 10805, pp. 291–308. Springer, Cham (2018). https://doi.org/10.1007/978-3-319-89960-2_16. ISBN 978-3-319-89959-6
20. Walukiewicz, I.: Monadic second-order logic on tree-like structures. Theor. Comput. Sci. **275**(1–2), 311–346 (2002)
21. Zielonka, W.: Infinite games on finitely coloured graphs with applications to automata on infinite trees. Theor. Comput. Sci. **200**(1–2), 135–183 (1998)

Author Index

Printed in the United States
By Bookmasters